Second Edition Volume 2

The "Who Is Johnny Dollar?" Matter

A Character Profile and Program Synopsis of
*"America's Fabulous Insurance Investigator,
The Man with the Action-Packed Expense Account"*

"Yours Truly, Johnny Dollar"

by **John C. Abbott**

THE "WHO IS JOHNNY DOLLAR?" MATTER
A CHARACTER PROFILE AND PROGRAM SYNOPSIS OF
"AMERICA'S FABULOUS INSURANCE INVESTIGATOR,
THE MAN WITH THE ACTION PACKED EXPENSE ACCOUNT"
"YOURS TRULY, JOHNNY DOLLAR"   VOLUME 2
© 2018 JOHN C. ABBOTT

All rights reserved.

No part of this book may be reproduced in any form or by any means, electronic, mechanical, digital, photocopying or recording, except for the inclusion in a review, without permission in writing from the publisher.

Published in the USA by:

BEARMANOR MEDIA
PO BOX 71426
ALBANY, GA 31708
www.BearManorMedia.com

ISBN: 978 1 62933 326 7 (alk. paper)

BOOK DESIGN AND LAYOUT BY VALERIE THOMPSON.

Table of Contents

V1	I. THE GOLDEN AGE OF RADIO	1
V1	II. WHO IS JOHNNY DOLLAR?	3
V1	BACKGROUND	3
V1	THE DIFFERENT INVESTIGATOR	5
V1	PERSONAL DETAILS	6
V1	OCCUPATIONAL HAZARDS	8
V1	RECREATION AND HOBBIES	9
V1	SOURCES OF INCOME	9
V1	III. THE FINAL CHAPTER MATTER	13
V1	IV. PROGRAM RELATED INFORMATION	23
V1	THE CASES	23
V1	THE ACTORS	24
V1	THE WRITERS AND PRODUCERS	24
V1	RECURRING CHARACTERS	26
V1	V. CASE SYNOPSES	29
V1	CHARLES RUSSELL	31
V1	EDMOND O'BRIEN	89
V1	JOHN LUND	259
V1	BOB BAILEY (5-PART)	435
V2	BOB BAILEY	683
V2	BOB READICK	1043
V2	MANDEL KRAMER	1099
V2	THE AUDITION PROGRAMS	1237
V2	VI. SO, WHO WAS THE BEST JOHNNY DOLLAR?	1251
V2	VII. REPORTS	1253
V2	EXPENSES BY ACTOR	1253
V2	EMPLOYERS AND AGENTS	1254
V2	RECYCLED PROGRAMS	1286
V2	VIII. THE CANONICAL JOHNNY DOLLAR LIST	1295
V2	THE DICK POWELL PROGRAMS	1300
V2	THE CHARLES RUSSELL PROGRAMS	1300
V2	THE EDMOND O'BRIEN PROGRAMS	1301
V2	THE JOHN LUND PROGRAMS	1304
V2	THE GERALD MOHR PROGRAMS	1306
V2	THE BOB BAILEY PROGRAMS	1306
V2	THE BOB READICK PROGRAMS	1318
V2	THE MANDEL KRAMER PROGRAMS	1318
V2	THE UNPRODUCED PROGRAMS	1320
V2	THE MISSING PROGRAMS	1321
V1&2	INDEX	1325

Dedicated to:
All those wonderful actors, actresses, writers, directors, producers, technical staff and sponsors, who made radio a wonderful place for almost 40 years.

Special thanks also go out to Stewart Wright, Dr. Joe Webb, J. David Goldin, and the late Bill Brooks for their support, and encouragement and most of all, for answering my many questions. Thanks guys.

Support for this project was also provided by Jeanette Berard and Klaudia Englund of the Thousand Oaks Library, Anthony L'Abatte at Eastman House, and Janet Lorenz at the National Film Information Service.

Bob Bailey

THIS IS THE START OF THE 30-MINUTE SERIES OF BOB BAILEY PROGRAMS.

Show: The Markham Matter
Show Date: 11/4/1956
Company: Western Life & Trust Company
Agent: Ed Porter
Exp. Acct: $968.20

Synopsis: Ed Porter returns Johnny's call, and Johnny would like to see him. Johnny tells Porter that he is always in a rush when he thinks someone is gypping us out of $100,000.

Johnny travels to San Francisco, California and gets a room at the St. Francis Hotel. Johnny walks to Ed Porter's office where Ed is nervous.

Johnny asks Ed about Floyd Markham, who is the husband of Mrs. Markham. Mrs. Markham is wealthy and the husband is an industrial engineer who depends on her for money.

Johnny shows Ed two checks for $50,000, full payment for two endowment policies. Johnny tells Ed that Mrs. Markham's payment history is up to date, but why would she forget about a third policy for $50,000? Johnny tells Ed that Floyd had called the company and told them that he was calling for Mrs. Markham.

Ed tells Johnny that they have a strange relationship, and each spends their own money. Ed tells Johnny that when he called to deliver the first check, Mrs. Markham was ill, and the second time she had just stepped out, and the check was given to Floyd. Ed has not seen Mrs. Markham since last spring.

Johnny checks with the bank and since June, the deposit slips were initialed by Floyd Markham and no unusual withdrawals had been made. Johnny checks with a hairdresser, and a car mechanic, but Mrs. Markham has not been there for months. Johnny also learns that Floyd had called to resign Mrs. Markham from the bridge club.

Johnny calls the residence three times and gets a different reason each for Mrs. Markham not being there. Johnny visits Floyd's business address and tells the receptionist, Iris Bidler, that he is Steven B. Harris with the Cleveland Pump Company. Iris tells Johnny that Mr. Markham has not been in the office for 6 months.

Johnny goes to the Markham house on Fiorella Street in Ed Porter's car. Floyd answers the door and Johnny asks for Mrs. Markham. Johnny tells Floyd that he has a check for the third policy. Floyd tells him he will take it but Johnny tells him that he has to deliver it personally. Floyd tells Johnny that Mrs. Markham is ill with severe anemia. Reluctantly Floyd goes to see Mrs. Markham and Johnny notices his rich clothes.

Johnny is directed to the room where Mrs. Markham is sitting by the window with a glazed look in her eyes. She asks how Mr. Porter is and asks Johnny not to tell Porter that she is ill, as she does not want to worry her friends. She is insistent that she wants some sherry, but Floyd tells her it is against her doctor's orders. Mrs. Markham tries to tell Johnny something but is too tired.

Johnny calls Ed to confirm a description of Mrs. Markham and tells him that Floyd is slowly killing her.

Johnny picks up Ed and tells him that Floyd is forcing his wife to sign money over to him and about her plea for some sherry so that she could be alone with Johnny. Johnny sees Iris drive up in a Cadillac and then leaves with Floyd. Johnny tells Ed to be an investigator and follow her.

Johnny walks to the house and makes sure that no one is there and enters the house. In her room, Johnny sees Mrs. Markham on a couch "doped to the ears". Johnny tells her that he is going to take her out of there and she remembers Johnny and does not want her friends to know that she is ill, Floyd had told her to say exactly that. She begs Johnny not to fool her and to help her get out of there. Johnny carries her to his car and takes her to the St. Regis Emergency hospital and tells the interns what has happened.

Johnny drives back to the house and meets Ed who tells Johnny that they went straight to the Bank of America to deposit the check and then he followed them to Angelo's where they are eating dinner.

Johnny and Ed drive to Angelo's on Stoker Street where the Cadillac is still parked. When Iris and Floyd leave Johnny follows them to a bar where he and Ed wait for 2 hours. Then they follow Floyd to a dark hill where Johnny and Ed watch Floyd and Iris necking.

They then follow Floyd back into town where he drops off Iris. Ed follows Floyd and Johnny goes in to talk with Iris. Johnny tells Iris who he really is, and invites himself in. He tells her that he has been investigating Floyd Markham, and that she will be in jail with him unless she has some information to give Johnny.

She tells Johnny that Mrs. Markham is out of town divorcing him. They had planned to move to a country estate in England to live a quiet country life, and Floyd had told her that she could start packing tonight.

Johnny takes Iris back to the Markham house and meets Ed. Johnny rings the bell and tells Floyd that his wife is in a hospital, and that Iris is in a cab. Floyd asks Johnny why he did not come around next week and Johnny tells him that next week she could be dead. Floyd tells Johnny that is the way she should have been for 16 years — dead.

"Remarks: This one will wind up in court. Mr. Markham's charges will include attempted homicide, attempt to defraud, attempt to…In the end, it was his attempt to run away, and it didn't work. It never works. Even if you get a way you find something new to run from."

Notes:
- This program is the beginning of the new series of 30-minute programs.
- This program contains a commercial for Jack Benny's new seasonal return program.
- Johnny notes that he carries Mrs. Markham to his car, but he does not have one, he was using Ed Porter's car, and Ed is following Floyd. Later he takes Iris to the Markham house in his car but tells Floyd that she is in a cab.
- Bob Bailey offers a thanksgiving message: "Thanksgiving, now there is a day that deserves celebration, and heartfelt thanks to the God who made us, for being able to live in the most free, and peaceful and bountiful country in the world. And yet, why wait for next Thursday, or any Thanksgiving Day? For American's, it seems to me that Thanksgiving Day should be every day. Think about it, won't you?"
- Based on the "air date" on the script, and the note from last week that the show will move to Sunday, the next show would be on 11/4/56, which agrees with the air date.
- The preview is for New Orleans but *The Big Scoop Matter* takes place in New York.
- Roy Rowan is the announcer.
- Music supervision is by Amerigo Marino.

Producer:	Jack Johnstone	Writer:	John Dawson
Cast:	Lois Corbett, Frank Nelson, Virginia Gregg, Bert Holland, Paula Winslowe, John Dehner		

◆ ❖ ◆

Show: **The Big Scoop Matter**
Show Date: **11/11/1956**
Company: **Northeast Indemnity Affiliates**
Agent: **Joe McNab**
Exp. Acct: **$187.40**

Synopsis: Joe McNab calls Johnny with high blood pressure. Joe may have to pay off on a $100,000 policy on a reporter friend of Johnny's, Art Wesley. Art is working on a story someone does not want him to report on. Art was beaten two days ago in an alley, and yesterday a car made a pass at him at high speed and it is still early today.

Johnny travels to New York City to meet with Art and finds him in a bar. Art tells Johnny that he is working on a story and cannot have anyone protecting him. Art tells Johnny that his departed wife is the beneficiary of the policy. Art tells Johnny that the story is about a national gambling syndicate run by someone in New York. He has the man's name written in a safe deposit box just in case.

Johnny goes to see Joan Wesley, who is not cooperative at all. Johnny cabs to see Det. Lt. Restelli, his old friend who knows about the attempts on Art's life. The phone rings and Art is calling for Johnny.

Art tells Johnny that he is leaving town and this might be it. Johnny cabs to Art's apartment and finds "Watika" written on a pad by the phone — a reference to Lake Watika, New York where Art has a lodge.

Johnny rents a car and drives to the lake through a heavy rainstorm and finds a mass of mud on the road to the lake. Johnny drives up the road to Art's place, finds Art's car and Art is lying dead in the doorway. Johnny drives to the sheriff and reports it.

Johnny meets the sheriff the next morning and they go over the known facts, including a hole in the roof over the foodstuffs. The coroner has reported that Art was killed about 10:30, while it was still raining. Johnny tells the sheriff about the story Art was working on, and Johnny is told that the only place to stay in the area is the Watika Inn.

Johnny drives to the inn and talks to the desk clerk who tells him that there were only two guests last night. One of the guests, Mr. Cooper, is sitting on the porch and the other has gone.

Johnny goes to talk to Cooper, who tells Johnny that he enjoyed the rain by sitting in front of his fireplace and reading a book. Johnny gets a description of the other guest for the sheriff and goes back to New York.

Johnny visits Joan Wesley, who knows about Art's death. Johnny asks if Joan had known that Art had gone to the lodge. She tells Johnny that she was at home all the previous evening.

Johnny checks the garage and finds that her car is clean. Johnny learns from the garage attendant that the car had been washed because the wheels were full of mud from last night.

Johnny confronts Joan with the mud on her car, but she is adamant that she was not at the lodge. Johnny tells her that the switchboard operator got a call from Art yesterday, and she admits she spoke to Art, but went out to meet someone else, which is why she wanted a divorce. The man is Ted Nash.

Johnny calls the apartment of Nash who is not there and goes to see Lt. Restelli to update him on the events of the case.

Lt. Restelli tells Johnny that he will check up on Nash and he tells Johnny that a man named Cooper was involved in some rumors of a gambling ring earlier that year. Johnny and Lt. Restelli go to Art's apartment and find the key to the safe deposit box, but it only has a number on it. Lt. Restelli starts a search of the banks, and Johnny goes back to Lake Watika.

At the lake, Johnny finds Cooper still there by the fire place. Johnny tells him about the story Art was working on, and that he thinks Cooper is part of the gambling ring. Lt. Restelli calls and tells Johnny that the name in the safe deposit box was Cooper.

Johnny tells the clerk to call the sheriff. The clerk tells Johnny that he had taken a drink to Cooper at 10:40 the previous night, and had talked to him for fifteen minutes, so Cooper could not have killed Art Wesley. Johnny talks to the clerk again and he remembers that Cooper had called for a drink at 10:40, and that he had gotten back to the desk at 10:55. Johnny gets a call from the sheriff, who tells him that the other man has been found, but he is not the right man.

Johnny drives to Art Wesley's place and reviews the facts, including the hole in the roof and the sugar bowl. Suddenly Johnny has the solution.

Johnny drives back to the lodge and goes to Cooper's room, where he finds a picture out of place. Behind it Johnny finds what he is looking for.

Johnny finds Cooper on the porch and sits down at his table. Johnny tells him that he was the man Art Wesley was looking for. Cooper recounts his alibi about the time and Johnny tells him that Art was not killed at his lodge. Johnny tells Cooper that he killed Art in his room, called the clerk and talked to him, and then took the body to the lodge and planted it there. You remembered that the slug that killed Art hit the wall, so you fired one into the ceiling to make it look like the killing took place there.

Johnny tells Cooper about the sugar in the cabin, and how it was not crusty, but dry. The hole was made after the rain had stopped, and Johnny tells Cooper that he has found the hole in the wall of his room.

Cooper tells Johnny that he has him covered with a gun under the table, and Johnny tells him the same thing. Cooper tries to run, but Johnny stops him and Cooper discovers that Johnny does not have a gun. "A big-time gambler bluffed right out of the game. Cooper you're slipping".

"Remarks. Cooper is awaiting trial. About Art Wesley, well I guess that sugar bowl was a dead man's revenge. Come to think of it, that revenge was pretty sweet."

Notes:
- Lt. Restelli was a character in *The Imperfect Alibi Matter* broadcast on 9/17 through 9/21/1956.
- Based on the "air date" on the script, *The Big Scoop Matter* should follow *The Markham Matter*.
- Dan Cubberly is the announcer.
- Music Supervision is by Amerigo Marino.

Producer: Jack Johnstone Writer: Robert Ryf
Cast: Virginia Gregg, Russell Thorson, Barney Phillips, Stacy Harris, Larry Thor, Parley Baer, Les Tremayne

♦ ❖ ♦

Show: **The Royal Street Matter**
Show Date: **11/25/1956**
Company: **Providential Fire & Marine**
Agent: **C. D. Binford**
Exp. Acct: **$517.20**

Synopsis: Angie Orsatti calls Johnny, and he wants to go to Andre's for dinner while Johnny is in New Orleans. Johnny tells Angie that he is in town for an insurance claim for $16,000 that someone wants to turn down.

Johnny travels to New Orleans, Louisiana and gets a room at the Roosevelt Hotel, and calls Angie Orsatti, an old friend who really knows the French Quarter. Johnny arranges for dinner with Angie and then calls Mr. C. D. Binford, who issued the policy.

Johnny meets with "CD" and learns that the fire was last Thursday night. The insured is Henry Dupass, and the $48,000 policy covers his antique shop on Royal Street and the policy was issued just three months ago. Dupass had always told CD that he did not have money for the policy, but suddenly he had money for the policy, in cash, shop improvements and a receptionist, a real good looker.

An antique lamp fell over and caused the fire. Henry told the fire marshal that he was talking to a customer and the lamp fell over, but Dupass has not told CD anything, and that is why he is riled. CD had stopped by and saw the damage, but Dupass did not even ask for a claim form. CD talked to the fire marshal and typed up the claim but Dupass refused to sign the claim and told CD to get out.

Johnny walks to Canal Street and goes to the antique shop, which looks like all the others in the area. Johnny knocks and Dupass opens the door. Johnny tells Dupass who he is and Dupass asks why "you people" are always bothering him. He tells Johnny to leave him alone. Johnny goes down the alley to the back of the store but cannot see anything.

Johnny has dinner with Angie, and Johnny asks what he knows about Dupass. Angie knows Dupass, and he had heard about the 24 or 25-year-old blond he is hanging with. Angie will try to find out who the blond is for Johnny.

Johnny buys a flashlight and goes back to the shop, where a small truck is parked in the back with a bunch of bananas in the bed. A man comes out and yells at Johnny to stop. Dupass comes out and tells the man that "Dollar" is with the insurance company. The man tells Johnny that Dupass will have to do something to keep Johnny away, and he tells Johnny to leave.

Johnny goes back to the hotel and is called by Angie in the morning. Angie tells Johnny that everyone knows the girl, but no one has seen her since she started working for Dupass. Her name is Rose Ellen, and she used to be a dancer.

Johnny gets the address from Angie and goes to see the girl. When Johnny gets there another girl, May Garbo, tells Johnny that Rose is not there and invites Johnny in. She tells Johnny that she and Rose moved in together and complements Johnny on being so polite. May tells Johnny that Rose does not come home for days sometimes and has not mentioned a fire. May last saw Rose last Thursday, but she never came home again. May tells Johnny that Rose has never stayed out this long, and that she is going with a man she had never met.

Johnny goes to CD's office and waits for him to come back. Johnny wonders if something happened that Dupass is trying to cover up. When he comes back, CD tells Johnny that Dupass had called and cancelled all of his policies to keep Johnny away, so now the case is over. Johnny has a scotch with CD and Johnny tells CD that Dupass is still covered until he returns the policy, so he can still snoop around. CD tells Johnny that the customer in the shop was Andrew W. DeLong, so Johnny goes to visit him but Johnny discovers that there is no such person in the city.

Johnny asks CD to check on Dupass, and they go to the bank to check up on Dupass. Johnny learns that Dupass has banked over $11,000 in the past month. Johnny goes to the hotel and gets a message from May to see her.

Johnny goes to May's apartment and she tells Johnny that a man called and told May that Rose is OK, and that he would come by and pick up her clothes. The man came at 4:00, and his name is Grant, the man she was seeing while she is dating "the old antique". All she could say was "Carl this, and Carl that." Johnny calls Angie and they rush to the antique shop.

Johnny breaks down the front door and they go in to find Carl on the floor with stab wounds. Carl tells Johnny that Dupass is going to kill Rose because she found out what Dupass was smuggling in the banana shipments. She has been taken to the old Spanish fortress on the Bayou Slidell only 10 minutes ago.

Angie gets his swamp buggy, and they head out to the fortress. At the fortress, Angie beaches the boat and sees Rose in a doorway.

Johnny and Angie go in and call for Rose, who answers and asks for Carl. Johnny tells her that Dupass tried to kill him and she tells Johnny that she was tied up on the night of the fire and that Dupass had told Carl to kill her, which is when the lamp fell over. She tells Johnny that Dupass was smuggling small boxes of powder in the bananas. Dupass comes in and shots are fired. Johnny does not have his gun, so he uses a brick to bean Dupass.

Remarks: Well where he is going, Dupass wouldn't have any use for the insurance money anyway. Carl Grant turned state's evidence and clinched the smuggling charges against him. Because of that, Carl may get off easy. I hope so. He and Rose could make a very happy couple.

Notes:
- This program contains two commercials about the need for volunteers for the Ground Observer Corps.
- Dan Cubberly is the announcer.
- Music supervision is by Amerigo Marino and Carl Fortina.

Producer:	Jack Johnstone	Writer:	Charles B. Smith
Cast:	Virginia Gregg, Forrest Lewis, Lou Merrill, Lawrence Dobkin, Frank Gerstle		

♦ ❖ ♦

Show: **The Burning Carr Matter**
Show Date: **12/2/1956**
Company: **Tri-State Life & Casualty Insurance Company**
Agent: **Earle Poorman**
Exp. Acct: **$385.26**

Synopsis: Earle Poorman calls Johnny, but Johnny is adamant that he is going on vacation to get away from the cold weather in Hartford. Earle is insistent that Johnny comes to work on an arson case in Sarasota. Johnny tells Earle that he has had a rough year and has made reservations for Sarasota and can't do it...umm, where did you say your branch office was? Sarasota. Florida.

Johnny travels to Sarasota, Florida and the office of Earle Poorman. Earle tells Johnny that Mike (his wife, Gertrude) will want him to come for dinner. Johnny notes that "poor man" is a misnomer for Earle as they drive out to his "shack" in his "jalopy", a brand new 1956 Cadillac.

The house is next to a quiet bayou, with a speedboat at the dock. The "big fat overbearing broad" Earle is married to is a cute petite blond who gives Johnny a strange look. Mike, who is a former dancer, gets Johnny a Martin's V.V.O. Scotch and soda, and Earle tells him that they will have to wait until Arnold Carr gets back.

Carr runs the lumberyard business, and his brother Ed just shares the profits. The lumberyard in Orlando is the one that just burned, and a claim for $120,000 has been filed. Mike tells Johnny that Arnold is in Orlando straightening things out.

Earle tells Johnny that he and Arnold suspect arson. There have been some other small fires in other yards, but no sign of arson has been found. Earle has never met Ed Carr, who lives in Orlando.

Arnold Carr calls and tells Earle that it was arson to night in Arcadia. The whole yard went up, and he has proof it was arson. "Do not come here, I will come to your place".

Johnny and Mike are suspicious that Arnold might be setting the fires. After a 30-minute wait and several calls to the Carr home, Arnold never shows up.

Johnny, Mike and Earle drive to Carr's home and see him through the window. Johnny notes that Arnold looks enough like him to be his brother. When Carr does not answer the door, Johnny looks again and Johnny sees that Arnold is dead. Johnny breaks down the door to find Arnold Carr shot in the forehead.

Earle calls the police and Johnny looks the place over. The police arrive and Johnny tells them what had happened. The policeman finds a bullet hole in the window and tells Johnny that he does not need his help and tells them to leave.

Johnny, Earle and Mike leave, and Johnny tells Earle that he had seen the hole in the window, but the shot came from inside the house, to make it look like it came from outside. Someone was trying to keep Arnold from talking. Earle confirms that Ed Carr will inherit the business and Johnny borrows a car from Earle and drives to Arcadia.

At the scene of the fire, Johnny trips over an old man sobbing over losing a part of his life. He had helped build up that business. He and Arnie had found a fire last week, and that is why he came here tonight. Arnie had seen a white car pulling away and said, "I knew that he would be involved". The car was a big Buick and Arnie told him not to tell anyone.

Johnny tells the man that Arnold is dead, and the man tells Johnny that he knows him, and that Johnny was responsible for setting the fires, and the old man shoots at Johnny. Johnny slaps the old man and takes his gun. The old man, the police officer and Johnny all see a family likeness to Carr.

Johnny goes to see Lt. Harkness in Orlando, who wants to tell Johnny that his brother is dead. Harkness suddenly sees the difference. Johnny tells him that Ed Carr is the firebug, and a killer. Harkness puts out an APB for Carr, and Johnny drives to Ed's house.

Johnny learns from Mrs. Harper, a neighbor, that Ed has parties and girls visit there. Johnny learns that Ed drives a white car. Mrs. Harper tells Johnny about a blond who keeps coming into the house and drives a white car. She dresses like some showgirl. She comes from Sarasota based on the license plate and has green eyes. Johnny realizes that the description is that of Mike Poorman.

Johnny calls Earle, and he tells Johnny that Mike is out. She was talking to Betty, they did a sister act, and was gone when Earle came down for breakfast.

Johnny drives back to Ed Carr's house and enters via the backdoor. Johnny suddenly feels a gun in his back and a voice telling Johnny that he owes him $5,000, and Johnny is slugged.

Johnny wakes up later that night as a woman runs up to Johnny and tells him that Tony hit him for not paying for the Arcadia job. She tells "Eddie" that she was trying to raise money to pay Tony and wonders why he is there. She tells Johnny that he had to kill Arnold.

Johnny calls her Mike and turns on the light, at which time neither is who they think the other is. Ed Carr arrives and takes Johnny's gun. The girl tells Ed that Mike had told her that Johnny was coming up there. Ed tells her that he has to get rid of her and Johnny. He is going to call Tony Ricardo and get him to the house. Then he will call the police and kill all of them just before they get there and blame it all on Tony by using Johnny's gun.

Ed shoots Betty and Lt. Harkness walks in and shoots Eddie Carr. Mike Poorman comes in and tells Johnny that she had come alone and brought Lt. Harkness there. She knew that Betty and Ed were going together and had not told Earle. Johnny and Mike drive back to Sarasota.

"Remarks: Betty of course has already paid for her part in the deal. And I guess it is pretty obvious what will happen to Ed Carr and Tony Ricardo. The insurance money and the Carr estate will be distributed according to Florida law. Further remarks: The apparent friction between Earle and Mike was only part of a normal married life. They are really a pretty nice pair. Oh, and I thoroughly enjoyed three days of fishing in the Gulf, thanks to Earle."

Notes:
- The date of this program has been changed to 12/2/1956 so that it will align with the air date on the script.
- The program for the next week, 12/9/1956 was preempted for a Jack Benny program.
- This is the first appearance of Earle and Mike Poorman, who end up becoming close friends of Johnny's.
- This program contains a commercial for the program *Jukebox Jury*, and a commercial for the United Community campaigns.
- This story is done as *The Case of Trouble Matter*, broadcast on 8/5/1962, but the location and business and names are changed, but the plot is the same.

- Dan Cubberly is the announcer.
- Music supervision is by Amerigo Marino.

Producer:	Jack Johnstone	Writer:	Jack Johnstone
Cast:	Virginia Gregg, Parley Baer, Vic Perrin, Bob Bruce, Harry Bartell, Vivi Janiss, Tony Barrett, Junius Matthews		

♦ ❖ ♦

Show: The Rasmusson Matter
Show Date: 12/16/1956
Company: Universal Adjustment Bureau
Agent:
Exp. Acct: $1,965.00

Synopsis: Hardy, returns Johnny's call to Mr. Ellis Rasmussen. Johnny instructs Hardy to tell Mr. Rasmussen that he is investigating a matter concerning a member of his own family. Hardy tells Johnny that Mr. Rasmussen will send a car at 6:00.

Johnny travels to Los Angeles, California and is stonewalled on the case after three days. At 6:00 the chauffeur, Stouffer, arrives for Johnny at his hotel and drives him to the Rasmussen home. Hardy meets Johnny at the door and takes him to see Mr. Rasmussen.

Mr. Rasmussen asks Hardy for 4 fingers of sour-mash and gets Johnny the same. Johnny tells Mr. Rasmussen about the blanket policies issued on his son by Imperial Rubber. Johnny tells Mr. Rasmussen he is looking for the widow. Mr. Rasmussen does not know where the widow is as he has never met her.

Johnny is told that his son married her in Elko, Nevada one night and then left for Malaya. The rubber plantation was raided, and now he does not have a son. The widow has never contacted him, and he wants to see her. He lost the best son a man ever had.

Johnny stays for dinner and hears the story of Ellis Rasmussen and of his son. On the way out, Hardy tells Johnny that everyone wants to meet Mrs. Rasmussen, and they hope he finds her. On the way to the car, Johnny asks Stouffer if Mr. Rasmussen approved of Fred's marriage. Stouffer tells Johnny that Mr. Rasmussen approved of Fred, and if he loved the girl, that was enough. They were real people.

Johnny wires Imperial Rubber for information and calls the San Francisco agent to learn that the widow arrived in San Francisco and has disappeared.

Johnny rents a car and makes a number of stops to get information on Laura Olsen Rasmussen. Johnny receives the folder from Imperial Rubber, and now has a picture to go on.

Johnny visits a boarding house and meets her mother. She does not know where Laura is, and she has not been here for 5 years. Johnny receives a list of passengers from the flight and tracks down a Mr. Oberlin who traveled with Laura Rasmussen. He remembers her, she was pretty chummy on the flight, and had not mentioned the death of her husband.

Johnny is called by Hardy, and Johnny is told that Mr. Rasmussen is dying and they want Johnny to see him. Johnny is afraid to tell him that so far all he knows is that his daughter-in-law is a big fat bum!

Johnny arrives at the Rasmussen house and the family doctor is there. Johnny talks with Mr. Rasmussen and updates him. Mr. Rasmussen tells Johnny to level with him and tell him what he has found. Johnny tells him that they will find her. Mr. Rasmussen tells Johnny that he wants to see her.

Johnny receives a call from officer Daly of the police, and they have Mrs. Rasmussen in the drunk tank. Johnny goes to see officer Daly and tells him that he has a check for Mrs. Rasmussen.

Johnny makes bail for her and Officer Daly shows Johnny her file, full of petty thefts and aliases. Johnny wires the other agents working on the case and tells them to halt their activities.

Johnny meets Laura and tells her he got her out of jail for a friend. Johnny buys her coffee and tries to find out about her life since she left Malaya. She tells Johnny that she did not call her father-in-law because she felt that she meant nothing to him. Johnny tells her about the check and takes her to his room to fill out the paperwork. Stouffer calls and Johnny tells him that he has found nothing, and Mr. Rasmussen is waiting for him. Johnny gives her the check and she leaves.

Johnny checks out and waits in the hotel lobby. Laura Rasmussen spots Johnny and tells him that she read that Mr. Rasmussen is dying. She tells Johnny that she wants to meet Fred's father and Johnny berates her for waiting.

She tells Johnny that she loved Fred and had met him at a cocktail lounge. He loved her with no questions asked. She told him of her past, but that did not matter to Fred. They went to Malaya and she learned what it was like to be loved, and then he was killed. She had gone to the Rasmussen house, but was afraid to go in, given her past. She still has her memories of Fred and cannot drink that away.

Johnny starts to leave and Stouffer arrives. Johnny introduces him to Mrs. Rasmussen, and he is mighty glad to meet her. On the way out to the house, Laura seems to change.

At the house, she meets Hardy, who is happy to meet her. Upstairs Johnny introduces her to Mr. Rasmussen. He calls her to his side, holds her as she cries and tells her that there is nothing that she has to tell him. She is his daughter, and that is all that needs to be said. Mr. Rasmussen calls for brandy and sour-mash.

"Remarks: The old man has a few weeks more. Laura is moving into the house with him, to take care of him. She will not be telling him some things about herself, she does not have to. You should have stood there and seen that big arm go around her shoulder when he said 'you are my daughter.' Yeah."

Notes:
- **This is probably one of, if not the most touching and heart-wrenching of all the Johnny Dollar stories.**

- This program contains a commercial for CBS News, and a commercial about the benefits of the "Letters Abroad" program.
- The scrip title page credits Lee Willway and Joan Mitchen as "Gals". Both work for CBS.
- Dan Cubberly is the announcer.
- Music supervision is by Amerigo Marino.

Producer: Jack Johnstone   Writer: John Dawson
Cast: Virginia Gregg, Jeanne Tatum, Eric Snowden, Roy Glenn, Will Wright, Frank Nelson, Jack Kruschen

♦ ❖ ♦

Show: **The Missing Mouse Matter**
Show Date: 12/23/1956
Company: Floyds of England
Agent: George Reed
Exp. Acct: $38.20

Synopsis: George Reed calls Johnny and asks if he has heard of Jodiah Gillis, the man who owns most of Rhode Island. George had written a special policy written on an object that has disappeared. George hopes that Johnny is sitting down, as the insured object is a mouse. What!?!

Johnny cabs to George Reed's office, and George is concerned about the policy, which is for "one unusually talented grayish-brown mouse". Floyds will insure almost anything and would not have issued the policy except that Gillis has all of his insurance through Floyds.

The mouse belongs to a man named Glaser, who is staying with him. The mouse is insured for $5,000. Gillis called last night and asked for the best investigator to be sent out. Gillis threatened to cancel his policies unless Johnny is sent out. George tells Johnny that he can write his own ticket on this case.

Johnny travels to the Gillis estate in Providence, Rhode Island. Johnny is met at the door by a tall, beautiful girl who is expecting him. She is Marian, Mr. Gillis' daughter.

Johnny is taken in to Mr. Gillis who is happy to see him. Bert Glaser is there, he is the Bert in "Bert and his Pals", a dog act. Gillis tells Johnny that the mouse has been kidnapped, and they know who did it. Bert tells Johnny that Gulliver is worth at least $50,000 because he can sing, he can carry a tune.

Johnny is doubtful, but Bert tells Johnny that it is a scientific fact that mice can sing, but Gulliver is a basso, so people can hear him. Bert and Jodiah take Johnny to a playroom where a cage contains two small mice, Hecuba and Esmerelda. They can sing also, but not as well as Gulliver. Bert tells them to sing "over the waves", and they sing. Johnny is still unconvinced.

Back in the library Johnny liberally samples the eggnog and learns that Harry McQueen has taken Gulliver. McQueen used to be Bert's agent, and has been here poking around, and was here long enough to take the mouse. Some children were there for the rehearsal for Bert's program, and McQueen could have taken him. McQueen was kicked out, and that is when the mouse was discovered missing.

Johnny calls George Reed, and asks him to find McQueen's home phone number. While Johnny is on the phone, he tells George that there is a big yellow cat there with a grayish-brown mouse between his front paws.

Johnny manages to get the mouse away from the cat just as Marian walks in. She tells Johnny that Rama the cat was out during rehearsal so the corpse could be Gulliver. Johnny promises not to say anything until after Christmas.

The next morning Johnny has breakfast and gets a call from Harry McQueen, and Johnny asks him about a missing mouse. McQueen tells Johnny that he has taken towels from hotels, but he has never taken a mouse.

McQueen tells Johnny that he was there to see Gillis about putting some of his people on the Christmas show. McQueen vowed a long time ago never to handle children, belly-dancers or animals. McQueen also tells Johnny that Bert Glaser does not have a dog act but is a topnotch ventriloquist.

Johnny goes out for a walk and thinks that Bert is running a con when he is hit by a snowball thrown by Marian. Johnny tells her that Rama probably got an ordinary mouse. Marian sees a boy on the front porch. When she calls to him, he runs away.

Johnny looks through the house and finds a leg clamp. The doorbell rings, and the boy is back. He had been there to see the show and Johnny asks him in.

Bobby is almost eleven and is not impressed with all this Christmas stuff, especially the presents. He and his mom get along OK without all the gifts. Bobby had followed a dog to the Gillis house and was invited in to see the show. He cannot have any pets where he is living now. Bobby tells Johnny that he had taken the mouse from the cage and decided to give the mouse back. Johnny tells him that Bobby has to give the mouse back himself.

Johnny, Marian and Bobby cab to the children's hospital and give the mouse back to Jodiah. Johnny asks Bert if Gulliver will sing, and Johnny tells him that he never sang for Bobby. Bert tells him that he did not sing because he was never asked to. Bert goes on stage with Gulliver. Bert leaves Gulliver on stage alone, and Gulliver sings Jingle Bells.

Bert tells Johnny that he would not believe that mice could really sing if Johnny knew Bert was a ventriloquist.

As for my separate and additional fee, as agreed upon before I took this matter, well there is a boy named Bobby Neves who lives on Skully Avenue over in Providence, see that he gets it.

Notes:
- Bob Bailey tells Dan Cubberly that "I just do not want to pass up the opportunity to do two things. First, well, Pam and Eric and Fran, Mr. and Mrs. Frolich, Helen Wills, Scotty, oh all the rest of you nice people who have written in to tell us how much you like the program. Thanks. I really appreciate hearing from you, and believe me, I will answer your letters as quickly as I can. Second, well, I am sure that you know what this is, and I want you to know that is comes from the heart. Merry Christmas to you. God Bless."

- This is the first appearance of George Reed, and the insurance company Floyds of England.
- This program contains a commercial for the *Robert Q. Lewis* program.
- Dan Cubberly is the announcer.
- Music supervision is by Amerigo Marino.

Producer: Jack Johnstone Writer: Charles B. Smith
Cast: Mary Jane Croft, Howard McNear, Parley Baer, G. Stanley Jones, Bill James, Lawrence Dobkin, Richard Beals

♦ ❖ ♦

Show: **The Squared Circle Matter**
Show Date: **12/30/1956**
Company: **Eastern Allied Casualty Insurance Company**
Agent: **Paul Kendrick**
Exp. Acct: **$491.20**

Synopsis: Paul Kendrick calls and Johnny asks if he has seen any good fights lately. Paul asks if Johnny remembers Al Coronado, and Johnny tells Paul that he lost $20 on Coronado. Paul tells Johnny to come over, as Eastern may lose $50,000 on him.

Johnny cabs to Paul Kendrick's office and finds him pacing the floor in his cubicle, worried about murder. Paul recounts how he and Johnny had followed the career of Al Coronado, and how Al used to have the quickest reflexes around. There is something wrong now. His manager took out an annuity for $50,000 and is trying to kill him. Paul wants Johnny to go to Joplin and watch Coronado fight. Paul has a hunch and wants somebody who knows Al to watch him.

Johnny travels to Joplin, Missouri and picks up a copy of the policy. Johnny then calls Paul and tells him that Ricky Malone had taken out the policy and paid the premiums, but the beneficiary is Frankie Fortina. Paul has been looking for Fortina but cannot find him. Johnny naps and then goes to the arena in Mt. Elba to watch the fight. The opponent in the main fight was a rank amateur. Frankie looked normal at first, but then Johnny noticed that Al was not connecting with his punches and Al almost misses his stool at the end of the round.

Al goes down for the count after a slight slap on the face and is hurried out of the arena. Johnny goes to the dressing room and Ricky Malone the manager will not let Johnny in to see Al. Johnny forces his way in and slugs Malone. Johnny talks to Al and realizes that Al is not well. Johnny tries to take him out and is slugged by Malone.

When Johnny comes to, the room is empty and Johnny goes to his hotel to call Paul. Johnny tells Paul that Al must have some sort of brain injury and that Malone is forcing him to fight.

Paul has a rundown on Fortina, and he owns Al Coronado. Al has not done well lately, and the only way Frankie will make any money is to kill him off.

Johnny goes to police headquarters and Sgt. Danny Ruskin tells Johnny that Malone and Al checked out this morning and flew to Monterrey, Mexico. Danny tells Johnny to look up Sgt. Romilio Garcia when he gets there, and to mention his name.

Johnny flies to Mexico via El Paso and goes to the policia, but Garcia is not there, he is at the fights. Johnny goes to the arena and has Garcia paged.

Sgt. Garcia is upset at being taken away from the fights, but when Johnny mentions Danny, Sgt. Garcia changes his attitude and tells Johnny that Al Coronado is fighting tomorrow and he will lose. The opponent is "El Toro Negro" who weighs 240 lbs. against Al Coronado's 181. El Toro is a killer and has thrown three men out of the ring. Johnny tells Sgt. Garcia about the last fight and who he is. Sgt. Garcia agrees to help Johnny find Al.

Johnny goes to his hotel and discovers that he is right next door to Al. Johnny talks to Al and he tells Johnny that he has insurance and will retire soon. Johnny notices a bottle of aspirin, and Al tells Johnny that he has been having headaches lately. Johnny tells Al that he has a brain injury and will get killed if he gets hit.

Johnny calls Sgt. Garcia and tells him to bring a doctor to the hotel. Frankie Fortina comes in and tells Johnny to hang up. Malone had called him in Joplin and they have checked up on Johnny. Frankie tells Johnny that he will be dead before Sgt. Garcia gets there.

Frankie tells Johnny that he has never been in Mexico, as his tourist card has a different name on it. Frankie tells Malone that Johnny has to have an accident, and that he has been stalling with Al. Frankie tells Malone that he will be taken care of after he takes care of Johnny.

Frankie tells Malone that he is to kill Al as well. The scene will look like a fight and all three will be killed. Malone agrees to kill Johnny and Johnny fights with him until Malone goes out the window. Johnny goes after Fortina, but Al had hit him with a clean left hook. Sgt. Garcia comes in and he wonders why Johnny thinks Al Coronado has lost his punch.

Johnny recommends that the company make some adjustment to the policy so that Al Coronado can start collecting immediately, as they never should have issued the policy.

Notes:
- Incidentals included a sport shirt loud enough to startle the entire state of Arizona, razor blades and a new toothbrush, and $3 for flowers for the stewardess who found him a bottle of champagne. Not very egregious by my account.
- Johnny makes reference to Paul working in a cubicle. That is kind of Dilbertesque!
- Dan Cubberly is the announcer.
- Music supervision is by Amerigo Marino.

Producer: Jack Johnstone   Writer: Jack Johnstone

Cast:	Harry Bartell, Herb Ellis, Vic Perrin, Jack Kruschen, Les Tremayne, Lawrence Dobkin

♦ ❖ ♦

Show:	The Ellen Dear Matter
Show Date:	1/6/1957
Company:	Western Maritime & Property
Agent:	Arthur Arthur
Exp. Acct:	$453.95

Synopsis: Pat McCracken calls about the sleek lovely *Ellen Dear*. She is loaded with $325,000 in jewels. Johnny is interested until he finds out that she is a boat. Pat wants Johnny to find out what is going on.

Johnny cabs to Pat's office and Pat is not smiling. Johnny is to bill Western Maritime & Property. Pat tells Johnny about Randolph Burrman, who everyone thinks is a crook, but seems to handle some of the finest jewels in the world. He is involved with the Betanhouse collection out of Hungary. A man in Mexico sold the collection to Burrman.

The boat is a 72-ft. motor-cruiser, and Burrman was sailing in the pacific. When Burrman heard about the jewels, he bought them. He had Western Maritime insure the jewels after he had them appraised by a gemologist named Jacques Giampiere in Guadalajara. So far there is no problem, but there have been incidents in the past, but Burrman got out of them. Western is worried and Johnny is to watch the jewels until they get to the states. The boat is in Mazatlan undergoing some engine work.

Johnny flies to Los Angeles, California where he is paged in the airport. Johnny goes to the PanAm desk and meets Arthur Arthur, the local Western Maritime agent, and Jacques Giampiere who had appraised the Betanhouse collection in Mexico. Giampiere has bad news.

He had tried to buy pieces of the collection and knows all of the stones. While in Mexico Giampiere watched a friend, Garcia Hernandez, work on a mount for a stone from the Betanhouse collection, the Calabar diamond. He is sure of the identity of the stone. Arthur thinks that maybe the jewels are not on the boat. Burrman is now on his way to Los Angeles, but Arthur is not sure where he will dock.

Johnny and Arthur drive to Burrman's office and Johnny notices a vault in the wall of the office. Johnny meets Mr. Corello and he gives Arthur a revision to the policy to exclude the Calabar Diamond, which has been sold. Corello tells Johnny that the boat is due in San Pedro tonight, and Johnny arranges to go with Corello to meet the boat. The phone rings and Corello learns that the *Ellen Dear* has sunk in 600 feet of water.

Johnny cabs to Coast Guard headquarters and meets Capt. Barney Thorson. Capt. Thorson tells Johnny that the passengers have been rescued and brought to the Coast Guard station. They had received a call and the boat was sinking when they got there. The engine was too big and had broken loose and destroyed the boat. There was a big safe on board and the owner was crying like a baby over the loss. The only thing Burrman saved was two hats, a fishing rod, some nylons and a hat box. Johnny is told that the Burrman's are staying at the Beverly Wilshire hotel.

Johnny calls the police in Mazatlan to make sure the jewels were on board when they left. Johnny then cabs back to Burrman's office and the Burrmans have not been there, but they are due in soon, and have asked for claim forms to be brought in.

Johnny gets a wild idea about something that happened when the *Andrea Doria* sank, the passengers were brought in without going through customs. Johnny wonders that if he could think of it, maybe Burrman could too.

Johnny calls Capt. Thorson who tells Johnny that the Burrman's did not go through customs. Johnny calls Arthur and tells him to get to Burrman's office to make sure that Burrman does not bring in the jewels, and to keep him there as long as possible.

Johnny goes to the hotel and watches Burrman leave, and then goes to his suite on the 9th floor. Vi Burrman opens the door, and she tells Johnny to leave, as Randy does not want anyone in the apartment. Johnny tells her that Garcia Hernandez sent him and she lets Johnny in.

Johnny tells her that Randy had sold Hernandez the wrong stone, and she tells Johnny that Randy gave Hernandez the diamond so he could make a legitimate looking change to the policy. Johnny tells her that he has to switch the diamonds when Randy gets there. Johnny tells her about the other diamonds in the hatbox and she asks if Johnny had read about the Andrea Doria just like Randy did.

Vi starts to wise up and Johnny forces his way into the apartment to search it and threatens to call the police if she continues to scream. Vi tells Johnny the jewels are in the closet and Johnny gets them. There is a knock at the door and Burrman tells Vi to open it.

Johnny opens the door and tells Burrman who he is and why he is there. Burrman pulls a gun and threatens to kill Johnny and Vi, "that dizzy blonde". Vi runs out with a bottle and hits Burrman with it as he tries to shoot her.

"Remarks: By way of getting off as easily as possible, Vi sang like a canary and incidentally cleared up a couple of other of his shady deals. Result, by the time his prison term runs out, he'll be too long dead to collect the insurance on his yacht."

Notes:
- The Star of Capetown diamond and the Kamandu Emerald are mentioned in the story. The Star of Capetown was featured in the five-part program *The Star of Capetown Matter*, broadcast on 7/16 through 7/20/1956.
- This is an AFRTS program that contains a story about the economies of democratic countries.
- $245 was spent for a couple of days of relaxation in the California sun. Now that is padding the expense account!
- The *Andrea Doria* was an Italian ocean liner built in Genoa and launched in 1951. On Wednesday, July 25th 1956 she collided with the *MV*

Stockholm near Nantucket, Massachusetts and 46 passengers and 5 crewmen were killed.
- This story was used for an audition program for potential sponsors. See the Auditions in Volume III.
- Dan Cubberly is the announcer.
- Music supervision is by Amerigo Marino.

Producer:	Jack Johnstone	Writer:	Jack Johnstone
Cast:	Virginia Gregg, Lawrence Dobkin, Howard McNear, Jay Novello, Jack Edwards, Barney Phillips, Raymond Burr		

♦ ❖ ♦

Show: **The Desalles Matter**
Show Date: 1/13/1957
Company: **Continental Insurance & Trust Company**
Agent: **Hillary Fuchs**
Exp. Acct: **$416.00**

Synopsis: Hillary Fuchs calls Johnny and asks how his time is? Hillary has a claim for a $100,000 straight life policy he wants investigated. He is afraid that they will be taken this time.

Johnny notes that everyone has heard of Dave Desalles, the industrialist. Johnny meets with Hillary Fuchs in his office and has two drinks with Hillary who tells Johnny that he is not going to give $100,000 to anyone.

Desalles drowned four days ago on the west coast. The policy is designed for people with big money who look at it for the accident-double-indemnity features. Desalles bought one of these policies three months ago, and now he is dead. Hillary is not sure that it was an accident, and the widow has filed a claim. The inquest in San Medio was inconclusive, as was the police investigation.

Bert Kenyon was assigned to the case and has recommended paying the claim. Johnny is to go out and reinvestigate the accident.

Johnny flies to Los Angeles, California and meets Bert in the airport. Johnny muses over having worked with Bert before on the San Antonio case in New Orleans, and how he seems nervous now.

Bert and Johnny drive to the hotel and Johnny tells Bert that Hillary does not like the report he submitted. Bert tells Johnny that the widow is worth $8 million, and that Desalles had bought the policy at the racetrack because his agent had given him a tip on a horse. Bert is insistent that the widow does not need the money and is nervous about why Johnny was sent out to help him.

Johnny gets a room in San Medio, and goes over the reports and meets with Mrs. Desalles who tells Johnny that she and her husband were on their boat having drinks with friends, and Dave had gone up for some air. A Mr. Burke came looking for Dave and was told he was on the deck. They went up to find Dave's hat floating in the water. They looked around and found Dave's body in the water. They tried artificial respiration, but to no avail.

Back in his room, Johnny is visited by Bert while reading the reports and Johnny tells Bert that the wife had help killing Desalles, as Desalles was an ex channel-swimmer and could have easily made it to shore. And why did he not yell? And suppose that the bruises on his head were there before he was in the water.

Johnny suggests getting and exhumation and Bert tells Johnny that Mrs. Desalles offered him the $100,000 to let the case go. Bert tells Johnny that Desalles means nothing to them, and Bert offers to split the money with Johnny. Bert pulls his gun and slugs Johnny. Johnny tries to get up but can only watch Bert leave before he faints.

Johnny slowly wakes up and thinks about Bert and how there is no way that he will collect the money. There is a knock at the door and two men are there. One is named Blair and the other is Sgt. LaFreeda. They ask Johnny why he is in town and if the has a license for his gun.

Johnny tells him who he is and about the case he is working on. They ask where Bert is and Johnny tells them that he had last seen Bert last a couple hours ago. Blair asks Johnny what is new on the case? They think that Johnny is there because there is something new on the case. They tell Johnny that Bert is dead and they go to the site of Bert's killing.

Blair asks a witness name Posey if he has ever seen Johnny, and he tells Blair that he has not, and then Blair and Johnny drive off. Blair tells Johnny that Posey heard shots and then saw Bert staggering in the road. Johnny tells Blair that he and Bert have not been friends for three hours.

Johnny buys coffee for Lt. George Blair who apologizes for being so hard on him in his room. Lt. Blair asks Johnny for help. He tells Johnny that his deputies are incompetent and had messed up the crime scene by hitting Desalles head on the dock while they were recovering the body.

Lt. Blair is sure that Desalles was murdered. The coroner runs a drug store and would tell you, with enough scotch, that a man was dead. Bert Kenyon's going along with the coroner's report confuses Lt. Blair. Johnny tells him that Bert had sold out and about the covered-over reports which Johnny was sent out to look into.

Johnny and Lt. Blair drive to the Desalles home and tell the butler to tell Mrs. Desalles that the police are there. Sgt. LaFreeda is there and he is upset that Johnny is giving assistance in the case, so Lt. Blair sends him home.

Lt. Blair gives Johnny his gun and tells Johnny that Tom was the first one there on the night of the killing. Lt. Blair and Johnny walk into Mrs. Desalles bedroom to find her crying and beaten up.

She tells them that Tom beat her and had helped her get rid of her husband. He beat her because he did not want her to talk to anyone.

Tom comes back in and opens fire on Lt. Blair and Johnny, but Johnny gets him. Lt. Blair tells Johnny that he thinks that all the "knickknacks" in the Desalles home were an enticement to Tom.

Johnny calls Hillary and tells him of the events, buys flowers for Bert and has a drink with George Blair.

Notes:
- This is an AFRTS program that contains a story about the origins of democracy.
- Hillary Fuchs was also the agent in *The Tears of Night Matter.*
- Dan Cubberly is the announcer.
- Music supervision is by Amerigo Marino.

Producer:	Jack Johnstone Writer: John Dawson
Cast:	Virginia Gregg, Harry Bartell, John Stephenson, Will Wright, James McCallion, Ben Wright

♦ ❖ ♦

Show:	**The Blooming Blossom Matter**
Show Date:	**1/20/1957**
Company:	**Inter-Allied Insurance Company**
Agent:	**Paul Brannon**
Exp. Acct:	**$61.55**

Synopsis: Paul Brannon calls and tells Johnny that he has troubles. Alfred W. Winkler has disappeared with an emerald worth $100,000. Well? Sure.

Johnny cabs to Paul Brennan's office and is told that Winkler was a partner in a New York jewelry firm. They got a hold of a stone called the Green Eye of Calcutta, it is big enough to choke a horse. The stone is insured for $100,000 and Winkler is insured for $10,000. Winkler took the stone home to work on in preparation for a show in Chicago.

His partner tried to call him on Sunday, but there was no answer. He went to the office but the stone and Winkler were not there. The police called him while he was there and they are looking for Winkler too. The apartment manager had called them after the maid found Winkler's apartment ransacked. Sgt. Randy Singer has been assigned to the case.

Johnny returns home to pack and is called by Wilbert McKenworthy Blossom, who is pleased that he will be working with Johnny. Blossom follows all of Johnny's cases on the radio and the newspapers and is Johnny's biggest fan. He is calling about Winkler and Blossom will be waiting for Johnny in New York at 875 East 73rd street.

Johnny travels to New York City and the brownstone home of Mr. Blossom who is expecting Johnny. The inside of the home is filled with Victorian furniture, old books and all sort of old junk, "you never can tell when you might need something" Johnny is told. Interspersed among the junk are priceless art works. Blossom tells Johnny that he bought them all at auction sales, he cannot resist a bargain.

Blossom tells Johnny that he knows Winkler very well and has seen him at his office. Blossom tells Johnny that he was going to go to an auction on Saturday but did not feel well and stayed home. A friend sent him something from the auction that will solve the case for Johnny. The item is an old trunk. Blossom tells Johnny he wanted to call the police but called Johnny instead.

Johnny opens the trunk, finds a body inside, and calls Randy Singer. Randy arrives with the lab crew and interrogates Blossom to get the names of the friends who were going to the auction with him.

Johnny cabs to the apartment of Elwood Bluett, the partner of Winkler. Elwood tells Johnny that Winkler often took jewels home with him as he felt it was safer. Bluett tells Johnny that Mr. Blossom was in the office often looking at the jewelry, but he never bought any. Blossom was last there on Friday and insisted on seeing the emerald.

Johnny calls Randy and is told that nothing has turned up with Blossom's friends who went to the auction. Johnny tells Randy he is going to the Winkler house, and wants a picture of the trunk, and wants Blossom watched. Johnny goes to Winkler's apartment and the officer guarding the house tells Johnny that Randy is on the phone. Randy tells Johnny that someone has attacked Blossom and beaten him.

Johnny cabs to 18th Precinct headquarters and meets with Randy, who tells Johnny about Blossom getting beaten. Johnny gets the picture of the trunk and the names of the friends from Randy. Johnny wonders who killed Winkler and then shipped the body to Blossom.

Johnny cabs to the offices of the railroad in New Jersey and talks to a Mr. McKenny about their auctions of unclaimed baggage. McKenny remembers the auction and Johnny shows him the names on the list, but none had been there. McKenny remembers selling the trunk to a man named Albert Winkler.

Johnny cabs back to Randy's office and learns that the prints from Blossom's attack belong to a "Carlo Bernasconi", who was in on a hijacking a couple years ago and drove the truck. He is being held, and Randy is sure that he killed Winkler and beat up Blossom.

Johnny calls McKenny who gives a detailed description of the man he sold the trunk to. Johnny and Randy talk to Bernasconi, and they learn that he delivered a trunk for Winkler and gives him a description, but he never saw Blossom, and just left the trunk in the lobby. He heard about the missing stone and went back to Blossom's to look for the rock but was scared off by a prowl car.

Johnny cabs back to Blossom and tells him that he can help him. Johnny reviews the facts with him, about the house full of junk and fine things, and that Johnny was told that Blossom would do anything to own the emerald. Blossom had reached the same conclusion. When Blossom learned that Inter-Allied was involved, it would be smart for the killer to bring Johnny in as a cover-up, wouldn't it?

Johnny tells Blossom that the body was packed in old newspapers, the kind the house is full of. Johnny tells him that Winkler was a small man, but the man that bought the trunk and ordered it delivered had thick old-fashioned glasses and Blossom's build. Blossom goes to a box and gives Johnny the emerald. Blossom would have bought the stone if Winkler would have sold it at a bargain price.

"Why? Just this overpowering passion to have things? Maybe, or maybe it was a reaction, a desperate attempt to some way, any way break from a lifetime of lonely, dull, drab loneliness. I dunno, and I'm sorry for, well, the funny little old character who turned killer."

Notes:
- This is an AFRTS program that contains a story about democracy.
- This is the first time where the publication of Johnny Dollar's cases is mentioned.
- Dan Cubberly is the announcer.
- Music supervision is by Jerry Goldsmith.

Producer: Jack Johnstone   Writer: Jack Johnstone
Cast: Howard McNear, Herb Ellis, Herb Vigran, Junius Matthews,
              Herb Butterfield, Frank Gerstle, Johnny Jacobs

♦ ❖ ♦

Show: The Mad Hatter Matter
Show Date: 1/27/1957
Company: Floyds of England
Agent: George Reed
Exp. Acct: $870.40

Synopsis: George Reed calls with a riddle and a blond photographer's model. The model married the former owner of the Preen Hat Company, but she has disappeared and took nothing with her. The riddle is whether Preen told the truth or not about her disappearance.

Johnny cabs to George Reed's office to find George reading a copy of Playmate magazine, where Mrs. Preen, Bridget Randall, is the center attraction. George tells Johnny that Mrs. Preen had been a very successful model, but after she married Preen she retired. Johnny notices that the magazine is the current issue and assumes that the photo is an old one.

George tells Johnny that Mr. Preen is twice her age and has a lot of money and has been living near Los Angeles. Det. Steiner is handling the case, and Preen carries no life insurance on his wife, but her face is insured. She bought a policy while she was modeling and renewed it 10 days before she disappeared. Johnny buys a copy of Playmate and goes home to pack.

Johnny flies to Los Angeles, California and gets a room at the Statler. Johnny calls Det. Steiner and then drives to the Preen home. At the front door, a knockout blond nurse meets Johnny. She tells Johnny that Mr. Preen can see no one, as he is in shock and cannot be disturbed. Mr. Preen calls out and tells Johnny to come in and meet him in the orchid room.

In the heat of the orchid room Preen tells Johnny that he is pollinating his plants. He has over two hundred different varieties. Preen is anxious that Johnny find his wife. Preen tells Johnny that he is not satisfied with the actions of the police and will cooperate totally with Johnny. Preen tells Johnny that his wife disappeared 10 days ago after coming back from their home at Lake Arrowhead. Mr. Preen was in bed when she returned and later that night she was gone. A search of the house turned up nothing. She had said nothing about going out but mentioned that she wanted to go back to Arrowhead the next day. Preen has no idea what happened to her.

On the way out, Johnny feels that something is wrong. Helen, the nurse, tells Johnny that the police feel that his wife's body is buried somewhere on the property. Helen hated the wife and feels that Mr. Preen was a kind man. She tells Johnny that Mrs. Preen would kill herself if anything happened to her face. Mrs. Preen has no friends, and Helen is sure that she is dead. She shows Johnny a set of plastic dental caps and tells Johnny that Mrs. Preen would never leave the house without them. Helen had found them in the garage two days after she disappeared.

Johnny drives back to Los Angeles and suddenly realizes that he had not seen any pictures of Mrs. Preen in the house. Det. Steiner comes to Johnny's room and tells him that the case is sewed up. They have been checking up on Mrs. Preen, and she had been taking a lot of weekend trips. They figure she has a new man and disappeared with him and left her clothes at home because she was too proud to take anything from Preen.

Johnny tells Steiner about the dental caps. Steiner shows him her dental records and tells Johnny that they are going to arrest Webster Preen for murder.

Johnny calls Playmate Magazine and asks Mr. Howitt about the picture of Bridget Randall Preen in the current issue. Howitt tells Johnny that Russell Tracy, who lives in Lake Arrowhead, took the picture in the magazine. Johnny drives to Lake Arrowhead and asks the post office about Tracy's address, which turns out to be right next to the Preen house.

Johnny drives to Tracy's house and meets with him. Johnny asks about the picture in the magazine and Russell tells Johnny that all he did was take pictures of Bridget and has no reason to kill her. When Johnny asks him why he thinks she is dead, Russell opens up and tells Johnny that Bridget loved to model, and when she found out that he was a photographer, she was always visiting him.

He had been in trouble with the law once and needed money. He had the picture of Bridget and sold it to the magazine without her knowledge. Other photographers called the house and Preen answered one of the calls. Preen wanted to get back at him and killed his wife and threw her body in an old well on his property. He moved the body before the police got there. Preen killed her because she loved Russell and was going to divorce Preen. Johnny tells Russell to bring his camera and film and they go to the gravesite.

Johnny calls Los Angeles and then picks up Russell and they drive back to town. Johnny calls Helen and learns that Det. Steiner has arrested Preen, but he was released two hours later. Johnny tells her to stay there and keep out of the way, as he is on his way over.

Johnny drives to the Preen house after leaving Russell with Det. Steiner. Helen offers to fix Johnny dinner as he goes up to see Mr. Preen. Johnny meets Preen in the hothouse and tells him that he has something just as beautiful as his orchids and shows him pictures of his dead wife.

Preen tells Johnny that he had to kill her as she was going to leave him, like everyone else has. He could not let her go.

Johnny notes that Preen had removed all the pictures of his wife from the house after he killed her. One photograph caused his death, the others put him away for the rest of his life.

Notes:
- This is an AFRTS program that contains a story about democracy and farmers.
- Dan Cubberly is the announcer.
- Music supervision is by Amerigo Marino.

Producer: Jack Johnstone Writer: Charles B. Smith
Cast: Parley Baer, G. Stanley Jones, Charlotte Lawrence, Forrest Lewis, Stacy Harris, Russell Thorson

♦ ❖ ♦

Show: **The Kirbey Will Matter**
Show Date: **2/3/1957**
Company: **Tri-State Life & Casualty Insurance Company**
Agent: **Danny Newcum**
Exp. Acct: **$331.25**

Synopsis: Buster Favor calls Johnny from Lake Mohave Resort. Do you remember Mike Kirbey, the guide? Buster tells Johnny that Mike has died, and Buster thinks it was murder.

Johnny makes reservations to fly to Las Vegas and gets a handful of American Express Travelers Checks. Danny Newcomb calls and wants Johnny to work on a case, but Johnny tries to turn the case down until he learns that it is at Lake Mohave Resort.

Johnny flies to Las Vegas and gets there at 7 a.m. and comments on the cacophony of the casinos at that hour. Johnny rents a car and drives to Lake Mohave Resort and meets Buster Favor, who is sure that it was murder.

Johnny is told that Mike Kirbey owned a string of restaurants and retired a few years ago and settled down here to go fishing. He often acted as a guide, but usually forgot to charge for his services. About six months ago he transferred title to all of his property to the resort, he did not like his relatives, as they were just waiting for him, to die to get his money. He also paid Buster $10,000 for rent on his cabin for as long as he lived.

Last Friday a rental boat came in and reported finding Mike dead beside his boat. Buster and Ham went out and found him, and Ham saw a rattlesnake bite mark on his leg. Chief Harding was called and he agreed about the snakebite. Buster felt that something was wrong, as there are not too many rattlers in that part of the country because of the heat.

Buster tells Johnny that he went back to the spot and could not find anything that Mike could have hit his head on, or signs of a snake trail. Buster noticed where another boat had been beached, and how Mike looked as though he had been rolled out of a boat. Buster tells Johnny that the relatives will be there soon.

Miss Martha Woodbury arrives and announces her presence as "primary heir" and expresses her desire to have the will read as soon as possible. Johnny asks her about her job, and she tells Johnny that she teaches toxicology at Armond College. Chester Kirbey, the "heir to the fortune" arrives, and then Henry Kirbey the black sheep of the family arrives. The only one missing is Lolita LaVerne, Martha's sister, who is a nightclub dancer. Chester is a playboy and a gambler according to Martha. Hank is a roust-about at circuses and carnivals. He is working at a rare animal show now and is in charge of the snake pit.

Chief Harding calls and tells Johnny and Buster that the venom was injected into the armpit and that the fang marks were fakes. Johnny asks him to determine if the venom was injected before or after Kirbey died. Buster arranges for rooms and Johnny tells them all to stay put.

Buster and Johnny go back up the lake and reminisce about the Midas Touch Matter. Buster sees a boat in the landing where Mike's boat was, and then bullets start hitting their boat.

Buster and Johnny return to the landing and confirm that the three heirs are still there. Buster tells Henry that the Kingman operator has not been able to reach his party. Henry tells them that he was trying to call Lita, and she is on her way.

Johnny calls Armond College, and confirms that Martha had left last night, Chester's private club verified he had been there when Mike was killed, and the carnival where Hank worked said he had been there, and Lita had not missed a show in weeks.

Johnny realizes that the other boat came from Cottonwood Landing and calls them to learn that they had rented a boat to a Lucy Hancock on Friday.

Lawyer Gilford arrives and the heirs assemble for the reading. Gilford tells them that the estate is valued at $10,000 that has been transferred to the resort. The rest of his estate was converted to cash years ago. There is an insurance policy for $5,000 meant to cover burial expenses.

In the will, Mike Kirbey has carefully spent every dollar he has ever owned. Martha wishes that Lucy, Lucy Hancock Woodberry, had been there to see them make fools of themselves.

Johnny leaves and acts on a hunch. He tells Buster to change the number of Chester's room to his on the register, and then goes to wait in his room. After midnight a car arrives and Johnny hears feminine footsteps approaching. A woman enters his room and calls him darling and tells him he was stupid to shoot at the boat and that the police will never find the needle she used as it is at the bottom of the lake. Johnny turns on the lights and Lita screams and tries to leave, but Buster stops her from leaving.

"Yeah, all four of them had wanted to see old Mike dead, but Hank the only honest working man of the lot didn't have the brains. Martha wouldn't have used the means that tied in with her toxicology work and probably didn't have the nerve. So, Chet, who lived by his wits, and Lita who was a real cheap no account, well the courts will take good care of them. And I still have to chuckle over poor old Mike's will, 'Being of sound mind, I have spent all my money.'"

Notes:
- This is an AFRTS program that contains a story about democracy and how it effects the lives of everyone.
- The script title page for this program has "Kirbey's" with the "'s" typed over with "xx".
- Dan Cubberly is the announcer.
- Music supervision is by Amerigo Marino.

Producer: Jack Johnstone   Writer: Jack Johnstone
Cast: Virginia Gregg, Barney Phillips, Shirley Mitchell, Stacy Harris, Carleton Young, Forrest Lewis, Frank Nelson, John Dehner

◆ ❖ ◆

Show: The Templeton Matter
Show Date: 2/10/1957
Company: Mid-Eastern Indemnity Corporation
Agent: Lud Barlow
Exp. Acct: $413.28

Synopsis: Lud Barlow calls and tells Johnny that he is in a pinch. The Templeton House was robbed last night and they have a $100,000 loss. Johnny is going to check on the plane situation, but Lud tells him to rush to hangar 12 at the airport, he is chartering a plane for him.

Johnny cabs to hangar 12 where a twin-engine Bonanza is being fueled. Lud Barlow is there and gives Johnny all the necessary paperwork. Lud tells Johnny that Templeton House is the biggest jewelry house in Boston and was burgled during the night, and that Mid-Eastern has a blanket policy. Lud tells Johnny to see Lt. Roebuck as the engines start.

In Boston, Massachusetts Johnny gets a room at the Independence Hotel and goes to Templeton House. The police are there and Johnny meets Lt. Roebuck, who is watching the ambulance crew working on an injured man.

The man was a special patrolman who must have walked into the robbery. When the ambulance leaves Johnny is shown where the door was jimmied to get in so that the thieves could open the vault and take the most easily moved things from the safe.

Johnny gets an inventory of the missing goods from Mr. Dorian Templeton. Johnny tells him that the insurance company will pay once the claim is filed, and that recovery is slim. Johnny tells him that whoever pulled the job opened the safe like his front door, and they have probably disappeared by now. Shooting the policeman complicated their getaway. Lt. Roebuck takes Dorian for his statement and tells Johnny that the policeman has died.

The usual gang of suspects is collected, and Johnny buys dinner for Lt. Roebuck who tells him that one of the employees, the janitor named Tabor, has a record, but denies being involved.

Johnny goes to visit Tabor in jail and he tells Johnny that he does not know anything about the robbery. Johnny tells him that he can offer him legal assistance if he can provide information which would incriminate him. Tabor tells Johnny nothing other than he will not get a fair deal from the police. Johnny tells Lt. Roebuck to turn Tabor loose and then follow him.

By the next morning three witnesses to the shooting have been found, but no one saw the killers. A police audit revealed no financial problems and that Dorian Templeton was the only person who had the combination to the vault.

Several days later a check for the full claim is given to Templeton. Lt. Roebuck picks up Johnny and tells him that a man was found in the harbor who was killed with the same gun which killed the police guard.

Johnny goes to the morgue to see the body, which has no labels in the clothing, and the finger prints are sent to Washington. Lud calls and Johnny updates him and tells him that there might be a recovery, but Johnny needs time.

Johnny rents a car and drives to the company that manufactured the vault. Mr. Grantland is standing in a new vault destined for South America. Beauty, strength. That is how he describes the vault. Johnny asks him for the records on the Templeton vault and learns that Mr. Keating had set the final combination, and that Grantland has a record of the combination in his vault, and no one else other than Mr. Templeton has the combination. Johnny asks to see Keating, but that is impossible as Keating is dead.

Later that day Dorian Templeton calls and asks to have lunch with Johnny. Templeton tells Johnny that the previous evening he and Mrs. Templeton had gone to a dinner dance at the country club and noticed a girl with a handbag that was sample stock, and one of those stolen. That morning he got the bag back in a package. Templeton had later learned that the girl was Helen Tabor.

Johnny calls Lt. Roebuck to check on the Tabor tail and then goes to see Tabor. The daughter lets Johnny in and he tells her that he saw her last night at the dance.

When Tabor comes in Johnny tells about Templeton being at the club last night and noticing the bag. Tabor tells Johnny that he borrowed the handbag two days ago and had been borrowing things for two years. He did it whenever his daughter needed something nice, and the goods were always brought back in good shape. He did it so that his daughter would have the best chances, and Johnny tells him he believes him and will not take him in. On the way out, Tabor tells Johnny that the man in the harbor is Billy Kiley from Philadelphia, he used to know him.

Johnny and Lt. Roebuck drive to Kiley's apartment but find nothing. On the way out, the phone rings and Johnny answers. Johnny mumbles some answers to the caller, who knows that he is not Tim, but Johnny recognizes the voice.

Johnny and Lt. Roebuck drive to the Grantland vault plant and are met with shots. Grantland asks Johnny what he is doing there and Johnny tells him he is looking for jewels. Johnny tells him he is alone while Lt. Roebuck circles him. Lt. Roebuck shoots Grantland and he dies before making a statement.

Johnny figures that Grantland opened the vaults with Kiley's help, and that Grantland killed him. The identity of Tim was never discovered.

"Remarks: Put that against the $100,000 the insurance company didn't have to pay off." Lud Barlow calls and tells Johnny that there are no jewels at the plant. Johnny tells him that there is a Grantland vault in the harbor of New York and if Lud hurries over there...Lud suddenly hangs up.

Notes:
- This is an AFRTS program that contains a story about Dr. Tom Dooley.
- This story is a variation on the Edmond O'Brien program *The Eighty-Five Little Minks*, broadcast on 3/14/1950, in which the janitor borrowed a mink coat for his daughter.
- The original program was written by E. Jack Neuman and John Michael Hayes. This story is by John Dawson, an alias of E. Jack Neuman.
- Cast Information from the KNX Collection at the Thousand Oaks Library.
- Dan Cubberly is the announcer.
- Music supervision is by Amerigo Marino.

Producer: Jack Johnstone   Writer: John Dawson
Cast: John Dehner, Peter Leeds, Vic Perrin, James McCallion,
              Stacy Harris, Virginia Gregg, Marvin Miller

◆ ❖ ◆

Show: **The Golden Touch Matter**
Show Date: **2/17/1957**
Company: **Providential Life & Casualty**
Agent: **Steve Kilmer**
Exp. Acct: **$240.00**

Synopsis: Steve Kilmer calls Johnny from New York City. Steve has a report about the death of Mrs. Martha Mayfield Merryman "the girl with the golden touch". Steve has a $500,000 policy on Mrs. Merryman and wants Johnny to investigate how she died. Johnny is told that Mrs. Merryman holds a controlling interest in "Consolidated Tire and Rubber Co."

Johnny trains to New York and goes to the residence of Mrs. Merryman, only to find her alive and kicking, and the perpetrator of many a practical joke. Johnny is told that the report of her death is false but has touched off a steep decline in the value of the company stock, which is being bought up for a song. When Mrs. Merryman hears this, she falls into a dead faint and winds up in the hospital.

Her hospitalization causes the price of the Consolidated stock to drop even further. Johnny wonders if this was all the work of "the Syndicate" which has been trying to acquire the Consolidated stock? Maybe it was Mrs. Merryman's son, Edgar?

Johnny discovers that Mrs. Merryman has been merrily buying up all the devalued stock to stop a takeover by "the syndicate."

Johnny reports that Mrs. Merryman now owns her company, that she and her son are on good terms and actually worked together to pull off the stunt.

And to celebrate, Mrs. Merryman and Johnny go out and paint the town red. The matter is closed, and changed names mean no problems with the Securities commission.

Notes:
- Music Direction is by Amerigo Marino.
- The announcer is Dan Cubberly.
- Story information obtained from the KNX Collection in the Thousand Oaks Library.

Producer:	Jack Johnstone	Writer:	Jack Johnstone
Cast:	Virginia Gregg, Lucille Meredith, Lillian Buyeff, Forrest Lewis, Herb Butterfield, Edgar Barrier, Chester Stratton		

♦ ❖ ♦

Show:	**The Meek Memorial Matter**
Show Date:	3/3/1957
Company:	**Assured Equity & Trust Company**
Agent:	**Max Green**
Exp. Acct:	**$98.30**

Synopsis: Max Green calls and wonders where Johnny has been for the past twenty minutes. "I was in the shower" Johnny tells Max. "For twenty minutes?" "Ok, so I'm a shiny dollar!" Ugh! Max quotes the Gettysburg address and asks if Johnny knows about the Meeks. Mariah Meek has lost her copy and it might cost them $100,000.

Johnny cabs to Max's office where he asks Johnny how many words are in the Gettysburg Address; the answer is 268. Two drafts only have 266, with the two words "under God" added at the time of the speech. Mrs. Meek has a copy without the two words and it is insured for $100,000. It was bought from Jason Penrod and has been kept under glass in the Meek Memorial. Max tells Johnny that he is going to run newspaper ads and a reward to try and recover the document. Max tells Johnny that some people would keep the document in a safe, just for pride of possession.

Johnny cabs back home and then travels to New Bedford, Massachusetts and gets a room. Johnny calls Mrs. Meek, who arranges for a car to pick Johnny up. There is a knock at the door and someone asks for "Mr. J".

Johnny opens the door and the man tells Johnny he got the wrong room. Johnny watches the man and then travels to the Meek home, and is met on the stairs by Paul Meek, the grandson of Mrs. Meek.

Paul and his wife Janet, who is having another drink, tell Johnny that Mrs. Meek is blind. Paul wonders how Johnny is going to find the document, and Janice is concerned about the money that the old woman is spending.

Paul and Johnny go up to Mrs. Meek's room where Martha wants to speak with Johnny alone. Martha wants to know when Johnny is going to arrest the crook that took the document. She tells Johnny that only the guard was there, and he got hit on the head that night. The memorial is not open to the public.

Mr. Penrod was there on the night of the theft discussing business. He is probably either in his room or in the memorial. Mrs. Meek asks Johnny for a cigarette. When Johnny asks about her son and daughter-in-law she asks if Johnny suspects them, and he tells Mrs. Meek that he suspects everyone, including her. "Well, bless you boy!" she tells Johnny.

Johnny speaks with Pete Vesuvio the guard, who knows his history by reading the documents in the memorial. Pete offers to repeat the Gettysburg Address to Johnny, he knows it by heart and learned it from the president's own writing.

Johnny then meets with Mr. Penrod in the memorial. He is taking inventory of the things Mrs. Meek cannot see. Penrod tells Johnny that he was there on the night of the theft and was the one who discovered the manuscript was missing. Mrs. Meek has given out too many keys to the memorial in his opinion. Penrod tells Johnny that Mrs. Meek had asked him to come up and take inventory. Johnny asks Penrod if he had stolen the document, how would he sell it. Penrod tells Johnny that he would sell it in Europe. He also tells Johnny that Paul and Janice are going to Paris in a few days.

Johnny goes to the house and Paul tells him that they have flight reservations to Paris, but he is not sure they are going to go. They have friends there, so it will not cost too much to live there, and they will pay for it when they get back, fly now pay later Janice calls it. Janice thinks that Mrs. Meek is using her heart condition to keep Paul there.

Johnny goes to his hotel and wires Max to check into the Meek's finances and then gets a phone call from a man calling about the ad in the paper about something missing from a memorial. He tells Johnny to meet him in the alley behind the Borne Whaling Museum, alone.

Johnny cabs to the museum and finds a man curled up dead in the alley. It was the man who had knocked on his door. Johnny calls the police and goes back to the hotel to ask who had his room before he got there. Johnny shows the clerk a $5 bill and the clerk shows Johnny the register. Johnny recognizes the name, and files it away until he finds some proof.

Johnny goes back to the Meek house and meets with Janice who tells him that Mrs. Meek is ill, and not expected to live and she wants to see Johnny. Pete is with Mrs. Meek and she asks Pete to finish quoting the Gettysburg Address.

Pete leaves and Mrs. Meek tells Johnny that she lied to him. She is broke and only has the house and the memorial. Mr. Penrod is going to purchase the memorial and is evaluating the contents.

Johnny leaves and asks Pete why he lied to him about learning the address from the original document. When Pete protests, Johnny tells him that he was just testing him. Johnny tells Paul that he knows which one of them stole the document, and that one of them hired Leo Jones to help them. Leo had called Johnny because he did not like the deal he was getting but one of you killed him.

Johnny asks Penrod if he was trying to blackmail Leo, because he came to the hotel room looking for him. Johnny tells Penrod that he switched copies of the address document after Mrs. Penrod started losing her sight and closed the museum. Pete had learned from the document that had been switched after the sale. Penrod pulls a gun, and Pete lunges for him to protect the family and Penrod shoots him. Pete tells them to tell Mrs. Meek he is a much better guard now.

"Pete Vesuvio will live to apply for his second papers, and in time probably will open a spaghetti joint in New Bedford. Penrod will be tried for murder. As yet he hasn't disclosed the name of the person who purchased the stolen manuscript, but in time I'm sure he will. As for the Meeks, well Mariah passed on later that night, but as she said, there was nothing left for her, but to rest."

Notes:
- This is an AFRTS program.
- On several occasions Mrs. Meek is called Mariah. When Johnny first meets her, he calls her Martha. Also, Paul describes himself as a grandson, but later Johnny asks Mrs. Meek about Paul, her son.
- Based on the Library of Congress web site, there are several different versions of the speech, some of which do not include the phrase "under God" as noted in the story.
- Cast Information from the KNX Collection at the Thousand Oaks Library.
- Dan Cubberly is the announcer.
- Music supervision is by Amerigo Marino.

Producer:	Jack Johnstone	Writer:	Charles B. Smith
Cast:	Lawrence Dobkin, Marvin Miller, Bert Holland, Virginia Gregg, Peggy Webber, Jack Moyles, Hans Conried		

♦ ❖ ♦

Show: The Suntan Oil Matter
Show Date: 3/10/1957
Company: Surety Mutual & Trust Company
Agent: Dave Lawler
Exp. Acct: $474.84

Synopsis: Dave Lawler calls and asks if Johnny owns sunglasses and some real loud sport shirts? Johnny tells him his are so loud he has to keep them in a sound proof drawer. Dave tells Johnny he is going where "the summer spends the winter", Palm Springs. Johnny tells Dave this will be expensive and Dave tells Johnny it will cost $75,000 unless he can prove the bracelet Dan Galloway gave to his child-bride wasn't really stolen. Johnny tells him that, for a trip to Palm Springs at this time of year, he can prove anything.

Johnny flies to Palm Springs, California and registers at the La Casa de Paz Hotel, and then goes to lunch with Det. Sgt. Lacey. Sgt. Lacey tells Johnny that he doubts that the bracelet was stolen. Dan Galloway is drilling down by the Salton Sea, he figures that if there is oil in the Gulf of Mexico salt domes, there is oil under the Salton Sea, which is all salt deposits.

Sgt. Lacey does not know how Dan can afford the jewelry, or the expensive Italian sports car she got two weeks ago. Roberta, his wife, is much younger that Dan by about 35-40 years, and there is talk about their relationship. There is talk of her and Sonny Wyman who is about her age and a playboy who always has something intriguing to interest his rich friends. This season it is Italian sports cars, Cosmo Romas they are called.

Johnny rents a car and drives to the Galloway house and sees a sports car in the driveway. The houseboy gets his name and takes him to see Mrs. Galloway. On the Lanai, she cannot tell Johnny anything about the bracelet other than it was stolen. She asks Johnny how he will recover the bracelet, and Johnny tells her that they might offer a reward. She asks Johnny how much he will get, and he tells her 10-30%. Johnny hears a door close and then the sound of a loud car leaving, but Roberta hears nothing.

Johnny drives back to town to meet with Wilhoit van Hooke the jeweler but is stopped on the street by Sonny Wyman in his sports car. Sonny tells Johnny that he must have heard him out at Roberta's and offers to sell him a Cosmo Roma. Sonny offers to help and tells Johnny that he sold van Hooke a Cosmo just like his. They are going to be in a rally next weekend. He also offers to take Johnny to see Dan Galloway.

Johnny meets with van Hooke and gets a complete set of records on the bracelet. Van Hooke tells Johnny that the bracelet was an exception to what he normally carries and had ordered it on consignment.

He asks Johnny to keep it quiet that Dan had come in and asked for cash and wanted him to refund the money on the bracelet, but van Hooke did not have the money as he had paid off some overdue bills. Dan needed money for his test well, something had broken on the rig necessitating a costly repair job. Berta probably does not even know about the well, and Dan has competition.

Sonny drives Johnny to the well site in his Cosmo Roma and tells Johnny that there is talk about him and Berta. There is nothing serious, they just have fun together. The house is always open, so anyone could have taken the bracelet. Sonny tells Johnny that recovered stolen jewelry usually gets a reward of 20 cents on the dollar, but Johnny tells him sometimes it gets you twenty years.

Sonny tells Johnny that the car business is great and he is going to work on the race course for this weekend. Van Hooke is quite a racing fan, and they are running a match race on Saturday.

Sonny drops Johnny at the drilling site office where Johnny meets Mrs. Flora Galloway, the first and former Mrs. Galloway. She has been waiting for three hours and is upset about $18,000 in back alimony. Johnny tells her the gun in her handbag will not help. She tells him that killing would be too good for Dan, so Johnny takes the gun from her. They drive to the well in her car and find Dan Galloway in the road, run over several times by a car.

Johnny calls Sgt. Lacey and drops Flora off at the Galloway house with Roberta. Sgt. Lacey tells Johnny that whoever ran over Galloway did it several times. Sgt. Lacey thinks that Flora might have run him down, but Johnny reminds him that the tires on her car do not match the tracks. Officer Levine calls and tells them that the tire prints match those on Sonny Wyman's car, so Sgt. Lacey orders Sonny picked up.

Johnny and Sgt. Lacey drive to Roberta's, and they learn that Sonny has not been there. There is a phone call for Sgt. Lacey and he is told that Wyman has been found. His car ran over a cliff and he is dead.

Johnny and Sgt. Lacey go to the site of the wreck and Johnny notices that the car looks as though it had been sideswiped, but Sgt. Lacey notices that there is no paint on the fender, and Johnny tells him he is wrong if the car was sideswiped by a car of the same color.

Johnny finds a phone and calls several jewelers in Los Angeles. After several calls, Johnny asks a Mr. Mencken if he had shipped a bracelet to van Hooke. He tells Johnny that he had sent three bracelets, but he sent two back immediately and the last one last Thursday.

Johnny and Sgt. Lacey drive to van Hooke's ranch. On the way, Johnny tells Sgt. Lacey that the paint on the two cars matched, which is why Lacey had seen nothing. Also, van Hooke had told Johnny he used the money from Galloway to pay off his bills, but he also bought an $8,000 sports car. Van Hooke had seen Johnny drive off with Sonny, so he had to cover his tracks and must have killed Galloway.

At the ranch the police surround the house. They hear a car start up and call to van Hooke to turn off the car. He speeds out through the garage doors and gets away.

Johnny and Sgt. Lacey follow along the main road. Sgt. Lacey spots van Hooke trying to squeeze through two trucks, but, as Johnny notes, "he squeezed through alright. Squeezed right through the pearly gates.

"Remarks: Well, justice is done in pretty strange ways is sometimes. Kinda makes you think. Maybe it pays to tread the straight and narrow, doesn't it?"

Notes:
- Johnny makes note of his commission on recovered jewelry, which ranges from ten to thirty percent. On this case alone, that would be $7,500 to $22,500   not bad for several days work even today.
- Dan Cubberly is the announcer.
- Music supervision is by Amerigo Marino.

Producer:	Jack Johnstone	Writer:	Paul Franklin
Cast:	Barbara Eiler, Paula Winslowe, Forrest Lewis, Frank Nelson, Sam Edwards, Austin Green, Shepard Menken		

◆ ❖ ◆

Show: **The Clever Chemist Matter**
Show Date: 3/17/1957
Company: **Philadelphia Mutual Life & Casualty Insurance Company**
Agent: **Harry Branson**
Exp. Acct: $84.35

Synopsis: Harry Branson calls and has a case for John. It is somewhat unusual. Harry is apprehensive about one of his clients, Dr. Walter Merrill the scientist and Nobel Prize winner.

Johnny travels to Philadelphia and Harry Branson's office where Harry meets Johnny on the sidewalk. Harry has rented a car so Johnny can drive to New Jersey where Dr. Merrill and his colleague Dr. Theodore Nash have a lab. They are working on some top-secret project, probably missiles or satellites. Dr. Merrill has a $25,000 policy and has made Dr. Nash the beneficiary. Dr. Nash also bought a $10,000 policy and made Merrill his beneficiary. Harry has received a letter of protest from Dr. Merrill's daughter who feels her father has been coerced into changing his policy.

The rental car arrives and Johnny drives to Malaga, New Jersey. At the post office, Johnny gets directions to Wampusbung where Dr. Merrill has a cottage. Johnny is told to announce himself at the gate or he will get shot at.

Johnny drives to the cottage, honks his horn at the gate and Dr. Merrill opens the door. He lets Johnny in and tells Johnny that Dr. Nash is in the lab. Dr. Merrill tells Johnny that they should talk in private, but Dr. Nash comes out and wants to know what is going on.

Johnny tells him he is making a routine check on the insurance policies and Dr. Nash takes Johnny into the lab and tells Merrill to finish his experiment. The molecular balance check is ready, so Dr. Merrill tells them to leave and locks the door to the lab, and Nash bolts the door. Johnny questions it, so Nash says it is force of habit and undoes the bolt.

Johnny tells him that he is there about the change in the policy and Nash tells Johnny that Merrill's daughter is married to a day-laborer that is waiting for him to die. Johnny leaves with the excuse that he needs to get a room, and leaves with the feeling that something is wrong.

Johnny drives back to the cottage and hears someone calling for help and finds the bolt to the lab locked. The door is unlocked and Dr. Nash comes out and tells Johnny that a man beat him and threw acid on him and killed Merrill with a gun.

Johnny calls Dr. Foote, who comes out and Dr. Merrill is pronounced dead. The sheriff is called and he gets the state police. Dr. Foote tells Johnny that Dr. Nash has lost the use of his left eye because of the acid.

Johnny speaks with Dr. Nash who tells Johnny that he saw the man and describes him as a young stocky man with black curly hair and working man's hands. Johnny gives Dr. Nash a drink of water and Nash tells him he tried to stop him but could not. Johnny goes back to the cottage and finds a copy of a wedding picture with a perfect match for the description of the killer, Howard Harding, Dr. Merrill's son-in-law. Johnny thinks about Nash's comments and of the conversation in the doctor's office.

The police arrive and find a .38 Luger that has no prints. No Prints! Johnny rushes back to Dr. Foote's office and picks up the water glass and goes to Harry's office to get the Harding's address and tells Harry to send the glass to Ray Kemper at the Bureau.

Johnny drives to the Harding residence and Mrs. Harding meets him. Johnny tells her who he is, and she tells Johnny that someone is poisoning daddy's mind. Howard is an officer of Columbia Aviation and is off fishing alone today.

She tells Johnny that there is something wrong with Nash. Her father always worked alone and is such an alert, bright-eyed busybody in spite of his age. Johnny tells her that when he saw Dr. Merrill, he seemed to be in a daze.

Howard comes home and tells Johnny that he has heard about him. Howard has been fishing at a private lake near Mount Holly. Johnny tells Howard that he has been identified as Dr. Merrill's killer, but Howard tells Johnny that Nash was the killer. Johnny gets a phone call and Harry tells him that Ray Kemper must see him immediately. Johnny tells Howard to stay put and Johnny goes to see Ray Kemper at the Bureau.

Ray tells Johnny that he found three sets of prints on the glass, Johnny's, Dr. Foote's and those of Theodore Nashevsky, a chemist from one of our not-so-friendly countries who is an expert on explosives. Ray has pictures of Nashevsky and one shows a picture of a boy with a patch on his left eye.

Johnny rushes back to Malaga with an FBI tail. At the state police office Johnny learns that Dr. Nash is in the clear because of Johnny's testimony that he was in the locked lab. At Dr. Foote's office, Johnny gives him some instructions and then goes to talk to Dr. Nash.

Johnny tells Nash that his government does not pay him too well. Dr. Merrill was doing important work and you would have been paid well by your country. Johnny tells him he gave himself away when he reached for the water and did not hesitate because he had lost his sight long ago. Nash tells Johnny that he found him locked in the lab. Johnny tells him he found the cord that was looped over the door, so that it could be locked from the inside. Nash tells him that he could not have, he destroyed it in a vat of acid and Johnny tells him he was bluffing and made a lucky guess.

Nashevsky tries to swallow a capsule but Johnny prevents him and closes his other eye with his knuckles and Nashevsky is saved from Johnny by the police.

"Remarks: Don't beef on this one Harry. The criminal, in spite of being the named beneficiary doesn't get paid."

Notes:
- Ray Kemper was a CBS sound man who worked on a number of programs, including Gunsmoke.
- This is an AFRTS program that contains a story about democracy and free choice.
- Johnny mentions a .38 caliber Luger. I searched the web and found one article noting that there were some Lugers manufactured in .38 caliber but they are very rare. The most common calibers for a Luger are 7.65 mm or 9 mm.
- Dan Cubberly is the announcer.
- Music supervision is by Amerigo Marino.

Producer:	Jack Johnstone	Writer:	Jack Johnstone
Cast:	Virginia Gregg, Harry Bartell, Howard McNear, Forrest Lewis, Jack Kruschen, Russell Thorson, Frank Gerstle, Bob Bruce		

Show:	**The Hollywood Matter**
Show Date:	**3/24/1957**
Company:	**National Marine Indemnity**
Agent:	**Abe Sandstrom**
Exp. Acct:	**$618.45**

Synopsis: Abe Sandstrom calls Johnny and tells him to go to Los Angeles. This is urgent, $1,000,000 urgent.

Johnny goes to Abe's office and Abe asks Johnny if he knows about guarantee policies, also called good faith policies where the insurer acts as a bond for the business venture. Abe tells Johnny that Sidney Sperry, who has been in Hollywood for 25 years, has organized the "Best American" company to make a motion picture. The film has been delayed and he wants his money.

Johnny flies to Los Angeles, and goes to Beverly Hills, California and gets a room at the Beverly Wilshire Hotel. During a downpour, Johnny notes that he always seems to go to Beverly Hills during the rainy season.

Johnny calls Sperry who tells Johnny that he will pick him up for lunch. Johnny buys a copy of Variety and sees a note about the movie. Sperry picks up Johnny and they go to lunch.

Sperry tells Johnny that a man from New York had called about the delay, and he had blamed the weather. The star of the movie is Booth Templeton, but he will not come to the studio. Templeton signed a contract but did not show up. He has made over 300 movies and even his agent cannot get in to see him.

Johnny rents a car and drives to the Templeton house. As the butler goes to get Booth, Johnny spots a woman and a much younger man at the bar. The butler returns and tells Johnny that Mr. Templeton is not there. Johnny asks to see Mrs. Templeton and the woman at the bar tells Johnny that she is Mrs. Templeton and tells Johnny to get out.

Johnny explains who he is and Mrs. Templeton gives Johnny a phone number to call. Johnny leaves and calls the number, but there is no answer. Johnny goes to Sperry's office and tells him about the man at the Templeton house and learns that the boyfriend is named Tyler, and that Templeton puts up with it. Johnny wants to call in the police, but Sperry tells Johnny to find Templeton.

Johnny calls the number, Hollywood 6-2289, and a woman answers. Johnny asks for Templeton, and the woman tells Johnny to come to 1224 Berendo.

Johnny drives to the address and Judith Ford answers the door. She tells Johnny that she is an actress and a good friend, and that Templeton is out getting some food. Templeton is staying there because he has no place else to go. Templeton returns and Johnny tells him why he is there.

Johnny leaves with Templeton and on the drive, Templeton tells Johnny all about his many films, and that his first wife Laura died at 25. They stop for a drink and Templeton tells Johnny that he cannot go back. Johnny and Templeton arrive at his house and Sarah and Tyler are surprised to see him. Templeton tells Johnny that he is 61 and seeking peace. He agrees to go to the studio, and then come back and go to bed while Sarah plays. Templeton tells Johnny that he has been looking for contented moments all his life, but he has not found many.

"Remarks: The advertising notices say that *The Best American* is a smash hit and Templeton's greatest performance and a cinch for an Academy Award. I hope he gets it. I hope he gets something better that what he's got as an excuse for a life."

Notes:
- The announcer is Dan Cubberly.
- Music Direction is by Amerigo Marino.
- Story information obtained from the KNX Collection in the Thousand Oaks Library.

Producer: Jack Johnstone   Writer: John Dawson
Cast: Herb Ellis, Virginia Gregg, Alan Reed, Jay Novello, Carleton Young, Jeanne Tatum, John Dehner

♦ ❖ ♦

Show: **The Moonshine Murder Matter**
Show Date: 3/31/1957
Company: **Philadelphia Mutual life & Casualty Insurance**
Agent: **Harry Branson**
Exp. Acct: **$299.50**

Synopsis: Harry Branson calls Johnny and asks if Johnny knows what Moonshine is. Johnny tells Harry to send him a case and is told that it may cost him $30,000.

Johnny travels to Philadelphia, Pennsylvania where Harry has a bus ticket ready for Johnny to go to Pine Grove, Pennsylvania where Harry has already made reservations for Johnny at the Sterling Hotel. While Johnny tries to remind Harry that he makes his own travel arrangements, Harry rattles on about all of the wonderful adventures Johnny has on his assignments. Harry even tells Johnny that when he took his last vacation, he came into the office to work. Johnny invites Harry to come along to see what it is like on a case. Harry checks with his boss and surprises Johnny by getting authorization to accompany him.

Johnny rents a car and they drive to Pine Grove. Harry tells Johnny that Horace Eckert has a policy for $30,000 and the beneficiary is his daughter Elaine. Horace has had his life threatened but has not called the police because he was a bootlegger a long time ago.

Johnny and Harry have a big dinner in Reading and drive to Piney Grove where they meet Elaine, who recognizes Harry and is very glad to see him. Horace arrives and, after introductions, he tells Johnny and Harry that he has had several car problems, the last of which was loose wheel nuts. Horace has not called the police because he hates them. Horace tells them that he used to make moonshine but has stopped and has been doing good works for the commission.

Horace tells Johnny that Mug Malloy killed a revenue agent and got thirty years and said that he would get even with Horace, and that Elaine has been seeing Al Hartwell. Elaine tells Horace that he really should call in the police and there are shots fired through the window. Elaine tells Johnny that the shots might have been meant for him. When Johnny notes that they might have been meant for Harry, he faints.

Johnny calls the police to try and locate Mug Malloy and tells them about the attempt on "Stoopy Eckert". Johnny is told that Mug is in Frackville, so he drives there and meets Mug's parole officer who tells Johnny that Mug is a miner now and is clean.

Johnny meets Mug and he tells Johnny that he has not heard about Eckert, and admits to having killed the officer, but what is past, is past. Johnny gets a phone call from Harry who tells Johnny that Horace is mad and wants to go after Mug, but Harry is holding a gun on him. Mug tells Johnny that the revenue agent was named Barney Hartwell.

Johnny rushes back to Harry and tells Horace that Mug is not after him. Johnny gets an idea after being told that Al Hartwell is a police officer. Johnny goes to Al's house where Al tells Johnny that his father was killed when he was just a boy, and that he had planned revenge for a long time. He was trying to scare Eckert into killing Malloy. He knew that his father was a cruel man and destined to die, especially for what he did to his mother.

Al's mother enters the room carrying a rifle and tells Johnny that she is not crazy and shoots out the window. She tells Johnny that she did the things to Eckert. She aims the rifle and there are shots, and the gun is shot from her hand.

Harry rushes in and tells Johnny that he had shot the gun from outside the window. When Elaine tells Harry that there is a hole in his coat from the first shot, Harry faints.

Notes:
- **The announcer is Dan Cubberly.**
- **Music Direction is by Amerigo Marino.**
- **Pine Grove and Frackville are both in Eastern Pennsylvania, northeast of Reading.**
- **Story information obtained from the KNX Collection in the Thousand Oaks Library.**

Producer:	Jack Johnstone	**Writer:**	Jack Johnstone
Cast:	Harry Bartell, Virginia Gregg, Will Wright, Herb Butterfield, Bob Bruce, Peggy Webber, Vic Perrin		

Show:	**The Ming Toy Murphy Matter**
Show Date:	4/14/1957
Company:	Floyds of England
Agent:	George Reed
Exp. Acct:	$225.70

Synopsis: George Reed calls and tells Johnny it is a bad morning. Jodiah Gillis has talked them into issuing another special policy. This time it is on an articulate canine, a talking dog. Oh, No!

Johnny cabs to George's office and learns that Iron Mike Murphy is the former owner of the dog. Gillis bought the dog three weeks ago and bought a $7,500 policy on the dog. Johnny wants to refuse the policy as his commission is not worth it, but Gillis wants Johnny. After finding his mouse, Gillis thinks Johnny is a miracle worker. George offers Johnny liberal expenses but Johnny has to find the dog or keep Gillis happy. If he cannot, the auditors will be all over Johnny's expense account. It is a real sucker bet, but Johnny accepts.

Johnny travels to New York City and gets a room at the Statler Hotel. Johnny calls the Gillis number and Marian answers the phone and tells Johnny to come over for the celebration.

Johnny cabs to Marion's apartment on the East River, and she takes Johnny in through the kitchen because her dad wants to see Johnny alone in the den. The celebration is for her engagement to Bill Fisher, who is with the Powers Advertising Agency, and who just talked a client into a new TV show. Bill walks in and meets Johnny and then Josiah walks in and tells Johnny to get to work.

Johnny calls the missing object a dog, and Gillis chews him out, she is a lady, a canine and her name is Ming Toy Murphy. She is a Chinese, er, a Pekinese. She was locked up in the den and disappeared from the apartment. The front door was left open when they got back from breakfast.

Gillis tells Johnny that all dogs can speak, but she can talk! Gillis tells Johnny that Ming Toy will be on a new TV program that is called "The Big Shock". They were looking for a dog that could say "Happy Hollow Dog Food, yum yum yummy!" Gillis was going to take Ming Toy to the studio and claim the $50,000 reward for a dog that could repeat the slogan.

Gillis bought the dog from Murphy before the ad came out because Murphy had told Gillis that the dog could talk. Marian had told Jodiah that Bill had talked the Happy Hollow people into looking for the talking dog for their show. Gillis starts the tape and Johnny hears a dog talking, sort of. Gillis has looked for the dog and posted a reward. Gillis feels that Iron Mike stole the dog back. Mike thinks that Gillis cheated him, which he admits to. Gillis tells Johnny that the window to the den was open, but there is nothing below but the East River.

Johnny cabs to his hotel and next morning gets an appointment to see Iron Mike Murphy. Johnny goes to Marian's apartment to get Gillis and meets the janitor. He tells Johnny that they are out for breakfast. He also tells Johnny that he picks up the trash every morning at nine o'clock. He did not see anyone who did not belong there on the morning the dog disappeared, but he did see

Miss Gillis' future husband carrying a present for her.

Johnny goes down stairs and meets the Gillis's. Johnny asks Marian to go to lunch with him and she suggests "21" at 12:30, and then he and Gillis cab to Iron Mike Murphy's house on Long Island. Mike tells Johnny how Gillis stole a beautiful dog from him and Gillis accuses him of stealing the dog back after the ads appeared. Gillis and Murphy square off at each other and a black eye and bloody nose result.

Johnny goes to "The 21 Club" to meet Marian for lunch. Johnny tells Marian about going to Iron Mike's and is about to tell Marian about meeting Morris the janitor when Bill arrives. Johnny asks Bill about being at Marian's at 9:00 and he swears he was not there.

Johnny leaves and calls Bill's secretary and learns that he had lied. Johnny cabs to his hotel, makes some more calls and waits.

Bill calls and asks Johnny to meet him at a bar where he accuses Johnny of calling his secretary and the agency. Bill tells him that the whole thing was for publicity and the $50,000 was safe, as dogs could not talk. He admits getting rid of the dog. He was going to take her out in the box but ended up throwing the dog out of the window into the river when it made too much noise. After all, it was only a dog.

Johnny calls Marian and, in a park near the apartment, tells her what happened. Johnny hears an ambulance heading towards the apartment and they run there where a policeman tells them that it sounds like a little girl is stuck in a drain. It has to be a girl, as it sounds like she is talking about a dog food being "yum yum yummy". Johnny goes down with the power and light men, stays a minute and then leaves.

Gillis arrives and Johnny takes him down to hear Ming Toy barking and talking. When they get to her, Gillis finds out that Ming Toy has had puppies. "She disappeared to have her family! And she called him Papa! Johnny, I am a grandfather!" Gillis tells Johnny.

"I never did tell Gillis exactly how the dog had been helped out of the apartment, all he knew was that Marian, for reasons of her own, had called off her engagement to Bill. Ming Toy spent a week in bed recovering from her ordeal, and naturally since Gillis refused to allow her to appear on TV that night, the $50,000 went unclaimed. And, alas, the long-suffering public has yet to hear the dulcet tones of a talking dog named Ming Toy Murphy."

Notes:
- **Johnny calls the janitor "Morris", even though he had not told Johnny his name.**
- **Dan Cubberly is the announcer.**
- **Music supervision is by Amerigo Marino.**

Producer:	Jack Johnstone	Writer:	Charles B. Smith
Cast:	Virginia Gregg, G. Stanley Jones, Herb Ellis, Joseph Kearns, Jay Novello, Bill James, Howard McNear		

Show:	The Marley K. Matter
Show Date:	4/21/1957
Company:	Intercoastal Maritime & Life
Agent:	Byron Kay
Exp. Acct:	$81.00

Synopsis: Byron Kay calls Johnny from Boston. "Remember Meg McCarthy?" he asks Johnny. Byron tells Johnny that Meg may not be long for this world, but he is not sure what is wrong.

Johnny flies to Boston and goes to Byron's office to learn that Meg had been calling hourly, but the calls have stopped. Meg is living in Fortescue, New Jersey now and is running a hotel. Meg has a $10,000 policy on her hotel and a $10,000 policy on her life.

Johnny flies to Philadelphia and rents a car. Johnny recounts his other cases with Meg McCarthy as he arrives at Meg's Palace Hotel, a real dive. On the way in Johnny is passed by three men being thrown out. Meg is yelling at them but as soon as Meg sees "her ever lovin' darling boy" she quiets down and is glad to see Johnny. Meg tells Johnny that she has no trouble, but just stopped calling Byron to scare him and get Johnny there.

Meg tells Johnny that Capt. Billy towed in a boat called the *Skate*. The skipper of the boat went to Port Norris while the boat is being repaired. Meg thinks that he is Blackie Harmon, a crook from Cod Harbor. Meg tells Johnny that Blackie lost a boat called the *Marley K* in a storm and was paid $18,000. Meg is sure that the *Skate* is really the *Marley K*.

Johnny and Meg go to look at the *Skate* and find a new paint job and new brass on an old boat and Johnny is able to see the letters "Mar" along the bow. While they are looking, Blackie appears with a gun and his assistant Alec.

Johnny and Meg are put on the boat and told that they are "going for a ride" while Alec starts the engines. Blackie tells Meg that he thinks that she brought Johnny in to get him and tells Johnny that the waters are full of sharks. Meg tries to get up and Blackie hits her causing Johnny to react and get hit as well.

Blackie yells at Alec about the course and tells him that Johnny is going to be thrown overboard. Johnny tries to scare Alec about being involved in murder and Blackie shouts at Alec, allowing Johnny to slug Blackie, who shoots Alec and then knocks Johnny out.

Johnny wakes up tied up in the cabin. Megs tells Johnny that Alec has been thrown overboard. Johnny spots a set of duplicate controls and an engine switch.

Johnny gets up and fakes being dizzy so that he can fall on the switch and kill the engine. Blackie comes in and aims his gun at Johnny, causing Meg to give him a body slam. Blackie falls to the deck and Johnny kicks him several times. Blackie is tied up and Meg drives the boat back to port.

"Remarks: Meg should get a couple of grand for the return of the *Marley K*."

Notes:
- The announcer is Dan Cubberly.
- Music Direction is by Amerigo Marino.
- Story information obtained from the KNX Collection in the Thousand Oaks Library.

Producer: Jack Johnstone   Writer: Jack Johnstone
Cast: Byron Kane, Virginia Gregg, Vic Perrin, Ben Wright

♦ ❖ ♦

Show: **The Melancholy Memory Matter**
Show Date: **4/28/1957**
Company: **Providential Assurance Company**
Agent: **Bert McGraw**
Exp. Acct: **$579.12**

Synopsis: Bert McGraw calls and tells Johnny about Hailey's comet. Harry Hailey the pitcher for the Spartans, whose fastball is called "Hailey's Comet", has disappeared. He is making $60,000 but has disappeared right in the middle of spring training. Bert has a $50,000 policy on him.

Johnny cabs to Bert's office. Bert is described as a big man who played ball in the bush leagues and played with the Spartans for a year. Bert wants Johnny to find Hailey. The policy was sold 6 months ago and Mildred Womac, his sister in Omaha, was the original beneficiary, but his wife is on the policy now. Harry has been married since he started spring training but no one has seen him for a week. Harry only thinks about baseball, but Johnny reminds Bert that he did get married. Bert has a telegram from Mildred and she is sure that Harry has been murdered. She sent the wire from Tucson, where the Spartans are training.

Johnny buys a paper to read a story about Harry Hailey, and then flies to Tucson, Arizona and gets a room at the Westerner Hotel. Johnny rents a car and goes to meet Mildred Womac at her hotel.

Mildred is sure that Harry's new contract is the reason why he is dead. She had hired a detective to see what her brother was doing when he stopped writing to her. He is twenty-five years old, but much younger mentally. With his new contract, Mildred is sure that he is like a ripe melon for some young chippie to pick off the vine. It was the detective who told Mildred that Harry was married. "How would you feel if you woke up some morning and found out you were married to someone named Juanita Torres?" she asks Johnny.

Johnny tells her that he has never met the lady, and Mildred tells him that she isn't a lady, she is Mexican. The detective Oglethorpe told her that Juanita worked for a nightclub as a dancer, and Harry must have been really drunk to marry her. She is a gold-digger, a horrible cheap tainted dancing girl! Changing her to the beneficiary was like putting a gun in her hand. Mildred is sure that she murdered Harry.

Johnny goes to visit Oglethorpe who is not in, and then to the police where he meets Lt. Snyder who offers Johnny a hard-boiled egg. Lt. Snyder has no idea what has happened to Harry. Nothing has turned up, and his car is missing. Lt. Snyder tells Johnny that Harry's wife is missing also.

Johnny goes to the ballpark and talks to Crawfish Crawford, the catcher. Johnny is told that Harry roomed with Crawfish and that Harry left everything behind when he disappeared. Johnny mentions his wife, but Crawfish claims to not know about her. Johnny learns that Harry's pitching was off this year, he must have been in love.

Back at his hotel Johnny is met by Lt. Snyder who tells Johnny that Harry's car was found abandoned south of Nogales, and dried blood was found on the front seat.

Johnny goes to his room and returns a call to Oglethorpe. Johnny him asks about Mrs. Hailey, and Oglethorpe tells him that she is from Magdalena, about fifty miles south of the border.

Crawfish comes to Johnny's room and tells him that Harry had been going to a doctor in Tucson, a Dr. Wolfe. Johnny checks the phone book and realizes why Harry disappeared. Johnny drives to Mildred's hotel, where she has been thinking about Harry. She has given up hope ever since he married that girl. Johnny reminds her that she had said she would change her mind about Juanita if there was a good reason for him to disappear, and Johnny tells her that he has a reason, and she should be ready to go with him in the morning.

Johnny and Mildred drive to Magdalena over rough roads and through loose chickens. Mildred does not care for the Mexicans because they are poor and dirty. She points to some children in a field as an example, and Johnny stops and talks to one of them. Johnny asks who taught them to play baseball with five bases, and a boy tells Johnny that a lady taught them, Senora Torres.

The boy takes them to the Torres house and a servant takes them to the living room. Mildred is sure that her brother is dead because of the blood in his car. Johnny tells her to ask her brother what happened, he is standing in the doorway.

Mildred is ecstatic to see Harry and wants him to pack his things and go back with them to civilization. Harry tells Mildred that he wanted to get away from her for good and hates her for what she said about his wife. Harry tells Johnny that Mildred tried to get him to leave Juanita and called him names. Mildred has been bothering over him since he was a kid. Harry tells her that she needs a husband, but she tells him that a husband would only leave, like Joe did. Harry tells her that Joe left because she was always looking after him, and never even cooked a meal for Joe.

Harry tells Johnny that the blood in the car was from a chicken that they hit. They had not taken his clothes, mainly because Mildred had bought them for him. He tells Mildred to go back to Omaha and stomps out of the room. Juanita comes in and tells Mildred that she really loves Harry. He is not well and has gotten bad news from a doctor in Tucson. Harry calls to her and she leaves. Johnny tells Mildred that Harry had been going to a specialist for eye diseases, and that Harry is going blind.

"Some people, you just can't figure. Mildred Womac stayed on in Magdalena. Yeah, she rented a small adobe house and did what she could to help her less fortunate neighbors. Harry Hailey never played ball again, but he retained enough of his sight to show the junior Magdalena Spartans the difference between four bases and five."

Notes:
- Chippy is slang for a woman prostitute.
- Dan Cubberly is the announcer.
- Music supervision is by Amerigo Marino.

Producer: Jack Johnstone Writer: Charles B. Smith
Cast: Virginia Gregg, Lillian Buyeff, Richard Beals, Barney Phillips, Frank Nelson, Harry Bartell, Richard Crenna, Lawrence Dobkin, Tom Hanley

◆ ❖ ◆

Show: **The Peerless Fire Matter**
Show Date: **5/5/1957**
Company: **Four-State Mutual Insurance Company**
Agent: **Henry Willowby**
Exp. Acct: **$14.46**

Synopsis: "Do you smell smoke Johnny?" asks Henry Willowby. The kind of smoke that $5,000 makes when hit goes up in flames. The fire is at the Peerless Junkyard in Cranford, Connecticut. "If it is only a $5,000 loss, how can you afford me" asks Johnny. Because Henry smells arson.

Johnny cabs to Hank's office and learns that the policy was issued four years ago to Oscar H. Lehman, the owner. The fire started at 4:00 a.m. and the claim was in Hanks office when he got there. Johnny calls Mr. Lehman and he wants to know if Johnny has the check.

Johnny trains to Cranford and cabs to Lehman's home. Johnny comments on the new development of Cranford after the closing of the big clock company after World War II. The cabby stops at the site of the fire and tells Johnny that he hates to see the junkyard gone, as that is where he got the parts for his cab. The cabby mentions that with the junkyard gone, the whole area can be residential, like it ought to. When the cabby tells Johnny that he should burn up his cab and get the insurance money, Johnny tells him to be careful who he talks to, especially to an insurance investigator!

Johnny gets out and looks at the yard with the fire chief, Dale Marley, who agrees that the residents of the area are glad to see the eyesore go up in flames. Johnny sees where the fire started, and the owner of a store next door reported that the fire started with a boom. The chief suspects arson and has called for the experts from New Haven. Johnny has an idea and relates how lumberyards and furniture factories are the worst place to look for signs of arson. Johnny goes to the store next door and buys a loaf of white bread. Johnny tells the chief to chew on a piece of bread and swallow it. Johnny drops a piece into the ashes and then uses the taste of the bread to find traces of kerosene. The chief wants to arrest the owner, but Johnny tells him to hold off.

Johnny cabs to Lehman's address, located in a has-been area. Lehman tells Johnny that he is waiting at home for the insurance company to pay him and that he did not know about the fire until 7:00 a.m. He did not want to sit around and wait, so he filed the claim. Johnny asks why he burned the yard, and Lehman tells Johnny that he did not burn the yard, and that he has a conditional license. If he is not in business every day, he loses his lease and the development company will take the land away. Johnny thinks he has already met the arsonist and was too blind to see it.

Johnny remembers something the cab driver said about the neighbors beefing since the junkyard got its license. Back at the junkyard chief Marley shows Johnny where a sliding door on the shed is still locked, and the window on the Howard Street side was open. Across the street are a number of houses with nice gardens surrounded by rocks. The chief has found a rock inside the remains of the shed. He thinks that someone broke the glass with a rock, climbed in, spread the kerosene, climbed out and threw in a light and left in a hurry. Johnny tells him he has a good suspect and goes across the street to talk to the neighbors.

At the first house Johnny talks to Howard McNeal who yells at Johnny for trying to sell him insurance. McNeal tells Johnny not to investigate the fire, as it was a blessing. It was the only way to get rid of the junkyard. But hate it enough to set it on fire? "Oh, no, not me". McNeal would never do that as he does not believe in insurance. McNeal tells Johnny to ask that Nazi Lehman. He is German, isn't he? Ask him if he had insurance. Mr. McNeal mentions the widow Cummings, and Miss Gertrude Mary Anastasia Conroy, the nice spinster, they would like to see it gone too. What spirit Miss Conroy has. McNeal will ask her for a date one of these days.

Johnny visits Miss Conroy, an Irish woman who is cleaning her house. She wants to see Johnny's badge and is tired of answering questions. She had wanted to get rid of the junkyard for years. But now that poor Mr. Lehman has lost everything, she could cry her eyes out. And the horrible things that Hitler did to him. He escaped from Germany and put all his savings into that "lovely second-hand lot" so he could earn an honest living. Such a gentleman he is. And the way he would click his heels and bow when he came to visit on Sunday afternoons. She used to hate the lot until she met Mr. Lehman, and now she has "set her cap" for him. She will marry him before she is through.

Johnny mentions Mr. McNeal and she calls him an old coot. She tells Johnny that Mr. Lehman was not in need of money, and the accident will help bring them together. She is sure that Johnny thinks that Lehman burned the shop, but he is wrong. She had told him to get the claim in real early. She is going to fix him corned beef and cabbage for dinner tonight. "What an offbeat insurance matter" Johnny muses.

Johnny visits the widow Cummings and the door slowly opens to show a small woman in a wheelchair. She has been waiting and listening to what the neighbors had told Johnny. She tells Johnny that he must take Rudolph, her stepson away. He is keeping her there until she dies to get the money her husband left her. He is smart and thought the fire would burn down the house and trap her there, but the wind changed.

He had told her that he would be away at work all night but came home early. She saw him take the kerosene can across the street, put it in the shed and run away after he lit the fire. She had lied to the police, as she hoped that he would give up when he saw she was still alive. Johnny is glad she told him, and she tells Johnny that Rudolph would just find some other way.

Johnny stays an extra day to clear things up, and for Rudolph to return. Johnny finds the kerosene can in the basement, and the chief finds the top in the ashes, with only Rudolph's fingerprints on it.

Rudolph is in the city jail and Johnny is sure that Mrs. Cummings will testify against him, after all her life is at stake. And Oscar Lehman's claim will be paid in full and Johnny hopes he and Miss Conroy will live happily ever after.

Notes:
- This is an AFTRS program that contains story about the flag of Missouri.
- Dan Cubberly is the announcer.
- Music supervision is by Amerigo Marino.

Producer:	Jack Johnstone	Writer:	Jack Johnstone
Cast:	Virginia Gregg, Peggy Webber, John Stephenson, Herb Vigran, Hans Conried, Forrest Lewis, Parley Baer		

♦ ❖ ♦

Show: **The Glacier Ghost Matter**
Show Date: **5/12/1957**
Company: **Tri-Western Life & Casualty Company**
Agent: **Walter Bascomb**
Exp. Acct: **$431.60**

Synopsis: Johnny is called by Walter Bascomb. Walt has a $100,000 claim to pay but can't. Walt wants Johnny to find the body.

Johnny flies to Los Angeles and gets a room at the Ambassador Hotel. The next day Johnny goes to see Walt who tells Johnny that the insured was Raymond R. Shelton, who was part of Rycoff-Shelton Plastics. The beneficiary of the policy is his wife, Gloria, who lives in Westwood. Ray and his partner loved to hunt and fish and had gone to a lake up near Palisade Glacier, California. They had gone to Lone Horse glacier and got caught in a blizzard. They made camp, but Ray fell into a crevasse. His partner came out two days later. Johnny's assignment is to find Shelton's body. Search parties have gone out, but they cannot find the body. The wife really needs the money and must wait for a year without the body. Walt also tells Johnny that he is in love with Gloria.

Johnny goes to the plant and talks to Al Rycoff, who tells Johnny the same story, and tells Johnny that he owes his position to Ray Shelton and will get the business.

Johnny goes to see the widow and she tells Johnny that her husband worked hard, but they were never close. He was thirteen years older and it was her social connections that got him his financing. Gloria tells Johnny that Al Rycoff was in love with her, and became like a member of the family, but now she is in love with Walter Bascomb.

While they are talking, Al comes in with a gun and tells Johnny that he will not let Johnny intimidate Gloria. He tells Johnny that he knows that he is the most likely suspect because he has the most to gain, but Johnny cannot prove that he killed Ray. Johnny calms him down and they arrange to go to the Sierras in Al's plane the next day.

Al flies Johnny over the glacier and they spot a body, but Johnny cannot prove it is Ray. Al and Johnny land at Forrest Lewis' Pack Station and Forrest tells Johnny that there is no way that he can get to the body to get it out, so it must stay there. Al leaves when Johnny tells him that he has accepted an offer from Forrest to stay and fish for a couple days.

After Al leaves Johnny gets some dynamite, some .30-30 cartridges and makes an impact fuse. After testing it, Johnny arranges with Joe Gracey to fly to the glacier with the dynamite. Joe and Johnny fly over the glacier and Johnny drops a bomb onto the glacier, causing the ice ridge with the body to fall into the lake. Joe lands his plane on the lake and they retrieve the body to discover a bullet hole in its back.

Joe takes off and heads back to the pack station when he spots Al Rycoff's plane, which buzzes them and shoots at his plane. Joe tells Johnny that he will head for Anchor Pass, which has very bad downdrafts if you do not know how to fly there. Joe gets his plane through, but Al crashes.

"Remarks: Justice was done in its own strange way."

Notes:
- The announcer is Dan Cubberly.
- Music Direction is by Amerigo Marino.
- Story information obtained from the KNX Collection in the Thousand Oaks Library.

Producer:	Jack Johnstone	Writer:	Jack Johnstone
Cast:	John Dehner, Herb Ellis, Virginia Gregg, Forrest Lewis, James McCallion, Tom Hanley, John James		

◆ ❖ ◆

Show: **The Michael Meany Mirage Matter**
Show Date: 5/19/1957
Company: **Floyds of England**
Agent: **George Reed**
Exp. Acct: **$420.10**

Synopsis: George Reed calls, and it is not a good morning, even though the birds are singing and the bees are buzzing for Johnny. George asks Johnny if he knows anything about whales. Neither Johnny nor George nor the agent in Gulf Port, Mississippi does. Floyds has a floater policy on 80 pounds of ambergris, which is used in the manufacturing of perfume. The ambergris is worth $20,000 and has disappeared. The agent is W. C. Owen. George tells Johnny that the ambergris will be easy to find as it "smells worse than a hound dog which has caught a skunk."

Johnny flies to Gulf Port, Mississippi and calls Owen, who visits Johnny in his hotel room to tell Johnny to find the ambergris within the next 48 hours. It is packed in dry ice that will last that long, and Michael Meany, Owen's client, was promised that Johnny could find it in that time. Meany has told Owen that the ambergris is worth upwards of $60,000. Billy Fisher, who works for Meany, found it. Meany puts his boats out on share, and takes a share of everything that is caught, so the ambergris belongs to Meany. Owen tells Johnny that Meany is waiting to talk in Mississippi City.

Owen takes Johnny to see Meany, a huge man and Johnny tells him he is an investigator. Johnny is told that the ambergris was stolen from the platform of the American Express office in Tuscaloosa, Alabama. It was being sent to an agent in New Orleans. The freight had not been paid, as the delivery person, Meany's nephew TJ, spotted a girl and neglected the box. Meany tells Johnny that he has forty-five hours to find the ambergris.

Johnny and Owen leave and Owen tells Johnny that Meany owns most of the businesses along the beach. Owen takes Johnny to Billy Fisher's boarding house where Billy is in his room with Jane Higgins.

Jane and Billy come out and Johnny wants to talk to him alone. Billy tells Johnny that he found the ambergris floating in the channel. He took it into the boat, not realizing it would belong to Meany. Cliff Dillinger, the checker for Meany, spotted the ambergris and took it away from him.

Johnny turns down dinner with Miss Harvey and goes to his hotel where he has a message from George that tells Johnny that a friend of a man in the office is an ichthyologist. He has told George that ambergris comes only from the sperm whale, and there never has been a sperm whale in the Gulf of Mexico. Well, if there never has been a sperm whale in the gulf, what is the stuff that is insured?

Johnny calls Owen, and he is shocked when he finds out what has happened. Owen is sure that Meany is not pulling a fraud as a chemist in Biloxi analyzed the ambergris, and said it was real. Owen tells Johnny that he should have checked on the chemist, and Johnny feels sorry for him, as the company might pull his franchise.

Next morning Johnny walks up the street looking for a place to eat breakfast when he meets Jane. She is on a shopping spree looking for something to get married in, and the lucky man is Billy Fisher. Jane tells Johnny that her father will be angry, but there is nothing he can do, as she is over eighteen. And he is going to change his mind about Billy. Johnny asks her to join him for breakfast, but she suddenly remembers something important she has to do.

Johnny enters the "All Night Diner", and orders ham and eggs over easy and coffee. The counterman is TJ, Meany's nephew and his uncle has told him about Johnny. He tells Johnny that he was waiting to put the package on the train when a girl drove up and gave him a great big come-on. TJ went across the street to talk to her and she told him that her name was Betty Lou Miller. TJ tells Johnny the he was just talking to her on the street.

After breakfast Johnny meets Owen and they go to the depot where the agent remembers everything, including the name of the woman who bought the ticket. Johnny goes to see Meany and tells him he thinks he knows who has the ambergris, and Meany wants the name. Johnny tells him he will know for sure, if Meany will help him.

Johnny asks Meany for the letter from the chemist who analyzed the ambergris and then leaves to see a lady. Johnny drives Owen's car to the Harvey boarding house. Johnny tells her what he knows and she tells Johnny that it was her fault.

She had put Billy up to it and had bought the train ticket. She knew that TJ would leave the package, because he has a weakness for girls. Johnny tells Miss Harvey that she timed it just like a professional as Billy was in the woods waiting for Jane to get TJ all mixed up, and then he grabbed the package and ran back to the woods where Jane picked him up later. The ambergris was shipped to Atlanta, where a man will sell it for Billy. Johnny tells her that he had run into Jane, and Miss Harvey tells Johnny that they will get married, even if the ambergris turns out to be something else.

Meany drives up with Owen calling for Johnny and asking what he is doing. Meany wants to arrest Billy and Jane for stealing the ambergris, and Miss Harvey tells Meany that Billy took the ambergris because it belonged to him all the time. Johnny agrees, if it was ambergris.

Owen has called the chemist, but he has quit his job, and no record was found of the tests. Meany tells them that it was ambergris, and Miss Harvey tells Meany he was seeing a mirage. Johnny tells Meany that the contract he had with Billy only covers fish and fish by products, which belong to Meany. But, the ambergris does not, because a whale is not a fish, it is a mammal.

"They say that young love can work miracles, and I guess it must be true, because later that day a huge sperm whale was sighted about three miles offshore near the Cat Island channel. Proving as I have always said, you can't figure whales any more than you can people."

Notes:
- This is an AFRTS program that contains a story about the flag of New Mexico.
- Ambergris is a fatty or pitch-like substance produced by sperm whales. Ambergris is typically found floating in the water, or on the seashore. When fresh, ambergris smells strong and unpleasant. It is used as a fixative in expensive perfumes.
- Dan Cubberly is the announcer.
- Music supervision is by Amerigo Marino.

Producer: Jack Johnstone Writer: Charles B. Smith
Cast: Virginia Gregg, Jeanette Nolan, G. Stanley Jones, Junius Matthews, Gil Stratton, Richard Crenna, John Dehner

Show: The Wayward Truck Matter
Show Date: 5/26/1957
Company: Tri-Western Indemnity Company
Agent: Ted Orloff
Exp. Acct: $501.05

Synopsis: Ted Orloff calls from Los Angeles and he wants Johnny to come out right away. The problem is a wayward truck insured for nearly $20,000. The driver disappeared, and he is insured for $10,000 and the cargo of copper tubing is insured for $9,500. Johnny will grab the next plane.

Johnny flies to Los Angeles, California and is met at the airport by Ted. Ted tells Johnny that a truck carrying copper tubing used in airplanes has disappeared. It was shipped from Marlowe Copper Products in East Los Angeles. Jackie McCallion was scheduled to deliver the tubing and made the run at night to avoid the heat of the desert. After midnight, Jackie signed out the shipment and by the next morning Belden Aircraft was screaming about the delivery.

The market for copper tubing is good because it is expensive and hard to get. Lockheed and Belden have built plants in the area and subcontract to smaller companies. The tubing would be worth its weight in gold to the smaller plants.

The driver is an honest man according to the employer, and they would trust him with a load of pure gold. Johnny infers that Jackie would know where to sell the tubing and could make a lot of money for himself.

Johnny meets Mr. Marlowe and Willie, the night watchman. Johnny is told that Jackie left at 12:05 and has not been seen since. When asked about how much money Jackie makes, Mr. Marlowe tells Johnny he is dead wrong if he is thinking that Jackie stole the tubing, and that Marlowe will take care of whoever has done him in, as that is the only way he would give up the goods.

Johnny asks Willie if there was anything unusual about Jackie when he got the truck and is told that everything seemed normal. When Willie leaves Johnny tells Mr. Marlowe that he needs a better night watchman. Johnny is told that the hijackers could get the information on the shipment from a lot of different sources. The route has been gone over by the police, and nothing had been found.

Johnny gets Jackie's address and borrows a well-marked company car. At Jackie's house the front door is open and Jackie's apartment is open. Inside someone is emptying the dresser drawers. Johnny enters and asks what is going on and fights with the man. Johnny overpowers the man who turns out to be Jackie McCallion.

Jackie tells Johnny that he is handy with his dukes for a skinny guy. Johnny tells Jackie who he is and he tells Johnny that the shipment was called off. It was supposed to go out Wednesday night, on "Betsy" his truck, but a girl in the office called and told him that the order got cancelled out and Jackie was told he could start his vacation right away. Jackie was in San Diego fishing for Yellowtail.

Jackie is surprised when Johnny tells him that the shipment went out and has not been heard of since. Jackie tells Johnny that he was in San Diego by 1:00 a.m., ask his sister. "And if some dirty guy took my Betsy out, I'll kill him!"

As Johnny and Jackie drive back to the Marlowe warehouse, Johnny is sure that Jackie is on the level, and Johnny wonders who could be enough of a double to fool the night watchman? Or could Marlowe himself have contrived to take the copper.

At the plant, Mr. Marlowe is happy to see Jackie. Marlowe tells Johnny that Jackie helped Marlowe build the company. Jackie tells Johnny that he only wanted to be a truck driver, even with the big retirement Marlowe gave him, he just wants to drive Betsy, and go fishing once in a while. Johnny asks to talk to Willie, and Marlowe calls him to the office.

Johnny remembers that there was something unusual in the way Willie had said Jackie picked up the truck. There were no positive answers. Marlowe tells Johnny that Willie carries a time clock and Johnny asks for the record and the manifest and the shipping order for the copper tubing.

Willie arrives and Johnny takes him to the watchman's booth and is told that it is Willie's "own private office". Willie tells Johnny that he had not talked to Jackie, as he had no reason to. Johnny tells Willie that he knew what time Jackie was coming and did not see him or see him sign the manifest or drive out with the truck. Knowing Jackie or someone was coming, Willie had left the gate open, and was a partner to the theft as Jackie did not pick up the truck.

Johnny takes out the time clock record and goes over the record of the checks. Johnny looks at the time clock record and tells Willie that he was on the far side of the plant when the truck went out. Willie admits that he had often left the gate open, like he usually does. He had left the catch on the main gate so it would look like it was set. He did that for the other drivers, but not for Jackie because he was too close to the boss. Johnny tells Willie he is in trouble and turns him over to Marlowe, but Johnny is no closer to finding the truck.

Over lunch, Jackie tells Johnny that the only ones who would know when the load was going out were Willie and Red Kingsley. Johnny remembers he had borrowed Red's car, and Jackie is about to tell him about Red when Marlowe rushes in and tells Johnny that the sheriff in Victorville has picked up some of the tubing. Johnny is told to borrow Red's car and Jackie goes with him.

Johnny rushes to the area, past Edwards Air Force Base as Jackie checks out all the trucks. As Johnny passes a truck the driver yells at him and Jackie recognizes the truck as Betsy. Johnny realizes that the driver had yelled "Hey Red" because of the car.

The truck catches up and rams the car and Johnny is awakened by a man slapping him. The man tells Johnny that he had edged the other truck off the highway, and it flipped over spilling its load. The police had seen the truck ram Red's car and had chased him, but it took a big truck like "Clara-belle", his tractor-trailer, to do that. It's not the first time he has helped the police."

"Yeah, they've given a lot of people a hand, those boys who drive the big interstate trucks and trailers. They're a pretty fine bunch to have on the road. Well I guess it's pretty obvious that Red Kingsley in Marlowe's shipping department was back of the hijacking operation. The two who were aboard the stolen truck turned state's evidence and sang plenty, and the courts will take care of them."

Notes:
- This is an AFRTS program that contains a story about the flag of New Jersey.
- Dan Cubberly is the announcer.
- Music supervision is by Amerigo Marino.

Producer:	Jack Johnstone	Writer:	Jack Johnstone
Cast:	Forrest Lewis, John Dehner, Junius Matthews, Stacy Harris, Jack Kruschen		

♦ ❖ ♦

Show: The Loss of Memory Matter
Show Date: 6/2/1957
Company: Continental Insurance Company
Agent: Les Crutcher
Exp. Acct: $95.00

Synopsis: Johnny is called by Les Crutcher who asks Johnny if he knows about the Preese expedition that went to the city of Ur, in the valley of the Euphrates. Les has the insurance on the collection, but nothing has happened yet, but come on over.

Johnny goes to the library to read up on Babylon, which is now part of Iraq, so that he can be ready for a trip to the middle east.

Johnny goes to Les' office and learns that the relics are located not in the middle east, but in Lakeview, Connecticut, and are owned by Alvin Peabody Cartwright, who is a crackpot of the first order. Johnny is told that the Preese expedition contains rare scrolls and tablets, some up to 4,000 years old and very valuable. Johnny is shown a pillow made of mud with some hieroglyphics on it and is told that it is a receipt for 24 fat sheep, 12 oxen, and 12 goats that dates from 2,350 BC and is typical of the collection. Alvin has sold the collection to the museum, and his step-son Alfred Hocking is going to deliver it, but Alvin is worried. There is a $20,000 transit policy, but Alvin wants Johnny to act as a guard for $250 plus expenses.

Johnny rents a car and drives to Lakeview and meets Alvin at the front door and is asked for his credentials. In the study is a sealed box with the relics. Johnny meets Alfred as Alvin tells the museum that there will be two people delivering the carton, and they are not to accept it if it has been opened. Alvin tells Mr. Waring to give Mr. Dollar the money because he does not trust his half-wit son. Alvin tells Johnny that he wants the cash brought back tonight!

Johnny leaves for Hartford with Alfred. In the car. Alfred tells Johnny about a back road and tells Johnny that if he were alone he would take the money because scrooge never let him have any, even though he has a safe full of money in the basement.

The car crashes, and Johnny regains consciousness with a headache, and amnesia. Al tells Johnny that Johnny is really Alfred Hocking, and they are making a delivery and will part company later. Johnny looks at this wallet, and his driver's license says he is Alfred Hocking.

A moving van stops and picks up Johnny and Al and takes them to the museum, where Al shows the director, Mr. Waring, his credentials. Al leaves the box and gets the $21,000 in cash from Mr. Waring.

Al and Johnny go to a car rental office and Al rents a car. Al and Johnny drive towards Danbury and Al tells Johnny that he is taking Johnny to a hospital in New York, but Johnny realizes that something is wrong when "Johnny" mentions his father. Johnny asks for Al's gun permit, looks at the picture and into the mirror, when Al slugs Johnny.

The car stops on a gravel road above a ravine and Johnny calls Al by name. Johnny starts to remember what had happened and Al fights with Johnny and three shots are fired before Al falls into the ravine.

Johnny gets the money back to Alvin, and Alfred is arrested. Johnny gets a $500 bonus from Alvin.

"Not bad for just a couple of wallops on the head, eh?"

Notes:
- This is an AFRTS program that contains a story about the experiences of Fred Hargesheimer who was shot down in New Guinea and later built a school for the natives who had rescued him.
- The announcer is Dan Cubberly.
- Music Direction is by Amerigo Marino.
- This is the first appearance of Alvin Peabody Cartwright.
- Alvin lives in Lakeview in this story, but later stories put him in Lakewood.
- Parley Baer plays Alvin, but he is later played to a "T" by Howard McNear.

Producer: Jack Johnstone Writer: Jack Johnstone
Cast: Les Tremayne, Parley Baer, Shepard Menken, Joseph Kearns, Barney Phillips, Tom Hanley

◆ ❖ ◆

Show: **The Mason-Dixon Mismatch Matter**
Show Date: **6/9/1957**
Company: **Providential Assurance Company**
Agent: **Bert McGraw**
Exp. Acct: **$319.00**

Synopsis: Bert McGraw calls Johnny about Darla Mason, niece of Sylvester Mason of Mason Steel and Iron. She disappeared six weeks ago, and Bert has a $25,000 policy with double indemnity on her. A body washed up on Newport

Beach yesterday and her father says it is Darla. Bert was going to pay off the policy until a man named Dixon showed up and claimed the body as his daughter.

Johnny cabs to Bert's office where Bert is in the process of hanging a picture of himself pitching for the Valgusta Lions. He did not win the game for them, the umpire cheated. Bert tells Johnny that so far, the authorities have not been able to identify the body. Bert gets a call from Capt. Miller of the Newport police, and he tells Bert that the body was shot with a .38. The Steel girl has been missing for six weeks and the Mason girl for three months, so Johnny is going to find the living girl.

Johnny cabs to his apartment and travels to Newport, Rhode Island and gets a room at the Ogden Hotel. Johnny rents a car and drives to the Mason estate where Darla's sister Joan meets him at the door and takes him to see her mother. But if Johnny wants to know about Darla, talk to her.

Mrs. Mason tells Johnny that he is there for nothing, as her husband has released a statement to the press saying that the body was not his daughter. Mr. Mason comes in and tells Johnny to talk to him if he wants answers. He tells Johnny that as soon as his wife found out that the girl had been murdered his wife felt that it was not her daughter, as their kind of people only die in bed. He tells Johnny that his daughter was a real nice girl. He is certain that the body is his daughter as she had no reason to leave. He had given her everything she could want. She was last seen at the Newport Yacht club. Joan saw her talking to a stranger, and she has never been seen since.

Johnny tells Mr. Mason that he is going to find her, or the Dixon girl. Mr. Mason is sure that Darla did not know the other girl, as his wife had drilled it into her daughter to not mix with people who were beneath her. Johnny gets a small picture of Darla and drives to town.

Johnny calls Henry Dixon and then goes to visit them. Mr. Dixon tells Johnny that this thing has not been easy on his wife, and they are almost sure that the body is not their daughter. Lucille comes in and they sit on the porch.

They only have a small insurance policy on their daughter. Henry had been a schoolteacher but had to slow down for health reasons. They have been in Newport for five months. Lucille tells Johnny that Ruth was spoiled and they moved to Newport hoping they could find some friends on her own level. She mentioned once that the Mason girl had been at the store where she worked. Ruth seems to be happy with her job as a hostess. Johnny gets a picture of her that was taken at the Newport Yacht Club where she worked.

At his hotel, Johnny has a message from Capt. Miller and goes to see him. The Masons are in Capt. Millers' office, and she is happy about the good news. She has proof that Darla is alive. Mrs. Mason got a bill for Darla from Kennedy's Department Store over in Providence. The bill came today, and a fur wrap had been charged by Darla just last week.

Johnny gets the sales slip with Darla's name on it. Capt. Miller arranges to get a copy of the driver's license to compare the signature and then Johnny and Capt. Miller drive to Kennedy's.

The clerk in the fur department is sure that it was Darla, even though she had not met her before. Johnny shows her the photographs after altering them slightly with paper hats. With the hair covered up the two girls look almost identical. Johnny and Capt. Miller go back to the office and compare the driver's license signature and are sure what had happened.

Johnny goes to his hotel and is called by Joan, who comes up to his room for her date. She tells Johnny that everyone knows about Darla charging the fur. Johnny asks about the day at the yacht club and the need for a guest pass to get in. Joan tells Johnny that the man was Peter Hansen, their tutor.

Next morning Johnny calls the employment agency which referred Hansen to the Masons and gets a Providence address and drives to the address followed by a battered blue sedan. Three addresses later Johnny stops and Mr. Dixon gets out of the car. He tells Johnny that he just had to do something.

Johnny goes to the house and finally Peter Hansen opens the door and laughs when Johnny tells him he is with an insurance company. Peter tries to close the door and Johnny pushes his way in and knocks Pete out while Darla screams about finding them. She tells Johnny that she would be happier if they thought she was dead. She left because she was bored of living the way her family wanted her to. She shows Johnny some sea birds that are free, just the way she wants to be.

Johnny tells Darla that he found her because of the bill sent to her house, and she tells Johnny that it was supposed to be sent to the beach house. Mr. Dixon comes in and is disappointed and tells Darla he wishes she was dead.

"Like Bert McGraw told me a long time ago, someone has to handle the rough ones, for me, this was it. Henry Dixon was in no condition to drive his car, so he rode back with us, and on the way, well Darla Mason will never forget the things he said to her, neither will I. As for Ruth Dixon, who murdered her and why, well that's up to the Newport police."

Notes:
- This is an AFRTS program that contains a story about a bull that threw a man.
- Dan Cubberly is the announcer.
- Music supervision is by Amerigo Marino.

Producer:	Jack Johnstone	Writer:	Charles B. Smith
Cast:	Virginia Gregg, Mary Jane Croft, Jeanette Nolan, Jean Tatum, Frank Nelson, Will Wright, Austin Green, Marvin Miller		

♦ ❖ ♦

Show: **The Dixon Murder Matter**
Show Date: 6/16/1957
Company: **Providential assurance Company**
Agent: **Bert McGraw**
Exp. Acct: $968.20

Synopsis: Bert McGraw greets Johnny with "The Bases are loaded, and there is nobody out, and you're pitching, Johnny boy!" as Johnny answers the phone. Bert is calling about the job Johnny did not finish, the Mason-Dixon Murder. Johnny tells Bert that it is up to the police now, but Bert tells Johnny that police want to talk to Johnny about the case and so does Bert. Ruth Dixon was insured for $1,000, but if Johnny will come up, they will foot the bill. Johnny is interested now.

Johnny cabs to Bert's office and thinks about the case in Newport Beach where two families had claimed a girl's body. Bert tells Johnny that Ruth had a $1,000 policy, and that the police have a lot to do with the company. Capt. Lewis of homicide, called and he is very unhappy with Johnny for not giving them up all the information on the Mason girl. The police chewed out the company, the company chewed out Bert, and Bert is chewing out Johnny.

Bert tells Johnny to go build up the good will, and keep Capt. Lewis informed. "I hope you understand. No hard feelings?" Bert asks Johnny. Johnny tells Bert "for an expense account like the one you are going to get, I could understand the theory of relativity!"

Johnny travels to Newport, Rhode Island, gets a room and calls Capt. Pete Lewis, who is not in. Johnny calls Darla Mason and asks if she can have dinner with him.

Johnny buys roses for Mrs. Lucille Dixon and then drives to the Dixon home, which has the scent of oriental incense coming from a burner on the mantle. Lucille tells Johnny that Ruth will like the flowers, and she will take them to her. She thinks that those who pass on never really leave us, and that Ruth is still there. Lucille asks Johnny to come with her to visit Madam De Salles. She has wonderful occult powers and she will help talk to Ruth when the time is right.

Henry Dixon comes home and Johnny is invited to dinner. Henry tells Johnny that the mantle looks like a heathen altar and would not blame Johnny if he were afraid to stay. Johnny asks Henry about men who Ruth might have been seeing, and he tells Johnny that she dated too much. She did have an older friend, Sam Hood who runs a small-craft repair shop on Viking Beach.

Johnny drives to Viking Beach and finds the repair shop and an old PT boat. A fat man with thick glasses and dirty clothes on the boat tells Johnny that Sam Hood is on vacation. Johnny goes down to the boat, the Conomore, to talk to Sam's brother, Leroy.

Leroy tells Johnny that he found the name in a book, and that the name fits him and the boat. Leroy opens a plug of Brown Mule Chewing Tobacco and tells Johnny that the boat belongs to him and Sam. Sam is visiting their folks in Augusta. Johnny asks about Ruth Dixon, and Leroy tells Johnny that Sam and Ruth used to talk a lot. Leroy thinks Ruth was a two-timing woman, and that Sam left town after her death. Leroy tells Johnny that Sam owns a .38 revolver like everyone else with a boat. Leroy is sure that Sam did not kill Ruth.

Johnny goes to meet Darla for dinner, but she does not show up. Later Capt. Lewis pounds on Johnny's door and tells Johnny that Darla Mason was shot tonight by the same gun that shot Ruth Dixon.

Johnny buys coffee for Capt. Lewis, who tells Johnny that Darla had gone to the boathouse to take the cruiser to the yacht club, and someone shot and wounded her. Capt. Lewis tells Johnny that the Masons have their boat repaired by Sam Hood, but he is still in Georgia. Capt. Lewis arranges to call the Georgia police, and Johnny suggests he tell them about Darla. Johnny has a hunch but wants to sleep on it.

The next day Johnny runs into Mrs. Dixon in the lobby and she wants to talk. Last night Madam De Salles let Lucille talk to Ruth. Ruth told her that a young woman with dark hair, brown eyes, and a big red scar on the back of her left hand shot her, so all Johnny has to do is find a girl with that scar.

Johnny calls Capt. Lewis, and learns that Sam is in Georgia, and that they service the Mason cruiser. Capt. Lewis asks Johnny about his hunch, but Johnny asks Capt. Lewis to call Augusta again and ask Sam Hood who named his boat.

Johnny goes to the library, finds what he is looking for and goes to Capt. Lewis' office to tells him of his hunch. Sam Hood calls with the answer to Johnny's questions, and Johnny goes to see Leroy.

Johnny asks how long it would take to go over to the Mason home and Leroy answers "no time at all". Leroy admits to hearing about Darla Mason being shot, and Johnny asks why he tried to kill her. Johnny tells Leroy that Darla told him that he had shot her, and Leroy tells Johnny that it was too dark.

Johnny tells Leroy that Sam told the police that Leroy cannot stand to have a woman laugh at him, and when they do he tries to make them sorry for it. Johnny tells Leroy that Sam left to think about what to do with his brother, and that Johnny is going to take Leroy in.

Leroy runs into the shop and comes out with a gun and shoots at Johnny. Capt. Lewis arrives and shoots Leroy. Johnny tells Capt. Lewis that Leroy wanted to be a lady-killer, but they all laughed at him. Also, the name of the boat, Conomore is the name of a real lady killer, Bluebeard.

"I saw Mrs. Dixon late that same afternoon. I am afraid she was a bit disillusioned. Having been so sure that the person who killed her daughter was a woman. But there was one funny thing. On the back of Leroy's left hand was a long red scar."

Notes:
- This is an AFRTS program that contains a story about the symbols in a town in Spain and an Air Force helicopter used to repair a statue.
- Bluebeard is a fable about a man who marries a series of wives and kills them all.
- Thanks to Jeanette Berard at the Thousand Oaks Library for helping me find out that Conomore (who was King of Breton [Brittany] in the 6th century) was known as the Breton Bluebeard.
- Brown Mule was a chewing tobacco made by R.J. Reynolds.
- Now this is a case with a padded expense account!
- Dan Cubberly is the announcer.
- Music supervision is by Amerigo Marino.

Producer:	Jack Johnstone Writer: Charles B. Smith
Cast:	Jeanne Tatum, Jeanette Nolan, Frank Nelson, Russell Thorson, Sam Edwards, Austin Green

◆ ❖ ◆

Show:	**The Parley Barron Matter**
Show Date:	**6/23/1957**
Company:	**Tri-State Life & Casualty Company**
Agent:	**Earle Poorman**
Exp. Acct:	**$421.50**

Synopsis: Earle Poorman calls Johnny from the land of "infernal sunshine". Earle may have a case for Johnny, maybe it's murder.

Johnny flies to Sarasota, Florida and goes to Earle's office where he gets a promise of a fishing trip before he goes home.

Earle tells Johnny that a long-time customer named Parley Barron retired bought a property near him on Lido Key, and he is insured for $50,000. His wife Laura is the beneficiary. On Friday, Parley left on some errands and his car was found on the fishing docks at 11 p.m., but he was not out fishing. Barron was a sweet old guy who got along well with everyone and has no enemies, so Earle thinks that Barron is dead.

Johnny goes to Lido Key and meets Mrs. Barron, a fragile woman who is clutching her Bible. She tells Johnny that only prayer can help now. She is very religious, but her husband loved to fish but worked in a sinful job, he was a chemist who made explosives for the Dufresne Chemical Company and retired in 1951. Johnny is told that Barron went fishing every day but never caught anything, and she feels that it was retribution. As Johnny is leaving, Mrs. Barron gives him a number of religious pamphlets to read. Johnny thinks that maybe he left because of the stifling atmosphere in the house.

Johnny calls Sgt. Brackett, who is out, so he goes to see Earle. Johnny and Earle go fishing to talk over the case and spot a hat and a body in the water. The body is unrecognizable, but Earle is sure that the body is Barron as they take it to the police.

The police take the body into the morgue for the autopsy surgeon and Johnny goes to the dock of Will Bright and he tells Johnny that he had been in Gainesville, and that Barron only rented his boat from him. When he got back, he found the boat, but in a different spot and wondered if someone else brought it back.

Johnny looks at the boat and notices a tackle box that had not been moved in months and the reel could hardly be moved. Johnny goes to the police and talks to Sgt. Brackett who tells Johnny that the autopsy showed that the body was dead before it went into the water — that means murder. A kid told the police that he saw Barron leave alone, but the skiff was back that night. Johnny is not sure that the body is that of Barron.

Sgt. Brackett tells Johnny that he is waiting for Barron's dentist, Dr. Dayner, to come from Tampa. Johnny asks if he is the same Jerrod Dayner who got so much publicity for the Atomic Radiation studies and the effect on teeth.

Johnny has lunch and calls Mrs. Dayner posing as Mr. Larkin from the Federal Bureau and asks if her husband followed his instructions and she mentions Dufresne.

Johnny buys gas and drives to the Dufresne Chemical Company and goes to the office of the president where he bursts into the conference room, where Johnny meets Mr. Dufresne, Dr. Dayner, and Mac McLaughlin from the Federal Bureau, all of whom are expecting Johnny.

Johnny is told that he has been followed and is a very sharp person, something they were not expecting. Johnny is told that Parley Barron is alive, and is making a valuable contribution to national security, and that his fishing trips were a cover for his work. Johnny is told that during the war, Barron made vitally important contributions to our national security and that Barron is alive and healthy and working on a nuclear project, somewhere in New Mexico.

Barron would go out every day to a remote area where he would be picked up and taken to Tampa to continue his work, and the Dufresne Chemical Company was used as a cover to mislead enemy agents. The body was that of a derelict. Johnny is told that Dr. Dayner will identify the body with reservations, and that Johnny is to prevent an insurance claim. Johnny will make sure that Earle does not push for a claim.

"For obvious reasons, I have used fictitious names through out this report, and of course, delayed filing it until obtaining official clearance."

Notes:
- This is an AFRTS program that contains a story about the candy dropped during the Berlin Airlift.
- The announcer is Dan Cubberly.
- Music Direction is by Amerigo Marino.

Producer:	Jack Johnstone	Writer:	Jack Johnstone
Cast:	Lawrence Dobkin, Jeanette Nolan, Will Wright, Harry Bartell, Virginia Gregg, Barney Phillips, Stacy Harris		

◆ ❖ ◆

Show: The Funny Money Matter
Show Date: 6/30/1957
Company: Floyds of England
Agent: George Reed
Exp. Acct: $171.25

Synopsis: George Reed calls Johnny and tells him that things are going bad. An old client, Durango Laramie Dalhart just made his $4,500 premium payment in crisp $100 bills. They are still on my desk. Every one of these bills is counterfeit. "Ah, I'll be right over." Johnny replies to George.

Johnny cabs to George Reed's office and sees the money. All of the bills look like they were made with washed out ink. Johnny notices that the serial numbers are all different and the paper is very good and the engraving is almost perfect.

George tells Johnny that Durango is as honest as the day is long. He lives on a ranch in a place called Bum Spung, Oklahoma. Johnny suggests calling the Secret Service, but George wants Johnny to handle it. Durango has always paid his premiums in cash.

George wants Johnny to handle this on an expenses plus special fee basis. Every year Durango comes east for a spree, drops off his policy premiums and heads back. Johnny agrees to take the case, but only to see what kind of a place deserves the name Bum Spung!

Johnny uses a ticket from George to fly to Enid, Oklahoma, eats and heads for Bum Spung. Johnny spots a sign and heads up a dirt road to an old farm house and old barn, two sad-looking bovines, chickens and other old animals and a brand-new Cadillac.

On the other side of the house Johnny spots a young lady who (rowf!) is really pretty. She calls to Johnny and tells him to come in. She is Carol Dalhart, Durango's niece.

She tells Johnny that Bum Spung means bad water. Durango liked the name and bought the place. Johnny asks to meet Durango, and suddenly Carol pulls a .45 and shoots a gopher snake twice.

She tells Johnny that she looks after the place for Durango from time-to-time. Durango buys her a new car every year and supposedly has a barrel of money. When he dies, she will get his money and can sell her filling station. Durango says a girl has to do something.

Carol asks Johnny why he is there and suddenly she trips and sprains her ankle and Johnny is forced to carry her inside. Inside the ramshackle shack is a thoroughly modern house, with all the latest appliances. Johnny cares for the ankle and starts to fix some dinner while Carol naps. Durango comes in ready to kill and shoots at Johnny several times.

Durango accuses Johnny of robbing his house until Carol calls him off. Johnny is able to take Durango's gun away from him, and Durango tells Carol he was having some fun with her boyfriend.

He gives Carol $500 to buy a new stove and other destroyed goods. Durango offers Johnny a jug and tells Johnny he gets tired of sitting around and has to go out to get some excitement. Durango tells Johnny that he has spunk, not like Carol's other boyfriends.

While Durango starts to fix dinner, Carol and Johnny "talk" on the sofa. Carol wants to know why Johnny is there, and he manages to put her off, while Durango constantly interrupts. After dinner Johnny learns of Durango's past, and how he has made more money than he can ever spend.

After retiring for the night, Johnny hears Durango go out of the house and follows him to an out-building where Johnny hears the noise of what he thinks is a printing press. Suddenly Carol surprises him and Johnny tells her he is looking for what is in the building.

Carol tells Johnny not to break Durango's heart, he thinks that no one, not even she, knows what is going on in there. He does not mean any harm to anyone. Durango comes out and Johnny pulls his gun on him. Johnny tells him to open the door so he can see what is going on.

Durango tells Johnny that he always goes to the bank and gets brand new $100 bills, but the banks did not have any the last time he was there. Johnny goes into the building to find where Durango is washing, starching and ironing his money to make it look brand new.

"Well, there you have it George, full report on the funny money that turned out to be only cleaned up a bit. And the next time, call in the Secret Service will ya? No, no, I didn't mean that. Just don't question the charges on this account for the extra week I spent out here. If you could see this pretty little Carol, oh that Carol. And it I ever get enough money so help me, I think I'll retire to Bum Spung, Oklahoma."

Notes:
- This is an AFRTS program that contains a story about Rev. Eugene Wood and his service to German POWs.
- This is the first appearance of the Dalhart clan, Durango and Carol.
- Dan Cubberly is the announcer.
- Music Direction is by Amerigo Marino.

Producer:	Jack Johnstone	Writer:	Jack Johnstone
Cast:	Virginia Gregg, G. Stanley Jones, John McIntire		

◆ ❖ ◆

Show:	**The Felicity Feline Matter**
Show Date:	7/7/1957
Company:	**Continental Assurance Company**
Agent:	**Henry Parker**
Exp. Acct:	**$407.20**

Synopsis: Henry Parker calls Johnny from Reno, and things are terrible in Nevada. Parker turns the phone over to a man who addresses Johnny as a "sloth-eyed Pinkerton". Johnny recognizes the voice as that of cantankerous old Jodiah Gillis, and he wants Johnny to get there before a feline friend of his gets killed. The cat has inherited $60,000 but someone is trying to make sure that he does not live long enough to spend it.

Johnny flies to Reno, Nevada and wonders about what Gillis is doing in Reno. Gillis meets Johnny at the airport with a tall, cadaverous man, who is Gillis' friend and business partner Henry Parker.

Parker tells Johnny that Gillis is quite concerned about Felicity and goes to get Johnny's bags. Johnny tells Gillis that no one has heard of Continental Assurance, and Gillis tells Johnny that it is a local company, and Parker is the president and Jodiah is the Chairman of the Board. He used to be covered by Floyds but dropped them when they told him he could not insure an African anteater named Archie. Archie over indulged on a house full of termites and died of acute indigestion.

Gillis tells Johnny that Continental paid off on the anteater and on the policy that Felicity inherited from poor old Mrs. Hammelmeyer. She left a brother, a nephew and a niece, but Felicity was the beneficiary. Mrs. Hawkins, a trusted friend of Mrs. Hammelmeyer is the trustee, but there have been two attempts on Felicity in two weeks.

Johnny is taken to the Mapes Hotel and then goes to the Hammelmeyer residence where Oscar Emmett, the nephew of Mrs. Hammelmeyer answers the door. Johnny and Jodiah go in and Johnny is told that Emmett does not work and spends his time in the casinos picking up change left in the slot machines.

Suddenly there is a scream when Johnny steps on Felicity's tail. Mrs. Leona Hawkins comes in and Jodiah is talked into getting Felicity calmed down for her dish of scallops. Leona is happy to see Jodiah and is pleased to meet Johnny.

She tells Johnny that a week ago Wednesday the cat was let out and when it started to rain, Mrs. Hawkins opened the door to let him in. It was then that she heard a big car zoom right for Felicity.

Last Thursday Felicity was poisoned. According to the vet, somebody put arsenic in Felicity's lobster. Johnny is told that Mrs. Hammelmeyer left instructions that Felicity was to have lobster once a week, steak three times and boiled chicken every Sunday. As long as she does that Leona can live there rent-free just like her kin, the Emmets. No one knows who gets the money if Felicity dies, and Mrs. Hammelmeyer left a sealed envelope to be opened only when Felicity dies. Leona is sure that the Emmets will get all of the money.

Joyce Emmett comes in and she bets eight-to-five that Johnny will not find the cat killer. Joyce tells Johnny that Aunt Mildred had no business leaving the money to that cat, and everyone else feels that way too. Mr. Emmett asks what interest Johnny has, and he tells him that Gillis sent for him. Emmett tells Johnny that he is a dog man, and it costs $23 a week to keep the cat, including the weekly appointment at "The Pretty Kitty". It will take 50 years to spend that money.

Felicity comes in and everyone is sure that Felicity thinks he owns them. Johnny goes back to the hotel and feels that the cat should be taken out of the house. At 3:30 a.m. the phone rings, and Leona tells Johnny that Felicity was let out and has disappeared, and she is sure he has been killed!

Johnny and Jodiah rush to the house and Joyce and Leona meet them, but Oscar is not there. Leona tells Johnny the she first noticed Felicity was gone an hour ago. Joyce and Mr. Emmett tell Johnny that they were at a movie, so Johnny decides to cruise the nightspots looking for Oscar.

Johnny visits all the casinos and finds Oscar at a roulette wheel with a large stack of chips. Oscar had been around town all night, and when he tries to leave after missing a winning spin, he pushes Jodiah down and then apologizes. Oscar tells Johnny that he did not mean to push Jodiah, but Mrs. Hawkins had been making a fool of Gillis. He has heard what is going on, and she has been giving the same line to Mr. Emmett, and she really loves him.

Johnny takes Jodiah to his room and then goes to the Hammelmeyer house where Joyce and Mr. Emmett and Leona are hunting for Felicity. Joyce offers Johnny coffee and tells her that Oscar was down town and asks what will happen if they cannot find Felicity.

Mr. Emmett calls them to the garage and Johnny sees a hatchet, blood and cat fur. Johnny takes Joyce out and Leona asks Johnny to tell Jodiah. Johnny returns to the hotel and tells Jodiah about the events of the night. Johnny then calls the local banks and gets the information he was after.

Back at the Hammelmeyer house, Jodiah calls Leona a miserable Jezebel and Johnny tells her it was for the way she planned to use Jodiah to get her out of trouble in case her scheme failed. Johnny tells Leona that she killed Felicity, and that Jodiah is having copies made of all her bank deposits since she moved in with Mrs. Hammelmeyer fifteen years ago and started paying her bills, buying her food and medicine and pocketing a good share of the money for herself.

Johnny tells her that she has $47,000 in the bank, and Leona asks why not, as Mildred did not pay her a salary. Leona tells Johnny that she will pay it back and that her name is in the envelope.

Joyce comes in with the envelope and everyone sits down. The envelope is opened and the codicil states that the unspent monies shall go the descendants of the original heir. Since Felicity was the original heir, the money goes to his descendants. Since he was a tomcat who loved to go prowling at night, did he ever have descendants! Hundreds of them!

"Well what happened later proves that miracles can happen. For at one o'clock on Friday afternoon, we got phone call from The Pretty Kitty Beauty Shop. A large tomcat with a bad cut on the back of his neck has shown up for his usual shampoo and manicure. Maybe they do have nine lives."

Notes:
- This is an AFRTS program that contains a story about the various types of milk issued to servicemen.
- Dan Cubberly is the announcer.
- Music Direction is by Amerigo Marino.

Producer: Jack Johnstone Writer: Charles B. Smith
Cast: Jack Edwards, Howard McNear, Edgar Barrier, Chester Stratton, Virginia Gregg, Will Wright, Joan Banks, Bill James

♦ ❖ ♦

Show: **The Heatherstone Players Matter**
Show Date: **7/14/1957**
Company: **New Jersey State Mutual Life Insurance Company**
Agent: **Garrett Reynolds**
Exp. Acct: **$51.25**
Synopsis: "Ah, how weary stale flat and unprofitable seem to me all the uses of this world" greets Johnny when Garrett Reynolds calls. "Alas I would a tale unfold whose lightest word would harrow up thy soul, freeze thy young blood, make thy two eyes like stars start from their spheres, thy knotted and combined locks to part and each particular hair to stand an end, like quills on the fretful

porpentine". "Garrett, have you gone off your rocker?" asks Johnny. Come on down and see.

Johnny trains to Trenton, New Jersey and cabs to Garrett's office. Garrett tells Johnny about the Heatherstone players and Cyril Peter Saint George Heatherstone who is just as bad as he sounds and is on his way over spouting his Shakespearean quotes. Heatherstone travels around teaching and performing, and after he gets the local money he leaves a lot of enemies and broken hearts behind. He is back in Trenton and is putting on a festival over radio station WVGR.

Johnny thinks he could join the cast, but Garrett tells Johnny that everyone there hates Heatherstone, except Joanie Carter who was picked to play the lead and promised a career. Heatherstone did it to lure her away from Charlie Cubberly, also a cast member. The cast would leave but Heatherstone has them under contract until the festival is over, or he is killed. Garrett has had to change the beneficiary on the policy so many times because Heatherstone uses it as a come-on.

Heatherstone walks in quoting King John, Act III scene I. Johnny is introduced and Heatherstone is told that Johnny is going to be his bodyguard until the festival is over. Three threats have been received, and the police have said nothing, which is why Johnny was called. Garrett notes that Charlie is mad with jealousy. Johnny mentions that Heatherstone has a reputation of being harsh with the cast, and Heatherstone tells Johnny he must be cruel to only to be kind. They are so ambitious, but so inadequate.

Johnny considers all of Heatherstone's associates as a threat, but Heatherstone does not believe it. Johnny is told that the festival will go on, and the next rehearsal is this afternoon. Johnny is going to be there to check up on the threats, but Heatherstone is sure that they are real, but nothing can touch him. Heatherstone leaves and Garrett wants a drink.

Garrett arranges for Johnny to sit with the engineers, and Johnny accuses Garrett of wanting to kill Heatherstone himself.

Johnny cabs to the studio and enters the control room and meets Gordon Mitchell. Johnny gets the layout of the microphones and Gordon phases in the mike on the table where the cast is rehearsing. Gordon tells Johnny that Heatherstone is the most hated man in town and a fast dealer. He convinced Gordon to invest all his savings in the festival, and it is only Beneficial Finance that is keeping him on his uppers.

Gordon phases in the mike when Joan is talking, and it is clear that Heatherstone is definitely using her. Gordon slips and tells Johnny that he had sent notes to the insurance man that someone would kill Heatherstone.

Heatherstone goes into the isolation booth to show the cast how to do something when the other sound effects man, Dan Ringo enters. Heatherstone starts speaking and suddenly falters in his speech and collapses. Joan run into the room and screams that he is dead.

Johnny runs to the isolation booth and finds Heatherstone dead. Johnny searches the stage and booth and finds nothing. Charlie is glad he is dead, and Don tells Joan that he was taking her, the way he took everyone else. Johnny tells Gordon to call the police and notes that the door to the isolation booth is open. Joan tells Johnny that she opened it, and inside it Johnny smells something and suddenly Johnny knows what killed Heatherstone. There is a faint odor of peach blossoms in the isolation booth, the odor of potassium payatin, a deadly poison.

Johnny talks to the cast and tells them what killed Heatherstone, and Don wonders if Heatherstone killed himself. Johnny tells Don that he was the last one near Heatherstone, which angers Don. Johnny asks Charlie if anyone had a better reason than he did, and Gordon tells Johnny he would like to have killed Heatherstone. Johnny notes that the only one who admits to wanting to kill Heatherstone was nowhere near him and had been with Johnny the whole time.

Johnny suggests one of the others could have slipped Heatherstone the drug but Johnny had searched the booth and found nothing. Johnny is told that Joan went in and could have removed any evidence. Joan tells Charlie that she thought she was in love with him, but now realizes she was not.

The police and the doctor arrive and agree with Johnny's conclusion on the death, but no evidence is found. The police suspect everyone but Gordon, but Johnny notes that he should be the most likely suspect.

Gordon asks if he can put his equipment away and starts picking up the cables. Johnny tells Gordon that the booth mike cable is thicker, and Gordon notes that it is an older cable with more wires. They go to the booth and take the faceplate off of the mike. Johnny thinks that the poison, potassium payatin, a crystal of potassium thayatin was vaporized in the booth.

In the mike, Johnny spots the remains of a small heating element that was used to vaporize the poison, thanks to the extra wires in the cable. Johnny shows the police the chemical discoloration and tells the police that only one man was vocal enough to admit that he wanted to kill Heatherstone, and who had an alibi because Johnny was with him.

Johnny tells Gordon he disconnected the power leads when he called the police, and Gordon tells him he is right. But it was a good try. "No flight of angels will sing him to his rest".

"So, that was it. And the company will have to pay the claim."

Notes:
- This is an AFRTS program that contains a story about the US ship HOPE.
- The first opening quote is from Hamlet, act I, scene ii. The second is from Hamlet, act V, scene v. The closing quote is Hamlet, act V, scene ii.
- Dan Cubberly is the announcer.
- Music Direction is by Amerigo Marino.

Producer: Jack Johnstone   Writer: Jack Johnstone
Cast: Virginia Gregg, Lawrence Dobkin, Richard Crenna, Sam Edwards, Frank Gerstle, Herb Vigran, Hans Conried

Show:	The Yours Truly Matter
Show Date:	7/21/1957
Company:	Universal Adjustment Bureau
Agent:	Pat McCracken
Exp. Acct:	$528.00

Synopsis: The operator calls Johnny with Johnny's call to Pat McCracken and Johnny tells him that the Kincaid case is finished. Johnny asks him to OK a case for his most important client, who holds several policies, and the one deserving the most attention — me!

Johnny travels from Los Angeles to Las Vegas, Nevada and gets a room at the Flamingo Hotel. Johnny calls Buster Favor to tell him he is on his way to Lake Mohave Resort. Buster is going to have work done on his car, so he will ride back with Johnny.

Johnny rents a brand-new air conditioned 1957 Cadillac. After dinner with Buster, they leave for the Lake Mohave Resort. Buster tells Johnny not to drive too fast, or the police will stop him. Johnny comments on the old roads along the main road, and Buster tells Johnny that they go up to mines in the hills. Buster sees lights approaching from behind him and they turn into a red flashing light.

Johnny stops and waits for the officer to walk to the car, but the door opens and a man with a gun gets into the back seat. He tells Buster that he used a flashlight to stop them. Johnny tries to upend him by starting in reverse but it does not work. He tells Johnny that this is just a stick up.

After driving down the road for a while, the man tells Johnny to pull off onto a side road and Buster whispers to him this is the road to the McKinney mine. They drive up the road until they get to a wide spot and the man tells Johnny and Buster to get out. As they turn around, the man frisks them and takes their money and jewelry. When a card falls from Johnny's wallet, the man laughs at holding up a private dick. Buster tries to attack the man, but he is shot. The man drives away and Johnny runs to help Buster.

Johnny gets to Buster, who is OK, the man was a lousy shot. Buster wanted to get onto the ground so he could bury some sharp rocks under the tires and work on the tire with his knife. Buster tells Johnny that the tire will go flat soon, so they start walking back to the road, picking up some rocks along the way for ammunition.

As Johnny and Buster walk down the mountain they spot lights coming up the road. They hide and wait for the car. Buster notices that the car is not the Cadillac. Johnny hails the car and it stops.

Buster recognizes the driver as Mack McKinney, a miner friend. Mack tells Buster that he helped the man change his tire a few minutes ago. Buster tells Mack what happened to them. Mack feels bad that he forgot to tell the man that the gate to the main road is locked. So, he cannot get back on the highway without wrecking his car. Mack remembers seeing a bulge under the man's coat, so he had an urge to get back to the mine and call the police. Johnny gives him the license number for a 1956 gray and white Chevy, license plate number CGJ-158, the car the crook is using, and tells Mack to walk up to the mine and call the police.

Johnny and Buster take Mack's jeep and drive cross-country down to the main road. Buster asks how Johnny got the plate number for the crook's car, and Johnny tells him that is why he started up in reverse, to turn on the back up lights and illuminate the plates.

When they get to the gate they find the Cadillac crashed into it. Johnny searches the Cadillac and the man is not there. Buster searches the jeep and finds wire cutters in the toolbox which will allow them to cut the fence and reach the main road. As they are driving back to the Chevy, Johnny thinks he sees a car under a storm bridge.

Suddenly the man has the gun in their backs again, he tells Buster that he got in the jeep while they were at the gate. At the man's car, he takes the keys for the jeep. He tells Johnny that his plans are messed up now, and he cannot take a chance with them getting away so he is going to have to kill them.

Johnny tells Buster that there was a car under the bridge, a police car. Johnny tells the man that there is a police officer in the back seat of his car, and Johnny throws a rock he had been carrying into the windshield. The man fires at the car until Johnny hits him. The police arrive and Johnny tells Buster he really did think he saw a car under the bridge.

"Expenses include $50 to Mack McKinney for the use of his jeep, and $81.50 for repairs on Buster's car as a way of thanking him. The car rental company will bill Pat separately. Oh, the windshield on the Chevy will have to be replaced, and it was covered by one of Pat's companies. So, Pat, you can just charge off this whole case to the recovery of that car."

Notes:
- Dan Cubberly is the announcer.
- Music Direction is by Amerigo Marino.

Producer: Jack Johnstone   Writer: Jack Johnstone
Cast: Virginia Gregg, Lawrence Dobkin, Barney Phillips, Chester Stratton, Junius Matthews

♦ ❖ ♦

Show: **The Confederate Coinage Matter**
Show Date: 7/28/1957
Company: **Providential Assurance Company**
Agent: **Bert McGraw**
Exp. Acct: **$405.10**

Synopsis: Bert McGraw calls and tells Johnny that Henry Samson, a newspaper owner in the south, collects confederate currency. He has a 50-cent piece worth $20,000 and it has disappeared.

Johnny cabs to Bert's office where Bert is reading a magazine about an old friend of his, Bob Feller. Bert tells Johnny that he helped Bob out many times until Johnny reminds Bert that he never played for the Cleveland Indians. Bert chokes and tells him it was Bob Faller of the Apalachicola Alligators.

Bert tells Johnny that Samson's secretary had called to tell that the coin was stolen. The coin was minted in New Orleans, and the mint only produced 4 such coins. Samson lives outside of Birmingham, Alabama at a place called Shade Mountain.

Johnny travels to Birmingham and is met by Mike Kopek, Mr. Samson's secretary, who will take Johnny to Zora, which is named after Samson's village in the Bible. The estate is large with a number of buildings, pools, a zoo and a turkey farm.

In the library, Mr. Samson is standing beside a large desk accompanied by a most beautiful woman named Delilah, who is Mr. Samson's wife. Samson shows Johnny the display case from which the coin was stolen. The thief did not try to pick the lock but broke the glass. Delilah tells Johnny that Mr. Samson suspects her. There were no visitors that night, and Samson did some work and then they played casino until 10:00. The only people in the house were the Samsons, Kopek, Mary Williams the maid and Digger the manservant.

Samson tells Johnny that only four coins were made because the Confederacy did not have the bullion to make more, that "dirty union blockade". The coin was a regular 1861 Union 50-cent piece. The reverse side was ground off and stamped with the shield of the confederacy.

Delilah offers Johnny a drink, again, and then fixes one for herself. Kopek is called and told to take Delilah to her room where Samson will have her dinner sent. Johnny is told that Jefferson Davis gave the coin to his great grand-pappy personally. He refused $10,000 for it in 1879 so it must be worth more now. Samson tells Johnny to earn his pay and find the coin. The gates to Zora have been locked and no one can leave until the coin is found.

Johnny goes to his room, unpacks and calls Bert. Johnny wants Bert to find out how many of those coins were made. There is a knock at the door, and Marry Williams and Digger are there.

They tell Johnny that they have snuck off to see him. They are glad he is working for a company instead of the police, and Digger is scared to death. Digger tells Johnny that Mr. Samson needs a lot of help here to run the farm, and he gets them from the prison. When someone is ready to get out, they get a job working for Mr. Samson. If they do not like it, they are sent back to prison. Johnny tells them that this is 1957, and things like that do not happen anymore.

Digger tells Johnny that he does not want to go back to that place. Mary tells Johnny that they want to get married, and they are afraid Samson will send Digger back if they ask him to let them get married. Digger will not tell Johnny anything unless he promises not to send him back. Mary tells Johnny that Digger knows who took that half dollar piece.

After dinner in the dining room Samson goes off to work. Kopek asks Johnny about his progress, and Johnny tells him he has not started yet. Johnny asks Kopek about the servants. He knows everything about them and will have their records sent to Johnny.

Kopek goes off to see Samson and Delilah calls to Johnny and asks if he likes to ride. Johnny says yes, and she tells him to meet her at the stables before breakfast. In his room, Johnny gets the files on Mary and Digger and all the facts about prison are true.

Next morning, Johnny goes riding with Delilah down by the river. At the river, Delilah just stares and tells Johnny that she married Samson for his money, but Samson is a collector. He married her because she is named Delilah.

At 11:00 Johnny calls Bert and he tells Johnny that the coin is only worth $5,000. A man named Scott had the dies and made 500 copies back in 1879. That lowered the price of the original. There are 504 in total. Johnny tells Bert he is out $20,000 unless he lets Johnny try something.

Johnny sends word to Digger and Marry. Johnny tells digger that he cannot promise he will not be sent back to prison, but Johnny will help him all he can. Mary reluctantly tells Johnny that Digger had stolen the coin. Digger broke in because Delilah threatened to tell Samson something really bad about Digger. Digger took the coin and ran down to the river to meet Mrs. Samson, but he tripped and lost the coin. They looked everywhere, but there is a good reason why they cannot find it. They take Johnny to the site and he agrees that there is a good reason.

Johnny goes back to the house and tells Kopek he wants to see Samson. Delilah comes down and notes that Johnny's bags are packed. He tells her he knows where the coin is and how it got there. He asks her why she did it, and she tells Johnny that the reason was money to get away. Johnny tells her that he has to tell Samson and she leaves.

In Samson's office Johnny tells him what he knows. Samson orders Kopek to take Digger to the place where the coin was lost, and Johnny and Samson meet them there.

In the middle of the turkey farm, Johnny tells Samson that Digger lost the coin in the field and one of the 2,000 turkeys ate the coin. Samson tells Johnny that they will have to pay him the insurance money. Johnny tells Samson that he will buy the turkeys from Samson for $5,000 and will guarantee return of the coin in 90 days, provided he lets Mary and Digger leave the estate and be responsible for the recovery of the coin. Johnny tells Samson that he is going to give them the turkeys. Samson agrees, and Johnny gets his 2,000 turkeys.

"A couple weeks after I left Birmingham, I received a letter from Mr. and Mrs. Digger telling me that they found the coin in the craw of the bird they killed for their first Sunday dinner together. Which proves once again, miracles do happen."

Notes:
- This is an AFRTS program that contains a story about the value of books and a library given to a village in Africa.
- The announcer is Dan Cubberly.
- Music Direction is by Amerigo Marino.

Producer:	Jack Johnstone Writer: Charles B. Smith
Cast:	Virginia Gregg, Eleanor Audley, Herb Ellis, Herb Vigran, Forrest Lewis, Vic Perrin

♦ ❖ ♦

Show:	**The Wayward Widow Matter**
Show Date:	8/4/1957
Company:	**Philadelphia Mutual Liability & Casualty Company**
Agent:	**Harry Branson**
Exp. Acct:	**$365.50**

Synopsis: Harry Branson calls and tells Johnny that there is no case. Harry wants Johnny to take a motor trip with a most important client, Betty Charlene Winters, a very wealthy client. Harry wants Johnny to accompany Mrs. Winters to her summer residence on Lake Wawayanda in New Jersey. Johnny will be on expense account along with a fee of $1,000 for the week. Johnny runs to grab the first train.

Johnny trains to Philadelphia, Pennsylvania and Harry is waiting for him. Johnny is told that Mrs. Winters lost her husband a short time ago, and she is very wealthy. She got half a million from her husband's insurance alone. Their home is an art gallery and she is going to give her art to the museums and sell the family estate. She is taking some things to the house in Lake Wawayanda. Johnny is going to take Mrs. Winters and a statue to the summerhouse.

Harry drives Johnny to the Winters house and Harry tells Johnny that Mr. Winters died in a car accident and that his body was never recovered. Johnny is expecting a young, rich widow, but Eric the butler takes Johnny to the library to meet Mrs. Winters, all 70 years of her.

Haskins, the chauffeur and handy man is there, and he starts to take the statue to the car. The statue is a "cherub" and really ugly. Haskins takes the statue to the car where it will be placed in a special box. Mrs. Winters asks Johnny if he can drive a Pierce Arrow. Haskins is going on vacation, and she is not sure if he will come back.

Mrs. Winters calls Harry a rascal for bringing a detective, especially such a young good looking one! Johnny gets a tour of the house and the art works. Johnny inspects the 1928 Pierce Arrow, and the car is immaculate.

At 5:00 cocktails are served. Johnny tells Harry that the statue is junk, and this case is very strange. At midnight Johnny retires and waits for everyone to go to sleep so he can get a look at the car. Johnny leaves his room and a door opens in the hallway and Johnny is knocked unconscious.

Johnny wakes up in the morning in his pajamas and in his bed. Johnny gets up and checks out the room down the hall, but it is empty. At breakfast Mrs. Winters is concerned and they go out to check out the car.

In the trunk is the box with the statute. Haskins is not there, and Johnny wants to inspect the box, but Mrs. Winters talks him out of it. She tells Johnny that Eric the butler has been with her for 30 years and is a gentleman, more so than her late husband.

She tells Johnny that she married her husband for his money and to get out of the chorus line. For the last few years they stayed buttoned up in the house while her friends were traveling. The summer-house was her idea, and it was a relief from the main house. Mrs. Winters wants to call the police, but Johnny tells her not to, he does not want to scare the attacker off. Besides, Mrs. Winters tells Johnny that the house has a very sophisticated burglar alarm system, which was turned on the previous evening. There was no one else in the house but the cook, who is as old as Mrs. Winters.

Eric serves breakfast and gives Johnny a strange look. Eric tells Johnny that he found him while inspecting the house and put him in his room. He thought Johnny had imbibed too much brandy, but Johnny tells him he was slugged. The burglar alarm was set, so whoever did it was inside the house. Johnny tells him it was dark, so the attacker may have been after Eric.

Mrs. Winters comes in and is ready to leave. She will be happy to leave and get the estate settled so she and Martha can live in peace at the lake. Johnny starts getting a wild idea on the drive to the lake, and Mrs. Winters talks the whole trip.

Johnny buys gas at the sign of the flying red horse and calls Harry and asks him to go to the Winters home and call him back at the lake.

At the lake, outside of Andover, New Jersey Johnny has to drive up a steep hill overlooking the lake to get to the garage. When Johnny mentions that he hopes the brakes will hold, Mrs. Winters mentions that the lake is over 100 feet deep at the end of the driveway. Mrs. Winters goes in to answer the phone while Johnny unpacks the car.

The box in the trunk is very heavy and Johnny leaves it perched on the trunk door to go to the phone. On the phone, Harry tells Johnny that it is terrible. How did Johnny know that Eric the butler is dead? He fell down the main staircase and Martha is beside herself. Johnny tells Harry to call the police.

Mrs. Winters calls from outside and Johnny runs out to see the box rolling down the driveway and into the lake. Mrs. Winters tells Johnny that she must have bumped it. Johnny offers to get a diver to come to the lake but she declines and decides to leave the box there in the lake, it would only be another memory of the old place. Johnny tells her she is wrong, they will get it back and whatever is in it.

Johnny hires a diver and gets the two boxes. One box has the body of Haskins, the other has the body of Mr. Winters who was supposed to have been washed out to sea. Mrs. Winters tells Johnny that Haskins had helped to get rid of Charles, so she and Martha had to do something with him. Haskins was the one who had hit Johnny, and Eric stopped him. Martha killed Eric, she had to, as Eric is the one who killed Haskins. She and Martha had planned so many wonderful things together. And now, oh dear.

"Remarks: Well, I would rather not say how I feel about a case like this, Harry. A whole crime wave by a couple of apparently sweet old ladies. The legal procedures, and there will be plenty of them, are up to you and the company, as well as recovery of the insurance paid on poor old Charles Winters. Hey, next time give me a case that does not turn my stomach, will ya?"

Notes:
- This is an AFRTS program that contains a story about the kaleidoscope and the value of sight.
- Andover, New Jersey is in the northern part of the state. There is a Lake Wawayonda and a park close to the New York state line.
- The announcer is Joe Walters.
- Music Direction is by Amerigo Marino.

Producer:	Jack Johnstone Writer: Jack Johnstone
Cast:	Virginia Gregg, Harry Bartell, Eric Snowden, Frank Gerstle

♦ ❖ ♦

Show:	**The Killer's Brand Matter**
Show Date:	8/11/1957
Company:	Universal Adjustment Bureau
Agent:	Pat McCracken
Exp. Acct:	$528.00

Synopsis: Pat McCracken calls and tells Johnny that Cooper's Bend, Nevada is having their big celebration, Frontier Week. Pat suggests that Johnny start growing a beard and get a ten-gallon hat. Cooper's Bend was just a sleepy western town, dying on its feet until last week. A publicity man, Bill Williams is trying to wake the town up with Frontier Week, and somebody is trying to put Bill Williams to sleep, the hard way.

Johnny cabs to Pat's office where he tells Johnny that this case is worth looking at. There is a big policy on William's life and Pat is worried. Williams does freelance publicity, and someone has taken a shot at him. Johnny thinks it might have been an accident, but Pat tells Johnny that the folks in Cooper's Bend are asleep at two in the morning, so watch yourself.

Johnny flies west and rents a car to drive to Cooper's Bend, Nevada. The town could pass as a set for a western movie, complete with a horse trough in front of the hotel.

A crowd gathers and tells Johnny that anyone without a ten-gallon hat goes into the water trough. Johnny is thrown in, welcome to town! Johnny looks for Bill Williams and is directed to the newspaper office where Johnny meets "Miss Cooper's Bend Frontier Week", also known as Lois. Johnny is told that Bill is with the editor, Fred Kirby, and should be back soon.

Fred comes back and Johnny tells her that Fred had helped him take a swim earlier. Fred laughs and tells Johnny that Bill is out making arrangements for the rodeo later that day and should be back soon. Lois takes Johnny to get a cup of coffee, and Fred tells her to take her time.

Johnny suspects an undercurrent between them as they drink their coffee. Lois tells Johnny that today is the last day of the celebration, and she is going away, as far away as possible. Dan Biggers comes in looking for Lois. He tells her that he is going to go to the dance with her, and a frustrated Lois leaves. Dan tells Johnny that Lois and he are engaged, so stay away from her.

Bill Williams comes in, and Johnny recognizes him as the ring leader of the dunking committee. Bill tells Johnny to get a hat to protect himself. Bill tells Johnny that he was driving through and saw the possibility of waking the town up, for the money.

Bill shows Johnny his car where a bullet hole is in the windshield. Bill feels that Dan Biggers did it because he smiled at Lois and she smiled back. Bill tells Johnny that Biggers is so jealous he cannot see straight. Johnny tells him that Fred has been watching them, so maybe he is interested in Lois too? Bill tells Johnny that after the dance tonight, he is getting his money and leaving town. Johnny tells Bill that Lois mentioned leaving town too, and Bill tells Johnny that she probably does not mean it. Bill leaves and Johnny goes to buy a hat but is caught by the swimming team again.

Johnny goes to the dance and spots Bill, who is excited about cleaning up. Johnny goes back to his hotel and has a message from Lois to see her. Johnny drives to her house on a back road. When no one answers the door, Johnny goes in and finds Lois very dead in front of the hearth.

Johnny finds Lois in front of the fireplace with a poker lying nearby. Johnny sees where she had hit her head after what looked like a struggle. Johnny hears a noise and eases outside to see a station wagon driving away with the lights off.

Johnny calls the sheriff and they go over the facts. Johnny tells him about the message and how it ties into the attempt on Bill's life. The sheriff tells Johnny that Biggers had beat up another man for asking Lois for a date. Johnny tells him about Lois' comment about leaving town and they drive to Dan's ranch.

At the Biggers ranch, they are shot at by Dan. He tells them they are not going to take him in until he finds out who killed Lois. Johnny tells him that he could not know about it unless he was there, but he tells Johnny that a deputy had told him when the call came in. Johnny tells Dan that he found out about her leaving and hit her, but Dan tells him he is crazy and fires at him.

Johnny and the sheriff leave and head back to town. The sheriff tells Johnny that Dan does not own a station wagon, and that there are a lot of them in the area.

Johnny ponders the facts over a drink and decides to talk to Fred. At the newspaper office, Bill and Fred are talking. Fred is sure that Dan did it, and he had heard Lois tell that to Dan in the office. Johnny asks Bill if he and Lois were planning on leaving together, and he tells Johnny that there was nothing to it, they had only joked about it in the office.

Bill leaves and Johnny tells Fred that he is trying awful hard to pin this on Dan, and that he has been carrying a flame for Lois. Johnny tells of spotting a station wagon at the house, the same kind of car Fred drives. Fred finally admits that he had driven to the house to talk Lois out of leaving but did not go inside. The sheriff is called and Fred is taken in.

Next morning Johnny meets Bill and he has his money and is ready to leave when the sheriff tells him he is finished. The crowd gathers and is ready to throw the hat-less Bill into the trough, but he tells them he is sick of the whole idea and they leave. Johnny realizes that the hot poker was the key to the murder. Johnny tells Bill that he is going to throw Bill into the trough and rips off his shirt to find burns and scratches.

Johnny tells Bill that Lois did that and Bill tells Johnny that he has a gun in his pocket. Bill tells Johnny that he was trying to shake Lois off, as he did not want to take someone like her to San Francisco. He told her that, and she attacked him. Bill starts to take Johnny to the alley when Johnny splashes water in his face from the trough and gets the gun from him and slugs him into the trough. Bill got dunked after all.

"Remarks: About Dan Biggers, he really wasn't such a bad guy except that he had a knot in his brain about Lois. He sold his ranch and moved away. About Bill Williams, you better cancel out his policy, Pat. He is due to go on trial soon, and in my book, he is a pretty bad risk."

Notes:
- The announcer is Bud Sewell.
- The script title page does not list anyone for musical direction.
- This is an AFRTS program that contains a story about helping one's neighbors around the world, and a story about the flag of Oklahoma.

Producer: Jack Johnstone Writer: Robert Ryf
Cast: Mary Jane Croft, Harry Bartell, Joseph Kearns, Lawrence Dobkin, Frank Gerstle, Barney Phillips

♦ ❖ ♦

Show: **The Winnipesaukee Wonder Matter**
Show Date: **8/18/1957**
Company: **International Life & Casualty Company**
Agent: **Christian Albeck**
Exp. Acct: **$0.00**

Synopsis: Johnny is called from Boston by Christian Albeck who has a routine matter for Johnny concerning a $100,000 policy, and Christian will be checking the expense account on this one.

Johnny flies to Boston and goes to Christian's office, only to be told that he should have driven to Lake Winnipesaukee, near Center Harbor, New Hampshire. Johnny is asked if he is familiar with Hardon, Carmon & Fisher, the big brokerage house, but Johnny tells Christian that he has only bought Allis Chalmers, and Sonocy Mobil. Johnny is told that Franklin Hardon is the senior partner in the firm, and that he summers in Lake Kanasatka, which is next to Lake Winnipesaukee. He went to the lake in June with his daughter Grace, and his sons Anthony and Ben. Franklin went fishing and a storm blew in and he has not been seen since and has been pronounced dead. The policy is double indemnity and the children have filed a claim. Christian is suspicious, so he wants Johnny to investigate.

Johnny drives to Center Harbor and gets a room at the Garnet Inn. Early the next morning, police chief Mike Sharp calls and arranges to meet Johnny for breakfast. Johnny meets the chief who tells him that the storm was really bad, just like the one that is brewing now. Frank knew the lake, but his boat was found on Bear Island. A search was made and Frank's hat was found. Three weeks later his fishing vest was found, and his coat was found all eaten by fish. The chief tells Johnny that he should go talk to the kids.

Johnny goes to the Harden cottage in a rainstorm and spots three sports cars out front: a Mercedes-Benz, a Jaguar and a Maserati. As Johnny reaches the door he hears gunshots. After knocking on the door, a boy comes out and holds Johnny at gunpoint. When the boy tells Johnny that he was expecting someone else, Johnny takes the gun and slugs him.

The others come out and Johnny is introduced to them. Tony recognizes who Johnny is and tells him that the gunshots were target practice that they did on rainy days, it was a suggestion from their father. Tony tells Johnny that they were expecting a friend, and the gun was a gag.

Grace tells Johnny that she is sure that their father is not dead and tells Johnny that all of them are adopted children, and they want their father back very much. She tells Johnny that filing the claim was the idea of the family attorney, Mr. Webster. Johnny is told that all of the children work in the business, and their father makes them work really hard. They tell Johnny that they have agreed to sign over their inheritances if their father is ever found alive.

Johnny is convinced that the children are on the level and is ready to leave when Grace spots her father's face in a window. They all rush outside to their father, who is standing on a bucket, and falls in the mud. Johnny goes outside to find Mr. Harden and the sheriff hiding outside the house. Johnny is told that the stunt was the idea of their attorney to test the faith of the children. He thought that the kids cared more about the money than their father. There is a big party that night, and everyone is happy.

Notes:
- The announcer is Bud Sewell.
- There is the first of several veiled references to Harmon-Kardon & Fischer stereo equipment.
- Story information obtained from the KNX Collection in the Thousand Oaks Library.

Producer:	Jack Johnstone	Writer:	Jack Johnstone
Cast:	Bob Bruce, Forrest Lewis, Virginia Gregg, Gil Stratton, Stacy Harris, Edgar Stehli		

♦ ❖ ♦

Show:	**The Smoky Sleeper Matter**
Show Date:	**8/25/1957**
Company:	**New Jersey Fire & Casualty Insurance Company**
Agent:	**Fred Larkin**
Exp. Acct:	**$130.49**

Synopsis: Fred Larkin calls early in the morning and tells Johnny that things are fine in Trenton, but not fine in Vineland, New Jersey. There was a fire there and

Fred suspects arson in a fire that destroyed $83,000 in mattresses and box springs.

Johnny travels to Trenton and Fred's office where he is told that the total loss in the fire was for $83,000. Ben Murray, who is the owner of the BenMur stores scattered around the Philadelphia area, filed the claim. The warehouse was in Vineland, where storage costs are lower. Murray has had a lot of inventory insurance and is a good client. They specialize in specialty sales. The inventory in the warehouse was for his next sale.

Murray is famous for switching: advertising one product and selling something else in its place. He is also suspected of label switching, putting a recognized label on inferior goods. The insurance was based on the invoice of goods as provided by the manufacturer's bills. The order was made up by one manufacturer for this sale.

Johnny calls his friend Adam Boles and leaves a message to meet him in Vineland, New Jersey. Johnny trains to Philadelphia and meets with Ben Murray. Murray is a real wheeler-dealer, not afraid of setting up deals in front of Johnny.

Murray tells Johnny that he works on volume and narrow margins, but the prices Johnny hears discussed tell him otherwise. While Ben is on one phone, Johnny answers the other phone for Ben, where a salesman is complaining about a dissatisfied customer who did not get what she bought and is threatening to go to the authorities. Ben grabs the phone and tells him to give her anything she wants. Ben is accusative of Johnny's reasons for talking to him, but Johnny tells Ben that they always investigate fires of this size. Ben calls Johnny a punk and tells him to leave.

Johnny rents a "drive your own" car and drives to Vineland, in the heart of the agricultural area of South Jersey. Johnny goes to the police in Vineland and meets Sgt. Luis Tomaso, who agrees to take Johnny to the fire scene. Sgt. Tomaso tells Johnny that they have been over the building with a fine-toothed comb, and Adam Boles has been helping them.

At the scene, Johnny finds a totally destroyed building. In some of the mattresses Johnny finds the best possible evidence for burning up the building. Ad Boles arrives and greetings are exchanged. Ad: You didn't send for a half-wit like Dollar, did you? Johnny: Well hold on "Stinky."

Ad tells Johnny that he is too late, Ad knows who started the fire. It was Jerry Cumber, the town wino. Ad tells Johnny and Sgt. Tomaso that Jerry was wandering around and went to sleep off a bottle of wine in the warehouse with a lighted cigarette. Ad tells Johnny to pay the claim and go home, but Johnny tells him that the case is just starting.

The fire looked accidental, but Johnny has doubts. Johnny calls Fred and tells him that he can prove fraud. Johnny asks Fred to read off the information on the invoices. Johnny asks for the label information on the "Night Cloud Sleep-rest" mattresses. The invoice shows a cost of $25.50 each. Johnny tells Fred that the labels showed a retail price of $69.00 each and Johnny remembers hearing Murray give a different cost when he was in the office. The "Night

Cloud Super Sleep" is listed at $26.20 each. The "Perfection Sleep" is $27.14 each. The manufacturer is the Golden Bedding Corporation in Woodbine.

Johnny asks for the name of another bedding company in some other city, and Johnny gets the name of Lauder Brothers, a very disreputable firm in New York.

Johnny drives to Woodbine and finds the Golden Bedding plant. Johnny goes in and presents himself as Barney Lauder. Mr. Golden tells "Barney" that he knows his father. "Barney" is now in the business and wants to talk business.

Golden tells Johnny/Barney that he has a really good business in Philadelphia, but will do business with him, and will pre-ticket the merchandise for him — he will put any price on the merchandise Barney wants.

Golden can put any name on them, and they each have 196 springs however the demonstrator model has 392 springs. The price for 10,000 units is $14.93, but Johnny tells him the price is too high. Golden agrees to bill him on the books for $29.96. That way, it looks like he paid twice as much for the units.

The phone rings and Ben Murray is calling. Golden describes his customer as wearing a blue shirt and a bow tie. Oh, no! Golden now knows that Barney really is Johnny Dollar, insurance investigator.

Johnny tells him that both he and Murray will be out of business soon when the Better Business Bureau and the Federal Trade Commission get hold of this case. Golden offers Johnny a $10,000 "commission", and Johnny tells him that he is going to get it. Golden calls Johnny a "dirty crook, a faker, a liar, a cheating dirty conniving chiseling...you ruined me!"

"Yes Fred, I am afraid your 'nice client' Ben Murray based his insurance claim on a lot of values which didn't exist. On hiked up prices, hiked up to cheat you and the income tax boys. And if that is not outright fraud, I'll eat my shirt. So, you can just forget about paying that claim, or any part of it. And I hope that you and the company will take what every legal step necessary to put these guys out of business."

Notes:
- This is an AFRTS program that contains a story about the earth shrinking because of faster transportation, a story about helping one's neighbors, and a story about the flag of Kansas.
- The announcer is Bud Sewell.

Producer: Jack Johnstone   Writer: Jack Johnstone
Cast: Russell Thorson, Jack Edwards, Will Wright, Paul Dubov, Lawrence Dobkin, Vic Perrin

Show:	**The Poor Little Rich Girl Matter**
Show Date:	9/1/1957
Company:	Masters Insurance & Trust Company
Agent:	Bert Major
Exp. Acct:	$317.75

Synopsis: Bert Major calls about a poor little rich girl who wants to take out a $200,000 straight life policy on her husband effective in two weeks. And hush — hush, it is a surprise. Nice piece of change for the company and for the girl, if she is playing a game. All the arrangements have been through the girl's lawyer.

Johnny flies to Los Angeles, California with a new pair of sunglasses to meet Roger Hackey the local agent, a repressed comic. Johnny goes to the Beverly Hilton and finally gets the details of the case from Roger.

The girl is Cynthia Dervin, and she is a strange one, like a chameleon. Roger met her in the office and she is a real trim and expensive person. She asked about various policies and how they paid off. She is a fixture in the society pages in Hollywood. Her husband, Peter, is a public figure ever since they got married three years ago.

Cynthia told Roger that her husband had just had a physical and gave Roger the report and the name of her attorney, Crane Collins. Roger went to see him and he just asked routine questions, about expediting the procedures and the importance of secrecy. Roger could not ask any questions as Cynthia was there sitting like "a mouse waiting to be pounced on" while the papers were filled out, and she signed them like they were a death warrant.

Johnny cabs to Collins' office and Collins does not understand why Johnny is there. Johnny tells him that insurance is not a surprise gift to the covered person. Collins tells Johnny that he has known Cynthia since she was born and is her guardian since the death of her parents. The husband plays an excellent game of golf and gets on with people when he wants to. Collins does not like Peter but tells Johnny that he only represents people and does not have an opinion on them or their wishes. Johnny gets the address for Cynthia and tells Collins not to tell anyone he was there, or the policy will not be issued.

Johnny makes a call and then cabs to Roger's office to borrow his car. Johnny drives to the Dervin home and meets Cynthia, who is all Johnny expected. As soon as Johnny starts asking questions she gets edgy. Johnny joins Cynthia by the pool and asks her the questions he needs to. Johnny learns that the issue date of the policy is Peter's birthday. When Johnny notes that Peter would be worth a lot of money, Cynthia gets a headache and leaves.

Johnny has seen both sides of her personality and her actions seem compulsory and not natural. The phone by the pool rings and Johnny listens in to hear Cynthia crying to a man named Eric, who tells her to meet him.

Johnny leaves and drives down the block to watch the house. Cynthia leaves and Johnny follows her, only to lose her within ten blocks.

Back in the office, Roger has no idea about Eric's identity. Roger shows Johnny a newspaper article on Peter who is playing in a golf tournament.

Johnny runs out to interview Peter, posing as a reporter.

Johnny spots Peter and asks him where his wife is, only to learn that she never watches Peter play. Johnny asks Peter about his upcoming birthday, and he tells Johnny that he is going to drive in the annual western road races that day. He has won the last two years.

Johnny cabs to Crane Collins' office and he is still there. In the office are voices, which stop when Johnny enters. Johnny waits in the lobby until Collins comes out and closes the door to his office.

Johnny asks about Peter being a racing enthusiast, and Collins tells him he did not think to mention it to him. Johnny tells him that no company will issue a policy on a racing driver. Johnny asks who Eric is and then barges into the office to find Cynthia gone.

Johnny eats and regrets not writing a report and going home. In the society page of the paper Johnny sees the answer to Eric's identity.

Johnny cabs to the police and chats with the captain who is on duty, and then goes to rent a tuxedo. Johnny cabs to the Hilton with a special pass that gets him into a society benefit, where he runs into Collins.

Johnny spots Cynthia who tells Johnny that she is glad to see him. They dance and she tells Johnny that Peter is resting up for his golf tournament. Cynthia is warm and wants to go to the terrace. On the way to the terrace Johnny spots a hawk-nosed man following them. Cynthia tells Johnny he is charming and she tells Johnny that she wishes…

Johnny asks Cynthia who Eric is. He tells her that she is planning an accident to kill her husband during the upcoming race and she screams. Johnny turns and ducks and then slugs Eric as Cynthia sobs on the floor.

"The house dick and I got them out of there, hawk-nose to police headquarters, Cynthia to a hospital. Eric turned out to be a quack psychiatrist who preyed on unstable rich women, and who was wanted in New York and Florida. He had a perfect setup in Cynthia Dervin, until he went for murder and the big money. Mrs. Dervin? Well the doctors tell me she ought to be normal mentally in a couple of years with proper psychiatric treatment."

Notes:
- This is an AFRTS program that contains a story about the value of people talking to each other all over the world, and a story about the flag of North Carolina.
- Bud Sewell is the announcer.
- The script title page does not list anyone for musical direction.

Producer: Jack Johnstone   Writer: Allen Botzer
Cast: Virginia Gregg, Herb Ellis, Frank Nelson, Marvin Miller, Peter Leeds

Show:	**The Charmona Matter**
Show Date:	9/8/1957
Company:	**Inter-Coastal Maritime & Life Insurance Company**
Agent:	**Byron Kay**
Exp. Acct:	**$103.80**

Synopsis: Byron Kay calls and asks if Johnny remembers hurricane Audrey. They have paid all the claims to the people in Louisiana and the neighboring area, as they really needed it. They just got a claim the other day from Buffalo, New York, and Byron wants to talk to Johnny.

Johnny flies to Byron's office in Boston where he is told that Charles Francis Keeley used to be a crooked promoter, who has been trying to change his life since the FTC and the SEC cracked down on him. Keeley has enough money to live comfortably with a nice wife, home and a 62-foot cruiser the *Charmona*, and the boat is the problem.

Early in June he took his boat to Detroit for some work to be done on it. A couple of weeks later on the way back, hurricane Audrey was working its way north. His wife was not worried that he had not come home, as he had often stopped in Cleveland in the past to see old friends. When he was not home by July 20th she got worried. Calls to friends and the Coast Guard turned up nothing. A few days later the life preservers from the boat turned up on the south shore of Lake Erie near Linsey. Keeley had a $35,000 policy on himself and a $106,000 policy on the boat.

Johnny travels to Buffalo, New York, gets a room at the Statler Hotel, and goes to the Keeley home. Johnny is pleasantly surprised at Keeley's wife Mona, who is young and attractive, and tells Johnny that he could have stayed at the house, it is so empty and she gets lonely.

Mona tells Johnny that every effort has been made to find the boat and Paul the pilot, who was very nice. The phone rings, and Johnny senses that something is wrong with this case. The call was from the Coast Guard, and Mona tells Johnny that Charles is all right, he has been found. Johnny is sure because of the look in her eyes, that she is lying through her teeth.

Mona tells Johnny that a farmer had picked up Charles and took care of him. Charles was out of his mind because of what had happened to him. Johnny tells Mona that she is not glad he is alive, and she agrees.

They were married nine years ago, but the things he did to make his money were not quite right. But who worries about a conscience when things are going right. Charlie started giving monies to religions and charities, money she could have used. He got moody and would not pay attention to her. And Paul, that is why she is not overjoyed that Charlie is alive.

Mona goes upstairs to change clothes for the drive to Cleveland and Johnny waits and wonders about the case as he walks through the house. In the den Johnny sees a piece of paper sticking out of a desk drawer on the desk.

The paper is a bill from an exclusive New York shop, for some very expensive gowns. In the drawer are thousands of unpaid bills, many with firm but polite warnings on them. No wonder she wished he was gone, and maybe she had a hand in getting rid of Charles. Johnny hears a noise and turns to find Mona in the doorway with a pearl handled .25 Colt in her hand.

Mona tells Johnny he should not have looked in the drawer. Johnny surmises why the wreck was no accident. Maybe he did not anticipate the storm. Mona tells Johnny that Charles is in the hospital. They are going for a ride but not to the hospital.

Johnny tells her to put down the gun and she tells Johnny that Charles did not sink the boat. Mona tells Johnny the Paul must have gone down with the boat. When the boat sank, she hoped she could take the money and run away with Paul.

Johnny shows her a gold paperweight and throws it into a mirror. Mona is distracted, and Johnny takes the gun away from her, the gun with the safety on. She tells Johnny that she could not have killed him.

The phone rings, and a man asks for Charlie. Johnny tells him that Charlie is in the hospital. The man tells Johnny that he was going to buy the *Charmona* for $98,000 when he got back from Detroit, but since the boat is lost, he wants his deposit back.

Johnny drives Mona to Cleveland and Mona says nothing on the five-hour trip. At the hospital, there is a police lieutenant and a stenographer. Mona sinks to a chair and is handcuffed to it.

Charles talks and makes the case crystal clear. He tells them that Paul refused to come on the trip back with him. The police were notified and have picked up Paul and found where he bought the various parts for the device. Charles knew that he and Mona were carrying on behind his back. He wanted to get back to sell the boat, but the boat exploded after leaving. He was lucky that he was sailing close to shore, as it saved his life. The Coast Guard divers have found the boat and there is a hole as big as a house in it. The storm might have taken a lot of lives, but it really saved Charles' life.

"I am glad there are courts to take care of situations like this. I myself would hate to dirty my hands any further. Yeah, it probably does take all kinds to make a world but believe me, the world would be a lot better off without some of those kinds. The claim on the yacht, sure it will have to be paid, and to a man who is honestly trying to live a decent life for a change."

Notes:
- Dan Cubberly is the announcer.
- This program introduces a three-act program. All previous programs in the series, except for the 5-a-week programs, had been two acts.
- This is an AFRTS program that contains a story about Dr. Tom Dooley, and a story about the flag of Wisconsin, and a story about friendship and the effort to provide medicine for a Spanish youth.
- Cast Information from the KNX Collection at the Thousand Oaks Library.

Producer: Jack Johnstone   Writer: Jack Johnstone

Cast:	Les Tremayne, Mary Jane Croft, Harry Bartell, Vic Perrin, Bob Bruce

♦ ❖ ♦

Show:	The J. P. D. Matter
Show Date:	9/15/1957
Company:	Floyds of England
Agent:	George Reed
Exp. Acct:	$204.80

Synopsis: George Reed calls, and Johnny wonders what Floyds of England has insured this time, more singing mice, wayward cats, or counterfeit money? Maybe they did a switch and insured someone against living this time? George tells Johnny that they have such a policy, but this case is something else. Floyds has a policy on a small brewery near Tamaqua, Pennsylvania. The Dortmund Brewery is insured against damage from a nearby construction project. George tells Johnny to come over and get the details.

Johnny cabs to George's office where he shows Johnny a map of the area around Tamaqua, near the Pixatawney Creek. The brewery is near the creek. Johnny tells George that he will rent a car in New York, but George tells him that he can get most of the way there by train, anything to save a dollar on the expense account. The plant is insured for $820,000. A new brewery is being built next door, and J. P. Dortmund is afraid of what might happen.

Johnny travels to New York, rents a car and drives to Tamaqua in the evening. The next day Johnny goes to the brewery, which needs a coat of paint. On top of a cliff behind the brewery, a construction project is in full swing.

At the door, a large raw-boned woman in a faded dress meets Johnny. She is J. P. Dortmund, and she accuses Johnny of being a lawyer for the outfit up on the hill. Johnny tells her he is there on behalf of the insurance company and she takes him into her private office, which is run down, just like her. Johnny is told that there is nothing fancy here, all they care about is the beer. Gretchen is called and told to bring Johnny a pitcher and a glass.

J. P. tells Johnny that the creek is the secret to their beer, it is the finest water for beer in the country. That is why the Carlson-Kemper bunch is building up on the cliff. But all their fancy equipment cannot make a beer equal to hers. J. P. tells Johnny that she ages the materials for three full months, and they come up with a better brew. They are getting ready to blast up on the hill, and the whole thing will come down and wreck her equipment. She tells Johnny to see if he can stop them. Johnny thinks that maybe she is on to something.

Johnny drives to the construction site on the cliff and talks to James Carlson. He tells Johnny that they are not going to do any harm to the Dortmund brewery. He cannot understand how she stays in business, her methods were out of date fifty years ago. He had offered to buy the plant for half a million (well it was actually $450,000), but she would not sell.

Carlson shows Johnny the permits and he tells Johnny that he has hired one of the best blasters in the country. The blast is scheduled for tonight. Johnny meets Sidney Crutchfield, who is working with a slide rule. Johnny learns that he has done the blasting on some of the biggest construction jobs in the country.

Sidney tells Johnny that he will set the charges tonight at two o'clock, and no one is to be there. Sidney gives Johnny a tour of the site and shows Johnny the entire layout of the charges and how they will be set off. Johnny is sure that this man could do nothing wrong.

Johnny drives to the brewery and finds the place totally deserted. Johnny slips the lock on the door and goes into the office to find it in shambles. Someone had been taking papers from the files. Johnny hears J. P. say "I'm sorry Johnny" and then she knocks him out, takes some papers and leaves.

Johnny comes to with a bad headache wondering why J. P. hit him. On the floor, Johnny finds a bill addressed to J. P. personally for 21 cases of dynamite. Johnny looks at his watch and it is 1:52 a.m. Johnny now knows where the rocks will land and why he was left there to be crushed by the rocks.

Johnny phones the operator and tells her to call the construction site, but she tells him that their lines were disconnected earlier that day. Johnny stumbles to his car and somehow drives to the top of the cliff. Johnny yells at Sidney to not blast and pulls his gun to stop him. Sidney realizes that something is wrong when Johnny faints.

Johnny realizes that Sidney saw the bill for dynamite that Johnny had taken with him, and good sense told him to stop the blasts. Later that morning, Sidney finds where J. P. had set a charge, which would go off from concussion and divert the rocks onto her brewery. No one would have ever known. When the police catch her, she has the books to the brewery with her, and they showed that she was broke.

Notes:
- Tamaqua, Pa. is about 30-40 miles NW of Allentown, Pennsylvania.
- This is an AFRTS program that contains a story about the flag of Massachusetts, a story about milk served to servicemen, and a story about the flag of Hawaii.
- The announcer is Dan Cubberly.

Producer:	Jack Johnstone	Writer:	Jack Johnstone
Cast:	Eleanor Audley, Jeanne Bates, G. Stanley Jones, Alan Reed, Austin Green		

◆ ❖ ◆

Show: The Ideal Vacation Matter
Show Date: 9/22/1957
Company: Universal Adjustment Bureau
Agent: Pat McCracken
Exp. Acct: $115.25

Synopsis: Pat McCracken calls, and Johnny thought he was on vacation. Pat was, but Ned Grant the Broadway columnist has forced him to cancel his vacation. Grant is heavily insured and is taking his vacation. He has made a lot of enemies in his time and one of his enemies is trying to make Ned's vacation permanent.

Johnny cabs to Pat's office where Pat is waiting for him. Johnny is told that Ned prints some pretty blunt stuff some time. He dug up some evidence on Willie Bemis a couple years ago, and Bemis went to jail. Bemis broke out last night, and Grant probably does not know about it. The police want to protect Grant but no one knows where he is to protect him. Johnny is to find Grant before Bemis does.

Johnny heads to New York City and talks to the manager of Grant's apartment. He has no idea where Grant went on vacation and was only told to hold his mail. Grant is unpredictable and has phone calls all the time and strange people seeing him at all hours. Grant had his phone disconnected before he left. Johnny tells the manager about Bemis' escape, and the need to find Grant before Bemis does. Johnny is referred to Doris Anthony, a close friend of Grants'.

Johnny hails a cab, but sees Willie Bemis going into the service entrance. Johnny runs back to the manager's office, breaks down the door to find the manager on the floor. He tells Johnny a man had barged in after Johnny left, and that he only told the man what he told Johnny.

Johnny looks up Doris Anthony's address and cabs there. She does not know where Grant is. Doris looks familiar to Johnny and she tells Johnny that Grant helped her in his column. She thinks the ideal vacation for Ned is where ever girls are. Johnny tells her about Bemis, and she becomes anxious. She remembers Ned stopping at a travel agency last week.

Johnny stops in to see a friend at the newspaper. In the morgue Johnny finds a picture of Doris sitting at a table with Willie Bemis. Johnny rushes back to Doris' apartment, but she is gone and the manager tells Johnny that she left with a suitcase.

Johnny goes to the travel agent and he tells Johnny that he had made a number of reservations for Grant. Grant always makes reservations and then never shows up. Doris calls Johnny at the travel agent's office and tells Johnny that she is no longer a friend of Willie's. She thinks that Ned might be at a ski lodge in Vermont. He has gone there before to get away from things. It is called Hastings Lodge, and is located about 20 miles beyond Bradberry.

Johnny travels to Hastings Ski Lodge and arrives after dark to find the lodge dark. Johnny goes into the lodge and senses that someone is there with him. Johnny calls for Grant and Bemis tells Johnny that he has the wrong person, that Ned is not there yet.

Bemis takes Johnny's gun and tells Johnny that Doris had told him where Grant was, after a little talk. Johnny wishes he had stayed at home and realizes what the ideal vacation is and where Ned Grant is. A car drives up and Bemis tells Johnny to answer the door. Johnny opens the door and Doris is there.

Johnny throws open the door against Bemis, grabs Doris and they drive to New York in her car. Johnny calls the local sheriff to have them pick up Bemis and arrive in New York at dawn.

Johnny rings the doorbell at the manager's office and he does not answer. Johnny tells Doris to call the police and goes to Grant's apartment. No one answers the door, so Johnny climbs out on a ledge and goes to the bedroom window to see Ned Grant asleep, with an empty bottle beside the bed. So, the ideal vacation is to tell everyone you are going out of town, and then lock yourself in your apartment where no one will bother you.

Johnny lets himself in and opens the door to let Doris in, along with Bemis, who has a gun. Bemis thanks Johnny for finding Grant for him. Bemis starts to shoot Johnny when the hallway is full of police who shoot Bemis' gun away from him. Ned wakes up and asks what is going on, and why Bemis is there? Johnny tells him to write it off as a bad dream.

"Look, the next time you send me out to protect a guy, don't pick one who is going to sleep all the way through the deal, huh. I don't know, it kind of takes the sport out of it. And Pat, since I didn't find a man who ran away for you, on account of he never really ran away, well how about sending my fee on this one to the community chest."

Notes:
- This is an AFRTS program with the typical stories edited out.
- Johnny donates his fee to the Community Chest on this one.
- Dan Cubberly is the announcer.

Producer:	Jack Johnstone	Writer:	Robert Ryf
Cast:	Mary Jane Croft, Lawrence Dobkin, Joseph Kearns, Jack Edwards, Barney Phillips Byron Kane		

♦ ❖ ♦

Show:	**The Doubtful Dairy Matter**
Show Date:	9/29/1957
Company:	**Tri-Western Property & Casualty Insurance Company**
Agent:	**Peter Hardy**
Exp. Acct:	**$418.00**

Synopsis: Peter Hardy calls and tells Johnny that there is trouble with the Amenian dairy farm near Reno. A year and a half ago Amenian lost a silo and it cost Peter $21,000. Amenian just lost a compound Silo and the cost is $56,000. Peter thinks it is arson.

Johnny travels to Reno, Nevada and meets with Peter. The Amenian dairies are just north of Reno, and the silos are specially made for him. The claim was filed the same day for the last one.

Johnny rents a car and drives to the Amenian dairy and is impressed with its size and efficiency. Johnny is shown the silo remains, which only has the concrete base left. Johnny is told that only Mr. Barnwell and Amenian know how the silo was built. The secret was in the ventilation. He is building a new one based on a better design.

Johnny tells Amenian that it was to his benefit to lose the silo, and that the fire came at just the right time for a new and better silo. Amenian tells Johnny that he does not think the silos were burned, and if they were, Johnny will never be able to prove it.

Johnny calls police Lt. Brady and he tells Johnny that he could find nothing to prove arson. Johnny remembers an old trick and buys a loaf of white bread. Johnny goes back to Amenian's ranch and drops a piece of bread in the ashes and then puts it in his mouth. Amenian is confused until Johnny tells him that it was a sure test for the presence of kerosene. Amenian tells Johnny to leave and not come back.

Johnny calls Herb Calbert at the bank and then goes to see him. Johnny asks Herb for information on Amenian. Herb tells Johnny that Amenian banks with him, and is the biggest account they have, and his financial condition is excellent. Herb tells Johnny that he is wrong when Johnny tells him that he has found evidence of arson. Herb tells Johnny that his employees love Amenian, as do his competitors. Johnny has dinner and drinks with Herb and gets a list of firms who do business with Amenian.

After visiting a casino with Herb, Johnny goes back to his hotel where the clerk tells Johnny that a man had been waiting for him, but it was not Amenian. The clerk spots the man leaving the hotel and Johnny follows. Johnny runs down the street after the man and follows him down an alley where the man attacks Johnny and beats him.

A moving van interrupts the beating and the driver carries Johnny back to the hotel. The hotel doctor patches up Johnny and notices a ring from the YMCA Johnny got for helping with a softball team. The doctor gives Johnny a shot and Johnny vaguely hears the doctor mentioning that the ring must have made a mark on the man who hit him as he goes out for the night.

The next morning Johnny goes to see Herb, who tells him that a man Johnny is curious about is in need of money and owes the bank money and did so last year. Herb tells him that the man must be at the Amenian ranch.

Johnny and Herb drive to the ranch and meet Amenian coming out of the pasteurizing plant. Amenian tells Herb that he heard a car and thought it was Barnwell. Johnny is about to apologize to Amenian until he sees a bandage on his face. Amenian tells Johnny that he cut himself shaving.

Johnny is about to pull the bandage off when Barnwell comes up and Johnny tells him that he knows Barnwell because of his bruised and bandaged face. Johnny rips off Barnwell's bandage and there is a mark on his face where Johnny had hit him. Johnny beats Barnwell to get him to talk about burning Armenian's silos.

"Yeah, he talked alright, plenty, about a racket so old I hadn't heard of it in years. A crooked businessman who burned out his own clients to get himself more work. And in this case, a natural, because he was the only one who shared Aram's secret construction plans. And by the time I was through with him, he blabbed about some of his other clients he had taken the same way."

Notes:
- **This is an AFRTS program that contains a story about Lt. Fred**

Hargesheimer, and his friendship with natives on an island, and a story about mercy and truth meeting each other via help given to earthquake victims in Chile.
- The announcer is Dan Cubberly.

Producer:	Jack Johnstone Writer: Jack Johnstone
Cast:	Paul Dubov, Will Wright, John Dehner, Harry Bartell, Parley Baer, Forrest Lewis

♦ ❖ ♦

Show:	**The Bum Steer Matter**
Show Date:	10/6/1957
Company:	**Tri-Western Life & Casualty Insurance Company**
Agent:	**Hal Verski**
Exp. Acct:	**$0.00**

Synopsis: Jake Denim calls Johnny from Colorado. He has a cattle ranch there and a policy with Tri-Western in Denver. He has no trouble, but his brand is the "Lazy JD", and "JD" are Johnny's initials. Jake listens to the radio programs every week, and he is sure that Johnny would want to come out and get some local color for his program. Johnny hems and haws about some reports that are due and Jake tells him that he will be expecting him. Johnny feels that Jake is lying through his teeth.

Johnny calls Hal Verski in Denver and asks him to OK and expense account for him. Hal tells Johnny that Jake has about $40,000 in insurance and Johnny tells Hal about the call from Jake. Hal tells Johnny that if he finds something they will pay for it, otherwise Johnny will have a nice vacation to pay for.

Johnny clears up the paperwork in four days and flies to Denver, rents a car and drives to Jake's ranch in Craig, Colorado. Johnny eats lunch at the hotel in Craig and gets directions to the ranch. The waitress asks if Johnny is a relative, tells him it was real nice and that everyone was there and then runs off.

Johnny drives to the ranch and sees a piece of black crepe on the doorframe. A woman meets Johnny at the door and asks Johnny why he did not come earlier. Jake was buried this morning, and she thinks he was murdered.

The girl was dressed in black and had been crying. The girl is Virginia, Jake's daughter. She tells Johnny that Big Mike Craven who owns the "C Lucky Star" ranch, and who wants to own all the other ranches in the area, was responsible for Jake's death. Jake died from anthrax, at least that is what they said it was.

Johnny talks to Virginia and she confirms that she thinks someone is trying to infect her herd. A young man comes in and asks Johnny who he is. The man tells Virginia that the hands will take their orders from her now, and he asks her to marry him. He will give up medical school to marry her, and she needs him to help run the ranch.

Johnny asks who he is, and he is Peter Trimmer, and his father owns a small ranch nearby. Pete tells Johnny that Jake died from "galloping anthrax" that he got from a steer. Pete tells Johnny that the steer has been buried on orders of the vet and the state inspector.

Johnny leaves and calls the state inspector, who tells Johnny he has never seen the steer as he was confined to bed at the time. Johnny calls the vet, who is out at the moment.

In the hotel, Johnny reads an article in a magazine that makes him call the vet again. The vet tells Johnny that he was going to see Mike Craver, an old college roommate. The vet had spotted the anthrax, which was only in one Hereford steer. He tells Johnny that the steer is buried in a far corner of the "Lazy JD" property. Johnny tells him that they are going out to look at the steer.

Johnny gets two assistants to handle the shovels, some flash lights and then they all go to dig up the steer. Once the cow is uncovered the vet tells Johnny that the color is not right, that there is no sigh of anthrax in the cow. Johnny asks if a poison could have caused it, and tells the vet that strychnine often produces signs similar to tetanus or lockjaw.

The vet tells Johnny that he remembers a poison from his school days, quintanigen sulfide. He tells Johnny that it still would not explain why Jake died. Johnny notices that the brand looks like it was put on over another brand. Johnny asks the vet to skin off the hide to determine what the original brand was. The vet tells Johnny that only a small amount of the poison would have killed Jake. The vet gets the hide off, and the original brand was the "C Lucky Star".

Johnny and the vet drive back and discuss the implications. The vet is sure that Big Mike did not do it. Instead of going to the Craven ranch, Johnny drives to the "K bar K" ranch and the vet tells Johnny that Carl Trimmer is just holding on.

At the ranch, Pete calls out and Johnny opens the door and they go up to Pete's room. Johnny tells him that the "Lazy JD" would be a nice place to get hold of. Johnny asks Pete where he got the quintanigen sulfide, and Pete tells him he does not know what he is talking about. Johnny shows him a marker in a toxicology book, and Pete is speechless. When Johnny asks how he gave the poison to Jake, Pete pulls a gun and the vet hits Pete with a chair.

"Expense account item 8, $55.95, living expenses incurred while waiting for the autopsy on Jake Denim. And yes, the same drug was used on him as on the Hereford steer. A small bottle of the rare drug was found in Pete Trimmer's trunk. So, Pete's not only lost a chance on a nice ranch, but also for living very long. Expense account total, including incidentals and fare back to Hartford, $618.50. Ah, on second thought, hows about sending that check to the Community Chest, then I'll feel a little better about this case, and myself too."

Notes:
- This is an AFRTS program that contains a story about the value of books sent to Tanganyika, and a story about friendship and how the Armed Forces uses friendship to aid others.
- This is the second case where Johnny requests that his expenses be donated to the Community Chest.
- Quintanigen sulfide is another Jack Johnstone original poison.

- The announcer is Dan Cubberly.

Producer: Jack Johnstone Writer: Jack Johnstone
Cast: Virginia Gregg, Jeanne Tatum, Will Wright, Jack Edwards, Howard McNear, Sam Edwards, Forrest Lewis

♦ ❖ ♦

Show: **The Silver Belle Matter**
Show Date: **10/13/1957**
Company: **Floyds of England**
Agent: **George Reed**
Exp. Acct: **$317.10**

Synopsis: George Reed calls Johnny with a $25,000 possibly $50,000 problem. Mercedes Crabtree has had a policy for 30 years. Someone took a shot at her and missed, and last night she disappeared.

Johnny cabs to George's office and he tells Johnny that this case is important. Mrs. Crabtree was one of the first American clients of Floyds, and Mr. Murdock Morton, the president of the company personally sold the policy. At the time, they became good friends and still correspond regularly.

Mrs. Henrietta Scott, the only friend of Mrs. Crabtree's in Silver Gulch, Montana, wrote to Mr. Morton to tell him of the problem. Mrs. Scott was supposed to have dinner with Mrs. Crabtree but she was not there. After two days, she wired Mr. Morton. The beneficiary is Mrs. Crabtree's favorite charity.

Johnny travels to Butte and takes a bus to Silver Gulch, rents a car and drives to the home of Mrs. Scott, who thinks Johnny is from an antique shop. Mrs. Scott tells Johnny that Mrs. Crabtree is still missing, and that the sheriff is still looking for her. Most of the residents in town have no use for her because she is stopping progress.

Charlie Greenpaw is trying to turn the town into a tourist attraction and Mercedes will not sell any of her land. She owns half of Main Street and the Silver Belle mine, the richest silver mine in Montana at one time. Mercedes was walking up to her mine when she was shot at. Mrs. Scott looks out the window and "well I'll be first cousin to a stink bug", she sees Charlie Greenpaw and Slim Richards, the sheriff's deputy walking towards the mine.

Johnny drives to the mine and introduces himself to them at a new "No Trespassing" sign which they take seriously. They are not going in but are considering it seriously. They tell Johnny if he wants to go in, there is nothing stopping him. Johnny goes into the mine and walks down a tunnel only to be shot at.

Johnny throws a rock into the tunnel, gets a shot in return and feigns being shot. When a woman calls out, Johnny calls out to Mrs. Crabtree and tells her that Mr. Morton is worried about her. Johnny walks up to her and tells her that Mrs. Scott had written to Mr. Morton. She tells Johnny that she came into the mine and hurt herself, and Johnny will have to carry her out.

Johnny takes her to her cabin and Mrs. Scott comes in. Mercedes tells Henrietta to go get the doctor. Johnny asks her why she shot at him, and she tells Johnny that she thought Johnny might be one of Charlie's men. She will not sell the mine because that is where her husband and his men are buried. She told everyone that if anyone sets foot on her property, she will shoot first and ask questions later.

Johnny goes to his hotel for dinner and is stopped by Charlie Greenpaw. Johnny asks him why he did not go into the mine. Charlie tells Johnny that his wife put him up to looking in the mine for Mrs. Crabtree otherwise it might look like he was responsible for hurting her. Charlie tells Johnny that Mrs. Crabtree has taken a shine to Johnny, as that was all she could talk about when the doctor was there.

Charlie tells Johnny that he will give him $1,000 if he will get Mrs. Crabtree to sell him the mine and the acreage beside Mrs. Scott. Johnny tells Charlie that he really wants the property and he tells Johnny he wants to open a dude ranch. The fire bell rings, and Slim Richards runs in to tell Charlie that Mrs. Crabtree's cabin is on fire.

Johnny rushes to the cabin, and finds Mrs. Crabtree wrapped in a blanket beside the sheriff's car. She tells Johnny to tell Charlie that she will sell to him, as there is nothing left to stay for. Charlie comes up and Johnny asks him for a map of the area.

In Charlie's office Johnny looks at the map and gets sick to his stomach. Johnny drives to Mrs. Scott's and knocks at the door. She lets Johnny in and he asks to see Mrs. Crabtree, but she cannot do that, as the doctor does not want her disturbed.

Johnny accuses her of burning the cabin with her in it. "She trusted you, she thought you were the only person she could trust. When she found out different she decided to sell her land and get away from here." Henrietta calls them lies.

Johnny tells her that she owns most of the property along the Crabtree property, and Charlie would not buy hers without buying Crabtree's as well. And when Mrs. Crabtree would not sell, you decided to get the land the hard way. Johnny tells her that she shot at Mrs. Crabtree to set up her alibi.

Johnny forces his way into the bedroom and wakes up Mrs. Crabtree. Henrietta comes in with a gun and tells Johnny to get back. Mercedes tells Johnny that Henrietta started the fire and there is a struggle and Johnny gets the rifle away from Henrietta. Henrietta yells at Johnny for ruining the whole thing.

"I was ready to leave Silver Gulch the next day, but I stayed over an extra week for a little English gentleman named Murdock Morton to arrive and claim his bride. Yeah, just about everybody in Montana came to Mrs. Crabtree's, excuse me, Mrs. Morton's wedding, everybody that is except her old friend Mrs. Henrietta Scott."

Notes:
- This is an AFRTS program that contains a story about Dr. Tom Dooley, a story about British divers who dive to the bottom of the ocean and find Portuguese relics.
- There was a Silver Belle mine in Montana, which operated in the 1880's.

- The announcer is Dan Cubberly.

Producer:	Jack Johnstone	Writer:	Charles B. Smith
Cast:	Virginia Gregg, D. J. Thompson, G. Stanley Jones, Frank Nelson, Sam Edwards, Will Wright		

♦ ❖ ♦

Show: The Mary Grace Matter
Show Date: 10/20/1957
Company: Mid-Eastern Life & Casualty Company
Agent: Ben Perrin
Exp. Acct: $0.00

Synopsis: Randy Singer calls and tells Johnny he is not doing so fine. You better come down here on account of Mary Grace Marshall. Oh, you know her too? I just spent a weekend with her in New York and we had a ball. Johnny, your little girlfriend has been murdered. I'll grab the first plane. Yeah, you better.

Johnny makes reservations to fly to New York City and then calls Ben Perrin at Mid-Eastern to tell him that a policy holder, Mary Grace Marshall has been killed. Ben tells Johnny that he has to wait until authorization has been obtained. When Johnny tells him that she was a personal friend, Ben approves the expense account.

Johnny thinks about Mary Grace on the flight to New York, and it hurts. Johnny wanted to marry her some years ago, but she had a career, and Johnny was not really the marrying kind anyway, so they remained friends, good friends.

Johnny cabs to the 18th precinct and Randy tells Johnny that all the clues point to the one person who was known to be with her when she was killed. She struggled and fell and hit her head on the fireplace. Randy offers Johnny a cigarette and lights it with a lighter.

Randy tells Johnny that the coroner says that she was killed late Sunday night by someone who spent several hours with her. Johnny realizes that he was with her late Sunday night. Randy is flicking the lighter and Johnny recognizes it. Randy tells him that it was left in the apartment by whoever killed Mary Grace Marshall.

Randy reads the inscription on the lighter, and Johnny tells Randy that he must have left it there. The wife of the building superintendent saw Johnny leave, fingerprints and cigarette butts prove that Johnny was there.

Randy asks Johnny what he was doing there and Johnny explodes at him, and then apologizes. Johnny tells Randy that they spent the afternoon at the Bronx zoo and had dinner and drinks in the apartment and listened to music. Johnny had picked up a bottle of scotch and had one or two light drinks, but Randy tells him the bottle was almost empty. Mrs. Walker the wife of the building super found the body. She went up to the apartment when she heard the screams. Randy tells Johnny that he ought to go see her. Randy tells Johnny that he is the prime suspect until he can help Randy prove he is wrong.

Johnny and Randy drive to the apartment and Johnny sees the signs of the struggle in the apartment. Johnny finds the bottle of scotch in the living room and tells Randy that he left the bottle in the kitchenette. In the refrigerator, Johnny finds a bottle of soda almost full. Nobody drinks that much scotch straight unless they are a lush, or unless you need a jolt for your nerves adds Randy.

Johnny and Randy talk to Mrs. Walker, a young doll with too much makeup. Johnny notices a strange spicy odor but forgets about it. She tells Randy that her husband has been sick and stays in bed. He heard screams, and she asked him what to do about it, but he told her to go back to sleep. She tried to sleep and heard noises later, like her husband was trying to get up.

At 2:00 a.m. she went upstairs and found the body. Johnny asks to talk to the husband, and she says sure, if he is sober enough. Johnny smells the odor again as he goes into the wife's bedroom.

In the husband's bedroom Johnny smells the odor of stale booze and finds the walls plastered with pinup pictures and photos of Mary Grace. The husband tells his wife that he does not want any more of that stuff. He tells Johnny that he heard screaming in the apartment, and then it stopped and he wrote it off as a nightmare and the wife tells him that he was dreaming about the doll upstairs instead of paying attention to her and about sneaking around to see her.

The doctor comes in and reprimands everyone for disturbing the patient. He has a serious heart condition and an infection. Johnny tells Randy to come back upstairs and he can clinch the case.

Johnny shows Randy the scotch bottle and the smears where someone tried to hide the prints. In the living room, Johnny shows Randy the hi-fi with the same record they were listening to Sunday night, the Dolorema by Vinghetti still in it. They had shut it off because it became too noisy with the screams during the death scene.

Randy tells him that the husband was responsible for it and killed her because she would not have him. He sees you with Mary Grace, he hears the screaming and he wakes up his wife and does not let her go up. After you leave he goes up and kills her. The wife ties it all up with the screams.

Johnny and Randy go back down stairs and Johnny tells him the same circumstances would work for her if she killed Mary Grace. Johnny tells Randy that the strange odor is cardamom, the drunkard's friend. You can drink all night, chew on some and no one will know. The odor was so strong in her room, maybe she is the lush.

In the hallway, the doctor tells them that the husband does not even drink and could not have gotten out of bed. The wife comes out and she tells them that the husband is dead. She asks if they are going to try and pin the murder on her, and Johnny tells her that she has already pinned it on herself. "You thought you left no fingerprints on the bottle" Johnny tells her and she blurs out that she used a handkerchief.

She pulls a gun and admits killing the dame on the second floor and the doctor slugs her from behind. Randy is happy now, but it does not bring back Mary Grace.

"I took on this case myself because of Mary Grace, and whatever she may have meant to me is none of the company's business. Oh, sure you will have to pay the claim on her policy, so let it go at that, will ya? The rest is on me, I want it that way understand? For old time's sake."

Notes:
- Another AFRTS program with the typical stories edited out.
- I searched through Groves Musical Dictionary and have come to the conclusion that the composer and opera noted in the story are another excellent piece of Jack Johnstone fiction. In reviewing the script, the original reference was to "Electra" by {Richard} Strauss.
- Johnny waives his expenses for personal reasons on this case.
- The announcer is Dan Cubberly.

Producer:	Jack Johnstone	Writer:	Jack Johnstone
Cast:	Vic Perrin, Les Tremayne, Paula Winslowe, Frank Nelson, Byron Kane, Jeanne Tatum		

♦ ❖ ♦

Show:	**The Three Sisters Matter**
Show Date:	**10/27/1957**
Company:	**Tri-State Life & Casualty Company**
Agent:	**Earle Poorman**
Exp. Acct:	**$351.20**

Synopsis: Earle Poorman calls from Green Mountain Falls, Colorado. Earle wants Johnny to join him. An important client has disappeared.

Johnny travels to Colorado Springs, Colorado where Earle meets Johnny at the airport. Earle tells Johnny that Green Mountain Falls is just east of here. Earle is staying at the Lucky 4 ranch, the last place that Misha Rolonov, the pianist was seen. He has a place up on the mountain where he and his three daughters, Olga, Maria and Ada — actually they are stepdaughters, live. They all got here ten days ago, after a concert tour of Europe.

Misha likes to take long walks and left on one three days ago. He stopped in at the Lucky 4 for coffee and has not been seen since. There has been snow, which covered up the any tracks he might have made. Earle knew him well, and Misha really loved the girls.

At the Lucky 4 ranch Johnny meets Ray Smischny who tells Earle and Johnny that Rolonov's body has been found near a bear cave with a bullet in the back of his head.

Johnny and the others go to the cave in a jeep, and Ray tells Johnny that the bear ate off of the garbage every day and he was going to kill it, but he has not seen it for several days before Rolonov was killed so maybe someone else has killed the bear.

Ray has also found a .257 Roberts cartridge near the cave. All the hunters in the area use either a .30-06, a .270 or a .30-30. The only .257 belongs to one of the girls at the Rolonov cabin, and one of the daughters is a good shot. Ray cannot believe that it was one of them.

Earle and Johnny drive to the Rolonov cabin and Earle cannot think of anyone who would kill Misha. The policy has no direct beneficiary, it is based on his will, which no one knows the location of. Misha had made it clear that the will would show up at the proper time.

At the cabin, Johnny meets a beautiful girl dressed like a model from Charles of the Ritz. She is Olga, the oldest sister, and she is very glad to meet Johnny. Johnny tells her that they had not found out anything about their father.

Johnny meets another sister, Ada who is at the piano playing a piece that her father had written on the morning her father left. She thinks it has some special meaning. Ada bristles at Olga when Olga mentions that Ada thinks she should be the pianist in the family.

Johnny asks Olga where she was on the morning her father left, and Olga tells Johnny that she was in Colorado Springs shopping. Maria and Ada were doing the dishes when she left. Maria arrives and meets Johnny. Johnny is surprised as Maria is dressed in hunting clothes and carrying a high-powered rifle.

Maria gives Johnny the rifle and Olga tells Johnny that all she does is tramp around and shoot at things. Johnny notes that the rifle is a .30-06, and she tells Johnny that she has another rifle, a .22. Johnny finally tells them that their father's body has been found, shot by a high-powered rifle.

Maria and Olga yell at each other while Ada is playing the piece her father wrote. Johnny tells her to play the piece again and notes that the first three notes are "A D A". She plays the rest of the piece to spell out the message "D E F A C E E D G E C A G E B E D", the canary cage.

Johnny opens the canary cage and finds the Last Will and Testament and a note. The note tells Johnny that Rolonov has fingered his killer. The note reads "and my reason for deliberately omitting her from my will is not only because of the self-centered life she has always led, not only because of her constant completely selfish extravagance, an extravagance which finally led her to forging my name on checks. Then when I discovered that she was sneaking out and practicing with the old rifle over the mantle".

Suddenly Olga has the rifle. She tells them that the rifle has five shots in it, one for each of them, including one for her. There is no other way out. She tries to fire the rifle but it is empty. Maria attacks her and takes the gun from her. Maria and Ada tell Johnny that they had taken the bullets from the gun and suspected Olga.

"Why, why, what kind of a mind can be so twisted?"

Notes:
- This an AFRTS program with all of the stories edited out.
- The .257 Roberts was introduced in 1934, and was a very popular and versatile cartridge.
- Cast Information from the KNX Collection at the Thousand Oaks Library.
- The announcer is Dan Cubberly.

Producer: Jack Johnstone   Writer: Jack Johnstone

Cast:	Joseph Kearns, Vic Perrin, Virginia Gregg, Lucille Meredith, Lillian Buyeff, Bill James

◆ ❖ ◆

Show:	**The Model Picture Matter**
Show Date:	11/3/1957
Company:	Universal Adjustment Bureau
Agent:	Pat McCracken
Exp. Acct:	$103.00

Synopsis: Pat McCracken calls Johnny about a beautiful model, Dorothy Blair. Johnny recognizes her as the girl with the million-dollar face who is on a lot of people's minds. "Well she is no daydream to me — she is a nightmare" replies Pat. That face of hers is insured for $100,000 and someone is trying to tear it up. She got slugged last night.

Johnny cabs to Pat's office where Johnny gets the address for Dorothy Blair and heads for New York City. Johnny arrives at Dorothy's apartment just as the doctor is leaving. Dorothy tells Johnny that there will not be any permanent scars.

She came home last night and a man hit her inside her apartment and then he left. She does not think it was a burglar. She is sure that it was Jerry Dunsmuir, a real creep, the real article. She modeled for him a year ago and swore that she never would again, but she did so just the other day. He wanted to take some street shots of winter clothes. After the second picture, he started up on her, and she left.

Johnny goes to see Jerry Dunsmuir, but his office is closed. Johnny contacts an old friend, Lt. Al Ricco at 18th precinct. Ricco tells Johnny that he has an unsolved murder with no leads. Johnny tells Ricco about Jerry Dunsmuir, but Lt. Ricco does not know anything about him. Ricco gets a phone call and learns that Jerry Dunsmuir has been found floating in the river.

Johnny cabs to Dorothy's apartment, and Edward Chandler is there. Edward leaves and Johnny asks Dorothy about the picture shoot, then tells her about Jerry. Dorothy asks if Johnny suspects her, and he tells her no. She can prove that Jerry took pictures, and she gets the envelope with prints of the pictures taken. Dorothy tells Johnny that Jerry looked strangely at her when she told him not to bother her anymore. After leaving Johnny vaguely remembers Ed Chandler's face but cannot remember where.

Johnny goes to Dunsmuir's studio where the secretary Susan Billings is closing up and does not want to answer any more questions. Johnny buys her a drink and she tells Johnny that she does not know who would want to kill Jerry. Susan tells Johnny that Jerry had changed about women and does not know Ed Chandler. She tells Johnny that she and Jerry were going to be married.

Johnny goes to see Lt. Ricco, who tells Johnny that Dunsmuir had a weakness for women. Johnny and Ricco go to see Dorothy and observe Dorothy coming out of her apartment with Ed Chandler. Ricco tells Johnny that the man is Ed Chatsworth and then Johnny remembers seeing his picture in the paper.

Now Johnny has two murders on his hand and a connection to the two of them. The first victim was Edith Summers, who the police believe was killed by her boyfriend Ed Chatsworth. Dorothy is now seeing Edith's boyfriend. Maybe Chatsworth was to get out of town while Dorothy handled Edith Summers. Dunsmuir found out and tried to blackmail her. She or Chatsworth or both of them decide to close Dunsmuir's mouth for keeps, it is a possibility.

Johnny thinks over the case in his hotel, but there is something wrong. Johnny goes back to see Dorothy at 10:00 p.m. and she is just coming home. She has a business meeting with Ed, and he is on his way up. Johnny tells her that Ed's real name is Chatsworth.

Johnny mentions Edith Summers, but Dorothy did not know her and she tells Johnny that Jerry was not trying to blackmail her. Dorothy tells Johnny that she met Ed yesterday. He told her he was organizing a big promotion and wanted to include her in it and wants to see some outdoors pictures. Dorothy tells Johnny that the pictures were taken on the same day Edith Summers was killed.

Johnny looks at the pictures sent from Dunsmuir and spots a shot in front of an apartment house, the Blackton Arms, the same place where Edith Summers lived. Dorothy spots a man in the background coming out of the building.

Johnny hears a sound and asks about a service entrance and tells Dorothy to get down as he turns off the lights. Johnny throws a cigarette lighter into the kitchen and the intruder shoots. Johnny shoots and hits Ed Chatsworth.

Johnny tells Dorothy that Ed was the one who killed Edith Summers. He had an alibi but spoiled it by getting into the picture that Dunsmuir took. He also was the one in her apartment the other night. Most pictures do not do people justice, but I guess this one will do him all right.

"Remarks: Well, there is a little snapper to the story Pat. You know that picture Chatsworth was knocking himself out to get? He did not realize it, but his face in the background was far too blurred to make an identification."

Notes:
- This is an AFRTS program with the stories edited out.
- The cast information is from the script in the Thousand Oaks Library.

Producer:	Jack Johnstone	Writer:	Robert Ryf
Cast:	Virginia Gregg, Lillian Buyeff, Lawrence Dobkin, Herb Ellis, Harry Bartell		

◆ ❖ ◆

Show: The Alkali Mike Matter
Show Date: 11/10/1957
Company: Western Life & Trust Insurance Company
Agent: Bill Kemper
Exp. Acct: $525.00

Synopsis: Meg McCarthy calls her lover boy Johnny Dollar. She is in trouble in Port Hopeful. Port Hopeful, Nevada. There is insurance trouble out here. The company is Western Life & Trust, the very company that insured what is lying dead at my feet. But I did not do him in. Ah, forgive me lover boy, my skirts are clean. Don't be putting those handcuffs on me now. Oh, Johnny boy, I am in trouble now.

Johnny calls Bill Kemper at Western Life and flies to San Francisco. The next morning Bill asks Johnny if he knows about Alkali Mike Murphy, who discovered gold out in the desert, built a house and named it Port Hopeful.

The original Alkali Mike was a ship captain who died, supposedly of suicide. His son, Alkali Mike Jr. has lived there for 40 years, and he has died, and how he died will affect the pay out on the policy of $200,000.

The beneficiaries are two nephews, a niece and an old housekeeper, all sharing equally. Johnny tells Bill that if Meg McCarthy is guilty, he will handle the case for nothing and quit the insurance business.

Johnny flies to Reno, rents a car and drives to Winnemucca and visits the police. Sgt. Otis Framley tells Johnny that they have the number one suspect, Meg McCarthy. If she did not poison Alkali Mike, he will eat his shirt. Johnny asks him how he wants his shirt cooked, because he knows Meg.

Sgt. Framley tells Johnny that she has been at Port Hopeful about six months and already she is a beneficiary. In her jail cell, Meg is pitching a fit until she sees Johnny. Meg tells Johnny that she will tell him all she knows, but the evidence she can give is enough to hang her.

Meg tells Johnny that she got tired of all the drunken sailors on the east coast. When she heard that Alkali Mike was looking for a housekeeper she took the job, and they got along just fine. She told him that she did not need the money. She knows the other beneficiaries and they are just hanging around waiting for Mike to die.

Edgar Murphy has a job at the bank over at Lovelock. Margaret is a disgrace to her name, playing around from one man to another, looking for the man with the most money. And Danny is always gambling. They are all out at Port Hopeful trying to cheat each other out of what is left.

The doctor says that Mike died of poison from something he ate, but Meg was the only one with him and the only one to touch his food. And Meg ate the same things Mike did. The doctor called the poison quintanigen sulfanate. Johnny remembers that the poison is related to the old Indian arrow poisons. Johnny wants to go to the house with her. Johnny gets a local attorney to get Meg released into Sgt. Framley's custody.

Johnny, Meg and Sgt. Framley drive to Port Hopeful, which Johnny thinks should have been called Port Hopeless, as the place was a mess and poorly built. Johnny notices three new cars in the driveway when they arrive. Sgt. Framley tells Johnny that none of the family killed Mike because people out here have too much respect for their kin.

At the front door, Edgar complains to Sgt. Framley about bringing Meg back. Sgt. Framley tells them who Johnny is and Margie recognizes Johnny, and is sure that everything will be all right, won't it, Johnny?

Inside, Margie gives Johnny a seat and Danny comes in and complains about Meg being there and the argument starts among them. They all agree that they wanted Mike gone, and that it was Danny who talked Mike into the insurance. Johnny tells them that Meg was probably the only one who showed Mike any kindness in years, and Edgar concedes that Meg probably deserves the money as much as anybody. Somebody killed their uncle, and they have all tried to make it look like Meg did it. Johnny is going to play a hunch that maybe he was not murdered after all.

Johnny tells Sgt. Framley that maybe Mike committed suicide. They all start quibbling about Meg paying attention to Mike. Edgar tells Johnny that Mike's father committed suicide by drinking an old Indian poison.

Meg mumbles something about a cup and takes them to the dining room where she shows them a cup in the china closet, the one old Mike used to kill himself. Meg tells Johnny that Mike would have his whiskey every night from a different cup, but he would never touch that one, he called it the death cup and joked about it. The night before he died he talked about the cup again and said it was making a superstitious old fool out of him.

Edgar gets the cup and gives it to Johnny. Meg tells them that Mike said that his father drank from it and died, so he was going to drink from it and live to show everyone he was not superstitious.

Johnny finds a deposit of deep purple quintanigen sulfanate in the bottom of the cup after forty years. Meg tells Johnny that she had tried to wash it, but that did nothing. Johnny tells them that the alcohol in the whiskey would have released enough to kill Mike.

"The police took a long time over this one, but they finally reached the same conclusion I had, accidental death. So, the relatives will collect the insurance, and Meg, bless her heart. But I am afraid that mere money will never take the place of her friend, Alkali Mike."

Notes:
- This is possibly another AFRTS program as there are no credits at all.
- Winnemucca is north east of Reno, and Lovelock is halfway between Reno and Winnemucca.
- Cast Information is from the script in the KNX Collection at the Thousand Oaks Library.
- The announcer is Dan Cubberly.

Producer: Jack Johnstone   Writer: Jack Johnstone
Cast: Harry Bartell, Virginia Gregg, Dick Kieth, Peter Leeds, Jeanne Tatum, Frank Gerstle

Show:	The Shy Beneficiary Matter
Show Date:	11/17/1957
Company:	Universal Adjustment Bureau
Agent:	Pat McCracken
Exp. Acct:	$410.00

Synopsis: Pat McCracken calls Johnny with a problem. "Did you ever have trouble getting rid of money? I have $25,000 and have been trying to get rid of it for two weeks and can't". Johnny tells Pat, "Boy, you do have a problem, I'll be right over".

Johnny cabs to Pat's office and learns that Helen Gazeworth died, and Pat cannot find the beneficiary, Elijah Summers. Pat has advertised in the New York papers and has found nothing. Also, Helen has no relatives. The landlady told the Universal Adjustment Bureau that Miss Gazeworth was an eccentric who lived all alone and felt the world was against her, except for Summers who was nice to her sometime in the past. "Pat, you don't have much to go on" Johnny tells Pat. "Correction Johnny, YOU don't have anything to go on."

Johnny travels to New York City and visits the landlady where Miss Gazeworth lived, and then a previous landlady only to learn that Helen moved from place to place. Johnny finds a first landlady who thought that Gazeworth came from San Francisco.

Johnny flies to San Francisco, California and places ads in the local papers. On the first day, Johnny gets results, with blond hair and blue eyes. The woman is Janet Blake, and Johnny tells her that he has not heard from Elijah. She is a friend of Elijah's and tells Johnny about a small town called South Fork on the Yuba River in the Sierra's. He might be up there, just call it a hunch.

Johnny rents a car and drives to South Fork, California, a barely populated town. Johnny finds the local law, a deputy named Rollins. Rollins tells Johnny "good luck" on finding Elijah, but if you find him let me know, he is wanted for murder. Johnny tells Rollins that Elijah is the beneficiary of an insurance policy.

Rollins tells Johnny that the killing took place last year at Jess Tyler's place. Elijah worked at the Tyler place as a hired hand. He and Jess got into an argument and Elijah shot him and took off into the hills. The widow took it hard for a year and Ben Watts pulled her out of it and married her last month. She and Ben are living on the ranch.

Johnny asks where Elijah might have gone and Rollins tells Johnny that he might have gone to Tough Luck Canyon where some hermits are panning gold. Rollins has been up there, but a man has to be careful, as Elijah is a dead shot with a .30-30, and there are a lot of places to hide up there. Rollins has not given up on Elijah. The longer he stays up there, the more curious he will get. One of these days Rollins will get him.

Johnny drives to the Tyler ranch and they are expecting Johnny. Mrs. Watts has gotten over the killing, and feels sorry for Elijah, as Jess had kept him on when it did not pay to. No one knows what the argument was about. Johnny asks Ben how to get to the canyon, and Ben tells him it is dangerous. Johnny gets directions and Johnny is warned that Elijah is a good shot. Ben was winged by Elijah on the night Jess was killed.

Johnny gets some camping equipment and follows the road to the timber line and starts hiking. When Johnny starts into the canyon he stops when he hears someone following him. Johnny lunges at the stalker who turns out to be Janet Blake.

She tells Johnny that her name is Janet Tyler, and Jess Tyler was her father. She wants to find Elijah and bring him back. She thinks that she can find Elijah, as he had a favorite spot up there and had brought her to it once. Shots ring out, and Johnny thinks that they have found Elijah the hard way.

Janet tells Johnny that Elijah is shooting at them with a .22. She found a .22 cartridge that came from Elijah's gun on the night her father was killed.

Janet calls out to Elijah and he recognizes her voice and Janet tells him that she and Johnny, who is a friend, want to talk to him. Johnny is told to throw his gun out and come into the open.

Johnny tosses out his gun, and Elijah comes out and he looks terrible. He had seen the deputy snooping around and could have gotten him. He remembers when Janet gave the .22 to him for ground squirrels. He has never used any other rifle. Johnny remembers that Jess was killed with a .30/30, and Janet tells Johnny that she saw someone pull the .22 slug from Ben's shoulder on the night her father was killed. She heard Ben tell everyone he had been hit with a .30-30. She is sure that Ben Watts killed her father and that Elijah was trying to protect Jess.

Elijah remembers that there was a big fight and he ran away. Ben has been poking around too with his .30-30. A shot rings out and Elijah is hit. Johnny scoops up his automatic and circles around behind the shooter. Johnny slips but is able to draw the fire of the shooter and hits him, it is Ben Watts.

"Remarks: Well I turned Ben Watts over to the local law, and I helped old Elijah fill out his claim for the $25,000 of insurance money Miss Gazeworth gave him. It ought to keep him real comfortable for the rest of his life. You know Pat, once in a while I get the feeling this job of mine is worthwhile after all."

Notes:
- Johnny notes in this episode that he is carrying an automatic.
- This is an AFRTS program that contains a story about the flag of Rhode Island, a story about the people of Spain and an angel on top of a church steeple, and a story about the flag of Alabama.
- Cast Information from the script on file in the KNX Collection at the Thousand Oaks Library.
- The announcer is Dan Cubberly.

Producer: Jack Johnstone Writer: Robert Ryf
Cast: Lawrence Dobkin, Virginia Gregg, Jack Kruschen, Jeanette Nolan, Russell Thorson, Howard McNear

Show: **The Hope to Die Matter**
Show Date: **11/24/1957**
Company: **Floyds of England**
Agent: **George Reed**
Exp. Acct: **$0.00**

Synopsis: A very hesitant George Reed calls Johnny. Johnny is glad that George has called because he has no assignment, and therefore no expense account to pad. "Remember you had asked me once if we had issued a policy against living" George asks Johnny. "Oh, don't tell me". "I am afraid so. The company is saddled with a death insurance policy". Floyds has insured someone against living.

Johnny cabs to George's office where he is pacing the floor. George tells Johnny that Harry Baxter issued the policy while George was on vacation. Usually they pay the face value when the insured dies, but on this policy, they will have to pay $250,000 if the insured does not die. Floyds is proud that they will insure anything.

George does not know what the policy is about and Floyds has paid Johnny some nice fees in the past. Johnny wants to turn the case down, but George tells Johnny that he will OK the expense report without even reading it. Johnny tells George that "there are some things a conniving, chiseling unprincipled rascal like myself…won't…even…" "Unlimited expense account, Johnny" adds George. "Okay, George, I'll take it."

Johnny is taking this case because of his friendship with George Reed, and the promise of an unlimited expense account. The insured is Mary Ellen Markham, who lives in New York. Albert Schwinner has taken out the policy, and is the beneficiary, but George does not know who he is, except that he is a doctor. You have to find out who he is, what he is and why he has bought insurance against this woman living beyond November 10th which is only a few days from now.

George wants Johnny to find some legal reason to cancel the policy. The paper work lists Dr. Schwinner, CL in Union City New Jersey, and Johnny wonders what "CL" is? Johnny gets an address for Harry Baxter in New York City.

Johnny travels to New York City and Harry Baxter's address, which is luxury from stem-to-stern. Harry has heard of Johnny from George, and he tells Johnny that he has so many social events to keep up.

George gave him no chance to explain why he sold the policy, and George will have to calm down before Harry will tell him. Harry will tell George, but not Johnny, as to why he issued the policy.

Johnny puts his foot in the door and asks Harry how Dr. Schwinner fits into this, and Harry tells Johnny that he is a close personal friend and slams the door.

Johnny calls George Reed, but he is out. Johnny tells the receptionist to tell George he wants a complete rundown on Harry Baxter. The receptionist tells Johnny she can tell him all there is to know, but Johnny wants George to do it.

Johnny cabs to Miss Markham's apartment where Johnny meets a pale, wan, tired woman who looks to be 65 or 70, in a room full of flowers. Johnny tells Miss Markham that someone has taken a policy out on her, and she tells Johnny that it was nice of Harry Baxter to do so. She is suffering from a rare incurable disease of the blood, and will not live long.

Johnny asks about Dr. Schwinner and is told that he is a great friend. Johnny asks her why he would take out a policy hoping she would die. She tells Johnny that November 10th will be her fiftieth birthday, and Dr. Schwinner is her physician.

Johnny leaves and calls George who has just tried to call Harry Baxter to apologize for getting upset. George tells Johnny that Baxter is the majority stockholder and Chairman of the Board of the company. Johnny tells George that Harry has left for Europe. If Mary Ellen Markham dies before November 10th, Floyds pays out $250,000 to Dr. Schwinner who is the physician of Miss Markham. Johnny thinks that there is something wrong with this deal.

Johnny cabs to Dr. Schwinner's office and learns that CL is for the Albert Schwinner Clinic for the Study of Rare Diseases of the Blood. The doctor is at Miss Markham's, so Johnny cabs back to her apartment, and meets the doctor.

He tells Johnny that Miss Markham is better. Johnny tells Dr. Schwinner that if she lives, he loses out on $250,000. But he corrects Johnny and tells him the clinic will lose the money.

Dr. Schwinner tells Johnny that when Miss Markham first became ill, she had only 5 years to live. But because of the work of the clinic, she has lived much longer. She has told them that if she lives to be 50, that would prove that the methods of the clinic are right, and they could prolong and possibly save lives. If she lives to 50, she will give the clinic $250,000, money which is much needed. She is the one who suggested the policy.

Dr. Schwinner tells Johnny that Harry Baxter's own mother died of the same disease, so he knew how necessary the money is, and that is why he chose the policy as a means to guarantee the money. Dr. Schwinner tells Johnny that it is probably his duty to try and cancel the policy. Johnny tells him that his duty is to do just exactly nothing.

Mary Ellen Markham did live to see 50, but only by a few days. Just long enough to make the gift to the clinic. Harry Baxter and the company? Well, Harry came back from Europe and he said he found some 'mistake' in the policy that required the company to payoff anyway. Eccentric? We should have more like that. Expense account total, are you kidding?"

Notes:
- Johnny mentions singing mice (*The Missing Mouse Matter*), and old alley cat (*The Felicity Feline Matter*), and a sick whale (*The Michael Meany Mirage Matter*) as the whacko things Floyds has insured.
- **Cast Information from the KNX Collection at the Thousand Oaks Library.**
- **The announcer is Dan Cubberly.**

Producer:	Jack Johnstone Writer: Jack Johnstone
Cast:	G. Stanley Jones, Ben Wright, Virginia Gregg, Shirley Mitchell, Marvin Miller

♦ ❖ ♦

Show:	**The Sunny Dream Matter**
Show Date:	12/1/1957
Company:	**Universal Adjustment Bureau**
Agent:	Pat McCracken
Exp. Acct:	$12.00

Synopsis: Frank Skinner, who operates the Sunny Dream home in Buckland Center calls Johnny. Something is wrong and they have never had anything like this before. Most of their residents are well insured, but they have been having a lot of deaths lately, too many. These have been accidental deaths and Mr. Skinner tells Johnny that he does not think that they were accidents. If something is not done to stop this... well, I think you better come up here.

Johnny calls Pat McCracken and tells him he will not be available for a few days, he is working on something that interests him. Pat tells Johnny that he has an assignment in Buckland Center. The Sunny Dream Home for the aged? How did you know? Pat tells Johnny that the number of deaths over there have made the actuarial tables look like a big mistake. Pat had promised the insurance companies that he would send Johnny to look into things. Also, the beneficiary of all the policies has been the Sunny Dream Home for the aged.

Johnny gases up his jalopy at the sign of the flying red horse and drives to the Sunny Dream Home. Frank Skinner comes over and greets Johnny in a wheel chair. Frank asks Johnny to act like he is looking over the place, like he is going to send an old relative there.

There have been five deaths in the past six months and they all look like accidents. Miss Epp died in a small fire in her cottage, Mr. Pearly had food poisoning the doctor called it, Miss Sharmley fell down the main stairs to the living room, Miss Lizzy Belle fell out the window of her bedroom, and Miss Betsler fell down the stairs too.

Frank tells Johnny that most can handle the stairs, and the others had their rooms on the first floor and Miss Lizzy Bell never left her room. Johnny tells him that so far there is no reason to suspect anything.

All of the accidents happened late at night, when the guests would have no reason to be up and about, when there was no one to help them. Each had their own bathrooms and if they wanted anything, all they had to do was ring the buzzer.

Mrs. Skinner comes in and tells Frank he is blabbing his mouth off. She tells Johnny to get out or she will throw him out, and she is strong enough to do it. Johnny asks if she is strong enough to push someone down the stairs or out of a window, and she tells him to get out.

Martha Skinner, the real manager, was a big strong woman, much younger than Mr. Skinner. She tells Johnny that she does not want anyone snooping around. She tells Johnny that she has nothing to hide, and his snooping will ruin their reputation, and that all the deaths were accidental. Johnny tells her that Frank thought they were accidents until a minute ago. She said a lot of things because the people who died were her friends.

She mentions that the police had been there and found nothing. Martha mellows and asks Johnny if she could possibly do anything to these kind people. Johnny mentions the insurance and Martha tells Johnny that making them the beneficiary was their guest's idea.

Johnny starts to leave for town and is told he will stay there for dinner and can have a room. Walter comes in and complains about having another room to take care of. Johnny is introduced, and Walter recognizes the name from the radio programs he listens to all the time. "So, what is your business here?" he asks.

Martha tells Walter that Frank had called Johnny, and Walter tells Johnny that his mother has enough trouble without him being here. He is sick of this nonsense and taking care of these old fogies. He takes care of the place while Frank handles all the money. He mentions how Frank keeps talking about getting enough money to move away from here. Johnny tells Walter he is pretty husky, and Walter asks Johnny if he would like a demonstration of how strong he is. Johnny tells them he will stay until he is satisfied. Walter tells Johnny that he will not be there for long, if he can help it and Martha apologizes for Walter. Martha is the owner, and if anything happened, the place would go to Walter and Frank. "You can't think that Walter would do anything to get the money, would you?" asks Martha.

At dinner Johnny talks to as many guests as possible, and they feel sorry for Walter, who stays to help his mother who is really devoted to them. Mr. Skinner was the one who convinced them to make out their insurance to the home.

Frank wheels up and asks Johnny if his room, at the top of the stairs is OK. Johnny tells him that he found something, marks from some kind of struggle, and a piece of cloth. He is going to leave them there for the police, as they might be clues to the killer.

Johnny waits in his room to see if his hunch will pay off. He remembers Pat telling him that he had notified Frank Skinner that he was coming, so maybe that is why Skinner called him, to allay any concern Johnny might have had.

Johnny hears a noise at midnight and opens his door to see Frank standing there on his own two feet. Johnny surprises him and tells him that there is nothing there. He had a nasty racket, convincing people to sign over their insurance and then pushing them down the stairs. Franks jumps at Johnny and is thrown down the stairs.

"Yeah, he will live to go to trial, and whatever sentence they hand him will be much too short. The Sunny Dream Home, well I hope it will be the quiet, peaceful place his wife wants it to be."

Notes:
- **This is an AFRTS program that contains an episode of "The Bellweathers", a story about Thomas Jefferson, and an organ serenade at the end.**

- This program contains another reference to Johnny's radio programs.
- The announcer is Dan Cubberly.

Producer: Jack Johnstone   Writer: Jack Johnstone
Cast: Junius Matthews, Lawrence Dobkin, Virginia Gregg, Bert Holland, Peggy Webber

♦ ❖ ♦

Show: **The Hapless Hunter Matter**
Show Date: **12/8/1957**
Company: **Tri-Mutual Insurance Company Ltd.**
Agent: **Gerald Holland**
Exp. Acct: **$13.13**

Synopsis: Gerald Holland calls Johnny and asks if Curtis Randall means anything. He is a big banker in Hartford, isn't he? Well, Randall and Byron Peters went deer hunting over near Kingman, New York and hired a local guide who was an alcoholic. They raised cane with Curly because they had not found any deer and got into a big argument. Curly got drunk and shot Randall and himself. Jerry asks Johnny to investigate, it is typical on policies over $500,000. The beneficiary is Byron Peters. Johnny tells Jerry that this case looks too easy.

Johnny cabs to Gerald's office where Gerald meets him at the door. Gerald tells Johnny that Byron Peters is in the hospital, he was shot by Curly too. Gerald rebukes Johnny for going off half-cocked on this case. The local police told Gerald that Peters supplied all the arrangements for the trip and arranged the guide. Gerald wonders if Curly had it in for Randall.

Johnny gets the address for Peters and learns that Randall only had an occasional drink before dinner but does not know about Peters. Johnny suspects Byron Peters based on a hunch.

Johnny drives to Kingman, New York and goes to the hospital where Peters is sedated after the police had questioned him. Johnny asks the chief resident doctor if the police suspect that Peters killed Randall and Curly and wounded himself, and the doctor there calls it ridiculous. The doctor tells Johnny that the extent of Peter's wounds makes that impossible, as he narrowly escaped death.

Johnny looks at Peter's wounds and x-rays, and then talks with police captain McManus. The police had talked to Peters, and McManus tells Johnny that Peters had lunged at Curly and was hit in the head. Peters called McManus from the cabin when he came to by dragging the phone to the floor. Randall was near the front door, and Curly was between Randall and Peters.

McManus tells Johnny that Curly was the town drunk who worked odd jobs and used the money to buy cheap booze, but he never drank during hunting season. He was a good guide and made a lot of money, and that is why McManus cannot explain him getting drunk during hunting season.

Johnny and McManus go to the coroner's office and Johnny finds something suspicious. Peters had a powder burn on his forehead, and Randall had none. But Curly showed no powder burns, even though he was supposed to have shot himself upwards through the jaw with his .30-30. Johnny asks, for the sake of argument, what if Randall shot first? Or suppose Peters started the whole thing? Johnny gets directions to the cabin and drives there.

The cabin is a shack surrounded by cheap liquor bottles but is comfortable inside. In the kitchen is a case of Prince Francis scotch, nearly full. On the floor, Johnny notices the angle of entry of the slug that hit Peters, and a heavy cord hanging from the rafter. Suppose that someone had hung a rifle up there and carefully fired it at himself?

McManus and the doctor call and tell Johnny he might be right. The doctor tells Johnny that Peters has left the hospital. Peters had asked the doctor who was in to see him, and a few minutes later the doctor heard his car leaving. McManus tells Johnny to leave the cabin just as Johnny hears the door opening and Peters walks in.

Peters was not as badly injured as Johnny thought. Johnny tells Peters how he rigged the incident, but Peters sticks to his story about Curly being drunk. Johnny tells him that he made a mistake by bringing up expensive scotch to the cabin, because Curly only drank cheap liquor.

Johnny tells Peters that he did not plan on the accident and came back because he remembers leaving the cord in the ceiling. Johnny tells him that the angle of the bullet was all wrong for what supposedly happened.

Johnny tells Peters that there were no powder burns on Curly when there should have been, because Peters had killed both Randall and Curly. Peters pulls a .38 and Johnny tells him he will not get away with it. Peters tells Johnny that he had forced Randall to make him the beneficiary because he knew of some shady business deals and had been blackmailing Randall.

Johnny tells Peters that he hopes McManus will slug him before he shoots, and Peters calls it a ruse — until McManus calls out and shots are fired. McManus yells at Johnny for not leaving.

"Remarks: Why? Why don't they ever learn?"

Notes:
- Cast Information from the KNX Collection at the Thousand Oaks Library.
- The announcer is Dan Cubberly.

Producer:	Jack Johnstone	Writer:	Jack Johnstone
Cast:	John Stephenson, Parley Baer, Forrest Lewis, Carleton G. Young		

• ❖ •

Show:	The Happy Family Matter
Show Date:	12/15/1957
Company:	Estate of E. P. Watkins
Agent:	Pat McCracken
Exp. Acct:	$73.00

Synopsis: Johnny is called and told to come over here right away. "Who is this, and where is here" asks Johnny. The man is Ellis P. Watkins the industrialist, and here is Broad Acres in Fairfield, Connecticut. Watkins has $100,000 to give away, Johnny is going to tell him who to give it to.

Johnny cabs to the Universal Adjustment Bureau and talks to Pat McCracken, who had talked to Watkins. Johnny is told that Watkins has a $100,000 policy, and the beneficiary was his wife, but she died several months ago. Watkins wants a new beneficiary, and he wants Johnny to do it. Johnny tells Pat he wants no part of this case, but Pat tells Johnny that Watkins does not have much time to live, so Johnny relents.

Johnny drives to Broad Acres and is shown into the library, where Mr. Watkins is sitting by the fire. Watkins tells Johnny that he has from one week to one year to live. Johnny tells him he is sorry, but Watkins tells him that he is not, his wife is gone, his business is failing and his children are strangers, so there is no reason to be sorry.

He has three possible beneficiaries: Sheila, a 28-year-old daughter, Michael, a 26-year-old son, and Elizabeth, a 24-year-old daughter, and he does not want to divide up the policy among them. Watkins also tells Johnny that the policy is the only estate. He wants the money kept in the family and only to one member of the family. He intends to leave the other two out in the cold.

Watkins tells Johnny that Sheila seems to think that she should be managing her father's affairs. Michael prefers the life of an artist. Elizabeth is stubborn and is married to James Lovett, who thinks he knows more about business than Watkins does. Johnny tells Watkins that the others are not going to like the decision Johnny makes, so Watkins is going to pay Johnny a considerable fee, but he will earn it, every penny of it. This is a weird assignment, but Johnny feels sorry for Ellis Watkins, as he is really alone.

On the way out, Johnny meets Sheila, who tells Johnny that her father was not always like he is now. He feels that his children have let him down. He resents Sheila as the oldest, because she is not a man. She is more like father and could have taken over for him, but he resents her helping him. Elizabeth is in Cranford, New Jersey, and Michael lives in New York. Johnny senses that Sheila is under a great deal of stress.

Johnny goes to see Michael in Greenwich Village. Michael tells Johnny that he does not want the money. He is doing what he wants to do — paint. Sheila is trying to hold the family together, but it will not work. Father had been trying to shove the business down Michael's throat, but he wants no part of it, but that did not matter to him. Michael tells Johnny that Sheila deserves to have the money.

Johnny goes to the Lovett home and talks to Elizabeth. She thinks that this is some kind of scheme. Her husband tells Johnny to give the money to Elizabeth so he can buy a controlling interest in the company and rescue it. James tells Johnny that he once worked for the company but Watkins is running the company the way he did 30 years ago, and that will not work today, so he left.

James tells Johnny that Watkins tried to get Michael into the company, but all he wants to do is paint his lousy pictures. James had sent Watkins a written contract guaranteeing the financing necessary to fix the company and asked for six months but Watkins would not even listen to him. He tore up the contract and told Jim to leave.

Johnny looks for an art dealer and learns that Mike really is a lousy painter. Johnny gets a message to visit the Watkins attorney in his hotel. Halfway into the room Johnny feels a gun in his back. A voice tells Johnny to drop the case, or he will get dropped.

Johnny asks the voice who hired him. When the man tries to slug him, Johnny anticipates what will happen and deflects the gun butt, but the man gets away. Johnny turns on the light and sees something that tells him that the truth was under his nose all the time.

Johnny calls the family members to a meeting and drives to Broad Acres. Ellis Watkins resents the theatrics, but Johnny tells him that it is necessary. Theirs is not a happy family because someone in the family does not want Johnny to finish his job.

Johnny asks Mike why he quit and started painting, and Mike tells him that his father was trying to shove the business down his throat. He could not take it any longer and quit when Sheila said it was best. Sheila tells Johnny that Mike should have a life of his own. Watkins tells Sheila that she had said she begged Mike to stay. Sheila says that she was acting in the best interests of the family.

Johnny asks Jim why he quit, and Jim tells him about the contract, but Watkins tells Jim that he never saw a contract. Jim had given it to Sheila, who said that her father had refused to look at it. Johnny notes Sheila's habit of shredding cellophane, and how he found some in the hotel room. Watkins asks her why, and she is not sure.

Johnny tells Sheila that she was trying to punish her father, but she is not sure. She tells them that everyone had a life of their own but her, and she could not help it. Watkins is bewildered and asks if Sheila was trying to tear the family apart to punish him, and Johnny agrees. Johnny asks if she was ever allowed to have a life? Watkins tells Johnny to suspend further action as the matter requires further thought.

"Remarks: Sheila is now undergoing treatment, and the outlook is favorable. Elizabeth's husband Jim is managing the affairs of Watkins and Company, Mike is helping him, and I guess he is doing a good job. Mr. Watkins, well he is still alive and his doctor tells me that now that the old gentleman has found some reasons to be alive he'll probably be with us quite a while and make all three of his children his beneficiaries."

Notes:
- This is an AFRTS program that contains an episode of "The Bellweathers", and a story about Daniel Webster.
- Cast Information from the KNX Collection at the Thousand Oaks Library.
- The announcer is Dan Cubberly.

Producer: Jack Johnstone   Writer: Robert Ryf
Cast: John Dehner, Lawrence Dobkin, Peter Leeds,
              Virginia Gregg, Shirley Mitchell, Paul Dubov

◆ ❖ ◆

Show: The Carmen Kringle Matter
Show Date: 12/22/1957
Company: Universal Adjustment Bureau
Agent: Pat McCracken
Exp. Acct: $0.00

Synopsis: Pat McCracken calls Johnny and asks how the weather is in Palm Springs. Pat has a matter nearby and wants Johnny to work on it, as it will only take a day. Johnny tells Pat that he is spending this Christmas in Palm Springs, not freezing like he did last year. Johnny wants to decline the case, but Pat mentions the bonus list in the office, and Johnny's name might be on it. Pat tells Johnny about an old ghost town named Calico. An old prospector named Kringle is breathing his last and wants to change the beneficiary on his $50,000 policy, but a nephew, Ned Kringle will sue if he does. Contact our agent in Barstow, Jean Craig. The new beneficiary is Carmen Kringle, a burro.

Johnny wires Jean Craig of his arrival plans, rents Al Sterner's plane, and flies to Calico, California located in the Mohave Desert. The plane lands on a dry lakebed and Johnny waits for his contact. Johnny gets the old feeling he is not alone. Then Johnny sees a car approach and a herd of burros disperses.

A man tells Johnny to walk towards him with his hands up. Johnny sees another car approaching as Johnny recognizes the marshal's badge. Jean Craig arrives and tells the marshal who Johnny is. Jean tells Johnny and the marshal that Kris has had another setback, and that someone has let his burros loose.

Jean and Johnny drive back to Calico, and Jean tells Johnny all about Kris who every year loads up his burro with gifts for the families of the miners in the area. This year will not be very joyful with Kris ill. Ned seems to be OK, but Willie Dagostino seems to do all the talking for Ned. Jean asks if a burro can be a beneficiary, and Johnny tells him that Kris can leave his money to a boat if he wants to, but a trust will have to be set up. Johnny asks what will happen when Carmen dies, but Jean tells him that there will always be burros in Calico.

In Calico, Johnny sees a page from the past. Walter Knott of Knott's Berry Farm had bought the town and restored it to its colorful past. Jean asks Johnny to spend the holiday with them and is very disappointed when Johnny tells her that he has other plans. At Kris' place, Doc Spangler asks Jean to drive him back to town. He has not seen Kris because he will not argue with a gun.

Johnny pounds on the door and a nasty Willie Dagostino tells Johnny that there will be no changes to the policy at this late date and just family will be admitted in the hour of the old man's demise. Johnny puts his foot in the door and pushes the door open and shoves Willie aside and is hit on the head.

Johnny wakes up to Jean fussing over him. Jean asks Willie to go up to see Kris and Ned wants to go also, but Willie tells them to go away. Willie tells them that the old man always was borrowing money from Ned to give to other people, and who loaned Ned the money? Willie. Now, Willie is going to get his money back.

Ned tells Johnny that he had loaned his uncle the money, as he was sure his uncle would hit a big strike some day. Willie tells them all to leave but the marshal comes in with his rifle and tells Willie to drop his gun. The marshal tells Willie to leave as he is guilty of carrying a gun and threatening people. Willie leaves, but Ned says he will stay.

Doc calls Johnny, Jean and Ned upstairs to hear Kris tell them something, but Johnny hears a shot outside and rushes out with Jean and the marshal to find Carmen dead, killed by Willie as he left town.

The marshal tells Johnny that he figured that Willie would do something like this as he takes the bells off of the dead burro and puts them on the real Carmen. The marshal stays to tend the $50,000 jackass while the others go inside.

Kris tells them that he is not going to scratch Ned's name off the policy, he just wanted to scare off Dagostino. He was afraid that he would have to die to square off the gambling debts. Johnny is asked to take a heavy bag from a footlocker and Kris tells them that the bag is full of uranium.

The last batch assayed at $900 a ton, and he has a whole mountain of it in his and Ned's name. Kris tells them that the bank will extend credit on the assay value and asks Jean if she can spend the next two days buying presents for the folks in the area.

Johnny calls four major cities where Willie Dagostino might be remembered and Johnny gets a long list of reasons why he is remembered. That was Johnny's present to them. Johnny rents a truck to haul the presents back to Calico so Ned could give them away.

And then there was Christmas Eve. We sat on the Kringle porch and watched the procession up to the Maggie mine, the flickering lights from the miner's lamps reflecting on the faces of the happy children.

"Old Kris was bundled up in blankets, his little eyes twinkling and chuckling to himself like he knew all of the answers to the universe. Jean was there too. Marshal Ed Noler was one of the wise men in the procession, I could recognize the sideburns. And Doc Spangler couldn't hide his height, and he wore an awful beard. Ned Kringle lead the burro that carried the blessed mother. Yeah, you guessed it, the burro was Carmen Kringle."

Johnny tells Pat that the $275 in expenses are on him.

Notes:
- Bob Bailey wishes everyone "From all of us to all of you, may this be your very merriest Christmas ever."
- This Christmas program was written by Bob Bailey, under the pseudonym of Robert Bainter, Bainter being his middle name.
- Calico, California is north east of Barstow, about half way between Los Angeles and Las Vegas.
- Walter Knott was the founder of Knott's Berry Farm and helped develop the Boysenberry. In 1952 he purchased Calico, California which had once been a prosperous silver mining town in the 1880s.

- The announcer is Dan Cubberly.

Producer:	Jack Johnstone	Writer:	Robert Bainter
Cast:	Herb Vigran, Howard McNear, Jeanne Tatum, Junius Matthews, Lawrence Dobkin, Forrest Lewis. Jack Kruschen, Richard Crenna, Bill James		

◆ ❖ ◆

Show: **The Latin Lovely Matter**
Show Date: **12/29/1957**
Company: **Universal Adjustment Bureau**
Agent: **Pat McCracken**
Exp. Acct: **$0.00**

Synopsis: "I love you" Johnny is told on the phone. A nervous Johnny wants to get together, to which she agrees. The woman identifies herself as Carmela Jocares. Johnny tells her that he usually gets calls on Sunday night for an insurance problem. Carmela tells Johnny that she has an insurance problem and it will not be dull. Tell your friend Pat McCracken that I called.

Johnny tries to call Pat McCracken on Monday and finally cabs to his office. Johnny mentions Carmela Jocares and Pat snickers. Johnny asks if she is like she sounds on the phone and Pat suggests that maybe special investigator Martha Mayberry Balderdale should handle her case.

Pat tells Johnny that Carmela is a dancer, but not a very good one, and Pat will put Balderdale on the case to have someone objective on the case. Surety Mutual has issued a $50,000 retirement policy on Carmela. If she dies, her beneficiary gets the money.

She dances in nightclubs and usually has a new partner every month. Her partner is the beneficiary of the policy. The cost of servicing the policy is getting ridiculous. The company has tried to stall making changes but she just yells at them. Surety has turned the case over to Pat and Carmela has specifically asked for Johnny.

Pat tells Johnny that Carmela heard about Johnny on the radio, and you are her dreamboat. Get her married or settle her down. Married? Yes, that's it Johnny, marry her. Johnny tells Pat that there is no way, but Pat laughs and tells Johnny that the Universal Adjustment Bureau will not defend him in case of a breach of promise case.

Johnny flies to New York City and Carmela's apartment where the doorman asks for his credentials. In the lobby the doorman calls Carmela but she does not answer the phone.

Johnny and the doorman walk up and he tells Johnny that Carmela had been fearful of something lately. Johnny pounds on the door and then gets the pass key, enters the apartment and finds Carmela lying on the floor, barely alive.

The doorman discovers the service entrance open and Johnny sends him for a doctor as he gives her a drink to wake her up. Johnny puts her on the sofa and she tells Johnny that a man hit her. She found him in the apartment looking for something and he hit her. He was short and dark.

She tells Johnny that a man from Mexico has been threatening her, telling her that "she has done it one time to many". "Oh, hold me tight, Johnny" she tells him. She tells Johnny that she only wants one little change to the policy.

The doorman comes back and she tells Billy the doorman to cancel the doctor. Johnny is suspicious, as there are no marks on Carmela.

Johnny leaves and goes to see Randy Singer to get a run down on Carmela. Johnny cuts down an alley and gets a gun in his back. The man takes him into a doorway and tells him that he is Federico. He was listening at the back stairway, and Johnny will not help Carmela, as he will kill Johnny first.

Federico will kill Johnny before he lets Johnny help Carmela and ruin his son. He will not let Johnny change the beneficiary. Johnny distracts him and takes the gun from him.

The man tells Johnny that he is Federico Gomez, and is the father of Armando Gomez, the next fly in the web of the spider. Armando is a dancer and Carmela is going to make him her next victim. Armando is a fine dancer, and she will charm him and bring him to the city to dance with her. She will bring boys to the city to dance with her, they will fall in love with her and she will name them as the beneficiary to dazzle them.

She has blinded so many young boys and taken their money. She laughs and spits at them when they want her to marry them. Federico tells Johnny that Pedro Fernandez, and the son of a friend committed suicide when she rejected him. The boys are unwise to the ways of the world and Carmela, and he will do anything to protect his son. Johnny tells him to go back to his hotel and stay there until he hears from Johnny.

Johnny goes back to Carmela and she admits that she had used the insurance money to lure the dancers to further her career and was proud of the broken hearts and minds she left behind.

Johnny tears into her and tells her about the death of the two boys. Johnny tells her that the police will be after her no matter where she goes. Johnny tells her that the insurance will be canceled unless she changes the beneficiary to someone she cannot hurt. Carmela promises to make up for the things she has done.

As Johnny finishes his report the phone rings and Pat McCracken tells Johnny to forget the expense account. Pat has just gotten a copy of the new and last rider, which cannot ever be changed ever again. And you, you sly dog, you are the beneficiary!

"Yours Truly, Juanito Peso."

Notes:
- This program contains another reference to Johnny's radio programs.
- This program contains commercials for Chef Boy-ar-dee Pizza, for Vic's Medicated Cough Drops, and for 4-Way cold medicine and Fitch Dandruff-Remover Shampoo.
- The announcer is Dan Cubberly.

Producer:	Jack Johnstone		Writer:	Jack Johnstone
Cast:	Lucille Meredith, Lawrence Dobkin, James McCallion, Harry Bartell			

♦ ❖ ♦

Show:	**The Ingenuous Jeweler Matter**
Show Date:	1/5/1958
Company:	**Philadelphia Mutual Liability & Casualty Insurance Company**
Agent:	Harry Branson
Exp. Acct:	$181.00

Synopsis: Harry Branson calls Johnny and tells him that this thing has him really upset. Harry wants Johnny to come to Philadelphia. If Johnny can clear up this matter, I mean $985,000, well any criminal could have done it. But the murder, it just does not make sense. What do you think Johnny? Johnny suggests the butler, and Harry is confused.

Johnny travels to Philadelphia, Pennsylvania and goes to Harry's office. Harry tells Johnny that the Beaufort Collection, which is insured for almost a million dollars, has been stolen from J. Harold Whipset. Johnny remembers that Whipset was tagged by customs for trying to smuggle jewels into the country several years ago. Harry had some misgivings, but Whipset is in the clear now. Miss Winkle is Whipset's secretary, Miss Perri Winkle, she was almost killed in their office last night on Walnut Street. The collection has several emerald and diamond brooches made up of small stones that could easily be remounted.

Johnny and Harry start to go to the office and Harry tells Johnny that Miss Winkle was shot and Whipset was not. Johnny gets the whole story on the jewels on the cab ride, but Johnny wants more information on Whipset.

Lt. Bart Stanley is in Whipset's office and he tells Johnny that they know nothing. Stanley knows about the reputation of Whipset. Johnny is told that Whipset and Miss Winkle were there late last night working on the books. A man knocked on the door and Whipset let him in, and the man demanded the Beaufort Collection. Whipset gave him the jewels, but Miss Winkle tried to run and was shot.

The man tied Winkle up, tore out the phone line and locked him in his office. Johnny asks how, as the door locks from the inside? Stanley shows Johnny a rubber door stop that proves that Whipset could not have rigged the deal.

Stanley shows Johnny how all the doors open out into the corridor. The man slammed the door on Whipset and used the wedge to hold the door closed. The harder Whipset pushed, the more the door was blocked. A policeman heard the shots and they got there quickly. Whipset was more upset about Winkle than the jewels. They thought that she was dead at first, but she is unconscious and will probably not make it.

Mr. Whipset comes in with officer Conroy, and he is upset about Miss Winkle. Whipset tells Johnny that Miss Winkle was his secretary, and he is in love with her. Johnny tells Whipset that Miss Winkle has not regained consciousness, but she will recover, and Whipset acts glad. Johnny told the lie to gets Whipset's reaction.

Whipset leaves to go home and Stanley asks Johnny about his recovery story. Johnny tells them he is going to the hospital in case she recovers. Harry talks Johnny out of going so Johnny calls the hospital and the doctor tells him that Miss Winkle has just died.

Johnny tells Bart and Harry that the girl is dead, and Johnny asks for a key to the office. Johnny tells Bart to go to the hospital in case Whipset goes there.

Johnny goes to the office and looks at the doorstop. Johnny notices a burr where a tiny hole has been pierced into the rubber. Johnny finds a piece of platinum wire in a desk.

Whipset returns and tells Johnny that he did not like his attitude. He sees Johnny has found the wire that Whipset had used to pull the wedge against the door. Johnny asks if the gloves he is wearing and the gun he has are the ones he used to shoot Miss Winkle and leave no prints.

Whipset tells Johnny that Miss Winkle was against him taking the stones and remounting the jewels at home and claiming the insurance. Whipset tells Johnny that he will kill him with the gun and lock him in the office, a kind of a trademark of the killer.

As Whipset tells Johnny to turn around Stanley comes in and tells him that he has a better idea. Stanley knew Johnny had an idea, so he decided to come back up. Johnny does not tell Stanley how it was done. He will let Whipset do it, he loves to talk.

"Harry, I think I will have to figure out some way to pad my expense account out even more than usual in cases like this. I mean where a .38 slug nearly ends up in me. After all, fun is fun, a job is a job, but some of these laddies carry thing too far. Come to think of it, I'll have to run down to New York again to appear against Whipset, so expense account total, including that and transportation back to Hartford, and all the incidentals I could possibly think of, $181, even."

Notes:
- This an AFRTS program with the typical stories edited out.
- The announcer is Dan Cubberly.

Producer:	Jack Johnstone	Writer:	Jack Johnstone
Cast:	Harry Bartell, Byron Kane, Vic Perrin, Joseph Kearns, Austin Green		

♦ ❖ ♦

Show: The Boron 112 Matter
Show Date: 1/12/1958
Company: Floyds of England
Agent: George Reed
Exp. Acct: $2,431.00

Synopsis: George Reed calls and Johnny shudders because of the wild crazy and impossible policies George issues. George tells Johnny that he has a normal policy he is worried about now. The insured is Josef Hantler, who is an inventor, and the invention is what is Floyds has insured. The invention is for making some sort of boron-based compounds, the sort of things the government is interested in for airplane and rocket fuels. "Can you come over?" "Yeah, I think I better. I'm on my way."

Johnny cabs to George Reed's Hartford, Connecticut office and George calls Louise on the intercom. Johnny is told that the policy on Hantler's device is for $20,000. The device is for making Boron 112 and is used for high-powered fuels.

George tells Johnny that many things once used as explosives are now being used as fuels. George has never seen the device, and Johnny calls it a pig-in-a-poke. George has had Dr. Hugo von Brauer look at the machine, and von Brauer says that Hantler is on the right track. George is worried about Hantler.

George introduces Johnny to Louise Larkin, who goes gaga over Johnny. Louise tells Johnny that a couple years ago, some of the kids she went around with had some pretty funny ideas. They thought they were smart by attending meetings that the FBI watched. She went to one meeting with her boyfriend Charlie White and the meeting was awful. They left in a hurry and the FBI later busted up the meeting.

This morning she saw the name on a policy, and Josef Hantler was one of the men she had seen at one of those meetings. Hantler had told George that the machine was vital to the government, but George is suspicious as to which government is involved. Johnny thinks about calling the FBI but decides to investigate first.

Johnny rents a car and drives with Louise to rural Connecticut and the Salmon Branch stream, where the lab of Josef Hantler is located. Johnny tells Louise to just nod if she remembers the man. Hantler calls out for them to stop and Johnny tells him he is an insurance investigator and Floyds has sent him to look at the machine, but Hantler tells Johnny that no one will see it. Johnny asks to see his government contract, but he has none. He will allow no one to see his laboratory. Hantler pulls a gun and tells them to leave, as they are trespassing.

Johnny takes Louise back to the office and calls Lee Hauk of the FBI to meet him for lunch. Louise tells Johnny that Charley would go out and kill that man. Johnny leaves for lunch as Louise answers the phone and talks to Charlie about meeting her dream man.

At lunch, Lee tells Johnny that Hantler is just a crack pot and they know he attended one meeting. Lee mentions that Louise was at one of those meetings too, and he also tells Johnny to watch out for her boyfriend, as he is the kind to take the law into his own hands. Lee tells Johnny that Hantler is harmless and usually makes crackpot inventions. Lee tells Johnny that von Brauer had a breakdown last fall. If George sold the policy to Hantler on von Brauer's OK, he is in trouble. Johnny knows that he needs to see the machine.

Johnny drives to the lab and blows his horn but gets no response. Johnny hears a thud and then the building explodes.

Johnny drags himself out of his destroyed rental car and sees Louise walking towards him with a husky football type who tells Louise that Hantler must have gone up with the building. Louise introduces him as Charley White and Johnny asks if he killed Hantler, but they say that they just got there and that they were going to give him to the FBI.

Hantler walks up and tells them that it was wonderful. He introduces Johnny to Dr. Bernard Steiner from "the commission" in Washington. The final test was final proof that is invention works. Dr. Steiner tells Johnny that they had watched the explosion from a hill, and that Dr. Hantler has developed a controlled power source from his compounds of great importance to the government's rocket program, but he cannot understand why it is called Boron 112.

Hantler tells them it was experiment 112 with his wonderful converter process. Dr. Steiner tells Charley that he is from Washington and that the government will take over the project immediately. Hantler tells Johnny that the converter went up with the building, and now he can build a bigger one for the government. Johnny tells him that now he will have the money to build another one, but Hantler tells Johnny that he is a great man now and is above such things and does not want the money.

"There you are George, full report, payment on the policy is up to you and if you do pay, at least it's in a good cause. Also, I guess both you and I have learned a lesson about jumping to conclusions."

Notes:
- Expenses include replacement of the rental car.
- In the script, the character of Dr. Steiner is named "Smithwyck".
- The announcer is Dan Cubberly.

Producer:	Jack Johnstone	Writer:	Jack Johnstone
Cast:	Shirley Mitchell, G. Stanley Jones, Parley Baer, Russell Thorson, Frank Gerstle, Lou Merrill		

♦ ❖ ♦

Show: The Eleven O'Clock Matter
Show Date: 1/19/1958
Company: Eastern Trust & Insurance Company
Agent:
Exp. Acct: $21.40

Synopsis: Pat McCracken calls and asks Johnny if he has heard of A B and C? Not the alphabet, but the ad agency. The "A" stands for Alfred Appleton, 55 years old and Eastern Trust has his life insured for $100,000. It is an annuity, which pays off at 65, and Pat thinks someone doesn't want him to make it. He thinks someone is trying to kill him. He is staying at his place up on Skeleton Point.

Johnny drives to Skeleton Point, Connecticut in a rainstorm. At the Appleton home Johnny is met at the door by Mrs. Gregory, who bluntly tells Johnny that Mr. Appleton only leases the house. Mrs. Gregory is the housekeeper, and she shows Johnny to the library where Mr. Appleton and his lawyer John Hillman are meeting.

Hillman tells Johnny that Mr. Appleton has received some crank letters. He did not report it to the police because he did not want any bad publicity in the middle of landing a new account. Tom Baker is the "B" and his only partner but there is some question as to whether he still is. Appleton will not accuse anyone until he has seen the books. The "C" stands for nothing.

Mrs. Laura Appleton comes in and Hillman goes to get something from his room. Mrs. Appleton seems not too happy to have Johnny stay overnight. Johnny asks if she was expecting someone else. Johnny sees someone outside in the lightening and goes out to see who it was. Johnny comes in to call the police, but the phone lines are dead.

Hillman asks Johnny if he saw anyone, and Johnny tells him the rain was coming down too hard. Mrs. Gregory announces Tom Baker, who is introduced to Johnny. He is soaked because he had to walk to the house when his car stalled in a deep puddle. Hillman suggests that they all go to the beach house and have some fun.

Everyone goes down on the stairway, but no one seems to have fun. The intercom buzzer rings, and Mrs. Gregory is told she can go to bed. Baker asks Appleton if they can have their talk, so Johnny and Hillman go to the house.

Johnny asks Hillman about accusing Baker of anything. Hillman is not sure, but Appleton thinks that there are some irregularities in the books. Hillman manages most of Appleton's affairs, so if anything is wrong it may be his fault. Hillman asks Johnny to call him at midnight to go over the books when Johnny is suddenly hit on the head as the clock is chiming 11:00.

Johnny comes to while the clock is still chiming. Hillman tells Johnny that he tried to grab the attacker but he got away. Johnny and Hillman search the house and end up at an open window. Mrs. Gregory comes in and Hillman tells her about the attack.

Johnny buzzes the beach house, gets no answer and goes to the stairs and hears a scream. Mrs. Appleton is standing at the top of the stairs where some of the railing is broken away. Alfred Appleton's body is at the bottom of the stairs on the beach.

Johnny looks at the body and Mrs. Gregory takes Mrs. Appleton back to the house. Johnny and Hillman go down to find Appleton's watch stopped at 11:10. Both Hillman and Johnny wonder where Tom Baker is.

Johnny goes back and calls the police, and they will get someone out as soon as possible. Hillman tells Johnny that the books seem to show a shortage of up to $50,000.

Johnny goes to see Mrs. Appleton and asks her what happened. She tells Johnny that after he left, she and Tom sat there for a while and then Tom left. Mr. Appleton was called on the intercom and left a few minutes after eleven. She went to the top of the stairs and she saw the broken rail and looked down to see his body.

Johnny asks why Baker was there and he tells her that she had been trying to signal Baker all night. Also, Appleton suspected a shortage and Hillman has confirmed it. Johnny suggests that maybe Baker came up to square things with Appleton.

Mrs. Appleton tells Johnny that Baker came up because she was going to ask her husband for a divorce so she could marry Baker, and they wanted everything to be in the open. They did not know that Johnny and Hillman were going to be there and that is why she tried to signal Baker.

Hillman comes in and tells Johnny that Baker has just come back. Hillman is told by Johnny to question Mrs. Gregory, who could have made the call to Appleton around eleven, while Johnny questions Baker.

Baker tells Johnny he had taken a walk on the beach and did not know that Appleton was dead until Hillman told him.

Johnny calls the police again and they will have someone there as soon as possible. Johnny notes that the policeman on the phone is not the same one he talked to earlier, and is told that the other officer, Harris, went off duty at 1:00 a.m.

Hillman tells Johnny that Mrs. Gregory denies making the call to the beach house. Suddenly Johnny thinks of something. Johnny checks everyone's watches and all of them read 12:50, but according to the sergeant it is after one a.m.

Johnny goes to his car and looks at the clock in his car where it reads 1:10. Johnny sees a gun and knows he had found the answer. Hillman tells Johnny that he had a foolproof plan until Johnny locked his car. Johnny tells Hillman that he had knocked him out, killed Appleton, reset all the clocks and woke Johnny up 15 minutes later as the clock was chiming. Johnny was only out for 15 minutes. Johnny hits Hillman with the car door and holds him for the sheriff. Hillman was not too happy to see them.

"Remarks: Hillman's motive was money of course. It was he who had taken the $50,000 from Appleton's agency."

Notes:
- This is an AFRTS program that includes a story about "The Bellweathers", a story about Harry Emmerson Fosdick, and ends with an organ selection.
- The announcer is Dan Cubberly.

Producer:	Jack Johnstone Writer: Robert Ryf
Cast:	Eleanor Audley, Paula Winslowe, Lawrence Dobkin, Will Wright, Ben Wright, Harry Bartell

♦ ❖ ♦

Show:	The Fire in Paradise Matter
Show Date:	1/26/1958
Company:	Four State Fire & Casualty Insurance Company
Agent:	Fred Hanley
Exp. Acct:	$241.28

Synopsis: Fred Hanley calls Johnny, and he has a routine case for Johnny in

Paradise, New Jersey. Johnny is told to go to Philadelphia, rent a car and find out how much insurance is due to Joshua Trimmings, who was hurt in a fire.

Johnny flies to Philadelphia, rents a car and drives to Paradise, while commenting on the drab colors of January in southern New Jersey. In Paradise Johnny meets sheriff Luther Hopkins and he tells Johnny that Joshua might have been hurt, but how bad is something else.

Johnny is told that the fire started on Friday and burned too fast to save the house. Joshua jumped from a window, and the sheriff is sure that the old skinflint did it for the money. Johnny learns that Joshua is retired, but that he spends his money somewhere else. Johnny gets directions to Joe Pasquale's house and drives to the fire scene, where he sees some interesting things.

Johnny goes to Joe Pasquale's house where Johnny meets the doctor. The doctor tells Johnny that Joshua is staying there because he loaned Joe money for seeds and fertilizer, and that he told Joe he might lower his fees on the loan if he could stay there. Johnny is told that Joe had to give Joshua free produce last year, and that no one likes him. Johnny is told that Joshua fights with everyone, and that his house was a dump. Johnny is also told that Joshua charges 10-20% interest on his loans, but there is never anything in writing.

Johnny goes in to meet Joshua, who tells the doctor that he will pay him for once, and he tells Johnny that the policy is unique, it requires payment if Joshua is incapacitated. Johnny leaves with the doctor, and he tells Johnny that there is nothing wrong with Joshua.

The doctor tells Johnny that Joshua calls the sheriff at all hours and even makes him clean up the trash around his house, and that the sheriff is fed up with him. Johnny is told that the fire started in several places, and that maybe he was burned out. Doc tells Johnny that the sheriff is a good man though, and has a sense of duty for everyone, even Joshua.

Johnny goes to the local store and buys a loaf of bread and goes to the fire scene while it is raining. Johnny finds some bills in the mailbox that provide clues to arson.

Johnny calls Fred to learn what Joshua had done for a living and then goes to Pasquale's house with the sheriff after learning that this was not Joshua's first fire. Johnny tells Joshua that he has been investigating the fires, and Joshua accuses Luke of setting the fire.

Johnny tells Joshua that the unpaid bills in the mailbox were a sure sign of planned arson, why pay the bills if the house were going to burn? Johnny tells everyone that Joshua ran a business that made celluloid dolls, and that his business had also burned. Johnny tells them that celluloid was used to burn the house. Joshua stands and tells Johnny that he is ready to be arrested. Johnny tells him that he was just guessing.

Notes:
- **The announcer is Dan Cubberly.**
- **Story information obtained from the KNX Collection in the Thousand Oaks Library.**

Producer:	Jack Johnstone	Writer:	Jack Johnstone	
Cast:	Vic Perrin, Forrest Lewis, Virginia Gregg, Will Wright, Parley Baer			

• ❖ •

Show:	**The Price of Fame Matter**
Show Date:	2/2/1958
Company:	**Four State Mutual Insurance Company**
Agent:	
Exp. Acct:	$2,341.00

Synopsis: Vincent Price calls Johnny from Hollywood, and Johnny is sure it is a crank call. The Vincent Price? Vincent tells Johnny that he has a problem with one of his paintings that is insured for $100,000. The painting has disappeared and Bert Parker the Four State Mutual agent is never there. Vincent has learned that no one knows where Bert is. Johnny will grab the first plane.

Johnny flies to Los Angeles, California on a Constellation. In the airport, Johnny spots Vincent in a crowd of autograph seekers. Vincent tells the crowd that this is the great Johnny Dollar and Johnny is beset by the throng of autograph seekers.

Johnny finally gets out of the airport and goes with Vincent to his home in Beverly Hills where the house is filled with fine art. Vincent shows Johnny a Goya called "The Old Man in Red", and a McManner called "Fright", and "Nightwind" by Jean Baptiste which is not lighted like the others. Vincent tells Johnny the lack of light is to accent the somber mood and has allowed the thief to make a substitution.

Vincent discovered the substitution when he came back from a tour, and has not contacted the police, that was Bert's job. Vincent tells Johnny that only a few friends knew of the painting, the house was not broken into and visitors were tracked while he was away. Johnny sees the list of visitors and spots Bert Parker's name on the list twice. Vincent does not know Bert very well and Johnny tells him the company will cover the loss.

Johnny and Vincent go to Bert's office and are told that he has not been seen there for two weeks. Johnny gets Bert's home address and Vincent offers to drive Johnny there.

At Bert's apartment, the landlord lets Johnny into the apartment, and they discover that Bert is gone. Vincent finds a travel folder for Paris, France in a desk drawer. Johnny and Vincent go to the travel office and learn that Bert has traveled to Paris, first class, and is staying at the Hotel du Louvres. Bert had wanted something close to the Montmartre. Vincent tells the agent to make the same reservations for him and Johnny.

Johnny and Vincent fly to Paris, France and check into the Hotel du Louvres where the manager tells them that Mr. Parker has left after a disagreement with the management. "You mean he ran out of money?" Johnny asks, only to get a shrug of agreement. Johnny is told that Bert had been at the Montmartre most of his time. Vincent tells Johnny that paintings are often sold in strange ways and tells Johnny that he will see what he can dig up.

Gay romantic Paris, and Johnny is waiting in his room. Vincent comes in later with some packages containing props for Johnny. Vincent gives Johnny a ten-gallon hat and tells Johnny he is in oil and his name is Matthews. Johnny ends up all dressed up and is told he will go to the Bal Macabre. Remember you made your money in oil, and Johnny is put in a cab.

At the Bal Macabre Johnny sees a lot of dirty people screaming at each other. A sly man comes to the table and tells Johnny that he is Les Chat Gris, the gray cat. He asks if Johnny likes the nightlife, and Johnny tells him he wants to buy some paintings, like a Baptiste. Les Chat Gris tells Johnny that he has friend who can help him and tells Johnny to wait at the corner for a cab.

Johnny goes out and the cab takes Johnny to a disreputable apartment where Johnny is to meet a dealer. Les Chat Gris tells Johnny that he only will ask for 10% of what Johnny pays for the painting.

At the door, Les Chat Gris knocks and Bert Parker opens the door to find Johnny standing there. When Les Chat Gris hears that Johnny is an investigator, he remembers someone waiting for him elsewhere. Vincent comes in as Les Chat Gris leaves.

Bert offers to give the painting back, and Vincent tells Johnny that he has a secret. Les Chat Gris was the one who got him the paining in the first place, but he only paid $300 for it. Johnny asks Vincent why he is not an investigator and Vincent asks Johnny why he is not an actor. Um, er, ah... let's get out of here.

The disposition of Bert Parker is up to the company. Vincent, now that he has the painting back does not care one way or the other. However, from the company's standpoint, this is not the kind of black eye that is good for you.

"Remarks: To Vincent price my eternal thanks not only for the help on this case, but most of all it has given me a chance to really know him."

Notes:
- The announcer is Dan Cubberly.
- The Hotel du Louvre is now a museum.

Producer:	Jack Johnstone Writer: Jack Johnstone
Cast:	Vincent Price, Virginia Gregg, Howard McNear, Junius Matthews, Forrest Lewis, Tony Barrett

♦ ❖ ♦

Show:	**The Sick Chick Matter**
Show Date:	**2/9/1958**
Company:	**Star Mutual Insurance Company**
Agent:	
Exp. Acct:	**$0.00**

Synopsis: Ben Pringle calls Johnny. Ben has retired and is running a poultry farm in Vineland, New Jersey. Things are going terrible. Someone is trying to put him out of business. Ben wanted to make sure Johnny was available before calling Star Mutual.

Johnny travels to Philadelphia and rents a car for the drive to Vineland, New

Jersey. Johnny gets directions to Ben's farm at a Mobil station. After searching an area full of chicken farms, Johnny pulls into a farm house to get further directions, and he ends up next door to Ben.

The neighbor, Mrs. Renzulli tells Johnny that Ben does not know anything about raising chickens. He should sell and move out. He is like all the other city people who retire, buy chickens and lose their money. Mrs. Renzulli tells Johnny that they buy up all the places that go out of business. Johnny asks if Mrs. Renzulli would benefit from Ben going out of business, and Johnny is thrown out.

Johnny gets to Ben's farm and learns that Ben has spent $40,000 so far. He has lost almost all his herd to bugs, and diseases and other things. Ben feels that the birds are being poisoned by someone who wants to see him go out of business. He is right next door — Joe Renzulli.

Ben tells Johnny he has the sickest herd of chickens anyone has ever seen. He has talked to the vet who has cured the chickens of all sorts of diseases. The vet gave Ben a book so he would know how to care for his chickens and feed them. Ben has looked in the book for the latest problem, and there is nothing in there.

In the chicken house Johnny sees a bunch of sad looking chickens staggering around. Johnny asks if Ben had been spiking the water with some of his private stock. Ben shows Johnny the feed he bought from Jake Romanov. Ben tells Johnny that Renzulli had helped him, and Ben has seen Renzulli spread something on this yard at night.

Johnny goes to talk to Joe Renzulli, who is building an elevated cage for his chickens. Joe tells Johnny that he tried to help Ben by throwing vitamin supplements to his chickens. Johnny asks about poison, but Joe gets defensive when Johnny mentions the police.

Johnny gets a sample of the vitamins to have analyzed. Joe tells Johnny that he has to be on good terms with his neighbors, and Joe tells him to find out for himself, because he does not live here. Johnny wonders if he has stumbled into something more than sick chicks.

Ben makes dinner for Johnny and the canned beans look, um, interesting? Ben tells Johnny that if neighbors tell on their neighbors they are outcasts. Johnny asks about Ben's other neighbor, the one with the new Lincoln out front.

Ben tells Johnny that he is John Culpepper, who came up from the south, a real nice young man. He has a lot of parties and women. Ben has been there, but Culpepper just gives him a bottle and tells him to enjoy it at home. There is a big barn out back, but Culpepper does not keep horses or other livestock. Ben also tells Johnny that he has heard trucks going in late at night. Johnny asks for a flashlight and goes exploring.

Johnny sees Ben's chickens hanging out by the fence, and there is a path from the fence to the barn. Johnny climbs the fence and goes to the barn and notices a faint piercing odor he first smelled in Kentucky. Johnny looks into the barn and sees cases of bottles and a copper still.

Culpepper comes up on Johnny with a gun and accuses him of being a revenuer. Culpepper looks at Johnny's ID and Johnny tells him that he is only interested in what is happening to Ben's chickens. Johnny is able to get the gun away from Culpepper, who offers Johnny money to go away.

Johnny realizes that whiskey is made from mash, and Culpepper tells Johnny that he has been dumping his mash over the fence, and Johnny realizes that Ben's chickens are just drunk.

Ben and Culpepper talk, and Culpepper agrees to pay Johnny's expenses, Ben's veterinary bills, and to move out of the county. Johnny should have turned him in, but that is a job for the company. And you know something? The stuff that Culpepper was turning out in that barn wasn't half bad.

Notes:
- This is an AFRTS program that contains an episode of "The Bellweathers" a story about freedom of the press and an organ serenade at the end.
- The announcer is Dan Cubberly.

Producer:	Jack Johnstone	Writer:	Jack Johnstone
Cast:	Lucille Meredith, Howard McNear, Gil Stratton, Jack Moyles, Sam Edwards, Bill James		

♦ ❖ ♦

Show:	**The Time and Tide Matter**
Show Date:	**2/16/1958**
Company:	**Universal Adjustment Bureau**
Agent:	**Pat McCracken**
Exp. Acct:	**$403.50**

Synopsis: Pat McCracken calls Johnny, and Johnny asks him what is new. Pat tells Johnny that Edward J. Rollins III is new. One of Pat's companies has a hefty policy on his life. Rollins requested a change to his policy, and then disappeared. "And you want me to go looking for him?" "That's the general idea." "Look Pat, you could be wasting dough sending me, chances are he will pop up again by himself." "I know, of course it involves a little trip to the Caribbean, but if you're not interested." "Caribbean! I'll be right over".

Johnny cabs to Pat's office. Pat tells Johnny that six months ago, Rollins decided to marry a girl named Virginia Blake and took out the life insurance policy. Apparently, he has changed his mind. He called from Nassau asking to remove Virginia from the policy. He was supposed to go to Miami to sign the papers but never showed up. He was in Nassau on his cabin cruiser with three of his friends, and Virginia Blake is among them.

Johnny travels to Nassau, Bahamas and finds a man who had refueled the boat and remembers hearing them mention Crooked Island. Johnny charters a plane, flies to Crooked Island and spots the boat in a cove. The plane sets down and Ed Rollins comes out to meet Johnny in a skiff.

Johnny tells Rollins about not meeting the agent in Miami, and he tells Johnny that he changed his mind. Johnny asks Ed about taking out the policy and changing his mind. Ed tells Johnny that he has just changed his mind. He tells

Johnny that he thinks Virginia has been two-timing him. He has not asked her because he might not like the truth. Rollins invites Johnny to come along with them to Jamaica.

On the boat are Virginia, Bill Winslow who handles the boat and Tony Atherton, who introduced Ed to Virginia. Johnny tells Rollins to introduce him as an old friend.

Johnny describes Bill as a man who looks at home on a boat, and Tony as someone who looks at home with a drink in his hand. Virginia, well one look at her and you forget where home is.

Johnny waits on deck with Tony and Virginia while the others skin dive. No matter what Tony says to Virginia, she tells him to lay off. Ed and Bill finally surface and Ed is in trouble. Ed tells them that there is something wrong with his air supply. Johnny finds a scraped spot on the air supply, and Ed says he must have scraped it on something.

Ed considered the event an accident, so Johnny did too. That night Johnny goes up on deck for a smoke and sees Virginia kiss Bill. Ed comes up and tells Johnny about cutting Virginia out of the policy, he has decided to marry her, as he cannot live without her. Ed sees Virginia up with Bill and figures she is navigating. Ed tells Virginia to turn in and takes over the helm.

Johnny asks Virginia why Tony feels she did not want to make the trip and she just says that she has known Tony for a long time. Bill tells Johnny that they should reach Jamaica the next night. Bill tells Johnny that he belongs on a boat, and Tony is just a passenger type. Virginia, well she can handle anything.

In Jamaica, Johnny calls Pat to have him check up on the three passengers on the boat. After dinner Bill goes to the boat and Tony goes bar hunting. Virginia is edgy and talks to Ed on the terrace.

Pat returns Johnny's call and tells him that Virginia has been sending regular $1,200 checks to Tony Atherton. Johnny goes to the terrace and then looks for Atherton in some nearby bars.

Back on the boat, Johnny wakes up Tony and asks why he is blackmailing Virginia. A policeman comes on board and tells them that Ed has been slugged and robbed. He may not live.

Johnny is taken to the location of the assault and learns that Ed had been hit with a piece of pipe and his wallet and valuables were gone. Next morning on the boat Johnny asks Tony again why he was blackmailing Virginia.

Tony tells Johnny that she was helping him with some bad investments. Tony points to the porthole and tells Johnny he saw Ed walking on the pier with someone following him, Bill Winslow.

Johnny questions Bill, who tells him he was just taking a walk and did not see Ed. Johnny mentions him and Virginia, but Bill insists he did not see Ed. Johnny talks to Virginia and she tells Johnny that she and Ed just walked around after dinner. Ed had business so she went back to the boat in a cab and went to bed.

She tells Johnny that Ed had talked to her about his doubts about her, and that he still wanted to marry her. She told him that he had to know some things about her. For one, she was once attracted to Bill, but it did not work out. She also told Ed that Tony had been blackmailing her. She had a roommate once who was stealing and went to jail because she could not prove she was not involved.

Johnny walks around for a while and looks at the boat sitting low in the water and gets an idea. Johnny goes back to the boat and checks the tide table to confirm that it was now low tide, and looks up the previous low tide, yeah!

Johnny goes to talk to Tony and he confirms that she has been paying him to keep quiet. Johnny tells Tony that Ed's business was to take care of Tony. Tony spotted Ed on the pier and hit him and probably figured you had killed him.

Tony recounts how he saw Bill following Ed, and Johnny tells Tony that he just hung himself. Johnny tells Tony to look out and Tony can only see the pilings. Johnny tells Tony he was lying and could not have seen over the pier last night. Tony tries to run and Johnny slugs him. Johnny tells him that Shakespeare is more right than he knew, "There is a tide in the affairs of man which sometimes leads to fortune." In your case brother, you missed.

"Remarks: Tony Atherton is in jail where he belongs. Bill Winslow is on a boat, where he belongs. Ed Rollins pulled through and he and Virginia will get married next month."

Notes:
- This is an AFRTS program that contains two episodes of "The Bellweathers" and an organ serenade at the end.
- The announcer is Dan Cubberly.

Producer:	Jack Johnstone	Writer:	Robert Ryf
Cast:	Virginia Gregg, Tony Barrett, Lawrence Dobkin, Herb Ellis, Frank Nelson, Ben Wright		

♦ ❖ ♦

Show:	**The Durango Laramie Matter**
Show Date:	2/23/1958
Company:	**Floyds of England**
Agent:	**George Reed**
Exp. Acct:	**$1,460.00**

Synopsis: George Reed calls and asks if Johnny remembers Durango Laramie Dalhart. Johnny asks if Durango has ever forgiven George for thinking he was counterfeiting money. George tells Johnny that Durango had written to say that he would be in the office on the 10th of last month to pay his $4,500 premium. That was six weeks ago, and he has not shown up. George has wired and written and is afraid that something may have happened because of the way Durango flashes around all his cash. Johnny tells George he will let him know what he finds out in Bum Spung.

This case from George looks like serious business. Johnny travels to Enid, rents a car and drives to Bum Spung, Oklahoma. When Johnny arrives at the broken-down shack he gets shot at. Johnny yells out to Durango and a voice tells Johnny that Durango is not there, and to go away. More shots are fired and Johnny notes that the man has shot out one of his tires.

When the man comes out to look at the tire Johnny gets his gun from him. The man is Sidewinder Wilson and Durango had sent him a telegram telling him to take care of the ranch for him. Sidewinder is an old friend of Durango's. Sidewinder tells Johnny that Durango left the house unlocked when he left, and no food was left for the animals and the tractor was left in the field, and that is funny. Sidewinder knows that Durango was loaded with money when he left, and his not showing up means that Durango was waylaid somewhere.

Sidewinder tells Johnny that he has not heard from Carol. Sidewinder helps fix the tire so that Johnny can drive back to Enid to see Carol Dalhart, when sidewinder spots Carol's convertible coming up the road. Carol drives up and grabs Johnny and gives him a great big hug and a kiss while Sidewinder just laughs.

Carol tells Johnny that Durango has gone to Hartford and has $50,000 with him. She got a postcard from Chicago, which is not like him as he usually goes straight to Hartford.

Sidewinder mentions a real estate man from Chicago who had been there. The card said the Durango was going to look at Ong's Hat. Johnny drives to Enid and calls Phil Avery, an old wire service friend, to see if the wires had picked up anything on Durango, but Phil has heard nothing. Johnny mentions Ong's Hat and Phil laughs.

Phil stops laughing long enough to tell Johnny that Ong's Hat is a town in southern New Jersey. Johnny and Carol grab a flight to Chicago to visit J. Harry Cramlan, the real estate promoter, who admits selling Durango some property in New Jersey for $35,000. Durango bought the property because he thought there was oil on the property. Johnny warns Cramlan that if Durango has been swindled, he is in trouble.

Johnny and Carol fly to Philadelphia where Johnny rents a car and drives to Mount Holly where they stop for lunch. Johnny notices a local newspaper article about an oil development in Ong's Hat.

Johnny drives to Ong's Hat and finds a large number of cars and people surrounding Durango and yelling at him. Johnny also notices two oil derricks. Johnny fears for the worse as he gets Durango's attention. Durango asks Johnny if he has snuck out to Enid and married Carol, which he had been hoping for.

Johnny tells Durango that he is on business. Durango accuses Johnny of transporting Carol across state lines, which means that they have to get married, and his six-gun will see to it.

Johnny tells Durango that he has been swindled, but Durango laughs and tells Johnny that he knows the area is not oil land. He tells them that as soon as the locals heard that he was an oilman they have been demanding that he sell them land even though he tells them that there is no oil there.

So far, he has made $65,000. Durango asks if Johnny is there to buy land or marry Carol? Johnny starts to back-pedal and Durango tells him it better be both.

"Expense account item 7, $1,000. The company now owns a small piece of land in Ong's Hat, New Jersey. As for Carol, that ever-loving doll, well someday."

Notes:
- This is an AFRTS program that contains two episodes of "The Bellweathers" and an organ serenade at the end.
- There is an area called Ong's Hat in the Pine Barrens area of southern New Jersey.
- The announcer is Dan Cubberly.

| Producer: | Jack Johnstone | Writer: | Jack Johnstone |

Cast: Virginia Gregg, G. Stanley Jones, Junius Matthews, Alan Reed, Frank Nelson, John McIntire, Bill Verdier, Tom Hanley

♦ ❖ ♦

Show:	The Diamond Dilemma Matter
Show Date:	3/2/1958
Company:	Masters Insurance & Trust Company
Agent:	Bert Major
Exp. Acct:	$284.30

Synopsis: Bert Major calls and asks Johnny if he knows anything about spacemen. Bert knows someone who thinks they have contacted him. The company is betting $2,000,000 that the man is either a liar or pulling one of the biggest hoaxes in history. Conrad Billings, ever hear of him? Billings, the Texas oil man and one of the richest men in the country? Right, and presently living in a mountaintop ranch in California minus $2,000,000 in diamonds he took up there with him. The diamonds were insured against theft by persons or things unknown on this earth. "You're serious, aren't you?" "You bet I'm serious". "Alright, I'll see you in your office".

Johnny cabs to Bert's office and Bert is really excited over this thing. Bert tells Johnny that it is impossible for diamonds to disappear, but it has happened. Billings is staying in his mountain-top lodge, and the police verify that no one could have gotten to the stones.

Conrad Billings called two weeks ago, and wanted the diamonds insured immediately. Bert is sure it was Billings as he had the call traced. Billings called Bert because he had done some business with a friend of his in Dallas. Billings had the diamonds with him, and he lives in one of the most isolated spots on earth.

Billings loves diamonds and plays with them like they are marbles, and he can afford to. Johnny tells him that an amateur could get to the diamonds. Bert recounts that he had insured the diamonds against theft by persons or things unknown on this earth. So, if a person took them prove it.

Bert tells Johnny that Billings must be in his right mind to run his empire, so they insured the diamonds. Johnny is to go out and make sense of this. Johnny gets the contact names and leaves.

Johnny flies to San Francisco, California and meets with Norton Shields at the Billings company headquarters. Norton has been with Billings for 10 years, except for Korea and he tolerates Billings. Norton tells Johnny that Billings has foibles, like diamonds. Norton saw Billings put the diamonds in a bag to be taken to his lodge before they disappeared. Norton tells Johnny he will have a plane ready for him in the morning.

Next morning a plane takes Johnny to Clear Lake, California where he is met by a car and driver, which takes him to Billings. The driver tells Johnny that he waits for Billings when he is not busy, and that no one lives at the lodge but Billings.

After passing through a series of gates and "Private Property" signs, Johnny is delivered to a wire gate. Johnny gets out and the car vanishes back down the mountain. A voice tells Johnny that he will be electrocuted if he touches the gates. If he is Mr. Dollar, the voice wants to know where he was yesterday, and Johnny tells him he was with Bert Major, and the gate opens. Johnny is told to drive a car up the road to the lodge.

At the top Johnny is met at the lodge by Billings who is short, bald and dressed in baggy clothes and hard of hearing. Johnny is shown the view from the lodge and he tells Johnny that he wants to collect on the diamonds.

On a control panel, Billings shows Johnny how electronic devices monitor the whole property with video monitors. Fences and sensors that allow Billings to detect anyone who comes in surround the whole mountaintop. Billings tells Johnny that he leaves nothing to chance, and that diamonds would be invaluable to other civilizations. Billings defies Johnny to find how the diamonds were stolen. Billings has a direct line to Andy Prentice, the sheriff if Johnny needs it.

Johnny drives down the mountain and sees no loopholes in the security setup. In Lakeview, Johnny is expected in the sheriff's office. Sheriff Prentice gets into the car and tells Johnny to drive to the lake so they can talk privately.

Johnny tells him that he does not believe aliens took the diamonds. Johnny notes that Billings does not wear a hearing aid, and Andy tells him he does not need one — he just turns up the volume on the equipment. Johnny asks about a parachutist landing there, but no one could get out, and they found no signs of entry or exit when they searched. Andy has no ideas how it happened. Johnny suggests a plane ride over the mountain and Andy goes along.

Johnny asks the pilot to fly around the mountain between the two fence lines, and he gets an idea. Johnny goes to San Francisco airport, talks to the captain of the airport police and at dusk he is where he wants to be, walking towards the Billings' lodge.

At the front door, Johnny surprises Billings who cannot understand how he got there. Johnny tells him that the sensors are in the wrong place as there is one spot that is not covered by sensors, and Johnny has a helicopter waiting there. They landed below the line of sight and hearing, so no aliens took the diamonds. Billings confirms that Norton Shields was a pilot while in Korea and flew rescue missions in…a helicopter.

"You know, in some ways I felt sorry for him. He'd spent millions of dollars to insure his diamonds and his privacy. Came a real showdown and it turns out he had neither. Oh, he will get his diamonds back sure, and will probably buy more. But privacy is a pretty hard thing to come by, at least in this man's world."

Notes:
- This is an AFRTS program with the usual stories edited out.
- The announcer is Dan Cubberly.

Producer:	Jack Johnstone Writer: Allen Botzer
Cast:	Edwin Jerome, Paul Dubov, Frank Gerstle, Junius Matthews, Marvin Miller

♦ ❖ ♦

Show:	**The Wayward Moth Matter**
Show Date:	3/9/1958
Company:	**Tri-State Life & Casualty Insurance Company**
Agent:	**Earle Poorman**
Exp. Acct:	**$204.00**

Synopsis: Earle Poorman calls and wants Johnny to come down over a $2,000 claim. Johnny wonders how Earle can afford for Johnny to come down, and Earle tells him that sometimes more is required than just paying off a claim. Earle tells Johnny that national security is involved in this case. Johnny will grab the first plane.

Johnny flies to Sarasota, Florida where Earle meets him at the airport. Earle has another new car with all the options. Earle tells Johnny that he cannot talk about the security issues here, and Johnny hopes Earle got him down here to go fishing.

Earle finally tells Johnny that he has insured the chemical plant of Dr. John C. Allworth at the request of Todd Swam of the Chamber of Commerce. Earle does not know what kind of chemicals Allworth is involved with. Earle does not know where the plant is and took Todd's word that the claim was valid.

Earle takes Johnny to Todd's office and leaves the keys to his car with Johnny. Inside Todd tells Johnny that he knows all about Johnny, and he knows that Johnny has worked with the FBI. Todd tells Johnny that he works with the Chamber of Commerce and also to be of service to the people.

Dr. Allworth is a retired chemist and has developed a key rocket fuel ingredient in his hidden chemical plant. He and an assistant work alone and Todd thinks the accident was sabotage.

Todd and Johnny drive in separate cars to the Everglades and the Cypress Swamp area. At the end of a dirt road, an Indian with a rifle meets Johnny. The man lowers the gun when Todd gets there. Todd introduces Johnny to Ben Osceola. Todd tells Ben that Johnny is to be allowed there anytime he wants.

Ben drives Todd and Johnny in an airboat to the site of Allworth's lab. Johnny meets Dr. Allworth and he takes them to the lab vault, which is where the accident occurred. Todd is sure that an enemy agent is responsible.

In the vault, Allworth keeps the finished rocket fuel component and an apparatus to finish the production process. No one has ever seen the apparatus, which was ruined by the explosion. In the vault the highly corrosive rocket fuel covers the floor. The secret apparatus has been destroyed and is lying on the floor.

Allworth tells Johnny that the glass flagon holding the rocket fuel was on a marble slab ready to be shipped to, well to its destination. The flagon exploded yesterday morning. Todd asks where his assistant Leon Salkoff is.

Johnny notes that an infamous man named Salkoff was involved in a series of industrial bomb plots, and Allworth tells Johnny that he is the same man, but he was cleared in the trials. Besides, Allworth tells Johnny that Salkoff does not know the combination to the vault. Allworth tells Johnny that Salkoff has gone to Ft. Meyers for supplies but has not come back.

Todd is sure that Salkoff has kept on going. Johnny asks about the windows to the lab and if a gun could have been used to break the glass flagon, but the windows are all in place and not damaged. Johnny goes outside to check to see if the windows could be removed from the outside and is stopped by a man with a gun.

Johnny tries to identify himself when Dr. Allworth comes out and tells Leon that Johnny is OK. Leon tells Johnny that he took so long because he was puzzling over how the flagon exploded. Johnny mentions Salkoff's conduct during the war, and Leon hopes he will be forgiven for what he was forced to do. He hopes working for this country will help him make up for what he did.

Leon has phoned the glass company and there is a way the glass could have crystallized. The formula from the company has given him the answer to the puzzle. They have a lot of work to do before morning.

The vault is cleaned thoroughly, and a new flagon is placed in the vault, and everyone waits. Early in the morning Johnny notices the rays of the sun coming through the window toward the flagon. Allworth holds a piece of paper in the light, and it bursts into flames. Allworth tells Johnny that the light could have caused the glass to crystallize, but it should have occurred by now.

Todd is positive that Leon is guilty until Allworth notices a tiny moth attracted to the light on the flagon. The moth circles and finally dives at the flagon and sets off an explosion. Todd is forced to apologize.

"Yeap, a tiny moth triggered the reaction that disintegrated, crystallized that bottle into a million tiny grains, like sand. And simply because of the difference in temperature of his little body. Seems impossible, but it happened."

"Remarks: Pay up on this claim in a hurry. The more help we can give to people like Dr. Allworth and Leon Salkoff, the better."

Notes:
- This is an AFRTS program with the usual stories edited out.
- The announcer is Dan Cubberly.

Producer:	Jack Johnstone	Writer:	Jack Johnstone
Cast:	Vic Perrin, Herb Ellis, Paul Richards, Lou Merrill, Leon Belasco		

Show:	**The Salkoff Sequel Matter**
Show Date:	**3/16/1958**
Company:	**Tri-State Life & Casualty Insurance Company**
Agent:	**Earle Poorman**
Exp. Acct:	**$0.00**

Synopsis: Johnny is paged in the airport and takes the call in the office. Todd Swam is calling to tell Johnny that he has to come back there to Sarasota, Florida. Johnny tells Todd that the company will pay the claim on the lab, but Todd asks if the company will pay a claim on Salkoff? Todd tells Johnny that it looks like murder.

Johnny expenses the no-show penalty on his flight to Hartford and Earle picks him up at the airport. Earle tells Johnny that Salkoff has just disappeared, and it looks like murder. Earle tells Johnny that Salkoff was involved in subversive activities during the war but has been given a clean slate. But if some of his old pals knew he was working for us, they would probably try to catch him, torture him for the formula and kill him. The details will have to come from Todd.

At the Chamber of Commerce building Johnny meets Todd, who gives him his car and tells him to go the lab. Todd has called the FBI, and they are going to send someone to assist Johnny. Johnny drives to Ben Osceola's shack and Ben takes Johnny back out to the island and Dr. Allworth is there.

Allworth takes Johnny inside and updates him. After Johnny had left, he and Leon worked to make the fuel additive lost in the accident. Leon had mentioned a man he had seen in Ft. Meyer the day before, someone he had known in Europe who would like to sabotage our effort.

Johnny is shown Leon's room, which is torn up from a struggle and Johnny spots blood on the floor. Allworth had heard voices in Leon's room and heard him call for help. He tried to open his door, but a chair blocked it. Allworth heard shots and the sound of Leon's body being drug out of the building. Allworth got out of his room by bracing his bed against the door and forcing the door open. Allworth chased after the men but they were gone, and they took Leon's airboat.

Allworth rushes off on his airboat to call the FBI, but he cannot hear Johnny tells him that they are already on the way. Johnny looks around the island and finds nothing. Johnny notices that the front door is closed, but he had left it open. Johnny walks in and is knocked out.

Johnny wakes up in Allworth's bed and plays possum while watching a man go through Allworth's files. Johnny pegs him as a subversive and starts to wonder about Allworth's story. Johnny groans and the man calls him by name.

They tell him they are concerned about him and did not know who he was until they searched him. He is Walter Bremman of the FBI. They had hoped that Johnny was one of the men they were looking for. Bremman tells Johnny that Salkoff is not dead. Bremman reminds Johnny of the Parley Barron case where a scientist had disappeared.

Johnny remembers that the reports of his death were to throw off their pals behind the iron curtain and now they have done the same thing with Salkoff. His partner Mike Kruschen is searching the lab. Bremman tells Johnny that there are two groups, agents from behind the iron curtain, that want to get to Salkoff either to get the secrets or to kill him. By reporting him dead, both will think the other did it. Allworth does not know, so do not tell him. Drag out your investigation to help us.

Bremman tells Johnny that the agents probably already know about Salkoff. Kruschen comes in and tells Bremman that he found nothing in the lab. Mike and Walt leave and tell Johnny that he knows what to do if anyone shows up. Also, tell Allworth that they have been there and will be back.

Johnny is confused and then hears their airboat leave, but not by the normal channel, there is something wrong here. Johnny checks his gun but it is empty, and his airboat will not start.

Johnny hears another airboat and sees Mack McLaughlin of the FBI and Dr. Allworth. Johnny tells Mack his boys had been there, and Mack gives a description of the two men. Mack tells Johnny that they are the ones who kidnapped and killed Salkoff. Their real names are Bremenoff and Kruchinski, spies and killers from you know where.

Mack gives Allworth a gun and tells him to shoot anyone he does not know. Johnny and Mack take off in the airboat and Johnny tells him what had happened. Mack tells Johnny that the men have not killed Salkoff because they do not have the formula. They did not kill Johnny because they need every option they can get. They left because they could not find the formula and are going back to Salkoff to get it from him.

Johnny tells Mack that they even knew about the Parley Barron case, and Mack reminds him that Johnny broadcast it on his radio show. Mack tells Johnny to keep quiet about this case until the space boys can launch a satellite successfully.

Back at Ben Osceola's shack they take Mack's well-armed car to chase after the two men. On the road heading south Johnny sees a police car going north and notices the two men are driving it. A fast U-turn and Mack is after them at over 100 mph. As Mack pulls up, there are shots, and Mack tells Johnny to use the tommy gun rather than his lemon squeezer to shoot the tires. Johnny fires and the car hits some cypress trees and the men are dead.

"Leon Salkoff, well I am afraid that he gave more than his skill and effort to the country he loved, that had taken him under its wing. His body was found trussed up and floating face down in the bayou from which Bremenoff and Kruchinski had launched the airboat.

Dr. Allworth? Now that a US space satellite is carrying out its mission, he is safely and officially working in a government laboratory.

Expense account total including incidentals and the trip back to Hartford, ah, forget it. If in any way it helped to get the Explorer out in space in orbit, it's on me."

Notes:
- This is an AFRTS program with the usual stories edited out.
- Once again, Johnny is using his "lemon squeezer".
- The announcer is Dan Cubberly.
- The U.S. Army put America into space by launching the Explorer 1 satellite into orbit on January 31, 1958, six weeks before this Johnny Dollar story. Talk about fast writing! The satellite carried a set of Geiger counters that discovered a zone of radiation around the planet known now as the Van Allen belt.

Producer:	Jack Johnstone	Writer:	Jack Johnstone
Cast:	Herb Ellis, Lou Merrill, Stacy Harris, Jack Kruschen, Vic Perrin, Harry Bartell		

♦ ❖ ♦

Show: **The Denver Disbursal Matter**
Show Date: 3/23/1958
Company: **Paramount Insurance Adjusters**
Agent: **Perry Jaimerson**
Exp. Acct: **$391.80**

Synopsis: Perry Jaimerson calls and Johnny accuses Perry of neglecting him. Perry tells Johnny that Four State in Denver has had a lot of large claims on young policies. There was $60,000 on one policy, $35,000 on another, $70,000 and a cool $150,000 on one last week. The beneficiary has been the same man. Johnny tells Harry to leave the door open, he is on his way.

Johnny cabs to Perry's office where the door was wide open. Perry has reservations for him on TWA at 6:00 p.m. and Johnny is to charge is expenses to Paramount. The local agent is William Whitney. Johnny asks how well Perry knows Whitney.

Perry tells Johnny that Whitney is a mild type and is not in with Don Ricardo, who was the beneficiary on the policies. Also, Whitney's wife is an ex-chorus girl who probably thought he had more money that he does. Perry is suspicious and is willing to pay Johnny to find out what is going on.

Johnny flies to Denver, Colorado and cabs to the Brown Palace. Johnny calls Pete Packer at the Denver Post newspaper, and Pete is ready to help Johnny tie one on. Johnny asks Pete if he knows Don Ricardo. Pete tells Johnny that he does not want to say anything without reason, but Don Ricardo was involved with Capone back in Chicago.

Johnny goes to get a drink and gets more information from the bartender about Ricardo. Johnny is told that Ricardo lives well and gives a lot of parties for people from out of town. The bartender spots a well-dressed man and clams up. Johnny leaves and notices he is being watched.

Next morning, Johnny looks up the Four State office on Broadway and meets Whitney. Johnny tells Whitney that the adjusters are concerned about the policies they have had to pay on.

Johnny is told that the policies were issued to some old miners who paid the premiums. Johnny gets the names of the miners and Whitney tells him that clearing up this matter will take a load off of his mind. Whitney has only seen Ricardo when he gave him the checks.

Johnny reviews the files, and then takes a cab to Golden. Johnny notices a foreign car following him, but it disappears. At an old frame house Johnny knocks on the door as the cab driver yells to him that the place looks deserted. The door opens and Johnny walks in only to be shot at twice.

The cab driver runs up and sees that Johnny is hit, but it is only a flesh wound. Johnny tells him to get out of the line of fire. A car drives off and the cabby spots it as a black foreign car. Johnny tells the cabby to take him to Millville and the home of Don Ricardo. The cab drops Johnny off at the front gate and drives off.

Johnny meets Don Ricardo and introduces himself. Ricardo has been expecting someone like Johnny to call because of his good luck lately. Johnny asks him who paid the premiums on the policy, and Ricardo tells him that the miners did. He had grubstaked them, and they made him his beneficiary. The miners were in their late 60s and died in mine accidents.

Johnny tells Ricardo that he was shot at in Golden and tells Ricardo that "you are a lousy shot". Johnny tells him about the dust on his small car and Ricardo tells him he might be right and pulls a gun on him and they struggle. The police rush in with Pete who tells Johnny he brought the police because he was sure Johnny would find something on Ricardo. Johnny tells him they will go out on the town when he finishes this job.

Johnny and Pete search the house and find the cancelled checks. Johnny "borrows" a car from Ricardo and drives to a house in the south end of town. Johnny gets out and at the front door Johnny hears loud voices and goes to a bedroom window to listen to the Whitneys getting packed to move out. Whitney tells his wife that she would still be in Ricardo's clubs if it were not for him.

Back at the front door Johnny knocks and Whitney opens it. Whitney is glad to see Johnny. Johnny notices the bags and Whitney tells Johnny that he had investigated Ricardo, and he is a gangster. He knew that Ricardo would know that Whitney had Johnny investigate him, and he is scared. He is leaving until this thing blows over. Whitney tells Johnny that he is going where Ricardo cannot find him and Johnny adds "to where I could not find you" and Whitney says yes.

Johnny remembers Whitney leaving him alone earlier, probably to call Ricardo, and shows Whitney the cancelled checks that show that 20% of the insurance policies were paid to Whitney one day after he paid Ricardo. Whitney struggles with Johnny and loses. Johnny tells him his milquetoast behavior may have sold insurance, but it has not sold Johnny.

"Oh, I guess you find them in every trade, but that doesn't justify them even being alive though. Fortunately, in the insurance business they never get away with it for long, even a team like Whitney and Ricardo. I wonder if they are sharing the same cell? Expenses include a doctor's bill, a night on the town with Pete Packard, and a gift to the cab driver."

Notes:
- Johnny is shot for the 8th time.
- This is an AFRTS program with a story about the flag of Vermont, a story about the heroism of Cpl. Ronald Rosser in Korea, and a story about the flag of Idaho.
- The announcer is Dan Cubberly.

Producer:	Jack Johnstone Writer: Jack Johnstone
Cast:	Virginia Gregg, Forrest Lewis, Barney Phillips, Edgar Barrier, Frank Gerstle, Peter Leeds

♦ ❖ ♦

Show:	**The Killer's List Matter**
Show Date:	3/30/1958
Company:	**Inter-Allied Life Insurance Company**
Agent:	**Pat Cummings**
Exp. Acct:	**$146.50**

Synopsis: Pat Cummings calls and asks if Johnny has heard of Everett Benton, the New York investor. Pat has a $100,000 policy on him. Last night he fell from a 14th story window — and Pat thinks he was pushed.

Johnny cabs to Pat's office where Pat tells Johnny that something does not smell right with this case. Benton had been doing well, his company is successful, and now he falls, or is pushed from a window. The beneficiary of the policy is his wife, a redhead who is 12 years younger than Benton.

Johnny travels to New York City and the expensive Benton apartment. Mrs. Benton fixes a drink as they talk. Johnny notes that she is bearing up well. She tells Johnny that they did not have an ideal marriage and she knows that Everett committed suicide. He had no enemies and will file a claim on the policy in the morning. And, she has an alibi for the other evening, and it is air tight.

Johnny goes to see Lt. Tovich at the police to discuss the case. Johnny is told that the company finances seem to be OK, and Benton was worth a lot of money. Benton had let himself into the office with his own key, and Mrs. Benton was with Larry Santos at his supper club.

Johnny goes to see Santos who is not too friendly. Santos tells Johnny that Mrs. Benton was in his office all night, and that she did not kill Benton. Johnny tells him that maybe Santos killed Benton, and is told to let the matter drop, as publicity is bad for business. Johnny is told he has a nose problem and better get over it, it could be fatal.

Johnny visits Tovich again and recounts the conversation with Santos. Tovich tells Johnny that they found a cigarette butt in the office that was different from Benton's. The phone rings and Tovich is told that Arthur Mayfield has been killed. He fell out of a 10th floor hotel room.

Johnny goes to the hotel and nothing was in the room to indicate anyone was with him. Johnny goes to see Mrs. Benton who tells Johnny that she does not know anyone named Mayfield. Mrs. Benton has an alibi for last night too, she was with Larry Santos. Tovich and Johnny discuss the similarities of the deaths, but there is nothing to connect the two men.

Johnny mulls over the case when someone knocks on his door. A man is there and asks if Johnny is the one investigating the two murders. He tells Johnny that he is Alvin Whiting, and he has information for Johnny.

Alvin looks out the window and tells Johnny that three men had bought an oil lease from a man named Tom Nolan. Nolan was eccentric and needed money so he sold the lease to Mayfield and Benton. Whiting feels that the killer is Nolan and he is getting revenge. Oil has just been discovered on the land and the property is worth millions and Noland feels he has been cheated. Whiting was in on the deal, he was the third man, and he is certain he is next.

Johnny takes Whiting to see Tovich where he tells his story. Tovich confirms the lease and tells them that Nolan has served time recently. The phone rings and Tovich gets the hotel where Nolan has been staying.

At the hotel, the clerk tells Johnny that he has not seen Nolan since he rented the room. They open the door and the room is empty. A cigarette butt is found that matches the one found in Benton's office.

The room clerk describes Nolan as a man with a wild look to him. A guard is posted and Johnny reviews Nolan's records. Johnny notices an item in the files and goes back to see Santos. Johnny tells him of the oil lease and Nolan's revenge. Johnny asks Santos why he put up bail for Nolan when he was arrested last. Johnny learns that Nolan is Santos' uncle, and is supposedly harmless.

Santos had arranged the lease to get money for his uncle, who was broke. Noland has been living in Coopersville and Santos has not heard from his uncle for six months.

Johnny calls Tovich and learns that Whiting has disappeared. Johnny goes to Coopersville and locates a woman who recognizes the picture of Nolan, but she tells Johnny that the man's name is Niles. He had been living there until last week when he left us. Johnny thinks that is when Nolan went to New York, but the landlady tells Johnny that he left them, he died.

Johnny realizes what has happened and goes to the graveyard to find the grave of Tom Niles, right where he had been. A shot rings out and hits Johnny's flashlight. Johnny fires back and hits Alvin Whiting. Alvin tells Johnny that he had to have the money as he was in debt and was desperate. Johnny tells him that he rigged the story to get the money from the lease. Too bad Noland was dead.

"Remarks: I turned Whiting over to the police and he made a full statement. Yeah, his motive was money. He was in the hole, gambling debts and bills, the high cost of living you might say. I guess he knows now that it is a real bargain compared to the high cost of dying."

Notes:
- This is an AFRTS program with the usual stories edited out.
- The announcer is Dan Cubberly.

Producer:	Jack Johnstone Writer: Robert Ryf
Cast:	Jack Edwards, Virginia Gregg, Jack Moyles, Tony Barrett, Parley Baer, Carleton G. Young, Lillian Buyeff

❖

Show:	**The Eastern Western Matter**
Show Date:	4/6/1958
Company:	**Tri-State Life & Casualty Company**
Agent:	**Earle Poorman**
Exp. Acct:	**$207.00**

Synopsis: Earle Poorman calls and Johnny tells him he is ready to grab his fishing rod and come to Florida. Earle tells Johnny to grab his Levi's, boots, a saddle and his six-guns. Earle tells Johnny that the freezing weather has hit the cattle ranchers really hard. A rancher has just hit Earle with a $78,750 claim on his entire herd.

Johnny flies to Sarasota, Florida and Earle drives Johnny to the ranch of Bart Trimball. Along the way, Johnny notices how the vegetation is brown and withered.

On the ranch, Johnny sees dead steers, 525 head in total, rotting in the sun. Earle called Johnny because Trimball had waited a month after the other claims to file his.

In the new tidy ranch house Johnny and Earle meet Betty Trimball and Bart, who is expecting a big check from Earle. Bart recognizes Johnny as an insurance investigator and asks Earle of they suspect him of killing off his herd. He does not like it and tells them so. Earle tells Trimball that Johnny has to approve the claim before it is paid, and Trimball gets upset. He tells Johnny to poke around all he wants and not to tell him he is a crook.

A man named Shorty comes in and tells Bart that the truck for the hides is there, and Bart leaves with Shorty. Mrs. Trimball tells Johnny that Bart had waited so long to file the claim because he was trying to salvage as much as possible. Johnny gets the name of their vet and tells her that the vet will have to look at the animals.

Bert changes his tone at dinner and apologizes for his comments. He had lost so much that he was just angry.

Bart tells Johnny that during the last cold spell, he had been trying to get feed for the cattle. They were all bunched up along the fence and would not move. The next morning, they were dead. Earle comments that he has seen Shorty somewhere.

Johnny is told that Bart and Betty have put everything they had into the ranch, even Betty's money from nursing, and have lost everything. All the hands are gone except Shorty. Johnny asks if they had thought of leaving and Bart tells that they had thought of going to California and farm there with relatives.

Johnny goes to bed and listens to Earle snoring. Johnny puts a pillow over his head, which almost turns out to be a deadly mistake. Later that night Earle wakes Johnny up and tells him to breathe, and the odor of chloroform is all over the pillow. Someone had come in and poured it on Johnny's pillow.

Earle recounts to Johnny how he had fallen out of bed and saw someone leaving and smelled the chloroform and threw Johnny's pillow outside. Earle tells Johnny that he had seen Shorty on a chain gang and remembers him throwing mud on his new 1958 Cadillac. Earle is sure that it was Shorty who put the gas on him. Johnny tells Earle he will handle things.

At breakfast the Trimballs are upset over what has happened. They go to the bunkhouse, but Shorty is gone. Betty tells them she never did trust Shorty but Bart says that he was the only one that stayed on when his wages could not be paid. Bart thinks that the chloroform came from a locker in the barn, they had used it to put an old sick horse down. Betty finds a note that Johnny reads, "I'm tired working for no pay. I will leave you know where to send my pay when you collect on that there insurance. Shorty". Bart mentions that Shorty thought that he would collect his pay if he poisoned the herd. Johnny asks if it was poison, now that he has someone to pin it on.

The vet arrives and Johnny, Earle and Bart go out with the vet to inspect the cattle, but they are too badly decomposed to tell anything. The vet notices a pale purple line on a water trough. The vet tastes it and tells them that someone used penorphic acid to kill the herd. The poison is used almost exclusively in laboratory experiments.

Johnny goes to the house to call the state police to round up Shorty Skinner. Johnny then calls the local police, and in Lake Wales the police have Shorty in their jail. They picked him up last night for vagrancy, and he put his "X" on the police blotter.

Johnny sneaks into Mrs. Trimball's bedroom and finds letters from the relatives urging them to come out to California. The letters were addressed to only one of the Trimballs.

As Johnny notices a diploma from the Lippenwald School of Nursing, Mrs. Trimball walks in and Johnny tells her that Shorty has served time, and she is sure that he had poisoned the herd. Johnny asks how she is certain now that the herd was poisoned, and she tells Johnny that it was just understood.

In response to Johnny's question, Betty tells Johnny that Shorty had given them a home address when he came to work for them. She shows Johnny the paper and Johnny tells her that Shorty cannot write, and the handwriting on the notes matches the handwriting on the return address note.

Johnny tells her that she learned of the poison in Nursing School and used the chloroform to try and kill Johnny to blame it on Shorty. Johnny tells her that Shorty was picked up before he had gone to bed. Bart walks in and asks Betty if she killed the herd, and she tells him that she hated this place. Bart would not do anything, so she did, and she failed.

"Expense account item 3, $50 to a lawyer at the county seat who took my deposition. It will be used in the trial against Betty Trimball. As for Bart Trimball, well I'm sorry for him."

Notes:
- This is an AFRTS program with a story about Maj. Smedley D. Butler, a

story about the flag of Wyoming, and a story about the code of conduct of Lt. Claude A. Jones.
- The announcer is Dan Cubberly.

Producer: Jack Johnstone   Writer: Jack Johnstone
Cast: Virginia Gregg, Marvin Miller, Herb Vigran, Jack Moyles, Vic Perrin

♦ ❖ ♦

Show: **The Wayward Money Matter**
Show Date: 4/13/1958
Company: **Northeastern Indemnity Association**
Agent: Fred Norwood
Exp. Acct: $104.70

Synopsis: Fred Norwood calls and he has a case for Johnny in Baltimore. Johnny just loves the thought of all that Chesapeake Bay seafood. Fred tells Johnny if he can get them off the hook on this one, he will approve the expense account blind. Over $100,000 is missing from a safe at the Trillingham Tobacco company.

Johnny travels to Baltimore, Maryland and the Sheraton Belvedere hotel. Johnny calls Mr. Trillingham, who will see him.

Johnny cabs to the company on Charles Street and meets Trillingham. He tells Johnny that someone opened the office safe and took the money. Johnny is told that they keep large amounts of money on hand because the farmers who sell their tobacco demand cash for payment. Also, Johnny is told that business is not as good as Trillingham would like.

Trillingham knows who opened the safe. It was Elmer Cockerley the bookkeeper. Johnny is told that Trillingham has just bought the company, and that he made his money in Florida real estate. Trillingham describes Cockerley as a mild, timid man who has been there for 30 years. At tax time, Cockerley discovered that some of the records were missing. During that time Cockerley had his house painted and bought a new car.

Johnny tells Trillingham that he should have been called then, but Trillingham tells Johnny that by the end of the year things seemed to work out. Johnny learns that Cockerley has not come in today and did not go home last night. Johnny rents a car and drives to Cockerley's home and discovers a reason why he might have disappeared.

At the front door, Johnny is met by Mrs. Cockerley who is very gruff and tells Johnny that she has not filed a claim yet, but she will. When she gets the insurance money she will not have that worthless worm under foot any more.

Johnny asks if she knew that the money was missing and she tells Johnny that they are just making due, and if it were not for Beneficial Finance they might not have made it. She had told Elmer if he was not so worthless he would have helped himself to some of that money, but he would just scream like a baby. Elmer had given her the combination to the safe and told her to go ahead and take the money. She tells Johnny to just try and put the robbery on her.

She shows Johnny a picture of Elmer and calls him a baby. Johnny tells her that there is something behind her gruffness, and that she is trying to cover up for her husband. He needed her to take care of him and make him toe the line, and she liked it. She tells Johnny that she does not know where Elmer is. Johnny is told to ask August Trillingham where he is, they used to go fishing together.

The phone rings, and Sgt. Macklin is calling for Johnny. Sgt. Macklin tells Johnny that they have found Elmer Cockerley and what is left of the money. Johnny is told to go to Hance's Bridge, about 9 miles north of town so he can identify the body.

Johnny drives to the bridge to meets Sgt. Macklin and wonders, which he always does when there is only one suspect. The wife tried to confuse him, and then there was Trillingham. Sgt. Macklin tells Johnny that most of the money must have floated down the creek, and that Cockerley was driving too fast making his getaway and went into the creek. Johnny identifies the body and notices a scrap of paper in one of Elmer's pockets that says "night Hance cat". Johnny also notices a bruise on Elmer's head, a bruise left by only one thing. Johnny tells Sgt. Macklin to call the coroner and leaves.

At Trillingham's office, he tells Johnny that the money was too much of a temptation for Elmer. Johnny tells him that it was a temptation for any man, including him.

Johnny now remembers that Trillingham had sold a lot of swampland in Florida and is still a crook and a killer. Johnny mentions the note asking Cockerley to go fishing for catfish with him.

Johnny tells Trillingham how he met Cockerley there at the bridge, hit him, put him in his car and pushed it into the creek. Johnny tells him about the bruise on the back of Elmer's head from a .38 Special, which Trillingham pulls from his desk.

Mrs. Cockerley comes in and accuses Trillingham of killing her husband. Trillingham goes to close the door, and Johnny slugs Trillingham and tells Mrs. Cockerley that Trillingham will pay for it.

"Well, so ends another chapter in the dirty history of crime. I hope that the insurance on Elmer makes up in some small way for Mrs. Cockerley's loss of her, well I was going to say husband. But I guess Elmer was kind of a baby to her. To manage, to brow beat, and to love."

Notes:
- There are two versions of this AFRTS program. One version has stories about the bravery of Capt. Douglas T. Jacobson, the flag of Alaska and the Boxer Rebellion. The other version has these stories edited out.
- The announcer is Dan Cubberly.

Producer: Jack Johnstone   Writer: Jack Johnstone
Cast: Virginia Gregg, Edgar Barrier, Alan Reed, Vic Perrin, Frank Nelson

Show:	**The Wayward Trout Matter**
Show Date:	4/20/1958
Company:	Universal Adjustment Bureau
Agent:	Pat McCracken
Exp. Acct:	$815.00

Synopsis: Pat McCracken calls and tells Johnny he has done a magnificent job for the company and has saved them a lot of money. He wants Johnny to take a vacation, at company expense, at Lake Mohave Resort where Johnny loves to fish. Johnny will grab the first plane but tells Pat to wait until he sees the expense account, because if Johnny ever smelled a rat, it is now!

Johnny flies to Las Vegas, rents a car and drives to Lake Mohave Resort. Johnny muses over the travails of the early explorers as he drives along at 60 mph. Johnny arrives at the resort and meets Buster Favor, who tells Johnny that the fish are really biting.

Johnny is rooming next to Gordon Hatch, an old-time confidence man who was never nailed for doing anything big. Buster tells Johnny that he and Ham would have told Hatch they were full up, but figure they are doing a public service by having Johnny come here. Buster got a call on Tuesday from some wealthy folks from Los Angeles, and Tuesday afternoon Hatch came busting in. The people from Los Angeles have been here before, and their wives always bring a lot of furs and jewelry. They also bring a lot of cash so they can go up to Vegas at night to gamble.

One of the guests is a lawyer who got Hatch sent up. Hatch swore he would get even, but Buster does not think he would do anything rough. There is no insurance angle unless some of the jewelry disappears.

Gordon Hatch walks in and tells Buster about the 10-pound fish he caught and is keeping in a live box. Even the worst crook in the world would not touch another man's catch. Hatch invites Johnny to come to his room for a drink and Johnny tries to beg off but goes to the room to size up Hatch and talk about fishing. Hatch tells Johnny that his past is past and that he is trying to make amends. Johnny drinks a night cap and goes back to his room and passes out, victim to the oldest trick in the world, and anything could happen before he wakes up.

Johnny wakes up in the morning when Buster pounds on his door at 9:00. Buster tells Johnny that Hatch is out fishing, and the guests have arrived. Johnny tells Buster that Hatch claims to have turned over a new leaf. Buster tells Johnny that Hatch may not be after Mr. Fellers after all.

Johnny has a bad headache from a mickey the night before but goes to join Buster in the café for breakfast where the other anglers are bragging about their morning exploits. Mrs. Feller rushes in and tells Buster that all their jewelry has been stolen, along with their money. Someone broke into the cabins and stole everything. Ham Pratt walks in and learns of the thefts. Johnny tells Ham to search Hatch's room and car while he and Buster go for a boat ride.

Johnny and Buster take a boat and find Hatch in a deep cove. Buster sees Hatch doing something near his boat. When they beach their boat, Johnny and Buster are told by Hatch that he has moved his live box.

In the box, Johnny sees a bunch of bass and a dead trout on the bottom. Hatch tells Johnny that he is going to leave later to get the trout mounted in Los Angeles.

Johnny wants to talk to Hatch, and Hatch tells Johnny that he wants to keep their fishing date, so Buster loans Johnny a rod and reel. They walk back to Buster's boat and Buster tells Johnny that there is nothing in Hatch's boat.

Suddenly Johnny has an idea and wants another look at the trout. Johnny wonders why the trout is not floating on the surface belly-up. Johnny pulls out the 10-pound trout, and it must weigh 20 lbs. because the trout is stuffed full of jewels and cash!

Hatch pulls a gun and tells Johnny to put the jewels in his boat, so Johnny offers Hatch the whole fish and slugs him with the wet trout.

The expense account includes the cost of five days of really great fishing.

Notes:
- This story mentions Fast-Strike minnow hooks, which were invented by Jack Johnstone.
- This is an AFRTS program that contains an episode of "The Bellweathers", a story about the Department of Justice and an organ serenade at the end.
- The announcer is Dan Cubberly.

Producer:	Jack Johnstone	Writer:	Jack Johnstone
Cast:	Lawrence Dobkin, Alan Reed, Russell Thorson, Edgar Barrier, Junius Matthews, Barney Phillips, Eleanor Audley		

◆ ❖ ◆

Show: The Village of Virtue Matter
Show Date: 4/27/1958
Company: Continental Insurance Company
Agent: Ben Orloff
Exp. Acct: $100.00

Synopsis: Ben Orloff calls and asks if Johnny has ever heard of a place called Virtue. "Do you mean Virtue, South Carolina? You want me to go down there?" "Yes, if you will." "Do you have a bulletproof vest and a couple of extra handguns I can take along?" "My one suggestion is that you do not take along any firearms. Our agent has an office in Georgetown. His name is Joseph Picatello." "Smokey Picatello, the guy that was linked with Murder Incorporated a few years back? I tell you this Mr. Orloff, if you do not have to pay off on my insurance policy before I'm through, well mister this is going to cost you a whopping big expense account.

Johnny travels to Georgetown, South Carolina and goes to see Joe Picatello. Joe tells Johnny that he used to be a bright young punk and studied law but gave up law when Dewey took over New York and broke up the rackets. Joe tells Johnny that in spite of his past, he is clean. Joe tells Johnny that he better be careful with his clients or he could be plain wrong, or dead wrong.

Joe tells Johnny that some of the boys saved their money and leased the old Carraway plantation near Virtue on the Pee Dee river. They all went respectable, and it has been 20 years now. Joe signed up with the insurance company and talked the boys into buying insurance and has policies on everyone, including the town.

The problem is that Buddy McGoon had his fishing boat stolen. Mr. Avery, who runs the general store had his boat stolen too. Ever since then somebody has had something stolen every day. The people blame the boys, and the boys blame the people. Joe tells Johnny that there is going to be civil war unless you can stop this and the company will be in trouble with the losses, so he sent for Johnny. Joe tells Johnny to take off his lemon squeezer and they will go to Virtue to check out the situation.

Joe and Johnny drive to the Carraway plantation, which is full of flowers and a fine old mansion. Johnny and Joe are shot at and Joe yells at the boys so he can identify himself.

Joe introduces Johnny to "Bull" McGoon, "Lefty" Stemper and "Flippy" Lacavitch who takes Johnny's gun. Lefty does not want Johnny there and tells him they will find their own stuff, like in the old days. Johnny asks for his gun back, and Flippy threatens Johnny, so Johnny puts a judo flip on Flippy and gets his gun back.

Johnny tells them he will try to stop what is going on and will bring in the police if necessary. Lefty tells Johnny that the boys are nervous after what has been going on. Lefty tells Johnny that they only have their hunting weapons, and Johnny tells them that the police will be there if anything happens to him. Johnny tells them he will have them thrown off of the plantation, and they start to cooperate.

Johnny is told that the boys all love the plantation and have been straight. But now after 20 years the people are after them. Johnny is told that Mr. Carraway, who owns the plantation, is the mayor of Virtue and the chief of police.

Joe and Johnny leave to visit Carraway. In Virtue Johnny finds a quiet town, with no hint of hostility. Johnny tells Joe that he hopes the boys continue to believe that he has protected himself.

Johnny finds Parley Carraway, the mayor, who is police chief, and who has not found out who is stealing the things, but he is sure that the gangsters on the plantation are responsible. He tells Johnny and Joe that he will have to evict them if the trouble does not stop. Johnny is told that the boys have started making the plantation a paying proposition.

Johnny notices a diamond ring and a new car outside, which belong to the mayor. He tells Joe that he tries to have a new car every year. Carraway tells Johnny that he can take care of things by himself. Johnny notes that he has made lot of money from the plantation, and Carraway slips and tells Johnny that he has been offered $124,000 for the plantation.

Johnny now knows that the mayor has been robbing the people to rile everyone up so that he can have the boys thrown out. Johnny threatens to call the state police and have Carraway locked up and to have Joe bring fraud charges. Carraway tells Johnny that all the stolen property is safe and stored away, and Johnny tells him he will call in the police unless Carraway returns the stolen goods and lets the boys continue their lease. Johnny leaves to go to the plantation to have a drink with some "respectable" people.

"Yeah, this insurance business really has some funny ones. And I guess it is the funny ones that balance out the bad, tragic cases. Anyhow, I like it. Expense account total including the trip back to Hartford, oh call it $100 even. And in view of our little secret Joe, maybe you better pay it out of petty cash! And those pals of yours, you better drop in on them to make sure that they stay on the straight and narrow, as well as that old coot Carraway."

Notes:
- This is an AFRTS program that contains a story about the flag of Florida, a story about Cpl. Charles L. Gilliland, and a story about the flag of Michigan.
- There is another reference to Johnny's "lemon squeezer", carried in a shoulder holster.
- The announcer is Dan Cubberly.

Producer:	Jack Johnstone	Writer:	Jack Johnstone
Cast:	Frank Nelson, Billy Halop, Jack Kruschen, Peter Leeds, Gil Stratton, Will Wright		

♦ ❖ ♦

Show: The Carson Arson Matter
Show Date: 5/4/1958
Company: Worldwide Mutual Insurance Company
Agent: Jim Paris
Exp. Acct: $56.90

Synopsis: Jim Paris calls and Johnny tells him he can smell the smoke from his apartment. Jim tells Johnny that the Cash and Save Market has burned. Jim wants Johnny to look closely at the store, it is part of a chain, and this is the fourth store to go up in as many weeks. The owner is John Wakefield Carson.

Johnny cabs to Jim's office in Hartford, Connecticut but learns little, other than getting a list of the stores that have burned. The coverage is for $106,000 on the latest store. Carson has his office in Boston, and his latest store is there also.

Johnny cabs to the scene of the fire, and the building is a total loss. Johnny notes that the store is as far as possible from a fire station. Johnny meets Hal Gibbons of the arson squad who tells Johnny that something inflammable had been used to start the fire. Hal tells Johnny that the other stores were far from a fire department as well. Carson has never showed up at any of the fires, he just files a claim. Carson is a millionaire who like to quote from the classics.

Margaret Carson shows up and is introduced to Johnny who she recognizes by name. Margaret introduces Walter Smitten, the company lawyer who wants nothing to do with the grocery business. He feels that someone is trying to put Carson out of business. Margaret leaves to file a claim, and Johnny wonders about Walter's intentions to marry Margaret and get to her money.

Johnny calls Jim Paris to get information on the policies. Jim calls back and Johnny gets a list of the markets and the store with the next largest coverage, which is in Salem.

Johnny cabs to his apartment and drives to Salem, Massachusetts and the local Cash and Save Market. At the store, Johnny spots a man in the back of the building. Johnny hears someone enter the building and follows him into the storeroom. Johnny turns on the lights and calls to the man and is hit by a falling object.

Johnny wakes up in the Salem police department and learns that he was hit with a gallon jug of pickles. Johnny learns that Mr. Carson was the man who hit him and brought him to the police.

Johnny drives to the Boston office and meets with Carson. He tells Johnny that the fires were set in the order of value, and he had been at the Salem store to inspect the store to prevent spontaneous combustion. Johnny tells him that the fires were set, and Johnny thinks Carson had them set.

Johnny asks if Carson is going to rebuild his stores in areas more convenient to the new real estate developments. Carson tells him that he will do what he wants with the insurance money. Johnny tells Carson that he knows who set the fires and leaves.

Johnny calls Hal Gibbons, who tells Johnny that the Hartford fire was arson started by an amateur, as were the other fires. Hal tells Johnny that Walter Smitten could not have started the fires, or Margaret the step-daughter. Johnny tells Hal to send the police to Carson's office and goes there to try a bluff.

In the office, Johnny tells Carson that he will be taken to court unless he talks. Carson tells Johnny that he likes Walter Smitten like a son. But, he has a stepdaughter, and he had promised his wife that all money from the business is to go to Margaret, and he regrets that promise. Margaret has made too many monetary demands of him since coming of age. Carson would distrust her every move were it not for Walter. She demands that he be in love with her to use his legal skills to take the stores away from him.

Johnny tells Carson that he has proof that Margaret has started the fires, and Carson is relieved. Margaret comes in with a gun and tells Johnny that he should make a deal with her. Johnny tells her that a man from the police is behind her but she tells Johnny that it is a bluff, until the police shoot the gun from her hand.

"Yeah, the company will not have to pay on the four markets, and the courts will have to deal with Margaret. I am sure they will. And next time, well give me something clean to work on, I hate this kind of stuff."

Notes:
- This is an AFRTS program that contains a story about the flag of South Dakota, a story about the Ploesti raid, and a story about the flag of Oklahoma.
- The announcer is Dan Cubberly.

Producer:	Jack Johnstone	Writer:	Jack Johnstone
Cast:	Byron Kane, Harry Bartell, Virginia Gregg, Jack Edwards, Joseph Kearns, Forrest Lewis		

❖

Show: The Rolling Stone Matter
Show Date: 5/11/1958
Company: Universal Adjustment Bureau
Agent: Pat McCracken
Exp. Acct: $146.00

Synopsis: Pat McCracken calls Johnny and he has $75,000 on his mind. Have you ever heard of the Savalla Diamond? "Yeah, matter of fact I have". It is a pink Diamond". Pat tells Johnny that the owner is trying to sell the diamond, but it was stolen last night.

Johnny cabs to Pat's office where Pat updates Johnny. Johnny then travels to New York City and the apartment of Joseph Wentworth, the owner of the diamond.

Wentworth tells Johnny he had been hit on the head and had borrowed heavily to get the stone. The insurance will barely cover the loans, as the diamond was not insured for its full value. Wentworth had a customer who was going to pay $100,000 for it.

Eloise Barns, his fiancée, had come by for dinner and Wentworth was putting the diamond into his safe when he was hit. Eloise came back up to the apartment and woke him up. Wentworth has known Eloise for a year.

Johnny cabs to Eloise Barnes' apartment, where she looks more expensive than the diamond. Eloise tells Johnny that she was looking for a cab when Wentworth was hit. She does not care for diamonds, only money or mink.

Eloise tells Johnny that Wentworth is not her fiancé as she is not the "engaged" type. It interferes with her hobby, having fun, and she hopes Johnny finds the diamond real soon.

Johnny goes to see Gerald Mantell, the customer for the diamond. Mantell tells Johnny that he was stalemated over the price and knows what the diamond is worth. He wants the diamond recovered by Friday because he is leaving for Europe on an impulse. Anything wrong with that?

Johnny reviews the case in his room and is called by a man who asks if he is looking for the Savalla Diamond. He knows where it is and wants money for the information. He will show Johnny it's case to prove he knows where the stone is.

Johnny goes to Antonio's Bar and waits for the caller to arrive when Eloise comes in. Johnny sits with Eloise and then Mr. Mantell arrives. Johnny is told that they have been friends for years, and Eloise is the one who told Mantell about the diamond. The waiter signals for Mantell and he leaves. Eloise tells Johnny that she is only having a drink with Mantell while she waits for Wentworth. She tells Johnny that Mantell is very impulsive and she thinks they both have been stood up.

Johnny starts to leave when Wentworth comes in. As Wentworth tells Johnny that he has spent too much time with Eloise, Johnny is paged and the waiter gives Johnny a package that was given to him by a stocky man in a gray suit. The note on the package tells Johnny "Couldn't take a chance contacting you, someone was following me. Contents of the package will show you I know what I am talking about. Will contact you later". In the package is the empty case that Wentworth had kept the diamond in. One the way to the corner for a cab Johnny spots a body in an alley, Mantell.

Johnny slaps Mantell awake and he tells Johnny that a cab driver was waiting for him. He went out and no one was there. Johnny suggests that Mantell had stolen the diamond and someone was trying to get it back from him. He swears he does not know where the diamond is.

Johnny goes to his hotel to think when Wentworth comes to his room. He apologizes for flying off the handle about Eloise. A man had called Wentworth at his apartment and would tell him where the diamond is for a price. Wentworth tells Johnny that he heard an operator say "Hotel Maysfield" in the background.

Johnny goes to the Hotel Maysfield and learns that the man was named Krause but he had left. Johnny looks in the room and finds a note pad with the imprint of the Cathcart Hotel on it.

Johnny goes to the hotel and goes to Krause's room. Johnny tricks him into admitting that he had talked to Wentworth, and Johnny figures that the robbery was staged and Wentworth was using Johnny to find Krause. Wentworth comes in and mentions blackmail.

Johnny tells them that Krause was supposed to turn the stone over, but instead tried to blackmail Wentworth about the fake robbery and called Johnny to frighten Wentworth. Wentworth tells Krause he made a mistake blackmailing a desperate man, as he has no money. He needed the money for Eloise to hold on to her. He is willing to add murder to keep Eloise.

Johnny tells Wentworth that Eloise only wants mink and money and takes the gun from Wentworth. Wentworth tells Johnny that he was right about him.

"Remarks: Krause handed over the diamond. He and Wentworth are both in custody. It was Wentworth who beat up Mantell for hanging around Eloise. And Eloise, the last I heard, she was going her merry way, having fun she called it. I never did accept her offer to join her after the diamond was recovered and I am not about to."

Notes:
- This is an AFRTS program with a story about the flag of the state of Alabama, a story about the heroism of Richard Antrim, a story about the flag of Hawaii.

- The announcer is Dan Cubberly.

Producer:	Jack Johnstone	Writer:	Robert Stanley
Cast:	Lawrence Dobkin, Forrest Lewis, Virginia Gregg, Edgar Barrier, Don Diamond		

♦ ❖ ♦

Show:	**The Ghost to Ghost Matter**
Show Date:	**5/18/1958**
Company:	**State Unity Life Insurance Company**
Agent:	**Oscar M. Trimley**
Exp. Acct:	**$31.50**

Synopsis: Art Price calls Johnny very early in the morning. Art has received a call from an insurance man who wanted Johnny's phone number. He said it was a big emergency and probably called the first person he thought of.

Johnny is called by Oscar M. Trimley, who is in Lake City, New Jersey. He is upset and wants Johnny to come there right away. Ian McAndrews, the man who founded Lake City is dead, or rather he isn't. Anyway, he died five years ago. The $55,000 life policy was paid off, but you have to come here. Ian McAndrews has come back, or his ghost has come back. Johnny tells Trimley he will think about it and starts making plans to travel to Lake City so he can catch the ghost off-guard.

Johnny calls Art and updates him. Johnny then calls Nancy Turner, a young old-flame who investigates the supernatural. Nancy tells Johnny that she has given up the supernatural. Johnny tells her that he has to go to New Jersey to investigate a haunted town, and Nancy tells Johnny that she is going with him.

Johnny and Nancy travel to New York City and rent a car for the drive to New Jersey. Nancy talks the whole way about her studies about the supernatural, and Johnny is almost convinced.

Lake City is a small quiet has-been town in northern Jersey, which was based on a mill that has closed. Johnny locates Trimley's office where Johnny and Nancy are introduced to Charlie Reed, Bill Foster and Tony Greg who are members of a businessmen's club in town.

They tell Johnny that they are worried about this thing. Johnny is told that he will have to see and hear what is going on at midnight. Charlie fixes up Johnny and Nancy with a boat and fishing equipment, while Charlie goes to get rooms for them. Everyone is mum about what is going on and Johnny thinks that there is something screwy going on.

After an afternoon of fishing, Johnny and Nancy meet with the others for dinner at the hotel where the talk is about Johnny's fishing. Later, Tony drives Johnny and the others to the middle of town where the things are about to happen.

As the clock chimes, Johnny is told that old McAndrews died at midnight. Suddenly the lights dim, bats fly from the clock tower and the town is filled with an eerie wail as the clock chimes 13 times.

Johnny goes to the McAndrews' house where the door slams in their faces. Johnny goes in with a flashlight and hears footsteps and all sorts of noises.

Suddenly they see a green light moving outside and a rocking chair rocking. Johnny looks at the chair and finds no wire or strings and the noises stop. Johnny tells everyone that he wants to investigate in the daylight.

The next day Johnny is helped by the others as he inspects everything and finds nothing other than the town being mobbed with people. A man takes a picture of Johnny and Johnny recognizes him as a New York reporter. Johnny tells them that he is leaving and drives out of town to wait for nightfall.

Johnny sneaks back to Oscar's office where they are all talking about notes inviting them to Oscar's office. Johnny is spotted and tells them that too much help was handicapping him. They tell Johnny that they just wanted to make sure that Johnny did not overlook anything.

Johnny tells them that the ghost is no more, and that it is one of them. Johnny tells them that he has found the sub-cellar in the McAndrews house with all of the complicated electrical equipment that was making the sound effects. Bill admits to making the equipment. Johnny tells them that it was a wonderful stunt, especially after the press was notified, and that everyone would benefit from the publicity. Johnny tells them that he will not give them away as long as the ghost of Ian McAndrews never walks the streets again.

"I don't know. I suppose I ought to really hit you over the head with this expense account. But, uh, after all the cause was a kind of worthy one. So, I will be honest with it for a change. And it was fun to have Nancy Turner along."

Notes:
- There are two versions of this AFRTS program. One has an episode of "The Bellweathers", a story about need for vigilance to preserve liberty. The second has a story about the flag of Kansas, a story about William B. Halyburton's actions on Okinawa during World War II, and a story about the flag of North Dakota.
- Charlie mentions "fast strike" hooks, which were an invention of Jack Johnstone.
- Next week's program is billed as the most dangerous, exciting incident in Johnny's career.
- The announcer is Roy Rowan, however the script page on file at the Thousand Oaks Library lists Dan Cubberly.

Producer: Jack Johnstone   Writer: Jack Johnstone
Cast: Virginia Gregg, Forrest Lewis, Joseph Kearns, Russell Thorson, Sam Edwards, Bob Bruce

◆ ❖ ◆

Show: **The Midnite Sun Matter**
Show Date: **5/25/1958**
Company: **Northwest Surety Company**
Agent: **Bill Chadwick**
Exp. Acct: **$600.00**
Synopsis: Bill Chadwick calls from Seattle and asks if Johnny has ever fallen

under the spell of the Yukon. Bill has a mine that he would like Johnny to take a look at. It is a gold mine in Alaska. Come on out and bring your gun.

Johnny flies to Seattle, Washington on a Mainliner and goes to Bill's office. Bill tells Johnny that the men who moil for gold are a pretty tough bunch. Even the management at the Universal Consolidated Mining Corporation can be tough.

Universal is located north of Fairbanks, above the Arctic Circle. The mine is located at the foot of a glacier, and the glacier is changing its course. They seem to think that the glacier is going to sweep over the mine and town and leave the company with a big claim. Bill wonders if the company might be causing the glacier to change course because the gold has run out.

Johnny thinks that it is a far-fetched theory, but Bill wonders why the glacier would change course all of a sudden and head for some well-insured property. Johnny arranges to fly out the next morning on a company plane, a two-engine Speedcraft Transport.

Johnny gets a room at the Benjamin Franklin hotel, and after a night on the town Johnny goes to a tiny airport and wonders why there is no one on the plane but him and the pilot. Yup, he should have wondered.

Johnny goes to the airport and meets Cliff Murray and they take off and Johnny learns he is the co-pilot. Johnny notes that the only things he has flown since the war have been piper cubs. Cliff tells Johnny that these planes are really easy to fly.

They took off from the remote airport because of the cargo and to save time. The miners are worried, and there have been some ice quakes this spring. The engineers think they can change the glacier, and Cliff is carrying the TNT for the job.

Johnny flies the plane for a while and they land at Anchorage for mail and food. After taking off again Cliff starts to experience pains in his stomach. Cliff calls the mine airstrip and alerts them of their course. As the pains grow worse, Cliff tells Johnny to take over. Cliff tells Johnny that he will have to land the plane, and he can do it.

Johnny is too busy to make notes on the rest of the flight, so the airport records make up the rest of the report.

2:35 — Johnny calls the tower and tells them that Cliff is sick. Cliff manages to tell them that they cannot dump the TNT because Johnny cannot leave the controls. The tower gives Johnny heading instructions from the Snake River marker, and they wait for the plane. Johnny calls for an engineer and tells Paul Foster that the landing gear will not come down. Johnny will try to use centrifugal force to get it to come down and might have to make a belly landing. Charlie tells Johnny that during a fly-by he saw that the landing door is partially open and Johnny is told to fly off the fuel.

2:41 — Paul asks Johnny if he has tried to shear the lock pin on the gear, and Johnny has not tried that, and has full hydraulic pressure. Paul tells Johnny that he might have to go to Fairbanks if he needs to make a belly landing, but Cliff has told Johnny that they would not want him to go there because of the cargo.

2:50 — Don Wilkins the chief engineer asks if Johnny has tried cycling the gear handle, and Johnny tells him he has. Don tells him to continue trying.

3:00 — Paul asks about the fuel, and Johnny still has 950 pounds, and Fairbanks is backed up and cannot take him. Don tells Johnny to feather the #2 engine and try to snap the gear down as he unfeathers it, but Johnny has tried that. Paul tells Johnny that they will ready the strip for a belly landing. Don asks Johnny to unload the hydraulic system and free-fall the landing gear, but Johnny has tried that.

3:28 — Paul tells Johnny that they are going to foam the runway to reduce the friction and prevent fire. Johnny is told to make a pass over the runway to get the feel of it.

3:31 — Don asks Johnny to raise the gear handle and then slam it down and hold it there.

3:46 — Johnny is told they are laying foam and he should be ready to land at 3:55.

3:51 — Paul asks Johnny how things are and Johnny asks if there is a doctor for Cliff. Johnny is told not to feather the engines when he sets down. Johnny tells them that he will make a final pass and Don tells Johnny that Paul will talk him down.

3:54 — Johnny makes a wheels-up landing. The doctor reports that Cliff had a successful appendectomy.

"A hard-bitten bunch of miners did you say? Those boys up in that lonely outpost are the salt of the earth. And as for trying to pull something on your insurance company, well you should have seen how just one good load of TNT put that glacier back on its course. Yes sir, I hope that the vein of gold never runs out for those boys. Expenses include gifts for the boys in the tower."

Notes:
- There are two versions of this AFRTS program. One contains an episode of "The Bellweathers", a story about the State Department. The other version contains a story about the flag of Louisiana, a story about the national flag and the Congressional Medal of Honor, and what they stand for, and a story about the flag of Oregon.
- This story is based on a real event, the belly-landing of United Flight 101 on October 31, 1957. It was dramatized by Jack Johnstone for a convention of airline pilots with Jimmy Stewart playing the part of the pilot, Charles C. Dent
- The "Midnite" spelling agrees with the script title page.
- The announcer is Roy Rowan.

Producer:	Jack Johnstone	Writer:	Jack Johnstone
Cast:	Jeanne Tatum, Frank Nelson, Russell Thorson, Barney Phillips, Harry Bartell, Forrest Lewis		

Show:	**The Froward Fisherman Matter**
Show Date:	6/1/1958
Company:	**Continental Insurance & Trust**
Agent:	**Clark Thorness**
Exp. Acct:	**$181.00**

Synopsis: Clark Thorness calls Johnny from Fort Wayne, Indiana, and he wants Johnny to come and see him. Clark asks Johnny if he knows Bertram R. Halsworthy, the fisherman. He has disappeared and a claim has been filed on his $160,000 policy. Clark wants Johnny to find him.

Johnny catches a mainliner to Fort Wayne and goes to Clark's office. Johnny is told that Bert Halsworthy lives in Angola, near Lake James and invented some fishing tackle. Johnny asks if it was the Fast-Strike hook and is told that some guy on the East Coast invented that. Johnny is told that Bert left in February for the Gulf of Mexico and came back in April, only to leave again. The police have investigated and have learned nothing.

Johnny drives to Angola to see the widow and she is sure that Bert is dead. He loved to fish in salt water, and they were not happy. Johnny is told that Bert took about $1,000 with him when he left in February. He sent postcards and came back once to get more money and left a note on the freezer.

Johnny goes to see Lt. Bascomb in Ft. Wayne and sees the note: "Be home one of these days, maybe. Meanwhile going back to get more of these beauties. You will be happier with me away, Martha, so will I. Bert". Johnny learns that the fish were striped bass, but the season is too early for them, and Lt. Bascomb has checked everywhere. He is sure that Martha killed Bert. Johnny tells Lt. Bascomb that stripers are running now in California, so Lt. Bascomb will check there.

Johnny talks to the family attorney who tells Johnny that Bert was a froward fisherman, and maybe it was his wife's fault. Johnny checks on the wife and is sure that she is not guilty of killing Bert. Johnny checks with Lt. Bascomb who tells him that the fish are the only clue, but stripers are not running now. Lt. Bascomb tells Johnny that Dr. Kindle at the University could probably tell them how long the fish had been in the freezer.

Johnny leaves and runs into Emmett Gowan, a sports writer who is looking for Lake James. Emmett tells Johnny that he met Bert last winter, and that he was a real non-conformist, he would use the wrong bait in the right place and catch fish.

Johnny drives through the night to get to Lake Moultrie in Columbia, South Carolina. At the lake, Johnny meets an old man with a load of fish. The man tells Johnny that stripers have been released into two lakes in South Carolina, Moultrie and Monroe, and that soon everyone will know about them. The man tells Johnny that he just like to do things differently.

Bert tells Johnny that his wife henpecks him too much. He thinks that if he makes her worry, she will be more tolerant of him, and maybe they can be happy like they used to be.

Johnny sees Mrs. Halsworthy in a fishing magazine, holding a 9-pound pike she caught in Lake James.

Notes:
- The announcer is Roy Rowan.
- Emmett Gowan is also in *The Lust for Gold Matter* as a retired fishing guide.
- Froward is defined as stubborn or contrary.
- This story is commonly and incorrectly called *The Forward Fisherman*.
- Angola, Indiana is in extreme northeast Indiana, and Lake James is almost on the Michigan border.
- Story information obtained from the KNX Collection in the Thousand Oaks Library.

Producer: Jack Johnstone   Writer: Jack Johnstone
Cast: Byron Kane, Virginia Gregg, Harry Bartell, Will Wright, Forrest Lewis, Howard McNear

• ❖ •

Show: **The Wayward River Matter**
Show Date: 6/8/1958
Company: **Continental Insurance & Trust Company**
Agent: **Lee Harkins**
Exp. Acct: **$100.00**

Synopsis: Lee Harkins calls and Johnny wonders if he is still in Ohio, and wonders if the fishing is as great as he remembers. Lee tells Johnny that the Ohio is on the rampage and it is still raining hard. Lee needs Johnny to come out, but any fishing will be for the bodies of people.

Johnny travels to Cleveland in the rain and is met by Lee in the airport. They are on the way to Carterette, Ohio and Lee tells Johnny it has been raining for four weeks. Lee tells Johnny that he is from Carterette and has sold a lot of policies to the shopkeepers there, but you never hear about the small communities in the news.

Carterette has been lucky so far as the rains were elsewhere, so the flood control project has not been handled properly. Carterette is in a valley on the Crooked River, and some of the town is below the river. If the levees break, the town will be lost. Lee received a call from Fred Norlock, and he will lose everything unless the river goes down.

Johnny notices how the streams are all over the banks and it starts to rain as they get to Carterette, where everyone is working to build up the levee with sandbags.

Johnny describes how the river, full of flotsam and debris, is ready to tear everything apart. Johnny notices how a railroad trestle is clogged by debris and causing the river to back up. But how to break up the dam?

Johnny asks Lee about getting dynamite and Lee tells him that Fred Norlock has it. Norlock is the only one working on his own property and Lee tells Johnny that Norlock has opposed the flood control program.

Johnny goes to the hardware store and Lee tells Norlock that he should be working on the levee. Lee asks for dynamite and Norlock tells Johnny he is crazy. Norlock will not give Johnny the dynamite, so Johnny pulls his gun and demands the explosives. Norlock relents and Johnny gets what he needs.

Lee and two workers go with Johnny to the trestle. Johnny elects himself to go out on the trestle and plant a case of dynamite on it. The job is done and the dynamite is set off and the trestle goes up and releases the water and saves the town.

The dam is broken, the town is saved, the people go home, and the rain stops in defeat. Johnny and Lee go back to town and rest in the local hotel.

Johnny cannot sleep but worries and frets over why one person had worked so hard to save his own things and not help the town. Johnny wakes up Lee and asks about Norlock's business, and Lee tells Johnny that Norlock has $100,000 in coverage. Johnny tells Lee that $100,000 is too much for a town the size of Carterette.

Johnny is convinced that Norlock knew about the dam and went through the motions to save his property. And why did he fight them from getting the dynamite? Johnny is convinced that Norlock wanted the levee to break.

Johnny goes to look for Norlock and finds him by the river with a case of dynamite. Johnny tells him that the river did not do what he wanted it to, and Norlock tells Johnny he will kill him if he comes closer. Norlock is going to set off a small charge to break the levee and destroy the town. Johnny is told to walk to the river and Lee calls him. Norlock shoots, but Johnny fires back and Norlock is thrown into the river and disappears.

"Norlock's body was never recovered. He'd lived alone, he died alone, a crooked man in the Crooked River. Nor was he mourned in the little town he tried to destroy."

Notes:
- This is an AFRTS program that has an episode of "The Bellweathers", a story about Einstein and his distrust of Hitler and an organ medley at the end
- Tom Hanley and Bill James (as John W. James) are mentioned for their special sound patterns.
- The announcer is Roy Rowan.

Producer:	Jack Johnstone	**Writer:**	Jack Johnstone
Cast:	Chester Stratton, Frank Gerstle, Bob Bruce, Parley Baer		

♦ ❖ ♦

Show: The Delectable Damsel Matter
Show Date: 6/15/1958
Company: Mono Guarantee Insurance Company
Agent: Ralph Single
Exp. Acct: $230.00
Synopsis: Ralph Single calls from Hollywood and asks if Johnny knows who

Hildegard Ransom is? Johnny recognizes her as a debutante and asks if Ralph was not going with her sometime back. He was, but he threw her over because of her crazy antics. Want a date with her? Come on out here and you can have a date with her, at company expense.

Johnny flies to Los Angeles, California on a DC-7 Mainliner. Single is a good name for Rip, who has a knack for meeting wealthy important people, particularly women and then sells them insurance. Johnny is not surprised that Rip knows Hilde Ransom, heir to a fortune, but he has not mentioned why he wanted Johnny to meet her. Rip tells Johnny that he can live off the premiums on Hildegard's account.

Rip drives Johnny to the hotel in his little old truck, a brand new El Dorado Biarritz, with gold fittings and all the accessories, including a bar. Rip asks Johnny if he has ever heard of the Cape Star, an emerald in a gold brooch with diamonds worth $300,000. Hildegard has reported it stolen and wants Rip to come to see her. Rip does not want to see her after she had a fireplug blown up because she did not like the looks of it and ended up flooding most of the Bel Air Estates.

Rip gets a call on the phone in his truck and it is Hildegard who wants to know where he is. Rip tells her that he has told the police and she gets angry and threatens to cancel her other policies. Rip gives the phone to Johnny and Hildegard is happy that Johnny is on his way. Rip takes Johnny to an airpark where he keeps his plane to fly Johnny to Balboa, where he will go out to Hilde's yacht.

Rip flies Johnny to Balboa and learns that Rip got some of his money from a rich uncle. Rip tells Johnny that Hilde took the Cape Star with her on a trip and discovered the emerald missing that day. At the dock are a number of boats but the captain of the cruiser does not want to take Johnny out there, he will only take Rip. Johnny tells him to radio the *Hildemora* and straighten things out. Rip leaves and the captain tells Johnny that he is ready to sail.

At dawn the next morning Johnny gets to the Hildemora, and a beautiful Hildegard Ransom, "Rowf!" Hildegard welcomes Johnny and mentions that the "old tub" had been shot at off of Formosa. She was there just cruising around and wanted to visit Chou En-Lai.

Hilde tells Johnny that he is more handsome than she had heard and wants to find out if he is as much of a wolf as Rip says he is. While walking along the deck Johnny notices one of the crew duck out of the way, and Johnny remembers his eyes looking at Johnny over the sights of a gun sometime in the past.

Hilde tells Johnny that she will have to go through customs and notices a drawer open with the Cape Star back where she had kept it. Johnny asks if this is a gag, and she says no. So now they can have some fun, as she is tired of the other guests. Johnny wants to meet the guests and the crew.

The captain comes in and tells her that one of the men, McCarty, has appendicitis, and was sent ashore in the cruiser. Johnny wants to see the man McCarty and radios the cruiser and gets no response. Johnny notices a speedboat and takes it to follow the cruiser with the first mate. The mate spots McCarty on the bridge shooting at them. Johnny is shown a berry pistol used to shoot up flares. The mate swerves in and Johnny shoots the flare gun at him and hits McCarty who crashes his boat into them.

Johnny pieces things together after the Hildemora picked him up. By sheer luck, his shot with the flare gun had hit McCarty full on and he was badly burned. And after the smash up the mate had pulled Johnny out of the drink. By then the yacht had caught up with them.

Hilde tells Johnny that McCarty was smuggling narcotics and had stolen the Cape Star long enough to get the cruiser to come out to the yacht and then played sick to get back to shore. If they did not have to get him back to a doctor, they could just cruise around for a few days. Three days. And what three days!

"Remarks: "Heh, heh, it's funny isn't it. You never know what you are going to get into when you take on even the most routine kind of case."

Notes:
- There are two versions of this AFRTS program. One has a story about the flag of Mississippi, a story about Sgt. Thomas A. Baker on Saipan in World War II, and a story about the flag of Iowa. The other has an episode of "The Bellweathers", a story about Daniel Webster and an organ medley at the end.
- Chou En-Lai (Zhou Enlai) was the "Red" Chinese foreign minister during the 1950s.
- Formosa was the site of the government of Chiang Kai-shek and is now called Taiwan.
- The announcer is Roy Rowan.

Producer: Jack Johnstone   **Writer:** Jack Johnstone
Cast: Virginia Gregg, Chester Stratton, Barney Phillips, Jack Moyles, Frank Gerstle

♦ ❖ ♦

Show: The Virtuous Mobster Matter
Show Date: 6/22/1958
Company: Continental Insurance Company
Agent: Ben Orloff
Exp. Acct: $174.00

Synopsis: Lefty calls Johnny — you know, Lefty Stemper from Virtue, South Carolina. Lefty is not having trouble with old man Carraway, they bought him out and now own the plantation. The place is fixed up now and they need insurance. Johnny tells him to go to see Joe Picatello. Lefty tells Johnny that he talked to Joe but he never comes over and is never in his office. Lefty wants Johnny to come down and figure out what is wrong.

Johnny travels to New York City and talks to Ben Orloff. Ben complements Johnny on his previous report on The Village of Virtue Matter. Johnny asks Ben if he has heard from Joe Picatello, but Ben tells him that Georgetown, South

Carolina is a small office with little business. Ben tells him that he has not heard from Joe in some time. Johnny suggests that he go down to see if all is well with Joe and Ben tells Johnny to let him hear from him.

Johnny travels to Georgetown, South Carolina and rents a car and drives to Joe's office, which is dark. Johnny gets no answer when he knocks, but hears a door open inside. A voice sounding like Joe asks who is there and reluctantly opens the door and Johnny tells him who he is, you know, Johnny Dollar, the investigator.

Joe is very quiet until "Willie" attacks Johnny and punches him out. Joe hears a car coming and they leave. Lefty and Flippy come to the office and trip over Johnny on the floor. Lefty hears a car leave and wakes Johnny up. Johnny tells Lefty that Joe and Willie hit him. Lefty recognizes the name Willie as "Willie the Lump" who was a former partner of Joe's. That means the Joe has gone back to the old ways. Joe walks in and Lefty is ready to blast him.

The atmosphere is tense in the office as they discuss how Joe has gone back to the old ways when Joe walks in. Joe asks Johnny what happened and Flippy tells Joe that he has gone back to working with Willie the Lump. Lefty reminds Joe of their deal to take out anyone who goes back to the old ways. Johnny demands Lefty's gun and tells him it was not Joe who worked him over. Look at his hands.

Lefty remembers "The Twin", Shep Larco. The law called Joe and Shep the twins because they talked and acted like each other. Joe cannot tell them where he has been and Lefty is still suspicious.

Finally, Joe tells Johnny that the Secret Service knew that Shep and Willie had pulled a job in Baltimore and could not find them. So, they spread the word that Joe knew where they were so that Shep and Willie would look for them. Joe tells Johnny that he has been hiding in Washington. The feds sent Joe to the office as living bait.

They all agree to stay with Joe when Shep and Willie come in. Shep thinks that Johnny is with the Secret Service. Willie is told to shoot Joe when shots break out and Johnny has gotten them both with Lefty's gun. Johnny asks if anyone knows a good doctor.

"Yeah, I've said it before, and I'll say it again. In this insurance business, you never know what you'll run into."

Notes:
- There are two versions of this AFRTS program. One version has a story about the flag of Delaware, a story about Lt. Edward V. M. Isaac in World War I, and a story about the flag of California. The other version has an episode of "The Bellweathers" a story about Noah Webster and an organ medley at the end.
- Johnny is shot for the 9th time.
- The announcer is Roy Rowan.

Producer: Jack Johnstone   Writer: Jack Johnstone

Cast:	Jeanne Tatum, Jack Kruschen, Les Tremayne, Billy Halop, Frank Gerstle, Gil Stratton Jr.

❖

Show:	**The Ugly Pattern Matter**
Show Date:	**6/29/1958**
Company:	**Masters Insurance & Trust Company**
Agent:	**Barry Winters**
Exp. Acct:	**$101.00**

Synopsis: Barry Winters calls Johnny, and tells him that he has a problem with an account. Simplex Tackle, a small outfit in Danbury, Connecticut. They are a small partnership owned by nine people. The employees are covered by a group life insurance policy and they have had to pay off on three policies, and they all were murders.

Johnny cabs to see Barry Winters who gives Johnny more than he thought. The police think that one man is responsible because each of the people worked for the same company, died within a month of each other and died on the same day of the week, Wednesday. There has been no apparent reason for any of the murders.

The first was Adams, a vice president who was run over by a car. The second was John Bowers who was strangled. Frank Dalvers was shot in his own house. Hanley Thomas the president thinks that more is involved. Johnny gets a list of the officers and their salary, and a list of the employees. There are six officers left.

Johnny goes home and then drives to Danbury and the Simplex plant. Johnny meets with Hanley Thomas who agrees that there is a pattern, someone knew the habits of their victims. All of the employees were talked to, as they all knew the habits of the officers. There have been some hotheads who do not like the top-heavy management, and profits have been good lately.

Johnny notices from his list that the three men were killed in alphabetical order but the real pattern is by salary. Adams made $12,000, Bowers made $13,500 and Dalvers made $15,000. So, the next to go would be James Williams or Charles Hart who both earn $16,500 and ultimately Thomas. Johnny is told that Williams is on vacation and has not been heard from. Sgt. Dennis calls and tells Thomas that another partner is dead. John Williams has been murdered at Parvin's Pond.

Johnny drives to Parvin's Pond and meets Sgt. Dennis who tells Johnny that Williams came up alone last Monday. They think that Williams had just come in from fishing and was bludgeoned to death with an oar. An old lady from next door came by to give him some cookies and found him. There are no fingerprints on the oar, and no footprints, the tourists would have trampled them out. The police think that he came in off the lake on Wednesday night, a week ago tomorrow. Dennis thinks that the murderer is an employee, because the employees are not paid very well because of the recession even though the company was making money. Dennis has talked to everyone and the officers are all fine men.

According to Johnny's list, the next one will be Charles Hart, and Johnny asks Dennis to put a watch on him. Johnny drives back to the office of Charles Hart, and talks to his secretary, Miss Gregg. She tells Johnny that Hart has not been in since last Wednesday. Thomas comes in and tells Johnny that Hart often goes on sales trips.

Miss Gregg tells Johnny that Hart was the one who built up the company and developed and sold all of the products that made the money along with Mr. Adams, until Thomas came in with all of his relatives. Thomas tells Johnny that Hart and Adams did start the company and brought in some partners who decided on the expansion. They came to Thomas for financing which made the expansion possible. Johnny asks what happens to the shares of the dead partners and is told that the other partners will absorb them.

Johnny feels that Hart has plenty of motive and knew about the habits of the others. Johnny drives to Hart's address but no one answers. The super comes up and tells Johnny that Hart is at the factory.

A $10 bill gets Johnny into the apartment where he looks through the desk and finds a list of the officers. Hart comes from behind the door with a gun. Johnny asks if the gun was the same one that killed one of his partners and Hart says no.

Hart realized the pattern from the list, and he knows that he is next. Johnny asks about Hanley and the others coming in and he tells Johnny that they deserve to be at the top.

He is not an executive, just a worker and he is content with the others being in charge in spite of the prodding of his secretary. Johnny tells Hart to stay put and leaves to follow a hunch.

Johnny picks up Dennis and goes to the plant. With Dennis' handcuffs, Johnny goes to see Thomas and tells him he is under arrest. Johnny asks if he was going to kill off his relatives also. Too bad he covered up the evidence, except to the oar the used to kill Williams, because he left prints on it.

Johnny tells Thomas that he has found the gloves and his wife has told Johnny that he was not at home during any of the murders. Thomas blurts out that his wife helped to plan the whole thing. Johnny tells him he was bluffing and Thomas pulls a gun and tells Johnny that no one will know when he gets rid of Johnny.

Dennis comes in and tells Thomas that he has heard a clean confession. Thomas tries to shoot Dennis, who shoots him. Johnny comments to Dennis that "Sergeant, I haven't seen that fast a draw except on TV." and Dennis tells Johnny "That's where I learned it."

"There will be a lot for the courts to work on, about who else was involved with Thomas. The sergeant's bullet killed him by the way, and I'd call it good riddance. Or at least quick justice. Remarks: Why bother?"

Notes:
- There are two versions of this AFRTS program. One version contains an episode of "The Bellweathers", a story about a quote from Harry

Emerson Fosdick and an organ medley. The second version contains a story about a quote from Harry Emerson Fosdick, and an organ medley.
- The announcer is Roy Rowan.

Producer:	Jack Johnstone	Writer:	Jack Johnstone
Cast:	Virginia Gregg, Les Tremayne, Forrest Lewis, Herb Vigran, Junius Matthews, Frank Gerstle		

❖ ❖ ❖

Show:	The Blinker Matter
Show Date:	7/6/1958
Company:	Surety Mutual Ltd.
Agent:	Fred Wills
Exp. Acct:	$434.50

Synopsis: Fred Wills calls Johnny and San Francisco is on his mind. Andrew Forman is an importer there, and Fred has a $50,000 policy on him. Fred asks if Johnny has ever heard of an importer being exported? Last night he disappeared.

Johnny flies to San Francisco, California and studies the file on the flight. Forman is 51 and has a good business. His wife Martha is 35 and the sole beneficiary.

Johnny goes to the Forman apartment and Martha looks at home in the expensive apartment. Johnny notices Alcatraz across the bay and thinks of the people he has sent to that exclusive club. Martha tells Johnny that she has filled out the police paper work, and a missing person's report has been filed.

She tells Johnny that Andrew was visited the other night by a stranger dressed in rough clothes, like a seaman. The name he gave was Blinker, because he kept blinking his eyes. He was shown into the library, and then Andrew said he was going to drive Blinker downtown to find a hotel.

He was gone the next morning and has not been to the office. Andrew had never mentioned Blinker before, and Johnny gets a detailed description of Blinker. Johnny asks what if Blinker had nothing to do with the disappearance? Did Forman have any reason to disappear? The answer was a certain no, maybe too certain.

Johnny cabs to see an old friend Det. Lt. Scapella who tells Johnny that they have covered all the hotels. Maybe there is no Blinker and Scapella notes that Martha's story was strange. She had too good of a description of the man and maybe the story was a fake. Johnny mentions the insurance and Scapella gets a call from Wayne Arnold, Forman's attorney who received a phone call that morning from someone interesting, a man named Blinker.

Johnny has to back up and rethink the case. Johnny cabs to see Mr. Arnold as he is leaving for an appointment. He heard from Blinker just a little while ago. Blinker had wanted $10,000 and hung up. Arnold thinks that Blinker is holding Forman for ransom. Arnold has been Forman's attorney for 3 years and knows of no reason why Forman would want to disappear.

Johnny buys cigarettes on the street and watches Arnold leave. Johnny follows in a cab to Golden Gate Park where a woman gets into the car and kisses Arnold. The woman was Marsha Forman.

Johnny goes to wait for Marsha Forman and when she comes home, he tells her that she and Arnold made up the story of Blinker. And what about you and Arnold? Did you enjoy your visit with him?

She tells Johnny that she is in love with Arnold, and Andrew would not have cared. She tells Johnny that she did not make up the story and her husband has not been killed. "Killed? Who said anything about him being killed?" asks Johnny.

Johnny asks why her husband has disappeared, and she tells Johnny that maybe it is related to his business. He imports trinkets and curios from the orient and has made a lot of money.

Johnny gets a key to the office and looks over the papers where a shipment has just come in on the Indian Princess. Johnny goes to find the ship, but it has left, so Johnny goes into Gus' Cafe and talks to Gus, short for Gussie. Johnny asks her about the ship and she knows all the crews, and she knows a sailor named Blinker. Gussie tells Johnny that Blinker has disappeared.

Gussie tells Johnny that Blinker was mixed up in something. He had come in for coffee and seemed pleased with himself and said he was into something good. He showed Gussie a carved elephant that was going to make him a lot of money.

Johnny thinks that maybe the elephant was of part of the reason for Forman's disappearance. Gussie tells Johnny that Blinker has his stuff stored in her back room. Johnny goes through Blinker's sea bag and finds an elephant with a hollow leg filled with an envelope containing white powder. Johnny goes outside to the pier and Gussie stops Johnny to show him a body, Blinker.

Johnny rushes to the warehouse and thinks he is being followed. In the warehouse, Johnny locates the shipment and the elephants have the same hollow leg with powder in it. A shot rings out and Johnny ducks and waits for 10 minutes.

A shadow comes to the crate and they fire at the same time. Johnny hits Andrew Forman and Johnny tells him that Blinker had discovered what Forman was importing and was trying to blackmail him. Forman caught up with him and he killed him.

Forman tells Johnny that the narcotics were put there without his knowledge. Johnny tells him that Blinker's body has been found, and Johnny bets the slugs came from Forman's gun. Forman tells Johnny that he did not have any choice.

"Remarks: Andrew Forman made a complete statement to the police. The murder case against him is open and shut. So, it looks like he is going to beat the narcotics rap after all. The hard way."

Notes:
- There are two versions of this AFRTS program. One version has the stories edited out and an organ serenade at the end. The other version has a story about the code of conduct of POWs, a story about advances in weaponry and an organ medley.

- The announcer is Roy Rowan.

Producer:	Jack Johnstone	Writer:	Robert Stanley
Cast:	Paula Winslowe, D.J. Thompson, Harry Bartell,		
	Stacy Harris, Vic Perrin, Bob Bruce		

• ❖ •

Show: **The Mohave Red Matter**
Show Date: 7/13/1958
Company: **Greater Southwest Insurance & Liability Company**
Agent: **Jake Kessler**
Exp. Acct:

Synopsis: Johnny gets a collect call from Lake Mohave Resort. Red is calling, Red Barrett the fishing guide. The fishing is great but he cannot tell Johnny what the problem is over the phone. Johnny ought to come out as soon as possible. Johnny tells Red that he usually travels for an insurance company, and Red tells Johnny that Greater Southwest insured him. Hmmm?

Johnny calls Jake Kessler to investigate what is going on there. Jake tells Johnny that there is nothing going on there in Kingman. Johnny asks about an accident at Lake Mohave and Jake tells Johnny that the claim was legitimate, but Johnny is convinced that there is something wrong.

Johnny flies to Las Vegas with his usual description of the night lights of the southwest. Jake meets Johnny at the airport and agrees to tell Johnny all about the Hobbes matter. Jake tells Johnny that he will tell him all about the matter and then he can head on home at his own expense.

Elmer P. Hobbes was a real estate developer from Los Angeles who spent a few days fishing at Lake Mohave with Red Barrett. Elmer went out alone one day and was caught in a windstorm and his body was found the next day on the Nevada shore. A claim has been filed by one of his two business partners, Stuart Manley.

The police investigated and the verdict was accidental death by drowning. Jake tells Johnny that he can just head back to Hartford, but Johnny wants to stick around.

Jake feels that there is no reason for Johnny to be there but Johnny feels that at least he can go fishing and asks Jake to drive him to the resort. Jake asks if Johnny knows something and asks Johnny how he wants the crow that he is going to eat fixed?

Johnny is sure that something is wrong, based on the call from Red Barrett. Jake drives Johnny to the resort and goes back to Kingman. Johnny goes to the dock and boathouse where Ham Pratt meets him.

Johnny tells Ham that Red usually sleeps on the dock, but Ham tells Johnny that Red has not come back in yet, and it is after midnight. He and Buster were about to go out looking for Red. He pulled the same thing two days ago, and has been doing some strange things since Mr. Hobbes died. Buster Favor tells Johnny that he did not believe that the death was an accident either. Red has been looking for the boat, and Johnny notes that the rental boats have flotation tanks and should have been easy to find.

Johnny, Ham and Buster take a boat out to look for Red in the darkness. Buster spots a fire on the beach and they head for it. Red tells them it took long enough to bring Johnny there. Red tells them that he needs Johnny's help to prove that Hobbes was murdered.

Buster is sure that Red must have a good reason for thinking it was murder. Red is sure that Hobbes would never have let himself be caught on the lake with a high wind blowing. Red wants Buster and Ham to leave in case he is wrong. He does not want to be embarrassed by too many people. Buster and Ham leave and Red tells Johnny to get some sleep and that he will show him things in the morning. In the morning,

Johnny wakes up to frying bacon and eggs and sourdough pancakes. Red takes Johnny up the lake to a rocky cove where there are signs of someone climbing up the rocks and footprints going out into the desert. In the water is a sunken boat, the one used by Hobbes.

Johnny dives down to the boat and sees that Red is right. Johnny sees where the flotation tanks were slashed, but Hobbes did not have an axe to slit the tanks, so somebody must have done it.

Johnny is convinced that Elmer Hobbes was murdered. Johnny still has to find out who killed Hobbes. Expenses for the case so far, $159.20 including the shooting and retrieving of one crow. Jake, how do you want it cooked?

Notes:
- This is an AFRTS program that contains a story about the flag of Vermont, the heroism of Capt. John Phillip Cromwell during World War II, and a story about the flag of Oklahoma.
- The announcer is Roy Rowan.

Producer:	Jack Johnstone Writer: Jack Johnstone
Cast:	Lucille Meredith, Forrest Lewis, Parley Baer, Alan Reed, Barney Phillips

◆ ❖ ◆

Show:	**The Mohave Red Sequel Matter**
Show Date:	7/20/1958
Company:	**Greater Southwest Insurance & Liability Company**
Agent:	**Jake Kessler**
Exp. Acct:	**$307.00**

Synopsis: Johnny calls Jake Kessler at his office, but Jake thinks Johnny has gone home and could not prove that Elmer Hobbes did not die from an accident. Johnny asks if the claim has been mailed, but Jake tells Johnny that he still has it. Johnny tells Jake to tear up the claim, as Hobbes was murdered.

Johnny tells Jake that Hobbes was murdered, but Jake tells Johnny that the police could not find anything. Johnny tells him that he had found the boat with the evidence of sabotage to the floatation tanks.

Johnny talks to Buster and Ham, and updates them. Everyone agrees that they should have been suspicious. There is no real suspect, as Elmer did not really mix with the others. All of the boats from Lake Mohave were back in at the time of the storm, so the killer must have come from another landing up the lake.

Johnny relates how he found the anchor rope coiled like it had been wrapped around the body to keep it there. So far, everything is circumstantial. Johnny wonders about the motive. Red tells Johnny what Hobbes had in his boat, but Johnny asks again about motive, but Red knows of no one who would want to kill Hobbes. He was one of Red's best friends.

Johnny takes Buster to the office to call Jake and tells him that he has an idea that he does not like. Buster tells Johnny that Red and Hobbes were usually always fighting when they were together and Red was alone when he found the body. Johnny calls Jake and asks about the beneficiaries. There are two beneficiaries on the policy, Manley is one, and the other is Red Barrett.

Buster is not convinced that Red had any part in Hobbes death but Johnny wonders if Red's actions were to cover things up. Ham comes to the office and asks if Buster told Red to go somewhere, as Red was rushing out in a hurry. Johnny borrows Ham's car and Ham tells Johnny that Red had a new Silaflex rod and Mitchell reel in his room, the same outfit that Hobbes had. Johnny tells Buster and Ham not to say anything to Red and leaves to drive to Los Angeles.

Johnny goes to the home of J. Stuart Manley and slips the lock to get inside. As Johnny looks through the house he senses that someone is there in the den. Johnny goes to the den and is attacked, by Red Barrett!

Johnny tells Red that common sense told him that Red and Manley were in cahoots. Red tells Johnny that Hobbes gave the rod and reel found in his room to him so they would have matching rigs. Red has found Hobbes' rod in the closet, all set up the way it was at the lake. The rod has the initials "EH" engraved on it. In the closet Red has also found the ax used to slash the flotation tanks. Red had rushed there to look for these items.

Red tells Johnny that Hobbes had told him that he never really trusted Manley. Red had called Manley to tell him that Johnny Dollar was working on the case, and he should go to Lake Mohave to clear up any evidence he might have left there. Red attacked Johnny because he though Johnny was Manley and had had come back.

Manley walks into the den and tells Red he was right and introduces them to his wife who tells Manley to kill them as burglars. She accuses Hobbes of fishing all the time and taking the money. Now they will have the money and the business.

Johnny tells Manley that he was foolish to leave the evidence there. Manley tells Johnny that since he has a gun, that he will be shot first. Red asks Manley if he can shoot as well as Red can cast, and Red buries a lure in Manley's hand. Mrs. Manley is upset at that silly red-headed old man for hurting her husband. Red tells Johnny that he hopes that the fishing is really good up where Elmer is now.

"Manley and his wife, yeah, Red had figured right. The morning of the day Hobbes was killed, they had rented a boat out of Cottonwood Landing a few miles up the lake, then ambushed him there in the big basin. Bob Cole at Cottonwood had noticed the new rod and reel when they came back off the lake just before the big storm, and had noticed the ax too, and had wondered about it. Now he knows. So, from here on in, it is up to the sheriff's office and the courts."

Notes:
- This is an AFRTS program that contains a story about the flag of Illinois, a story about manhood and the actions of William H. Horsfall during the civil war and a story about the flag of New Mexico.
- The announcer is Roy Rowan.

Producer:	Jack Johnstone Writer: Jack Johnstone
Cast:	Virginia Gregg, Parley Baer, Forrest Lewis, Barney Phillips, Alan Reed, Russell Thorson

♦ ❖ ♦

Show:	**The Wayward Killer Matter**
Show Date:	7/27/1958
Company:	**Continental Insurance & Trust Company**
Agent:	**Paul Hemple**
Exp. Acct:	**$315.17**

Synopsis: Paul Hemple calls Johnny, and he tells Paul that he was beginning to think that they had hired someone else. Paul tells Johnny that they have hired some staff investigators, but Paul needs Johnny to work on this one. Paul R. Welton has had his life threatened. Johnny tells Paul that it is OK to hire someone else when there is a life at stake, so Paul tells Johnny that he will call Lt. Randy Singer and tell him the deal is off. Singer has told Paul that if they send Johnny, he will cooperate, send anyone else and he will not. Johnny is told that there is a $2,000 fee if he keeps Welton alive.

Johnny travels to New York City and goes to the office of Lt. Randy Singer. Randy tells Johnny that there is nothing he can do. Welton was a witness to the murder of a bookie, and there are no other clues.

On Tuesday of last week, Welton was walking his dog around 2 a.m. He passed an alley, saw two men struggling and heard a shot that frightened his dog. The dog ran around in circles and tied up his legs with the leash. The killer came out of the alley and tripped over Welton who got a good look at the man in the street light. The killer slugged Welton, and the dog got a piece of the man's pants before he ran away.

The dog kept howling until a patrolman came and found the bookie dead in the alley. Randy has not found the gun used and Welton has been shown the mug files. A reporter wrote up the story that Welton had seen the man and could identify him. When Welton connected the man in the alley to the bookie, he became afraid.

Johnny thinks that maybe the mob is involved in this case, and Randy tells Johnny that he is going to post a guard on Welton's apartment. Officer Conroy comes in and Johnny goes with him to Welton's apartment. At the apartment, they find a crowd gathered and several policemen there. On the side walk is Welton.

Johnny finds Welton sprawled on the sidewalk, but he is still breathing. Johnny is told that some kids heard some noise in the building, like a fight, with Welton yelling for help. Welton then comes flying out of the window. The apartment is a mess and the assailant made his escape out the back of the apartment.

The doctor arrives and Welton is taken to the apartment where the dog is yelping. Welton is sedated and Johnny is told that he can talk to him later. Randy arrives and goes over the crime scene.

Johnny goes to the alley and is glad he did, because there is a work crew there. Johnny calls an old friend that Randy would like to put in jail, "Smokey" Joe Sullivan, a man who has been picked up on more petty charges than you can name. In a city with an underworld like New York, Smokey was a good person to know, on occasion. Johnny offers Smokey $100 on the phone and arranges to meet him at the Lexington Hotel.

Johnny cabs to the hotel and waits for Smokey, who does not show. Johnny realizes that someone important is there in the hotel as a police car is out front. Johnny walks to 3rd Avenue and spots Smokey at a newsstand. Johnny asks Smokey if he is betting on the horses and using the syndicate. Johnny asks Smokey something that is muffled by a truck pulling away. Johnny tells Smokey he will double the money if the information exists.

Johnny goes back to Welton's apartment where Randy has found nothing. Randy tells Johnny that he has found the gun in a storm drain and has to push the dog off. Welton wakes up and Johnny goes to make a call.

Welton tells Randy that the same man he had seen in the alley had attacked him. Johnny talks to Smokey and mentions $23,000, which gets Welton's attention. Johnny then tells Randy he can make an arrest. Johnny gets the dog and tells Randy that the dog deserves the credit.

On the night of the killing the dog supposedly chewed up the killer's pants, but the killer did not shoot the dog. Also, the dog did not fight off the attacker earlier because there was no one to fight off. Johnny accuses Welton of faking the attack.

Johnny tells him that the electric company has finally fixed the streetlight where the bookie was shot; If had been out for three weeks. Johnny's phone call proved that Welton was in hock to the bookie for $23,000. Welton blurts out that the bookie had threatened him, so he had to kill him.

Johnny and Randy take a night on the town, Randy needed a break. Oh, don't forget the $2,000. Welton is still alive, for a while at least.

Notes:
- This is an AFRTS program that contains a story about the National Heart Institute and the heart-lung machine, a story about the Wright Brothers and the gains in aviation technology.

- Smokey Sullivan make his first appearance in this program.
- The announcer is Roy Rowan.

Producer:	Jack Johnstone Writer: Jack Johnstone
Cast:	Edgar Barrier, Herb Vigran, James McCallion, Paul Dubov, Lawrence Dobkin, John Dehner, Bill James, Vic Perrin

◆ ❖ ◆

Show:	**The Lucky 4 Matter**
Show Date:	8/3/1958
Company:	**Tri-State Life & Casualty Insurance Company**
Agent:	**Earle Poorman**
Exp. Acct:	**$224.95**

Synopsis: Earle Poorman calls and asks if Johnny remembers the Lucky 4 Ranch where he and Ray Smischny had investigated the death of the concert pianist and did some really good fishing. Remember the private lake behind the ranch owned by Bill Cherry? Well it is not there anymore, nor is Old Bill. According to the available information he was killed when the dam broke and sent his farm house crashing down onto the valley. Earle has the policy and will send it to Johnny at the Lucky 4. Ray has called and he thinks the breach of the dam was no accident.

Johnny calls Ray to tell him he is on the way.

Johnny flies to Colorado Springs, Colorado where Ray meets Johnny at the airport. Ray tells Johnny that they were poaching on Cherry Lake when they were fishing there. Bill was kind of ornery, and the creek used to water some pasture before he put in the dam. Because of the altitude, the lake fills with summer snowmelt. During a heavy summer rain, the dam burst like an explosion.

Ray takes a shortcut to his ranch and tells Johnny that he originally thought that the lake gave way naturally, but he has been poking around and found some things. Also, Ray had opened the package from Earle by mistake and had seen that the beneficiary was a worthless nephew of Bill's.

Ray's car starts acting up and he pulls over. When the hood is raised Johnny spots a lot of wiring and they hit the deck just as a bomb goes off. Somebody must have seen Ray poking around and knows that he sent for Johnny and did not like it.

A moving van driver takes Johnny and Ray to town where Johnny rents a car and drives to the "Lucky 4" ranch. Johnny and Ray take a jeep up to the lake site, and Ray shows Johnny a sample of the wiring that came from the car.

Ray shows Johnny that the flow of the creek is just like it was before the dam went in, and notes that he does not need the water as much as Ralph Kimble. Kimble is a neighbor and is a retired professor who keeps to his self and is ornery just like old Bill. Ray tells Johnny that Bill was found with a package of El Parro Cuban cigarettes in his hand, but Bill never smoked. Ray thinks Bill found someone snooping around the dam.

Johnny sees the remains of the concrete dam, and evidence of the dynamite used to build it. Ray tells Johnny that Bill did not use dynamite to build the dam, he was afraid of it. Ray shows Johnny a piece of dynamite label plastered on a rock: "Titan Super IXL Dynamite". That brand is only sold in one little store in Denver, and Bill never went to Denver, as he hated the place.

Johnny and Ray go to Colorado Springs to find Tommy Walker the nephew. At the Ace-High Radio Shop, where Tommy was last working, Johnny asks the manager for Tommy and is told that he has not been there for two days. Tommy was supposed to know all about electronics but could only turn on a radio, and the music he listened to! He was so dumb he could not attach wires to a plug correctly.

All he wanted was a place to sit and smoke those smelly Cuban cigarettes. Johnny shows the manager the wires from the car bomb and asks for some, but he does not carry that type of wire. Johnny goes back to the ranch to play a hunch.

Back at the ranch Johnny has lunch and reviews the policy from Earle in which Tommy would only get $1,000. Ray tells Johnny that no one liked Bill putting in the dam, but Ray has plenty of water now that he put in the pumps. Ray has used dynamite before, but not that brand. Besides everybody knows where to get it. Everybody? Including Ralph Kimble next door? Ray's wife tells Johnny that the Kimbles are not home as Mrs. Kimble had told her that they were going to Denver. Johnny goes over to look around with Ray.

Johnny searches a work shed and Ray finds a case of the Titan dynamite, a rock drill, some of the same type of wire used on the bomb, and the Cuban cigarettes. Ray thinks that the evidence is circumstantial, but Johnny reminds Ray that Kimble was a physics professor. Ray tells Johnny that Kimble knew about the shortcut from the airport and knew that Johnny was coming.

Ray notices mud on a pair of boots, and that type of mud only comes from around the lake. Johnny mentions that the law needs "seven points of similarity" for the evidence to stand up. Johnny quotes the odds of that happening as 1 in 38 billion.

Mr. Kimble comes in with a gun and tells Johnny to pray fast. Mrs. Kimble calls and tells him that Ray's wife is on her way over with a shotgun, and Johnny slugs Kimble.

"Well, it's up to the authorities now, the courts. And I don't think that there is much doubt as to the outcome. Kimble's attempt to kill us was the clincher. As for Tommy Walker, the heir, you will have to pay him off on old Bill's policy."

Notes:
- Most catalogs list this as *The Lucky Four Matter*, however the script title page has *The Lucky 4 Matter.*
- After the explosion, Johnny notes that he stowed his luggage in a cabin at the ranch. The bomb must not have been strong enough to destroy the car.
- Johnny mentions "seven points of similarity" concerning the evidence. This seems to have some basis in fingerprint evaluations.
- This is an AFRTS program that contains a story about Lt. Edouard V. M. Izac in World War I, and an episode of "The Bellweathers" and no credits.

- Cast information is from the script on file at the Thousand Oaks Library.
- Roy Rowan is the announcer.

Producer:	Jack Johnstone	Writer:	Jack Johnstone
Cast:	Ken Christy, Vic Perrin, Lawrence Dobkin, Virginia Gregg, Will Wright, Shirley Mitchell		

♦ ❖ ♦

Show: The Two Faced Matter
Show Date: 8/10/1958
Company: Northeastern Fidelity & Bonding Company
Agent: Nick Walters
Exp. Acct: $9.80

Synopsis: Nick Walters calls and tells Johnny that the problem is $58,000. Ever hear of Old Lang Syne Furniture? It is located up north, is run by a bunch of real characters, and produces some of the finest furniture in the world. Oh, and wear a dark suit, white shirt and dark tie and suspenders when you go there.

Johnny cabs to Nick's office in his most funereal clothes. Nick tells Johnny that the craftsmen at the factory are old-world types and the furniture is top-rate. One of their lads has run off with company funds, $58,433 to be exact. The police were never called in, and the theft occurred sometime in the past three and a half years. They discovered the theft last month and just let Nick know.

When Johnny brings up the timeliness of the claim Nick tells Johnny that he had waived a 60-day notification clause from the policy because the owners do not like to be rushed. Go talk to J. Worthington Keasley, the senior member of the organization, they do not have officers. Johnny is going up, on expense account of course, to take a look at these crazy characters.

Johnny takes a bus to Weldon, Massachusetts where the plant looks like it had been there since year one. On the walk up the driveway, Johnny notices horses and carriages parked besides the building. Inside Johnny meets Mr. Keasley, who looks like one of the Smith Brothers, sitting behind his roll-top desk. Keasley tells Johnny that all the workers wear beards, as did their fathers, so that they can continue the tradition of craftsmanship. The horses were good enough for their grandparents, so they are good enough for them.

Keasley suspects Roscoe J. Twiller of the theft. Johnny is shown a picture of Twiller in a group photo from 1941. Keasley should have known when Twiller bought a motorcar that he was not one to keep the traditions. Twiller was the one who took off with the $58,433.41.

Keasley is sure beyond a shadow of a doubt, as Twiller was the only one who had a key to the vault where the building funds were kept. When he suddenly left them 3 years, 5 months and 16 days ago, Keasley should have known then.

On June 21 at 10:04 when Keasley went to the vault to put some extra money in the vault, he found a note that said "Good luck suckers, signed Twiller". Johnny asks where to start after three years, but Keasley tells him that is up to Johnny unless the insurance company is going to pay the claim.

Johnny agrees that Twiller is the thief but is sure that the money has been spent by now. Keasley did not know where Twiller lived, as that was none of his business. Maybe Mr. Bottomly, who is working on a Hepplewhite table would know where Twiller lived.

Johnny walks through a shop equipped only with hand tools used by old men with long beards. Johnny meets Mr. Bottomly, who tells Johnny that he must find Twiller, who was his neighbor. Twiller drove Bottomly to work in his buggy until he bought the motorcar, at which time Bottomly bought a bicycle.

Twiller lived on Peach Avenue in East Weldon. When Johnny mentions that he will talk to the police, the shop is full of upset men who are worried about the blot on their name. Johnny tells them that he will use the police if necessary. Bottomly tells Johnny that the chief of police is the mayor, John Kenworthy Wilkins, but they have never dealt with him as he is not of their sort and they do not go into town.

Bottomly has a picture of the mayor he found in his carriage, he is running for reelection. When the picture is shown, all the men howl their disgust at the disgraceful image, as the mayor is bald and clean-shaven. But how to find Twiller?

Johnny finds the mayor, John Kenworthy Wilkins, on his porch sipping a gin and tonic. He tells Johnny that he had heard a rumor when he got to town, but did nothing, as a report had not been filed and that Twiller was gone before he got there. He was elected mayor when the towns people found out about his record of police work in Ohio. Johnny tells him that the factory has no idea where Twiller might be.

Johnny walks across town and meets a boy playing "cowboy". He is Jimmy Carter and asks Johnny if he wants to see his "artistical" drawings, and Johnny admires a beautiful moustache — on a picture of a girl advertising cigarettes. Jimmy tells Johnny that he needs a paint set.

Jimmy shows Johnny what he has done to the mayor's reelection poster by adding hair and a beard, and Johnny realizes how to solve the theft. Johnny takes the poster and tells Jimmy he does not know how good of an artist he is.

Johnny goes back to the mayor and asks him to make an arrest. He knows who took the money. Johnny tells Wilkins that he showed up just after Twiller left town. Twiller had a thick beard, and you have none. Johnny should have recognized from the red tint on his scalp that he had been using hair remover and accuses him of being Twiller. When Johnny tells him a search of his house would turn up the key to the vault, Wilkins blurts out that he threw the key away.

"I don't know why Twiller gave up so easily, I guess it was because I caught him completely off guard. He even signed a confession and promised to pay back what he could. So, from here on in it's up to the courts. And all thanks to a little kid who liked to draw moustaches on billboards. Expense account total, including the finest paint set I could find for my little pal Jimmy, oh, wait, I gotta pad this, it only comes out to $9.80!"

Notes:

- The Smith Brothers refers to the bearded Smith Brothers which was the logo for Luden's "Smith Brothers Cough Drops".
- George Hepplewhite was an 18th century English cabinetmaker.
- This is an AFRTS program that contains a story about the attack on Ploesti and a story about the changes in warfare.
- The announcer is Roy Rowan.

Producer:	Jack Johnstone	Writer:	Jack Johnstone
Cast:	Will Wright, Herb Vigran, Forrest Lewis, Edgar Barrier, Richard Beals, Bill James, Gus Bayz		

♦ ❖ ♦

Show: The Noxious Needle Matter
Show Date: 8/24/1958
Company: Worldwide Mutual Insurance Company
Agent: Waldo R. Westbury
Exp. Acct: $61.20

Synopsis: Waldo Westbury calls Johnny to investigate the death of a client, J. Lamont Scofield, the theatrical producer who was world famous for the beautiful girls in his productions. He died yesterday of "natural causes", but Waldo has doubts, based on the beneficiary of the $750,000 estate. Please come over and see me.

Johnny cabs to the office of Waldo Westbury and is shown the policy which provides $750,000 on Scofield's life. The beneficiary has constantly been changed. Goldie Laverne, an old burlesque queen, Toodles Tempest, Baby Boodles Baker, Bubbles Jones, Pepper Caprice Carstairs, and Cupcake Delond are listed as former beneficiaries on the riders. Mary T. Smith is the current beneficiary, the T. stands for "Torso". Waldo thinks that Scofield was killed, bumped off. At the time of his death, Mary Smith was his nurse.

Johnny is asked to prove that Mary Smith killed Scofield. Johnny is also told that, because of the amount of the policy, there will be no questioning of his necessary expenses, no matter how high! Scofield died in Cranford, New Jersey, and Mary Smith is still there. She used to be a showgirl before becoming a nurse. Westbury knows nothing about the doctor, Leonard Foote.

Johnny travels to New York and rents a "drive your own" car for the drive to Cranford and the office of Dr. Foote. In Dr. Foote's office, Johnny is told that Scofield had a heart condition which required digitalis and intravenous injections of sadilinid. His nurse gave him the injections under his orders, and Mary is a registered nurse. Dr. Foote tells Johnny that his tentative opinion is natural causes.

When Johnny tries to infer that Mary could have injected something to hasten death, Dr. Foote questions Johnny's tactics and wants an apology, but Johnny is insistent that Dr. Foote might be involved in a possible cover up or conspiracy. Dr. Foote tells Johnny that he learned this morning that Mary is the heir to the estate, which he did not know before, and he has held the body for an autopsy. Johnny is forced to apologize to Dr. Foote, who offers a towel to Johnny to wipe the egg off of his face.

Dr. Foot tells Johnny that he has realized that it is possible that Mary Smith might have hastened the death of Scofield. Dr. Foote thinks that Scofield could have lived for many years. Dr. Foote has called in Dr. Stanley, a toxicologist to examine the body. Dr. Foote tells Johnny that the police have found no poisons, and the autopsy is because the most possible cause of death would be an over dose of medication.

Johnny goes to Scofield's house and meets Mary Smith, a very young Mary Smith. There was only one word that did Mary justice: WOW! Johnny tells Mary who he is, and she has heard of Johnny and asks him in. She wonders why Johnny is there and Johnny tells her that it is a routine investigation.

Mary pours drinks and tells Johnny that she is not grief stricken. Mary asks if Johnny has any money and tells him that she knows she was the heir to the estate. She has been on 24-hour duty for 2 solid years, and there were times she thought Monty would live forever, even times when she wished she could help him out of this world.

Johnny tells Mary he thinks she killed Scofield and is there to make sure she does not skip out when the autopsy report comes in. Mary utters an "oh", and Johnny asks if that concerns her. Johnny tells her that someone with an attitude like hers is either completely innocent, or guilty as the devil.

She tells Johnny that she wanted Monty dead and wanted his money. When Johnny mentions an overdose, she tells him that an overdose or poison would be stupid, as no one had been with Monty for a week except her and Dr. Foote. Mary offers to sign a confession if it will confuse Johnny.

The phone rings and Dr. Foote calls to tell Johnny that the autopsy showed no signs of poison or overdose. "I guess you cannot build a case out of thin air.", she tells Johnny and hands him the "confession". Johnny thinks about the phrase "thin air" and has an idea and thanks Mary for saying that.

Johnny calls his own doctor in Hartford and talks about some ideas he has for the "perfect crime" and gets some enlightening ideas. Johnny drives to the coroner's office and talks to Dr. Stanley and asks if Scofield could have died of an embolus in the brain and asks Stanley to check on it over Dr. Foote's objections.

Later Dr. Stanley tells Johnny that he was right, an embolus in the brain killed Scofield. Dr. Foote has the medical kit used to give Scofield his injections. Dr. Foote tells Johnny that only the small needle was used and the others never contained anything but air. Dr. Stanley tells Johnny that 50cc of plain air could cause an embolus, and Johnny asks him to look for traces of tissue on the other needles.

"Yes, the microscope showed that needle had been used on J. Lamont Scofield recently. Pretty slim evidence I know, but when Mary was faced with it, well I am still not quite sure why, maybe we scared her, but she broke down and confessed the murder. Yeah, she had been wrong, sometimes you can build a case on nothing but thin air."

Notes:

- An embolus is an air bubble in a vein or artery.
- This is an AFRTS program that contains a story about hope in the face of great odds and the attack on Ploesti, and a story about David Bushnell and his "Turtle" submarine and the nuclear-powered Nautilus.
- The announcer is Roy Rowan.

Producer: Jack Johnstone   Writer: Jack Johnstone
Cast: Virginia Gregg, Bartlett Robinson, Marvin Miller, Junius Matthews

♦ ❖ ♦

Show: **The Limping Liability Matter**
Show Date: 8/31/1958
Company: **Universal Adjustment Bureau**
Agent: **Pat McCracken**
Exp. Acct: **$1,020.20**

Synopsis: Johnny gets a collect call from Smokey Sullivan, and reminds him of all the cases he has helped Johnny with. Smokey has information about an insurance racket, but they do not even know that they are being taken. Smokey wants Johnny to come down to New York.

Johnny addresses this case to the Universal Adjustment Bureau, even though he has not been assigned to it, but he is sure that they will OK the expense account, and Johnny describes Smokey's checkered past.

Johnny goes to New York City and meets Smokey by a newsstand near the Lexington hotel. Smokey wants Johnny to go to a bar and talk, but Johnny threatens to get Randy Singer involved.

Smokey tells Johnny that Jake Fortina is paying drunks to have accidents and gives him the details. Johnny calls Pat McCracken and tells Pat that Fortina puts up the rum, gives the drunks money and insures them and then kills them after they get the money. Fortina will break an arm or a leg, and then take the drunk to a department store and fake an accident and threaten to sue. Pat tells Johnny that he has noticed a series of unrelated accidents from different insurance companies. Pat tells Johnny that Fortina is smart, so be careful.

Smokey and Johnny go outside to think and Smokey tells Johnny that while he was on the phone a man came in, saw Johnny and ran out. Smokey tells Johnny that he had made a deal with Fortina to break his leg to keep him interested. Smokey called Johnny because he has been playing it straight and has helped Johnny before. Smokey tells Johnny that he will go back and talk to the bartender, who knows Fortina. Smokey gives Johnny his room key at the Brakley Hotel and tells Johnny to wait for Fortina to come there.

Johnny goes to Smokey's room and finds Fortina waiting for him with a .38 automatic and a huge man named Benny McGurn who tells Johnny that he had sent his brother to prison. Johnny is sure that it is a double-cross, and Benny is ready to kill Johnny and break his bones.

Benny tells Johnny that they are there because he saw Smokey talking to Johnny in the bar. Benny grabs Johnny's leg and tries to break it. Johnny jumps up and grabs Benny, only to be squeezed in a bear hug. The door bursts open and there are shots. Randy Singer walks in and tells Johnny that Smokey had called him and brought him there.

Johnny adds $1,000 for Smokey on the expense account.

Notes:
- The announcer is Roy Rowan.
- Story information obtained from the KNX Collection in the Thousand Oaks Library.

Producer:	Jack Johnstone	Writer:	Jack Johnstone
Cast:	Virginia Gregg, Vic Perrin, Tom Holland, Lawrence Dobkin, Jack Moyles, Shepard Menken, Herb Vigran		

♦ ❖ ♦

Show:	The Malibu Mystery Matter
Show Date:	9/7/1958
Company:	Western Maritime & Property Insurance Company
Agent:	Peter Hanley
Exp. Acct:	$101.50

Synopsis: Peter Hanley calls Johnny at 4 a.m. He had to call all the way across the country only to discover that Johnny is right there in Beverly Hills. Johnny is ready to head back to Hartford, but Hanley wants Johnny to work on a claim for him. The claim is for $150,000 to $250,000 for the loss of a yacht. Hanley will meet Johnny at the Malibu Pier.

Johnny has breakfast at his hotel, the Beverly Hilton and rents a car to go to Malibu, California. Johnny notices that cars are lining the road to the pier and parks where an ambulance has pulled out.

Hanley meets Johnny and shows him the accident. The Coast Guard is circling where the $150,000 diesel yacht the *Tatus* has blown up. Mr. and Mrs. Merrill, the steward, and a deckhand escaped, but the skipper went down with the boat.

Johnny is introduced to Capt. Rollins of the Coast Guard, who has found no sign of the *Tatus*, and it seems that the boat just blew up. The explosion was about 2 hours earlier, and someone along the beach notified the Coast Guard. Hanley confirms that the Merrills are OK, but Johnny wants to talk to them. The claim could be much higher than just for the boat because of the jewelry Mrs. Merrill had on board. Hanley tells Johnny that he had been notified of the explosion by a friend.

Johnny follows Hanley to the home of the Merrills. Mr. Merrill tells Johnny that he had sold his plastics business and bought a smaller house in a less fashionable neighborhood, as they do not do a lot of entertaining anymore. Mr. Merrill was thinking of selling the *Tatus* for economic reasons.

Mrs. Merrill tells Hanley that the jewels are safe, they were the first things she grabbed when the engine started making noises. Johnny looks at the jewels and then gets the story of what happened. The engine was making noises and the skipper ordered them off while he looked into a fuel problem. Then the boat exploded. While playing with the jewels Johnny discovers that this case needs investigating and needs it bad.

Johnny recalls how mercury could coat gold and make it look like silver, and how a diamond would scratch glass. While listening to the Merrills talking Johnny was toying with the jewels and dragged them across the glass coffee table, and they did not cut the glass. The jewels are fakes! On the way out, Mr. Merrill tells Johnny and Hanley that he needs the money but would never sell the jewels.

Johnny drives back to Malibu and tells Hanley that the jewels are fakes. Hanley tells Johnny that Merrill was quite a promoter and bit off more than he could chew with the plastics plant.

Johnny drives to the Coast Guard for a navigation chart and a topographical map of the area, and hires a surveyor named Bartley. Johnny goes to the house of Mr. Dobken, Hanley's friend, who tells them that he heard the boat's whistle in the fog and then heard the explosion and shows Johnny where the explosion was. Bartley takes a bearing and plots the line on the map. Dobken thinks that the neighbors would have heard the explosion also.

Johnny and Hanley continue to interview Mrs. Grey, and Mr. Phillips and another woman, who saw the explosion while Bartley plots the lines. Johnny goes to the Coast Guard with his maps to tell them that the boat went down in a different area where it is accessible to divers.

Johnny waits in his hotel until the Coast Guard calls to tell him that the wreck of the boat was not found, but something that looks like a raft was found, a raft with explosives and oil to make it look like the boat went down. Johnny tells the Coast Guard to search the ports along the coast for the Tatus and goes to see the Merrills.

Johnny tries a bluff on the Merrills. Johnny tells Mr. Merrill that the Coast Guard has found the remains of the skipper and there are signs that they killed him. Mrs. Merrill blurts out that the skipper is still alive. She tells Johnny that the skipper is in Mexico with the yacht and Mr. Merrill calls his wife a fool.

Johnny tells Merrill that his wife's fake jewelry tipped him off. Mr. Merrill tells Johnny that he will fight the insurance company, but Johnny tells him that he will not get to first base.

"Yeah, when a crook tries to pull a fast one on an honest insurance company, well, you'll see when the courts get through with Merrill and his wife."

Notes:
- This is an AFRTS program that contains an episode of "The Bellweathers", and a story about the advances in warfare.
- Interestingly Lawrence Dobkin and Barney Phillips play characters with their own names in this program.
- The announcer is Roy Rowan.

Producer: Jack Johnstone   Writer: Jack Johnstone

Cast: Paula Winslowe, Eleanor Audley, Jeanne Tatum. Ben Wright, Harry Bartell, Will Wright, Lawrence Dobkin, Barney Phillips

♦ ❖ ♦

Show: The Wayward Diamonds Matter
Show Date: 9/14/1958
Company: Western Maritime & Property Insurance Company
Agent: Peter Hanley
Exp. Acct: $218.00

Synopsis: Peter Hanley calls Johnny again and is returning Johnny's call. Johnny tells him how he is enjoying Malibu, California and the Beverly Hilton on expense account. Hanley tells Johnny how Merrill has agreed to plead guilty, but Johnny tells him that he will change his mind. Johnny reminds Hanley that it was the fake jewelry that tipped Johnny off, and Mrs. Merrill is not being held because her husband signed a statement saying that she was not involved. Now she is on the loose. A worried Hanley will come right out to pick Johnny up.

Johnny buys drinks for himself and Hanley who tells Johnny that he had forgotten about the fake jewels. Johnny tells Hanley how he discovered that the jewels were fakes by dragging them across the coffee table. Hanley wants to call in the police but Johnny is sure that the diamonds have not been sold yet, and the Merrills still have them.

Johnny is sure that Mrs. Merrill will sell the diamonds to pay for the legal fees. Johnny tells Hanley that he is having Mrs. Merrill tailed to figure out how she will dispose of the jewels. Johnny reminds Hanley of how proud Mrs. Merrill was to show them the fake jewels to get their minds off of them. Johnny gets a call from the detective who has been knocked out by Mrs. Merrill, who is gone.

Johnny and Hanley drive to the Merrill home and are let in by Sam, the detective. Sam tells Johnny that he was casually walking up and down the street all morning and saw Mrs. Merrill go out to the garage. Mrs. Merrill got into the car and ran Sam down in the driveway and got away. Sam does not know what kind of car she was driving and got into the house to phone Johnny by climbing into an open window.

Johnny fires Sam and tells him to get out. Hanley calls his office to get the information on the Merrill car and Johnny searches the house. In a desk, Johnny finds a bill from a jeweler that could have covered the substitution of the jewels. Johnny sends Hanley to the police to have them issue an APB, and then heads to the jeweler.

Johnny drives to Howards Hillcrest Jewelers and asks for the owner but is told by a sales clerk that Mr. Howard is busy with a very important client. While the clerk is distracted by another client Johnny searches the back rooms to find Mrs. Merrill talking with Mr. Howard about putting the real jewels back into the mountings. She tells Howard that she must go through the motions of getting a lawyer for her husband.

When Mrs. Merrill mentions that Johnny Dollar is working on the case, Mr.

Howard is alarmed because he knows about Johnny. Howard tells her that he has already disposed of the jewels and mentions other cases where he has helped people cheat their insurance companies. Howard tells her that he knew the boat thing would not work.

Mrs. Merrill is sure that no one else knows that the jewels were fakes. Howard tells her that now he must get rid of Johnny and gets his gun. Johnny walks in and Howard threatens to kill Johnny there. When Johnny tells him that there are customers out front, Howard tells Johnny to go to a private vault in the back of the store.

While Johnny is trying to stall for time the clerk pounds on the door and tells Howard that the police are there. Johnny grabs the gun from Howard and slugs him after shots are fired. Hanley comes in with the police who tell Johnny that they have been trying to catch Howard for years.

"Expense account item 2, $50 in legal fees to make a deposition, so I won't have to hang around for a trial or two or three. And I have a sneaking suspicion that Howard, Merrill and his wife are going to have a long, long time to think things over."

Notes:
- This program is an ARFS program that contains a story about Pvt. Robert Von Schlick, who won the medal of honor during the Boxer Rebellion, a story about the flag of Kentucky and a story about the heroism of Lt. Frank Luke in World War I.
- The announcer is Roy Rowan.

Producer:	Jack Johnstone	Writer:	Jack Johnstone
Cast:	Paula Winslowe, Ben Wright, Jack Kruschen, Jack Edwards, Marvin Miller, Joseph Kearns		

◆ ❖ ◆

Show: The Johnson Payroll Matter
Show Date: 9/21/1958
Company: Universal Adjustment Bureau
Agent: Pat McCracken
Exp. Acct: $526.50

Synopsis: Pat McCracken calls and tells Johnny he has been working too hard, and needs an all-expenses paid vacation in southern California. Johnny tries to turn Pat down, but Pat tells Johnny that the job is really simple. All he has to do is go out to the coast and bring back $100,000.

Johnny cabs to Pat's office and gets the details of the case. Pat tells Johnny about the Johnson Payroll robbery in New York, and the payroll was insured by one of Pat's companies. One of the robbers was wounded and told them that the others were going to split the money elsewhere. Pat has received a call from a man in Los Angeles who could give them a lead, for a price. Pat wants the money and tells Johnny that the man will contact him at his hotel.

Johnny flies to Los Angeles, California and cabs to the Hotel Nestor where he has been told to go. When the cab arrives, a woman gets into the cab and falls onto Johnny. Johnny wants to give her the cab but she leaves.

Johnny goes in to register and has a message from the informant to drive to Corrado Beach and meet him on the pier, so Johnny rents a car, drives to Corrado Beach and gets a motel room. The next morning Johnny goes to the pier and talks to a man who tells Johnny that the fishing has been fine lately. Johnny tells him that he is supposed to meet someone and the man points to a man next to a boat on the pier. They walk out to the boat as the first man tells Johnny the bass fishing has been fine. As they get to the second man, they discover that he is dead.

Johnny searches the man but finds no identification and the police are called. The police arrive and they know nothing either. Johnny waits in a local bar and then calls Pat McCracken to update him. Johnny tells him that he got the mug shots that Pat had sent and then sees someone at the bar.

Johnny walks over to the woman who had gotten into his cab and wants to go outside and talk. As Johnny holds her elbow, the bartender comes over and tells Johnny to let go of the girl, and she walks out.

Johnny leaves and looks around for the girl and discovers that there is a motel key in his coat pocket, but not to his motel. Johnny goes to the motel and opens the door, to discover a gun in his back.

Johnny is ushered into the room by one of the men in the mug shots, a man named Slattery. Slattery tells Johnny that Blake was the one who killed the man on the pier, and that he has the payroll dough. Slattery knows that Blake's girlfriend got into Johnny's cab in Los Angeles and probably slipped him the key. Slattery wants the money or he will kill Johnny.

Slattery searches the room and does not find the money and slugs Johnny to find out where the money is. Johnny tells him that a man had called from Los Angeles, and Slattery tells Johnny it was Hollis, the dead man on the pier.

Slattery tells Johnny that Blake engineered the robbery, and then ran out on him and Hollis, and Johnny is in league with him. Johnny tells Slattery that he does not know anything about the girl or where the money is. Johnny manages to slug Slattery and runs out of the room with Slattery in pursuit.

Johnny gets back to his car and goes to look for the girl. Johnny finds a Myrna Grant in the third motel in town and goes to see her in room 8. The girl tells Johnny to leave and he tells her about the key, the robbery and the double-cross. She tells Johnny that she did not know Blake that long, but he had told her he was in trouble and that he had told her to put the key in Johnny's pocket and the meet him at the beach. She did not know that Blake was a criminal and agrees to help Johnny find Blake.

Johnny and Myrna go back to the bar and Johnny asks the bartender if he knows Fred Blake. The bartender does not know Blake. When Johnny mentions that fishermen must come in here, the bartender mentions that there has been no fishing here for months because of a chemical plant nearby. Johnny realizes that the man at the pier was Blake.

Johnny goes to the pier, with a car following him with its lights out. At the pier, Johnny gets the drop on Blake and tells him that he killed Hollis and hid on the pier. Slattery arrives with his gun and wants the money. Blake pulls a gun and is shot by Slattery, and Johnny slugs Slattery.

Remarks: The payroll money is back where it belongs and Slattery and Blake are back where they belong, with Blake facing a murder rap to boot. Funny, I probably wouldn't have nailed him if he had not told me that phony story about the fish biting near the pier. Teaches me a lesson, Pat. I'm not going to tell any more fish stories, they can kill ya.

Notes:
- This is an AFRTS program that contains a story about the flag of Georgia, a story about the actions of Cpl. Raymond Rosser in Korea, and a story about the flag of Ohio.
- The announcer is Roy Rowan.

Producer:	Jack Johnstone	Writer:	Robert Stanley
Cast:	Virginia Gregg, Lawrence Dobkin, Forrest Lewis, Shepard Menken, Frank Gerstle		

♦ ❖ ♦

Show:	**The Gruesome Spectacle Matter**
Show Date:	**9/28/1958**
Company:	**Tri-State Life & Casualty Insurance Company**
Agent:	**Ed Barrett**
Exp. Acct:	**$148.00**

Synopsis: Ed Barrett calls and is sick. He tells Johnny that he was going to go to a fishing lodge of a friend, Tommy Hargrave, and had just received word that a car rolled over on Tom and killed him. Since the policy was for $70,000 double indemnity and an accident was involved, Ed has to order an investigation. His wife Mary was the beneficiary but they did not get along. The place is called Shadow Hill and is near Bethel, New York. The police force is a man named Skinner, and he had notified Ed. Ed is sure that there is nothing amiss with this case.

Johnny travels to New York City and rents a car to drive to Bethel, gets a room in Emmer's hotel and then goes to Shadow Hill. On the way up the long driveway, Johnny stops at the accident scene and a man levels a .30-30 at him. Johnny is told to get out of the car but slams the door into the man and gets the gun from him.

Johnny is told he will be locked up, as the man is Amos Skinner, the chief of police. Johnny tells Skinner that he has come to see him. Are you "the" Johnny Dollar he asks. Amos shows Johnny the wreck site and tells Johnny that he had called the insurance company for Mrs. Hargrave. Amos thinks that Hargrave took the turn too fast and the car rolled over and killed him.

Amos has just come from Doc Walton's and he is worried as to why Hargrave would have an accident on a road he knew too well. Johnny notices that the sedan has the windows closed yet Hargrave was under the car. Amos realizes that Hargrave was murdered. Now to discover who did it and why.

Amos tells Johnny that he learned of the accident from Mary while he was at the gas station talking about the Hamiltonian and how much money Barney Martin has made taking bets on the race. Johnny is flabbergasted that there is a bookie in town. Mary had just driven back from New York, drove back to the gas station and told Amos what had happened.

Amos and Johnny go down to the car and realize that the keys are in the ignition, which is turned off. Johnny puts some fine dust on the steering wheel, but there are no fingerprints there. Johnny asks if Hargrave wore glasses and Amos tells Johnny no. Johnny wants to see the body now and goes to see Doc Walton.

In the doctor's office Johnny is shown how the clothes were torn like there had been a struggle, and the mark at the base of his skull. Johnny recognizes the mark as coming from a .38 automatic, of which he has seen plenty. Everyone agrees that Hargrave was murdered.

Doc Walton tells Johnny that Mary Hargrave wears glasses and shows him a pair that he had found in the car. Doc agrees that they could be Mary's, and Johnny wants to see Mary Hargrave.

Johnny, Amos and Doc Walton drive to the Hargrave home, where the evidence points to her. Mary answers the door and is introduced to Johnny, who is expected. She tells Johnny that she was slow to answer the door because she has misplaced her glasses, and the old pair she is wearing are hard to see through. She tells Johnny that she mislaid her glasses a few days ago.

Johnny notes that Mary is not grieved and she tells Johnny that all Tommy cared about was fishing and betting on the horses. She is going to sell the house and go to the city. Mary notices the glasses Doc is holding, but Doc realizes that the glasses are not Mary's as the lenses are wrong.

Mary tells Johnny that Tommy had been playing the horses while they were there and had been bragging about the big killing he had made. Johnny takes the glasses and looks at the optometrist's mark. Johnny leaves and tells the others to stay put, and tells Amos not to arrest anyone, as he might be sorry.

Well, that really is just about all there is to this case. Oh, except for the fact that the optometrist in Monticello had no difficulty at all in matching the glasses I had found with the prescription of, yeah, you guessed it. They had belonged to the bookie chief Skinner had told me about, Barney Martin.

Of course, Barney wanted to put up a fight when we faced him with the facts, but then he couldn't seem to explain the various sundry bruises he was carrying around until we reminded him of the fight he had had with Tommy Hargrave. Yeah, he'd killed him and pushed the car over on top of him. The reason for it all was simple. Tommy had won a cool $25,000 from him, had threatened to put him out of business if he didn't pay, which he couldn't.

So, Barney killed him and tried to fake the accident, and you know something? I have a sneaking suspicion chief Amos Skinner isn't going to stand for any bookies operating in Bethel, New York from her on out. Oh, and Mary found the glasses she had mislaid.

Notes:

- This is an AFRTS program that contains a story about the flag of Rhode Island, a story about the Boxer Rebellion and a story about the flag of Kansas.
- The announcer is Roy Rowan.

Producer:	Jack Johnstone	Writer:	Jack Johnstone
Cast:	Virginia Gregg, Harry Bartell, Junius Matthews, Joseph Kearns		

♦ ❖ ♦

Show:	The Missing Matter Matter
Show Date:	10/5/1958
Company:	Universal Adjustment Bureau
Agent:	Pat McCracken
Exp. Acct:	$0.00

Synopsis: Jack Johnstone, the writer who dramatizes Johnny's cases calls. He tells Johnny that he sent a copy of the latest report to Mary Ann Hooper, his secretary. Jack tells Johnny that she went to Hollywood, but never got there. Now there is no material for the show. Jack wants Johnny to come out and look for the script and Mary Ann.

Johnny makes reservations to fly to Hollywood, and on the way out meets Pat McCracken at his front door, and Johnny tells him that he has a problem with his radio program and is in a real hurry to get to the airport.

Pat tells Johnny that his program is very important to the insurance industry, as it discourages insurance fraud and false claims, etc. Pat tells Johnny that he wants Johnny to get out to California. Pat has his car, so he drives Johnny to the airport, and gets a speeding ticket on the way.

Johnny flies to Los Angeles, California and calls Jack's office from the airport, and Mary Ann Hooper answers the phone. Mary Ann knows nothing about the script, and tells Johnny that Jack had called her, but now he has disappeared.

Johnny cabs to Jack's office and runs into Joan, the receptionist, who tells Johnny that Mary Ann has not been in the office for several days. Now two people are missing.

Johnny is taken to the phone switchboard and is introduced to the girls. One of the operators remembers talking to Mary Ann recently, but she has not been there for several days. Johnny is told that Mary Ann works at home until the scripts are ready and has phone calls routed to her home.

She calls Mary Ann, but there is no answer. Johnny calls Pat McCracken, but he is in a conference. Johnny calls his home later, but he is not there.

At 10:00 Mary Ann arrives and she tells Johnny that she is not sure where Jack is. Jack had told her on Tuesday that he would have a script for her, but she has not seen it. Johnny realizes that things do not add up.

Johnny flies back to Hartford and goes to the garage behind his apartment house to get his car, but it is gone. Johnny cabs to Pat McCracken's office and he is told that he is expected.

Johnny goes in to find Jack Johnstone in Pat's office. Jack explains to

Johnny that his programs help the insurance companies to save money, and they are grateful for his three years of service via his programs.

Pat tells Johnny that they had to get him out of town so that they could reinstall his two-way radio. Pat takes Johnny to the window where he shows Johnny a brand new yellow hardtop, with air conditioning and all the accessories, including his two-way radio.

The car is a gift of gratitude from all of the insurance companies. Jack wishes Johnny a happy anniversary and tells him to drive the car in good health.

Johnny thanks all of the many people who help to make this program possible.

Notes:
- The announcer is Dan Cubberly.
- The script secretary for this program is Mary Ann Hooper.
- This is the only reference to a two-way radio in the series.
- Story information obtained from the KNX Collection in the Thousand Oaks Library.

Producer: Jack Johnstone Writer: Jack Johnstone
Cast: Jack Johnstone, Lawrence Dobkin, Virginia Gregg, Jeanne Tatum, Shirley Mitchell, Forrest Lewis

♦ ❖ ♦

Show: **The Impossible Murder Matter**
Show Date: **10/12/1958**
Company: **Tri-Western Life & Casualty Company**
Agent: **Walt Bascomb**
Exp. Acct: **$516.25**

Synopsis: Walt Bascomb calls Johnny from Los Angeles and has a case for him. The case is either an accident or murder. The victim is Paul W. Ranken, who was insured for $100,000, double indemnity. Walt suspects murder, but if Ranken died as reported, it is impossible.

Johnny flies to Los Angeles, California and goes to Walt's office where Johnny is told that Paul W. Ranken was a real estate promoter, and the beneficiary is his wife Grace. Ranken was on vacation with his business partner in the Sierra Nevada mountains, and had gone to Forrest Lewis' fishing camp.

Ranken had packed in to Lone Horse Lake and was supposed to be picked up by a guide named Shorty in three days. When Shorty went back, Ranken was dead. Walt had been asked to change the beneficiary on the policy because Ranken had discovered that his partner, Al Warren, had been seeing his wife on the sly. The details of the murder are impossible, so Johnny will have to go there and see for himself.

Johnny flies to Forrest Lewis' camp and learns that Grace and Al were openly in love with each other, even in front of Ranken, who did not approve. Forrest tells Johnny that Ranken had brought them up here so he could leave them alone together without any luxuries.

Johnny talks to Grace and Al, who tell Johnny that they are glad, as it will be better for both them and the business. Johnny is told that Ranken was a crook and ran phony real estate promotions and had gotten letters from his victims. Johnny is told that the body is at the coroner's office in Big Pine, and that they are staying until the autopsy.

Johnny goes to his cabin to discover that someone had searched his bags. Johnny then rides up to the campsite at Lone Horse Lake.

Johnny is shown where the tent was, and the footprints that led to the body. Johnny is told that Ranken was found in the snow and had been hit with a blackjack and there were no other tracks there. Johnny returns to the camp and tells about his bags being searched.

Dr. Wilson arrives and tells Johnny that the murder was caused by just one mark on Ranken's head, and that Forrest provided all of the evidence. Johnny gets everyone together and goes over the reasons why Grace and Al would benefit from the death of Ranken, but Johnny is told that everyone was in camp the whole time. Shorty tells Johnny that he has to leave to feed his mules.

When Johnny hears mules, he gets a hunch. Shorty tells Johnny that he came from Missouri and is a muleskinner who uses a long whip. Johnny is sure that Shorty used the whip to kill Ranken. Shorty cracks his whip and tells Johnny that Ranken had stolen his father's money. Shorty tells Grace to move away from Johnny, and then hits both her and Al. Johnny gets to Shorty and slugs him.

Johnny reports to Walt that the death was not an accident.

Notes:
- The announcer is Dan Cubberly.
- Forrest Lewis' camp also figured in *The Glacier Ghost Matter*.
- Story information obtained from the KNX Collection in the Thousand Oaks Library.

Producer:	Jack Johnstone Writer: Jack Johnstone
Cast:	Edgar Stehli, Forrest Lewis, Virginia Gregg, James McCallion, Bartlett Robinson, Vic Perrin

◆ ❖ ◆

Show:	**The Monoxide Mystery Matter**
Show Date:	**10/19/1958**
Company:	**Philadelphia Mutual Life & Casualty Insurance**
Agent:	**Clarke Bender**
Exp. Acct:	**$74.65**

Synopsis: Clarke Bender calls Johnny and tells him that he got a call form Saticoy City, Pennsylvania from Mrs. Abbey Norton, who cared for Rufus W. Harper, her brother-in-law, and is the beneficiary of his $25,000 policy. Mrs. Norton found Rufus in his car, dead, and the death was called suicide, but she is not convinced.

Johnny flies to Philadelphia and goes to see Clarke who tells Johnny that on the first call, Abbey was told about the suicide clause in the policy, and later Clarke was told that the death was not a suicide. Clarke tells Johnny that he will get a fee of $1,500 if Abbey is right and $1,000 if she is wrong. When Johnny asks if the fees are not reversed, Clarke tells Johnny that he is concerned about providing good service to his customer.

Johnny rents a car and drives to Saticoy City and goes to see Abbey. She tells Johnny that the body is with the coroner, who is also the local carpenter and a coffin maker. Abbey tells Johnny that she wants the money from the policy. She also tells Johnny that Rufus had just sold a lot for $1,600, and the money was gone from his pockets and warns Johnny to be careful.

Johnny calls on Dr. Lehman, but he is not in. Johnny then goes to see the coroner, who tells Johnny that Tim Otis, the police in the town, is in bed with a hangover. Johnny is told that when the body was found, the car door was open.

Johnny looks at the body and Dr. Lehman arrives. Johnny asks the doctor if the face and neck were cherry red, which is typical of carbon monoxide, and is told that they were not. Doc Lehman also tells Johnny that there was evidence that Rufus was hit on the head with a bottle, either at Paddy's Bar or on the way home. Johnny is also told that Jake Quest has $1,600.

Johnny and Doc Lehman go to see Tim Otis, who is in bed with a headache. Tim tells Johnny that Rufus was at a party at Paddy's and was buying drinks, and that the Durkin boys were also there. The Durkins are Paddy's nephews, and local troublemakers. They tried to get Rufus to gamble with the money he had, and Doc tells Tim that Rufus was murdered.

Johnny goes to Paddy's, and Doc Lehman insists on coming with him and tells Johnny that Paddy's is closed tonight. When they get there, Johnny sees a light on and hears the Durkins inside. Johnny goes to the door to listen and hears Bo tell Paddy that he slugged Rufus, and the he is afraid of an investigation. Bo hears a noise and they grab their guns and go outside and find Johnny.

While they are threatening Johnny, Doc Lehman uses his voice to create the presence of other police officers. Bo drops his gun, and Johnny drives Bo to the jail from the back seat of Bo's car.

The state police are called and the insurance is to be paid to Abbey. And, Johnny will be paid more!

Notes:
- The announcer is Dan Cubberly.
- Story information obtained from the KNX Collection in the Thousand Oaks Library.

Producer: Jack Johnstone Writer: Jack Johnstone
Cast: Russell Thorson, Virginia Gregg, Lawrence Dobkin, Harry Bartell, Lillian Buyeff, Forrest Lewis, Alan Reed, Billy Halop

Show:	The Basking Ridge Matter
Show Date:	10/26/1958
Company:	Eastern Trust & Insurance Company
Agent:	Stuart Smith
Exp. Acct:	$29.55

Synopsis: Stuart Smith calls Johnny from New York, and tells Johnny that David Rockwell Winters lives in Basking Ridge, New Jersey, and collects fine art. Winters has reported that the Victoria Ruby has been stolen, and is afraid he will lose something else, his life.

Johnny drives to Basking Ridge and meets Winters, who is glad that Johnny got there before he was murdered. Winter tells Johnny that he has sold his art collection, and that the money is in a vault in the basement, and that there is only one key. Winters also tells Johnny that his nephews and niece want his money, but he does not want them to get it because it will spoil them.

Winters tells Johnny that his nephews are Ronald and Bill Tatum and their sister Bettina. When Johnny asks why Winters did not just change his will, he tells Johnny that he never thought of that. Johnny tells him that he will stay until the changes are made.

Winters tells Johnny that several attempts have been made on his life, and that they started two weeks earlier. The relatives had come in a green car to visit and ask for money, and Winters threw them out. Then Winters found a loose step, ground glass in his sugar, and was almost hit by a green car.

Johnny goes to nearby Bernardsville to visit the relatives and finds a green car outside the house. Johnny meets Ronald and Bettina, who is really cute. Both think that their uncle is crazy and want Johnny to look into the insurance for them.

Al arrives and they tell Johnny that Winters had promised them an education, and that Bettina has become a nurse, and Ronnie and Al were told that they could go to Rutgers, but now they are living off of Beneficial Finance. Johnny agrees that something is wrong, and that the kids seem to make sense.

Johnny goes back to Winter's home and finds him groaning on the floor. Johnny gives him a brandy and he tells Johnny that he was hit just after Johnny left. The vault key is still in his pocket, but they go to the vault and open it to find the money gone. Johnny finds footprints and calls the police.

Johnny makes some calls and then goes to a gun shop and makes a purchase. Johnny then goes back to Bernardsville where Bettina is home and the boys are gone. Johnny draws the blinds and places his gun on a table and talks to Bettina.

Johnny tells her that he found her footprints in the basement and asks her why she did it. Bettina grabs the gun and tells Johnny that their uncle was cutting them out of the will, and so she stole the money. She shoots Johnny three times, but the gun contains blanks. Johnny determines that the brothers are not involved.

Notes:

- The announcer is Dan Cubberly.
- Basking Ridge is in north-central New Jersey, south of Morristown.
- Story information obtained from the KNX Collection in the Thousand Oaks Library.

Producer: Jack Johnstone   Writer: Jack Johnstone
Cast: Frank Gerstle, Will Wright, Jeanne Tatum, Sam Edwards

◆ ❖ ◆

Show: **The Crater Lake Matter**
Show Date: **11/2/1958**
Company: **Northwest Indemnity Alliance**
Agent: **Peter Wilkerson**
Exp. Acct: **$495.60**

Synopsis: Peter Wilkerson calls Johnny from San Francisco and tells Johnny that he has a claim on a $300,000 life policy. Johnny is on his way.

Johnny flies to San Francisco, California and goes to the Huntington Hotel and then to Pete's office. Pete asks Johnny if he knows Sam Arnold, the man who writes for all of the pulp magazines. Pete sold Arnold his first policy in 1939 and he has regularly increased his coverage. The beneficiary of the current policy is Vonnie Revell, the stripper.

Three months ago, Arnold increased the coverage to $300,000. Arnold recently went to Crater Lake and rented a boat and disappeared. The body was found, but was only a skeleton, and his wife based the identification on a ring, but Pete is suspicious of the wife.

Johnny flies to Klamath Falls, Oregon and goes to Crater Lake to talk to the park ranger, who is sure that Arnold was murdered. Johnny is told that the body was found in 1960 feet of water while they were taking depth soundings. Joe thinks that Arnold was on the lake when a big wind came up, and he was thrown overboard and caught his foot in a rope and was pulled down with the boat.

Johnny looks at the rope from the body and is sure that Arnold was murdered because the rope is knotted and there is cloth in the knots. Johnny is told that Gimpy Joe Larson, a bad character from San Francisco was at the lake at the same time Arnold was there, and he disappeared at the same time, leaving his camping gear. Joe wonders if Arnold was murdered for something he wrote.

Johnny goes back to San Francisco and meets with Vonnie, who is upset. She tells Johnny that she met Arnold when she was in burlesque and gets upset when Johnny suggests that she had him killed. She also tells Johnny that she does not know anyone named Gimpy Larson. She tells Johnny that she is going away as soon as she gets the money, which gives Johnny a hunch.

Johnny goes to see police Lt. Dubov and learns that Gimpy is not in town. Johnny gets a photo of Gimpy, and he is a dead ringer for Sam Arnold. Johnny leaves and buys some old magazines with articles written by Arnold in them. Johnny then goes to see a man named Ah Lee, who is suspected of selling fake passports.

Ah Lee denies making fake passports but for $100 he agrees to help

Johnny by telling him where to look for a special forger's mark on fake passports. Johnny calls Vonnie and arranges to have dinner with her.

Johnny then goes to Vonnie's and breaks in after she leaves. Johnny searches and finds Vonnie's passport and a fake passport under another name with Sam Arnold's photo on it. The door opens and Arnold walks in with a gun.

Johnny tells Arnold that he had built up his insurance so that he could disappear. Johnny tells Arnold that he killed Gimpy and put the body where the rangers were going to do depth soundings so that it would be found. Vonnie comes in and tells Arnold to kill Johnny. Arnold pulls at Vonnie and Johnny slugs him.

Notes:
- The announcer is Dan Cubberly.
- Bob Bailey welcomes station WABI in Bangor, Maine to the CBS network.
- Story information obtained from the KNX Collection in the Thousand Oaks Library.

Producer:	Jack Johnstone Writer: Jack Johnstone
Cast:	Peter Leeds, Barney Phillips, Virginia Gregg, Herb Vigran, Lawrence Dobkin

◆ ❖ ◆

Show:	**The Close Shave Matter**
Show Date:	**11/9/1958**
Company:	**Universal Adjustment Bureau**
Agent:	**Pat McCracken**
Exp. Acct:	**$383.20**

Synopsis: Pat McCracken calls, but Johnny tells Pat that he is going on vacation. Pat tells Johnny that he has a case for him at Lake Mohave. Johnny cabs to Pat's office and is told that Jim Barker from Western Maritime had called about his client Jules Maitland, who is insured for $250,000. Pat wants Johnny to go to Lake Mohave and investigate.

Johnny flies to Lake Mohave Resort and gives his usual description of the desert area as he goes to meet with Buster Favor. Buster tells Johnny that Maitland is worried that he is about to be murdered for his insurance money. Maitland's beneficiary is his wife Betty Jane, who lives on their ranch. Their stepson Charles Warren is no good and would kill Betty to get the money. Buster tells Johnny that Maitland has letters with him threatening his life.

Johnny goes out and sees a new car in the parking lot and is sure that Charles is there. Johnny meets Charles, who knows who Johnny is, and tells him that his stepfather told him that the letters are gone. He tells Johnny that he came to the lake to ask for money to go to school.

Buster notes that Charles seems OK, and that the threats must be all talk. Johnny remembers a newspaper article about a car used in a robbery in Los Angeles, and the license plate number is similar so Johnny raises the hood and adjusts a valve on the engine.

Johnny goes to see Maitland and tells him to stay in his room and then calls

Sgt. Hacker at the Los Angeles police and is told that the car matches except for the license plate number. Johnny goes out and sees that the car is gone.

Johnny goes to see Maitland, who has just finished shaving. Johnny fixes them a drink and then Maitland starts to stagger. Johnny calls Buster who gets a doctor who is staying at the lodge. The doctor examines Maitland and finds that he was poisoned with potassium peyotin.

Maitland tells Johnny that Charlie had given him a new shaving soap to use. Maitland tells Johnny to follow Charles, but Johnny does not have to. He tells Maitland and Buster that he had opened the drain valve on the engine, and Charles' radiator should be empty by now.

The police are called and they pick up Charles on the road and find the poison in his car.

Notes:
- The announcer is Dan Cubberly.
- Story information obtained from the KNX Collection in the Thousand Oaks Library.

Producer:	Jack Johnstone	Writer:	Jack Johnstone
Cast:	Lawrence Dobkin, Barney Phillips, Ralph Moody, Carleton G. Young, Jack Edwards		

♦ ❖ ♦

Show: The Double Trouble Matter
Show Date: 11/16/1958
Company: Tri-State Life & Casualty Company
Agent: Earle Poorman
Exp. Acct: $178.70

Synopsis: Earle Poorman calls Johnny and tells him he is moving to California to get away from the insurance business. He has a wild case trying to get rid of $65,000, which Albert Schuyler Kingman left to his only son, Henry. The trouble is, Earle has found two sons.

Johnny travels to Sarasota, Florida and goes to Earle's Office. Earle tells Johnny that Kingman was a widower who lived in North Carolina, and the company has waited 20 years to settle the policy.

Kingman was killed during a hurricane in 1938 when Henry was 10 years old. After the storm, Kingman's body was eventually found, but Henry disappeared. The insurance case is still open and they are waiting for the beneficiary.

The company had advertised for the beneficiary, and two men have claimed the policy. They are staying here in Sarasota, and both seem to have iron clad stories. Earle gets the file on the father and the family for Johnny to review. Johnny and Earle drive to Earle's house for dinner. Johnny reviews the folders and thinks he knows how to expose the phony claimant.

Johnny goes to a motel to question Henry #1 but gets nowhere. Henry #1 tells Johnny all about his buddy Obie O'Brien and evades a trap about Miss Albertis the supposed Sunday School teacher. Johnny thinks that Henry has too good of an alibi. Henry #1 tells Johnny that he did not have much education and wandered around after the storm. He saw the ad and thought it would be a chance to get an education. Johnny is unable to trip up Henry #1.

Johnny drives to another motel to see Henry #2, who answers all of Johnny's questions. He tells of being adopted by a family named McGovern after the hurricane. His parents knew who he was but never told anyone. Henry #2 was told he was adopted on his 21st birthday, and his foster parents died about seven years ago. Unfortunately, Bridgeton, where he lived, was destroyed by a storm, and no one is there to tell Johnny who Henry #2 is.

Over dinner, Johnny tells Earle and Gertrude about his lack of progress. Earle wonders if the men knew each other, but they each deny knowing of the other. Johnny has an idea and goes to see Doc Crutcher, an old friend of Earle and Johnny. On the way, Johnny is slugged by a man who comes from behind a tree.

Earle is talking to Doc Crutcher as Johnny is given smelling salts. Gertrude brings a cup of tea for Johnny, but Doc suggests brandy, and Johnny changes the order to scotch. Johnny tells Earle to get the two Henrys and bring them there while Johnny asks Doc about heredity.

Johnny talks to the two Henrys, who Earle had found in the same hotel room. Johnny looks at their hands and Henry #1 has bruised knuckles, but Doc notices that Henry #2 also has bruises. Both claim they were hurt opening a window.

Johnny tells them that he has realized that the laws of heredity can solve this case. Johnny tells Earle about talking with Doc Crutcher and checking the insurance records, where he learned that both parents had brown hair and brown eyes.

Johnny tells them that when parents have the same hair and eye colors, the offspring will as well. When Johnny tells them of their varying hair and eye colors, Henry #1 tells Henry #2 that he was a crazy fool and knew it would not work. But Henry #2 is afraid that Henry #1 would cheat him out of the money. Henry #2 pulls a gun and Johnny out draws him and shoots him after Gertrude hits Henry #1 with an old vase.

"Yeah, my heredity gag was just that, a gag. But it certainly brought things to a head in a hurry. How did they know so much about the real Henry Kingman? Well listen: As soon as we locked them up, I called the national press services and had them put the story of this attempted fraud in the headlines all over the country. Result: a phone call from the head of an orphanage where the real Henry had been taken in as a child, where he still lived. And yeah, the phonies were a couple of kids who had run away from that orphanage after he palled around with them, told them all about himself. As for why they both appeared to make the claim? Sure, each of them saw the company's ad and tried to get in ahead of the other. Well they are in alright. For a long time."

Notes:

- This is an AFRTS program that contains an episode of "The Bellweathers", a story about Pvt. Robert Von Schlick, who won the medal of honor during the Boxer Rebellion, and a story about the new American warrior who uses technology to do his job.
- The announcer is Dan Cubberly.

Producer:	Jack Johnstone	Writer:	Jack Johnstone
Cast:	Virginia Gregg, Vic Perrin, Sam Edwards, James McCallion, Parley Baer		

♦ ❖ ♦

Show:	**The One Most Wanted Matter**
Show Date:	11/23/1958
Company:	**Trinity Mutual Insurance Company**
Agent:	**Bob Tank**
Exp. Acct:	**$3,995.00**

Synopsis: Bob Tank calls and tells Johnny that he will put him on the map with all the publicity from this case. Johnny tells Bob that he has another more important case, but Bob tells Johnny that Pat McCracken had given him Johnny's number. Johnny calls Pat, who tells Johnny that he has never heard of Trinity Mutual but tells Johnny to look into the matter.

Johnny goes to meet Bob Tank, who offers Johnny a drink and tells Johnny that he used to work in advertising but inherited the company from his father. Bob tells Johnny that a policyholder died and left $25,000 to his son Albert Siedel. Johnny recognizes Albert as Skippy Siedel, who is on the ten-most-wanted list, and is wanted for arson, murder and bombings, although Bob insists that he is only wanted in six states.

Johnny calls the police all over the country and learns that Skippy's wife is living in Palmdale, California. Johnny goes to the airport and sees a headline in the papers "Famous Insurance Investigator on Siedel Case".

Johnny calls Bob and accuses him of tipping Skippy off, but Bob tells Johnny that it is just local publicity. Johnny flies to Los Angeles and goes to the police and then to Palmdale, just north of Los Angeles.

On the way, Johnny spots a stopped train and a crowd of people around an ambulance. Johnny stops and learns that the train had hit a man, who turned out to be Skippy Siedel. Johnny talks to the state police who are sure the man is Skippy, because the car was stolen in Reno by Skippy.

Johnny goes to see Skippy's wife Sandra, who is in seclusion but agrees to talk to Johnny. Johnny gets in and Sandra is so beautiful that Johnny can only stare.

Sandra tells Johnny that she runs a beauty shop and is glad that her husband is dead. Skippy had wanted to hide there but she had told him no, so he was going to leave the state.

Johnny asks about a local motel, and Sandra suggests McKenny's Ranch Motel, but insists that Johnny have dinner with her. After dinner Johnny leaves, buys gas and a local paper that has an article about a prospector who has disappeared.

Johnny drives to the motel over a very remote road. The car starts to cough and Johnny opens the hood to find a bomb. The car explodes and Johnny realizes that Sandra was only a diversion while Skippy planted a bomb in the car.

A car drives up with Sandra and Skippy in it. Johnny hides and hears Skippy mention killing the prospector as he starts to burn the car. Johnny surprises Skippy and hits him.

Johnny wonders if Bob got his publicity as he adds the cost of the rental car to the expense account.

Notes:
- The announcer is Dan Cubberly.
- Story information obtained from the KNX Collection in the Thousand Oaks Library.

Producer:	Jack Johnstone Writer: Jack Johnstone
Cast:	Jerry Hausner, Lawrence Dobkin, Tom Hanley, Bill James, Virginia Gregg, James McCallion

♦ ❖ ♦

Show:	**The Hair Raising Matter**
Show Date:	**11/30/1958**
Company:	**Star Mutual Insurance Company**
Agent:	**Fritz Melchior**
Exp. Acct:	**$47.50**

Synopsis: Fritz Melchior calls Johnny, who is glad to hear from Fritz, as his cases usually put a lot of money in his pocket, and he needs a few extra bucks, quite a few. Fred was not thinking about a fee on this case but will pay Johnny's expenses.

John Wakefield Edwards is a retired businessman who lives outside of Albany. Nothing has happened yet, but he has a lot of insurance, and his wife died a few years ago. His beneficiary is his adopted daughter Maralyn, who lives in Troy. Edwards had called last night and demanded that Fritz send Johnny over and not to tell Maralyn. Johnny tells Fritz he will go over first thing in the morning.

Johnny decides to drive to Albany, New York that night and calls Mr. Edwards from the hotel. Edwards tells Johnny to see him first thing in the morning, as nothing will happen in the meantime. "Be here at seven sharp for breakfast" Johnny is told.

Johnny leaves the next morning and drives to the Edwards mansion. Johnny sees a new sports car in the driveway with a pretty girl getting in. Johnny introduces himself, and Maralyn Edwards recognizes who Johnny is. She tells Johnny that she thought daddy would call someone like him. She is a model she tells Johnny as they go into the house.

Maralyn calls for daddy and then Durkin, the housekeeper. Durkin comes in and tells Maralyn that she has rung for breakfast three times but Mr. Edwards has not come down. Johnny and Maralyn go upstairs and knock on the bedroom door. Johnny thinks he smells cordite, and they open the door to find Edwards dead.

Johnny finds the body with Maralyn and calls the police. Sgt. Christy and Dr. Lincoln arrive, and examine the body. Durkin tells them that Edwards has not been sick, and the doctor thinks it was a heart attack. Maralyn does not want an autopsy, so doctor calls the cause of death "natural causes". As Durkin closes the windows, the doctor goes back to the morgue.

Johnny thinks that something is wrong and wonders why the windows were open. Did Maralyn really just arrive? And what about Durkin?

The undertaker gets the body around noon, and Johnny questions Maralyn and Durkin. Maralyn tells Johnny that no one else would benefit from her father's death, but Durkin tells them that he left her some money in his will, and a codicil in the will says that Maralyn has to share the insurance money with her, if she collects.

Durkin tells Johnny that Maralyn and her foster father did not get along, and Maralyn had not seen him for several years.

Johnny goes to search the room and only finds a few bottles of hair tonic, and a funny looking hat stand on the dresser. Maralyn rushes in with a .38 she found in a myrtle bush. She gives the gun to Johnny, so now the gun is covered with her prints and Johnny's. Suddenly Johnny has an idea.

Johnny is sure his hunch is right. He tells Maralyn and Durkin to stay at the house and goes to see the undertaker. The undertaker takes Johnny to the body, and Johnny examines the body.

Johnny pulls up a hairpiece that covers a small bald spot. Johnny realizes that the stand was for the hairpiece, and that no one probably realized he had used one. Johnny gets a solvent to remove the hair piece and finds a bullet hole.

Back at the house Johnny questions Maralyn and tells her that her father was murdered. Johnny asks about the stand, and Maralyn tells her that it was a hat stand she played with as a girl. Johnny asks her how long her father had worn a toupee, and Maralyn replies "never" as he was proud of his hair. Johnny tells her of the hairpiece and the bullet wound.

The attention turns to Durkin and Johnny decides to try a bluff. Durkin comes in and Johnny tells her of the line click he heard on the phone when he talked to Edwards the previous night. Johnny tells Durkin that he was at police headquarters checking her prints from a water glass against the prints he found on the .38.

Johnny tells her that the fingerprints match, but Durkin says it is a lie, she had wiped off the gun. She confirms she opened the windows to get rid of the gun smoke and wiped off the prints. At least she thought she did.

"Don't worry, there will be no part of the insurance or any other money for Durkin. The courts will take care of that and probably with vengeance. And for Maralyn, well you know something, there is a gal I think I would like to see again, and I do not mean because of her fortune."

Notes:

- The announcer is Dan Cubberly.

Producer:	Jack Johnstone Writer: Jack Johnstone
Cast:	Virginia Gregg, Shirley Mitchell, Jack Edwards, Ralph Moody, Junius Matthews, Parley Baer

♦ ❖ ♦

Show:	**The Perilous Parley Matter**
Show Date:	**12/7/1958**
Company:	**Universal Adjustment Bureau**
Agent:	**Pat McCracken**
Exp. Acct:	**$8.00**

Synopsis: Johnny gets a call from Sam Hodge who asks what is wrong, isn't $10,000 enough? The deal was for $5,000 if the job was done today, but it wasn't. Sam will give Jimmy one more day to take care of Parley. When Johnny says "Huh?" the caller hangs up.

Johnny wonders who Sam is, and what kind of parley is involved, maybe a parley at a race track? Pat McCracken calls Johnny and tells him that he has Johnny's check for *The Love Shorn Matter*, and is going to add an additional $500. Johnny tells Pat about the strange call he got, and Pat tells Johnny that he is going to send the check by messenger, so don't parley it on the horses.

Later there is a knock at the door with a special delivery package. Johnny opens the door and falls instinctively when he sees the gun. Johnny wakes up in the hospital where Pat McCracken tells Johnny that he was shot, but the bullet just creased his arm.

A police sergeant comes into the room and tells Johnny that they do not know who shot him. Johnny mentions the call about the parley and is told to come to Hartford, Connecticut headquarters when he is able. Johnny tells Pat all he knows and then goes to see the police.

When Johnny mentions the call and Jimmy, he is told that the police just closed a case on Jimmy Waller, a hood from Chicago and New York, who just left town.

Johnny goes to see Pat who tells him that they have a policy on Parley Barnes, who is a retired businessman who runs the "Clean Business Association". Johnny wonders who is trying to kill Barnes.

Pat tells Johnny that Barnes came from Corpus Christi, New Orleans and Memphis where he had been plugging his business. Johnny goes to the police and tells them to send an officer to 14325 Euclid Ave. to protect Barnes.

Johnny calls Wayne Stockseth, an old friend in Corpus Christi, and Wayne tells Johnny that Barnes was following a boiler room operator named Samuel Truesdale Hogerston. Johnny gets an address for Sam Hodge and calls the number and gets the same voice as the previous call.

Johnny calls the police and then calls again acting as Jimmy. Sam takes the call and yells at his secretary for confusing Jimmy Waller with Johnny Dollar. Sam asks if Parley is dead and tells Jimmy to leave town. Hodge is arrested in his office and Jimmy is arrested at Barnes' home.

Johnny wants a fee on this case!

Notes:
- The announcer is Dan Cubberly.
- Johnny is shot for the 10th time.
- The following programs:
  The Allanmee Matter #103 (11/28/58),
  The Telltale Tracks Matter #108 (12/28/58),
  The Hollywood Mystery Matter #109 (1/4/59),
  The Deadly Doubt Matter #104 (11/30/58),
  The Love Shorn Matter #106 (12/14/58), and
  The Doting Dowager Matter #105 (12/7/58)
  were reordered by script number and air dates and were aired in the following order:
  The Allanmee Matter #106 (12/14/58),
  The Perilous Parley Matter #107 (12/21/58),
  The Telltale Tracks Matter #107 (12/28/58),
  The Hollywood Mystery Matter #108 (1/4/59),
  The Deadly Doubt Matter #109 (1/11/59),
  The Love Shorn Matter #110 (1/18/59),
  The Doting Dowager Matter #112 (1/25/59).
- The script mentions *The Love Shorn Matter*, which was recorded on the same day but, as noted above, not broadcast until January 18.
- Story information obtained from the KNX Collection in the Thousand Oaks Library.

Producer: Jack Johnstone   Writer: Jack Johnstone
Cast: Virginia Gregg, Alan Reed, Lawrence Dobkin, Frank Gerstle, Tony Barrett

◆ ❖ ◆

Show: **The Allanmee Matter**
Show Date: **12/14/1958**
Company: **Greater Southwest Insurance Company**
Agent: **Fred Brinkley**
Exp. Acct: **$341.10**

Synopsis: Johnny is called by Myrna Dodd who tells Johnny that she has tried to call Fred Brinkley at Greater Southwest, but he has not returned her call. Myrna tells Johnny that she has been robbed, and that he must come to Corpus Christi and she will pay his expenses if necessary.

Johnny flies to Corpus Christi, Texas where Myrna, a living doll, meets Johnny at the airport. Myrna tells Johnny that her husband Al is out fishing on the Gulf of Mexico as she drives Johnny to their home.

Myrna tells Johnny that the robbery occurred on their boat, the *Allanmee*, which is a 52-foot cruiser. They have a guard, but the jewels and the guard were gone when they returned from a trip. She also tells Johnny that the *Allanmee*'s crew usually comes from her husband's shrimp boats.

On the boat, Johnny finds that it had been torn apart, and the jewels are gone. Johnny also finds a secure compartment where a metal strongbox has been pried open. Johnny tells Myrna to call the insurance company and she leaves.

Al Dodd returns and hits Johnny and accuses him of robbing them. Myrna returns to the boat and explains to Al who Johnny is, and Al apologizes. Myrna tells Al what has happened and that Toby Rich, the guard, is gone.

Al tells Johnny that he does not want to call the police, and that he will buy his wife new furs and jewelry, and that no claim will be filed, and that he will pay Johnny's expenses. Al offers to take Johnny fishing, but Johnny declines the offer.

Johnny is suspicious and calls Fred from the airport. Fred tells Johnny that the jewels were insured for $7,000, but the furs were not insured. Johnny calls police Lt. Culpepper who tells Johnny that they have nothing on Al Dodd who works as a deck hand on a fishing boat. Al does have a boat with twin diesel engines and usually fishes in Mexican waters.

Johnny tells Lt. Culpepper about the robbery and learns that Toby has been arrested in East Humble, Louisiana. Johnny flies to East Humble and inspects the car driven by Toby. In the trunk, Johnny finds the furs and the jewels along with a bag containing $320,000.

Johnny returns to the Dodd house to find the boat pulling away from the dock. Johnny jumps on and slugs Al. Myrna tells Johnny that Al told her to leave without packing.

Johnny tells Myrna and Al that he has located Toby, and about the jewels, furs and money in his car. Johnny tells Al that he is really smuggling heroin from Mexico, and Al offers Johnny a bribe.

Al is arrested and charged with smuggling and tax evasion.

Notes:
- The announcer is Dan Cubberly.
- Story information obtained from the KNX Collection in the Thousand Oaks Library.

Producer:	Jack Johnstone	Writer:	Jack Johnstone
Cast:	Virginia Gregg, Russell Thorson, Harry Bartell, Sam Edwards		

• ❖ •

Show: **The Telltale Tracks Matter**
Show Date: **12/28/1958**
Company: **Continental Insurance & Trust Company**
Agent:
Exp. Acct: **$0.00**

Synopsis: Alvin Peabody Cartwright calls Johnny, addled as usual, and tells Johnny that he has been robbed. Johnny is told to come there or he will cancel all of his insurance.

Johnny drives to Lakewood, Connecticut on Christmas day. When Johnny gets to Alvin's house Alvin gives Johnny his present, a diamond studded watch and wishes Johnny a happy new year as he escorts Johnny to the door. When Johnny mentions the robbery, Alvin takes Johnny to see his tree and explains that his niece and her two children came to see the tree, but all the presents were gone.

Johnny is told that a mink coat, some jewels and toys and an envelope with $25,000 were taken. Alvin shows Johnny the window the burglar used and tells Johnny that the police have not been called. Alvin tells Johnny to follow the footprints in the snow and get his presents back. Johnny follows the tracks, but notes that he would not have, if he had known.

Johnny follows the tracks to a shack where he sees a girl sick in bed taking some medicine, and a boy wearing some fancy clothes. Johnny also sees a woman in a tattered dress, wearing a mink coat and wearing a jeweled watch as she counts the money.

Johnny goes into the shack and asks for directions to Alvin's house, and the woman offers Johnny some hot cider. She tells Johnny that she is Betty Rogan, and that her daughter will recover. She tells Johnny that her husband Ricky left for New York and eventually moved all over and had stopped writing.

She tells Johnny that she and her daughter Nancy got sick, but now they will be all right because Ricky came home last night and left a note for them. The note said that things never work out, but he had left the gifts, and this is the last time he would say goodbye.

Johnny goes back to Alvin's house and remembers who Ricky Rogan is. Johnny calls Randy Singer to get information on Rogan, and Alvin tells Johnny that his desk was also broken into, and one piece of paper was taken.

Randy calls back and tells Johnny that Ricky Rogan is really Rick Marengo, who is a sneak thief and burglar. Rick had pulled a bank job in New York and killed a bank guard and was also injured.

Johnny gets a flask and a flashlight and follows a set of footprints leading away from the shack. Johnny finds Rick in the snow, takes his gun and gives him a drink.

Rick tells Johnny that he had stolen the things for his family from the house, and Johnny tells him that he knows what happened to him. Rick tells Johnny that he saw the situation of his wife and kids, and that he never did right by her.

Rick tells Johnny that he stole the things that mean nothing to that rich man but mean the world to his wife. Rick dies and Johnny goes to the police and tells them where to find his body.

Johnny mentions the recovery of the goods to Alvin who decides that he will get Betty a decent place to live, and will give her a job, maybe as her housekeeper.

Notes:

- The announcer is Dan Cubberly.
- Story information obtained from the KNX Collection in the Thousand Oaks Library.

Producer:	Jack Johnstone	Writer:	Jack Johnstone
Cast:	Howard McNear, Richard Beals, Virginia Gregg, Herb Vigran, Harry Bartell		

◆ ❖ ◆

Show:	**The Hollywood Mystery Matter**
Show Date:	1/4/1959
Company:	**Eastern Liability & Trust Company**
Agent:	**Hal Spidle**
Exp. Acct:	**$0.00**

Synopsis: Parley Baron calls from Hollywood. He knows that Johnny handles all investigations for the Eastern Liability and Trust. Baron is sure that Eastern will be calling Johnny about a $10,000 embezzlement from the Berkley Furniture Manufacturing Company in Hartford. Check with Berkley and the insurance company. "When you have learned the facts, you will realize it is of the utmost importance to contact me" Baron tells Johnny.

Johnny calls Hal Spidle, his usual contact at Eastern and Hal has not received a claim yet. Johnny is put on hold by Hal only to find that he has an assignment with Berkley Furniture, they just found out about the embezzlement. Johnny realizes that the informant knew something.

Johnny goes to the Berkley Company in Hartford, Connecticut and meets with the president, Mr. Berkley. Berkley tells Johnny that he wants the money back. It was taken by a bookkeeper that had been with them for 30 years. The man earned $65 a week, which was plenty of money. The bookkeeper was not married and could not afford a wife. Johnny realizes that the man was paid as little as Berkley thought he could get away with.

Berkley tells Johnny that the man went to see his doctor yesterday, and this morning Berkley discovered $9,984.75 missing from the safe. Berkley called the apartment of the bookkeeper to discover that the man had left the previous afternoon. So far, the police have not been notified. Berkley will not prosecute, he only wants the money.

Johnny gets the address of the bookkeeper. Johnny tells Berkley how an informant had called him on the phone. Berkley tells Johnny that the bookkeeper was Parley Baron.

Johnny cabs to the apartment of Baron and runs into a woman leaving who takes the taxi Johnny had come in. Johnny meets the manager who tells Johnny that Baron left the previous day.

Johnny is taken to the apartment and is assured that a nice quiet old man like Baron could not do anything wrong. Baron never had any excitement, except when his niece Virginia Lockhart came to visit. She looks in on him and cooks for him once in a while.

In the apartment, Johnny sees signs of a hasty departure. The manager tells Johnny that Virginia just left the apartment and shows Johnny a photo. Johnny spots a note that tells Virginia that Baron has less than a week to live and he is going to really live it up to make up for the things he has missed over the years, and for her not to try to follow him.

The manager calls Johnny a cab and Johnny goes to the airport just in time to see Ginny Lockhart heading for New York. Johnny catches a flight to New York and sees Ginny getting on a plane. Johnny dashes on the plane and uses his credentials to keep from being thrown off. The stewardess tells Johnny that his plane is going to Miami, Florida — not to California.

Johnny goes to the cabin and fumes over the rest of the flight. Johnny finds the only open seat is next to Ginny Lockhart. Johnny introduces himself to Ginny and tries to start a conversation, but she does not want to talk. She tells Johnny that she is going to try and save someone's life but does not want to talk about it.

In Miami Johnny takes a cab and follows Ginny to Hollywood, Florida and a hotel. Johnny overhears Ginny getting a room number and beats her to the room where Johnny thinks Parley Baron is.

At the door, Johnny tells Ginny why he is there and about what Parley did. Johnny tells her how he hates this assignment because of the way Parley has been taken advantage of by Berkley. Ginny tells Johnny that she will give him the money her uncle has spent if he will not arrest him.

She tells Johnny about the new doctor Baron went to, and how the doctor had told Baron he only had a week to live. The doctor later discovered that the lab reports had been mixed up and called Ginny after being unable to talk to Baron. She has been trying to find her uncle because he will be all right. "Well let's tell him the good news" Johnny tells her.

"Oh, I don't know. Maybe I am just a sucker for a good-looking girl. And, uh, maybe this makes me an accessory to the crime. But you know something, and you can blame it on the holiday season or anything you like, I don't care. Expense account total, including the trip back to Hartford, well a happy New Year to you too."

Notes:
- Bill Bailey mentions another Florida story in the February 1959 copy of Harper's Bazaar, just out.
- A salary of $65 in 1959 is equal to about $545 in 2017, or about $28,300 per year.
- The announcer is **Dan Cubberly,**

Producer:	Jack Johnstone	Writer:	Jack Johnstone
Cast:	Virginia Gregg, Jeanne Tatum, Parley Baer, Forrest Lewis, Junius Matthews, Frank Gerstle		

◆ ❖ ◆

Show:	**The Deadly Doubt Matter**
Show Date:	**1/11/1959**
Company:	**Universal Adjustment Bureau**
Agent:	**Pat McCracken**
Exp. Acct:	**$41.00**

Synopsis: Carol Carson calls Johnny at 1 a.m. and she tells Johnny that Bud Ralston had suggested she call Johnny at his hotel. She tells Johnny that maybe he can help, as she is in real trouble. She is at the apartment of Everett Reed, and she thinks she has killed him.

Johnny cabs to the New York City apartment of Everett Reed and Carol points to the body. Carol thinks that she is the one who killed him, and she feels light-headed and confused.

She tells Johnny that she came to see Everett around 11:00 because he sent for her and she had to come. He told her to have a drink and that is when she started feeling light-headed and dizzy. She left the apartment around 11:30 and walked the streets. She came back and does not remember anything else.

When she woke up she saw the body and the gun and called Johnny. Johnny tries to get her to remember where she was, and she remembers getting a cup of coffee near a neon sign on Third Avenue. She remembers someone following her and he told her his name: Tom.

Johnny calls Lt. Tovitch of homicide and then goes to get a drink and think about her story, it sounded so phony it might be true.

Johnny calls Pat McCracken and learns that Reed was insured by one of their companies. Johnny starts checking the local eating places, and at Eddie's Bar and Grill a man remembers seeing Carol around midnight. He also remembers seeing a man in the doorway. She was given the coffee and just left. She was in the bar for just a minute.

Johnny goes to see Tovitch and updates him. Johnny is told that the medical examiner says that Reed died between 11:30 and 12:30, and she called Johnny at 12:00. So far, her story only covers 5 minutes. Johnny tells Tovitch that Carol will not explain why she was at Reed's apartment, or how she got the lump on her head.

Tovitch tells Johnny that Reed was a big-time gambler who had been winning lately. Reed had been running around with Jack Visel and that crowd. Larry Bowman comes in and asks Tovitch what is happening with Carol, his fiancé. He does not know why she went to see Reed and Larry can prove that he was with her while she was walking the streets. She did not mention that Larry was with her because she was confused. The story he gives to Johnny is all wrong, but Larry is sure Carol did not kill Reed. Johnny buys coffee for Larry and he tells Johnny that he cannot stand by while nothing happens.

Johnny then goes to see Jack Visel, who tells Johnny that he had no reason to kill Reed. Visel tells Johnny that he did owe Reed money, two bits.

Johnny canvasses the area again and goes to his room. A man knocks at the door and tells Johnny that he is the man Carol had mentioned, Tom. He tells Johnny that he had followed her for an hour and gave up trying to meet her.

He was with her from 11:30 to 12:30.

Johnny takes Tom to police headquarters where he gives his story to Tovitch and Carol identifies him. After Carol is released, she thanks Tom, and tells Johnny she will call Larry from her apartment. Carol gets a cab and Johnny notices another cab following hers with Tom in it.

Johnny goes to Carol's apartment and discovers Carol paying off Tom. Tom tells Johnny that he had seen someone going down the fire escape and followed him. When the story came out, Tom figured he could make some money on it, but only after Carol got out of jail.

Carol screams "Larry!" and Johnny turns, deflects the gun as Larry shoots and then Johnny slugs Larry. Carol tells Johnny that Larry had been gambling with Reed and losing. She went to see Reed to square the deal and Reed drugged her. Larry killed Reed while she was gone, slugged her when she came back and planted the gun on her. She was not sure until Tom told her what he had seen.

"Yeah, Larry Bowman's gambling was a big fat mistake. First with Everett Reed, and then trying to frame Carol. I guess that's the trouble with gambling, you push your luck too far, and sooner or later you are bound to lose."

Notes:
- Station KRMG in Tulsa, Oklahoma is saluted as the newest CBS station.
- *The Doting Dowager Matter* is announced as next week's story   see the notes above at *The Perilous Parley Matter.*
- The announcer is Dan Cubberly.

Producer:	Jack Johnstone	Writer:	Robert Stanley
Cast:	Virginia Gregg, Junius Matthews, Paul Dubov,		
	James McCallion, Alan Reed, Frank Gerstle		

◆ ❖ ◆

Show:	**The Love Shorn Matter**
Show Date:	1/18/1959
Company:	**Universal Adjustment Bureau**
Agent:	**Pat McCracken**
Exp. Acct:	**$377.00**

Synopsis: Pat McCracken calls Johnny and wants him to play a long-shot for the insurance companies that have become part of a racket.

Johnny goes to Pat's Hartford, Connecticut office where Pat reminds Johnny that insurance companies use the Universal Adjustment Bureau to process difficult claims. Pat reviews the case of Mrs. Dorothy Conrad Shaw who died in an accident when she lost control of her car. Her new husband was Jeremy Alcot Shaw. Pat reviews several other cases where the beneficiary had the initials J. A. S., the policy holder had a new husband and died in an accident.

Johnny calls a number of insurance companies and alerts them to beware of changes in policies to widows with new husbands, and to report those changes to Johnny. Johnny gets his telephone service to take any calls and then goes to Danbury, Connecticut to see an elderly woman.

She tells Johnny that Mrs. Conrad lived there until she got married to a young man around fifty. Johnny is shown a photo of Mr. Shaw and learns that Mrs. Conrad placed a lonely-hearts ad that read "Charming middle-aged wealthy family. Would like to meet younger man". Before Mrs. Conrad got married, her insurance was to go to a charity, but she changed it before she was married.

Johnny takes the photo and visits the cities of the cases Pat had reviewed with him. Johnny learns that all of the women ran personal ads. Johnny calls Pat and arranges for the photo of Shaw to be mailed to companies all over the country. Johnny checks his messages but has no leads.

Johnny gets a call from Sam Nelson at Masters Insurance who tells Johnny that he got the photo, and one of his policy holders asked to change her policy, her prospective husband is the man, Jason Arthur Sharpless!

Johnny goes to the address and meets Dora Merrill and tells her about the aliases when Sharpless drives up. Sharpless comes in and Johnny tells him that he answered the personal ad and is after Mrs. Merrill's money. Sharpless pulls a gun and when Dora comes in to tell him that she had heard what was said, Johnny slugs him.

The courts will take care of this matter.

Notes:
- The announcer is Dan Cubberly.
- This is the first program where Johnny makes a reference to a call service.
- Story information obtained from the KNX Collection in the Thousand Oaks Library.

Producer:	Jack Johnstone Writer: Jack Johnstone
Cast:	Lawrence Dobkin, Frank Nelson, D. J. Thompson, Jeanne Tatum, Shirley Mitchell, Forrest Lewis, Virginia Gregg, Marvin Miller

♦ ❖ ♦

Show:	**The Doting Dowager Matter**
Show Date:	1/25/1959
Company:	**Floyds of England**
Agent:	**George Reed**
Exp. Acct:	**$17.80**

Synopsis: George Reed calls Johnny and tells him things are really good at Floyds. But George has a problem though with a small statuette owned by Dora Harkness Balin, a very wealthy but very eccentric woman. The statuette has disappeared. It is only insured for $26.50, but Miss Balin carries hundreds of thousands in other forms of insurance. George tells Johnny that the owner has placed particular value to the statuette. George is afraid she will take her insurance elsewhere, so Johnny tells him he will be in touch.

Johnny travels to New York City and goes to the Balin residence, an old Brownstone. Inside, the house is full of Victorian era furniture and art works.

Higgins the butler takes Johnny to the Library where Hal Winters, the nephew asks Higgins about the mail, and Higgins goes to check on it.

Hal tells Johnny that his aunt likes the pot-metal statue because it looks like her grandfather, because he was the only Balin who did anything on his own. Hall suddenly recognizes who Johnny is, and gets nervous and tells Johnny to forget the case. Johnny asks Hal about the statue, the servants, guests, etc., but gets no information.

Miss Dora Balin comes in and tells Johnny that he had better recover the statue, or she will cancel all of her insurance. Dora asks if the mail has come and Hal tells her that he was going out to check on it but is told to let Higgins do it. Hal wants to leave but is told to sit down.

Dora tells him he was going to call that girl, that Nancy Gavin, who is trying to take him away from her. Dora likes Nancy but will not let her take Hal from her. Johnny is told to leave no stone unturned just as Higgins comes back in with the mail. There is a letter with no postmark, addressed to Dora. The letter is a ransom note for the statue, and the thieves want $75,000.

Everyone is surprised at the ransom. Dora accuses Hal of thinking that the ransom would mean less for him to inherit. Dora is prepared to pay the ransom and has the money in the safe. The note tells her to give the money to Hal, who will be contacted. If the police are brought in, the statue will be destroyed. Dora tells everyone to stay in the house except for Harold who will do what the kidnappers tell him. Johnny is told to do as he is told.

Nancy Gavin arrives and gives Hal a big kiss. Johnny is introduced, and Nancy also knows who Johnny is. Nancy is told of the ransom, and glibly tells Dora to pay it. Nancy asks Dora when she will let Hal marry her and get out on his own. Dora tells Nancy that her precious Harold would not do that.

Johnny asks Hal what he would do and is told to stay out of the matter. Johnny tells Dora that he is on the right track and asks Hal again if he would leave. Johnny is sure Hal's answer will solve the case, but he is dead wrong.

Hal tells Johnny that he would leave his aunt if he could, and Nancy concurs. Dora tells Nancy that Hal needs her, but Nancy tells Dora that Hal needs a break and the chance to show what he can do. Hal tells Dora that he would leave if he could, and that Dora did not know that because Dora only cared for herself.

Johnny is sure that he knows where to look for the statue as Hal and Nancy leave. Dora tells Johnny that she had not called the insurance company, Higgins had called.

Johnny tells her that the note was poorly written and probably came from within the house. Dora tells Johnny that she had hoped that Hal would make a move to break from her, but it would have to be on his initiative. She tells Johnny that the cheap statue was chosen for the experiment. She pumped up the value of the statue so that Harold would think she would do anything to get it back. He finally got up the nerve to do something, and she is tickled pink that he did.

Johnny tells her that she is happy that she has made a thief of Harold. She tells Johnny that in the instruction note she will write she will tell Harold that she hopes he and Nancy will be happy and will even throw in a few extra thousand dollars as an extra wedding present. Also, she does not want Harold to bring that monstrosity back here! Harold comes back in and asks if Johnny has determined how he will proceed. Johnny tells Hal he is going to give up the case and leaves.

Johnny tells Dora to call the insurance company about the extra fee he is to get on the case, and she tells Johnny that she already has. As Johnny leaves Hal shows him the instruction note and asks if it is OK. Johnny realizes that Hal knew what was going on.

Hal tells Johnny that Dora was just being her eccentric self and could not just tell Harold and Nancy to get married, that would ruin her reputation. Hal offers to send Johnny the statuette when this is all over.

"Believe me, I have handled some pretty wacky cases over the years, but this was by long odds the wackiest. And yet, why complain, when it's a good living."

Notes:
- Johnny bemoans the lowly $17.80 on the expense account but does not mention the generous fee he will get.
- The next program is about the personals column in newspapers, which is *The Love Shorn Matter*   see the notes above at *The Perilous Parley Matter*.
- The announcer is Dan Cubberly.

Producer:	Jack Johnstone	Writer:	Jack Johnstone
Cast:	Virginia Gregg, Eleanor Audley, G. Stanley Jones, Eric Snowden, Sam Edwards		

◆ ❖ ◆

Show:	**The Curley Waters Matter**
Show Date:	2/1/1959
Company:	**Masters Insurance & Trust Company**
Agent:	
Exp. Acct:	**$0.00**

Synopsis: Curley Waters calls Johnny and tells him that he has busted out of prison and will come and get Johnny.

Johnny wonders if the call really was from Curley Waters, who Johnny had nabbed for the Mailey's Department Store job when Johnny found him asleep, but without the $84,000.

Johnny gets a paper and sees the story about Curley escaping. Johnny goes back to his Hartford, Connecticut apartment to make a phone call, and Curley tells Johnny to drop his gun. Curley empties the gun and gives it back to Johnny and tells Johnny that he came in the rear window.

Curley shows Johnny a priest's outfit and tells Johnny that he is going to help Curley get the $84,000, or he will die. Johnny tells Curley that he has a date with Betty Lewis and Al Matthews, but Curley shows Johnny a .257

Roberts Winchester Model 70 rifle with a 4X scope.

He is going to change clothes and drive to Myrtle's Steak House where Johnny is to go in with a note for Gimpy Taylor, Myrtle's husband. The note will be an order for 1 dozen hamburger rolls, 3 cartons of coffee and a broken thermos that has the money in it. Curley warns Johnny that he will be watching and will shoot Johnny if he does not cooperate.

Curley changes clothes and calls Gimpy to inform him of the plan. They drive to Myrtle's and Johnny goes in and sees a policeman sitting at the counter. Johnny gets the order and goes to the car and returns to his apartment with Curley, who tells Johnny that he is going to dye his hair, when the phone rings.

Johnny answers and tells Betty that he must cancel their dinner plans and asks her to apologize to Al and Bernice Matthews. Curley bleaches his hair and is ready to shoot Johnny when the police bust in and Curley is shot.

Betty rushes in and Johnny tells her that he is glad that she caught the clue, Mrs. Matthews is Marry Ann, not Bernice.

Curley Waters is behind bars, and there is no expense account, but what about a fancy fee on this one?

Notes:
- The announcer is Dan Cubberly.
- Story information obtained from the KNX Collection in the Thousand Oaks Library.

Producer:	Jack Johnstone Writer: Jack Johnstone
Cast:	James McCallion, Forrest Lewis, Lucille Meredith, Tom Hanley, Bill James, Bert Holland

♦ ❖ ♦

Show:	The Date with Death Matter
Show Date:	2/8/1959
Company:	Masters Insurance & Trust Company
Agent:	Bert Wells
Exp. Acct:	$47.00

Synopsis: Johnny dials a number on a phone and hangs up only to have the phone ring with Betty Lewis on the extension phone. Johnny explains to her how to check the extension by calling the number and hanging up. The phone rings again and reluctantly Johnny answers. Burton Wells has to see him in the office. Burt tells him that unless Johnny gets to the office, he will have a date with death.

Johnny leaves Betty with instructions not to leave and goes to Burt's Hartford, Connecticut office. Burt tells Johnny that the problem is Curley Waters. Johnny recounts how Betty Lewis should get credit for catching Curley after he escaped.

Burt tells Johnny that Curley was wounded but has escaped from the hospital. Lt. Howie Daily arrives and tells Johnny that with the help of Gimpy Taylor, Curley Waters has escaped from the hospital, even with three good men watching him. Lt. Daily tells Johnny that he is having a bodyguard assigned to him until

Curley is picked up. When Burt mentions Betty, Johnny calls Betty's apartment but gets no answer.

Johnny and Lt. Daily drive to the apartment, going up a one-way street the wrong way in the process, and climb the stairs to the apartment. The door to Betty's apartment is open and Johnny searches the apartment to find it empty. The apartment is searched and no trace is found except for a coat hanger on the floor where a coat was taken.

The phone rings, Johnny answers and officer Riley wants to talk to Lt. Daily, who is told that Gimpy Taylor has been caught. He plowed his car into a tree and survived. The police know that two men stole the car, but Betty was not in the car.

Johnny thinks that Curley is still in town and using Betty to get to Johnny. Betty comes into her apartment and tells Johnny that she got a call from the hospital telling her that Johnny had been shot by Curley Waters. Johnny tells Lt. Daily that Curley is smart and only Johnny can bring Curley into the open. Johnny is going to go to his apartment and wait.

Johnny goes to his apartment and waits. At 12:30 there is a knock at the door and Lt. Daily is there, he is just checking up and tells Johnny that he is taking too much of a chance. Daily leaves and Johnny brews a pot of coffee. There is a knock at the back door and Johnny hears Betty there. Johnny lets her in and she tells Johnny that she was worried and had to come and see Johnny.

There is a knock at the front door, so Johnny sends Betty to the bedroom and a voice tells Johnny that it is "Howie". Johnny opens the door to find Curley Waters there. Johnny is forced to drop his gun and Curley tells Johnny he has been waiting in an empty apartment across the hall.

Curley is sure there are no cops in the area, and Gimpy Taylor's wife is spotting for him, and will call if the cops show up. She will shoot into the alley to distract the police. The phone rings and Myrtle Taylor tells Curley that Johnny is not alone. The woman tells Curley to shoot if the bedroom door opens.

Curley goes into the bedroom, the door bursts open, Curley shoots, and Johnny slugs Curley with the phone. Johnny thanks Betty for remembering how to make the phones ring. Betty makes Johnny hold her when Johnny shows her where a bullet had nicked her arm.

"Yeah, Curley is back in the clink, and this time to stay. When the necessary papers were signed, I hauled him over to the state pen myself. So, expense account total, including transportation $47.00 even. Betty? Betty Lewis? Well, I tell you this: if I were the marrying kind, believe me..."

Notes:
- There are two versions of this AFRTS program. One version has the AFRTS stories edited out. The other version has an episode of "The Bellweathers", a story about Thaddeus Lowe and an organ serenade at the end.
- The announcer is Dan Cubberly.

| Producer: | Jack Johnstone | Writer: | Jack Johnstone |
| Cast: | Lucille Meredith, James McCallion, Russ Thorson, Sam Edwards, Herb Vigran | | |

♦ ❖ ♦

Show: The Shankar Diamond Matter
Show Date: 2/15/1959
Company: Providential Life & Casualty Insurance Company
Agent: Steve Kilmer
Exp. Acct: $50.00

Synopsis: Steve Kilmer calls and asks if Johnny would like to attend a wedding. Johnny says sure, as long as it is not his. Steve tells Johnny that he knows what Johnny means. Steve would be a bachelor too if it were not for a wife, four kids and a couple of grandchildren. Steve asks if Johnny remembers Martha Mayfield Merryman in New York City. Johnny reminds Steve of how he helped clear up a report of her death in 1957. Steve tells Johnny that her son Edgar is getting married, and she insists that Johnny be there. Johnny agrees to take the case.

Johnny travels to New York City and the Merryman brownstone on Sutton Place. Martha tells Johnny that her sprout is finally getting hitched, so what about you Johnny? Johnny politely turns her down, but Martha says she will wait, unless Betty Lewis is making time behind her back.

She tells Johnny that she heard the broadcast about the Curly Waters case. Martha tells Johnny that she has a lead because she has already proposed to Johnny, and if she were a couple years younger she would run Johnny ragged. Johnny reminds her of a night on the town after the last case. Martha calls Larkin the butler to get them a drink and accuses him of snooping in the hallway. Larkin is told to open the safe and bring her the ring. Johnny is amazed that Larkin has the combination to the safe. Martha tells him that there is not much in the safe.

The ring is the Shankar Diamond, which is worth a million and is supposed to bring good luck. Edgar is going to marry Mary Luann Melanie Beaufort Exumy Culpepper, and maybe it will bring them luck. Martha tells Johnny that he is going to escort her to the wedding in Greensboro, North Carolina. They will take a company plane together after Johnny goes home to get the proper clothes for a wedding. She is sure someone will try to take the diamond. Larkin brings in the Shankar diamond, all 34 carats of it, and Johnny feels that someone wants that stone bad, and might even kill for it.

Johnny goes home for his clothes and then back to Martha's, where the chauffeur takes them to the airport and flies them to North Carolina with the Shankar diamond in Johnny's pocket. Johnny accuses Martha of not leveling with him.

She tells Johnny that she feels her chauffeur Eric Chatterley took the job to get close to her. Eric is a distant relation of Larkin the butler. Larkin is retiring soon and did not know much about Eric. Martha has discovered that Eric's father is still serving time in England for jewel theft. Johnny remembers reading about him and his unsuccessful three-year plan to get to the crown jewels. She had found Eric alone in the study once and thinks that he was casing the safe. Johnny tells Martha that no one is to know that Johnny is carrying the diamond.

At the Culpepper mansion, the place is crowded and Johnny wonders if some of the guests might have designs on the diamond. Johnny is surprised when the local police hire Eric as a special guard. The wedding takes place without a hitch and the reception starts at 8:00 and Johnny dances with a number of lovely ladies. Johnny spots Eric outside a window and leaves Martha to investigate when the lights go out and Martha screams. Johnny gets back to Martha and the diamond is gone from her finger.

Martha is taken upstairs and examined by a doctor. Johnny has Eric taken into town by the police and investigates the window to find a fuse box which was used to turn out the lights.

Johnny drives to police headquarters and is told that Eric does not have the diamond and is going to be released. Johnny asks where the nearest hospital is and an x-ray of Eric Chatterley's torso shows the diamond in his stomach without the mounting. But Johnny tells the police that the stone is not the Shankar diamond.

Erick admits taking the stone, but Johnny tells him that it was an imitation. Eric tells Johnny that he was told Martha had the real stone when he wrote him to come over and apply for the job, then Eric clams up.

Back at the mansion, Martha tells Johnny that she is sure that Eric did not have the combination to the safe, and that she last wore the diamond last spring. Johnny and Martha fly back to New York and tell Larkin the butler about the theft.

Johnny goes to Larkin's room where he is packed for his trip to England. Johnny tells Larkin he will search all of his bags until he finds the diamond. Johnny tells Martha that she had forgotten that Larkin was also related to Chatterley and even gave Larkin the combination to the safe.

Johnny tells her that Larkin had an imitation made from strass, a highly leaded glass that looks like a diamond. Larkin conceived the plan to have his distant cousin Eric steal the fake diamond. If Eric were successful, he would settle with him later. If Eric were caught, Larkin would just leave. No matter what happened, Larkin would be clean.

Larkin agrees to give Johnny the diamond. Johnny tells him that the x-ray told Johnny that the diamond was fake as a real diamond is invisible to x-rays.

"So, the diamond is safe and sound, and Larkin and his dearly beloved cousin are in the clink. Martha was a bit upset about what Larkin had done, but she will get over it. Yeah, and I sure hope I get over this headache. That brawl she threw for me by way of a celebration was a dilly."

Notes:

- This is an AFRTS program that contains an episode of "The Bellweathers", a story about Herbert Hoover and the importance of freedom of the press.
- This story makes a reference to *The Golden Touch Matter*, broadcast on

2/17/1957. Mrs. Merryman was the main character.
- Strass is a brilliant paste, or fake jewelry, made out of lead glass and used to simulate various transparent gemstones. It is named after George Frederick Strass (1701-1773) who was born near Strasbourg, France.
- The announcer is Dan Cubberly.

Producer:	Jack Johnstone	Writer:	Jack Johnstone
Cast:	Lillian Buyeff, Jack Edwards, Barney Phillips, Forrest Lewis, Eric Snowden		

◆ ❖ ◆

Show:	The Blue Madonna Matter
Show Date:	2/22/1959
Company:	Floyds of England
Agent:	George Reed
Exp. Acct:	$620.00

Synopsis: George Reed calls, and Johnny is glad to talk to him, because of the fees he gets from Floyds. George tells Johnny that he just got a transatlantic call for Johnny from a man in France that only identified his self as "Les Chat Gris". Johnny tells George that he knows him and his real name is Louis De Marsac, and that De Marsac knows more about the dark side of Paris than anyone else. George tells Johnny that De Marsac mentioned the Blue Madonna by Bardot. Kingsley Holland, who lives in Philadelphia, owns the paining which hangs in the Gavin gallery, and is insured for $12,000. De Marsac has some interesting news about the painting. Johnny tells George that he should be willing to pay Johnny's expenses and pay him a big fat fee. Johnny is willing to bet 10 to 1 that the painting in the gallery is a fake.

Johnny calls De Marsac in Paris to talk about the painting. De Marsac wants $1000 but Johnny offers $50. De Marsac counters with $900 and Johnny with $75, then $750 and $100, $500 and $200 then $400 and $300 and finally De Marsac offers $200 which Johnny accepts. Fooled again!

De Marsac tells Johnny that the Blue Madonna is now in the shop of Duboisson, who is an evil crook, but an honest one. He is going to wait until the real Madonna is found missing before he raises his price.

Johnny calls his old friend Foster Harmond in Florida and arranges for him to go to Philadelphia and meet Johnny at the Belleview Stratford hotel. Johnny travels to Philadelphia and dines with Foster. Johnny arranges to go to the Gavin Gallery in the morning and look at the painting.

Johnny cabs to Kingsley Holland's apartment and Holland asks if Johnny wants to buy the painting. Holland offers Johnny the painting directly for $12,000 to save the commission to the gallery. Holland wants to go back to Paris and would be there except he has run out of money. Holland tells Johnny that his uncle had left him the painting and tells Johnny that the people in the gallery are crooks, but the Blue Madonna is real. Johnny thinks that Holland has recognized his name.

Next day Johnny and Foster go to the gallery and meet Mr. Gavin, who tells them that the price for the painting is $20,000. Johnny convinces Foster to leave and outside Foster tells Johnny that the painting is a fake. A man on the sidewalk asks Foster if the painting really is a fake. The man is a Rup Alloway, a reporter who also knows who Johnny is.

Foster tells Johnny that the copy is exactly the style of Bardot. Johnny tells Foster that Holland knows who Johnny is, and what he is doing. Johnny wonders if a switch was made before or after the painting was put in the gallery. Johnny tells Foster that both Holland and Gavin know what hotel Johnny is in, so he is going to go and wait to see who shows up.

Johnny sends Foster back to Florida and calls Sgt. Jerry Hawkins at police headquarters. Later Sgt. Hawkins calls Johnny back and tells Johnny that Holland is a lazy kid trying to live off of his parents, and that Gavin seems to be OK. Also, the story of the fake painting has hit all the wire services and papers. Johnny has an idea what has happened, and is going to play a hunch, and tells Sgt. Hawkins to read tomorrow's paper.

In the evening paper, Johnny sees that the prices for Bardot paintings are going through the roof. After Johnny places a call for De Marsac, Mr. Gavin comes to Johnny's room and is very angry because the police have closed his shop. He has had offers for all his Bardot paintings, and has wired Bardot to paint more.

Holland bursts in an accuses Gavin of starting the whole thing, but Gavin says he did not know that the painting was a fake until this morning. Holland tells Johnny that his grandfather had smuggled the painting into the country.

De Marsac calls Johnny back, and Johnny will have to pay him a vast sum of money, but Johnny tells him that he was going to tell Johnny that Bardot himself smuggled the painting into Paris. "How did you know?" De Marsac asks disappointedly.

Johnny offers De Marsac $200 to learn that Bardot is on his way to Philadelphia with the real Madonna. Johnny calls Sgt. Hawkins to have his boys pick up Bardot at the airport. Johnny is sure that Bardot has painted two of the Madonnas for the publicity, and anything he paints now will only make him a fortune. Johnny tells both Gavin and Holland that they will both benefit, and Johnny wonders if "Les Chat Gris" was in on this from the beginning?

"Sure, sure he was in with Bardot. And probably collecting plenty from him. Anyhow, the insurance company is not out anything. But I hope they will be a lot more careful the next time they insure a painting, any so-called original."

Notes:
- There are two AFRTS versions of this program. One version has the AFTRS stories edited out. The other contains an episode of "The Bellweathers", and a story about Noah Webster.
- The announcer is Dan Cubberly.

Producer: Jack Johnstone Writer: Jack Johnstone
Cast: G. Stanley Jones, Forrest Lewis, Harry Bartell, Joseph

Kearns, Bert Holland, Byron Kane

Show:	**The Clouded Crystal Matter**
Show Date:	3/1/1959
Company:	Tri-State Life & Casualty Company
Agent:	Earle Poorman
Exp. Acct:	$168.50

Synopsis: Earle Poorman calls Johnny from Sarasota, Florida and tells him that he has received a lot of claims for stolen property that were cancelled when the goods were found. Earle wonders if this some sort of racket, so come on down.

Johnny flies to Sarasota, Florida where Earle meets him at the airport. Johnny is told that he has a date with Miss Betty Charlene Churchill, and that he will also see Dolly Mae Winston, Edith Ann Devere and Linda Carol Keene, all of whom have placed claims that were cancelled. The losses range from $7 to $150 and were for wristwatches, handbags and rings, and all of the women know one another.

Johnny goes to Earle's office and meets Mrs. Valerie Hatch Kenworthy Froelich Tinsdale Dawson, who tells Johnny that she had a compact stolen from her car. She tells Johnny that Edith had her purse stolen from her home, and he told them where to find the items.

He is Shanu Yarba, a swami who uses his crystal ball to locate the stolen items. Johnny is told that Yarba lives behind a hardware store, but Valerie does not want Johnny to tell him that she told Johnny about the swami.

Johnny visits the other women and gets an idea that will use Mike Poorman as bait. Johnny wants Earle to stay with a neighbor while Mike poses as a wealthy widow who will go to the swami to ask his advice on investments.

Mike goes to the swami posing as Gertrude Mary Anastasia Conroy and then goes to the beauty parlor where her purse is stolen. Johnny watches the shop, and only sees another woman leave.

Mike goes to see the swami and notices that his suitcases are packed. The swami tells Mike where to look for the purse and invites the others to a séance. Johnny watches the store while Mike is with the swami.

Mike is told that the crystal ball senses some psychometric paramagnetic radiation and he invites Mike to a séance.

Johnny is at Mike's home when the swami opens the front door and does something. A woman named Dora comes to the house and tells the swami not to go in because Johnny Dollar is there.

Johnny comes out of the house and slugs the swami and Dora, his wife. Johnny relates that Dora Duggin was a pickpocket and a thief who used wax impressions of the house keys to get into their pigeon's homes.

Notes:
- The announcer is Dan Cubberly.
- Story information obtained from the KNX Collection in the Thousand

Oaks Library.

Producer:	Jack Johnstone Writer: Jack Johnstone
Cast:	Vic Perrin, Paula Winslowe, Peggy Webber, Shirley Mitchell, Don Diamond

♦ ❖ ♦

Show:	**The Net of Circumstance Matter**
Show Date:	3/8/1959
Company:	**Tri-State Life & Casualty Company**
Agent:	**Earle Poorman**
Exp. Acct:	**$151.50**

Synopsis: Earle Poorman calls Johnny, and he tells Earle that he just left him. Earle tells Johnny to bring his expense report with him. Earle tells Johnny that after Johnny had gone, Earle got a call from Bill Hall, who runs a men's clothing store called Webb's. Earle has insured both the clothes and the night watchman, and the police think the watchman was murdered. Johnny will catch the first plane.

Johnny flies to Tampa, Florida and is met by Earle. They drive straight to Bill Hall's store where Bill is trying to clean up. Bill estimates that over $9,000 in clothing and accessories have been stolen. They think that the watchman, Jimson Cooley may be dead, as there was sign of a struggle out back.

Bill tells them that more than one person was involved because the robbery happened between the regular police patrols. Also, three men had robbed the store last year. Two of the robbers were identified, and that is when Jimson was hired as night watchman. Johnny wonders about the third man. Bill tells Johnny that Jimson was an old man, and he had given him the job to help him out. Jimson used to run a shrimp boat but is too old for that now.

Sgt. Drummond arrives and tells them that they have new clues about the robbery. A drunk was picked up last night who remembers seeing something at around 2 or 3 a.m. The drunk saw a car come out from behind the building that he recognized, a pickup truck that was loaded down with something under a net. It was a 1930 model truck belonging to Jimson Cooley.

Everything seemed to point to murder until the truck belonging to Cooley was seen. All the police in the area have been notified, but Jimson's house has not been searched yet. Johnny goes out back of the store and gets a sample of cloth and goes to visit some friends.

First Johnny goes to see Doc Crutcher and gives Doc the cloth to examine. Johnny and Earle then go to see the Cooley home, a real broken-down shack surrounded with chickens. Mrs. Cooley wants to know if they have found Jim yet, and is anxious to get the insurance he has. He was a lazy bum and it was her chickens that made any money.

She saw a missing net and thought Jim was out shrimping or had sold it for booze. She thinks that the gang that robbed Hall's store did it, as Jim had seen one of the members around town lately.

Johnny asks Mrs. Cooley to sell him a chicken, and he gives her a dollar for it, and only takes the head. Back at the Doc's Johnny gives him the chicken head to use as a comparison.

Sgt. Drummond calls Johnny to tell him that Jimson Cooley has been found and is OK. He told them that a man made him open the store beat him and left him in the woods.

Johnny goes to headquarters and talks to Cooley, who is a disagreeable sort who had some cuts and bruises. Johnny goes to see Doc Crutcher who tells Johnny that the blood behind the store was not chicken blood. Doc discovered that there was human blood on the cloth, but not Cooley's. Johnny thinks that there was a fight, but Jimson did not lose the fight.

Johnny thinks that Cooley was helping the man who robbed the store and now they need to find the other man's body. Johnny suggests that he and Earle go fishing, to let their minds clear.

Earle takes his boat out to Humpback Bridge and City Island and Johnny starts to troll. Johnny has Earle troll very slowly in the area where Jimson used to run his shrimp boat. Finally, Johnny snags something and pulls up a net with a body in it.

"When Jimson was faced with the man's body wrapped in the net he had sunk, out there in the bay, he broke down and told us what had really happened. Even told us where the stolen stuff was hidden. Yeah, the dead man was one of the gang who had robbed the store a year ago. He persuaded Jimson to help him do it again and offered him a hundred bucks. But when he had the stuff, he tried to run out without paying off, so Jimson had killed him. Now the courts will have to take over. Incidentally, I understand that Webb's is installing a foolproof burglar alarm system."

Notes:
- There are two versions of this AFRTS program. One contains an episode of "The Bellweathers", and a story about Daniel Webster and the value of freedom and protective laws. The other version has these stories edited out.
- The story mentions radio station WSPD.
- The announcer is Dan Cubberly.

Producer: Jack Johnstone Writer: Jack Johnstone
Cast: Lillian Buyeff, Vic Perrin, Harry Bartell, Barney Phillips, Bartlett Robinson, Bill James

♦ ❖ ♦

Show: The Baldero Matter
Show Date: 3/15/1959
Company: Western Maritime & Property Insurance Company
Agent: Arthur Arthur
Exp. Acct: $0.00

Synopsis: Johnny receives a call from Pat McCracken while he is in Sarasota. Pat wants Johnny to go to the West Coast and See Arthur Arthur in Beverly

Hills. Piracy is the problem. Piracy? Johnny does not believe it but will go investigate.

Earle drives Johnny to the airport for his flight to Los Angeles, California and Earle tries to convince Johnny that piracy is still an issue.

In Los Angeles, Johnny cabs to the Beverly Hilton and then goes to see Arthur Arthur. Arthur tells Johnny that Mr. Balderston was cruising around near Mexico on his yacht the Baldero, which is over 100 feet long. The boat is kept in Balboa. The guests on the boat included Mrs. Balderston, Mr. and Mrs. Hooper, Richard Spidal and Lee Willway. They were going to cruise up to San Francisco for a charity ball, which is why they all had their finest clothes and jewels with them.

Arthur tells Johnny that $394,000 in jewelry was stolen, along with some other things, and that the robbery was reported by one of the guests. The pirates pulled up in the night, came on board with guns and took the jewels. Arthur is not sure where it happened, as Balderston was kind of vague.

Johnny rents a car and drives to the Balderston home. In the driveway, Johnny spots a sports car and a larger car with a man getting out. Mr. Balderston greets Johnny, recognizes who he is, and takes him in for a cocktail with Mrs. Balderston.

Balderston tells Johnny it took almost 12 hours to cruise back to Balboa. Johnny does not learn much other than the men came on board at night, held the passengers in their cabins and wore disguises. Only Lee Willway had seen the boat that was used. Balderston never did say exactly where it happened and Johnny grows more suspicious of Balderston.

Balderston is not sure where he was and was just killing time until he had to head for San Francisco. They did not take a position sighting because they were just going to follow the coast back to San Francisco. Lee said it was a long black speedboat. After the pirates left, they started the boat and motored back. They tried to call the Coast Guard, but the radio did not work. Johnny is sure that there is something funny about this case.

Johnny checks with the Hoopers, whose story matches Balderston's except they do not think it took 12 hours to get back to port.

Johnny goes to see Lee Willway, who is a real doll. Charles of the Ritz would have been proud of this one, but Johnny does not see her being on a cruise with the Balderstons. She tells Johnny that the she saw a long black boat and then went to the radio but it did not work. She had been at the radio earlier, but just to listen.

Lee tells Johnny that Richard Spidal could have stopped them, as his was the only cabin the pirates did not go into and there was a rifle right outside his door. Lee tells Johnny that the sports car he saw at the Balderston's belongs to Larry Balderston. After turning down an offer for more drinks and dinner with Lee, Johnny goes to see Richard Spidal. As Johnny gets out of his car another car rushes up, a man gets out and slugs Johnny.

Johnny recognizes the lights from his attacker's car as belonging to Larry Balderston. When Johnny wakes up, he is in his car with 5 $100-bills on the seat and a note which says "Take this money and get out of town. You have no case anyway, because the things that were stolen off the yacht have been returned. So, you may as well leave while you have your health."

Johnny goes in to see Richard Spidal, who gives Johnny a drink. Richard tells Johnny that the only reason Mrs. Balderston had brought Lee along (and Richard was to be her escort) was to shame the ladies at the charity ball. Lee is a beautiful, but a common person.

Mrs. Balderston hoped that by taking her to the charity ball, Lee would see that she had no place with them, and she would break off the romance with Lawrence Balderston. Larry probably found out and staged the piracy bit to keep the plan from being carried out, he was always doing crazy things like that.

When Richard heard the noise he just locked himself in his cabin. Richard thinks that Lee was in on it and was using the radio to guide Larry to the yacht.

Johnny goes to see Mr. Balderston and is told that the jewels have been returned. Johnny asks for Larry and goes to see him in the study.

In the study, Johnny slugs Larry while he is talking to Lee. Larry admits to Johnny that he rigged the whole thing because he was fed up with the way his mother was trying to run his life. But maybe she was right about Lee.

Larry tries to hit Johnny for hitting him, but Johnny gets the upper hand. Johnny apologizes to Mr. Balderston, but he tells Johnny that he had hoped someone would do that to Larry for a long time. He admits spoiling Larry but did not know he would go as far as he did.

"Fee on this case? Forget it. The $500 that Larry mistakenly tried to bribe me with, plus a nice fat check from Mr. Balderston, well much as the thought of it hurts me, let's forget the expense account too. Okay? Okay."

Notes:
- This program contains commercials for William Bendix for 4-Way Cold Tablets ($.29 and $.59), one for Fitch Dandruff remover shampoo, one for numbered Fram oil filters, one for Tums (rolls $.10 or 3 for $.25 or 6 roll pack for $.49), and one for Kentucky Club pipe tobacco and the Thoroughbred Derby contest.
- Lee Willway is the name of the script secretary.
- Bob Bailey offers belated congratulations to station WJLS in Beckley, West Virginia on its 20th anniversary.
- The announcer is Dan Cubberly.

Producer: Jack Johnstone Writer: Jack Johnstone
Cast: Virginia Gregg, Eleanor Audley, Vic Perrin, Howard McNear, Lawrence Dobkin, Will Wright, Carleton G. Young, Jack Edwards

Show:	The Lake Mead Mystery Matter
Show Date:	3/22/1959
Company:	Universal Adjustment Bureau
Agent:	Pat McCracken
Exp. Acct:	$196.45

Synopsis: Pat McCracken calls Johnny. "Greetings Master" is Johnny's reply. Pat gently asks about Johnny's trips to Sarasota, and the lack of fishing while he was there. Johnny tells Pat that he has been dreaming of Lake Mohave and its lunker bass. Pat asks what about Lake Mead just outside of Las Vegas? Pat wants Johnny to go fishing at Lake Mead for a slight case of murder. Johnny is told to contact Roscoe Trimmer in Las Vegas who has all the details on the $20,000 double indemnity policy.

Johnny cabs to the airport and travels to Las Vegas, Nevada. Johnny marvels at the night-time glow of Las Vegas. Johnny gets a room at the Flamingo and accidentally finds the casino. Johnny manages to win so much he will not expense the room and food.

Johnny meets Roscoe Trimmer the next morning and is told to take a rental car to Overton where a client, Thomas Mayfield Thomas came from Chicago and retired last year. A week ago, Thomas and a friend went out fishing with a local guide, Hob Fulton. They stayed over and went out the next day and were caught in a big east-wind. They did not get off the lake quick enough and Hob found their boat and the friend the next morning, but Thomas supposedly went overboard when the wind hit them.

Roscoe tells Johnny that the friend was Charlie Wentworth, who came from Chicago two weeks ago, and just hangs around the gambling joints, and supposedly is illegally making book. There is a lot of worry about people coming from Chicago, especially when they do not work and hang around the gambling joints. The police have looked for Thomas' body and they are not holding Wentworth. Roscoe thinks Johnny ought to investigate, and so does Johnny.

Johnny is suspicious of Charlie Wentworth. Johnny calls his friend Ken Bugby, a reporter in Chicago, to get information on Thomas and Wentworth. Ken tells Johnny that Thomas was a mouthpiece for the old Moretti mob. When they started the clean up some years ago, Thomas couldn't or wouldn't get them off the hook, and they all did time and Thomas retired to Elmhurst.

A year ago, he moved out west somewhere. Charlie Wentworth was a trigger-man, "Casual Charlie" they called him. Wentworth is in Joliet, no wait, Wentworth and Snooty Wilson were released about the same time Thomas moved.

Johnny goes to the library and looks up the Moretti mob. Johnny is sure that Charlie was getting even, but how to prove it without a corpus delicti.

Johnny rents some equipment from a sporting goods store and goes to Overton. Johnny arranges to meet Hob Fulton and goes out on the lake. Hob is sure Johnny does not need the stuff he has brought, but Johnny just wants Hob to take him to the same places where he took Thomas.

Hob tells Johnny that Thomas did not seem any too happy, and Charlie kept saying, "let bygones be bygones". Hob mentions that their tackle boxes got thrown over, even Charlie's which was really heavy.

At the Glory Hole (a tree and a half deep) Johnny starts to dive. Two hours later Johnny tries a hole by Goat Island that is five trees deep. Johnny dives, comes back up for a rope and pulls up the body of Thomas Mayfield Thomas with a bullet hole between the eyes.

Johnny takes the body to the Las Vegas police and learns that Thomas was shot with a .38. Johnny searches the gambling joints and finds Charlie Wentworth.

Johnny introduces himself and Charlie tells Johnny that he is really sorry about Thomas. Charlie asks Johnny to go up to his room where Johnny accuses Charlie of killing Thomas, but Charlie tells Johnny that he is through with crime and is clean. Johnny tells Charlie that he hated Thomas's guts and Charlie agrees, but he got over it.

Johnny asks Charlie why he killed Thomas, and Johnny is told that he cannot prove it. Johnny tells Charlie he as absolute proof, Johnny has Thomas's body with the bullet hole in it from Charlie's gun. Charlie pulls a gun and shoots, but Johnny nails him and takes his gun, the proof he needed.

"Down at headquarters, the ballistics team took less than an hour. Yup, the bullet they found in Thomas Thomas' body came from the same gun Charlie had tried to kill me with. So, it is back to prison for him for a long, long time. Oh, and the company will not have to pay double indemnity for accidental death."

Notes:
- This program contains commercials for Fitch Dandruff remover shampoo, Joan Bennett for 4-Way tablets, numbered Fram Oil Filters worth $1,000, a Pepsi commercial "Be sociable!", and the Rambler Ambassador compact luxury car.
- This program is from WRTW in Albany, and apparently was recorded on the air as it includes a station identification and a commercial for Old Gold cigarettes.
- The announcer is Dan Cubberly.

Producer: Jack Johnstone Writer: Jack Johnstone
Cast: Lawrence Dobkin, Bartlett Robinson, Frank Nelson, Harry Bartell, Gil Stratton Jr

❖

Show: **The Jimmy Carter Matter**
Show Date: 3/29/1959
Company: **Amalgamated Life Association**
Agent: **Waldo Bottomly**
Exp. Acct: **$117.00**

Synopsis: Jimmy Carter calls Johnny from East North Weldon, Massachusetts. Jimmy saved the money from his newspapers to make the call. Jimmy tells Johnny that he helped him solve the robbery case. Jimmy can help Johnny solve another case of murder.

Johnny recounts how he had gone to East North Weldon the previous fall to recover some money stolen from a furniture factory by the bald-headed mayor. Jimmy tells Johnny that he can help solve a murder. Jimmy saw someone throw Mr. Andrew Parkinson off of a bridge, but everyone thinks he just had an accident.

Jimmy's time runs out for the call before Johnny can get the name of the man Jimmy saw. Johnny calls the auto club for route information and then calls Pat McCracken and asks him to look up Andrew Parkinson's policy and find out who his company is, and Johnny will call him back.

Johnny buys gas and drives to Fitchburg and, after an argument with a highway policeman, Johnny calls Pat to get the name of the company, which Johnny learns does a lot of rural business. Waldo Bottomly issued the policy. The death was the day before yesterday and was called an accident. A claim has been filed by Lucius Weatherby the beneficiary.

Johnny drives on into North East Weldon and stops at the general store. Johnny asks a local man about where Jimmy Carter is, but he does not know where Jimmy is. Johnny is told that Jimmy lives on North Spruce Street, and Johnny asks the man to tell Jimmy that he is looking for him.

At the Carter house Johnny meets Jimmy's mother who wants to know where Jimmy is. She tells Johnny how Jimmy was agitated and had not gone to school or picked up his newspapers. She is sure that something has happened to Jimmy!

Jimmy is gone, disappeared, and his mother wants to know where he is. Johnny tells Jimmy's mother that he has not seen Jimmy. Mrs. Carter tells Johnny that Jimmy idolizes him and has been upset ever since Mr. Parkinson fell off the bridge. Johnny reassures her and goes out looking for Jimmy.

Johnny goes to the drugstore and talks with Waldo Bottomly, the proprietor, who has heard of Johnny. Waldo tells Johnny that he is also the coroner, and that the policy claim has been sent in. Waldo tells Johnny that Parkinson was an old man who had many problems and fell from the bridge. Bottomly tells Johnny that he saw Jimmy that morning when he made change for him.

Waldo tells Johnny that Lucius Weatherby, the town drunk might have seen Jimmy, as he usually sits on the front step by the phone booth. Waldo tells Johnny to take Lucius a bottle of medicinal brandy (that'll be $3.75 please) if he wants any information from Lucius, but Johnny prefers to the use the "pick him up by the lapels and yell" method. Lucius tells Johnny that Jimmy went off in a car, and Lucius could remember the name if he had a drink. Waldo comes out with the brandy and Johnny is forced to use it and pay Waldo for it.

Lucius gets a long drink and remembers Jimmy being forced into the car of Harvey Willman, who is not one of the more respectable people in town and was distantly related to Parkinson. Harvey lives on the old farm out on Winter Avenue.

Johnny drives to the farm and realizes he does not have his gun. In the front yard is a lot of new Allis Chalmers farm equipment. Johnny spots an old sedan outside as he bangs on the door.

Jimmy yells and Johnny breaks down the door. Once inside, Willman is behind Johnny with a gun, and Jimmy tells Johnny that he will kill them. Willman searches Johnny and fires once when Johnny uses jujitsu to throw him to the floor. Jimmy picks up the gun and starts to cry in fright as Johnny comforts him. Johnny tells Jimmy that he is a real hero for trapping the killer for Johnny.

"Item 6, $48.50 for a new sports jacket without holes in it. Yeah, Harvey Willman had managed to get off that one shot. Item 7, $67.00 for a brand-new bike for Jimmy. Why? Because he saved the company from having to pay double indemnity. Expense account total $177.00, unless you would like to tack on a little extra fee."

Notes:
- This program makes a reference to *The Two Faced Matter*, broadcast on 8/10/1958. This program also featured Jimmy Carter.
- This program contains commercials for this station being a CBS affiliate and the benefits thereof, a Fram oil filter commercial for their Silver anniversary, a Pepsi commercial, and a public service announcement for the new shorter form 1040-A for incomes below $10,000.
- The announcer is Dan Cubberly.

Producer:	Jack Johnstone	Writer:	Jack Johnstone
Cast:	Virginia Gregg, Richard Beals, Lawrence Dobkin, Forrest Lewis, Edgar Barrier, Jack Kruschen		

♦ ❖ ♦

Show:	The Frisco Fire Matter
Show Date:	4/5/1959
Company:	Greater Southwest Insurance Company
Agent:	
Exp. Acct:	$923.91

Synopsis: Smokey Sullivan calls Johnny at 5:00 a.m. He is living in Frisco now, and wants to know if Johnny has heard of the Barnwell warehouse fire that is still burning. Smokey knows who did it. Johnny tells Smokey that he will stay in the Huntington Hotel. That is too nice a place for Smokey, so he will call Johnny.

Johnny calls Pat McCracken to get some facts and figures. Pat calls Johnny back and confirms the fire at the warehouse of Peter H. Barnwell who has an office in town. The warehouse is insured for $340,000.

Johnny never gets an official OK, but flies to San Francisco on a jet flight on American. Johnny gets a paper at the airport and then goes to the Barnwell office. The receptionist is turning away all the reporters but Johnny gets in when he shows her his card. The other reports want to know what paper Johnny is with, and he tells them he is with the Bigsville Bugle near Bum Spung, Oklahoma.

Johnny goes into the office and meets Mr. Barnwell who is not upset at the loss. The building has been a loss for years, but he has kept up the insurance on it, so now he will be able to collect on it and be sitting pretty. The police have found no proof of arson, and neither will Johnny.

Johnny recounts how Smokey Sullivan had been an arsonist once but had gone straight after helping Johnny with a case several years ago. Johnny is sure that Barnwell had the fire set as he cabs to see Bill Mullen at the Arson Squad.

Bill is glad to see Johnny but tells him that a derelict named Stumpy Moran slept there on an old mattress, got drunk and set the place on fire with a cigarette. No more mattresses, no more warehouse, no more Stumpy. Bill is positive based on the evidence he has seen. Bill wants Johnny to call the papers and get them to get off of the police's back by telling them this was not arson.

Johnny leaves for his hotel and waits for Smokey to call. Smokey calls and tells Johnny that Stumpy was a friend of his. He knows Stumpy did not do it as Stumpy neither drank nor smoked. Johnny is told to go to the Hungry Angel Bar and go to a phone booth to meet Smokey. Smokey knows who did it, the only man who could do the job and not leave a trace, "Touchy" Thompson.

The police will not question Touchy because he has been straight. He lives in a nice house on Aldea drive, but he is not there because he has gone fishing. Smokey tells Johnny that he is the only one who knows what to look for and will show it to Johnny. There are shots, and the line goes dead.

Johnny goes to the phone booth to find the police going over it. Johnny is told that Smokey is in the hospital and will not live. The police tell Johnny that if the warehouse was arson, the only one who could have done it was Smokey, so good riddance. They have all the other firebugs nailed down so it had to be Smokey.

At the hospital, the doctor is amazed that Smokey will live, even though his heart was nicked. Johnny talks to Smokey who tells him that he did not talk to the cops. He did not see who shot him, but it must have been Touchy. Smokey tells Johnny that Touchy used special chemicals that did not leave a trace. You need a gas mask, and that is what killed Stumpy Moran. Johnny now has to find Touchy, and Smokey tells him to be careful.

Johnny cabs to Touchy's home, but no one is there. Johnny goes to see an old friend, Maury Webster at KCBS radio.

Johnny cabs to the studio and Maury tells Johnny all about their 50th anniversary celebration, they were the first radio station in the country and were proud of it.

Johnny asks Maury about their news broadcasts and Johnny scribbles a news item to read on the air. The news announcement is read "Dollar has proof that the fire was set by an old hand at that business, Smokey Sullivan, his reason, to kill another man named Moran, whose body was found buried in the embers. Incidentally, Sullivan himself has just died." Johnny tells Maury that he is going to stake out the house of Touchy Thompson.

Johnny goes to watch Touchy's house and waits for him to come home. When Touchy comes home, Johnny confronts him with the fire, but Touchy shows Johnny some trout he caught at Mono Lake. Johnny knows that trout cannot live in Mono Lake because of mineral deposits.

Touchy gets nervous when Johnny mentions the use of special chemicals and Barnwell walks in and tells Touchy that maybe Johnny does have proof. Barnwell tells Touchy that he fell for the fake news story, and thanks Johnny for setting the stage for him. Barnwell tells Johnny he came here because he suspects Touchy, and the police will find that they have killed each other.

As Barnwell starts to shoot, Bill Mullen breaks in with reinforcements. Johnny asks what caused Bill to come here, and Bill tells Johnny that Smokey Sullivan called him from the hospital because he was worried about Johnny. Do you mind? No, not a bit!

"Yeah, they were both in it up to their ears. Each, in trying to defend himself just put the other in that much deeper. By the time the courts get through with the two of them they will be sorry they ever lived."

Notes:
- This program is a four-act program format that includes commercials for Fram oil filter and their Silver anniversary, a Pepsi commercial, a Rambler commercial and a Lysol commercial.
- J. David Goldin notes that KCBS went on the air in 1909. While doing some internet research on this matter, it appears that, while KCBS did go "on the air" in 1909, the subject of the "first" radio station is one that is open to debate.
- The announcer is Dan Cubberly.

Producer: Jack Johnstone Writer: Jack Johnstone
Cast: Virginia Gregg, Gil Stratton Jr, Tony Barrett, Vic Perrin, Lawrence Dobkin, Alan Reed, Paul Dubov, Bartlett Robinson, Donald Mosley

♦ ❖ ♦

Show: The Fairweather Friend Matter
Show Date: 4/12/1959
Company: Floyds of England
Agent: George Reed
Exp. Acct: $203.50

Synopsis: Sidewinder Wilson calls Johnny from Bum Spung. He is a friend of Durango Laramie Dalhart. If Johnny should happen to come out to Bum Spung, Sidewinder can show something that will make Johnny's eyes pop out of his head. Come on out and I will tell you when you get here.

Johnny cabs to George Reed's office and tells George Reed about the call from Sidewinder Wilson. George tells Johnny that Durango was there a few days ago to pay the $4,500 premium for Carol Dalhart's policy in fresh $100 bills. George tells Johnny about a robbery-murder case near Enid. A messenger was killed and the securities were returned. Johnny gets George to pay his expenses (within reason) as he runs out the door.

Johnny flies to Enid and rents a car to drive to Bum Spung, Oklahoma and the weather-beaten old farm. Johnny sees an ancient Maxwell parked beside the house as Sidewinder shoots a welcome at Johnny.

Sidewinder tells Johnny that Durango went to Hartford to pay his insurance, and then to Washington to pay his taxes. Sidewinder tells Johnny that he called about the securities robbery. Johnny guesses that if Sidewinder thinks he can find out who returned the securities, he will have a lead on who killed the messenger. Sidewinder knows who sent the securities back, "it was me" he tells Johnny.

Sidewinder takes Johnny inside to tell him all about the robbery. Sidewinder tells Johnny that he returned the securities and then tells Johnny to stay still, as a sidewinder approaches Johnny. Sidewinder shoots the snake and takes the rattles for his collection. That snake is #425.

Sidewinder tells Johnny that the man who killed the messenger was the "ben-u-fici-ary" of his insurance policy. Sidewinder knew that because he lived in Fairweather with him. He knew that Claude Needles left his insurance to his no-good nephew Barney Gifford.

Sidewinder talked it over with Carol and Durango (you're kinda sweet on her aren't you) and if Durango finds out you have been here and not married Carol he is going to shotgun you into it! Carol rushes in and gives Johnny a great big kiss or rather a bunch of kisses. Sidewinder gets real antsy about Johnny and Carol smooching and threatens to call Durango. Carol is really ready to marry up with Johnny this time.

Carol tells Johnny that Sidewinder wanted to be a deputy in Fairweather when Claude Needles was killed, so he could hunt for the killer. The police said no, they did not need him. Sidewinder was sore so they all talked about who could have done it. And that is when Sidewinder remembered that Barney would get the money.

Carol arranged a date with Barney so Sidewinder could search his house. Sidewinder found the securities and tied up Barney and put him in a shed and had Old Pete watch him. That is when Durango told Sidewinder to call Johnny and get him out here to see Carol. The phone rings and Sidewinder tells Johnny that Barney has gotten loose, beaten old Pete and is coming there to kill Sidewinder.

Johnny realizes that Sidewinder is scared of Barney, so Johnny suggests that they leave. Johnny sends Carol to go get the police, but she will not leave.

Barney bursts in the front door with a rifle. Barney tells them to go outside so he can kill them. Barney searches them and takes Johnny's gun. Johnny asks sidewinder if this is retribution for the killing he did earlier today. Suddenly there is the sound of a rattlesnake and Johnny slugs Barney. Johnny thanks Sidewinder for using his rattles.

"You know, I really hated to leave that place, to leave Carol is what I really mean. But there was another phone call and Sidewinder answered it. Yup, it was from Durango, phoning from Enid. Durango was so tickled to learn I was still around he promised to come to the ranch as soon as he could." 'As soon as he can pick up the preacher' Sidewinder adds." "Well, much as I love that gal…"

Notes:
- This program contains a commercial for CBS and its popularity in a recent poll of radio programs, a commercial about polio shots and the need to take them, a commercial for Pepsi and a commercial for Lysol.
- The announcer is Dan Cubberly.

Producer: Jack Johnstone   Writer: Jack Johnstone
Cast: Virginia Gregg, Junius Matthews, G. Stanley Jones, James McCallion, Bill James

◆ ❖ ◆

Show: **The Cautious Celibate Matter**
Show Date: **4/19/1959**
Company: **Floyds of England**
Agent: **George Reed**
Exp. Acct: **$1,053.45**

Synopsis: George Reed calls Johnny and he is calling about something that might not even need an expense account. "Come on over to my office Johnny, and take your time."

Johnny cabs to George's office and is told to go right in. Johnny tells George that he rushed right over because George said not to rush. George seems to fumble over lighting Johnny's cigarette and tells Johnny that he got back from Bum Spung much earlier than expected. "Now what does Bum Spung mean?" George asks.

George notes that Durango would like to have Johnny marry his niece, Carol Dalhart. That Johnny tells him, is why he left as soon as he could when he heard that Durango was on his way back with a preacher. Johnny tells George that he is a confirmed celibate. He really likes Carol, and George asks Johnny why he does not marry Carol. Johnny tells George that he is not ready to marry right now.

George tells Johnny that marrying Carol would help his client relationship with Durango. Durango has asked George to get Johnny into the office and keep him there. Durango comes in the office and Johnny goes out the fire escape trying to out run Durango's bullets.

Johnny really runs down the fire escape and grabs a taxi to his apartment. Durango being in Hartford means only one thing, Durango is still obsessed with Johnny marrying Carol. Johnny packs his bags and calls George to see what has happened to Durango. George tells Johnny that the police did not even take his six-guns. Johnny tells George that he is leaving and putting the cost on Floyds. Durango gets on the phone and tells Johnny to stay in his apartment. "California here I come!" replies Johnny.

Johnny goes to the airport and gets a flight under the name "Bailey", just in case. Johnny puts the $146.85 for the flight to Los Angeles on his American Express credit card, but George is going to pay for it. The stewardess pages

Johnny Dollar on the flight and Johnny tells her that Mr. Dollar is a friend of his who missed the flight, but she will not give him the information.

When the plane lands in Chicago, Johnny is tempted to call George, but does not. On the flight to Los Angeles Johnny dreams of Durango chasing him. When Johnny tries to grab a cab in Los Angeles, Durango is there with a limousine for them to use. Durango had used a jet flight to catch up with Johnny!

Durango tells Johnny to get into the limo and Johnny uses a diversion to run into the airport and climb onto an airplane headed for Portland, Oregon.

In Portland, Johnny spots Durango, who had chartered a plane to get there ahead of him. Johnny runs out and gets a cab and ends up at a private airstrip where the pilot is told to fly ANYWHERE! Suddenly Johnny gets an idea and travels to a person who is in the same situation he is.

Johnny travels to Bum Spung and Carol, that lovely lovin' Carol Dalhart. After a few dozen welcoming kisses, Johnny tells Carol how Durango had gone to Hartford to get Johnny to marry her. Carol tells Johnny that she is not going to marry Johnny just because Durango wants her to.

Durango bursts in and Johnny tells Durango that he is not going to marry Carol. Durango tells Johnny that he chased Johnny, not because of Carol, but because Johnny had kept Sidewinder from getting killed. Now Sidewinder is the sheriff.

Since Johnny has been so good to Sidewinder, Durango had gone to Hartford to give him a $10,000 wad of cash. Just enjoy it. "Are you sure you don't want me to get the preacher up from Enid? No, I guess not?" Durango says dejectedly.

"This time I did stay over for a couple of days. Yeah, and it I ever take the leap... As for the expense account George, I will still argue with you about it but that's all."

Notes:
- Johnny mentions using an American Express credit card for the first time.
- The announcer is Dan Cubberly.
- The script title page credits Tom Hanley and Bill James for providing "Ad Libs".

Producer: Jack Johnstone   Writer: Jack Johnstone
Cast: Virginia Gregg, Jeanne Tatum, John McIntire, G. Stanley Jones

♦ ❖ ♦

Show: The Winsome Widow Matter
Show Date: 4/26/1959
Company: Greater Southwest Insurance Company
Agent: Herb Shilling
Exp. Acct: $250.00

Synopsis: Long distance calls Johnny with a call from Pat McCracken. Pat asks about his message and Johnny tells Pat he is in Los Angeles to confab with Jack Johnstone, the guy that dramatizes the cases he handles and puts them on the radio. Johnny wonders if Pat has anything for him to handle on the West

Coast. Pat tells Johnny to call Herb Shilling there in Los Angeles, California. "And Johnny, have you got a gun with you? Judging by Herb's wire, you may need it."

Johnny cabs to Herb's office and surprises Herb by getting there so soon. Johnny tells Herb that he was in Los Angeles when he got the news. Herb tells Johnny that the matter has to do with a not-so-little liquor store holdup.

Herb tells Johnny that bottled goods stores are prone to holdups, and they limit the number and amount of the policies they issue. The store of Willie Layman was opened in 1951 and he was first robbed in 1952. Willie bought some insurance from Herb, and there have been seven attempted robberies. Willie bought a gun and knows how to use it. Last night $400 was taken, and Layman was killed. Herb has his life insurance too, $30,000.

Johnny rents a car and drives to the West Los Angeles police and sees Sgt. Mike Kirby. Kirby tells Johnny about all the holdup attempts and that Willie was a good shot and quick on the draw. Just last month he killed one of the men who tried to rob him. Kirby thinks that if they find the other man, they will probably find Willie's killer. Kirby tried a stakeout, but nothing happened. As soon as the police left, the robberies started again.

Kirby and Johnny drive to the store and enter with a key. Johnny sees where the body was lying and the broken bottles. Kirby tells Johnny how the bullet went into Willie's shoulder and down through his heart. Mrs. Gloria Layman, who is thirty years younger than Willie, comes into the store. Johnny goes to a phone booth and calls Herb to ask who the beneficiary of the policy was. Johnny is told that it is his wife.

Johnny goes back into the store and Mrs. Layman is telling Sgt. Kirby that she is going to sell the store. She tells Johnny that Willie has some insurance for her, but who thought he would die this soon.

Gloria tells Johnny that she was upstairs in bed when the robbery occurred. She came down and saw Willie lying there on the floor. She tells Johnny that she married Willie because it made him happy, but what a bore he was, he always wanted to go back to the old country. She likes to have fun, and Willie did not know where she was half the time. Gloria married Willie last September.

Kirby gets a phone call and then he tells Johnny that they have picked up the man who did the killing. Johnny and Kirby go to headquarters to question a wino named Benny, who tells them that he took the money and ran but did not shoot Willie. He was only carrying a rubber gun. Bennie tells Kirby that he would not have gotten caught if he had not gotten drunk and told someone what he did. Bennie tells Kirby that Willie reached under the counter and came up empty so he gave Bennie the money.

Officer Conroy comes in with a negative paraffin test. The ballistics test is in, and the gun Willie had didn't have any prints on it. Kirby tells Johnny that the bullet that killed Layman and those that were in the wall came from Layman's own gun. If Bennie did not kill him, who did? Johnny thinks he better get some proof.

Johnny tells Kirby that Bennie was a shaky wino who could not have outgunned Layman or taken his gun. Johnny can get the killer, but he has to get her his way. Sgt. Kirby and Johnny go back to the store where Johnny goes in to see Gloria alone. Gloria asks if Johnny is getting the money for her. Johnny asks how she knows about the $30,000, when she had said she did not know how much insurance Willie had? Johnny thinks that someone would have had to tell others when the police were there, and Willie was too good with a gun, unless he did not have his gun.

Gloria shows Johnny where Willie kept his gun, and Johnny puts his gun there. Johnny tells Gloria to get behind the counter and tells her how a man came in and pulled a toy gun. Gloria tells Johnny that Willie would have grabbed is gun, and points Johnny's gun right at him.

Johnny tells her that she had taken the gun, and after the robbers left she had come down and shot Willie from the stairs. Gloria tells Johnny that it happened just the way he said, but he will never tell, and she pulls the trigger on Johnny's empty gun. "You tricked me, you dirty double crossing, lying cheat!"

"Pretty obvious I guess, right from the beginning as I said. But getting proof, or in this case a confession, isn't always so easy."

Notes:
- The opening of this program makes reference to a meeting in Hollywood with Jack Johnstone about the radio programs.
- This program has a CBS commercial which lists the seven winning daily dramas put on by CBS: *The Romance of Helen Trent, The Couple Next Door, Ma Perkins, Whispering Streets, The Right to Happiness, The Second Mrs. Burton, Young Doctor Malone*, a CBS commercial about the CBS News department using Fidel Castro as an example of their speed and accuracy, a commercial for Pepsi and a commercial for Sinclair Dino gasoline.
- This program credits Jack Johnstone as writer, Fred Hendrickson as producer and director and starring Mandel Kramer, Jackson Beck, Joseph Julian, Jack Grimes, Bob Maxwell, Peter Fernandez, and Ethel Huber as music supervisor and Walter Otto for sound patterns. These are the credits from *The Tip-Off Matter*, the last of the Yours Truly Johnny Dollar series and have been added to this program in error.
- Cast Information from the KNX Collection at the Thousand Oaks Library.
- The announcer is Dan Cubberly.

Producer: Jack Johnstone   Writer: Jack Johnstone
Cast: Lawrence Dobkin, Virginia Gregg, Bartlett Robinson,
              Paul Dubov, Frank Nelson

Show:	**The Negligent Nephew Matter**
Show Date:	**5/3/1959**
Company:	**Amalgamated Life Association**
Agent:	**Leonard Tillson**
Exp. Acct:	**$10.50**

Synopsis: Richard Coleman calls Johnny and tells him that Amalgamated insures him, and that he needs a witness. Johnny is told that Coleman has a horrible disease and the doctors cannot help him. Coleman says good bye and there is a gunshot.

Johnny goes to the Amalgamated office where Leonard Tillson tells Johnny that Coleman lives in Hartford, Connecticut, and is insured for around $40,000. Leonard gets the folder and tells Johnny that the policy is for $50,000, and gives Johnny Coleman's address, and the address of his nephew Bert.

Johnny goes to Coleman's apartment and finds a body in a chair with a .32 automatic beside it. Johnny calls the police and looks through the shabby and pathetic apartment. Sgt. Miller arrives and they agree that there is no sign of suicide, which gives Johnny a crazy idea.

Johnny calls Leonard and updates him. Johnny goes to see Coleman's doctor and learns that the case was hopeless even though he had the money to pay for a hospital. Johnny is told that the nephew was told of the condition and did not visit his uncle, because Coleman wanted it that way.

Johnny gets the address for Randolph Gifford, Coleman's attorney and the doctor tells Johnny that Coleman's eyes were bad, and he had to use contact lenses, but hated to. Without the contacts, Coleman could not see any closer than five feet.

Johnny remembers that Coleman had said that he looked Johnny's name up in the phone book. Johnny calls Sgt. Miller who calls the death suicide and tells Johnny that the body is still in the apartment.

Johnny goes to see Gifford and is told that the only relatives were two nephews, Paul and Bert Coleman. Johnny goes back to the apartment and the lab men are still there. Johnny looks at Coleman's eyes, and the contacts are not there. Johnny asks the police to see if Coleman's prints are on the phone book and tells them that he is sure that someone else fired the gun, because Coleman was blind as a bat without his contacts.

Johnny meets Rich who tells him that he is not sorry his uncle is dead. He had tried to help and has not talked to Paul for fifteen years. Paul was adopted and his uncle never liked him because he was a black sheep who stole things.

Johnny calls Leonard and is told that the policy had a suicide clause, and the police found a bullet in the wall. Johnny is told that Paul is on his way to the office.

Johnny calls Sgt. Miller and goes to Leonard's office to meet Paul. Johnny accuses Paul of murdering his uncle because he knew there was a suicide clause, but Leonard had not been told yet. Paul asks Johnny how he knew, and Johnny tells him that he knew Johnny's name. Paul admits that he hates Rich, who would get the insurance except in case of suicide. Paul pulls a gun, but the police arrive and he drops it and gives up.

Notes:
- The announcer is Dan Cubberly.
- Bob Bailey congratulates station WDBO in Orlando, Florida for their 35th anniversary.
- Story information obtained from the KNX Collection in the Thousand Oaks Library.

Producer:	Jack Johnstone Writer: Jack Johnstone
Cast:	Stacy Harris, Carleton G. Young, Herb Vigran, Parley Baer, Will Wright, Sam Edwards

♦ ❖ ♦

Show:	**The Fatal Filet Matter**
Show Date:	**5/10/1959**
Company:	**Continental Insurance Company**
Agent:	
Exp. Acct:	**$0.00**

Synopsis: Ray Connelly calls Johnny. There is no problem, Ray just wants to ask if Johnny can come over for dinner. He has a thick steak in the refrigerator. Be there at 6:30. Johnny is suspicious because of what Ray does not tell him.

Johnny feels that there is something funny about Ray's invitation because Johnny was familiar with Ray's problems with ulcers.

Johnny cabs to Ray's Hartford, Connecticut apartment and decides to let Ray bring up any problems. Ray pours Johnny a scotch and soda and Ray has one of his pills. Ray wants to tell Johnny something later. Ray tells Johnny that his wife is away and that he had some groceries delivered, including the steak.

Johnny and Ray sit down to dinner, and Johnny's steak is overcooked. Johnny goes to the kitchen to make a sandwich. Ray tells Johnny that he does not like being threatened when Ray starts having stomach pains. Ray collapses in pain and asks Johnny for his medicine. Johnny calls for Ray's doctor and after he arrives he calls for an ambulance. On the way to the hospital Ray dies.

Johnny is told by the doctor that Ray died of an internal hemorrhage. Johnny goes back to Ray's apartment and finds nothing. In the kitchen, Johnny finds the bag of groceries and a cufflink with "XD" on it.

The next morning Johnny goes to talk to Morris Bain the grocer. Bain tells Johnny that Mrs. Connelly was in just the other day and asks about her husband. Bain gets a list of the groceries that were delivered to Ray's apartment. The only item not on the list was the steak because Bain does not sell meat.

Johnny calls Dr. Ransom and asks for an autopsy and goes to Continental Insurance to get a list of people who might have threatened Ray. Johnny is told by the secretary, Grace, that there was a man in yesterday who lost a cufflink with "XD" on it. Johnny asks the secretary to find the policy for the man.

Johnny calls Dr. Ransom and is told that Ray's stomach was full of ground glass. Johnny calls Grace to get the name of the man who visited Ray, Xavier Denato. Johnny gets the address and is told that Xavier was the beneficiary on his father's policy, but his father committed suicide.

Johnny goes to the address but Denato has gone. Johnny calls Sgt. Jimmy Maxwell at police headquarters and listens to Jimmy yell at him. Johnny updates him with the information he has about Xavier, or "Zavier" and has an idea.

Johnny cabs to Bain's grocery store and asks about his clerk Zavier. Johnny finds him and shows him the cufflinks and tells him where he found them. Xavier tells Johnny that he got the steak and put the ground glass in it. He did not think it would kill Connelly. He did not run because he is smart, if you run, the cops think you are guilty.

He had to get even because of the insurance policy that Connelly would not pay. His father killed himself, as did his grandfather and great grandfather because they were off in the head. But Xavier is smart, he gets even with them. But he will not get caught. Johnny takes Xavier to the police.

"Prison, I doubt it, not with a family history like that. But there are institutions for his kind. I am sure he will spend the rest of his life in one of them. And maybe by studying his case, the doctors, the psychologists can learn more about helping such people before they go off the deep end. Expense account, forget it. Ray Connelly was my friend."

Notes:
- This program contains a rare opening: "Dan Slate, 107B" then Dan Cubberly says "This is Johnny Dollar for broadcast Sunday May 10, 1959."
- This program contains commercials for CBS News, for Lowell Thomas, for Pepsi, and the value of an education and the need for contributions to college funds.
- Ground glass was also used in the five-part story, *The Lonely Hearts Matter*. There are several articles on the internet that dispel the effectiveness of ground glass as a murder weapon. But it does make for a good story.
- The announcer is Dan Cubberly.

Producer: Jack Johnstone Writer: Jack Johnstone
Cast: Virginia Gregg, D. J. Thompson, Jack Edwards, Marvin Miller, Lawrence Dobkin, Harry Bartell, Frank Gerstle

♦ ❖ ♦

Show: The Twin Trouble Matter
Show Date: 5/17/1959
Company: Floyds of England
Agent: George Reed
Exp. Acct: $0.00

Synopsis: George Reed calls Johnny, and George has a client whose life is being threatened. Johnny tells him that he hates these kinds of cases. George tells Johnny that there are confidential matters involved, and George offers to go along with Johnny. The client is George's brother, Adam. Johnny is on his way.

Johnny cabs to George's office, and is told that the client is George's brother Adam. Eighteen years ago, Adam came to the states with his wife, and now owns a brokerage firm in New York. He lives in Upper Montclair, New Jersey.

Adam had traveled a lot when he first came to this country and met two men, Shockley and Baron in California who offered him a job. It turned out that the men were swindlers who sold worthless stocks. When Adam finally figured out what was happening, he called in the police and everyone, including Adam, went to prison. Now Shockley is out and is threatening Adam. If his clients ever found out that Adam had been in prison it would ruin the business, and Adam's wife is in the hospital with a heart condition.

Shockley has demanded $75,000 from Adam to keep quiet and not leak the past to the papers and kill Adam, making it look like suicide to void his insurance policies. He told Adam he had gotten away with it once before, and Adam cannot call in the police or risk his business. Johnny is not sure what to do yet, other than to not pad the expense account.

Johnny buys gas for his car and drives to Adam's home. Adam is a complete twin to George except for his accent. Adam had heard from Shockley earlier and had gone to the bank. Shockley is coming here tonight and wants $10,000 as an act of good faith. George tells Johnny he will take care of the matter and wants Johnny's gun.

The phone rings, and Johnny goes to an extension to listen in. Shockley is on the phone and he tells Adam that he does not trust him. He tells Adam to meet him at Cedar Knoll, at the shack on the top of the hill, and come alone in his car or someone will die. After the call, Johnny discovers that George has taken a gun and driven to Cedar Knoll.

Johnny gets directions to Cedar Knoll and realizes that Shockley will get there before George will. Johnny leaves to drive to Cedar Knoll in heavy traffic and frequent police patrols. Johnny spots the knoll and the shack with Shockley's car out front. Johnny spots a pair of lights in the cabin and tries to cut a rubber tube on Shockley's car.

George arrives and Shockley tells George to wait outside. George tells Shockley that he is going to end this thing and to throw down their guns. Shockley realizes that it is not Adam, but his brother George. Baron throws his gun at George and there are shots.

George is thrown onto Johnny, who fights with Baron and Shockley and is almost knocked unconscious. The men get into their car and Johnny warns them to not use it. The men drive off and Johnny tells George that he had cut the brake line as there is the sound of a crash in the distance.

"By the time the highway police got to the scene of the crash there on the back road, and of course their car exploded and burned, they had forgotten all about the gun shots, if they had heard them at all. So, George and I were able to leave by the main road unmolested. At the bottom of the hill I picked up my own car without attracting attention. I suppose I will have to make some sort of report to the police, but I do not see any reason why I should have to reveal the name of the man they were out to get, do you? It is certainly too late to need anyone to bring charges against them. As for the expense account, so what is a couple gallons of gas in so good a cause?"

Notes:
- Bob Bailey says thanks "to all of the good people who write in to say how much they like the show. It may seem like a little thing to you, but it means a great deal to all of us. Believe me, I'll answer your letters just as fast as I can get around to them. But you'll just have to be patient if it takes a little time."
- Bob suggests that for the next show the audience read *The Cask of Amontillado* by Edgar Allen Poe.
- In this program Frank Gerstle plays a man named "Baron", but the script lists his name as "Barrow".
- The announcer is Dan Cubberly.

Producer:	Jack Johnstone	Writer:	Jack Johnstone
Cast:	G. Stanley Jones, Alan Reed, Frank Gerstle		

♦ ❖ ♦

Show: The Casque of Death Matter
Show Date: 5/24/1959
Company: Philadelphia Mutual Liability & Casualty Company
Agent: Harry Branson
Exp. Acct: $101.20

Synopsis: Harry Branson calls Johnny, and he has a case for Johnny involving some important clients. Johnny suggests a nice fee, but Harry tells Johnny that he will pay Johnny's regular expenses and commission. There will be no fee, depending on what Johnny unearths. Johnny asks something or someone. Harry means facts. The clients have disappeared, and the police gave up years ago. Johnny tells Harry he is on his way, and to have a shovel waiting for him.

Johnny trains to Philadelphia, Pennsylvania and meets "old sober-sides" in his office. Harry tells Johnny that in the case of mysterious disappearance, the insured is declared deceased after seven years, and the policy is paid.

Seven years ago, Mr. Wilbur Davis of Goshenville disappeared. In checking the files Harry has determined that there have been eight disappearances in the same area, the last four months ago. The beneficiaries were all different persons. Johnny gets a list of the people involved and reviews the list that night.

Johnny rents a car and drives to Kirkwood, New Jersey where Charles Moody had disappeared. At the general store, Johnny learns that Moody had taken a bus to Philadelphia and disappeared. Moody left the policy and his money to his nephew. All of his property, except his wine cellar will go to the town. If Moody is dead, the wine cellar will go to a man in Philadelphia, he belonged to some sort of gourmet club. Moody had quite a collection of wines in his collection.

Johnny checks out all Moody's other friends and learns nothing but realizes later how much he did learn. Johnny travels to the other cities where the clients disappeared.

In Millmay, Pennsylvania, Johnny learns from the lawyer for Frederick Burton that Burton also had a wine cellar, which will be given to Edward Alden Poley in Philadelphia. Johnny realizes that the others also had wine cellars. The lawyer realizes that the list Johnny has are the other members of the epicurean club that Burton belonged to. The only missing name is Bradford W. Turner in Alloway.

The lawyer is stunned when he learns that all of the others have also disappeared. Johnny drives to the home of Bradford Turner who tells Johnny that the club has not been very active lately. Poley has a marvelous wine cellar, with some rare Amontillado. Turner has a rare bottle of Medoc to offer Poley now. Johnny is told that wine is a passion for Poley. Johnny tells Turner that he will take the bottle of Medoc to Philadelphia.

Johnny drives to Poley's house and is taken to the library while Poley eyes the package Johnny has. Poley tells Johnny that he has to have the best of everything. Johnny notices a large collection of Edgar Allen Poe, who shares Poley's initials.

Johnny shows Poley the bottle and Poley must have it, but Johnny tells him he only wants an appraisal. Poley tells Johnny he has a cask of Amontillado in his cellar, maybe they can swap.

Johnny goes with Poley to the cellar where Johnny is asked if he is a mason. Johnny remembers the story from Poe and realizes that Poley is living the story. Poley shows Johnny a vault where the other members of the club are buried. Poley tries to knock Johnny out to bury him, but Johnny shoots instead.

"The eight men who disappeared, yeah, they were all buried behind the bricks and mortar that walled up eight of the niches in that deep underground vault. Funny, I completely forgot to look to see if there was a cask of Amontillado in that cellar. Edward Alden Poley? When the courts get through with his case, I am sure that he will be committed to an institution for the rest of his life. Yeah, I told you in the beginning, this was the weirdest case I ever tackled."

Notes:
- *The Cask of Amontillado* was written by Edgar Allen Poe in 1846.
- Amontillado is a type of sherry made near Montilla, Spain, from which it derives its name.
- This may possibly be an AFRTS program, but it lacks any of the typical features.
- The tag for this program is for *The Wayward Heiress Matter*, and not *The Big H Matter*. On the scripts, the original script numbers and air dates have been reversed.
- The announcer is Dan Cubberly.

Producer: Jack Johnstone Writer: Jack Johnstone
Cast: Harry Bartell, Forrest Lewis, Bartlett Robinson, Parley

Baer, Marvin Miller

Show:	The Big H Matter
Show Date:	5/31/1959
Company:	Greater Southwest Insurance Company
Agent:	Royal J. Harkins
Exp. Acct:	$447.45

Synopsis: Helen Daner calls Johnny from Morro Bay, California. She has a policy with Greater Southwest Insurance Company. Helen tells Johnny that she always listens to Johnny's radio program and is his most loyal listener, which is why she is calling Johnny rather than the police. If the police nab these terrible people, they would know she told them and something terrible would happen. Helen starts to tell Johnny what is going on when the phone goes dead. "Oh, don't be a sucker now. But yet, I wonder."

Johnny calls Royal J. Harkins at Hollywood 8-2124 in Los Angeles and tells him he is coming. Johnny asks about Helen Daner and is told she is a spinster who called and demanded Johnny's phone number. Roy had called her back and got no answer.

Johnny flies to Los Angeles at 12:30 a.m. and is met by Roy with his rental car at 6:30 the next morning. Roy tells Johnny that he still cannot get hold of Helen, and Johnny is not sure that anything has happened, yet.

Johnny drives to Morro Bay and goes to Helen Daner's house, which has an expensive car parked out front and a decrepit dock out back. Bessie Daner, Helen's sister, answers the door and tells Johnny that Helen is at the market. Johnny leaves and feels there is something funny going on.

Johnny drives to the market and learns that Helen is not there, and that the market delivers groceries to her house, as she has not been out of the house in weeks.

Johnny drives back to the house and asks Bessie where Helen is and is told to come in. Once inside Johnny finds Helen tied to a chair and a .38 in Bessie's hand. Bessie takes Johnny's gun and they wait.

Bessie takes the gag out of Helen's mouth and Helen tells Johnny that these terrible people are smugglers who are bringing in narcotics from Mexico. A man named Pete had asked to use the dock, and Helen had watched them take out the heroin instead of fish. She had found some spilled on the dock and remember how Johnny had described it. Bessie tells Johnny that they will use some "H" on Helen to keep her quiet.

Pete comes in and tells Johnny that he made a mistake by coming here. Now, they are going to take a ride, Chicago style. Pete tells Bessie that they will have to wait until after dark to get rid of Johnny. Pete will take Johnny to a quarry in Cayucos Beach and leave his body there. Johnny attacks Pete when he hits Helen and is knocked out.

When Johnny wakes up he is in the car with Pete and Bessie. Johnny tries to get a cigarette and crumples the pack to get the tobacco out. Johnny asks Bessie for a match, and when she turns around he blows the tobacco dust into

Bessie's eyes and when she drops the gun Johnny grabs it, knocks Pete unconscious and the car crashes.

"It was a commercial trucker driving one of those big interstate trailer jobs who pulled off the highway to give us a hand. Yeah, somehow those boys are always around when you need 'em. And he used his head. When he found my credentials in my pocket he saw the whole picture in a flash. So, he hailed down the first police car that came along and turned both Pete and Bessie over to them. Miss Helen Daner, bless her heart? That spunky old character was tickled pink to be involved in the whole thing. Yeah, she just can't wait to go to court and testify against those two."

Notes:
- Next week is the wildest case Johnny ever got messed up with.
- Morro Beach and Cayucos are north of San Luis Obispo on the California coast between Los Angeles and San Francisco.
- The announcer is Dan Cubberly.

Producer:	Jack Johnstone	Writer:	Jack Johnstone
Cast:	Peggy Webber, Virginia Gregg, Bartlett Robinson, Joseph Kearns, Russell Thorson		

◆ ❖ ◆

Show:	**The Wayward Heiress Matter**
Show Date:	**6/7/1959**
Company:	**New Britain Mutual Insurance Company**
Agent:	**Al Turner**
Exp. Acct:	**$10.00**

Synopsis: Al Turner calls Johnny and tells him that an important client, Mrs. Virginia Haskell wants to get in touch with Johnny, she is an old friend of yours. Before she got married last year, her name was Van Doren. "Ginny Van Doren! Well that's something else again, and I mean something. She is one of the most delectable bits of feminine pulchritude I ever ran up against. Believe me, a young man's fancy didn't have to wait for spring to turn to thoughts of her!" Johnny tells Al that even he had serious ideas about her after college and marrying into the family fortune. Al tells Johnny that Virginia lives with Gordon Haskell on Birchbrook Road in Bronxville. Johnny remembers that she had a thing for Paul Snowden, a childhood sweetheart. She made it clear that she needed to see Johnny about the family insurance. Al tells Johnny that the sky is the limit for his expenses.

Johnny drives his car to Westchester County and Bronxville, New York. The Haskell home is old money and neatly kept. Virginia was just as beautiful as Johnny remembered her from college in the mid-west.

She tells Johnny that she is worried sick about Gordon, and Paul Snowden is who has her worried. She loved Paul and hoped he would marry her. When her father died and she inherited the fortune, Paul stopped seeing her. She had gone to visit him in his factory in Chicago and she proposed to him. She offered to finance his business, but he did not like that. Paul told her he had to work things out on his own, and to find herself a nice husband.

She fell in love with Gordon, but not as much as Paul, but in a different way. Gordon does not have as much money as she has, but they get along and she is a good wife to him. She thinks that Paul might kill Gordon, and that is why she sent for Johnny.

Ginny tells Johnny that Paul has come here to kill Gordon. Paul was angry when he found out and swore he would kill Gordon. She left Chicago to get away from Paul. She has helped Gordon start an importing business.

Ginny tells Johnny that Gordon's life is insured, and Johnny will have to protect Gordon. Paul has called her from New York and told her that he would come out when Gordon was there and to prepare for the worst. Now, Gordon is in Larchmont, hiding. Johnny agrees to help and tells her to have Gordon come home.

Johnny leaves and feels like an advice to the lovelorn columnist. Johnny is stopped at his car and a voice tells Johnny that he knows why he is here and shows him some papers he has collected from police files in the mid-west, and that he knows all about him. Johnny is hit and Ginny comes out calling for him. The attacker mumbles "oh no" and runs away. Virginia recognizes him as Paul and goes to aid Johnny.

Johnny has been convinced by Paul's actions how serious the situation is. Johnny mentions how Paul had some papers and photostats and goes back out again to look for Paul and the papers. Johnny drives away and sneaks back into the house. Johnny opens the front door and calls outside for Paul and tells him "this is Johnny Dollar, so stick around. I am leaving the front door is unlocked, so use your own judgement". Johnny comes back in to see Gordon there with Ginny.

Gordon tells Ginny that he is not staying around for Snowden to kill him and tells her to open the safe and give him the money in it. Gordon pulls a gun on Johnny, but Johnny takes it away after Paul shoots Gordon.

Paul tells Johnny and Ginny that Gordon has a police record "as long as your arm" under a variety of names. He marries wealthy women and takes their money and has killed some of them. Paul apologizes for slugging Johnny.

"Well, maybe Paul and Ginny will finally get together for keeps. I don't know. I do not even know if I care. I am just glad I was not involved, that is any more than I was."

Notes:
- The announcer is Dan Cubberly.
- This story is the only reference to Johnny having attended college.
- Birchbrook Road in Bronxville is also mentioned in *The Deadly Crystal Matter* and *The Wrong Ending Matter*.
- The tag for this program is for *The Big H Matter*.

Producer: Jack Johnstone   Writer: Jack Johnstone

Cast:	Virginia Gregg, Les Tremayne, Sam Edwards, James McCallion

♦ ❖ ♦

Show:	**The Wayward Sculptor Matter**
Show Date:	6/14/1959
Company:	Universal Adjustment Bureau
Agent:	Pat McCracken
Exp. Acct:	$26.15

Synopsis: Pat McCracken calls Johnny and remarks how he has not had to bleed through one of Johnny's fancy expense accounts for a month. Pat has a funny case now. Come on over and let's talk.

Johnny cabs to Pat's office and comments about Pat's previous wild cases. Pat tells Johnny that a big problem for him is preventing the prosecution of insurance fraud, and this has been going on for a long time.

Pat shows Johnny a case where a company received $520 and a note telling them that the money was taken and now the writer has a clear conscious and signed "detter". Companies get a lot of such payments but this case is different.

Johnny sees a list of payments received from the same person: $833.34 on 7/21/56, $833.34 on 8/21/56, same thing on the 21st of the month, every month for several years. There was a note saying that the payments were restitution for monies paid out on someone who will pay the money back if it takes five years. They have all come from the New York area, and Pat wants Johnny to find out who the payments are coming from.

Johnny calculates that $833.34 times 60 months comes to $50,000.40. But, $833.333 times 60 is exactly $50,000! Johnny wants Pat to find out who paid out $50,000 in June of 1956.

Johnny learns that there was only one policy paid in 1956, to Henry Davidson Pollock, the sculptor. Pat thinks that Pollock did not die, and the wife is paying the money back, but it is still fraud to Pat.

Johnny trains to New York City and the address of record for Pollock. The manager of the building tells Johnny that Mrs. Pollock died last fall. He had carried her in after the auto accident, and Dr. Maitland can verify it.

Johnny learns that Henry Pollock lived in the apartment also and died in a plane crash in the desert. He kept to himself and his wife was younger than he was. "But the money is still coming in" Johnny notes.

Johnny calls Pat to update him. Pat agrees that maybe there is no fraud, but Pat wants an answer.

Johnny cabs to Dr. Maitland who tells him that the woman definitely was Mrs. Pollock. Johnny checks with Randy Singer who confirms the death. Johnny checks the newspaper morgues and confirms the death of Pollock in the plane crash.

Johnny goes to a gallery mentioned by Dr. Maitland that Pollock used as an outlet. The owner, Mr. Bessem tells Johnny that he never met Pollock, as Pollock abhorred the public. His wife always brought in the art works and took the money. Bessem tells Johnny that anyone who saw the work of Pollock wanted to buy it.

Bessem has one piece in the gallery and shows it to Johnny. The price is $15,000. Johnny sees another piece similar in style but is assured that it is not a Pollock. John Wesley Collins, an admirer, has been making artwork in Pollock's style for the past two years.

As he leaves, Johnny watches Bessem make a phone call, so he goes back in to hear Bessem make a call to Henry to tell him about Johnny's visit, and Bessem agrees to leave the door open for him.

Johnny leaves and calls Dr. Maitland to ask if Pollock had a scar on the thumb of one hand, which he did. Johnny goes back to the gallery and meets Bessem.

Johnny asks Bessem if he wants to write a statement or go to the police. Johnny notes the similarity of the styles of Collins and Pollock. Johnny shows the similarity of thumbprints on the two pieces. Bessem pulls a gun as Henry Collins walks in and tells Johnny that he is giving up.

Henry tells Johnny that he wanted to get away from his wife. He was going to fly to the west coast and disappear. At the last minute, he gave the ticket to someone else. Knowing he was thought dead, he decided to disappear in New York.

He remembered the insurance money and decided to repay the insurance his wife had gotten. Henry tells Johnny that the works of John Wesley Collins have sold well, and the balance of the policy had been sent to the company that day.

"So, Pat, there you have it. And you can take whatever action you think is necessary. Pollock is waiting for the company or the courts, or whoever. And Walter Bessem is too scared to go anywhere. As for the expense account, I think the company can afford it."

Notes:
- The announcer is Dan Cubberly.

Producer:	Jack Johnstone Writer: Jack Johnstone
Cast:	Herb Vigran, Edgar Barrier, Carleton G. Young, Will Wright, Lawrence Dobkin

◆ ❖ ◆

Show:	The Life at Steak Matter
Show Date:	6/21/1959
Company:	Continental Insurance & Trust Company
Agent:	Bill Ferguson
Exp. Acct:	$0.00

Synopsis: Johnny receives a call from the Hartford operator. Johnny is connected to Bill Ferguson. Johnny tells Bill he was almost ready to leave Los Angeles and head home. Bill asks if Johnny remembers Alvin Peabody Cartwright? Johnny tells Bill how he had cleared up a robbery for him, and Cartwright insisted on giving him a small bonus of $3,000. Johnny is ready, willing and able to help Alvin if he needs help. Bill tells Johnny that Cartwright has a small place there in Los Angeles at 10321 North Roxbury Drive in Beverly Hills, and he must see Johnny right away.

Johnny calls "Crestview 3-2121" to speak with Alvin. Johnny has a very confusing call with Alvin, until Johnny tells him who he is. Alvin wants to know how Johnny got there so fast and hopes Johnny has not been fooling around with rockets. Johnny tells him he was in Los Angeles already.

Alvin and Jonathan Peebles both want to see Johnny, so get up there right away. Johnny gets an Avis rental car. and on the way out a boy with a hula-hoop causes Johnny to stumble. Johnny wakes up in the dispensary hours later and rushes out to the car. Johnny drives to Alvin's house to find the door wide open. Jonathan Peebles meets Johnny and tells him that Alvin is gone, and based on the evidence, Alvin has been murdered.

Peebles tells Johnny that he had been called by Alvin to come over, and he did not hurry as Betsy (his car) does not like to be rushed. Peebles tells Johnny that he found the door wide open, but Alvin often left the door open. Peebles tells Johnny that he is not a wealthy man and relies on Beneficial Finance to keep up the payments on his car.

Peebles had looked for Alvin but could not find him. He saw two men walking out of garage carrying a tour-robe, which is a big heavy suitcase like a small wardrobe trunk, and it was dripping something all over the driveway. As Johnny goes to look at the driveway Peebles tells Johnny that Alvin kept his tools and frozen foods in the garage. Johnny realizes that the driveway is full of blood.

Johnny inspects the garage and the house. Peebles remembers seeing the men's car and he has seen it before. It was a silver and cream sedan with license plates CFU-610. He has seen it at the Malibu docks where Alvin keeps the *Alpecar*, his yacht.

Johnny drives to the docks in Malibu and Peebles sees the car, but the boat is gone. A man named Whitey tells them that the boat left about ten minutes ago, and two men had a boat take them to the *Alpecar*. Whitey wants to sue them for making a mess on his dock with the drippings from the trunk.

Peebles fears that the men are taking Alvin's body out to sea to dispose of it. Johnny arranges to borrow a boat at the dock that belongs to a Larry Comstock, and has Whitey call the Coast Guard.

Peebles and Johnny speed out to the *Alpecar*, which is just cruising along. Peebles sees one of the men at the wheel, and the other coiling ropes, and Alvin! They have put him back together again!

Alvin welcomes Johnny and Peebles and tells Johnny that he had wanted to take him out for a ride on his nice new boat. He deserved it for all the work he has done for him over the years. He feels that Johnny deserves a nice long cruise. Peebles was invited to come along too.

Alvin realized something was wrong as soon as he left the dock. He forgot to wait for Johnny and Peebles. Alvin tells Johnny that he had also forgotten to take the trunk of thick juicy tenderloin steaks and had to send Gerald and Harold back to get them. Gerald and Harold are Alvin's new cook and butler. Johnny realizes that all the blood came from the steaks which had thawed out too much.

"You know something? It's crazy, it's wild. But it does my heart good to get tangled up in something like this sometimes. Helps keep away the ulcers. As for the expense account, forget it. Alvin Peabody Cartwright shoved a check into my hands before I left that would cover the expense account a dozen times over. As for Larry Comstock, the man whose boat I had appropriated? Well when he heard the story of what had happened, he wouldn't accept a penny for it. So, that's that!"

Notes:
- Bob Bailey congratulates station WDBJ in Roanoke, Virginia for their 35 years on the air.
- Johnny mentions that he was California working on a case in Morro Bay. That was *The Big H Matter*. The scripts for *The Big H Matter* and *The Mei-Ling Buddah Matter* have their air dates overwritten, hence the confusion over the previous case.
- The announcer is Dan Cubberly.

Producer: Jack Johnstone Writer: Jack Johnstone
Cast: Virginia Gregg, Jeanne Tatum, Howard McNear, Forrest Lewis, Joseph Kearns, Paul Dubov

♦ ❖ ♦

Show: **The Mei-Ling Buddah Matter**
Show Date: **6/28/1959**
Company: **Worldwide Mutual Insurance Company**
Agent: **Marty Bruce**
Exp. Acct: **$300.00**

Synopsis: Marty Bruce calls Johnny and asks if him if he has ever heard of the Mei-Ling Buddha, the most valuable piece of jade in the world. Marty has it insured for $40,000. He does not know if anything has happened to it, or if nothing has happened to it. Come on over and let's talk.

Johnny cabs to Marty's office and is told that Ray Kerner, one of Marty's agents knew that the Buddha was insured and should have investigated when he saw it in Europe. It was in a dingy old antique shop in Paris and Ray did not even have the sense to get the address of the place. It is supposed to be locked up in the house of Darryl Harcourt in Boston, but there has been no report of a theft.

Johnny calls his friend Louis De Marsac in Paris and tells him he will pay $200 for information on the Buddha. De Marsac has seen the Buddha that morning, and it had been smuggled in only a few weeks ago. The asking price is 32,000,000 francs, about $80,000. De Marsac offers to obtain (steal) it, but Johnny tells him he will send a check.

Marty tells Johnny that Mrs. Mary Haskell is taking care of Harcourt house. Only the contents of Mrs. Haskell's room and the study are still there. The study goes to a nephew the day he graduates from Harvard. The Buddha was the only thing of value in the room, and the house goes to Mrs. Haskell.

Johnny rents a car and drives to the Harcourt house in Boston, Massachusetts. Mrs. Haskell meets Johnny and comments on the dismal, desolate house. She will live in the house until the estate is settled. Johnny wants to see the study, but he is told that the room is sealed.

Mrs. Haskell tells Johnny that she last saw the Buddha before Mr. Harcourt died two years ago. After assuring Mrs. Haskell that he is authorized to go into the study, Johnny is taken into the room, which is covered with dust. Johnny trips over a fan and goes to a wooden casket on the desk, but the Buddha is gone.

Johnny searches the room, but there is no trace of the Buddha. But how could someone get in without leaving a track in the dust? Mrs. Haskell tells Johnny that she has the only key to the room and no one has been in it except the taxman and the appraiser. Mr. Bancroft in town is the attorney. Johnny has the room re-sealed and tells Mrs. Haskell he will be back.

Johnny stops to see Mr. Bancroft and is told that only Mrs. Haskell has access to the study. Johnny is told that Mrs. Haskell was paid very little over the years and that she deserved more. All the valuable things, the collection of tapestries have been willed to various museums, and they were kept in a hermetically sealed room.

When Johnny asks about the hermetically sealed room, Bancroft tells him that both the library and study had very thick doors and sealed windows. That information causes Johnny to wonder about the source of the dust in the study.

Bancroft tells Johnny that Charles Curtis the nephew is an admirable man. He is going to be a lawyer and is very wealthy. He plans to donate the Buddha to a museum. Johnny has an idea about the dust and the tapestries and goes to play a hunch.

Johnny searches Mrs. Haskell's room and finds a bankbook with a very low balance and a sudden deposit of $21,000. Johnny thinks it is the money from the Buddha.

Johnny takes her to the study and shows her that the dust is really fuller's earth, which was used to clean tapestries. Johnny tells her that the fan he tripped on earlier did not have any dust on it because that is what was used to spread the dust in the room.

Mrs. Haskell refuses to go with Johnny to the police and tells Johnny that she deserved more. Now she has money, plenty of money and offers Johnny a bribe of $10,000 or $12,000. Johnny tells her to think of a better way out, and she is going to have plenty of time to think.

"Yeah, I know, the Mei Ling Buddha still has to be brought back from Paris. Maybe I will get the assignment. Maybe it will go to one of our regular foreign investigators. As for Mrs. Haskell, well I am sure Mr. Bancroft will not waste any time in taking whatever steps are necessary."

Notes:

- "Next week, well, far be it from me to get up on a soapbox, but I hope you'll make a point of listening to it. It concerns a lot of money in the wrong hands, in the hands of a bunch of kids too young to meet responsibility. Too young to realize that cutting loose from family before they are ready can lead to trouble. In this case, murder. Yeah, I think you better hear it."
- Fuller's Earth is a fine clay like substance which is used to clean fabrics, and as a catalyst.
- The incorrect spelling of Buddha (Buddah) in the title is taken directly from the script title page.
- The announcer is Dan Cubberly.

Producer: Jack Johnstone   Writer: Jack Johnstone
Cast: Virginia Gregg, Paul Dubov, Will Wright, Forrest Lewis

♦ ❖ ♦

Show: **The Only One Butt Matter**
Show Date: **7/5/1959**
Company: **Eastern Liability & Trust Company**
Agent: **Fred Wakely**
Exp. Acct: **$25.55**

Synopsis: Fred Wakely calls Johnny because he thinks Johnny is the best private eye in the business. He wants Johnny to investigate something that may or may not fall under the heading of insurance. The matter concerns Sarah Balderson Barling, who is an important client. Johnny is told that in addition to his expenses he will get a $5,000 bonus for handling this case.

Johnny cabs to Fred's office and is told that Mrs. Barling is worried about her daughter, Truda Lynn Barling, who is just over twenty-one and threw herself a birthday party that cost $40,000, including the damage to the hotel. She is young, wealthy and rebellious and does not get along with her mother.

Truda packed up and left 5 days ago with Harvey Howard, who is a playboy. Lucy Taylor, a "playmate", also left with Truda. Johnny is told to bring Truda back or the company will lose all of its insurance. When Johnny starts to decide against the case, he is offered $10,000 to find Truda.

Johnny finds the taxi driver who took Truda and her friends to the train station where they went to New York City. Johnny calls Randy Singer in New York and he knows who Truda is. She and her friends have been raising cane around the nightclubs, and Truda is staying at an expensive apartment.

Johnny trains to New York and goes to the apartment Truda was renting. After getting past the doorman and the elevator operator, Johnny notices the door to the apartment is open. Johnny rings the bell several times and gets no answer. Johnny walks in to find the body of Truda, who had been beaten with a bronze candlestick holder, and calls Randy Singer. Johnny searches the apartment and notices a still-smoking cigarette butt. Johnny calls Randy back and tells him to pick up Harvey and Lucy on his way over.

Johnny questions the elevator operator and the doorman and learns that there is only one entrance to the building. Two people had been to see Miss Barling after she had been to see Doctor Thorson across the street.

Miss Barling came back and said she was going to leave. Then Miss Taylor came by about ten minutes before Johnny got there and left almost immediately. Then Harvey Howard had come there right after Miss Taylor left. He only stayed a minute also.

Johnny leaves to go to see Dr. Thorson, who tells Johnny that Truda had a mild ulcer and was a hypochondriac. She used the doctor as a confidant and came to see him to boost her courage. She told him she was now able to think for herself and had decided to renounce the two "leeches" that came with her and go back to Hartford. Johnny is sure one of them killed her, but who?

Johnny is told the police are there when he gets back. Randy has Miss Taylor and Howard locked in the bedroom. Randy calls Miss Taylor a "real looker" and tells Johnny that she was in her hotel room packing, as was Howard.

Johnny meets the two friends and questions them. Lucy tells Johnny that she came to see Truda every day. She admits that Truda called her to tell her that she was going home. When Lucy got there, Truda would not let her in. Howard tells them that he found the door open when he got there to talk to her. He came and knocked but got no answer. Howard then admits that he came in and found the body, and Lucy tries to get him to admit he killed her.

Randy tells Howard that he came in, found Truda sitting in a chair smoking a cigarette, put on his gloves and killed her, but Howard denies it. Lucy tells Johnny that she did not come into the apartment.

Johnny tells Randy that he had found a cigarette with lipstick on it, but it was Lucy's cigarette. Truda would hardly smoke a cigarette with an ulcer and her other "illnesses". Howard then tells them that Truda did not smoke. Johnny tells Randy to take Lucy's gloves, where the lab will probably find microscopic traces of bronze from the candle stick she was beaten with.

"Yeah, guilty as sin. But you know something, if that pretty-boy Harvey had found her alive when he'd arrived, I am not so sure he wouldn't have done her in. There are times I am glad I am not rich, with a bunch of these leeches around grabbing at my dough. Which reminds me, that nice extra fee you promised me on this case."

Notes:
- Jim Matthews is the announcer.

Producer: Jack Johnstone   **Writer:** Jack Johnstone
Cast: Virginia Gregg, Les Tremayne, Herb Vigran, Alan Reed, Frank Gerstle, Jack Edwards, Jack Grimes

Show:	**The Frantic Fisherman Matter**
Show Date:	**7/12/1959**
Company:	**Greater Southwest Insurance Company**
Agent:	**Roy Harkins**
Exp. Acct:	**$650.85**

Synopsis: Buster Favor calls Johnny from Lake Mohave and tries to bait him to come out and go fishing. Buster tells Johnny to come on out for a few days, as "the days a man spends fishing are not deducted from his life span". Johnny asks if Buster has some insurance problem to bill his expenses to, and Buster thinks that there might be something here, so Johnny relents. Johnny tells Roy that he had no notion that the company was involved, but the facts will justify paying the expenses, plus a big fat fee.

Johnny flies to Las Vegas and rents a car to drive to Lake Mohave Resort. When Johnny gets to the lake, Buster gives Johnny a room and a new Harnell rod with a Mitchell 300 reel. Buster tells Johnny that the insurance matter is out on the lake and leaves to meet Johnny on the dock.

Buster and Johnny take a boat to a narrow cove where another man is fishing with a large saltwater rod. Buster fakes a motor problem and quietly tells Johnny that the man is Otis Hellman from Los Angeles. Buster tells Johnny to watch him when he gets back to the dock. Johnny remembers that Otis has just gotten out of prison, and Buster tells Johnny that he has been at the same cove day after day, and he isn't after fish.

Johnny and Buster fish for a while and watch out for Hellman. Buster leaves to beat Hellman to the dock where Hellman tells them that he had caught nothing. Johnny notices the large treble hooks that Hellman is using. Later Buster tells Johnny that Hellman had told him he was trying to snag carp. Johnny is sure that Hellman is trying to snag something, and Buster thinks that there is a body in the lake, and that is why he called Johnny.

Johnny calls Roy Harkins and Roy tells Johnny that Hellman had taken $60,000 from a mine, along with his partner Oscar Kirkman. Kirkman has disappeared and so has the money. Johnny tells Roy he might be able to find Kirkman's body.

Johnny prepares to drive to Las Vegas to rent some special equipment when Johnny learns from Buster that Hellman had been watching Johnny that morning. In Las Vegas, Johnny rents a skin diving outfit and learns that a man had rented some gear a couple years ago from the same store and never brought it back. His name was Kirkman.

Johnny gets a topographical map and studies it in his room. Johnny shows Buster where the cove is and where a mine called Kirkman's Folly is at the end of the cove, right where Hellman had been fishing.

Johnny borrows Buster's boat and goes to the cove as Buster arranges for Hellman's boat to have troubles. Johnny dives into the cove and finds the entrance to the old mine. Johnny removes the boards on the entrance, finds a package of money wrapped in plastic and wax, which he takes it to the surface.

Johnny throws the money into his boat and is told "thanks" by Hellman, who is waiting for him. Johnny overturns Hellman's boat and drags him under the water until he faints.

"Buster, bless his heart had been worried when he saw Hellman follow me up the lake. So, he had borrowed a boat and was waiting for us there at the end of the cove. Otis Hellman, well that is up to the courts. The money of course, all $60,000 of it, will go back to the company."

Notes:
- The announcer Jim Matthews.

Producer:	Jack Johnstone	Writer:	Jack Johnstone
Cast:	Barney Phillips, Sam Edwards, Bartlett Robinson, Forrest Lewis, Ralph Moody		

♦ ❖ ♦

Show:	The Will and a Way Matter
Show Date:	7/19/1959
Company:	Greater Southwest Insurance Company
Agent:	Jake Kessler
Exp. Acct:	$3,280.00

Synopsis: Red Barrett calls Johnny from Lake Mohave Resort and tells him to come back out. He had been in Kingman when Johnny was there and has run into some trouble. When Avery Nicolette died, Red went to take care of his things, including his money. Red discovered that someone had changed the will, and the police and insurance company agree that the will was valid. Red tells Johnny to come out if he ever expects to see Red again.

Johnny flies to Las Vegas, rents a car and drives to Kingman, Arizona and goes to Jake Kessler's office. Jake tells Johnny that he had written Avery's policy and the beneficiary was to be named in the will, which is highly irregular. They were not sure that Avery had a will until Red showed them where it was.

Red was the only friend Avery had, and Red was supposed to get everything but the insurance, all of which amounted to a couple thousand in the bank, his clothes and things. Johnny tells Jake that the will had been tampered with, but Jake tells Johnny that the authorities were sick of Red badgering them about the will.

Jake tells Johnny that a man named Louis Marino was supposed to get the money according to Mrs. Turner, a nurse and housekeeper for Avery. She had heard Avery mention Marino. Also, the other witness, Tim Hanson had been killed in an accident. After startling Jake by telling him he is on expense account, Johnny leaves to talk to Red at Lake Mohave.

Red tells Johnny that Avery had shown Red the will and Marino was not in it. As Red tells Johnny that Marino got angry when he mentioned calling Johnny, shots ring out.

Buster knocks on the door and tells Johnny the shots came from up on the old mining road. Buster knows that Marino had been living in Vegas and working in a garage. Buster had used Tim from time to time, and tells Johnny that Tim never drank, even though he was supposedly drunk when he was killed.

Johnny learns that Avery had come to Kingman in January, and Mrs. Turner became his nurse in March when Avery got sick. The will was also made out in March and Marino came to Vegas in March. Tim Hanson died in April, and Red almost died in April in a car crash when his steering gave out.

Johnny leaves to see the surrogate of the will, lawyer Robbins. Johnny goes to Robbins' office and looks at the will, which leaves the insurance money to Mario. The handwriting seems identical, and the police have examined it. Johnny looks at the paper under a magnifying glass and bets that Marino was an addition to the will. Johnny asks Robbins to arrange a meeting with Red, Marino and Turner for the next morning. Johnny leaves to go back to Lake Mohave but stays in a motel after his rental car explodes in a bomb blast.

Johnny calls the police and learns from Sgt. Tommy Parker that the police have been suspicious of Marino too. Sgt. Parker tells Johnny that the police in Vegas had run a check on Marino, and he was recognized as "Louis the Penman", a forger for the mob in Chicago. Parker checked on Mrs. Turner, her real name was Polito, with a string of elderly husbands who died in car accidents. Interestingly, her first husband was Louis Marino.

Johnny goes to the meeting with Robbins and takes Sgt. Parker with him. Johnny arrives just as Red tells everyone that he will give the money to charity, and Marino gets angry. Johnny lets Mrs. Turner know that he knows about her former husbands and Marino tells Johnny that Hanson was drunk, but Johnny tells him that Hanson never drank. Johnny notes that someone could have tampered with the car, and that Louis is a mechanic.

Mrs. Turner tells Johnny that she and Hanson had seen Avery write the will. They all signed it, folded it and put it in an envelope. Johnny tells them that the paper is coated, and folding breaks the coating causing ink to bleed, like it has on the will. The part giving the money to Marino was added after Mrs. Turner found the will in the linen closet. Robbins looks at the paper and is convinced that Johnny is right, at which time Louis pulls a gun.

"Yeah, Louis pulled a gun and started making the normal fool of himself. Then Sgt. Parker quietly walked in and took over. And, you know something? I think that given time with Mary and Louis in the clink for this forgery, he will probably pin those other things I mentioned on him, as he is a good man."

Notes:
- Expenses include replacement of the rental car.
- The announcer is Jim Matthews.

Producer: Jack Johnstone Writer: Jack Johnstone
Cast: Virginia Gregg, Barney Phillips, Forrest Lewis, Parley Baer, Jack Moyles, Billy Halop, Byron Kane

Show: The Bolt out of the Blue Matter
Show Date: 7/26/1959
Company: Four State Mutual Insurance Company
Agent: Harry McQueen
Exp. Acct: $171.50

Synopsis: Harry McQueen calls from Gloucester and he has a funny one for Johnny. It seems that someone is threatening the life of Amos Weatherby, a retired sea captain. He lives on Cape Anne, and his niece is the beneficiary of his $50,000 policy. She is worried about her uncle and has asked for Johnny to come up. Harry is sure that the niece is not plotting to get the money. And, Harry assures Johnny, that she is the most gorgeous girl Harry has ever seen.

Johnny drives his car to Annisquam, Massachusetts on Cape Anne (at 10 cents a mile). Johnny arrives at the big frame house that looks over the bay. One corner has a tower with a brass rail and a weather vane.

The niece Thelma Jean, is a real vision who knocks Johnny out with her looks. Thelma tells Johnny that the captain has gone up to the bridge to check on the weather. He usually spends all his free time there, watching the ocean.

Thelma tells Johnny that she was engaged to a man named Roger Burton, who the captain never liked. The captain discovered that Roger had been married twice to rich women who died mysteriously. Thelma broke off with Roger and the captain threw him out. Roger threatened to kill the captain and bragged he could get away with it as he did with a couple of "nosey wives".

After Johnny tries to flirt with Thelma, she tells Johnny that Harry McQueen had called Johnny an old, dull, stodgy, pedantic bumbling person. Thelma tells Johnny that after Roger had been thrown out, someone started sneaking around the property at night, and it must be Roger Burton.

Thelma is sure that the prowler is Roger. Thelma tells Johnny that she had seen Roger poking around between the house and an old building called the cell, which was an old jail, but is now used as a transformer station for the house.

As a storm builds, Thelma tells Johnny that the captain loves to stay up on his bridge during storms, it reminds him of his sailing days. Thelma tells Johnny that she had found ladder marks by the house that morning.

The captain comes down and asks for the location of his sou'wester. Johnny is introduced as an old friend who will stay for the night. Thelma shows Johnny the ladder marks and Johnny finds a lightning rod that has been cut off, and a copper wire leading to the transformer station. Johnny goes to the bridge and finds the copper wire attached to the brass railing the captain was holding on to.

Johnny tells the captain to go below, but he refuses until Johnny slugs him. Johnny carries the captain downstairs and Thelma is upset. Johnny tells her about the cable and tells her to keep the captain off of the bridge.

Johnny goes to the transformer house and sees where the doors are open with Roger waiting inside with a .38. Roger tells Johnny how he will kill the Captain, and Johnny can only wait. Johnny sees that the cable on the railing is connected to a 22,000-volt transformer that Roger will use to electrocute the captain.

Roger tells Johnny that he will throw the switch when the captain goes out on the deck, and it will kill the captain and melt the copper wire, and everyone will think that lightening killed the captain. Roger points to the captain getting ready to go out and hold onto the rail. Suddenly a bolt of lightning strikes and Roger is electrocuted.

"Yeah, the bolt of lightning had struck the rod high up on the tower, had streaked down the wire into the blockhouse and fairly exploded inside of it. The force had blown me out through the door and it was a couple of hours later inside the house before I was able to move. Burton, holding the switch had been killed instantly. I am glad I hadn't tried to get any closer to him. It was a bolt out of the blue. It was justice in its own strange fashion."

Notes:
- The announcer is Jim Matthews.

Producer: Jack Johnstone   Writer: Jack Johnstone
Cast: Virginia Gregg, Carleton G. Young, Ralph Moody, James McCallion

• ❖ •

Show: **The Deadly Chain Matter**
Show Date: 8/2/1959
Company: **Continental Insurance & Trust Company**
Agent: **Bill Ferguson**
Exp. Acct: **$27.35**

Synopsis: A very addled Alvin Peabody Cartwright calls Johnny. Alvin is being threatened and he wants Johnny to look into the matter. Johnny is to come to Lakewood before he is killed. If Johnny does not come, and he is killed, Alvin will cancel all of his insurance.

Johnny recounts how Alvin has been taken advantage of in the past as he cabs to Bill Ferguson's office. Bill has heard nothing but tells Johnny to look into the matter.

Johnny drives to Lakewood, Connecticut in his personal car. Johnny knocks at the door only to have Alvin thank him for the unexpected visit.

Inside, Alvin tells Johnny that he will get killed like Hector Kenworthy and Alpheus J. Perrim if he does not carry on a chain letter. Alvin reads the letter that promises him money in a dozen-dozen hours (that is six days, Alvin figured it out all by himself!) if he forwards the chain letter. But if he breaks it, dire circumstances will come to him. His two friends broke the chain, and they are both dead. Alvin tells Johnny that Kenworthy died six days after he broke the letter.

Johnny tells Alvin about the nature of phony chain letters that have duped the general public. Alvin tells Johnny that this chain letter goes only to an exclusive group of retired people. Alvin tells Johnny that hit-and-run drivers killed both of his friends on the 6th day after they broke the chain.

Alvin tells Johnny that Admiral Parley Baron forwarded the chain letter and came into a fortune, and Adjutant Frederick Melchior was cured of cancer. Alvin tells Johnny that he is supposed to send $100 to a post office box in New

York, where the name at the top of the letters will receive it. Two other wealthy people in the area have received similar letters. Johnny is sure that someone has bought a list of rich people and is using it to bilk them. Johnny tries to call the police, but the phone is dead. Alvin is sure that someone has come to get him.

Johnny goes out to look at the phone lines and is slugged by a man. Johnny wakes up in the library with a headache and Alvin offering him a drink of brandy. Alvin tells Johnny that he had followed Johnny and hit the man with a cricket bat and has him tied up and locked in a closet.

Johnny questions the man, who was a "pug-ugly gorilla" who had been hired to beat Alvin and make it look like a burglary. After a night's sleep the phone is fixed and the man is still in the closet.

Johnny calls Randy Singer and gives him the address the letter was supposed to be sent to and asks him to have the box watched. Johnny visits Mrs. Templeton and tells her not to send any money or she could go to prison. Johnny and Alvin visit Mr. Winterbottom and tell him the same thing.

Johnny goes back to Alvin's home, where Randy calls to tell Johnny that he has nabbed Daniel Stringer, who has a number of aliases. He was opening a number of chain letters full of money and was getting ready to mail more. Johnny tells Randy he will get a postal inspector to prefer charges.

"Yeah, maybe some of those chain letters, the little ones, are harmless, but again, maybe they are not. And they are all against the law. But there is only one thing to do, avoid them like the plague. Or better still, if you get one, take it right down to your local postmaster. He'll know how to go about helping to stamp out this racket. And believe me, that's all it is, a racket."

Notes:
- This story appears to have originally been an AFRTS program with a public service announcement about the electors of the Electoral College. I have several copies, but only one has this PSA.
- The announcer is Jim Matthews.

Producer:	Jack Johnstone	Writer:	Jack Johnstone
Cast:	Virginia Gregg, Howard McNear, Paul Dubov, Frank Gerstle, Herb Vigran		

◆ ❖ ◆

Show:	**The Lost by a Hair Matter**
Show Date:	8/9/1959
Company:	**Worldwide Mutual Insurance Company**
Agent:	**Fred Starkey**
Exp. Acct:	**$162.70**

Synopsis: Fred Starkey calls Johnny from Columbus and wants Johnny to come out on a case. Mrs. George Hemingway Tilford is pretty wealthy since her lumberyard burned down. She insists on Johnny coming out to talk to her. Johnny agrees to come, as the company is going to cover his expenses and his usual fees.

Johnny flies to Columbus, Ohio and cabs to the Hilton for the night. Johnny visits Fred the next afternoon. Fred has nothing new to tell Johnny. The lumberyard fire was a total loss, and cost the company $330,000, but it was under insured. The yard was near Minerva Park. Her husband left Mrs. Tilford a quarter million in securities when he died several years ago. She is a great admirer of Johnny's. Fred is sure that the visit has nothing to do with the insurance, and bets Johnny $500.

Johnny rents a car and drives to Minerva Park and the Tilford home. Mrs. Tilford meets him at the door, and she is really glad to see Johnny. She tells Johnny that she listens to his program every Sunday on WBNS. She wrote Johnny for a picture a year ago, and wishes she was young again after meeting Johnny.

She sneaks Johnny into the library, past the three suspects in the living room. She tells Johnny that she has figured out why the lumberyard burned down. She is sure it was set. Mrs. Tilford tells Johnny that each of the three suspects could have gained from the fire. She has proof and knows Johnny can figure it out. She is kind of holding out for a big climax, and Johnny is going to help her make sure. Johnny goes in to meet the suspects.

First is Harry W. Shelder, the husband's business manager who is very clever about money. He could have burned the lumberyard down so that it could be replaced by homes and stores, making it worth millions. Second is Michael Tilford, an adopted son, who went to business college, but did not do very well and has been living at home. He wants to sell the property to a development company. Mr. Tilford's will stipulated that Michael would get half the income from the property if it were sold. Third is Nancy Willis, Mrs. Tilford's niece. Her parents were not wealthy but she is the heir to the bulk of the estate. Mrs. Tilford goes upstairs to wash her hair and Johnny meets the suspects.

Shelder tells Johnny that Mrs. Tilford does not have long to live. She can make millions if he manages the property for her. Michael calls Shelder's plans too risky. He wants someone else to take the risk while all we, er, mother has to do is sit by and share in the profits. Neither trusts the other for one second. Nancy tells Michael that she is tired of his plans and to let Aunt Grace handle things her way. Mrs. Haskell is called and told to bring in the portable bar for cocktails. Mrs. Haskell runs back into the living room and tells them that Mrs. Tilford is dead.

Johnny recounts how she had died sitting under the hair drier and knocked it over when she fell. The doctor arrives and he calls the cause of death a heart attack.

Harry and Michael continue to argue with each other. Michael tells Johnny how she gave everyone more than they deserved. Even Michael admits he took money from her. Nancy tells Johnny that she took care of her aunt because neither Harry nor Michael had been there for weeks. Mrs. Haskell tells Johnny how Nancy bought the hair dryer, and how much Mrs. Tilford loved it.

Johnny remembers a newspaper article about a freak accident with a hair drier just like Mrs. Tilford's, and how it had injured someone a month earlier. A wire had come loose, and there was a big noise about it. Harry tells Johnny that Nancy had bought the drier three weeks earlier as a gift, but she charged it to Mrs. Tilford's account.

Johnny inspects the drier and finds the bare wire that electrocuted Mrs. Tilford. Johnny tells them that Harry and Michael had not been there for weeks, and Mrs. Haskell was afraid of it. Johnny tells Nancy that she was there and Nancy pulls a gun and Michael tries to take it from her and is shot. Johnny takes the gun and the police are called.

"So, Nancy's wild shot busted one of his ribs, but Mike will recover. Nancy? I don't know what the penalty for murder is in Ohio, but believe me, she will find out the hard way. As for the estate, well that is up to the courts too. No doubt much of what might have been Nancy's share will go to the company for that payment on the fire."

Notes:
- The announcer is Jim Matthews.

Producer:	Jack Johnstone Writer: Jack Johnstone
Cast:	Virginia Gregg, Helen Kleeb, Shirley Mitchell, Ben Wright, Sam Edwards, Harry Bartell, Lawrence Dobkin

◆ ❖ ◆

Show:	**The Night in Paris Matter**
Show Date:	8/16/1959
Company:	Floyds of England
Agent:	George Reed
Exp. Acct:	$5,878.00

Synopsis: George Reed calls Johnny and tells him that he wishes he was going to France at someone else's expense. George tells Johnny that he has just received a collect transatlantic phone call from Johnny's friend Louis De Marsac, "Les Chat Gris". He wants to talk to Johnny about the Olney diamond, three quarters of a million in diamonds in a necklace that was stolen from the Earl of Olney in the states during a recent visit. George tells Johnny that he will not quibble over the expense account.

Johnny calls "Les Chat Gris" and learns, after a promise of $2,000, that he can help Johnny find the diamonds.

Johnny gets $1,000 in American Express Travelers Checks and flies to Paris, France. On the plane, Johnny sits next to Annette Dubov, a lovely young lady with money of her own. Annette recognizes Johnny's name from the radio and tells him that she has no definite plans, a situation Johnny promises to change.

In Paris, Johnny takes a cab to the Hotel du Louvres shaves and goes to meet Louis De Marsac. At Louis' apartment, Johnny notices that the door is open and goes in to find the apartment was in shambles.

The phone rings and Johnny answers, only to talk to Louis. Louis tells

Johnny to meet him at the Café Chez Macabre, a beatnik place. While Johnny is on the phone, a man comes in and slugs Johnny. Johnny wakes up in a chair next to a bottle of cognac and a note nearby saying "je regrette", "I'm sorry".

Johnny leaves and goes to the café to meet Louis. The Café is a really dirty place, full of strange people. Louis comes in and sits at Johnny's table. Johnny tells him what had happened and Louis tells Johnny the man must have thought Johnny was Louis and apologized.

Louis starts ranting something for the benefit of someone else. Louis tells Johnny that Francois Duboisson, the art dealer, has the Olney diamonds. Johnny remembers that Duboisson was involved in the Vincent Price painting case and the Blue Madonna case.

Louis tells Johnny that he has arranged for Johnny to pay Duboisson 50,00,000 francs, and that Duboisson will contact Johnny tonight at midnight. Duboisson will be looking for Johnny under the name Robert Matthews, a rich man from Texas. Johnny warns Louis about a double-cross and agrees to pay $3,000 if all goes well. Johnny relates how most crimes are solved, not by detectives, but by informants who must be paid-off.

Johnny arranges for another room and waits to meet Duboisson at midnight. Johnny realizes his gun is missing just as the phone rings. Duboisson is on the phone and Johnny tells him to come on up. Johnny is warned that Duboisson has a gun with a silencer, just in case.

Johnny rigs up a dummy in the bed and then waits behind the door. Duboisson comes in and tells Johnny that he is wise to him. Annette tells Francois that she is sure Johnny is here. Annette realizes that there is a dummy in the bed, and that Johnny has no gun.

Johnny throws a light bulb as a distraction and tackles Duboisson, only to find out that Annette has the gun. Louis De Marsac comes in and slugs Annette, only to raise his fee to $5,000 for saving Johnny's life.

"Of course, there will be some fancy international legal procedure necessary, but I am sure the company can arrange for return of the necklace to the United States. As for Duboisson, and the lovely but treacherous Annette, well the Paris police are making the arrangements for them, and I am sure that they will not be very pleasant ones. Incidentally, I met a luscious little blond on that return trip, and she...well let's not go into that."

Notes:
- This program makes a reference to *The Price of Fame Matter*, broadcast on 2/2/1958, and *The Blue Madonna Matter*, broadcast on 2/22/1959.
- The script lists John {Bill} James and Gus Bayz for providing "Ad Libs".
- The announcer is Dan Cubberly.

Producer: Jack Johnstone   Writer: Jack Johnstone
Cast: Virginia Gregg, Forrest Lewis, G. Stanley Jones, Tony Barrett, Bill James, Gus Bayz

♦ ❖ ♦

Show:	**The Embarcadero Matter**
Show Date:	8/23/1959
Company:	Floyds of England
Agent:	George Reed
Exp. Acct:	$1,174.00

Synopsis: The night clerk calls Johnny in his Paris hotel room, and George Reed is calling from Hartford, and Johnny has to tell the nosy night clerk to get off the line. George congratulates Johnny for recovering the Olney jewels, in spite of the money spent. Johnny is to contact Maurice Rigot in Paris. Rigot wants help recovering the Cellini Medallion, which has been stolen from the Louvre three weeks ago. Johnny tells George that he has a better idea.

Johnny calls Louis De Marsac, "Les Chat Gris", who tells Johnny that he has made only one small investment with the money he had gotten from Johnny, she was so young and beautiful, so why did she steal from Louis? Johnny offers Louis $100 for information on the medallion, and Louis agrees to bring the information for $200.

Louis comes to Johnny's room an hour later and tells Johnny that the medallion is on its way to San Francisco, hidden in a shipment of wine on the Klemperhol, a freighter out of Le Havre. It will arrive tomorrow, and the medallion is hidden in a bottle of wine. Frank Gerstel, a fence who used to operate in New York, is supposed to pick up the wine. The correct case has a circle with a Maltese Cross in it. Johnny pays Louis $200 and questions how he got so much information so quickly. Louis tells Johnny that he helped his friends smuggle the wine aboard the ship and marked the case himself.

Johnny flies to San Francisco, California and goes to the Huntington Hotel. Johnny walks to a restaurant for dinner and walks back to his hotel, only to be followed. The man following Johnny turns out to be his old friend Smokey Sullivan.

Smokey tells Johnny that he has been hanging around the docks and has learned that there is a lot of smuggling going on there, mostly narcotics. Johnny advises Smokey to go to the Feds, but Smokey is concerned about his past.

Smokey had seen Frankie Gerstel hanging around the docks waiting for a boat, and Smokey helped Frankie unload a shipment of wine this morning. Johnny and Smokey head for the warehouse where the wine is stored.

Johnny pounds on the door for a night watchman, only to find him dead, shot in the head. Johnny wonders if Frankie got there first and has the medallion. Johnny takes the guard's flashlight and goes into the warehouse to look for the medallion.

Johnny spots the cases of wine and goes to them in the dark. Johnny spots an opened case and hears a noise. There is a shot, and Johnny waits in the dark. Frankie calls to Johnny to give up and shoots several times. Johnny throws a cinch bar to distract Frankie. Johnny gets a bead on him and fires but misses.

Frankie walks to the crates to kill Johnny and is shot by Smokey, he had the night watchman's gun. The police arrive and Smokey wants to run, but Johnny reminds him that he is on the side of the police now.

"The Cellini medallion: in Frankie's pocket. It was pretty obvious that he'd killed the watchman, taken the medallion out of the wine case and was about to leave when we showed up. Smokey's shot had killed him. Had Smokey a bit worried too, when the police barged in on us, but now he is a public hero. Oh, sure, there will have to be some kind of hearing on the whole affair, my deposition is already in. But Smokey is really in the clear, as for the couple hundred bucks I gave him, well forget it George, it came out of my own pocket."

Notes:
- Bob Bailey welcomes stations KAAB in Hot Springs, Arkansas, WRIG in Wausau, Wisconsin, WOMI in Owensburg, Kentucky to the CBS network.
- Jack Johnstone uses a play on the name of one of the actors, Frank Gerstle as the name of the fence, Frank Gerstel.
- The announcer is Dan Cubberly.

Producer:	Jack Johnstone Writer: Jack Johnstone
Cast:	Forrest Lewis, Vic Perrin, G. Stanley Jones, Tony Barrett, Frank Gerstle

◆ ❖ ◆

Show:	The Really Gone Matter
Show Date:	8/30/1959
Company:	Universal Adjustment Bureau
Agent:	Pat McCracken
Exp. Acct:	$401.05

Synopsis: Pat McCracken calls Johnny about Percival Leslie Fairfoot, who is the head man at Tri-Western in Eugene, Oregon. He has $50,000 and wants to give it to the beneficiary of a policy, Mr. Jonathan Doe. Pat wants Johnny to find Mr. Doe, and Johnny wants his expenses and the usual commission based on face value of the policy. Pat tells Johnny that they usually make that deal based on what he is able to save the company. Johnny convinces him to stretch the point and give it to him on this case anyway.

Johnny flies to Portland and then gets a flight to Eugene, Oregon. In the Tri-Western office, Les Fairfoot welcomes Johnny. Les is a big-mouthed guy who offers Johnny a drink.

Les tells Johnny that Harvey Wakeman and his wife and son came here a few years ago to retire. Harvey bought a farm and did wonders with it. He left his insurance to John Doe, but Les does not know who Doe is. Johnny learns that Wakeman died in his sleep, and Doe had a farm just north of Wakeman's, and left Doe the money, but Les cannot find him.

The police cannot find him and want to wait. The policy stated that if the beneficiary cannot be proved to be alive, the money goes to the secondary beneficiary after seven years. Les wants Johnny to find Doe or prove him dead. Johnny is not sure how he will proceed.

Johnny rents a car and drives to the Wakeman farm. At the farm, Johnny meets Ben Wakeman, the son. Ben has no idea what had happened to Doe. Mrs. Wakeman is sure that Doe was so broken up about Harvey that he left after Harvey died. After all, Harvey had spent almost all of his time at Doe's farm, and their Allis Chalmers tractor is still there. Mrs. Wakeman wonders if Doe might have been murdered. Mrs. Wakeman has never met John Doe, nor has Ben. No one else in the area knew Doe either. Johnny is sure they are telling the truth.

Johnny goes to the police and gets the name of the man who worked the case, Sgt. Conroy. Johnny searches for other sources of information, but can find no trace of Doe, who has never owned a car, and has borrowed the Allis Chalmers tractor from Wakeman. Johnny searches for anything with Doe's name on it and finds nothing. Johnny wonders if Doe ever existed.

At city hall, Johnny is told that Mr. Waverley, the lawyer had signed all of Doe's papers, but Waverley is out of town. The next day Johnny goes to meet Sgt. Conroy but learns nothing. Conroy tells Johnny that Ben Wakeman was just like his father, very quiet. Conroy tells Johnny that Ben is the secondary beneficiary on the policy.

Johnny calls Fairfoot who tells him that Ben will get the $50,000 if he just waits. Johnny goes to the farm to talk to Ben, who has an answer for everything. Mrs. Wakeman just talks and talks while Johnny is there and threatens to call Mr. Waverley.

Johnny finally leaves to meet with Mr. Waverley. He tells Johnny that Mrs. Wakeman is the reason Harvey Wakeman spent his time on Doe's farm, to get some peace and quiet. Waverley cannot tell Johnny anything about Doe. He tells Johnny that Doe was never alive, he was a fictitious person. Harvey knew he would not live long and arranged for his farm to go to his wife and son.

We wanted to do more and arranged for Waverley to write the policy so that the money could not go to Ben until he is old enough. John Doe was a fictitious person for a sound logical reason. Harvey could leave the money to someone without slighting his wife or son yet have them benefit later. Waverley and Johnny agree it would be best for the Wakemans not to find out for about seven more years.

"So, Les, you can just hold this $50,000 payment outside and outstanding for a while. And don't forget to keep up the interest on it. Also, I think you have sense enough to keep your mouth shut about it."

Notes:
- This is the second story in which Jack Johnstone mentions Allis Chalmers farm equipment.
- The announcer is Dan Cubberly.

Producer: Jack Johnstone Writer: Jack Johnstone
Cast: Virginia Gregg, Lawrence Dobkin, Marvin Miller, Sam Edwards,

Junius Matthews, Stacy Harris, Bartlett Robinson

❖

Show:	**The Backfire that Backfired Matter**
Show Date:	9/6/1959
Company:	Universal Adjustment Bureau
Agent:	Pat McCracken
Exp. Acct:	$450.00

Synopsis: Johnny is called early in the morning by Betty Lewis, who asks Johnny to marry her, but gets the usual runaround from Johnny. Betty chides Johnny for missing her housewarming party. Johnny tells Betty that he was in Eugene, Oregon, and is concerned about the sound of shots in the background. Betty tells Johnny that they are backfires. Some kids have a hotrod and do it every morning at eight o'clock. Betty invites Johnny over for breakfast the next day to find out for himself. Maybe Betty can convince him to marry her. "So, why not?"

Johnny knows he has not been assigned to a case but urges Pat to read on. Johnny drives to Betty's house at 11325 Maple Drive in Hartford, Connecticut amazed at how many people are around early in the morning. Betty's house is a one-story house between two larger ones. Betty is amazed that Johnny is there before 8:00 and greets him with a great big kiss. She tells Johnny that if he had any sense he would marry her, but Johnny raises the same reasons why he cannot, the job, and Betty reluctantly agrees.

Betty tells Johnny that Barton J. Robinson, who is a bachelor, lives across the street. Johnny remembers that he prosecuted a big insurance fraud case a few years back. Betty tells Johnny that Robinson is very punctual, and always eats breakfast by the window at 8:00. Johnny tells Betty he is going to warn Robinson to stay away from Betty — she is his property. The hotrod shows up and the backfires sound off, but Johnny notes how the backfires stop when they pass Betty's house.

Betty tells Johnny that no one knows who the kids are who drive the car. Johnny remembers the tag number, 3CFU160, and calls Jerry Wilson at the motor vehicle office. Jerry tells Johnny that he must have made a mistake. Johnny tells Betty that the license was a phony, and the drivers were not kids.

Betty tells Johnny that Robinson has been away for a few weeks and this morning is the first time he has been there to eat his breakfast. Betty tells Johnny that the hot-rodders showed up a week after Robinson left. Johnny is sure that the drivers are casing the place.

Johnny leaves a very disappointed Betty with a kiss and a promise to take her out that night and goes to look into the matter of the phony tags and the drivers who were not kids. Johnny inspects tire marks left by the car and canvasses the neighbors to get information.

Later that afternoon the cook at a diner tells Johnny that he has seen the car take the cut-off to Biley's Swamp. Johnny drives there and sees the tire marks he is looking for. Johnny spots the car behind a shack and goes in, only to get slugged.

When Johnny wakes up he hears voices and a man is searching him. A man named Gil throws water on Johnny and a man named Ringer tells Johnny that the police must have given up on finding him after he got out of the clink and sent Johnny to find him.

Ringer tells Johnny that no one can stop him from killing the man who sent him up, Barton Robinson. Ringer tells Johnny that the backfires will cover the sound of the shots, and he only needs one. Ringer tells Johnny that Robinson has the place locked up tight, but tomorrow they will get Robinson as he eats breakfast.

Johnny is tied up with wet rawhide thongs as it starts to rain outside. After Ringer and Gil leave, Johnny rolls outside and puts the rawhide into a puddle to loosen the thongs and remove them.

Johnny hides behind the door as Ringer drives back and tells Gil that Robinson was not there at the window, and Johnny Dollar must have warned him. Another car drives up, and it is Betty.

Ringer shoots, but Johnny gets loose and slugs Gil as Betty hits Ringer with her car. She tells Johnny that when he did not come last night she was worried and had told Robinson to stay away from the window. Then she followed the car and rescued Johnny. Ringer gets up, but Johnny slugs him as he is kissing Betty to calm her nerves.

"It was Betty Lewis who really saved the life of that insurance attorney. So, most of this expense account covers some well-earned entertainment, plus a little gift for her. No, not an engagement ring, but a big jug of My Sin. But I must admit she certainly makes me think of the merits of…uh, yeah."

Notes:
- According to Google Earth, Maple Drive does exist in Hartford, but there is no 11315 Maple.
- The announcer is Jim Matthews.

Producer:	Jack Johnstone	Writer:	Jack Johnstone
Cast:	Virginia Gregg, Forrest Lewis, Barney Phillips, Tom Holland		

♦ ❖ ♦

Show: **The Leumas Matter**
Show Date: 9/13/1959
Company: **Worldwide Mutual Insurance Company**
Agent: **Les Walters**
Exp. Acct: **$89.50**

Synopsis: Les Walters calls Johnny and tells him that Elmer Leumas has disappeared, that there is nothing to go on.

Johnny goes to Les' office, and is told to go to Vineland, New Jersey, where Elmer was the owner of the Leumas Glass Company, from which he retired at 59 and lives with his younger wife Lena.

Johnny goes to Philadelphia and rents a car for the drive to Vineland, where he stops to see Sgt. Tomasso, who tells Johnny that Mrs. Leumas is not upset. She is a social butterfly but Leumas hated parties. Leumas left 10 days ago, took his luggage and sold his sailboat two days before he disappeared.

Johnny eats dinner with Sgt. Tomasso and then drives to the huge home of Lena Leumas, who is a real dish. She tells Johnny that she saw him in town and knew he would invite himself there. She tells Johnny that her husband was a big fan of his radio program and that she will get the insurance and a lot more money and she knows how to use money.

Johnny tells her that there are a couple of things that could put a crimp in her plans, but she tells him that "what Lena wants, Lena gets. That's why she married Elmer in the first place." When Johnny asks if she thinks that her husband was murdered, she asks who would want to kill sweet old Elmer?

She tells Johnny that she does not love Elmer, but she does try to keep him happy — that is the least she can do. She cannot understand why Elmer kept his moustache and goatee — with his shock of wiry hair it made him look older than he was, I mean is.

Lena tells Johnny that the boat was sold to Samuel Remle in Tuckahoe, New Jersey. Johnny changes his ploy and tells Lena that she had planned to kill Leumas, and she tells Johnny to leave. On the way out, Johnny meets Pete, who is protecting Lena. Pete calls Jerry and Johnny is knocked out. Johnny wakes up later and goes to his hotel.

The next day Johnny goes to the police and gets a hunch. Johnny goes to Tuckahoe and the boat, the *Lena*, is gone from Wilson's Landing. Johnny gets a description of the owner, who is clean-shaven with short hair.

Johnny calls the Coast Guard and learns that the boat is in Cape May. Johnny drives to Cape May and meets the owner of the boat, but is it Leumas or Samuel?

Johnny meets the owner and is told that "Leumas" spelled backwards is "Samuel", and "Elmer" spelled backwards is "Remle". As for Pete and Jerry, they are bodyguards he had left for Lena. Leumas tells Johnny that he is trying to figure out their relationship and does not know where he will go.

Pete and Jerry are arrested for assault, and as for Leumas and his wife, who knows?

Notes:
- The announcer is Jim Matthews.

Producer: Jack Johnstone Writer: Jack Johnstone
Cast: Virginia Gregg, Harry Bartell, Paul Dubov, Jack Kruschen, Sam Edwards, Russell Thorson

◆ ❖ ◆

Show: **The Little Man Who Was There Matter**
Show Date: **9/20/1959**
Company: **Universal Adjustment Bureau**
Agent: **Pat McCracken**
Exp. Acct: **$12.34**

Synopsis: Pat McCracken calls Johnny and tells him of 1, 2, 3 in a row, 3 mysterious disappearances in a row Johnny has worked on. First was the case of

John Doe, then Elmer Leumas who disappeared to get away from his wife. This case is in Kerr's Ferry, New York. The charges are perpetrating fraud against the insurance company.

Johnny cabs to Pat's office commenting on the three mysterious disappearances. Pat tells Johnny how Howard L. Edwards insured his life for $50,000, double indemnity, with his wife as beneficiary. The police are not sure he is dead, even though his car was found in the river. The police discovered that Edwards and his wife are stone-broke and living off the finance company.

The wife broke down and confessed that they had planned the disappearing act for some time. This type of fraud has been tried before. Johnny tells Pat that if he finds Edwards he will get a nice fat fee, which Pat almost chokes over. "Just find him", Pat asks.

Johnny drives to Kerr's Ferry and contacts Sgt. Ben Ringler at the local police department. Ringler tells Johnny that the Edwards car was deliberately run into the river. It was after midnight when his wife called and asked them to look for him. The next morning a kid spotted the car's wheels while fishing.

Edwards claimed to be an inventor and he had their house up for sale. That way she could leave as soon as she got the insurance money and no one would suspect her. Ringler is doubtful that Johnny can get anything out of Mrs. Edwards, he tried and got nothing, so what is Johnny going to be able to do?

Johnny visits Mrs. Edwards, but she does not want to open the door. When Johnny says he is with the insurance company, she lets him in. She hopes Johnny can find Howard, because the police can't. Ringler and his son-in-law have been pestering her.

She tells Johnny that Howard had been preoccupied with a machine and did not pay any attention to her. She is selling the house, as that is all they have left. The insurance would make up for all the skimping. She needs the money but does not wish her husband dead. Howard finally has found someone who would buy his invention, but everything is gone now.

Howard had been going to see the buyer, but the plans are now lost in the river. She had told Ringler, but his son-in law, Peter Barskin, said she was lying about them. Johnny infers that Howard would likely sell the invention and skip out on her, but she strongly disagrees, he would never do that. She told the police that Howard had talked of going away to work uninterrupted and they had told the insurance company.

Johnny goes back to police headquarters where Sgt. Ringler and Peter Barskin are playing checkers. Johnny tells them that they have not considered all the possibilities. Johnny is working on the possibility of murder.

Johnny calls Randy Singer and asks him to have a fingerprint expert come up to help him, and Randy agrees to have Marty Levit come up to help out. Marty arrives and they go to look at the car but Marty cannot find any fingerprints, including ones on the steering wheel and gearshift. The car had been wiped clean.

Johnny drives Marty to the train and goes to the Edwards house where Mrs. Edwards is very anxious. She shows Johnny how the house has been ransacked, and she had seen a man running out the back door. She tells Johnny that she has not called the police.

Johnny searches the house and finds part of a letter from a plastics company in a desk drawer. The letter seems to imply that the local authorities had recommended the man who Howard had gone to see. Johnny realizes that whoever had been there knew the value of those letters.

Peter Barskin walks in with a gun and tells Johnny that he will never find out. Johnny tells Pete that "this isn't Gunsmoke" and draws on Pete and shoots him. Pete asks how Johnny found out, and he tells Pete he was not sure until Pete came in with the gun.

Sgt. Ringler comes in and tries to arrest Johnny, but he is told to drop his gun or he too will get shot. Johnny is sure that Kerr's Ferry will get a new chief of police, and Ben and Pete might even share the same electric chair.

"Sure, it's up to the courts. But when the state police came in and found the papers on the invention hidden in Pete's house, oh, that invention now belongs to Mrs. Edwards, to say nothing of the insurance money, $50,000. So, Pat, I'll let you off the hook real easy."

Notes:
- This is an AFRTS program that contains a story about Cyrus W. Field, who laid a cable across the Atlantic, a story about the constitution and the 17th amendment.
- This program references *The Really Gone Matter*, broadcast on 8/30/1959 and *The Leumas Matter*, broadcast on 9/13/1959.
- The announcer is Jim Matthews.
- Most catalogs list *The Gruesome Spectacle Matter* as the next program to be broadcast on 9/27/1959. However, a check of the newspaper listings for 9/27/59 indicate that a special program with Maurice Chevalier was broadcast in the YTJD timeslot.

Producer: Jack Johnstone Writer: Jack Johnstone
Cast: Virginia Gregg, Lawrence Dobkin, Ralph Moody, Gil Stratton, Herb Vigran, Vic Perrin

♦ ❖ ♦

Show: **The Buffalo Matter**
Show Date: **10/4/1959**
Company: **Universal Adjustment Bureau**
Agent: **Pat McCracken**
Exp. Acct:

Synopsis: Pat McCracken calls and Johnny complains about not having an assignment for several days. Pat complains about the expense account from last week, which Johnny cannot clearly remember. Pat reminds him that the $12.30 was enough to make Pat worry that Johnny was sick. Pat tells Johnny that he has convinced the company to add on a $500 fee because he almost got himself killed. Pat tells Johnny to go to Buffalo and contact Edward J.

Macnear at Macnear's Emporium. Someone lifted over $400,000 from the safe over the weekend. Johnny is on his way.

Johnny flies to Buffalo, New York and meets with Mr. Macnear who totals the loss at $421,216 and he blames himself for the loss. John Harker had recommended changing the procedure, but he resisted.

Every Saturday night, each department head would bring the receipts to Harker who would issue a receipt and put the money in the vault. Johnny notes that it would have been better to have an armored car take the money to the bank, and Macnear agrees, and that is what Harker had suggested. As Johnny is told that Mr. Ellery was the last to knock on the door, there is a knock on the door and Mr. Harker enters.

Harker tells Johnny that Mr. Ellery knocked and told him who was there. Harker went to open the door but it was slammed open and he was knocked unconscious. When he woke up the money was gone from the safe. Ellery had been beaten and bound by the robbers. Ellery had told Harker that the robber was wearing a mask.

Macnear tells Johnny that Harker is taking his cruiser on a trip with a friend and is leaving that night. Johnny meets with the police and learns nothing.

Johnny meets with Mr. Ellery who tells Johnny that the events were just like Harker told the police. He usually had gone up, knocked on the door and given the money to Harker. That night, the man sneaked up on Ellery and threw him into the room. Ellery tells Johnny that Harker is working hard for the company and Macnear appreciated it.

Harker has been with the company for a year and has lived up to the recommendations from the big department stores. That is why Mr. Macnear has given him a much higher salary. Johnny wonders at the way Harker was sent out before he could be questioned, and the way the robber would have to know everything about the procedures.

Johnny goes to his hotel to unpack and notices his hand-bag was unlocked. He hears a sound he has heard before and throws the bag out of the window before it explodes. Johnny suspects that someone in Buffalo does not want him around.

Johnny explains to the police what had happened, and their theory is that the man in the mask planted the bomb. Johnny reviews how only three people knew he was there: Macnear, Harker and Ellery.

The next morning Johnny goes to the bank and meets an old friend named Barton, who is the Cashier and a Vice President. Johnny asks about the financial conditions of Macnear and his store and is told that Macnear is worth millions and the store pays cash for everything.

Johnny calls Macys, Gimbels and John Wannamaker's to check up on Harker. Johnny learns that none of the stores had ever heard of John Harker. Johnny goes back to Macnear and he has no idea where Harker has gone. Johnny suggests that by encouraging him to take his boat, Macnear played into his hands and allowed him to get away with his money.

Johnny tells Macnear that his friend is probably the man in the mask.

Johnny tells him that Harker had said, "he should have known by the tone in his voice that something was wrong" when Ellery knocked. But, Ellery did not know that the robber was there until after the door had been opened!

Johnny tells Macnear that he was a fool when he hired Harker, because his recommendations were fakes. He trained Harker how to fix the robbery and helped him get away. Johnny laments how he really needs a stroke of luck now, and luck shows up in the guise of a storm.

A big storm is approaching and the Coast Guard has notified all the boats on the lake. Harker responded and told them that they are riding out the storm in Canadian waters. Johnny asks, off the record, if he went out to get the men, would there be anyone who could do it. The Coast Guard remembers a man who has a converted sub chaser who might be able to take Johnny out. Johnny rents the boat and the skipper for $585 and relates how the case could have ended, but it will have to wait for the next report.

Notes:
- Pat chides Johnny over his $12.30 expense account for the previous case, but the actual figure was $12.34.
- The announcer is Jim Matthews.

Producer: Jack Johnstone   Writer: Jack Johnstone
Cast: Lawrence Dobkin, Bartlett Robinson, James McCallion, Richard Crenna, Junius Matthews, Gil Stratton

♦ ❖ ♦

Show: **The Further Buffalo Matter**
Show Date: 10/11/1959
Company: **Universal Adjustment Bureau**
Agent: **Pat McCracken**
Exp. Acct: **$1,800.00**

Synopsis: Pat McCracken calls Johnny and Pat has the expense report Johnny sent in, but why did he add return transportation when he is still in Buffalo? Johnny admits he got a little ahead of himself. Johnny tells Pat that he has not gotten the money back yet, but he knows where it is. It is impossible to get the money because of the storm. Johnny promises Pat that he will get the money back or die trying. Pat tells Johnny that he had better get the money back or he will gladly attend the funeral.

Johnny relates how the Coast Guard had prevented him from going out in the sub chaser because of the storm. Johnny was able to get half of the money back but will credit it to this report as the charge was on his American Express credit card.

Mr. Macnear visits Johnny in his hotel room. He tells Johnny that he does not want the crooks to get away with his money. Johnny tells him that the Canadians have been contacted, and there could be international problems if Harker does not have the money. Macnear tells Johnny he will ride Johnny out of Buffalo on a rail if he is wrong.

Johnny is not feeling so good but gets a call from Murphy at the Coast

Guard, and he has a weather report that the storm is subsiding. He can arrange a boat for Johnny once the weather clears. Johnny has an idea. He will be right on top of the crooks when the weather clears.

Johnny cabs to the municipal airport and spots what he needs. Johnny rents a helicopter from Tinker Barnham for $300. For $600, Johnny convinces Tinker to take off, even though the weather is not good. Johnny takes his first ride in a helicopter out over Lake Erie.

Tinker spots the Long Point peninsula and the cruiser. Johnny fastens himself to a winch as he spots Harker and a tough looking character on the boat. Johnny realizes he is outnumbered but tries a ruse. Johnny uses a megaphone to tell Harker that Macnear has found the man who took the money, but the money is still missing. Johnny mumbles something about Mr. Macnear and tells Harker he is coming down. Tinker eases Johnny down onto the cruiser.

Johnny is dropped onto the boat and Billy takes his gun from him. Harker tells Billy to shoot Johnny. Harker tells Johnny that he is not a fool and did not believe anything Johnny told him. Johnny is taken below, out of sight of the helicopter, and Harker signals to Tinker to leave.

As Tinker leaves Billy gets ready to shoot Johnny, but Tinker comes back. The boat starts up as Johnny looks at Billy's .38. Johnny is told to move to the front of the cabin and spots a duplicate set of controls as he moves forward.

Johnny stumbles and grabs the wheel, causing the boat to weave. Billy shoots, but Johnny slugs him and takes his gun. Johnny goes up on deck but Harker tells Johnny that he has a gun too.

The helicopter comes back and Harker shoots at Tinker and Johnny pushes Billy overboard. Johnny fights with Harker and overpowers him. Tinker calls to Johnny to make sure he is OK and then goes after Billy in the water. After all, Tinker had told the tower that this was a sea rescue operation.

"Yeah, like Billy had said, the stolen money, all of it, was stashed away in the forward chain locker. So, after tying up Harker with all the line I could find, I started the engine of that beautiful yacht but then suddenly realized, well put it this way: If Tinker and his copter hadn't stayed with me, so help me I never would have found my way back to Buffalo."

The expense account includes $1,000 for Tinker.

Notes:
- Johnny notes that this was his first ride in a helicopter, but in episode 3 of *The Star of Capetown Matter*, broadcast on 7/18/1956, Johnny was ferried to the Southern Empress in a military helicopter.
- Sam Edwards appears in this program, but the credits do not reflect it. RadioGOLDINdex notes that the ending of the program has been modified. Perhaps the original closing credits included the correct actors.
- The announcer is Jim Matthews on this and the previous program, but the scripts indicate that Dan Cubberly is the announcer.

Producer: Jack Johnstone   **Writer:** Jack Johnstone

Cast:	Lawrence Dobkin, Bartlett Robinson, James McCallion, Richard Crenna, Junius Matthews, Gil Stratton, Sam Edwards

Show:	**The Double Identity Matter**
Show Date:	10/18/1959
Company:	**Universal Adjustment Bureau**
Agent:	**Pat McCracken**
Exp. Acct:	**$20.00**

Synopsis: Johnny gets a call from a woman who tells him that she is home from her vacation and asks him to come over and propose. Johnny recognizes her as Betty Lewis. Johnny suggests he pop the question and asks, "so, will you marry me, Paula?" Betty wants to know who Paula is, and Johnny has to admit he was joking. Johnny suggests dinner, and Betty agrees to have the cocktails ready at 6:30. The phone rings again, and Randy Singer is on the phone. Randy has to see Johnny right now. Randy arranges for a squad car to pick Johnny up at Grand Central Station.

Johnny tells Pat McCracken that he has not been assigned to the case yet, but read on.

Johnny trains to New York City and meets Randy in his office. Randy tells Johnny that "they" are insurance matters, and Johnny should have been assigned to them. One case was Paul R. Brownfield who "committed suicide" by sleeping pills in the fall of 1956. Eastern Casualty and Trust paid $41,000 to his wife of two months, and she disappeared after she was paid off.

Franklin P. Ogborn died the same way in September 1957 and Tri-Mutual paid off $30,000. Peter William Gerheart died the same way in August 1958 and the widow collected $50,000. Last month William Earl Chadwick died and the company paid off $25,000.

In each case the marriage was only a few months old, and the wife was much younger, and the men were married to the same girl. Randy has found the girl, but she is out of his jurisdiction, but not Johnny's. The girl lives at 11325 Maple Drive in Hartford, Connecticut, and goes by the name of Betty Lewis!

Johnny reviews the files and the description of the girls is identical. According to Randy, the girl was Betty Lewis, the girl Johnny knows and almost took seriously. Randy wants Johnny to go back and get friendly with the girl and try to trip her up.

Randy tells Johnny that the sleeping pills used in each case were a special prescription. Randy has found a kid who delivered the pills, and the boy had letters telling him to make some more pills. Officer Conroy comes in and tells Randy that the reporter has been sent away. He had told him that Randy was busy with Johnny Dollar about the suicide cases.

Johnny is met at his apartment by Betty, who is anxious after her extended vacation. She is not going to give up on Johnny. Johnny asks how she got into the apartment, and she tells Johnny that the door was wide open.

Johnny asks about her vacation, and she tells Johnny that she had gone to several places, including New York. Johnny asks Betty what her hair color used to be, and she gets really irritated.

Johnny notices that his desk is all messed up and Betty asks Johnny if he always leaves the window to the fire escape and the front door open. Johnny goes in and finds where the window had been jimmied open, and Betty tells him that it looks just like her mailbox. Betty asks if Johnny's questions have anything to do with the article she saw in the papers about a number of suicides. Johnny is sure that Betty scared off someone when she got there.

Johnny realizes she had said her mailbox had been opened, and she tells Johnny that the lock was broken. Today, she came home from the office and there were high-heel footprints in the mud around the mailbox. Maybe someone was using her name and mailbox. Johnny wants a key to her house so he can solve four murders.

The next day, Johnny stays in the house after Betty leaves for work. At 10:30, the mailman leaves a package in the mailbox. Johnny goes out to get the package and it is addressed to Betty Lewis. A woman drives up and asks what Johnny is doing poking around her mailbox, and the girl looks a lot like Betty. She asks for the package, but Johnny tells her he needs it to pin the murders of four husbands on her. She pulls a gun and demands the package. Johnny takes the gun from her and puts her in her car for a drive to police headquarters.

"Sure, there is a lot more to be done, only by the police both in Hartford and down in New York. But there is not much doubt about the outcome, especially since the kid who supplied the drugs broke down and said plenty. The insurance companies? Well the money she had left can be prorated among them and that will be that. My problem of course will be explaining things to Betty. But, you know something, that may have its pleasant aspects, too." Johnny calls the expense total $20.00, provided there is a fee on this one.

Notes:
- This program contains commercials about the benefits of professional nursing, Stuart Erwin for 4-Way cold tablets, Fitch Dandruff Remover Shampoo, and Ex-Lax.
- Johnny notes that Betty Lewis is a blonde.
- This is the second reference to 11325 Maple Drive.
- The announcer is Dan Cubberly.

Producer:	Jack Johnstone	Writer:	Jack Johnstone
Cast:	Joan Banks, Lillian Buyeff, Herb Vigran, G. Stanley Jones		

❖

Show:	**The Missing Missile Matter**
Show Date:	**10/25/1959**
Company:	**Floyds of England**
Agent:	**George Reed**
Exp. Acct:	**$0.00**

Synopsis: George Reed calls John and asks if he has a security clearance. George cannot discuss the case over the phone, so Johnny goes right over.

Johnny cabs to the office of George Reed, who takes Johnny to an empty office. George tells Johnny that there is a small company in California that operated as the Smithwick Paint Remover Company. It really is a cover up and should be called the Smithwick Missile Company. The government does not recognize them, and Floyds writes the insurance based on orders from the top brass. Smithwick has reported that they have a missing missile. Dr. Smithwick will be waiting for Johnny.

Johnny flies to New York City and then to Los Angeles, California on a 707, rents a car and drives to the Smithwick Paint Remover building where Johnny notices a good-looking blond closing a door.

She is Gloria Snowden the secretary and knows who Johnny is. She tells Johnny that Dr. Smithwick has gone to Washington, and Gloria was told to have Johnny wait for him. Johnny gets directions to a motel and arranges to take Gloria to dinner. Johnny finds the motel and gets a room. There is a knock at the door and no one is there when Johnny opens it. There are two shots and Johnny groans.

Johnny gets up when the manager, Mr. Barnwell comes back and tells Johnny that he heard shots. Johnny asks how the manager knew they were shots and not a backfire. The manager tells Johnny that he did not see anyone, only a car pulling away. Johnny tells him not to call the police and arranges for another room without listing it on the register.

Johnny waits for a while and then goes back to get Gloria, but she is gone. Johnny sits in his second room and hears someone knocking on the other room. The visitor identifies himself as Bob McKenny, who used to work for CBS and handled his radio program, and he wants to talk to Johnny.

Bob had learned that Johnny was there from Mr. Barnwell, the manager. Bob has a tape recorder with some coded signals that he had recorded earlier that evening. Bob tells Johnny that he has an amateur license, W6BFG, and experiments with high frequency signals. Bob had crossed some wires and discovered signals on a frequency that is not supposed to be used by anyone. Bob recorded the signals and played it back real slow, and determined that it was international Morse code.

Johnny listens to the code and determines that is was not destined for anyone on this side of the iron curtain. Bob tells Johnny that the signal was very strong and probably originated nearby. Bob mentions that Kenny McManus has a direction finder and Bob will get him to help locate the signals. Johnny asks Bob to leave the tape recorder with him. Bob realizes that Johnny also had understood two words in the code: "Johnny Dollar"!

Johnny calls Lt. Harry Golden on the homicide squad, and he arranges for Alan Orloff, an interpreter, visit Johnny. Orloff tells Johnny that the tape had a threat against Johnny and secret plans for a missile and someone is holding them for an agent to pick up today.

Bob McKenny comes back and tells Johnny that the broadcast station is in North Hollywood. Bob gives Johnny the address and tells Johnny that there is no outside antenna. Johnny looks at the address and decides to go to the missile plant instead.

Johnny drives to the missile plant and Mr. Smithwick tells Johnny he was sure the missile plans were missing and had urged the government to send someone to look into the theft. The men should be here today. But when he returned from Washington, he found the plans in the proper place.

Johnny tells him the plans were stolen for the benefit of one of the big foreign powers. Johnny wants to call Gloria into the office, but Smithwick tells Johnny that the only reason she is there is because she is stupid.

Gloria is called into the office. Johnny tells Smithwick that Gloria was the only one who could arrange to have Johnny attacked and the last one to be suspected of copying the plans. Johnny prepares to play a tape of the signals taken from Gloria's home. Gloria pulls a gun and Johnny throws the tape recorder at her and gets the gun. Johnny hopes the G-men will keep the date with the contact Gloria was supposed to meet.

"The government boys were more than glad to take over, and I hope they can find some way to reward Bob McKenny who really solved this case."

Because this was so good a cause, Johnny waives the expense account.

Notes:
- This program has commercials for Camel cigarettes, Columbia Stereo One phonograph players, Mel Torme for 4-Way cold tablets, Fitch Dandruff Remover Shampoo, Swiss Vacation contest sponsored by the makers of Swiss watches, and Ex-Lax.
- Johnny mentions to Bob that he had "pounded a key" many years ago.
- Bob McKenny is listed as a technician on many of the Johnny Dollar scripts and was also a character in *The Wayward Kilocycles Matter* and *The Vociferous Dolphin Matter*.
- Kenny McManus is an associate director on some of the programs.
- Based on the closing preview in this program, it would seem that the order of this program and *The Double Identity Matter* may have changed at some point, although most catalogs place this program after *The Double Identity Matter*. Both script pages show an "Air Date" of October 18, 1959.
- The announcer is Dan Cubberly.

Producer: Jack Johnstone Writer: Jack Johnstone
Cast: Virginia Gregg, G. Stanley Jones, Forrest Lewis, Harry Bartell, Don Diamond, Bartlett Robinson

◆ ❖ ◆

Show: **The Hand of Providential Matter**
Show Date: **11/1/1959**
Company: **Providential Assurance Company**
Agent: **Ernest L. Whiteman**
Exp. Acct: **$0.00**
Synopsis: Ernest L. Whiteman from Providential Assurance Company calls, and Johnny tells him that he has never heard of him. Whiteman has a case of

embezzlement and wants Johnny to look into it. Johnny asks about the fee over and above his expenses, and is told he can name his own figure, up to $5,000 if he gets the $200,000 back. Johnny suggests that he should pad his expense account.

Johnny cabs to the Hartford, Connecticut offices of Mr. Whiteman where Johnny meets Elwood Sprague who is the owner of the company. Sprague tells Johnny that he made a lot of money in oil and started this company and is getting more money.

Mr. Whiteman and Sprague tell Johnny that his company is gaining a reputation by settling all their claims in cash without questioning them. Sprague tells Johnny that they hope to lose money in the business for tax reasons.

The money in question was stolen from the office and Tom Hauser was the one who stole the money. He kept the books and had the combination to the safe. Whiteman discovered today that Hauser had been juggling the books and now Hauser is gone.

Johnny wonders how they got a license, and Sprague tells Johnny that they do not have one yet. Johnny is told not to worry about it and to catch Hauser. When Johnny warns them of the problems that the Insurance Commission and the government can bring, Sprague just looks at it as a tax loss and tells Johnny to find Hauser. When Johnny tells Sprague that he does not worry about being fined millions, but worries over $200,000, Johnny is told that what Hauser did was illegal.

Johnny wants to beg off the case and tells them that he will have to notify the commission. Sprague tells Johnny he can do whatever he wants after he catches Hauser. With $5,000 dangling in front of his eyes, Johnny decides to take the case.

Johnny checks the last known address of Hauser and learns from the manager that Hauser left the previous night. Johnny gives the manager a five spot and gets the key to the apartment. At the door, Johnny hears a voice on the phone and realizes that Hauser is still there. Hauser tells the man on the phone that "he can take care of Johnny Dollar". Johnny opens the door and is beaten by Hauser.

Johnny wakes up with the manager putting a cold rag on his head. Johnny grabs the lamp he was hit with and cabs to police headquarters and talks to Sgt. Ed Wilson, who takes the lamp to the lab.

Johnny goes home and takes a shower only to be called by Wilson and informed that Tom Hauser is one of the 10 most wanted. Wilson tells Johnny that if Hauser thinks Johnny saw him Hauser will be back to finish him.

Pat McCracken calls Johnny and Pat wants him to look into a phony insurance company. Pat has a complaint about a small company who is stalling on a claim, and Johnny recognizes what is happening.

Johnny tells Pat that he is working for them, and Pat tells Johnny to stay away from them. Pat is told that the Commission is coming the next week to investigate Providential. Johnny is sure that Providential is a scam when Sprague calls Johnny. Sprague wants to see Johnny in his room at the Guilford Hotel.

Johnny senses the fear in Sprague's voice when Pat calls back to tell Johnny that he had talked to the police and cannot reach anyone at Providential.

Johnny goes to the hotel and meets Sprague in his room. Sprague admits that he never did make any money in oil and has used his wits to fool people. Whiteman was fooled and convinced Sprague to act as a front man. Whiteman was very good at selling policies, and when a claim came in, they stalled it. They were going to keep at it until the commission investigated.

Whiteman brought Hauser in to take the wrap because of his record, but Hauser took all the money. Sprague had heard Whiteman talking to Hauser to split the money and kill Sprague.

Johnny starts to take Sprague to the police when Whiteman comes in with a gun. Whiteman tells Johnny that he has killed Hauser and now is going to kill Sprague and Johnny. Sgt. Wilson and Pat McCracken come in behind Whiteman and there is a barrage of gunfire and Whiteman is killed. Sprague agrees to go with the police, real peaceful.

"So, the big fat fee that was promised doesn't get paid to me after all, and I am sure I might as well forget the expense account for a change. But you know something? It doesn't matter. Because the important thing was to have had some small part in wiping out this dirty racket. Me? I feel good."

Notes:
- This program contains commercials for Winston cigarettes, Columbia Stereo One phonographs, Mona Freeman for 4-Way cold tablets, Fitch Dandruff Remover Shampoo, and Ex-Lax.
- The announcer is Dan Cubberly.

Producer:	Jack Johnstone	Writer:	Jack Johnstone
Cast:	Virginia Gregg, Edgar Barrier, Junius Matthews, Jerry Hausner, Lawrence Dobkin		

♦ ❖ ♦

Show:	**The Larson Arson Matter**
Show Date:	11/8/1959
Company:	**Philadelphia Mutual Liability & Casualty Insurance Company**
Agent:	**Harry Branson**
Exp. Acct:	**$79.75**

Synopsis: John is called by Harry Branson who tells Johnny that they have not had need of Johnny's services for a while. Johnny asks Harry if the problem is murder, mayhem or arson, and Harry tells Johnny it may be all of them combined. Johnny asks if they have been selling insurance to gangsters. Harry tells Johnny that the policy was sold to a former gangster, Bertie Larson. Johnny remembers that Bertie had been up before a special investigating committee, the one that had been on the television investigating narcotics and killings. Johnny tells Harry to cancel the policies and pay Bertie off, but Harry tells Johnny that since the hearings, they have increased the amount of the coverage.

In view of the threats on Larson's life and family, Harry needs help. Johnny tells Harry that if Harry wants his help, there is going to be a big fee involved.

Johnny trains to Philadelphia and goes to see Harry. Harry tells Johnny that Herbert James Larson lives in Penfield, Pennsylvania in a nice home insured for $30,000 and his property is insured for $20,000. Larson's life is insured for $20,000. The beneficiary of all the policies is the wife, Nora. Bertie's life has been threatened over the phone ever since he started testifying.

Last week Bertie had found a can of gasoline sitting on his doorstep, as a threat. Bertie has continued testifying in spite of the threats. Harry is sure the threats must have come from gangsters. Harry wants Johnny to protect Bertie because the police protection is inadequate. Johnny agrees to help Harry.

Johnny gets a rental car and drives to Bertie's house where no one is home, and no policemen are around. Johnny spots lights in a window and walks up to the house. Johnny smells gasoline in the garage and heads there. Johnny remembers smelling the gas before he is slugged and shots ring out.

Johnny wakes up in a hospital room with a police sergeant and another man. The man tells the sergeant that he thought Johnny was one of the men who were threatening him, and the shots were to summon the police. Johnny is told how Bertie found Johnny sneaking around and had slugged him. Bertie tells Johnny that the hospital bill is on him.

Bertie tells Johnny that he is going up to the country to make sure his wife is OK. She is staying with friends in the Catskills. Bertie leaves and the sergeant tells Johnny that he is lucky that Bertie did not kill him. The sergeant tells Johnny he should have come to him first.

Johnny is told that Bertie is not the man the committee is after, as Bertie was only a messenger. The committee is using Bertie to flush out the others. Johnny is told that Bertie is scared, but he is reveling in the glory, and it is helping his used car business. The threats are only on Bertie's word. Johnny tries to tell the sergeant about the gas, but he just walks out.

Johnny feels that something is all wrong with this case. Johnny leaves his room and drives to Bertie Larson's house. Johnny spots a big car in the driveway and sees a man packing it.

Johnny surprises Bertie and is told that he had come home to get some things for his wife and he had spotted someone running away. Bertie tells Johnny he had smelled gasoline in the house and takes Johnny in to show him. Johnny notices the house is almost bare and tells Bertie that he would probably put in a claim for everything if the house burnt down. Bertie shows Johnny how gas had been poured in the carpet and Johnny notes that the window screen had been punched out from the inside.

Johnny tells Bertie that he had been losing money at the used car business and is using the threats as a cover for the arson he was going to commit. Bertie pulls a gun and Johnny gets the drop on him.

Nora Larson comes in and tells Johnny to drop his gun. Bertie tells Nora they can now torch the place with Johnny in it. They will also strip Johnny so the bones will be Bertie's, that's $20,000 more in insurance.

Nora tells Bertie she is leaving both of them there and shoots Bertie. The police rush in and shoot Nora. The sergeant tells Johnny that the hospital had called him when Johnny left, and Johnny is mighty glad.

Johnny's expenses include a stay in the Belleview Stratford hotel.

Notes:
- This program contains commercials for Winston cigarettes, for other CBS shows including *Gary Moore, Arthur Godfrey, Andy Griffith, Bob and Ray, Art Linkletter, Amos n' Andy,* the *New York Philharmonic* and the *Metropolitan Opera*, Mona Freeman with a commercial for 4-Way cold tablets and Fitch Dandruff Remover Shampoo, and Ex-Lax.
- The announcer is Dan Cubberly.

Producer: Jack Johnstone   Writer: Jack Johnstone
Cast: Virginia Gregg, Harry Bartell, Don Diamond, Bert Holland

♦ ❖ ♦

Show: **The Bayou Body Matter**
Show Date: 11/15/1959
Company: **Tri-State Life & Casualty Insurance Company**
Agent: **Earle Poorman**
Exp. Acct: **$168.65**

Synopsis: Earle Poorman calls Johnny from Sarasota. Earle reminds Johnny of how his house is on a bayou. Earle asks Johnny how he would feel if Earle sold $50,000 of straight life to a man, and then found his body under his dock three days later? Johnny agrees to catch the first plane to Florida, and not to go fishing.

Johnny flies to Tampa, Florida and is met by Earle at the airport. Johnny is told that Earle called Johnny before the police were called. Earle thinks the man had a heart attack.

The man was Ralph P. Carter and lived four houses up the bayou and used to live in New York. He was 64 and had some heart trouble and retired to Florida with his wife, and Earle knows that they are loaded. Johnny immediately suspects the wife until Earle tells him that she is in her fifties.

Earle tells Johnny that Carter owned several other policies, blue-chip stocks and bank accounts and that the policy means nothing. Earle tells Johnny that the wife did not know about the policy, and the beneficiary is a former stripper, Mitzi Taylor who lives in New York. Carter told Earle that he knew her rather well before he married his wife three years ago.

While waiting for the autopsy to be conducted by Dr. Phillips, Johnny talks with Sgt. Edwards. Johnny is told that the autopsy is being done because Carter was alone when he died. Also, Mrs. Carter is not home, and does not know about her husband's death. Edwards has checked with Carter's physician, Dr. Foot, and Carter's heart condition was serious.

Dr. Phillips, an old friend of Johnny's, tells Johnny and Edwards that Carter died from a heavy blow at the base of the skull by a poker the police took from the house. Edwards tells Johnny that he will issue an APB for Mrs. Carter.

Edwards tells Johnny that the APB is out, and Earle tells Johnny that the Carters did not get along too well. Edwards tells Johnny that the neighbors had reported a big fight the previous night. The neighbors also reported that Mrs. Carter was seen leaving about the same time the coroner says Carter died. Edwards is sure that Mrs. Carter did it because she was much younger and very attractive. Also, the lab reported finding lint from gloves on the poker. Earle tells Johnny that Mrs. Carter always wore a hat and gloves when she went out.

Johnny goes to Earle's for lunch and then walks to the Carter house. Johnny finds a door open and looks around. Johnny spots a locked desk and pries it open. In a folder are a number of checks made out to Mitzi Taylor, but three checks are missing. Johnny goes to Mrs. Taylor's desk and finds the missing checks.

Mrs. Carter comes in and Johnny gives her his credentials. She tells Johnny that she was upset and had been at a beauty parlor. Johnny asks her if she left before or after Ralph had died? She is shocked that Ralph is dead, but not sorry.

She tells Johnny that this was her second marriage and had hoped that he would be content with her money and settle down. The only woman he cared about was that horrible girl. She found the checks yesterday and told him that she was going to divorce him. She tells Johnny that she always wears special gloves made for her in France.

Sgt. Edwards returns and arrests Mrs. Carter for suspicion of murder. Johnny tells Edwards that the "suspicion" may save him from being sued for false arrest.

Johnny is taken to the airport and flies to New York and cabs to the neighborhood of Mitzi Taylor. Johnny phones her and pretends he is Louis. Mitzi tells Louis he should have stayed in Florida, but since he is here, come to the apartment and she will pay him off.

Johnny calls Randy Singer and he agrees that the wife would have caught on eventually, but Mitzi could not wait. Johnny arranges for Randy to come over when things are wrapped up.

Johnny goes to Mitzi's apartment and forces his way in. Johnny tells her that she will not collect on the $50,000 policy she did not know about. Mitzi tells Johnny he will be floating in the East River the same way Carter was floating in the bayou.

Louis comes in from the next room and Mitzi takes Johnny's gun. When Mitzi goes to close the door, Randy is there and Louis is shot. Randy comes in with a very sarcastic "Hi ya, Johnny, fancy meeting you here" remark, and Johnny thanks him for coming over.

"Louis managed to survive, and I understand the way he shot off his mouth in the hospital, well I understand he pretty much cinched the case against both himself and Mitzi.

Notes:

- This program contains commercials for Winston cigarettes, Columbia Stereo One phonographs, Mel Torme for 4-Way cold tablets, Fitch Dandruff Remover Shampoo and Ex-Lax.
- Dan Cubberly is the Announcer.

Producer: Jack Johnstone   Writer: Jack Johnstone
Cast: Virginia Gregg, Lillian Buyeff, Vic Perrin, Sam Edwards, Barney Phillips, Herb Vigran, Frank Gerstle

♦ ❖ ♦

Show: The Fancy Bridgework Matter
Show Date: 11/22/1959
Company: Tri-State Life & Casualty Insurance Company
Agent: Earle Poorman
Exp. Acct: $200.00

Synopsis: Earle Poorman calls Johnny from Sarasota, and Johnny complains about being called to Florida and only fishing bodies from the water. Earle tells Johnny that maybe he can get some fishing in when Johnny comes down to determine if a policy holder was killed or committed suicide.

Johnny flies to Tampa and then to Sarasota, Florida where Earle meets Johnny in his brand new air-conditioned car. Earle tells Johnny that if suicide is proved, Johnny can save the company $40,000.

The insured was a tin-horned gambler named Alfie Garver, and he only paid one premium. Alfie had been losing money at the dog track and is living on handouts. His wife told a doctor that Alfie was in bad shape and might commit suicide.

Alfie was out last night and got into a big fight with Luke Thrasher at the track. Luke has had several mysterious murders tied to him, but no one could prove anything. The fight was over a bet that Alfie had welched on and Luke told Alfie to get out of town or he would kill him.

Alfie's wife had been at the police at 2 a.m. asking them to find Alfie. She is the beneficiary and about as worthless as Alfie. Luke was arrested and is being held in jail.

As Earle approaches a police car, Earle tells Johnny that the police found Alfie's coat on the bridge and a boat found his hat in the water. Earle stops and they talk to Lt. Dodge, who tells them that they have something to work on. The evidence, including blood on the bridge, points to a struggle.

Johnny reviews the evidence and is inclined to agree until he looks at the jacket. Johnny spots a feather, and Johnny thinks that it is a clue that Alfie was not murdered. Johnny asks Earle to take him to Doc Crutcher with a little sample of the blood.

Dr. Les Crutcher pours Johnny and Earle a drink and then works on the blood sample. Doc Crutcher tells Johnny that the blood was from a chicken. Earle is now sure that the signs of a struggle were a fraud. Johnny will be sure when they find Alfie.

Johnny goes to see Lt. Dodge who tells him that Luke's alibi was airtight.

Johnny arranges to borrow a car and act as a chauffeur for Luke Thrasher. Johnny takes Luke to a dingy motel but does not get much help finding Alfie. When Johnny tells Luke that he is an investigator, Luke gets out of the car and reminds Johnny that he has killed others.

Johnny muses how his hunches do not always pan out, but he has a couple about Luke Thrasher. Johnny drives to Earl's house and answers a late-night phone call from Doc Crutcher.

Doc tells Johnny that the blood contains signs of a tropaniosis virus rarely found in the south. He had checked with a vet and discovered the chicken could only have come from Andy Polucci on Bee Ridge Road.

Johnny goes to see Andy and wakes him and asks if Alfie Garver bought a chicken the other night, and Andy tells Johnny that Alfie's wife bought the chicken, along with Luke Thrasher. Andy threatens to complain to the police, and Johnny tells him to go right ahead.

Johnny goes to the motel room of Mrs. Garver and invites himself in. Johnny tells her how she and Luke planned the murder of her husband. Since Luke was winning at the track, they decided to get rid of Alfie, and used the talk of suicide as a decoy. She spilled the chicken blood after Luke's alibi was established so she could collect on the insurance.

She tells Johnny that she did not kill Alfie, Luke did it. Luke comes in and she takes Johnny's gun. Lt. Dodge gets the drop on Luke from a window and makes Luke drop his gun. Dodge tells Johnny that he got a complaint from Andy Polucci for getting him up in the middle of the night.

"Luke Thrasher, in spite of all the pressure they put on him, still refused to talk. So, it was Lena Garver who finally broke down and told the police where they could dig up Alfie's body. Yeah, the bullets in him came from the gun Luke had held on me. So, it's up to the courts."

Johnny manages to get in some really great fishing with Earle Poorman this time.

Notes:
- This program contains commercials for Winston cigarettes, Stu Erwin for 4-Way cold tablets, Fitch Dandruff Remover Shampoo, and Ex-Lax.
- The virus Doc Crutcher mentions, tripaniosis appears to be another Jack Johnstone creation. There is a virus called trypanosomiasis that causes Chagas Disease, but I don't hear that many syllables in the word Doc says.
- The announcer is Dan Cubberly.

Producer: Jack Johnstone   Writer: Jack Johnstone
Cast: Virginia Gregg, Vic Perrin, Barney Phillips, Edgar Stehli, Peter Leeds, Frank Gerstle

Show:	**The Wrong Man Matter**
Show Date:	**11/29/1959**
Company:	**Floyds of England**
Agent:	**George Reed**
Exp. Acct:	**$1.00**

Synopsis: George Reed calls Johnny, and Johnny is glad for the assignment. The man in trouble is John Patrick O'Shea who is retired, lives in Hartford and is confined to a wheel chair. Last night someone broke in and beat him severely. He would have been killed if a neighbor had not barged in and scared the man away. George wants Johnny to pick him up so they both can go over, as George is personally involved in this case.

Johnny cabs to George's office and they drive to the Hartford, Connecticut apartment of O'Shea. George tells Johnny that Harry Marshall, a male nurse, had been sent over to change the beneficiary on O'Shea's policy. The only relative is a ne're-do-well nephew in Boston. O'Shea does not have much money, so he bought a policy and named Marshall as the beneficiary.

Marshall felt that O'Shea should have made provisions for the nephew and convinced O'Shea to make the changes. Marshall came over to talk to George, but George had gone to a movie with his wife. Marshall left a note in the door saying he had stayed until almost eleven and hoped George and his wife had enjoyed the movie and asked him to call Marshall in the morning. When Marshall got home, O'Shea had been attacked.

George and Johnny arrive and ring the bell. Harry answers the door and Lt. Barley is there. Barley shows Johnny a Harris tweed patch torn from a jacket in the window. Marshall blurts out that he could kill the man who hurt O'Shea. Johnny wants to sit down and talk to Marshall for a while.

Johnny learns that Marshall had left shortly before 10:00 p.m. and O'Shea was still up watching TV. Marshall waited at George Reed's house, and then returned to find the front door open. Mr. Wakely from next door, and the police were in the house. Mr. Wakely walks in and asks if Johnny wants to talk to him.

Wakely tells Johnny that O'Shea would be dead if he had not come over. Wakely got here 2 minutes after 11:00. He had been trying to listen to the news and came over to tell the man to turn down his TV. He does it every night and had called Marshall to have him turn it down. When he got to the porch, he hears O'Shea calling for help.

Wakely broke down the door and found O'Shea on the floor covered with blood and the window open, and then he called the police. Wakely tells Johnny that everybody on the block would be willing to kill O'Shea because of the noisy TV.

Wakely warns Johnny not to accuse him of anything and pulls a gun. Johnny takes the gun from Wakely and it fires once, then Johnny slugs him. Johnny tells Marshall to call the police as he goes up to talk to O'Shea. Johnny changes his mind and asks George when he had decided to go to the movie. George tells Johnny that it was after dinner, as he and his wife had no other plans.

Johnny checks on O'Shea who is out like a light, and then goes to search

Marshall's room. In Marshall's room Johnny finds receipts for the rental of a room several blocks away. Johnny gives instructions to George to look after Wakley and Marshall.

Johnny leaves and goes to the rooming house and the manager takes Johnny to Marshall's room. In the room, Johnny finds a Harris Tweed jacket with a missing piece.

Johnny returns to O'Shea's house and Lt. Barley is there. Marshall spots the coat and he is speechless. Johnny tells Barley that he found the coat in a rooming house on South Elm, and how Marshall was smart by adding another beneficiary to the policy, that way not too much of the money would be diverted away. If O'Shea were to die before the change was made, no one would suspect Marshall.

Johnny tells Marshall that he had been checking on George very carefully, as the note he left said "hope you and Mrs. Reed enjoyed the movie." Marshall congratulates Johnny on his skill.

"So, George, having saved your company from having to pay off the old man's insurance, well how much is my fee going to be? If it's big enough I'll forget all about the, wait a minute, what expense account? A lousy buck for the trip over to your office this morning? Oh, me."

Notes:
- This is an AFRTS program that contains a story about Walter Hunt who invented the safety pin and other things, and a story about Samuel Colt.
- The announcer is Dan Cubberly.

Producer:	Jack Johnstone Writer: Jack Johnstone
Cast:	Virginia Gregg, G. Stanley Jones, Chester Stratton, Sam Edwards, Junius Matthews

◆ ❖ ◆

Show:	The Hired Homicide Matter
Show Date:	12/6/1959
Company:	Tri-Western Life Insurance Company
Agent:	Horace. W. Milford
Exp. Acct:	$0.00

Synopsis: The Milford Advertising Company calls, and Horace W. Milford calls Johnny, and Johnny tells him that if he wants to buy time for his radio show he will have to call CBS Radio in New York. Mr. Milford tells Johnny that this is a personal matter, but that Tri-Western insures his life. Milford tells Johnny not to contact the insurance company, and that he will pay Johnny's expenses. He wants Johnny to help prevent a murder.

Johnny flies to Denver, Colorado and gets a hotel room at the Brown Palace. After getting some sleep, Johnny walks to the office of the Milford Advertising Agency.

Mr. Milford tells Johnny that the whole matter must be kept confidential. Johnny must prevent a murder. Milford tells Johnny that after his wife passed away, his daughter and his business have been his only concerns.

Until two years ago, he did everything at the firm. Then two years ago, he brought in Tony Ferringer, his son-in-law who brought in a major electronics firm as an account. Unfortunately, he did it in a rather unethical way and told Milford that he had sensitive information on the company executives. Tony constantly reminded him that he had brought in the account.

Tony had courted and eloped with his daughter and bragged how he would take the business away from Milford. Milford tells Johnny that Claire, his daughter, had killed herself because of Tony. Milford tells Johnny that he hates Tony.

Tony has now started his own agency and threatened to take the account away. Two days ago, the executives of the account came to Milford and told him that they had heard what Tony had said, and there was no truth in it and they would stand by Milford.

Milford tells Johnny that he had hired a professional killer to take care of Tony. He has no way to call the man off until he has murdered Tony.

Milford tells Johnny that he very carefully arranged with an underworld contact named Eric Blinker for a killer to contact Milford. The killer only told Milford that his name was Blackie. There is no way now to call off the killer, because Blinker's body was found in the Platte river yesterday.

Milford has never met Blackie and only talked to him from outside a window. He paid Blackie $5,000 and was told that Blackie would do the job by the end of the week. Milford has not talked to Tony, as that would allow him to bleed Milford dry. But how to stop the killer? Milford tells Johnny that Tony has insurance with some distant relative, not even his wife was named.

Johnny gets Tony's address and then Tony enters the room. Tony tells Milford he has heard that Milford ruined his chances of starting his own agency, that he conned Bonar Electronics to stay with him. Tony tells him that he finally caught on, and now he will make him pay plenty.

Tony leaves and Johnny gets an idea. Johnny gets a cab to follow Tony to his home. Johnny has the cab wait as he walks up to the house. Johnny rings the back-door buzzer and then hides. Tony comes out and Johnny slugs him and drags him inside.

Johnny pays the cabby to help him take Tony to a boarding house across town. Johnny pays the manager $10 to tell Tony a cabby brought Tony there.

Johnny cabs back to Tony's house to find Blackie there. Blackie has Johnny sit on a piano bench and Blackie tells Johnny that he knows he is not Tony, but Johnny knows too much. Blackie knows Johnny took Tony to the rooming house. Now Blackie has no choice.

Johnny tries to bluff Blackie as he prepares to shoot Johnny in the head. Johnny falls from the bench and gets the gun from Blackie and slugs him.

"Nailing Blackie for the murder of Eric Blinker, the stoolie, allowed me to keep Mr. Milford out of the picture completely. Nor did Blackie talk, some code of the underworld I guess. As for the expense account, in view of the fee that was handed to me, you can forget it. As for Tony Ferringer, he never did figure out what happened to him. Now will somebody please give me a nice clean case to work on?"

Notes:
- There seem to be two versions of this program. On one version, Bob Bailey welcomes WKNE in Keene, New Hampshire back to CBS, and WKVT in Brattleboro, Vermont is welcomed aboard. The other is an AFRTS version with the welcomes deleted.
- The announcer is Dan Cubberly.

Producer:	Jack Johnstone	Writer:	Jack Johnstone
Cast:	Virginia Gregg, Marvin Miller, Lawrence Dobkin, Russell Thorson		

♦ ❖ ♦

Show: **The Sudden Wealth Matter**
Show Date: **12/13/1959**
Company: **Universal Adjustment Bureau**
Agent: **Pat McCracken**
Exp. Acct: **$38.25**

Synopsis: Pat McCracken calls and Johnny tells his "Santa Clause" that all he wants is a million bucks, a new convertible, a bevy of beautiful blondes and two red heads. Pat laughs and tells Johnny that he has a case of pure old-fashioned greed plus a no-good Samaritan. Johnny inquires about the fee, but Pat tells Johnny he may end up being one of Santa's helpers.

Johnny cabs to Pat's office where Pat tells Johnny that some of the clients that Universal Adjustment Bureau handles cater to the farming community and issue annuity policies. Pat tells Johnny that he has received word of a lot of people cashing in their policies and borrowing against their farms to invest in the stock market. The money was given to a stranger who moved into town who promised to double their money in two weeks.

Johnny recognizes the scam where the early contributors are paid off by the later ones until the scam artist has enough money to leave town. The latest claims have come from Enterprise, New Jersey. The local authorities cannot do anything because the man is still paying off. Johnny is anxious to look into this, on expenses only, on account of Christmas.

Johnny flies to Philadelphia, rents a car and drives to Enterprise, New Jersey, a small run-down farming town. Johnny goes to the city hall and talks to police chief Walters. Johnny tells him who he is and chief Walters recognizes him and tells Johnny he listens to his programs on WCAU in Philadelphia.

Chief Walters tells Johnny that a lot of people have taken money from their policies and in a few weeks the folks will have a lot of money. Mr. Lowery who runs the paper says that John D. Morgan, the man who is putting a lot of money into the town, is a crook.

Morgan has told the townspeople that he belongs to the New York Stock Exchange and is related to the Morgan's and the "Rocyfellers". Morgan is being so generous because one of his ancestors, Jodiah Morgan, got his start in the town back in the 1800's.

Morgan is staying at the Parker House and keeps the money in a safe there in his third-floor suite. Johnny asks the chief to tell Morgan that he wants to see him, under the ruse of being a local boy who made good selling on the road.

Johnny goes to see Mr. Lowery at the newspaper, and he tells Johnny that he has tried to tell people that Morgan is a shyster, but then people would not buy the paper. Morgan keeps taking in money but will leave when he has all the money in town. Johnny suggests a plan to Mr. Lowery, but it will require his money, as they need to convince him that they are on Morgan's side. Johnny wants Lowery to stop the press and print an apology and then call on Morgan with his money to invest. Johnny will try to get some money himself. Once he gets the money, Morgan will try to leave town, and then they will get him.

Johnny goes to city hall and convinces the chief to search the records there, and the chief finds no record of a Jodiah Morgan. Johnny calls the New York Stock Exchange and they have never heard of Morgan.

Chief Walters and Johnny go to the local bank to get money to loan to Morgan and Johnny gets the bank president, Mr. Peterson, to cooperate. Johnny calls Pat and gets $10,000 wired to the bank. Johnny gets $1,000 from Peterson's personal account and tells the chief to head for Morgan's room. Johnny gets the location of Morgan's car and goes there.

In the garage, Johnny spots the car and uses an old trick. At the hotel, Johnny finds a room full of people and an empty safe. Chief Walters had the safe opened and it is empty. Lowery tells Johnny the people think Johnny is responsible for Morgan disappearing. Johnny runs out the back window and towards the garage with the crowd in hot pursuit.

John D. Morgan was sitting in the car with the money and a .38 Colt aimed at Johnny. Johnny tells him he took the distributor cap from the car. Morgan wants the distributor cap, but a crowd gathers and Morgan becomes afraid. He tells Johnny that the money is in the trunk and agrees to give it back to the people.

"That mob, slowly, menacingly moving in on us was something I won't forget for a long, long time. Matter of fact it was Morgan tossing out the money and shrieking out a confession promising to pay them back that saved me from them. And now, of course, he will be taken care of by the courts, yeah, plenty."

Notes:
- This program contains commercials for Winston cigarettes, Columbia Stereo One portable record players for $139.95 that play 45s, 78s and the new LP and stereo records, Stuart Erwin for 4-Way cold tablets, and Fitch Dandruff Remover Shampoo, and "Shop early and safely and buy a gift set from Yardley".
- The announcer is Dan Cubberly.

Producer: Jack Johnstone   Writer: Jack Johnstone
Cast: Lawrence Dobkin, Forrest Lewis, Junius Matthews, Edgar

Barrier, Russell Thorson

❖

Show:	**The Red Mystery Matter**
Show Date:	**12/20/1959**
Company:	**Universal Adjustment Bureau**
Agent:	**Pat McCracken**
Exp. Acct:	**$0.00**

Synopsis: Johnny is called by Red Barrett and told to come out to Lake Mohave Resort. Johnny tells him that he is too busy to come out and go fishing, as he has too much work. Red tells Johnny that Pat McCracken told him to call Johnny. Red tells Johnny that something will happen, and it will be very bad for Lake Mohave Resort. Red does not believe that Johnny would just sit there and do nothing, so Red tells Johnny to catch the next plane and hangs up.

Johnny decides to believe in Red's story and catches a plane to Las Vegas. Johnny opines on the desert sky at night and the lights of Las Vegas. Johnny rents a car and drives to Lake Mohave Resort, commenting on the desert.

Buster Favor meets Johnny and tells him that the police have not even gotten there yet, and that Red has disappeared. Buster takes Johnny to Red's room and it has been ransacked. Johnny spots signs of a cooked meal and blood on the floor.

Johnny reminds Buster of how Red had often talked of just leaving, but Buster tells Johnny that he had not said anything to anyone. Buster tells Johnny that Ham Pratt had come to talk to Red after dinner, and he was gone. So, why would someone want to do Red in?

Buster can think of nothing that could cause problems for the resort when Ham comes in to tell them that everyone in the area is looking for Red. Ham tells Johnny that he has received a tip that a car like Red's has been seen near Bolder City. Johnny is suspicious that he will have a score to settle with Buster and Ham.

Johnny thinks things are starting to add up, starting with Red calling Pat and the lamp with the unbroken bulb, and the fish scales in the blood on the floor. All very fishy.

Johnny looks over the room and notices that something important is missing from Red's room, and his boat is empty as well. Johnny tells Buster that he is going to do nothing until morning, and Buster suggests they go fishing, as Johnny is just a bundle of nerves, and Johnny agrees to go fishing.

Johnny recalls that he had been a little feisty, and the fishing did wonders for his disposition. First thing in the morning Johnny recalls not finding Red's tackle and personal clothes, and notes that the blood on the floor was from a bass. The road on which Red's truck had been seen led to a resort called Temple Bar.

Johnny drives to Temple Bar and waiting at the dock is Red Barrett, all ready for Johnny with an extra rod and bait. Red tells Johnny a smart man like him could track him down. Red had decided to move on to a different resort, and Ham was in on it too.

And the terrible thing that would happened to the resort? They would lose

the best guide in the area!
Red shows Johnny a letter from Pat McCracken telling them that Johnny needs some rest and relaxation, on the Universal Adjustment Bureau, and Merry Christmas!
"A very wise man once said that the time a man spends fishing is never deducted from his life span. And you know something? I for one am convinced that he was right. So, Merry Christmas to all of you too."

Notes:
- This program contains commercials for Winston cigarettes, Mel Torme for 4-Way cold tablets, Fitch Dandruff Remover Shampoo, and one on fire prevention during the holidays, and gifts from Yardley.
- The announcer is Dan Cubberly.

Producer: Jack Johnstone   Writer: Jack Johnstone
Cast: Forrest Lewis, Barney Phillips, Alan Reed, Lawrence Dobkin

♦ ❖ ♦

Show: **The Burning Desire Matter**
Show Date: **12/27/1959**
Company: **Universal Adjustment Bureau**
Agent: **Pat McCracken**
Exp. Acct: **$874.20**

Synopsis: Johnny is called by a man who just says "yeah". The caller turns out to be Pat McCracken who tells Johnny that "yeah" was the conversation during a call he just had. Johnny remembers that a friend in San Francisco talked like that, but Pat tells Johnny that the call came from Los Angeles. Johnny tells Pat to check his records, and he will find a lot of arson claims, and will have to pay his expenses to Los Angeles.

Johnny is sure that the call came from Smokey Sullivan and calls the number Pat had given him — Hollywood 8-3142. Smokey tells Johnny he has a legitimate job in Los Angeles. Smokey tells Johnny that he has helped Smokey in the past, and now Smokey has a chance to help Johnny.

Smokey tells Johnny that there have been a lot of fires in the area, and he has a lead. Smokey is at 322 S. Equity Ave. and Johnny tells him that he will meet Smokey there. Pat calls back and tells Johnny that there have been seven fires covered by seven companies, and the police reports suggest arson.

Johnny flies to Los Angeles, California and cabs to Smokey's address in a beat-up industrial area. Johnny knocks on the door of a rooming house and a woman opens the door. Johnny asks for Smokey and the woman asks if Johnny is the man Smokey is expecting. Johnny goes up and pounds on Smokey's door to hear glass breaking inside.

Johnny rushes in and finds Smokey lying beaten on the floor. The landlady gets towels, cold water and a bottle of cognac for Smokey. The landlady tells Johnny she thought the other man was the one Smokey was expecting.

Smokey comes to and tells Johnny that the man was "The Chimp", a strong-arm man for Mickey Fortina. Smokey tells Johnny that he has to stop Mickey or there will be more fires.

Smokey tells Johnny that he had scared off the Chimp when Johnny knocked on the door, and someone had tipped off Fortina about Smokey's call to Johnny.

Johnny takes Smokey to the Statler Hotel and gets a room and a doctor for Smokey. Smokey tells Johnny that all the fires were set for the insurance and set by different persons. Fortina is a go-between, he makes a deal to torch a place and brings in the people to do the jobs.

Fortina had sent for Smokey and asked if he wanted to work for him. Johnny is sure that Fortina knows Johnny was sent for. Smokey tells Johnny that Fortina's office is located at 1025 S. Spring. There is a knock at the door and a voice calls out "police".

Johnny opens the door to find an old friend, Sgt. Pat Nichols. Nichols tells Johnny that the room clerk had reported an injured man being brought in. Nichols knows who Smokey is and Johnny tells Smokey to talk to Nichols. Johnny convinces Nichols that Smokey needs a bodyguard, and then goes to talk to Fortina.

At Fortina's office, Johnny plans on acting like a man who needs a property burned down. Johnny goes into the "Fortina Friendly Loan Company" as Mr. Morris. Through the open door, Johnny hears Mickey ask about the Chimp and the hotel.

Fortina comes out and Johnny tells him that he owns a shoe store and that business has been bad. Fortina offers a loan and Johnny tells him that he has $180,000 in insurance on the property and wants it torched. Fortina tells Johnny that he needs to make a $10,000 deposit and Johnny tells him just to torch the place, and he will give Fortina $15,000.

The Chimp comes in and tells Mickey that he knows who Johnny is and that Husky is on his way to the hotel to take care of Smokey. The secretary warns them that the police are there and Mickey pulls a gun after Johnny slugs the Chimp.

Johnny turns out the lights, there are shots and a fight and Johnny gets the best of Mickey just as Sgt. Nichols and Smokey come in. Smokey had told Nichols what the deal was after Husky Costalini came to the hotel. Nichols took Husky to jail and then he and Smokey came here. Nichols is sure that the boys will talk to avoid taking the rap for everything.

"Yeah, they talked all right, and as a result the police in a couple of nearby states should have no trouble at all in picking up some of the other of Fortina's boys, his hired torches. Ah, funny isn't it? These stupid jerks just never seem to learn."

Notes:
- This program contains commercials for Winston cigarettes, Mona Freeman for 4-Way cold tablets, and Fitch Dandruff Remover Shampoo.
- This program was recorded live on WROW in Albany and has a long ad at the end for Veterans disability benefits.
- The announcer is Dan Cubberly.

Producer:	Jack Johnstone Writer: Jack Johnstone
Cast:	Virginia Gregg, Jeanne Tatum, Lawrence Dobkin, Vic Perrin, Paul Dubov, Don Diamond, Frank Gerstle

◆ ❖ ◆

Show:	**The Hapless Ham Matter**
Show Date:	1/3/1960
Company:	**Eastern Trust & Insurance Company**
Agent:	
Exp. Acct:	**$100.00**

Synopsis: Johnny is called by a man who needs Johnny's help. The man is Walter E. Lynch and Johnny must come out to Manchester and protect him. He implores Johnny that his life has been threatened, but Johnny wants to know what company his insurance is with. Lynch has not called the police and wants protection. Johnny hangs up and Pat McCracken calls and reminds Johnny that he was due in Pat's office for a disposition eight minutes ago at 10:00. Johnny asks Pat to look up the insurance on Walter Lynch.

Johnny cabs to Pat's office, signs the deposition, and Johnny tells him of the conversation with Lynch. The secretary brings in a copy of the policy that Mr. Bartell had located. The policy is for $50,000 with a nephew, Fred Lynch, as the beneficiary. Pat authorizes Johnny to pay Walter Lynch a visit.

Johnny drives to Manchester, Connecticut in his car. The Lynch house is a small Cape Cod with two police cars out front. A police sergeant asks for Johnny's ID and then tells Johnny that Lynch is dead, murdered.

Johnny goes in and confirms that Lynch had been murdered, and the police doctor shows Johnny where the knife had gone in. Officer Conroy comes in and reports that there were no footprints outside. The police sergeant tells Johnny that a neighbor, Mr. Halsey had called them. Halsey had come over to talk to Lynch about his nephew, saw what happened and then called the police.

Johnny learns that Lynch had been awarded custody of a fortune that had been left to Freddy by his mother, and Lynch had spent it all. Johnny is told that the police think that the Lynch tribe is no good. The knife wound troubles the doc. He tells Johnny that it came from a long, two-bladed knife.

Mr. Halsey comes in and recognizes who Johnny is, and tells Johnny that the nephew, Freddy, was a worthless bum who worked in the theater, and that Freddy was there that morning. Halsey does not blame Lynch for not giving Freddy any money, because he was living in New York, that pit of iniquity with all those sinful people, actors, chorus girls and the like!

Halsey tells Johnny that Freddy was there from around 9:30 to before 10:00. The doc fixes death at around 10:00. Halsey is sure of the time as he was listening to the radio, and Freddy left just before the WDRC announcer gave time signal at 10:00. Johnny is sure that Freddy did not kill Lynch because Walter was alive after 10:00, Johnny had talked to him at 10:08!

Johnny is sure that he was the perfect alibi for Freddy Lynch who had walked to catch a bus at 10:15. Freddy must have done it, because Halsey had seen no one else come in.

Johnny gets the address for Freddy and drives to New York City. Johnny gets into Freddy's room, which is covered with posters, playbills, and costumes. Freddy comes in and Johnny tells him he is Jerry Allen the agent, and that he has been trying to get in touch with Freddy. He has a part for Freddy, but Freddy tells Johnny that he is thinking of giving up show business but changes his mind when "Jerry" asks if he just inherited a fortune.

Jerry tells Freddy that the play is written by Johnstone, who has had a bunch of hits lately. The part is of a young man who ages 20 years in the second act and then is 60 in the third act. Freddy gives Johnny his best shaky old man's voice to prove he can do the part. Johnny gets Freddy to say the same things he had told Johnny over the phone.

Johnny tells him that he had killed his uncle and called him from the bus station to get Johnny to come there. Freddy pulls a long thin Arabian knife and Johnny shoots him in the hand. Johnny didn't think he was that good a shot.

"So now I will have to make another disposition for the sake of another trial. I am sure that hamming it up in court won't keep Freddy from playing out the rest of his life in front of a captive audience."

Notes:
- This program contains commercials for Winston cigarettes, Mona Freeman for 4-Way cold tablets, and Fitch Dandruff Remover Shampoo.
- The announcer is Dan Cubberly.

Producer:	Jack Johnstone	Writer:	Jack Johnstone
Cast:	Virginia Gregg, Chester Stratton, Lawrence Dobkin, Sam Edwards, Herb Ellis, Ralph Moody, Junius Matthews		

♦ ❖ ♦

Show:	**The Unholy Two Matter**
Show Date:	**1/10/1960**
Company:	**Tri-Western Life Insurance Company**
Agent:	**Jack Price**
Exp. Acct:	**$287.20**

Synopsis: The introduction to this program is missing.

Johnny flies to Corpus Christi, Texas and gets a room at the Robert Driscoll hotel. As Johnny is checking in, he meets Doug Johnstone, who is Jack Johnstone's younger brother. Doug offers to get together and talk about Jack, and offers Johnny any help he can give.

Doug asks if Jack Price called Johnny in, and Johnny confirms it but does not know anything about what case he is working on. Doug has some ideas about old man Peterson. Doug feels that Peterson did not die from a heart attack, but that he was murdered.

The next day Johnny goes to see Jack Price, who tells Johnny that he is looking into Sterling Peterson who disappeared just after his uncle died. Sterling did not know that he was the beneficiary of the policy. Paul Peterson, Sterling's half-brother gets everything else. Paul is a stockbroker and Jack does not know what Sterling does, only that he is gone. Jack also has not called the police. Jack confirms that the doctor said death was from a heart attack, and Johnny asks Jack to order an autopsy.

Johnny goes to see Doug Johnstone who knows Sterling from his activity at the Merrill-Lynch office. Sterling was always trying to get money from Paul, who was working the market by buying penny stocks and other speculative stocks, but he always made money. Sterling needed money to pay off his gambling debts.

Doug feels that Sterling was at the point where he would kill to get money. When he found out he would not get the property, he left not knowing about the insurance. Johnny cabs to Paul's apartment and then to the Merrill-Lynch office where Paul has not been seen for several days. A friend notes that Paul was out looking at investments.

Johnny goes back to Jack's office to learn that the autopsy is finished, and that death was from a drug that had been substituted for the old man's digitalis. Johnny cabs to Sterling's rooming house and learns from the landlady, Mrs. Toomey, that Sterling owed two months' rent.

In Sterling's room, Johnny sees that all of Sterling's clothes are gone, but the medicine cabinet has all his personal items. Mrs. Toomey tells Johnny that Sterling had waited all day for Paul to come. Paul did call and told Sterling to meet him at a dive. Sterling came back late that night but was gone the next morning.

Johnny goes to his hotel where there is a message from Jack Price telling him that the police are looking for Sterling, and the police want to talk to Johnny. Johnny is visited by Paul Peterson, who is answering Johnny's note to call him.

Paul shows Johnny a number of letters from Sterling, mailed from various cities. The typed letters seem to indicate that Sterling was running away. Johnny wonders if Paul had typed the letters and used his business trip to mail the letters. Johnny asks if Paul killed Sterling after he tried to blackmail Paul.

When Johnny mentions the personal items left in the medicine cabinet Paul pulls a gun and threatens to kill Johnny. The police come in with Doug Johnstone and Paul gives up.

"So, another day, another dollar, and I'm not talking about myself."

Notes:
- This is the first of 5 appearances of Doug Johnstone, the real-life brother of Jack Johnstone. Doug appears in *The Unholy Two Matter, The Canned Canary Matter, The Unworthy Kin Matter, The Perilous Parley Matter* and *The Skidmore Matter.*
- This program contains commercials for Camel cigarettes, Mel Torme for 4-Way cold tablets, Fitch Dandruff Remover Shampoo and Ex-Lax.
- The announcer is Dan Cubberly.

Producer: Jack Johnstone   Writer: Jack Johnstone

Cast:	Virginia Gregg, Jack Edwards, Forrest Lewis, Stacy Harris, Gil Stratton, Barney Phillips

• ❖ •

Show:	**The Evaporated Clue Matter**
Show Date:	1/17/1960
Company:	Four State Insurance Company
Agent:	Henry Bascomb
Exp. Acct:	$574.00

Synopsis: Henry Bascomb calls and asks Johnny to come down and look into a matter. The investigation is in New York, and the fees will be based on the straight life policy worth almost $200,000. Johnny is on his way.

Johnny flies to New York City and goes to Henry's office. The $189,000 policy is on Jonathan R. Kenworthy, a retired mine owner. Kenworthy was murdered, and the grandson, Carleton M. Kenworthy, is the beneficiary. The police feel that Carleton, who is the sole heir, did it because he has the motive and a perfect alibi.

Henry knows that Jonathan Kenworthy had no enemies and Carleton is about as useless as you can get. Carleton does not work and is generally a playboy. Carleton hangs around with Allen Barker, who is a real leech. The grandfather did not suspect what was going on, and believed his grandson was investing the money he gave him. The murder was last Tuesday, and Randy Singer is handling the case.

Johnny leaves to visit Randy who tells Johnny that he is sure that Carleton killed his grandfather, as he was up to his ears in debts. Kenworthy was killed with a poker from the fireplace, but Carleton has an alibi, he was in Alaska.

Randy tells Johnny that Carleton was in Alaska, and Randy has checked out everything. The lab report on the poker comes in and shows fingerprints from both Kenworthys. Carleton comes in and tells Johnny and Randy that he often made the fire for his grandfather. Carleton tells Johnny that he went to Alaska alone. Johnny asks for an address and goes to see Allen Barker.

Allen is almost a twin of Carleton, who tells Johnny that he and Carleton like the same things and are called "The Inseparables". Allen tells Johnny that he took a trip while Carleton was gone and has no idea where he went. Johnny tells him that he could benefit from Kenworthy's death, but feels Baxter is too weak natured to actually do it. Johnny gets an idea, an expensive idea.

Johnny flies to Juneau, Alaska via Seattle. In Juneau, Johnny realizes he should have brought a photograph. Johnny goes to the hotel and gets the same story that Randy had gotten. At dinner in the hotel Johnny gets the clue that will solve the case.

Johnny flies back to New York and goes to see Randy and Carleton in Randy's office. Carleton tells Johnny that he was in Juneau when his father was killed. Johnny asks if Carleton ate dinner at the hotel, which he did.

Carleton tells Johnny that he paid cash for the dinner of shrimp cocktail, salad, a steak and coffee. Johnny asks Carleton what he had in his coffee, and Carleton tells Johnny that he used the cream and sugar that was on the table.

Johnny tells Carleton that Allen went there posing as him. Johnny tells him that the hotel does not use cream, only evaporated milk. Carleton breaks down and tells Johnny and Randy that Allen helped him kill his grandfather.

"Believe me, if I were to put down all I think about the Allen Barkers and Carleton Kenworthys, and all the rest of that rotten, Ah! Why bother, what's the use."

Notes:
- This program contains commercials for Camel cigarettes, Stuart Erwin for 4-Way cold tablets, Fitch Dandruff Remover Shampoo and Ex-Lax.
- Bob Bailey welcomes stations WBRK in Pittsfield, Massachusetts and WKNY in Kingston, New York to the CBS network.
- The announcer is Dan Cubberly.

Producer:	Jack Johnstone Writer: Jack Johnstone
Cast:	Harry Bartell, Herb Vigran, Carleton G. Young, Herb Ellis, Jack Edwards

• ❖ •

Show:	**The Nuclear Goof Matter**
Show Date:	**1/24/1960**
Company:	**Floyds of England**
Agent:	**George Reed**
Exp. Acct:	**$0.00**

Synopsis: George Reed calls Johnny and tells him that he is all cleared, and though it is not covered by the insurance, it is OK to go on over. George just got a call from Dr. Paulus Rayburn, who runs Nuclear Processors, Inc. on the north end of Hartford, Connecticut. Floyds holds the other insurance, and George needs Johnny to look into something. Dr. Rayburn has reported something missing that is important to the space program, and Johnny is needed to look into it.

Johnny buys coffee and donuts on the way to the Nuclear Processor site. At the main gate three guards inspect Johnny's ID and let him into the plant. Another guard at the main building takes Johnny inside where he meets Dr. Rayburn who tells Johnny that the plant does scientific research, and that time is of the essence.

A small quantity of radioactive material has been stolen. Outside of the paramagnetic fields in the plant, the material will become dangerous within hours and can destroy a small city. The chain reaction could start in four to six hours, depending on conditions, which is why he could not wait for investigators from Washington. The time now is 9:34 a.m. and the material was stolen at 7:46 a.m. by Dr. Igor Ralinov who did not know the danger of the material.

Dr. Rayburn tells Johnny that he brought in Dr. Ralinov for another project, and that he stole the materials for a foreign government. Dr. Rayburn had employed Ralinov before a security clearance was obtained. Johnny gets a list of addresses and contacts and tells Dr. Rayburn to call the FBI. Johnny gets a detector that will react to the material that was stolen. The detector is very fragile, so Johnny must take care. Johnny buys gas and heads for town.

Johnny goes to Ralinov's address and realizes he does not have a picture or description. Johnny stops at a drugstore, and as he is trying to park he hits a young blond man who has just gotten off of a bus. Johnny takes the man and his briefcase to the hospital. Johnny leaves the man at the hospital and goes back to Ralinov's with the detector going crazy on the seat, it had fallen to the floor and cannot be turned off.

Johnny goes back to Ralinov's rooming house and knocks at the door. The landlady asks if Johnny is Mr. Parker. She tells Johnny that Ralinov has gone, and that he has rented the whole third floor. Johnny goes up and breaks down the door and enters the dark apartment and is slugged by a man who tells Johnny that he is not Parker.

Johnny is searched and the landlady is told to get some towels and water. The man is Stacey Ringler who Johnny knows from the FBI. He tells Johnny that he is with the Nuclear Processors security department now, and that Harry Parker came up from Washington this morning and is working with Stacey. They got into Ralinov's rooms and were waiting.

Stacey tells Johnny that the man he ran down at the drugstore is Ralinov. Parker followed Johnny to the hospital and has arrested Ralinov. Johnny wonders if someone in the mob at the drugstore has the material, so they go back to the bus stop.

Stacey notices the detector and Johnny tells Stacey how it was clicking, but now the battery is dead. Johnny suddenly realizes that the material must be in the briefcase on the back seat. The time is 11:38 a.m. and the material could go off in seven minutes. Johnny floors the car and heads for the plant.

"So, by some miracle we made it. But only seconds before that tiny mass of nuclear destruction was due to become critical. Yeah, we made it by the skin of our teeth. But after all, what more could you ask. Expense account total, oh so what. I needed a tank of gas anyway."

Notes:
- This program contains commercials for Camel cigarettes, Mona Freeman for 4-Way cold tablets, Fitch Dandruff Remover Shampoo, and Ex-Lax.
- Bob Bailey mentions that they are going to miss Dan Cubberly, who is the announcer.

Producer:	Jack Johnstone	Writer:	Jack Johnstone
Cast:	Virginia Gregg, G. Stanley Jones, Bartlett Robinson, Sam Edwards, Stacy Harris

Show:	**The Merry Go Round Matter**
Show Date:	**1/31/1960**
Company:	**Universal Adjustment Bureau**
Agent:	**Pat McCracken**
Exp. Acct:	**$0.00**

Synopsis: A glum Pat McCracken calls Johnny and mentions Alvin Peabody Cartwright and tells Johnny that now he has a problem. Johnny tells Pat about all the money he has gotten from Cartwright, and Pat almost gets Johnny to work on the case without expenses because he likes Alvin. Pat tells Johnny to drive up to Lakewood and see Alvin. Pat does not know what is going on, as Alvin tells something different to everybody he talks to.

Johnny notes how doing a job for Alvin is like riding a bunch of carnival rides. Johnny buys gas and drives to Alvin's estate in Lakewood. At the front door, Alvin tells Johnny to get inside and not to track up the house, and then he realizes who Johnny is. Alvin wishes Johnny a Merry Christmas and then gives Johnny a present, a diamond encrusted money clip. Alvin wants to wish Johnny a happy New Year before he leaves, and then Alvin remembers why Johnny is there and tells him that he is in terrible trouble.

Alvin tells Johnny that the problem is his new art gallery. Ever since he went to Paris and saw the Louvre, he has wanted an art gallery. Alvin takes Johnny to a room and shows Johnny an ornate gallery with a marble ceiling. The room is full of paintings, tapestries, sculptures and jewelry.

Alvin tells Johnny that he has been robbed. A sacred painting, an icon encrusted with jewels has been stolen. It was worth $90,000. Johnny notes it was small enough to be taken out under a coat. Alvin tells Johnny that he had a guard on duty. He was the first man who answered the ad, but Alvin has fired him. Alvin tells Johnny that only one person was allowed in at a time.

The other night a man dressed in rags came in to see the gallery, and another man, Alvin's friend Jonathan Peebles also came to visit and gave Alvin a lecture on security. When the old man left, he tripped on the stairs and the guard helped him up and drove the old man to town. Jonathan then noticed that the icon was missing. The guard was Gummy O'Bannon. Johnny recognizes the name as an old gangster from New York.

Johnny goes to Gummy's shack and listens outside. Inside Gummy and the old man are drinking beer and counting a stack of money. Gummy mentions that another man had given them money to have the old man fall. His name was funny, like some sort of building.

Johnny goes to New York and a fancy apartment house where the doorman has a note for Johnny. The note tells Johnny that Peebles has been trying to contact Johnny, and that he is to see Peebles before he talks to Alvin. The note tells Johnny that the icon is in an urn in the gallery.

Johnny drives back to Lakewood to find the door to Alvin's home open. Jonathan and Alvin are arguing with each other at the breakfast table. Jonathan wants Alvin to turn the gallery over to a museum. Also, Jonathan wants Alvin to get some legitimate guards for the gallery, and Alvin agrees that the whole thing is silly. Alvin will do anything to get the icon back.

Jonathan tells Alvin that he has the icon and will give it back if Alvin will do as he asks. He tells Alvin that he hid it to pound some sense into Alvin's head. Alvin promises to do as Jonathan asks, and the argument continues.

"And if you think for a minute that was the end of it, you are wrong. Those two wild old men sat there for the better part of an hour squabbling, shaking their fists at each other, and half dozen times they almost came to blows. But, finally they ran out of breath, put their arms around each other, shed some tears of repentance, and then as they have done so many times before, quietly solemnly swore undying friendship for each other. What a pair!" The expense account? Why bother. After all, by now Alvin Peabody Cartwright has probably forgotten he even sent for me."

Notes:
- This program contains commercials for Camel cigarettes, Mel Torme for 4-Way cold tablets, Fitch Dandruff Remover Shampoo, and Ex-Lax.
- The announcer is John Wald.

Producer:	Jack Johnstone	Writer:	Jack Johnstone
Cast:	Lawrence Dobkin, Howard McNear, Frank Gerstle, Will Wright, Forrest Lewis, Joseph Kearns		

♦ ❖ ♦

Show:	**The Sidewinder Matter**
Show Date:	**2/7/1960**
Company:	**Greater Southwest Life Insurance Company**
Agent:	**Jake Kessler**
Exp. Acct:	**$345.40**

Synopsis: Jake Kessler calls Johnny and tells him that a client, Rafe Chisolm, has a cattle ranch, and his cattle are being poisoned. Rafe found out who has been poisoning the cattle and there will be a killing. Can you come out and see what you can do?

Johnny calls Buster Favor to find out about the Circle RC ranch. Buster hopes Johnny can come out before someone is killed. Buster agrees to meet Johnny in Las Vegas.

Johnny flies to Las Vegas, Nevada where Buster meets him and drives Johnny to the Circle RC ranch. Buster comments to Johnny about the importance of water in the area to feed cattle. Buster tells Johnny that Rafe is pretty tough, and people call him "The Sidewinder". Local folks were not happy when he got a lease on the good ranch land with all the water on it.

Buster feels that an ex-partner, Jerry McCoy, is the one who is poisoning the cattle. Rafe had cheated Jerry out of the money he bought the ranch with, and Buster is sure that Jerry has caught up with Rafe.

At the ranch, Johnny notices the abundance of water. Mrs. Chisolm meets the car and she tells Johnny that her son Wayne told Rafe that Jerry McCoy was out fooling around with a water trough and he grabbed his gun and a knapsack and rode out after him.

Mrs. Chisolm does not know what is in the knapsack. She is clearly worried about Rafe and Wayne has gone out as well. With Rafe mad, he would shoot anyone, including his son. Buster and Johnny borrow horses and ride out to find Rafe.

Buster notices that the hoof prints of the horses indicate that someone is following Rafe. There are shots and Buster and Johnny ride to Block Canyon where Rafe has a windmill and shack. Buster spots a storm coming in and they ride for cover in a cave in Shadow Mountain.

The storm starts before they get to the cave, but they make it into the cave on foot. In the cave are a number of animals, all seeking safety from the storm. The winds finally subside only to bring a hailstorm, with hail the size of golf balls.

The storm is finally over and the animals leave. Buster notices Wayne lying under a rock in the cave and sees that he has been shot by Rafe.

Wayne tells Buster that he had followed Rafe, and when he spotted Wayne, he shot at him, but did not mean to shoot him as Wayne was hit by some wild shots. Wayne tells Buster and Johnny that he circled back to the shack where Rafe had found Jerry McCoy skinning a calf in the shack.

Wayne heard Rafe decide to let Jerry go if he does as he is told. Jerry was told to cut some thongs from the steer hide. Jerry was then told to tie Rafe to a post in the shack with thongs around his ankles and his neck. Rafe tells Jerry that his son will be there soon to let him loose. Jerry was told to leave and gives Jerry his gun.

Jerry left and took Rafe's horse just as the storm started. Jerry was told not to touch the knapsack, the same one he used when he was prospecting. Jerry opened the knapsack and screamed. Wayne tells Johnny that there were three sidewinders in the knapsack and that Jerry was bitten and died.

Wayne is sent home and Buster and Johnny ride to the feed shack. Johnny finds Jerry's body half buried in the sand. In the shack, they find Rafe Chisolm, the rawhide had dried out and shrunk, choking him.

"I don't know, I don't know. And who is to question the ways of justice?"

Notes:
- This program contains commercials for Pepsi (be sociable), Camel cigarettes, Stu Erwin for 4-Way cold tablets, and Fitch Dandruff Remover Shampoo.
- This program ends before the closing credits.
- The announcer is John Wald.
- Cast Information from the KNX Collection at the Thousand Oaks Library.

Producer: Jack Johnstone   Writer: Jack Johnstone
Cast: Joseph Kearns, Barney Phillips, Virginia Gregg, Sam
              Edwards, Junius Matthews, Ralph Moody, Bill James

♦ ❖ ♦

Show: The P. O. Matter
Show Date: 2/14/1960
Company: Mid-Eastern Indemnity Corporation
Agent: Harry McQueen
Exp. Acct: $397.70

Synopsis: Harry McQueen calls Johnny, and Johnny tells him he can't wait to come to New York and have some fun — on expense account of course. Harry mentions Dan Diamond and Johnny wants to work elsewhere and tells Harry he has another assignment and wants to live to middle age. Johnny reminds Harry that three people died in the last job Diamond pulled. Harry tells Johnny that Dan has retired and is growing orchids in Long Beach. Dan is in New York and has just lifted $75,000 from a jewelry store. Johnny wants to turn the job down, until Harry mentions the commission on a $75,000 recovery and the unlimited expense account.

Johnny does not want the case, but the bait is too much to resist. Johnny trains to New York City and meets with Harry. Harry relates to Johnny how Diamond robbed the cash from the jewelry store at closing time. The cashier told the police that Dan Diamond identified himself during the robbery. The police have him in jail but are going to release him today for lack of evidence. Harry tells Johnny that Randy Singer is assigned to the case, so Johnny goes over to talk to him.

Randy tells Johnny that he is working on the case due to the killings on the previous cases involving "Dapper Danny". Randy tells Johnny that there is no evidence and that Diamond has an ironclad alibi. Randy has found nothing, including the missing money. Randy tells Johnny that Diamond works alone and would not trust the money with anyone short of the government. Randy gets a call and learns that Diamond is on his way home, so Johnny decides to leave for California.

Johnny gets a photo of Diamond from Randy and flies to California only to find out he is sitting next to Danny Diamond, who is holding a dispatch case in his lap. Johnny identifies himself as "Jerry Reynolds", and Diamond tells Johnny that he probably has read about him in the papers. Diamond unsuccessfully tries to fool Johnny into answering to his real name. Johnny tells Diamond that he is going out to visit a friend, Jack Johnstone, who writes for the radio. Dan thinks the name sounds familiar, as he listens to the radio.

When Dan goes to the back of the plane to get a drink, Johnny tries to figure out how to get into the dispatch case and gets the latch open. Diamond comes back drink-less and tries to buy a bottle from a fellow passenger. Johnny moves the case and it falls open onto the floor. The case is full of newspaper articles about the robbery. Johnny wonders if the case is a decoy.

In Los Angeles, Johnny rents a car and drives to Long Beach, California and gets a hotel room. Johnny calls Western Union and has a telegram from Randy Singer that tells Johnny to "Make contact with P. O. Your man is Sgt. Wyman. Good Luck, Randy". Johnny is sure the "P. O." should be "P. D." as he drives to see Sgt. Wally Wyman who tells Johnny that he knows all about Dan

Diamond, but they can do nothing without evidence. If Johnny can find something against Diamond, the town will love Johnny.

Johnny arranges to have the police call Diamond in for a "talk" so that Johnny can search his luggage before he unpacks. The police call Diamond to come in while Johnny "takes a walk on the beach". Johnny drives to the neighborhood and sees Danny arrive in a cab, and then drive away in a sports car. Johnny jimmies the back door and searches the luggage and the house and finds nothing. Johnny feels that the money is still in New York. Johnny remembers Randy saying that Diamond would trust no one but the government and gets an idea.

Johnny goes back to Sgt. Wyman and mentions the "P. O.", which he thought was "P. D.". Johnny asks where the closest post office to Diamond's house is and drives there.

Johnny finds Danny's car parked out front, and inside Danny is in line behind a wino. The clerk tells Diamond that he has a package from New York for him. As Diamond leaves, Johnny lunges at the package and manages to tear it open exposing the money inside. Danny tries to shoot Johnny, but Johnny slugs him. Johnny tells Danny that now he has him for murder, as his wild shot killed the wino.

"So, from here on in of course, it's in the hands of the law, the courts. As to credit in solving this one, well actually it all goes to simple typographical error. Funny."

Notes:
- This program contains commercials for Mona Freeman for 4-Way cold tablets, Fitch Dandruff Remover Shampoo, Camel cigarettes and Ex-Lax.
- The announcer is John Wald.

Producer:	Jack Johnstone	Writer:	Jack Johnstone
Cast:	Virginia Gregg, Harry Bartell, Herb Vigran, James McCallion, Stacy Harris, Gil Stratton		

• ❖ •

Show:	**The Alvin's Alfred Matter**
Show Date:	**2/21/1960**
Company:	**Floyds of England**
Agent:	**George Reed**
Exp. Acct:	**$0.00**

Synopsis: George Reed calls Johnny, hesitantly. George understands that Johnny has handled cases for Continental Insurance and Trust Company. Johnny tells George that the crazy cases Floyds has given him are nothing compared to the ones from Continental, all because of one man: Alvin Peabody Cartwright. Johnny tells George that Peabody told Continental that he would drop them if they sent anyone else. Johnny tells George that, in spite of the crazy cases, he has come to like Alvin and would do almost anything to help him out. George hems and haws and hesitantly tells Johnny that his problem is, you guessed it, Alvin Peabody Cartwright!

Johnny muses how George's cases were bad enough as Johnny cabs to

George's office. George tells Johnny that he had managed to convince Alvin to change companies. George tells Johnny that they should have been more careful, especially on this one policy for Alfred Cartwright, a ward of Alvin's. Alvin has told George that Alfred has been abducted. Also, Alfred is a dog, a female dog. "Oh No!" cries Johnny.

George tells Johnny that Alfred has life, accident, injury, and mysterious disappearance insurance. Being a ward, Floyds never thought twice about the policy. George tells Johnny to go to Lakewood and find out what has happened. There is no limit on expenses and Johnny can name his fee. Johnny agrees to take the case if George keeps it quiet that Johnny Dollar was searching the country for a pooch!

Johnny buys gas and drives to Lakewood where Alvin is too upset to talk and slams the door on Johnny. Alvin finally recognizes Johnny and invites him in. Alvin tells Johnny that he must spare no expense to find Alfred, who was like a child to him.

Alvin shows Johnny Alfred's room, which is like a child's playroom, complete with a tree, fire hydrant, model train and a working seismograph. Alvin tells Johnny that some of the toys are his, things he never had as a child. Maybe he is silly, but now he has the things he wanted as a child. Johnny notes that his parents could not afford to buy him a model train.

Alvin feels that the problem with growing up is that people do not enjoy the simple things of life, or that someone would laugh at them if they did. Alvin had searched for a long time before he found the dog at the pound and is upset at losing his dog. He had hoped for a boy so he named the dog Alfred.

Alvin knows that Clarence Brickston, a servant he had fired yesterday, is the only one who could have done it. Alvin had gone to visit the widow Parkinson and no one was home except Alfred. Clarence had a key and came in and abducted Alfred.

The police say that Clarence has an alibi, his wife said that he was at home with her. Johnny has a crazy idea and borrows something of Alfred's.

Johnny drives to the address of Clarence Brickston. Mabel Brickston answers the door and Johnny walks in. Clarence tells Johnny to get out and that he is tired of everyone yelling at him for taking the dog. Clarence has scratches on his hands, and they seem to know an awful lot about the dog.

Clarence tells Johnny that the dog escaped to get away from Cartwright. Johnny tells Clarence that he had a key, but he forgot about the seismograph, which registered the footsteps while Clarence chased the dog. Johnny shows Mabel and Clarence the tape from the seismograph to prove it.

How's that for scientific investigation? Mabel tells Johnny that Clarence took the dog so that they could return it for a reward. Clarence gives up to Johnny as he is too smart for him.

"Oh sure, modern scientific investigation, but he fell for it. And Mabel brought the dog up from the cellar, and she was kind of a mangy little pooch, the dog I mean. But she meant the difference between keeping or losing Cartwright's insurance account, which reminds me, you can forget the expense account. Cartwright did well by me as usual. And he'll probably break down and take Clarence back. Oh Well."

Notes:
- This program contains commercials for Pepsi, Camel Cigarettes, Mel Torme for 4-Way, Fitch Dandruff Remover Shampoo, and for Ex-Lax.
- Bob Bailey welcomes WATV in Birmingham, Alabama and KSOB in Cedar City, Utah to the CBS Network.
- The announcer is John Wald.

Producer:	Jack Johnstone	Writer:	Jack Johnstone
Cast:	Virginia Gregg, G. Stanley Jones, Howard McNear, Frank Gerstle		

◆ ❖ ◆

Show:	**The Look Before the Leap Matter**
Show Date:	2/28/1960
Company:	**Universal Adjustment Bureau**
Agent:	**Pat McCracken**
Exp. Acct:	**$9,571.00**

Synopsis: "Thirty days hath September," starts the caller, and Johnny finishes with "April June and November. All the rest have thirty-one, except. So today is February 27, so this month we get cheated out of a couple days or two, so what? So, who is this?"

The caller is Pat McCracken. Pat tells Johnny that being near the end of February has something to do with a case Johnny could not solve almost six years ago. Johnny remembers Bernard Margot, "Barney the Bum", who jumped off the Tri-Borough Bridge. Johnny reminds Pat that the whole thing was a phony so "Big Mike" Killian could collect the $300,000 insurance. Pat reminds Johnny that he spent several thousand dollars to find Barney but could not prove it. Pat tells Johnny he can save the company a lot of money if he can find Bernie before March 1.

Johnny cabs to Pat's office. Pat tells Johnny that this is one he would like to close out, and that Continental should not have issued the policy, but Barney had already jumped before they could cancel the policy. A witness claims to have seen Barney jump, but Killian has not been paid the $300,000. Unless Barney is picked up before March 1, the courts will order the policy paid. Johnny bemoans that today is February 27.

Pat tells Johnny that the witness, Maidy Prescott just came back from Paris, where she saw Barney Margot. Pat tells Johnny that with all the diplomatic red tape cannot get him back in time. But if Johnny can somehow get him back in time, there is a $10,000 bonus plus expenses. Johnny tells Pat that it is impossible, which is why he is going to try!

Johnny goes to the New York City apartment of Maidy Prescott, who recounts her testimony about seeing Barney jumping from the bridge, but she must have been wrong. She tells Johnny that she saw Barney in Paris, France, in the antique store of Monsieur Duboisson. She is sure of it.

On the elevator, Johnny remembers that Duboisson is a fence. Suddenly two men stop the elevator. One of them tells Johnny that Big Mike does not like Johnny Dollar messing into things, and they slug Johnny and put him in the basement.

Johnny is found by the building super and then goes to send a wire, book a flight to Paris and then goes to see Randy, who tells him that the men were probably two of Killian's boys. Johnny wants Randy to stay put until he comes back from Paris.

Johnny flies to Paris, France and calls his friend Louis De Marsac who is not home. Johnny cabs to the shop of Duboisson who recognizes Johnny from previous cases. Johnny wants information on Margot, but Duboisson calls for Maurice and tells him to leave and arrange for the funeral of his friend.

Duboisson does not know anything about Margot and tells Johnny that he is wasting his time. Johnny calls Louis again and the phone is busy so he cabs there. At Louis' apartment, Johnny finds him on the floor. Johnny rushes in and Maurice slugs Johnny.

Johnny knows that his arrival is the only thing that saved Louis from being killed. After some cognac, Louis comes to and he tells Johnny that he has found Barney. Johnny agrees to $350 for the information on where Barney is.

Louis tells Johnny that he has Barney, so Johnny tells Louis that he will give him $1,000 if he can deliver Barney to Johnny. Louis asks for $2,000 if he can also arrange for transportation out of France to the states. Johnny agrees if he can get Barney back before midnight. Johnny agrees to $2,500 if he makes it back in time.

Louis takes Barney out of his closet and they drive to the airport where a plane is waiting. Johnny manages to get the pilot to fly to the states for $7,000. Johnny calls Randy to get clearance for the plane to land, and Randy agrees, reluctantly.

The plane trip was one not to forget. Johnny finally lands and an escort is waiting to take Barney back to jail. In Randy's office, Johnny is yelled at by Randy for what he did, but Johnny keeps falling asleep.

Randy tells Johnny that they landed at 12:07 a.m., which Johnny says is too late. He had to get Barney back by midnight, now he will have to pay the fees out of his own pocket. Johnny feels like blowing his brains out, but Randy reminds Johnny that 1960 is a leap year. So, Johnny got Barney in before midnight on the last day of February!

"You know something, I should have blown my brains out for forgetting that extra day this month, this year. But instead I'll just take that $10,000 in fees. As for the expense account, hold your hat — $9,571.00!"

Notes:
- This program contains commercials for Frito Corn Chips, Camel Cigarettes, Stuart Erwin for 4-Way cold tablets, Fitch Dandruff Remover Shampoo, Burgess Meredith for the Super 60 hearing glasses from Mako Electronics, and Ex-Lax.
- Closing comments: "Here is your star with something to think about on

account of its Brotherhood Week: Johnny." "John, it is a thought for this week, and every week, and it's simply this: In my job I run across all sorts of people, both the right guys and the wrong ones. And this much I am sure of, a crook is a crook, in any place, in any language, he's just no good. But an honest man, a man who respects the law and the rights of his fellow humans, regardless of his hue, his origin or his accent, well believe me, that one is yours truly with Johnny Dollar."

- The announcer is John Wald.

Producer:	Jack Johnstone Writer: Jack Johnstone
Cast:	Virginia Gregg, Lawrence Dobkin, Forrest Lewis, Frank Gerstle, Herb Vigran, Tony Barrett

♦ ❖ ♦

Show:	The Moonshine Matter
Show Date:	3/6/1960
Company:	Providential Assurance Company
Agent:	Clark Tracy
Exp. Acct:	$340.00

Synopsis: Clark Tracy calls Johnny and asks him to go to Kennett, Missouri. They have the wrong man there, Charles Kingsley St. Clair, a Harvard man who does not know how to deal with the people in that area. They are moving him out and closing the office, but they have one outstanding claim on the death of Casper Crump. The widow, Eupha Crump, has to be given the $5,000 due her, but St. Claire claims he cannot do it. Can you clear this thing up for us? Clark promises Johnny a fee and no questions on his expense account.

Johnny flies to Memphis and takes a bus to Kennett. St. Clair tells Johnny that he is glad to be going back to civilized country. The natives out in the country are poor white trash, ignorant, illiterate moonshiners who did not know what they were buying.

Mrs. Eupha Crump lives in the 20-mile swamp, which is a nest of moonshiners. A gentleman would never venture in there. The natives say it was murder and the police leave them alone.

Johnny rents a car held together by bailing wire and rope and drives out to the swamp. Johnny drives down a road along the swamp, past the water moccasins sunning themselves on rotting logs. At a shack on stilts Johnny is shot at, loses control of the car and crashes.

When Johnny comes to he is lying beside the car but does not have his gun. Johnny plays possum as two lanky men walk towards him. They do not think he is a revenuer, but do not know who he is. Johnny gets up and tells Cass Dingle and Morphy Teed that he has a check for Eupha Crump. They tell Johnny that Eupha is a mighty fine woman.

They agree to take Johnny to Eupha and notice his missing gun, too bad, as there are people here who will shoot first and find out about you later. People like Dade Wupper. He killed Casper Crump and he will think that Johnny is coming after him.

In Cass Dingle's cabin, a really squalid place, Johnny gets a drink of corn liquor right from Eupha Crump's still. Cass and Johnny take a dugout canoe up the slough. At the Crump cabin Morphy tells Cass that one of Eupha's kids has gone to tell Dade Wupper about Johnny.

Johnny notes that Eupha is a nice-looking woman of 20 with 4 kids. She takes the money and tells Johnny that most of the money will go to improve the still and buy Cass a new suit of clothes. Morphy rushes in to tell them that Dave is all liquored up and on his way with his shotgun loaded with slugs.

Johnny and Cass leave but Dade is right on their trail shooting at them. Dade shoots and kills Cass.

Johnny dives into the water and swims under water towards Dade's dugout. Dade yells at Johnny that he will get him like he got Casper. Johnny goes under and swims to Dade, grabs his legs and overpowers him.

"So maybe those people were pretty much a law unto themselves, but Dade Wupper went back to Kennett. There he will stand trial for two murders. And I will continue to poke along in this soft cozy little job of mine, yeah."

Notes:
- This program contains commercials for Pepsi, Camel cigarettes, Mona Freeman for 4-Way Cold Tablets (29 cents), Fitch Dandruff Remover Shampoo, Fritos and Ex-Lax.
- There is a Kennett, Missouri located in the extreme southern part of the state, near the Mississippi river north of Memphis.
- The Cottonmouth Water Moccasin (Agkistrodon piscivorus) and the Western Cottonmouth (piscivorus leucostoma) are the only poisonous North American water snakes. It is a pit viper and related to the Copperhead and the Rattlesnake. The moccasin has a reputation for being an aggressive reptile that will stand its ground or even approach an intruder. Given the location in Missouri, the snake referenced could be either.
- Johnny mentions swimming to some Tules (pronounced toolees) which is a type of reedy grass.
- When Johnny crashes his car, the sound effect is the typical car screeching on pavement. Too bad he was on a muddy dirt road.
- Johnny mentions going up the slough (pronounced slu), which is a creek-like channel in a swamp.
- The announcer is John Wald.

Producer: Jack Johnstone Writer: Jack Johnstone
Cast: Virginia Gregg, Harry Bartell, Ben Wright, Sam Edwards, Vic Perrin, Ralph Moody

Show:	The Deep Down Matter
Show Date:	3/13/1960
Company:	Continental Insurance Company
Agent:	
Exp. Acct:	$131.50

Synopsis: Ralph calls about Bertram Haskell who owns a small copper mine in Michigan. His partner Ben Oliver has been murdered, and Haskell wants Johnny to investigate. It is the insurance on Haskell that is motivating this investigation. Ralph tells Johnny that the country and the people are pretty rough up there.

Johnny flies to Chicago and then on to Houghton, Michigan where he rents a car. Johnny drives to the Haskell mine where there are a number of weather beaten houses and a big hole. Johnny goes to the office where Mr. Haskell is telling a man that he had better not throw Mrs. Oliver out of her house.

Haskell tells Johnny that Ben Oliver and he had worked together for years, and he is making a fortune. Ben did not want to be a partner, only a scientist. Ben was murdered in the mine exploring an abandoned area. It had to be one of the miners, but not one of the six could have done it as there was only one shot fired in total darkness.

Haskell shows Johnny a map of the mine, and where the ore comes up. Ben was killed 321 feet below the surface in a big room. Haskell takes Johnny down into the mine to show Johnny where Oliver was killed.

Johnny describes the ride down, past the various stopes in the mine. In the bottom stope, Johnny notices that the lights were on. Haskell tells Johnny that Ben was checking for uranium and had asked for a Geiger counter. Haskell went down with the equipment and the six others when the lights went off. When the lights came back on, Oliver was found dead from a pellet gun wound. There was no sign of a flashlight, and one of the men in the car did it. Johnny thinks he has a pretty big order.

Johnny arranges to stay with Haskell, and over dinner Haskell tells him that the uranium was not worth digging for. Haskell and the police have no clue. The pellet gun was a foreign make, which could have come from anywhere, as there is a big foreign population there. Johnny has a few ideas, and asks to talk to the six men who went down with Haskell.

Johnny questions the men and then talks to Mrs. Oliver. She tells Johnny that Bertram was always kind to Ben, but she tells Johnny that if he is going to work for Haskell, to look out and make sure he gets credit for anything he discovers. Ben was easy going and easy to be taken advantage of.

She typed the report where Ben was certain that there was uranium with great commercial possibilities in the mine. Mrs. Oliver tells Johnny that in the report, she made Ben say that he wanted to share in the profits, unlike the money he did not get from the copper finds.

Mrs. Oliver shows Johnny Ben's equipment that includes a scintillator and a black light. Johnny turns it on and Ben's clothes glow. Johnny is sure that the glow is the solution to the murder.

Johnny puts Ben's jacket on under his topcoat, takes the equipment and goes to see Haskell. Johnny gets Haskell to take him down into the mine. Haskell is asked to turn the lights off and Johnny moves to the place where Ben was killed.

Johnny removes his topcoat and turns his back to Haskell. Johnny tells Haskell to turn on the black light so he can see the target on the back of the coat Ben was wearing. Haskell shoots at the coat, but Johnny had taken it off. Johnny tells Haskell that he knew there was uranium in the mine and killed Oliver to keep the profits.

"The almost perfect crime. And he was so sure of it that he called me in to back up his story of loyalty to Ben Oliver so that no one would ever question his taking over the uranium that Ben had found."

Notes:
- This program contains commercials for Fritos with a free package of Burpee flower seeds to celebrate spring, Winston Cigarettes, Mel Torme for 4-Way cold tablets, Fitch Dandruff Remover Shampoo, and Ex-Lax.
- The announcer is John Wald.

Producer:	Jack Johnstone Writer: Jack Johnstone
Cast:	Will Wright, Virginia Gregg, John Stephenson

◆ ❖ ◆

Show:	The Saturday Night Matter
Show Date:	3/20/1960
Company:	Surety Mutual Insurance, Ltd.
Agent:	Peter H. Fillmore
Exp. Acct:	$301.01

Synopsis: Peter H. Fillmore calls Johnny from Denver, and he has just discovered a racket of grocery store robberies. They occur every Saturday night with most discouraging regularity. Fillmore is certain that a gang is involved, but Johnny should agree once he gets the facts. They will not quibble over the expense account and there is a fee and commission involved, on account of the danger to Johnny's life.

Johnny grabs a box of .38 shells and flies to Denver, Colorado. In his office, Mr. Fillmore tells Johnny that the robberies did not all not occur in Denver. But Fillmore has found a pattern.

The policies involved are for unlimited loss by robbery and have increased his business. Every robbery occurs on Saturday night, eight so far. The robbers enter at gunpoint just at closing time. The two robbers also wear stocking masks over their heads. There has been no police coordination, because of the different localities. Fillmore has just found a pattern.

The robberies occur in a pattern of decreasing city population. Fillmore feels that the next robbery will be in Wheat Ridge or Grand Junction, they have equal populations. Johnny must decide on which town. Johnny takes a quarter and flips it: heads Wheat Ridge, tails Grand Junction. "Can you think of a better way?" Fillmore is worried about paying off on another claim.

Albert Berry, Fillmore's assistant comes in and tells Fillmore to cancel the policies, but Fillmore does not want to. Berry tells Fillmore that he would rather leave than continue selling these policies. Johnny tells Berry that, at the flip of a coin, he is heading for somewhere, but he needs to get busy.

Johnny rents a car for the drive to Grand Junction but stops first at the police department in Wheat Ridge where Sgt. Keasley tells Johnny that they are watching the store in Wheat Ridge. Johnny is told to talk to Dick Spidel in Grand Junction.

Johnny drives on towards Grand Junction. Along the way, he spots a number of cold trout streams and thinks of coming back some day to fish. After lunch Johnny is watching the scenery when a car swings into him at a detour and runs him off the road.

Johnny is rescued by a state trooper and taken to a hospital where he is given a hypo and goes out. Johnny wakes up with Dick Spidel in his room. Dick tells Johnny that they know he was run off the road. The same car was used at a market robbery there in Grand Junction.

Dick tells Johnny that the owner of the market, Barnaby Shaltus has a record of stock manipulations and phony bankruptcies. Johnny realizes when Shaltus was robbed, he knew he would get the insurance. Dick tells Johnny to stay put and that he is being guarded until the doc says he can get up.

Johnny is out the next day and goes back to Mr. Fillmore. He tells Fillmore that the owners could arrange the robberies themselves and get a part of the robbery. Johnny is sure that someone is running a robbery ring. Fillmore realizes that someone must know who had the policies.

Johnny suggests that Al Berry is collecting both ways, by selling policies and arranging the robberies. Berry comes in and tells Johnny that he should not have gone through his files and made it so obvious.

Johnny tells him he was sloppy for pulling the robberies in the same order he sold the policies, from biggest to smallest. Berry pulls his gun, and Johnny tells him that the police are there. Berry is sure that he is joking, until a police sergeant comes in and takes the gun.

"Sure, in the hope it might make things easier for him, Al produced the punks who had been working with him, who had actually pulled the jobs. And then he came up with most of the dough from the robberies. But you know something? I doubt if it will do him any good, nor the store owners who had played along with him." Johnny will leave the car that was wrecked to Fillmore.

Notes:
- This program contains commercials for Pepsi, Winston cigarettes, Stuart Erwin for 4-Way Cold Tablets, Fitch Dandruff Remover Shampoo, Fritos, and Ex-Lax.
- The announcer is John Wald.

Producer: Jack Johnstone   Writer: Jack Johnstone

Cast: Bartlett Robinson, James McCallion, Forrest Lewis, Russell Thorson

♦ ❖ ♦

Show: **The False Alarm Matter**
Show Date: 3/27/1960
Company: Tri-State Life & Casualty Company
Agent: Earle Poorman
Exp. Acct: $161.00

Synopsis: Mike Poorman calls Johnny and tells him that she heard on WSPB radio about a man who was found dead in his car just off the Tamiami Trail. The radio report said the car was just like Earle's. Mike had called the radio station, and they did not know anything. Johnny tells her to call the station again. Johnny is going to see how quickly he can get there.

Johnny flies to the Poorman home in Sarasota. Mike meets Johnny at the door and tells him that Earle had run out that morning, and that the radio station had called back. They checked with the police in Bonita Springs, and they had reported the man, who was named Jansen or something like that, had suffered a heart attack. Johnny suggests that maybe he can get Earle to take him fishing, but Earle is not home yet.

The phone rings and Johnny answers it. Earle apologizes to Mike for not calling earlier, but he is on a murder case and asks her to call Johnny Dollar and have him meet Earle down here. Johnny asks "Down where?" Earle tells Johnny to meet him at an address near Venice. "Who is this?" asks Earle. Earle does not know who is on the phone because he does not know that Johnny had come down.

Johnny drives to the address given to him by Earle, and it is a huge expensive home. Johnny spots Earle's car and another that belongs to Doc Crutcher. Doc had called Earle to the estate.

Johnny learns that Doc Crutcher had been the family doctor for Linda since before she married Frank, but it is a bad marriage. Frank was only out for Linda's money. She had hired a bunch of other old boyfriends but ended up running the family chemical company herself. Doc shows Johnny the body of Linda on the bed, and even in death she is beautiful. Doc had found the body twisted in pain when they got there, but it looks peaceful now.

Johnny suspects cyanide, but Doc says it is something subtler, possibly potassium theramalicilate. PTM initially gives symptoms of cyanide, but later those symptoms are gone. The maid had called and said that Linda was having a heart attack. When they got there, Doc started running tests and found indications of the PTM, but no evidence of it. Doc has checked everything but cannot find the poison.

Johnny wants to question the servants, and they all convince Johnny that they were devoted and loyal to Linda. Linda's personal maid Irene tells Johnny that Linda was sitting at the dressing table and putting on some perfume when she clutched at her heart.

Johnny goes back to Doc Crutcher and they look at the empty perfume bottle.

Doc runs a test to see if the bottle ever had the poison in it. Earle thinks that Frank Hanson, her husband, is the likely suspect. He went to the plant this morning but has disappeared.

Doc tells Johnny that the poison had been in the perfume bottle. Johnny then remembers Mike telling him earlier that the man found by the police that morning was named Jansen or something like that.

Johnny calls the police in Bonita Springs and learns that Frank Hanson had been driving along smoking a cigarette and had a heart attack. Huh? Johnny tells them to run tests for the poison. The police call back to say that the poison was found in the cigarettes.

Johnny talks to Earle about Linda's love life, and one name comes up, one man who had promised to get even if Linda married anyone else. Johnny asks Doc to concoct something that would make a stain after a few minutes. Doc gets two chemicals which, when mixed, will produce a blue stain. Johnny wants to play a hunch and tells Doc to get the materials ready.

Johnny, Earle and Doc drive to the chemical plant and meet the chief chemist, Harry Forester. Johnny shakes hands with both hands and they go into the office. Johnny asks Harry, "if Linda were to die" and Harry interrupts to tell Johnny that he was in love with her at one time.

But Johnny continues that the money would go to her husband Frank. But if Frank were to die, would you not be next in line? And Harry knows where to get hold of PTM, but Harry tells Johnny that he is scared of it and never uses it.

Johnny takes out a bottle and spills some of it on Harry's hand. A bluish tinge appears and Johnny says that the stain is proof that he has been handling PTM, that he had put it in Linda's perfume bottle and Frank's cigarettes.

Harry admits to killing them both, and he tries to swallow a capsule to get out of going to jail, but Johnny slugs him. Doc thinks the capsule is full of PTM.

"So, it will be up to the courts whether Harry Forester likes it or not. And believe me, I would hate to be in his shoes. Yeah, I keep wondering, why don't they ever learn?"

Notes:
- This program contains commercials for Winston cigarettes, a public service announcement for the Red Cross, and Ex-Lax.
- The announcer is John Wald.

Producer:	Jack Johnstone	Writer:	Jack Johnstone
Cast:	Shirley Mitchell, Virginia Gregg, Vic Perrin, Lou Merrill, Paula Winslowe, Frank Nelson, Richard Crenna		

Show:	**The Double Exposure Matter**
Show Date:	4/3/1960
Company:	Masters Insurance & Trust Company
Agent:	Frederick Keeley
Exp. Acct:	$17.20

Synopsis: Frederick Keeley calls Johnny and he has a problem. One of their claimants has apparently never received a claim check. Johnny tells Keeley to call the bank and stop payment. However, Keeley tells Johnny that the claimant has cashed the check. Johnny thinks that someone may have gotten the check first, which would be forgery. Johnny agrees to look into the case.

Johnny cabs to Keeley's office and is told that a $3,000 claim is relatively unimportant (i.e. small commission for Johnny), but the claimant must be stupid to think that he can get away with it, but Peter Upman is not stupid.

Keeley is sure that the case is forgery, that someone else has taken the check. Keeley is sure that this could lead to larger crimes. According to the bank, they have proof that Upman appeared, cashed the check and left with the money. But Upman had signed a deposition that he never got the check. That is why Johnny has been called. Johnny accepts the challenge.

Johnny drives to Milford, Connecticut and the Peoples National Bank, which is closed. Johnny gets a hotel room the Milford Arms, has dinner and visits Mr. Upman, who is a nervous football type.

Peter is sure that Johnny has the replacement check and asks for it. Upman repeats his story that he never got the check, but Johnny tells him that they have a receipt. Peter tells Johnny that Alfred Price, the lawyer, took his statement, so ask him. Upman tells Johnny that he is a nervous person, and it might not be healthy to aggravate him. That is not a warning, it is a threat. Johnny is unable to reason with Upman.

Johnny goes to visit Mr. Price who tells Johnny that Peter comes from a wealthy family. He wanted to make something of himself, but his father cut him off. The other family members do not get along with him. Peter owns a small electronics shop and is the only one in the family who knows the value of money. He could use the money, but Price does not think that Peter would try to cheat the insurance company. But what about the check? Price asks if Johnny has talked to the teller or seen the photograph of the transaction. Price tells Johnny that the bank camera is a very clever device.

First thing in the morning Johnny goes to the bank to talk to the president, Mr. Oliver. The camera is a clever device, when it works. It takes a picture of everyone who steps up to a teller counter. It really helps stop bad checks.

Johnny asks to see the picture and Oliver gives it to him, but it is very fuzzy and could be a double exposure. The camera was an experimental model, and only Oliver and the head teller know that the pictures are fuzzy. The picture could be of anyone.

Mrs. Eberhardt, the head teller tells Johnny that Mr. Upman cashed the check. Mrs. Eberhardt is called to the desk, and Johnny casually pulls his gun and holds it across his chest as Mrs. Eberhardt approaches. Johnny now sees things a lot more clearly.

Mr. Oliver is told not to mention the gun as Mrs. Eberhardt comes in tripping over things and misidentifying the other employees. She notices that Johnny smokes a pipe too, just like Mr. Oliver. Johnny tells her to take a good look and she finally recognizes that the pipe is Johnny's pistol.

Johnny asks when she last had an eye exam and Mrs. Eberhardt gets upset. Johnny tells Oliver that she is blind as a bat. Johnny calls Price, has lunch and then goes to Price's office.

Price gives Johnny photos of Janet Upman and Edward and Paul Upman, who Johnny mistakes for a young Peter. They dislike Peter because of the hidden bequest in the will that Peter does not know about. Peter gets over a million in a few months, when he turns thirty-five, provided he stays out of trouble. Johnny is ready to try something with Price's assistance.

Johnny calls Peter and Price calls the other family members. When they are all assembled in Price's office Peter tells Johnny that he does not like Johnny. Johnny tells them about the check from Aunt Elizabeth and Paul tells them that Peter should be locked up.

Johnny tells Paul that it would be easy for him to pick up the check, forge the signature and take the check to half-blind Mrs. Eberhardt to cash. Johnny tells Paul that a little machine put the finger on him, a machine that took a picture of him.

Janet tells Johnny that the camera in the bank has not worked in years. Her boyfriend is a cashier at the bank and he told her so. Johnny asks Janet "he didn't tell you it has been fixed?" Johnny gives the picture to Price, who agrees that the picture is clear. Peter gets angry and goes after Paul and a fight breaks out. Price is sure that Peter will kill Paul, but Johnny asks Price if he can think of a better way for justice to be done?

"Yeah, Peter paid Paul on this one, but I mean royally. And I must confess it did my heart glad to watch him. And Pete, bless his fighting Irish heart, Yep, he'll be a millionaire one of these days. He's earned it."

Notes:
- This program contains commercials for Pepsi, Winston cigarettes, and Ex-Lax.
- The announcer is John Wald.

Producer: Jack Johnstone   Writer: Jack Johnstone
Cast: Ralph Moody, Peter Leeds, Virginia Gregg, Bartlett Robinson, Marvin Miller, Jack Moyles, Eleanor Audley, Sandra Gould

Show:	**The Deadly Swamp Matter**
Show Date:	**4/17/1960**
Company:	**Providential Assurance Company**
Agent:	**Charles Kingsley St. Clair**
Exp. Acct:	**$161.60**

Synopsis: Charles Kingsley St Clair calls Johnny from Kennett, Missouri, and Johnny tells him that he thought he was leaving the company. Charles tells Johnny that he is a changed man now. Johnny tells him that they make some powerful moonshine down there. Charles tells Johnny that Dave Wupperman has been tried and incarcerated, but his brother Dan'l, or rather Daniel has been making trouble. Charles wants Johnny to come back and help him. Johnny reluctantly agrees to come down.

Johnny flies to Memphis, Tennessee where Charles meets Johnny, and to Johnny, he has changed. Charles tells Johnny that he has decided to stay in Kennett. When he got there the swamp people were the only ones he had to deal with, but he has decided to stay. Johnny taught him how to deal with them on his last visit. Johnny has friends there now, and they will help.

Charles tells Johnny that there have been a series of murders, and the victims have been relatives of the swamp people. They view the insurance company and Johnny as a protection agency. These cases are not a matter for the local police, as they have no jurisdiction.

Charles tells Johnny that Eupha Crump, who Johnny helped on his last trip, was the latest victim. Johnny asks what else he knows, so he can start to work on the case.

Johnny remembers Eupha as a person out of place in the swamp, working hard to care for her family. Now Cass and Eupha are dead. But Charles tells Johnny that Cass is still alive and that he married Eupha.

Cass asked Charles to have Johnny help him. Johnny borrows Kingsley's car and drives to the 20-mile swamp. Johnny heads to Eupha's house when he is shot at. Johnny stops and waits on the floor.

Cass Dingle comes up and asks for "Mr. Johnny". He tells Johnny that he shot to make Johnny stop so he could not go to the house. Cass tells Johnny to hide his car at the old cabin. After getting the car out of a mud hole, Johnny does not find Cass at the cabin.

Johnny walks to the cabin and goes in. Inside he finds Cass tied up on the floor and Dan'l Wupperman standing there with a very old, large bore rifle. Three other men appear and Johnny gives up, even though he notes he took a course from the FBI on how to disarm a man with a gun in your back, but not four men. Paul Wupperman takes Johnny's "pretty gun" and is told to hold onto it while Dan'l kills Johnny.

Johnny notes he has been in some tight spots before, but never anything like this. The swamp people use their guns for survival, but he notes that survival is not for Johnny today.

Dan'l tells Johnny that he is going to kill him for sending his brother to jail. He tells Johnny that he has no business there. Dan'l killed Eupha because

Johnny gave her the money, and he knew that Johnny would come back. Cass tells Dan'l that this is all wrong.

Paul thinks that if you kill an outside man, the police will come after him. Dan'l cocks the gun, and Cass tells Dan'l to kill him instead. Cass asks Johnny if he talked long enough, and it should be five o'clock by now. Johnny agrees it is about time and starts to whistle his theme.

Dan'l wants to know what he meant, and Johnny tells him that if he is not out of the swamp, the state police will come in to get him. Dan'l thinks he is lying. Paul is told to go out and look for any one, along with two of the others. Now there is only one enemy to deal with.

Johnny tells him that he has not heard from the others because the police have them. Dan'l starts to look at Johnny's watch to see what time it is and Johnny knees Dan'l and gets his gun and slugs him.

"I knew the sound of the gun shot would bring the others back to the cabin, after all they certainly hadn't found any sign of those mythical state police out there. So, after setting Cass free, I laid down just inside the door looking very dead. And then when John and Paul and Peter came in one at a time, Cass, who was standing back of the door, very quietly and carefully took care of them, with the help of the butt of Dan'l's gun. So now four more of the swampers have left that region to spend a long, long time behind the bars."

Notes:
- Dave Wupperman's name was Dave Wupper in *The Moonshine Matter*.
- This program contains commercials for Pepsi, Winston cigarettes, and Ex-Lax.
- The announcer is Hugh Douglas.

Producer:	Jack Johnstone	Writer:	Jack Johnstone
Cast:	Ben Wright, Sam Edwards, Roy Glenn, Vic Perrin		

❖

Show:	**The Silver Queen Matter**
Show Date:	**4/24/1960**
Company:	**Inter-Coastal Maritime & Life Insurance Company**
Agent:	**Byron Kaye**
Exp. Acct:	**$58.35**

Synopsis: Byron Kaye calls Johnny and tells him that things are not well in Cod Harbor. Johnny reminds him of the case he had handled for Meg McCarthy and her greasy spoon restaurant. Byron tells Johnny that it is Meg who called him and insisted that Johnny come up to see her. Meg has told Byron that if Johnny does not come up, she will cancel her insurance on the restaurant. Johnny tells Byron that Meg is used to handling things herself, so something must be wrong, the last time she called it was a murder. Byron tells Johnny he will pay the expenses.

Johnny decides to drive to Cod Harbor, and buys a tank of gas. Johnny arrives just after noon and describes the town and Meg's Palace. Johnny describes the boats tied up in the harbor on his way to visit Meg.

In the Palace, Meg is yelling at someone who broke up some dishes while he was drunk. After the man leaves, Meg attacks Johnny who is hiding in the shadows. Then she recognizes her "darlin' Johnny boy". Meg tells Johnny that she has to take care of the boys who come to her restaurant.

Over a cup of terrible coffee, Meg tells Johnny about Marty Silver, who owns the *Silver Queen*. He sailed in several days ago from Gloucester and wants to sell the *Silver Queen*. Captain Andy comes in and mentions that several people have made bids on the boat. Meg tells Andy to make sure that no one buys the boat. Meg tells Johnny that if Marty finds out that she sent for Johnny, there will be a murder, hers.

Meg tells Johnny that she had called Tom Lavery in Gloucester, and he has never heard of Silver, and Tom has lived there a long time. Last night Meg took a good look at the boat and discovered that the boat was originally named the *Arctic Queen*.

Meg called Tom again and learned that the *Arctic Queen* was supposed to have been lost at sea, with both hands aboard lost, the captain and the first mate Marty Flag. She feels that Silver and Flag are one in the same. Johnny is about to go to the phone booth to call the Coast Guard when she tells Johnny that Silver is going to murder her for snooping around his boat.

Meg gets upset because she feels that Johnny is not taking care of her life, and cares more about the boat. Johnny tells Meg that he will let nothing happen to her and leaves to call the Coast Guard.

Johnny calls the Coast Guard who have never heard of Silver. They are sure that Silver killed the captain of the *Arctic Queen*, painted the boat, and is trying to sell it. Johnny tells them he will watch Silver and do nothing to scare him until they get there. But, Johnny has to break that promise two minutes after he hangs up the phone.

Johnny goes back into the café and hears some activity in the kitchen and a door slam. Johnny goes into the kitchen where Meg has been attacked. She is sure that Silver would have killed her if Johnny had not come back in. She tells Johnny that Silver was hiding in the kitchen.

Johnny hears foots steps coming in and Captain Andy rushes in. Andy had seen Silver running from the restaurant and Johnny tells him that Silver had attacked Meg in the kitchen. Andy is ready to kill him and tells Johnny that Silver has gone back to the *Silver Queen*.

Meg sees the *Silver Queen* leaving port and Johnny gets Andy to follow him. As they go out to sea they follow the running lights of the *Silver Queen*. Slowly they pull up on the *Silver Queen* and Johnny checks his .38 to make sure it is loaded.

Johnny realizes that Silver can see them as well and goes to turn off their lights, but Silver has turned off his now. Johnny turns on the spotlight and notices Silver turning to run them down. Johnny shoots and Silver is hurt. Finally, the *Silver Queen* hits their boat.

"Well, I suppose I ought to make some crack about it being a long swim back to Cod Harbor, but I won't, because it wasn't. The *Silver Queen* sank like a rock, and with the help of the spotlight we finally managed to find and pick up the body of Marty Silver. Then, with both Andy and me bailing like mad, we slowly limped back to port. And that is about it."

Notes:
- There are two versions of this program. One is an AFTRS program with the commercials edited out. The other version is a network version that contains commercials for Winston cigarettes and Ex-Lax. For the middle commercial, Bob Bailey breaks out of character to remind the audience that "Here in America radio is free, its products are truth and entertainment. But truth is often missing behind the Iron Curtain where seventy-six million people are fed a lot of controlled opinion propaganda. We can keep faith with those captive people through Radio Free Europe. They ask for more, risk their lives to listen so the least we can risk is the truth dollar. Send it now, send all you can spare to the Crusade for Freedom care of your post office. Do it, will ya, right away."
- Johnny makes reference to his .38.
- The announcer is John Wald.

Producer:	Jack Johnstone	Writer:	Jack Johnstone
Cast:	Virginia Gregg, Olan Soule, Ralph Moody		

◆ ❖ ◆

Show:	**The Fatal Switch Matter**
Show Date:	5/1/1960
Company:	Western Life & Trust Insurance Company
Agent:	Art Bascomb
Exp. Acct:	$386.21

Synopsis: Johnny is called very early in the morning. The caller tells Johnny the he has checked the plane schedules, and if he leaves now he can just make the early 707 to the West Coast. Johnny asks who is on the phone, and it is Art Bascomb. Art tells Johnny that he has to catch the plane, as this is a case of murder.

Johnny flies to Los Angeles and Art meets Johnny at the airport. They get in Art's car and head for Balboa, California. Art tells Johnny that one of the yachts there, a 42-foot cruiser, the *Leslyn*, is owned by Freebairn Electronics, which is owned by Lester Freebairn.

Freebairn owns the sales and manufacturing rights to a radio control device. Freebairn's partner, Edgar Porter, invented the device and owns the patent. Porter took the boat out for a cruise yesterday. Freebairn called him and during the conversation someone killed him. The Coast Guard is trying to find the boat. Porter was out there alone with no other boats around, but someone apparently killed him. Freebairn had recorded the conversation over the radio and has the recording. Johnny is confused.

The Freebairn home is smaller than most in the area, and Lester Freebairn is in his mid-fifties with a much younger beautiful wife. Freebairn tells Art and Johnny that the Coast Guard still has not found the boat, and that Porter told him that he was alone.

Freebairn plays the tape of the conversation and tells Johnny that he made the tape recorder himself. On the tape, Baron talks to both Mr. and Mrs. Freebairn and tells them that he is alone. Baron notes that the weather is chilly and Freebairn tells him to turn on the cabin heater and be sure to open the vent, and then there is a shot. Johnny tells them that it is impossible, except that it happened.

Johnny tells Freebairn that there is nothing that can be done until the boat is found. Mrs. Freebairn, who wants to be called Maralyn, notes that Baron had already put on the heater. Mr. Freebairn tells Johnny that carbon dioxide could build up quickly, but Baron knew that.

Johnny is told that Baron was meticulous about the boat, so no one could have stowed away on the boat. Freebairn tells Johnny that the noise could have been an electrical short, but he doubts it. Johnny is told that Baron was ready to get millions from the invention.

The policy was a partnership policy worth $250,000 and all of the patent rights revert to Freebairn if Baron dies. Maralyn met Baron at a party and asked him to bring the invention to Freebairn. Johnny is told that Adam Patrick is the contact at the Coast Guard.

Johnny borrows Art's car to go visit his old friend, Adam Patrick, who helped him on the Ellen Dear case. Johnny has a handful of ideas and wants to go alone. He will only tell Art that if he can get to the boat before anyone else, he can prove that two plus two equals five.

Johnny meets with Pat and gets on a cutter with him to go out to the *Leslyn*, the Freebairn boat. Pat has told Freebairn that the boat had been found and gave him the coordinates. Pat knows that the Freebairn's are quite a team, especially with Maralyn's "assets". Pat tells Johnny that Freebairn is in debt after building his plant and could use the money from the insurance.

They reach the boat and Johnny goes on board with Pat and a doctor to find Baron dead, laying over the radio. The doctor tells Johnny that it appears to be carbon monoxide poisoning.

Freebairn arrives in his speedboat and comes on board. He tells them that it was carbon monoxide poisoning and opens the vent. Johnny tells him that the vent was open when he got on the boat, which puzzles Freebairn. Johnny tells them that the carbon monoxide came from some other source.

Johnny tells him how convenient it is to get the invention, and how Baron must have had an eye on Maralyn, but his being dead would be even better. Johnny reminds Freebairn that he had been a chemist and knows how a crystal that had been heated could produce carbon monoxide.

Johnny shows Pat how Barton had to bend over the transmitter to use the radio, and how Freebairn had mentioned earlier that Baron fell against the transmitter. Johnny tells him that he knew that Baron would be leaning over the radio.

Pat finds a small coil on the transmitter, and Johnny tells him that it was used to heat up a crystal that produced the carbon monoxide. Pat agrees that all Freebairn had to do was call Baron on the radio, and the coil would heat up. "Well, Mr. Freebairn?"

"Yep, Lester Freebairn had suddenly run out of answers. And I am willing to bet that the best lawyer in the country can't get him out of this one. Best of all, of course, he won't collect a penny of the insurance on the partner that he murdered."

Notes:
- Johnny notes that Adam Patrick helped him with *The Ellen Dear Matter*, but in the script, the Coast Guard contact is Capt. Barney Thorson.
- The announcer is John Wald.

Producer:	Jack Johnstone	Writer:	Jack Johnstone
Cast:	Virginia Gregg, Olan Soule, Sam Edwards, Will Wright, Hershel Bernardi		

◆ ❖ ◆

Show:	**The Phony Phone Matter**
Show Date:	**5/8/1960**
Company:	**International Life & Casualty Insurance Company**
Agent:	**Art Ingles**
Exp. Acct:	**$1.35**

Synopsis: Art Ingles calls Johnny and asks if he is ready for a case. Johnny asks if it is murder, fraud or arson, and Art tells him that he does not know. A very important client wants to see Johnny, and no one else. Johnny tells Art that the last time he took a case like this he was slugged, shot at and thrown off a bridge, but he will take the case.

Johnny does not like vague assignments but International has paid him well. Johnny meets Art and they drive across Hartford, Connecticut to Mr. J. Ransom Wendell's office. Johnny is told that Wendell owns Crown Lithograph and that the company is worth millions. Wendell carries half a million on himself and his wife, and Wendell is used to having his own way, and Johnny remembers that he is called "Alimony Wendell".

Johnny thought that he had read where Wendell was supposedly through with the gold-diggers. Art tells Johnny that nine months ago he married LaVon Laverne (yikes! remarks Johnny) and now she has a ring in his nose and is making a dent in his bank account.

In Wendell's huge and lavishly appointed office Johnny is fooled by Wendell's appearance. He is not a doddering old man but a sharp businessman. Wendell is concerned about his wife, but not her insurance, and tells Ingles to leave. Wendell tells Johnny that he has had seven wives and has made a fool of himself. He should not have paid them off. But LaVon is a good wife, but she is afraid of being murdered.

Wendell tells Johnny that she is afraid that someone is going to kill her. Wendell wants Johnny to find out if there are grounds for her fear. Johnny asks if he has called in a psychologist, but Wendell will have no part of that. Wendell wants Johnny to come to their lodge on the Pequabuck River, posing as an old friend. They are going to meet LaVon there for lunch. Wendell calls for his car and Johnny is still not sure what he is supposed to do.

Wendell tells Johnny that he has followed Johnny's career for years on the radio and knows that Johnny knows how to get close to people and inspire confidence. Johnny adds that he also would be handy to have as a bodyguard.

Wendell drives Johnny to his apartment where he packs his bags and gets his .38 caliber lemon squeezer. They drive to the lodge and Wendell tells Johnny that he knows of no one who would want to harm LaVon, but her past career included dancing in some questionable clubs owned by gangsters.

They arrive at the 10-room lodge, but LaVon's car is missing. They go in and Wendell pours drinks and phones his home. LaVon is there and Wendell tells her that he is worried. Wendell mentions that she has a visitor and then the line goes dead. Wendell tells Johnny that she gave a strange gasp and dropped the phone. Johnny picks up the phone and has the operator connect him with the Hartford police homicide division.

Johnny and Wendell drive back to Hartford, and the police are at the Wendell home, and Lt. Billy Walker is in charge. LaVon is on the floor with the phone beside her. The police medic had removed a gruesome knife from her back, and Wendell is very upset.

Walker tells Johnny that the knife went through her heart and came from a collection over the mantlepiece. Walker tells Johnny that the servants were off for the weekend and were too old to have killed her. Also, the back door was ajar. Wendell regrets letting the servants off for the weekend. Johnny is told to find the killer.

Johnny tells Wendell to call his attorney, who is Harold Spidel, and Wendell tells Johnny that he will call soon after he is composed. Walker is on the phone and is told that the only prints on the phone were from LaVon, which is strange unless someone wanted it to appear that way. Johnny agrees and leaves.

Johnny borrows Wendell's car and drives to the office of Lawyer Spidel on a hunch, and Spidel will never know how much he did help. Spidel tells Johnny that it is too bad, but it does save Wendell the expense of another divorce. He was certain that the marriage was due to fail.

None of his wives was as expensive as LaVon was. Johnny is told that he is the perfect alibi for Wendell, as he heard him on the phone with LaVon.

Johnny calls Betty Lewis and she agrees to go along with a little stunt that might solve the case. Johnny goes back to Wendell's home where Wendell has calmed down and tells Johnny that what has happened, has happened. Johnny tells Wendell not to call his lawyer, as Johnny is expecting a call and that he has heard that Wendell was a pretty ruthless businessman.

The phone rings, Johnny answers the phone and Betty agrees to hang up. Johnny tells the phone that he will give it $500 if the information is accurate. He ups it to a $1,000 if the caller will come to the house and agree to appear in court. Johnny is "told" that the caller saw him through the side window. He saw him take the knife and open the back door.

Wendell tells Johnny to hang up and that the informer will get what Johnny will get, a bullet in the head. Johnny tells Wendell that his name is not Matt Dillon but if he thinks he can out draw him, then Johnny draws his gun and shoots Wendell. Wow!

"Well I hope that Wendell never finds out that my phone conversation with a mythical informer was just as phony has his, his talk with his wife after he had killed her and left her there at the telephone in his home and set me up as his alibi at the lodge. But what is the difference where he is going. Expense account total, $1.35? Let's talk about the fee on this one!"

Notes:
- This program contains commercials for Camel cigarettes, the CBS News broadcasts and the need for cancer checkups, and Ex-Lax.
- This program title was used twice, once on 5/8/1960, and again on 12/24/1961, but the story lines are different.
- The announcer is John Wald.

Producer:	Jack Johnstone Writer: Jack Johnstone
Cast:	Virginia Gregg, Harry Bartell, Marvin Miller, Richard Crenna, Lou Merrill

◆ ❖ ◆

Show:	**The Mystery Gal Matter**
Show Date:	**5/15/1960**
Company:	**Continental Insurance & Trust Company**
Agent:	**Fred Melchior**
Exp. Acct:	**$0.00**

Synopsis: A girl calls and asks Johnny why he doesn't get married to her. Johnny agrees to marry Janet, I meant Carol. The caller is Betty Lewis, and Johnny tells her that he knew it all along. Betty tells Johnny that if it were not for his business, she would trick him into a trip to the altar. "Yes Dear" Johnny answers and hems and haws about her badgering him about marriage. Betty tells Johnny that if he ever gets an honest job, she will marry him. She has called Johnny about insurance and must see him. She is not at home and tells Johnny to stay home until she calls him. She cannot talk and tells Johnny to wait for her call. Hmm, there is something very funny about this.

Johnny feels that there is something strange, as he had the same conversation with Betty a few days earlier. But why stall Johnny when he has another case.

Johnny waits an hour and then calls Betty's house and then her office where she has been all morning. Johnny asks Betty why she did not call him back, but she tells Johnny that she had not called him. Betty accuses Johnny of having so many girls on the line and getting them confused. Betty tells Johnny that she did not call. Johnny hangs up and wishes he knew what is going on.

Johnny cabs to Fred Melchior's Hartford, Connecticut office and Fritz tells Johnny that he did not expect him so soon. Fritz tells Johnny that Johnny had called him back and asked if it was OK to be late, and Johnny tells him that something screwy is going on. Fritz tells Johnny that he had called and he agreed to come over. After a while Johnny had called and told him that he should not waste time coming to the office. Johnny tells Fritz that he did not call.

Fritz is certain that Johnny had called and asked for all the details on the case. Fritz had told him everything about the case, but this means that Johnny has not been to see the client on East Maple Drive. Fritz grabs Johnny and they drive out there. Fritz tells Johnny that time is of the essence. Fritz tells Johnny that he had been called earlier by John Sawyer.

Johnny tells Fritz that Sawyer lives across the street from a friend. Sawyer had been in the district attorney's office in New York and had sent up "Andy the Actor" Rinaldi. Johnny recalls how he had a record and the skill to impersonate people.

Fritz tells Johnny that Andy has been paroled and is on the loose. Mr. Sawyer was awaked by someone prowling around and feels that it was Andy. Sawyer wants Johnny on the case. Johnny wonders how Andy could impersonate both himself and Betty Lewis. Johnny takes the wheel and they arrive at the Sawyer home. The door is open and there are shots and Fritz sees a body in the doorway.

Johnny discovers that the body was not Sawyer's. Sawyer comes out and gives Johnny a still-smoking .38. Sawyer had shot Andy, who is still alive. Johnny thanks Sawyer for saving his life. Johnny follows the ambulance but Rinaldi does not come too.

Johnny goes to his apartment where a man from the phone company is waiting for him. He tells Johnny that there had been a tap on his line, but Johnny would never have noticed it, but they did. Johnny knows who did it and goes in to test the phone with the repairman on the line.

Johnny dials Betty and tells the lineman to get off the phone. Betty tells Johnny to come over, but Johnny asks Betty what part of the movie they came in on several nights ago. She tells Johnny that it was right when Jimmy Stuart walked up to the judge. Betty tells Johnny to come out, as she has a big surprise for him, a really important one. She is really an important one.

Johnny rushes over and Betty takes him inside. She tells Johnny that she had come home early and saw Johnny and another man drive up, but she was too busy to call out. She went to the back door but it was open. In her living room, hiding behind a curtain was a girl with a gun. She aimed at Johnny and the other man. Betty ruined one of her nicest vases by hitting the woman with it and then tied her up. The girl came too and tried to talk, which is why she put the gag in her mouth. Johnny grabs Betty and kisses her. "Oh, honey, why don't we just get married" moans Betty as Johnny kisses her.

"Eh, what a gal. And maybe someday, um yeah, expense account total including... that's funny. Something or someone seems to have diverted my attention for the moment from anything as trivial as an expense account. Trivial?"

Notes:
- This program contains commercials for Pepsi, Camel Cigarettes, and Kellogg's All-Bran.
- The announcer is John Wald.

| Producer: | Jack Johnstone | Writer: | Jack Johnstone |

Cast: Virginia Gregg, Jerry Hausner, Parley Baer, Peter Leeds

♦ ❖ ♦

Show: **The Man Who Waits Matter**
Show Date: **5/22/1960**
Company: **Eastern Liability & Trust Company**
Agent: **Ted Bessem**
Exp. Acct: **$0.00**

Synopsis: Ted Bessem calls and Johnny is told that it might be a good time to take another crack at the diamonds. Ted has some new information on Rocky Harrison. Rocky disappeared after his probation, and Rocky is the only one who knows what he did with the diamonds. Johnny is on his way to see Ted.

Johnny, and Johnny alone could take credit for Rocky's trip to Sing-Sing seven years ago. But Johnny had not been able to recover the Olney diamonds. The fact he was new in the business was no excuse.

Johnny trains to New York City and Ted Bessem's office. Ted tells Johnny that Rocky had admitted everything to get a lighter sentence and told the jury that the diamonds had been stolen from him. They also believed that the servant accidentally fell down the stairs and was killed, which kept Rocky from being tried for murder.

Rocky behaved after probation and got a job and saved his money, which disappointed the police. Now that his probation is over, he has disappeared. Ted is sure that Rocky is here in New York, the easiest place in the world to get lost.

Ted talked to a paid informant named Soder, Whiskey Soder, and he told Ted that Rocky is in town. Johnny gets the address for Soder. Ted tells Johnny that Rocky has changed his appearance, but Soder had recognized him. Johnny is told to be careful. Here is a chance to make up for seven years ago.

Johnny cabs to the address and asks the manager for Soder. Johnny is told that he is the second man to ask to see Soder that day. Johnny goes to the room and knocks. Johnny breaks down the door to find Soder dead on the floor.

The manager tells Johnny that she did not hear anything, and Johnny tells her that the man used a pillow to muffle the shot. The manager tells Johnny only that the other visitor had gray hair. Johnny gives her $5 and tells her to call Sgt. Randy Singer and tell him that Johnny was there. The manager recognizes Johnny's name from the radio.

Johnny mentions how Rocky had changed his appearance once before, but Johnny used an old trick to catch him. Maybe it would work again.

Johnny stops at a drug store for some "goop" to plaster down his hair, some black hair dye, some peroxide to get rid of his suntan, which would take time. After several days Johnny has grown a mustache which he has dyed black as well. Johnny buys some new clothing including an apron, and a pair of thick glasses, which he can see through, but which give him a headache.

Johnny acts the part of a slow-witted waiter at bar and waits for several days for someone to show up. One night a man named Barney calls another one Rocky and is told his name is Tillson, Edward Tillson. Johnny is sure that he is on the right track. The man Tillson had been there for three nights, and Johnny had not recognized him. Rocky has a beard, gray hair, has put on twenty pounds and has had his teeth fixed. The partner must be Bernard Little, a fence known to the police.

Johnny stays near them but they clam up when he comes near. Tillson and Barney leave to go to see the owner. Pete Monister had been away when Johnny was hired, and probably knew all about Rocky. Johnny goes to change clothes and leaves when Pete comes in and tells Johnny that he is fired, as he is not needed. Johnny leaves and is met in the alley by Tillson, who hits Johnny while Barney tells him not to shoot. Tillson tells Barney he is just going to use the butt of his gun.

Johnny vaguely remembers something hitting him, and then noise and gunshots and sirens. Johnny wakes up in a hospital with a doctor holding a hypo. Sometime later Johnny wakes up and Randy Singer is there.

Randy tells Johnny that he will be OK. Randy did not know that it was Johnny who was being jumped. He had been following Rocky ever since Whisky Soder had told Randy where Rocky was. Randy tells Johnny that he had told Randy where to find Rocky seven years ago, at the Purple Hat bar. "Are you the only one who thought he could lead us to the jewels?" asks Randy.

Randy does not have the jewels, thanks to Johnny. Both Rocky and Barney are dead. They have searched Rocky's house and found nothing. Johnny has a hunch that he can fake his way into finding the jewels.

Johnny goes back to the Purple Hat and barges into Pete Monister's office. Pete recognizes Johnny as the waiter he fired. Johnny tells him that his desk is bugged, and Johnny tells him not to reach for a gun or he will shoot.

Johnny tells Pete that he heard Pete tell when to send Johnny out into the alley, but Pete plays ignorant as to the reason. Johnny tells Pete that he knows where the jewels are and tells Pete to open the safe. Pete wants to make a deal but Johnny tells him he wants the jewels or he will kill Pete. Pete agrees to open the safe.

"The fee on this one, for recovery of the diamonds, well maybe the department frowns on such things, but half of it goes to Randy Singer, NYPD. Good man. Good friend. Expense account total, including the ride back to Hartford, well it just about balances with what I made on my job as waiter."

Notes:
- This program contains a single commercial for Camel cigarettes.
- There is a reference here to Johnny having been in the business only seven years. But in *The Bennet Matter* of 1956, Johnny states that he had been an investigator for 14 years.
- The Olney Diamonds were also mentioned in *The Night in Paris Matter*.
- Cast Information from the KNX Collection at the Thousand Oaks Library.

Producer: Jack Johnstone   Writer: Jack Johnstone

| Cast: | Marvin Miller, Virginia Gregg, Forrest Lewis, Barney Phillips, Frank Gerstle, Herb Vigran, Peter Leeds |

♦ ❖ ♦

Show:	**The Redrock Matter**
Show Date:	**5/29/1960**
Company:	**Greater Southwest Insurance Company**
Agent:	**Jake Kessler**
Exp. Acct:	**$496.25**

Synopsis: The opening for this program is missing.

Johnny sends a telegram to Jake Kessler with his arrangements and then flies to Las Vegas. Jake drives Johnny to Kingman, Arizona and tells him that back in '52, Ralph Garrett and Jerry Bisbee were prospecting in these parts. Ralph was OK, but the town had hoped for years that Jerry Bisbee would go somewhere else.

They had gone over to Chloride to prospect near Mt. Tipson. A month or so later Jerry came back alone. He said that Ralph had left him to get a job in California. Ralph's wife claimed it was a big lie, and that Bisbee had killed Ralph in the desert.

She claims that Ralph had gotten suspicious of Bisbee and did not trust him, and he would not have just left her like that. The police were called in, but no one could find a body. Mrs. Garrett had Bisbee tried, but he got off.

Just last year the claim on Ralph's insurance was paid off. Bisbee moved and has not come back. Last week there was a windstorm that uncovered a body in the desert. The papers did not report that the skeleton had a bullet hole in the back of its head. A hole of the same size as the Winchester '94 Bisbee used to carry.

Jake tells Johnny that only Doc Blessing can identify the body, and he is waiting in Kingman. When Johnny and Jake get to his office, there is a note from Doc Blessing telling them to wait for him. Blessing had taken over his father's practice along with all the patient records.

Doc Blessing comes in and tells them that he has evidence that his father had repaired a broken femur on Ralph's leg with a steel plate back in 1942. On the skeleton is the same stainless-steel plate. The skeleton is Ralph Garrett's. Jake tells Johnny to find Bisbee and bring him back to justice, that's all!

Jake tells Johnny that Bisbee left right after the trial and has not been seen again. The Kingman police have notified the state police and bulletins are out. Bisbee was a prospector and worked in some of the mines to feed his drinking.

Johnny has an idea and makes a phone call to the Bureau of Mines in Washington. He gets a list of recent claims for Jerry Bisbee, and the last few have been in Nevada. Johnny is told that the Carson City office would have more information.

Johnny calls Carson City, and a lady there will not give out any information without the permission of Mr. Harker. Johnny rents an old and under-powered plane to fly to Carson City. Johnny goes into town to see Mr. Harker who is reluctant to give out information until Johnny mentions murder. Johnny rents a car and drives to Virginia City, Nevada.

Johnny describes Virginia City as a fabulous monument to the Comstock Lode. Johnny describes the buildings that still stand and the historical names of the times.

Johnny talks to a grizzled old man who tells Johnny that he should stay away from Bisbee, as he is crazy. He is up on Redrock Pass, but Johnny's car will not make it, he will have to rent a horse. But if Bisbee finds him up there, he will shoot.

Johnny rents a horse and heads out for the pass. Johnny finds the shack and no one is there. Johnny follows a trail to a mine and is shot at. A voice tells Johnny to get out. Bisbee tells Johnny that he knows why Johnny is there, but Johnny will not take him in.

Bisbee tells Johnny that they tried him once and cannot try him twice for the same crime. Johnny waits and then hears a rattlesnake at his feet and shoots it, but there is a nest of them. Johnny runs to another rock and Bisbee tells him that he can get Johnny at any time. As Bisbee approaches he tells Johnny to give up and throw out his gun. Johnny throws out his gun and Bisbee tells him he is going to shoot him. Bisbee runs behind the same rocks Johnny was behind and his bitten by the rattlesnakes.

"By the time I got over to him and hauled him out of that pit of death, half a dozen of the deadly rattlers must have struck him. He died before I could get him back to Virginia City. Yeah, justice again in one of her own inscrutable ways."

Notes:
- The script title page for this program calls it "Redrock", not "Red Rock".
- This program contains commercials for Pepsi, Camel Cigarettes, and Dennis James for Kellogg's All-Bran cereal.
- Tom Hanley and Bill James are the CBS sound men and are noted in the cast for "ad libs".
- The announcer is John Wald.

Producer:	Jack Johnstone	Writer:	Jack Johnstone
Cast:	Virginia Gregg, Parley Baer, Harry Bartell, Vic Perrin, John Dehner, Will Wright, Tom Hanley, Bill James		

♦ ❖ ♦

Show: The Canned Canary Matter
Show Date: 6/5/1960
Company: Providential Property Insurance Company
Agent: Jack Price
Exp. Acct: $1,121.00

Synopsis: Jack Price calls Johnny and he tells him that he is now working for Providential Property Insurance there in Corpus Christi. He has a claim for $465,000 that Johnny can help them with. Jack offers Johnny a big commission and expenses. Johnny agrees to grab the first flight he can.

Johnny flies to Corpus Christi, Texas and Jack meets Johnny at the airport and starts to take him to the Robert Driscoll Hotel. Jack tells Johnny that the case is the Canary Diamonds, the most perfectly matched set of yellow diamonds in the world. The diamonds are set in a necklace, a brooch and a solitaire on a ring. They were stolen from Mrs. Clara Barnes Smithwick Tyson Brownfield.

Jack tells Johnny that Mr. Tyson made his money in oil and died a few years ago, leaving his wife a considerable fortune in the stock market. A year ago, she married young Augustus Brownfield. He is about forty-five, ten years younger than his wife. Jack is sure that August Brownfield is on the level. He has a small cannery business that handles items for the fancy restaurants.

Jack tells Johnny that the diamonds disappeared a few weeks ago. Mrs. Brownfield had gone out that night and was placing a set of earrings back in the safe when she noticed that the diamonds were gone. But other items were left in the safe. The police found nothing, only that it was a professional job. Only the Brownfields knew the combination. Johnny wants to go visit the Brownfields that evening.

Jack and Johnny arrive at the mansion and Mrs. Brownfield is described as a real lady, and Gus a devoted husband. Mrs. Brownfield cannot imagine anyone taking the stones out to be sold. They tell Johnny that they had gone to a party that evening. On the way they passed the packing plant and Gus noticed the lights were on.

The party was boring so Gus had gone to the factory for a few minutes to turn off the lights and do a few odds and ends and then went back to the party. Johnny mentions that Mrs. Brownfield had mentioned the stones being broken up, and she refuses to talk to Johnny.

Gus tells Johnny that his business is not profitable and Johnny is told to leave. Johnny tells them that the notion of the stones being broken up has given him an idea.

Johnny leaves to play a hunch. The reaction of Gus Brownfield only seems to clear him in Johnny's mind. Johnny also agree that the job was done by a pro.

Later that night Doug Johnstone visits Johnny in his room. Doug had run into Jack Price and learned that Johnny was there, and he just had to stop in and give Johnny a hand. If he didn't, his brother Jack would not forgive him. Johnny tells Doug that he would like to drag Jack into the cases so he could help him solve them.

Doug tells Johnny that he has figured out the case, and the thief is in the local jail. Doug tells Johnny that Brownie is an old friend and he knows about Gus' cannery and the people who work there, especially one man in the shipping department. Doug had done some digging and found a story about a jewel heist that has a picture the man from the shipping dock. The heist happened fifteen years ago. The man is Les Murdock.

Johnny recognizes him as "Fingers" Murdock who went to jail in 1945 for twenty years. Doug tells Johnny that Murdock was paroled two years ago for good behavior. The police arrested him and he finally confessed. Doug has solved the case, but the police do not have the jewels, so Johnny's work is not done as he has to get the diamonds back.

Johnny visits the jail, but Murdock will not tell him anything. He would rather spend time, get out and then spend the money from the jewels. Johnny remembers Murdock's international connections.

Johnny calls Brownfield and learns that a shipment had been made recently to the Imperial Import Company in Paris, and it should arrive today. Johnny calls Louis De Marsac in Paris and Johnny asks him what he knows about canaries. Louis tell Johnny that they are for the birds. Louis has never heard of the Canary Diamonds. But for $500 he will find out about them.

Louis tells Johnny that the smuggler and fence Duboisson has closed his antiques shop and opened a new produce company, the Imperial Import Company. Johnny agrees to wire Louis $100 if he can tell Johnny where Duboisson is.

Johnny flies to Paris, France and goes to the Imperial Import Company warehouse with a 39-cent kitchen object to help solve the case. Johnny meets a surprised Duboisson and asks him to help find some stolen jewels. Johnny wants to look for the latest import of canned goods from the states.

Over Duboisson's objections Johnny goes into the warehouse and finds ten cases of fruit from Corpus Christi. Johnny tosses Duboisson a can opener and tells him to open the cans until they find the diamonds. Johnny tells Duboisson that his .38 is all the authority he needs, unless Duboisson wants Johnny to call the police. Reluctantly Duboisson shows Johnny which case has the dented can with the diamonds in it.

"Thanks to its Paris representative, the company was able to arrange for getting the stones back to the U.S. As for Duboisson, well I suspect he was long gone when the police arrived at his place. Expense account total, including the trip home, $1,121.00 and uh, don't forget about my commission on this one."

Notes:
- The Canary diamonds were mentioned twice, once in *The Double Deal Matter*, and here in *The Canned Canary Matter*.
- This program contains commercials for Pepsi, Camel Cigarettes, and Dennis James for Kellogg's All-Bran cereal.
- The announcer is John Wald.

Producer: Jack Johnstone   Writer: Jack Johnstone
Cast: Virginia Gregg, Jack Edwards, Russell Thorson, Stacy Harris, Jack Kruschen, Forrest Lewis, Tony Barrett

Show:	The Harried Heiress Matter
Show Date:	6/12/1960
Company:	International Casualty & Life Insurance Company
Agent:	Bert Larkin
Exp. Acct:	$7,604.25

Synopsis: Bert Larkin calls Johnny and he has a $300,000 problem which must be distributed shortly. Johnny tells him just to send the money to him and asks Bert if he is expecting a policyholder to kick the bucket. Bert tells Johnny that William Makepiece Everly lives in the Piney Woods part of Hartford, Connecticut. His doctor has told Bert that Everly does not have long to live, and Everly wants to see Johnny. Johnny thinks that there is something funny going on here, and Bert agrees.

Johnny buys gas and drives to the Everly estate. Dr. Thatcher meets Johnny at the door and Johnny is taken to Mr. Everly's room. On the way in, the doctor tells Johnny that he has contacted Everly's nephew but has been unable to find his niece. That is why Everly wants to talk to Johnny.

Johnny meets Everly and he tells Johnny that Doc Thatcher does not know what he is talking about, and that he will probably outlive both of them. He has willed everything to his niece. She has been kind and loving and has stood on her own feet. But, Everly does not know where Nancy is, and he wants Johnny to bring her there while he is still alive.

Everly tells Johnny that he wants nothing to go to his stepson Alfred Harker, a worthless no-good idle sponge who has even forged checks to get his money. If he finds out that Nancy gets everything there is nothing he would not do.

Everly gets upset and tells Johnny that Nancy does not know about Alfred, and Johnny must protect her from him at all cost. Everly is given a shot and goes to sleep. Dr. Thatcher tells Johnny that he had told Alfred that Nancy is the sole heir. But where to look?

Dr. Thatcher tells Johnny that Alfred had kept track of where Nancy is living. Johnny is sure that Nancy is a sitting duck for Alfred.

Johnny gets Alfred's address and heads for his apartment. The building super tells Johnny that Harker had packed and left on a trip the previous day. Johnny gives the super a five-spot to get into the apartment and it is obvious that Harker left in a hurry. Johnny finds a schedule for flights to Los Angeles and Nancy's address in Philadelphia.

Johnny flies to Philadelphia, Pennsylvania and goes to Nancy's apartment, but she is not there, but Maryanne Hooper is. Maryanne knows Nancy from the office, and she tells Johnny that Nancy has been transferred to the Los Angeles office of Hardon, Karmon and Fisher, the ad agency. Maryanne invites Johnny in for a drink, but Johnny runs to the airport to get a flight to Los Angeles, California.

Johnny goes to the Hardon, Karmon and Fisher office in Los Angeles, and Nancy is not there and will not come in that day. Johnny gets her address at 1308 Pandora Ave. in West Los Angeles and grabs a cab there. So, Nancy is in Los Angeles and so is Alfred, so there is no time to waste.

At Nancy's address the landlord tells Johnny that she lives there but left a few hours ago on a trip with a nice young man. They were headed for Las Vegas, probably to get married. Ouch!

Johnny calls the Las Vegas marriage bureau. He asks if Alfred and Nancy have been there and tells the clerk to keep them from being married. The clerk tells Johnny that he needs some legal grounds to not issue a license.

Johnny cabs to the Lockheed Air Terminal and charters a plane to Las Vegas, Nevada. Johnny cabs to the license bureau but learns that Nancy and Alfred have gone. The clerk tells Johnny that they left on foot, so they must have gone somewhere close to get married.

Johnny gets a list of nearby wedding chapels and people where the wedding could take place and starts to check them out. Johnny finally finds a wedding in progress for Alfred Harker.

Johnny interrupts the ceremony and tells Nancy that Alfred is marrying her for her money. Nancy tells Johnny that she has no money, but Johnny tells her that she will have plenty of money when her uncle dies. "Ask Alfred, as he knows all about it" Johnny tells her.

Johnny tells them that Uncle William is leaving Alfred nothing, so the quickest way to get the estate is to marry Nancy. Alfred tells Nancy he can explain everything and Nancy asks why Uncle William would write to Alfred and beg him to marry Nancy? Johnny asks to see the letter, but Alfred has thrown it away.

Johnny tells Nancy that the letter was forged, just like the checks Alfred had forged over the years and Alfred admits it. Alfred pulls a gun and tells them that nothing will stop this wedding. Johnny calls him foolish and Alfred pulls Nancy to him. Nancy struggles to get away from Alfred and he shoots at Johnny, but Alfred is slugged by Johnny.

"Pulling his gun was a big mistake. Yeah, the people there in Vegas, the police, just don't go for that sort of thing. As for any charges the company may care to make against him, well that's up to the legal department. The main thing is to keep him away from her permanently. Incidentally, I managed to get her home to see her uncle before he died.

Notes:
- This program contains commercials for Pepsi, Frito corn chips, and Dennis James for Kellogg's All-Bran cereal.
- Bob Bailey welcomes station KFBK in Sacramento, California.
- I find it interesting that Hardon, Karmon and Fisher is a wonderful play on Harmon-Kardon, which owns Fisher Electronics. These were very high-end consumer stereo components during the 1960's.
- Mary Ann Hooper is the name of the script secretary in 1958.
- The address "1308 Pandora Avenue" was used in three Johnny Dollar programs, *The Harried Heiress Matter, The Shadow of a Doubt Matter* and *The Urned Income Matter.* I have been told that the address was Jack Johnstone's home.
- The announcer is John Wald.

Producer:	Jack Johnstone Writer: Jack Johnstone
Cast:	Virginia Gregg, Jeanne Tatum, Lillian Buyeff, Marvin Miller, Russell Thorson, Bartlett Robinson, Forrest Lewis, Sam Edwards, Harry Bartell

◆ ❖ ◆

Show:	The Flask of Death Matter
Show Date:	6/19/1960
Company:	Western Indemnity Company
Agent:	Paul Peters
Exp. Acct:	$431.00

Synopsis: Paul Peters calls Johnny from Los Angeles and asks Johnny to come out and help the race to outer space. Johnny demurs on a ride in a space capsule, but Paul tells him that they have no proof that the deaths were not accidental, but if Johnny can prove otherwise...Paul tells Johnny that he is convinced that sabotage is involved.

Johnny flies to Los Angeles and cabs to Paul's office on the "miracle mile". Paul has rented a car for Johnny to drive up to Santa Barbara, California and the Bar-Bar Manufacturing Company, named after Dr. Joseph L. Barrum and Dr. Ralph T. Barnwell.

They are top grade scientists who are working on a capsule that will allow a man to return from outer space. They will make millions if the capsule works. So far two men have died during the testing of the device, but no one knows why they died. The doctors do not want Johnny poking around, but the insurance company insisted, so Johnny is expected.

Johnny drives to the plant and meets Dr. Barnwell who is pulling something from the ocean. He tells Johnny that the test must work this time. The last time the tests were successful, but the man inside died. This time Dr. Barrum is manning the capsule. Barnwell opens the capsule and discovers that Dr. Barrum is dead.

Barnwell tells Johnny that there was nothing in the capsule to kill him. An autopsy will be held, but he knows that the result will be death by suffocation. Johnny asks about the possibility of poisonous gas, but Barnwell tells him that any known poison would have been spotted. He tells Johnny that nothing would go into the capsule without them knowing.

Barnwell tells Johnny that oxygen is provided in the capsule, and that the tanks have been taken out. Johnny tells him that not knowing how the capsule works will be to his advantage. Johnny tells Barnwell that he has a hunch. "Do you believe in hunches, doctor?"

Johnny's hunch is a long-shot. Johnny gets a pass that allows him full access to the plant. Johnny looks at the rooms where the oxygen bottles are kept and talks with Pete Prosser. Pete tells Johnny that he opened the release valves on the capsule to equalize the pressure. Pete tells Johnny that the oxygen bottles come from his storeroom. He does not know who fills up the bottles. They are always full when they are needed.

The bottles used today were checked, and they were OK. Pete has the bottles ready to empty into the air and opens the main valves on the bottles. Johnny asks Pete to close the valves and offers to empty the bottles for Pete so he can go home.

Johnny goes to another lab and gets a couple of white mice and takes them back to the oxygen bottles where Johnny empties the tanks into a cage holding the mice. After a minute the mice keel over and die.

Johnny now knows how the others were killed and remembers the phrase "cui bono", who benefits. Johnny goes to Dr. Barnwell's office with an oxygen bottle and sets it on his desk. Johnny tells him that the bottle has a leaky valve.

Barnwell tells him that too much oxygen is dangerous in the room, but Johnny promises to be careful. Johnny asks if Barnwell got out of the government because the government found something on him. Johnny tells Barnwell that he opened the capsule today to dissipate the poison gas from the tank. Johnny tells Barnwell that now that the capsule works, it is worth millions that will all go to him.

Barnwell gets very nervous about the oxygen bottle and wants out of the room. He tells Johnny that the bottle has hydropenoxygen gas in it. Johnny tells Barnwell that if he moves he will shoot him, and Barnwell tells Johnny that he killed all of the others to get the money from the capsule and stars choking. Johnny tells him to relax, that all the tank has is pure oxygen, I hope!

"I don't know, of course, but I suspect that the government will take over. Maybe they will have something in that space rescue capsule. But as for money, royalties, I am sure that Barnwell won't be able to spend much of it in prison."

Notes:
- Hydropenoxygen gas is another Jack Johnstone invention.
- Tom Hanley and Bill James are mentioned again for their sound work.
- The announcer is John Wald.

Producer:	Jack Johnstone Writer: Jack Johnstone
Cast:	Paul Dubov, Parley Baer, G. Stanley Jones, Forrest Lewis, Tom Hanley, Bill James

♦ ❖ ♦

Show:	**The Wholly Unexpected Matter**
Show Date:	**6/26/1960**
Company:	**Universal Adjustment Bureau**
Agent:	**Pat McCracken**
Exp. Acct:	**$0.00**

Synopsis: Pat McCracken calls, but Johnny tells him that the answer is NO. His bags and fishing tackle are all packed. He has tickets and the answer is no. There is nothing that cannot wait a week or two until he gets back. Pat offers to drive Johnny to the airport, but the answer is no. "And, so help me, if he tries chasing me out to the airport..."

Johnny cabs to the airport in a cab that gets a flat tire and almost makes him miss his plane. Johnny gets on his shuttle plane to New York and the stewardess knows all about Johnny from his radio program. Johnny tells Claire that he is going to Lake Mohave to do some fishing.

Once airborne, Johnny moves to his assigned seat, right beside Pat McCracken. Johnny tells Pat that in New York, they will part company. "You want to bet on that?" asks Pat.

Johnny switches flights in New York, but Pat gets on at the last minute. Pat tells Johnny that he had checked with the airline to get the flight. Pat is betting that Johnny is going to the Lake Mohave Resort, and has brought his fishing tackle also. They can go fishing together, provided that there is no talk of business. Pat notices a man who looks familiar, and he was on the flight from Hartford also. "Are you sure you do not know him?" Johnny asks Pat.

Pat and Johnny get to Las Vegas with the same man on the flight. Pat and Johnny get a hotel room and visit the casinos, and Johnny manages to collect $365 at the dice table. Pat meets up with Johnny and tells Johnny that he has seen the man watching Johnny at the dice tables, but Johnny discounts it, lots of people from Hartford come to Las Vegas.

Johnny and Pat drive to Lake Mohave Resort across the colorful desert. Johnny and Pat get rooms and a promise of their limit every day. Buster Favor tells Johnny that a Mr. Malloy is there from Hartford also.

Pat gets a phone call and his secretary calls about the Morley Warehouse fire. She tells Pat that Johnny had told the police how to catch "Scar Face" Maloney. Well, Maloney has escaped and is after Johnny. Pat tells Johnny that he is now on the expense account. "Malloy, Maloney, hmm." wonders Johnny.

Buster tells them that Mr. Malloy does have a scar and had asked when Johnny was going to be arriving. Buster tells Johnny that Malloy has gone out fishing. Johnny and Pat go fishing as well.

Johnny gets a boat and searches the lake for Maloney. Johnny finally decides to do some fishing in a deep cove. Pat notices a man on the rocks over the cove and Pat sees blue steel aimed right at Johnny.

Johnny rocks the boat to the ledge and tells Pat to act like Johnny is still there. Johnny climbs the rocks up towards the man on the rocks with his gun drawn. Johnny finally spots the man with…an old pair of binoculars. Johnny trips and the man spots him.

He tells Johnny that he is Franklin J. Malloy, and he did not realize that Johnny was that jealous of his fishing secrets. Malloy tells Johnny to put his gun down and tells him he is a real fan of Johnny's.

A lady friend who works for the airline had told him that Johnny was going to Lake Mohave, so he came out to spy on Johnny hoping that he could learn to catch some of the nice big fish out here the way Johnny does.

Buster arrives and tells Johnny that the Hartford police have picked up Scar Face Maloney and he is back in the pen.

Johnny tells Buster to take Pat out where he can catch an old bluegill or a carp. "Mr. Malloy and I are going out for some real lunkers, a couple of secret spots I know. Okay, Mr. Malloy?" "Bless you, Mr. Dollar" replies a very happy

Malloy.

"Well, you sure can't win 'em all especially when there isn't anything to win. And at long last, I got in a full week of fishing at Lake Mohave. Expense account total? Well Pat, you add it up, you're paying for it!"

Notes:
- This is an AFRTS program that contains a story about Thomas Edison and the phonograph, a story about the seventh amendment and the right to a jury trial, and a story about the orbital aspects of the moon and Simon Newcomb's correction of lunar orbital data allowing a flight to the moon.
- The announcer is John Wald.

Producer:	Jack Johnstone	Writer:	Jack Johnstone
Cast:	Virginia Gregg, Shirley Mitchell, Lawrence Dobkin, Sam Edwards, Barney Phillips, Edgar Barrier		

• ❖ •

Show:	**The Collector's Matter**
Show Date:	7/3/1960
Company:	Floyds of England
Agent:	George Reed
Exp. Acct:	$371.20

Synopsis: George Reed calls and tells Johnny that he is in an embarrassing situation. A very important client of the company is Orson Ogleby Terwilliger. He is a collector and lives near Bethel, New York. Go on down and see him. He wants a change made to his policy for $500,000 double indemnity.

George tells Johnny that he is calling from the city jail. He was rushing and was speeding a little and argued with the officer, and his hearing is not until tomorrow. George offers to double the expenses and give Johnny $100 besides. All Johnny has to do is find out what the change is to the policy. Johnny tells George that every time George gives Johnny a simple assignment, he is lucky to get out alive.

Johnny flies to New York where he rents a car and drives to Bethel, New York at the foot of the Catskills. The town is very small, and Johnny is told how to get to Terwilliger's home by a local man who is interested in buying the property. He tells Johnny that maybe Mr. Terwilliger will show Johnny his gun collection.

Johnny drives up to the estate on a rough road. On the way, Johnny spots a wrecked car lying against a boulder by the road. Johnny finds a body, and the driver's license belongs to Mr. Orson Terwilliger.

Another car approaches from the house and a woman rushes to the car and collapses and cries in Johnny's arms. She is Blanche Terwilliger and she knows who Johnny is. She is glad that Johnny found him, because of all the awful things the people say. They drive to the house and call the doctor and the police.

Chief Allen and the doctor arrive and go to the accident site. They tell

Johnny that it was an unfortunate accident, and that the bruises on the body are all from the crash. Johnny tells them that one of the bruises, a round one behind the ear, was not made by something in the car. Johnny is told not to let his imagination run away with him.

They take the body to the house and the chief asks Johnny if Mrs. Terwilliger is a beautiful woman. Too bad she and Mr. Terwilliger never... Blanche calls to make arrangements for the funeral and to have the car removed.

Blanch asks Johnny to stay and help to fill out the insurance papers. Johnny wants to get a hotel room, but Blanche tells him to stay and have dinner. Johnny goes to get a room at Emmer's Hotel and calls George, who tells Johnny that Blanche is the only beneficiary. Johnny feels that Terwilliger wanted to change the beneficiary, but the beautiful Blanche played it smart.

Johnny notes that the only thing he has to go on are some rumors about the Terwilligers and the mark behind his ear. Johnny buys a flashlight and goes to search the accident scene. Johnny finds something with ordinary fletching and a big stone head.

Blanche walks up with a gun and threatens to shoot until she recognizes Johnny. Johnny takes the gun and tells her that there must have been some Indians in the area.

After dinner Blanche tells Johnny that she is glad to have him there. Johnny wants to see the weapons collection and tells her that with her figure she must have been an athlete in college. Johnny holds her hand and she tells Johnny that she was a girl athlete.

Johnny tells her that her husband must have had to drive slowly on the road, slowly enough so that someone could not have missed him with a pea-shooter. Johnny tells her that archery was her best event. He could tell by the calluses on her hand, which came from a heavy hunting bow.

Blanche admits that she killed her husband, "but if you knew what I had to put up with" she tells Johnny. Johnny tells her that she took a chance on murder to get a million bucks, but she lost.

"And according to the law, no person convicted of the murder of the decedent shall be entitled to any portion of the estate, including the insurance. But just don't forget my commission on that amount. Expense account, including room and board at Emmer's, and the trip back to Hartford, $185.60, doubled!

Notes:
- There are two versions of this program. One version is an AFTRS program that contains a story about Walter Hunt who invented the safety pin, and a story about the oath of office. The network version of this program contains commercials for Pepsi, No-Doz, Fritos, and Ex-Lax.
- The announcer is John Wald.

Producer: Jack Johnstone   Writer: Jack Johnstone
Cast: Virginia Gregg, G. Stanley Jones, Forrest Lewis, Vic Perrin,

Bartlett Robinson

◆ ❖ ◆

Show: The Back to the Back Matter
Show Date: 7/17/1960
Company: Continental Insurance & Trust Company
Agent: Ed Barrenger
Exp. Acct: $25.80

Synopsis: Ed Barrenger calls and he has made reservations for Johnny to fly to New York on the next flight. He will meet Johnny at the airport and give him the details. The reason is to prevent a murder.

Johnny buys gas and drives to the airport where Ed is waiting. Ed gives Johnny the address for Lucien R. Fletcher, who owns an ad agency. Ed tells Johnny that Fletcher had called him just before Ed called Johnny. The agency is a small one, and Fletcher's partner is William Spade.

Fletcher feels that Spade is out to murder him. Spade is out of town and is due back today. Fletcher is not the kind to go off half-cocked, so get to New York City. Johnny tells Ed to call Lt. Randy Singer, and Johnny leaves.

Johnny calls the 18th precinct and gets officer Conroy. Conroy calls Johnny a "private eye", and Johnny calls him a "copper", terms which neither like. Conroy tells Johnny that Randy is not there, and he does not know if Randy got any calls.

Johnny tells Conroy to tell Randy that he is at 614 East 52nd, and Conroy tries to tell Johnny that Randy has gone there with the police doctor but Johnny cuts him off. Johnny cabs to the address and goes to the Fletcher apartment, only to find Randy there. Randy takes Johnny to the library to see a dead Mr. Fletcher.

Randy tells Johnny that Fletcher was killed with one bullet through the heart. Fletcher must have known who did it to let the man get that close. Ed Barrenger had called, and Randy had tried to call Fletcher but could not get him at the office or at home, so Randy came over and found Fletcher. The doc thinks that death happened around midnight.

The bullet was placed just right to penetrate a back-support corset for his sacro-lumbar problem. The shot had to be placed just right or the steel ribs would have deflected it. Johnny reminds Randy that the .38 packs a lot of wallop, but Randy tells Johnny that it was a. 22. Barrenger had told Randy that Fletcher had been expecting problems and who he suspected. Johnny starts to tell him about the partner when there is a knock at the door.

Johnny opens the door to find Mr. Spade who has just arrived from Philadelphia with an urgent matter for Mr. Fletcher. Johnny questions Spade about his trip and Spade shoves his plane ticket into Johnny's hand. Randy tells Spade that he was in Philadelphia when his partner was shot. Spade wants to see Fletcher but Johnny tells Spade to go to the office to take care of his important matter. Johnny tells him that they will be in touch if they hear anything.

Randy wonders what is going on with Johnny, and Johnny tells him that he knew Spade was in Philadelphia and had checked the plane schedules when he arrived. Johnny is sure that Spade was on the plane. "So, it seems that there was no way for Spade to have murdered Fletcher" states Randy. "Wanna Bet?" asks Johnny.

Johnny calls the Fletcher agency and Spade is not there. The operator tells Johnny that Spade had called her from the airport when he arrived.

Johnny calls various airline offices and finally talks to the stewardess who remembers Spade because he was always punching the call button claiming he was airsick. Johnny wonders if he was purposely calling attention to himself.

Johnny calls the Belleview Stratford hotel and the desk clerk tells Johnny that Spade had come in around ten and gone right to his room. He left at eight this morning and mentioned the importance of catching a plane to New York.

Johnny is sure that Spade had murdered Fletcher, but where was he before he checked in? Johnny is sure that Spade went to New York under another name, killed his partner, came back in time to leave at eight. But how to trick him?

Johnny cabs to Spade's office and Spade tells him that he is busy with his new client. The desk is piled up with all the newspapers and Johnny tells him that the papers would only print a story if Fletcher were dead.

Spade tells Johnny that they ran the business together, but Fletcher was a difficult person. Spade blames the problems on the pain from Fletcher's back problem.

Johnny tells Spade that he had plenty to benefit from by killing Fletcher, and maybe Fletcher even gave him a key to his apartment. Spade tells Johnny that it is bad enough that Fletcher is dead.

Johnny corrects him by saying that is the second time you said Fletcher was dead. Johnny tells him that no one said that Fletcher was dead. Johnny tells Spade that he should have thought about the corset, and that little .22.

Spade tells Johnny that he saw him fall and that he was sure he had killed him as he had aimed for his heart. "Oh no!" gasps Spade. Johnny tells Spade that Fletcher is dead and makes a phone call.

"Ah, it's funny how a man like that can plan a thing so carefully, carry it out so carefully and then when he is caught, lose his head and blab all over the place. Heh, he even made a grab for the little .22 pistol he'd used and had right there in his desk. That will be good as evidence."

Notes:
- There are two versions of this program. One version is an AFTRS program that contains a story about the Electoral College, and a story about Thomas Hunt Morgan who studied fruit fly genetics. The network version of this program contains commercials for Pepsi, No-Doz stay awake tablets, and Dennis James for Kellogg's All Bran.
- In this program, Ed Barrenger calls Johnny (presumably in the morning), stating that Fletcher had called him just before Ed called Johnny. But the time of death is around midnight   before Fletcher supposedly

called Barrenger. Also, Randy notes that Ed had called him early in the morning.
- The announcer is John Wald.

Producer:	Jack Johnstone Writer: Jack Johnstone
Cast:	Virginia Gregg, Jeanne Tatum, Frank Gerstle, James McCallion, Herb Vigran, Jack Edwards, Forrest Lewis

♦ ❖ ♦

Show: The Rhymer Collection Matter
Show Date: 7/31/1960
Company: Mono Guarantee Insurance Company
Agent: Fred Porter
Exp. Acct: $35.50

Synopsis: Fred Porter calls and asks Johnny if he remembers the theft of the Rhymer collection, a set of miniature paintings done on porcelain. Six were stolen and the insurance company had to pay out $20,000. Wilbert Rhymer has contacted Fred and he wants to talk to Johnny. Fred is sure that Wilbert wants to talk to Johnny about the miniatures, as he demanded that only Johnny be brought into the case. Johnny questions why he should get involved and Fred reminds him that the company investigator was Jerry Pitcher, the investigator who was suspected of complicity in some of his cases. The police could never prove anything so the insurance company fired Jerry and warned the other companies. Johnny asks where Jerry is now, and Fred does not know. Johnny will take the first train.

Johnny takes a train to Philadelphia, Pennsylvania and cabs to the Rhymer Gallery, where Mr. Rhymer is described as "very, very British". Rhymer tells Johnny that he had wished Johnny had been assigned to the case originally, as he could have recovered the miniatures, which were vastly underinsured. Rhymer is sure that Pitcher was involved with the theft because of the way he handled the investigation.

Rhymer gives Johnny a check for $4,050 that he will mail to the insurance company that day. The amount is exactly what the insurance company paid him for one Pellegrini. Rhymer tells Johnny that the Pellegrini has been returned and that Rhymer has a buyer for it, Mr. Charles Cunningham who is a regular customer.

The painting was found inside the door under the mail slot tied up in some brown wrapping paper. The Pellegrini is very well known, and Johnny thinks that it might be too well known to sell, so it was returned.

Johnny wonders about the black market in Paris, and Rhymer notes that a lot of famous works have been sold there. Rhymer has no idea why the painting was returned, unless the thief was a connoisseur who could not destroy the paintings and realized he could not sell them. Johnny notes that the return rules out Jerry Pitcher.

Johnny asks for the string and wrapping paper but is told that it has been thrown out. Rhymer had called for Johnny hoping that he could return the rest of the paintings. Johnny jokes that he could just sit and wait for the others to be returned. When asked what his next move is, Johnny has no idea.

Johnny cabs to Fred Porter's office and updates him on the return of the Pellegrini. Johnny is told that a complete investigation was done at the time of the theft and Jerry Pitcher was assigned because he seemed to know something about art. Only Rhymer thought that Pitcher was involved in the theft and it was then that the insurance company learned of Pitcher's reputation. Fred is sure that Jerry has skipped the country.

Johnny has an idea and calls his old friend Louis De Marsac, who knows all about the black market. Louis asks for $1,000 but Johnny only asks if De Marsac has heard of Jerry Pitcher.

Louis has never heard of Jerry, but he knows that the Rhymer collection of miniatures was on the black market and for $200 Louis tells Johnny that the paintings were bought 3 years ago for a gallery in the states. For $250 Louis tells Johnny that Mr. Rhymer bought them himself. For $400 Louis tells Johnny that he last saw them six months ago in the gallery of his dearest friend, that scoundrel and crook Francois Duboisson who could not sell them because they were too hot.

Louis does not know to whom Duboisson was trying to sell the paintings for. Johnny is sure that Louis knows what the paintings are worth and tells Fred that that sort information would really cost.

Johnny has an idea and goes to the Museum of Art and talks to Mr. Kingman who tells Johnny that a fool stole the paintings, as they could never be sold without the thief being brought to justice. Kingman tells Johnny that the paintings were originally not worth much. But now that their history is known, they are worth around $200,000. Kingman tells Johnny that a Mr. Cunningham would pay dearly to buy a Pellegrini.

Johnny tells Kingman what has happened and gets the address of Mr. Cunningham. Johnny calls Cunningham, but he is out of town.

Johnny gets a room at the Belleview Stratford and next morning Johnny calls Cunningham again. Johnny is told that the value of the paintings has gone up recently. Johnny suggests to Cunningham that he could be part of a fraud investigation, so Cunningham tells Johnny that he is going to pay Rhymer $20,500 for the Pellegrini. Johnny suggests he call the bank and stop payment on the check.

Johnny cabs to Fred's office and they go to Rhymer's gallery together. Johnny asks Fred about Rhymer's policy premiums and Fred notes that there is a large one slightly over due. Johnny wonders how bad business is and how much Rhymer owes.

At the shop, Johnny is told that another of the paintings, a Lombardi, has been returned just like the other was. Rhymer has saved the string and wrapper for Johnny, but Johnny tells Rhymer that he was stupid if he did not wear gloves while he wrapped the paining up. Johnny tells Rhymer that he brought him in so that Rhymer would not be suspected.

Johnny asks about Rhymer's last trip to Europe and he confirms that it was in June. Johnny wants to look at Rhymer's bank statements for the past year, or would you like to talk to the police?

Johnny tells Rhymer that he bought the paintings on the black market and notes that he should have been alarmed when Rhymer noted that the paintings were under insured. Johnny tells him that they were insured before their real value was known. By the time he did know, Rhymer had already pulled the fake robbery and collected the insurance to keep his business going.

Rhymer is told he tried to sell the paintings in Paris but they were too hot. He needed money and now he could sell them for $200,000. He made them reappear one at a time and gave the cock-and-bull story about the thief not wanting to be caught. Rhymer asks Johnny if he returned the others and gave a full confession if the police would be gentler with him.

"Son of a gun, why do they do it? Won't they ever learn? What's the matter with people anyhow, some people, that is. Oh well. Expense account total including the tip back to Hartford, $35.50. And Freddy don't forget, a nice fee on this one, as well as a check to Les Chat Gris over there in Paris."

Notes:
- This is an AFTRS program, but only the AFRTS network identification at the end exists.
- The announcer is Dan Cubberly.

Producer: Jack Johnstone Writer: Jack Johnstone
Cast: Harry Bartell, Ben Wright, Forrest Lewis, Junius Matthews, Marvin Miller

◆ ❖ ◆

Show: **The Magnanimous Matter**
Show Date: 8/7/1960
Company: **Universal Adjustment Bureau**
Agent: **Pat McCracken**
Exp. Acct: **$0.00**

Synopsis: Johnny is called by an addled Alvin Peabody Cartwright, who offers Johnny the position of First Vice President of the Magnanimous Accident Insurance Company. Alvin tells Johnny that it is his new company and tells Johnny to come to Texas. Then Pat McCracken calls and tells Johnny that he has to go to Corpus Christi, Texas. Come on over, or else!

Johnny goes to Pat's office and is given a drink. Pat tells Johnny that he has a wealthy client named Alvin Peabody Cartwright who is running his own company in Texas but does not know what he is doing. Johnny is told that Alvin sells a policy and pays off for any accident, and Pat has proof. Pat has a claim to settle a case through the Universal Adjustment Bureau, and he is afraid that the racketeers will be involved soon.

Johnny goes to Corpus Christi, Texas and goes to Alvin's office, which is a madhouse. Johnny closes the office for the receptionist Laura, but Alvin tells her that he is waiting for his new Vice President.

Laura tells Johnny that she listens to the cases and is convinced that Alvin is crazy for selling insurance to people who do not deserve it. No one can argue with Alvin, but it must be stopped.

Johnny uses his American Express credit card to wire money to Smokey Sullivan in Los Angeles. Johnny calls Smokey who tells Johnny about a phony racket he used to pull with his trick knee, and Johnny tells Smokey to come to Texas. Johnny gets a room at the Robert Driscoll hotel and has dinner. That evening Johnny tells Smokey of his plan.

The next day Smokey buys a $10,000 injury policy. Johnny talks to Alvin who tells Johnny about his philanthropic company. Johnny warns him that crooks will take advantage of him, but Alvin tells Johnny that he is too smart for them and makes a bet with Johnny. If Johnny wins, Alvin will close the company and cancel all of the policies.

Later Smokey comes in and tells Alvin that he fell in a building and injured his knee. It is such a sad story that Alvin wants to pay immediately. Smokey signs a release and gets the money. Smokey pops his knee back into place, thanks Alvin for the money and tells him that he will tell all of his friends. Alvin agrees to close the company.

Notes:
- The announcer is Dan Cubberly.
- Story information obtained from the KNX Collection in the Thousand Oaks Library.

Producer:	Jack Johnstone	Writer:	Jack Johnstone
Cast:	Howard McNear, Lawrence Dobkin, Virginia Gregg, Vic Perrin		

♦ ❖ ♦

Show:	**The Paradise Lost Matter**
Show Date:	8/14/1960
Company:	**New Britain Mutual Insurance Company**
Agent:	**Al Turner**
Exp. Acct:	**$50.00**

Synopsis: Al Turner calls and asks how old Johnny is. Johnny tells Al that on his next birthday he will be thirty-uh, why? Al thinks that it is time for Johnny to enter a home for the aged. Al wants Johnny to go to the Mackley Rest Home in Frog Mountain, New York. Sudden death is the problem, four in a row and Al covered three of them. The beneficiary for all of them was the Mackley Rest Home.

Johnny buys gas and drives the Kingston area and then to Frog Mountain, New York. Johnny drives by a rest home and stops. A man introduces himself as Justin Perry. He asks if Johnny has some relatives to send to him at the Paradise Rest Home. Johnny learns from Justin's son Eddie that the Mackley place is a mile up the road.

Johnny drives up the road to the Mackley Rest Home, a new place but one lacking in warmth. The guests were just sitting around. In the office, Johnny meets Peter Mackley, who knows that Johnny is coming. Johnny notices that the place must have cost a lot of money, and Pete tells Johnny that the place will not pay for itself for years. Johnny tells him that a few more policies will really help in that regard. Pete tells Johnny that he is not the police, so get out!

Pete admits that it was too bad the four patients died. The deaths were unexpected, even by Dr. Nathan Way in Kingston. Pete tells Johnny that Mr. Partley slipped on the porch. The others were natural causes, and Johnny wonders if poison was involved.

Dr. Way comes in and Pete tells him that Johnny thinks the deaths were deliberate. Dr. Way tells Johnny that the financial debt is to be expected for a new place. Pete tells Johnny that he and his wife have been in the business for fifteen years, ever since his parents died. He started in Pennsylvania and moved to New York because the air is better and they had to close down, as the buildings were substandard according to some new code.

Dr. Way tells Johnny that some of the clients had moved with Pete from Pennsylvania. Dr. Way tells Johnny that he had suggested that people leave the insurance to the rest home, and they thanked him for the idea. Pete tells Johnny that unless he loses his reputation, he will do OK.

Dr. Way tells Johnny that he did not do autopsies as the victims were up in years. Johnny wants the bodies exhumed and autopsies done, and he is going to check on Dr. Way. Dr. Way leaves to start the process.

Johnny drives to Kingston and gets a room and meets with police Lt. Art Connelly. Art is glad that Johnny is looking into the deaths. Mackley is well thought of and Dr. Way is a fine man and the best one to do the autopsies. Johnny tells him that Mackley had a lot of guts to compete with Justin Perry, as a lot of the people in town were partial to Perry.

Doc Way comes in and tells Johnny that he can do the autopsies that night and that he will call Johnny when he is finished. Johnny goes to his room and falls asleep in an easy chair. Johnny hears the door close and the lights go out. Johnny is slugged and goes out.

Johnny wakes up the next morning with Dr. Way tending a head wound and offering some medicinal brandy. Doc tells Johnny that he has done the autopsies and came to tell him the results. Doc tells him that three of the deaths were from poison and Johnny calls Lt. Connelly.

Doc tells Johnny that the only drugs those people got were the ones he prescribed. Lt. Connelly calls and Johnny tells him that Pete Mackley had slugged him that night. Connelly tells Johnny that he is wrong as Connelly had Mackley at headquarters all night. Doc tells Johnny that the prescriptions were always made up at Mrs. Pearson's pharmacy and they go there.

Johnny asks Mrs. Pearson if she stocks a drug called sodium theramelicilate. She tells Johnny and Doc that she keeps a supply for the local vet. Johnny hears a motorcycle pull away outside and Mrs. Pearson tells him that it was the boy makes all the deliveries. She finds the bottle, and a lot of the tablets are missing.

Johnny and Dr. Way chase after the motorcycle on a winding mountain road. Young Edward Perry finally crashes while looking back. Doc and Johnny rush up to the wreck and Edward tells Doc that he knew they had gotten wise that he was putting the poison in the medicine, and that his father made him do it. Edward tells Johnny that if enough people died at the Mackley place they would come to the Paradise and put Mackley out of business, and then he dies.

"Ah, I don't know. I don't know what the courts will do. Ask me, Justin Perry murdered his son just as much as though he had done it with his own two, eh, I don't know."

Notes:
- The announcer is John Wald.

Producer:	Jack Johnstone	Writer:	Jack Johnstone
Cast:	Virginia Gregg, Harry Bartell, Edgar Barrier, Sam Edwards, Stacy Harris, Junius Matthews, Forrest Lewis		

◆ ❖ ◆

Show:	**The Twisted Twin Matter**
Show Date:	8/21/1960
Company:	Floyds of England
Agent:	George Reed
Exp. Acct:	$196.55

Synopsis: George Reed calls Johnny and asks if the name Franklin P. Franklin means anything. Johnny remembers that he was a World War I fighter pilot, "Franky the Flying Fool". George tells Johnny that Franklin died the other day, leaving $110,000 to be divided between the two sons. Randolph buried his father but George cannot find Phillip. Come on over and I will tell you what I know.

Johnny ponders how Floyds hands him some funny cases that really pay off as he cabs to George's office. George tells Johnny that Franklin was a daring aviator, and flying was an obsession for him. Franklin crashed into a mountain and was injured during the war. If it were not for his family's money, he might have ended up in a mental institution.

Franklin was able to recover mentally and physically and raise a family and manage the family money. The mother of the twins died when they were born. Both of the boys inherited some of their father's instabilities. Randolph is a salesman for a machine company, and Phillip is a henchman working for Carlo Frizetti in Chicago. Johnny remembers working on a case concerning Frizetti once.

According to Randolph, his brother Phillip died a year ago, but no proof has been offered. Johnny is told there will be a commission based on the face of the policy and his expenses — reasonable expenses.

Johnny goes to visit Randolph Franklin in Hartford, Connecticut and the doorman is not sure if Randolph is in or not, as he is always on the road. The doorman tells Johnny that the phone is broken so Johnny takes the elevator up.

Randy is in his thirties with shifting eyes and terribly nervous. His head shakes violently and his hands shake and he is constantly adjusting his tie.

Randy tells Johnny that Phillip is dead and it was his fault. Phillip worked for Carlo Frizetti and Randolph had gone to Chicago on business and met with Phillip. He told him to come home and get a job or dad would cut him out of the will. Randolph tells Johnny that he has to find Phillip.

He tells Johnny that the threat of losing some of the estate convinced Phillip to fly back with him, but when he thinks about the aircraft accident he gets blackouts and cannot remember things. Randy tells Johnny that the plane ran into a storm and crashed into a mountaintop. It was an accident just like his father's. When Johnny mentions that his father's crash caused him to lose his sanity, Randy tells Johnny that his father was not insane, only terribly scared.

Only Randy, the pilot and a little girl were able to crawl away from the wreckage of the airplane, each going in a different direction. Randy had been unconscious for several days when he was found. The plane was burned completely so there was no way to find Phillip's body. Johnny tells Randy that he seems to be the sole beneficiary of the insurance.

Johnny asks for his employer's name and address and tells him that he has a crazy hunch, a term that Randy hates. Johnny tells him that he is going to continue the search for his brother, so stick around.

Johnny goes to New York City and checks with Randy's employer. Johnny learns that Randy had been a good salesman, but since the accident he has not sold much, and has had long unexplained absences and they were seriously considering dropping him. Thus, he seems to have a need for the insurance money.

Johnny goes to Chicago, Illinois and meets his friend Smokey Sullivan, who takes him to Carlo Frizetti's hangout. Johnny knocks and Randy opens the door. The man tells Johnny that he is Phil Franklin. Carlo comes in and welcomes Johnny as a friend, for once.

Carlo tells Johnny that the man is Phil Franklin. Half the time he is there helping out, half the time the boys are out looking for him. Carlo tells Johnny that a year ago, he cracked up in an airplane accident. Phil brings cocktails and Johnny leaves quickly with a highball glass and flies back to Hartford.

Johnny drives to Randy's place, but he is not there. Johnny pays the doorman to call him when Randy comes back and to keep his mouth shut. Five days later Charlie the doorman calls Johnny and tells him that Randy is back.

Johnny stops at the police lab and picks up Lt. Tim Waverley and gives him the highball glass with instructions. They then drive to Randy's apartment. Johnny tells Randy that he has been away, and he seems confused.

Johnny introduces Lt. Waverley and asks Randy where he was. Randy does not know where he was. Waverley shows Randy the glass and he does not remember seeing it and gives it back to Lt. Waverley. Lt. Waverley looks at the glass and tells Johnny that the prints are identical.

Johnny tells Randy that since the crash he has been both himself and his brother Phillip. Randy tells Johnny that he had a blackout after Johnny was there and mentioned the crash, and Johnny tells him that he talked to him in Chicago, and the fingerprints prove it. Johnny struggles with Randy and ends up slugging him.

Johnny takes Lt. Waverley's gun and fires five times in Randy's direction until he faints. Johnny and Waverley take Randy over to see doc Parsons, the psychiatrist. Johnny confirms with the doctor that it was a guilt complex that brought about the nervous condition.

Doc Parson tells Johnny that Randy had built up the complex at the shock of his brother's death in the plane crash, and Randy felt responsible for Phillip's death. During the blackouts, he really felt he was Phil. Johnny is told the shots could have shocked Randy to death, and Johnny tells the Doc that he only did it after he realized what was going on.

Doc Parsons tells Johnny that the combination of the gunshots, the pain of being hit and the exposure as Phillip all acted to offset the terror of the plane crash. Dr. Parsons feels that Randy will probably recover with the proper treatment. "And, don't you ever try anything like this again, young man!"

"Yeah, Doctor Parsons was right. After this I'll leave the shock treatment bit to people like him, who really know what they are doing. Expense account total $196.55. There'll be no fee on this one."

Notes:
- The announcer is John Wald.

Producer:	Jack Johnstone	Writer:	Jack Johnstone
Cast:	G. Stanley Jones, Frank Gerstle, James McCallion, Jack Moyles, Herb Ellis, Russell Thorson		

◆ ❖ ◆

Show:	**The Deadly Debt Matter**
Show Date:	**8/28/1960**
Company:	**Tri-State Life & Casualty Insurance Company**
Agent:	**Don Boomhauer**
Exp. Acct:	**$200.00**

Synopsis: Don Boomhauer calls Johnny from Sarasota, and business is booming in the real estate market. Don mentions that Earle has gone to California, and it seems that he just might stay out there. With Earle out of town, Don has been holding down the Tri-State office, and now he has a problem. The client is Thomas Patterson. A few years ago, when he was living up in Jacksonville, Thomas was the sole witness to a murder. The killer was tried and sent to state prison. (Uh oh!) So now the killer is loose, and Don feels that Patterson's life is not worth a hill of beans. Johnny will catch the first plane he can.

Johnny flies to Sarasota, Florida and meets with Don Boomhauer. Don tells Johnny that the policy is for $70,000, and Johnny starts figuring his commission.

Young Tommy lived up in Jacksonville and worked as a milkman. One morning in 1951 he saw a man named Casey Carey kill a man named Harker who was busy shooting at him at the time with a .38. The jury did not buy self-defense because there was a feud between them, and Carey did not get life because Harker had a police record, so Carey was sentenced to ten years.

It was Patterson's testimony that convicted him, and he swore that he would get even. Patterson has a small family and the threats scared him. Later Tom was left some money and legally changed his name to Thomas K. Patterson and moved to Venice and started the Excellent Dairy Company.

In Jacksonville he bumped into a man on the street one day, looked into his face and started running. It was Casey Carey. Tom could not believe it, but he looked into the records and found that Carey had gotten out on good behavior. Tom feels that Carey is out to get him.

Don tells Johnny that Tom was not sure that Carey had recognized him. Tom went home and bought a Colt .32 and got a permit. Don tells Johnny that a couple months ago, Carey moved to Venice and got a job at a service station. Tom tried to avoid him, but when they met Carey was the one who avoided Patterson.

Johnny wonders if Carey is playing a cat-and-mouse game to build up the suspense and prolong the agony. Don is sure Carey is succeeding. Tom was a nervous wreck when he called and asked for Johnny to come down. Don reminds Johnny that Carey swore he would kill Tom, and Don is sure of it.

Johnny borrows a car and drives to Venice to see Tom and the police. Johnny finds Tom in his office and he is beside himself with fear. Johnny takes him to the police and the chief, Brad Younger, is cooperative and knows all about Casey Carey. Younger tells Johnny that he had learned all about Carey from his employer, and he had talked with Carey. There was no reason to tell Tom and get him upset.

Tom gets excited and tells the police that they should have done something. Tom demands protection when the chief tells him that Carey is OK. Younger asks Tom to turn in his gun and Tom refuses. Johnny won't help him, so he will have to help himself. Johnny promises the chief he will get the gun from Tom.

After lunch together, Johnny drives Tom to Carey's house for a showdown. Johnny knocks at the door and a neighbor tells Johnny that there is evil in there. The woman had heard a shot and has called the police. Tom and Johnny enter and find Carey shot through the head with a .32. Younger arrives and arrests Tom for murder.

Tom tells the chief he is wrong, but chief Younger has Tom's gun. Johnny tells chief Younger that he had to drag Tom to the house. The chief tells Johnny that a young officer named Billy Barker had given him the gun. It was found beside the road over by Midnight Pass. Barker had stopped to fix a tire and found the gun. Tom is insistent that he had left the gun at home.

The chief tells them that Tom had come over here and killed Carey after he left the chief's office. Johnny tells Younger that Tom had been with Johnny all afternoon. The chief tells them that the bullet and the medical exams will prove that Tom did it. Maybe Younger was right when the report proves that the bullet came from Tom's gun, and the neighbor heard the shot just a few minutes before they pulled up. Johnny decides to play a wild hunch.

Johnny calls Don Boomhauer and he tells Johnny that the man Carey killed was named Harker, not Barker. Johnny makes another call to Mike Kirby on the city room of the Jacksonville Times Press.

Mike searches the files and finds some revealing information. It seems that the boy was working on the police force there in Jacksonville, trying to live down the family reputation. A month or so ago he quit and moved. Johnny is sure that he is still a cop.

Johnny goes back to police headquarters and asks the chief to call one of his officers in. The chief calls Billy Barker and Johnny asks him why he changed his name from Harker, and why he moved here after the man who killed his father, Casey Carey, moved here? The man you swore you would get for killing your dad.

You worked on the force in Jacksonville, and then moved here when Carey did, biding your time. This afternoon you heard us talking. You got Tommy's gun somehow and went to the house and killed him. When Johnny asks Billy to go to Sarasota and take a paraffin test, he pulls his gun, but Johnny is able to get it away from him. Johnny asks the chief to release Tom.

Johnny goes fishing with the chief the next day. Remarks: "The fishing was great."

Notes:
- This is an AFTRS program that contains a story about Thomas Edison and his electric lamp, and a story about the importance of silver over gold in military insignia.
- The announcer is John Wald.

Producer:	Jack Johnstone	Writer:	Jack Johnstone
Cast:	Virginia Gregg, Russell Thorson, Barney Phillips, Sam Edwards, Bert Holland, Stacy Harris		

♦ ❖ ♦

Show:	**The Killer Kin Matter**
Show Date:	9/4/1960
Company:	**Floyds of England**
Agent:	**George Reed**
Exp. Acct:	**$0.00**

Synopsis: George calls Johnny and he asks if it is George Reed. Floyds of England? So that's the big insurance company that sent you out to nail Felix Caine a couple months ago? George tells Johnny that the insurance company must have paid him a lot of money to clear up the robbery and nail Felix. Maybe you even got a big bonus because now Felix is dead. That's killing for money isn't it. And his girl, you had someone trick her into telling you where to find him, so she's doing a stretch now because she was in with them. Remember when you tagged Felix and he fell on his own gun and killed himself? Is that the way you said it happened? Nobody could prove otherwise, and you were pretty lucky then. You got away with it because Felix's brother was on the lam on the west coast. They were awful close all their life. Now that Felix is dead, it means that the other one will get even with you. My name is George, George Caine, Felix's brother.

So, what if I hadn't killed Felix Caine. It does not make any difference now. But why would George call me to warn me? Johnny calls George Reed and asks if he knows where George Caine is, but George does not know where he is. Johnny realizes that George must be in New York City, so he is going to go there and contact Randy Singer.

Johnny trains to New York and talks to Randy. The police want George Caine for a charge of assault with intent to kill. Johnny reminds Randy that Felix fell on his gun, but Randy reminds Johnny that he will not convince George, as George is very clever and Randy does not know where he is. With the new direct dialing for long distance you cannot tell where a call is coming from. Randy is glad that Johnny is letting them look for George, now go on back to Hartford, and be sure you do go.

Randy threatens to call all the precincts in New York and tell them to arrest Johnny and bring him to Randy if they see him. Randy tells Sgt. Conroy to take Johnny back to Hartford. So be a good little boy. By the way, Conroy is a fan, so you can tell him all about your adventures on the way home.

Sgt. Conroy escorts Johnny all the way to his apartment, at Johnny's expense. Conroy (with a deep Irish accent) asks Johnny to finish a story and calls the office. The phone rings, and George tells him that the New York cops will not help him. "You killed my brother and I am going to kill you".

Then Betty Lewis, "the girl he is going to marry someday" calls and there is a click on the line. Johnny tells Betty he was out on business, but not with any other girls. Betty asks if Johnny has forgotten about their date in New York tonight? Betty is staying with Nancy Spaulding at 1624 McDougal Alley. The line clicks again and Johnny dismisses it. Johnny tells Betty not to be surprised if they have a police escort.

Johnny gets ready to fly to New York when there is a knock at the door. It is Mr. Perry, the building super. He tells Johnny that the young man who rented the room next door left in a hurry, and Mr. Perry has found a wiretap in the room. The man was named John Jones.

Johnny gets a description and calls Randy Singer. Johnny promises to call Randy when he gets to the Spaulding apartment. Johnny remembers that Betty had helped him get Felix, so Johnny rushes to get to New York ahead of George Caine.

Johnny flies to New York and cabs to the Spaulding apartment. Johnny knocks and asks for Betty, but Nancy tells Johnny that Betty left with a detective. From the description Johnny realizes it was George Caine. Nancy tells Johnny that they went to meet him. They went east, and the driver was Tommy, who sits at the cab stand on the corner.

Nancy spots the cab back outside and Johnny rushes down to the cab.

Tommy tells Johnny that he took them to the Bowery. On the way there, a police car stops them for speeding and Johnny tells officer Tim O'Reilly that he is in a hurry. O'Reilly tells Johnny to get into the squad car, and Randy is there waiting for him. Randy tells Johnny that everything is under control. George is not taking Betty anywhere. They had followed the cab and nabbed him at a boarding house and Betty is waiting for Johnny at the station house.

"The expense account, forget it, forget all of it. I only hope that someday, somehow, I can repay Randy Singer, over his dead body though, because all he cared about was getting his hands on Caine. And, for some silly reason he seemed to think that I'd been helping him. What a guy."

Notes:
- This program mentions direct dialing, which was starting to be implemented in the early 1960's.
- The announcer is John Wald.

Producer:	Jack Johnstone Writer: Jack Johnstone
Cast:	Virginia Gregg, James McCallion, G. Stanley Jones, Herb Vigran, Jack Moyles, Junius Matthews, Lillian Buyeff, Paul Dubov

◆ ❖ ◆

Show:	The Too Much Money Matter
Show Date:	9/11/1960
Company:	Floyds of England
Agent:	George Reed
Exp. Acct:	$0.00

Synopsis: George Reed calls and tells Johnny that he has just received a frantic call from Alvin Peabody Cartwright. Alvin is an important client, and he wants Johnny on the west coast immediately. Johnny tells George that the last time Alvin called someone was trying to kill him and the time before that was to give Johnny a Christmas present. Alvin is in Santa Barbara at the home of Rockland Rockwell, another extremely wealthy client of Floyds. If this case involves Mr. Rockwell, it will be plenty serious. Johnny will be in touch.

Johnny flies to Los Angeles and rents a car. Johnny drives to Santa Barbara, California and gets directions to the Rockwell home, which is on ten acres and is well tended. The house is like a castle built of native stone.

Alvin Cartwright meets Johnny at the door and tells him that he wants Rocky to sell him the house and that the situation is serious. Alvin tells Johnny that he has had reason to think his life was in danger in the past, but poor old Rocky. Rocky is very brave and keeping up with his parties, pretending that nothing is wrong. All Rocky does is entertain, what with all his money. Right now, Rocky and his friends are out on a foxhunt. Alvin is worried because Rocky is going to be murdered.

Alvin tells Johnny that Rocky will be murdered unless Johnny can do something about it, but first Alvin takes Johnny on a tour of the house. The house is fabulous with marble, wood paneling and other expensive appointments.

After the tour, Alvin tells Johnny that he might be able to buy the house for two or three million dollars. Alvin spots the party returning and Rocky is leading them.

Alvin goes to get Rocky, who turns out to be an obese, florid type of man who wheezes when he breathes. Johnny wonders how he (or the horse for that matter) survived the foxhunt.

Rocky tells Johnny that many years ago he pulled a fast one on Lord Jacob Hunter Ashley. Ashley never even knew that Rocky had done it. Rocky had put him out of business, ruined him. Now Ashley's son Marvin, an actor, has found out what Rocky had done.

A few months ago, Marvin had written to say he was coming to take revenge for the poverty of the family. Rocky got a call a few days ago that Ashley was in the states. Rocky told Ashley that he was a changed man, and would give him anything he wanted, but Ashley told him that he was going to kill Rocky. Rocky is sorry, but Johnny wonders if it is because he is in danger. Unless Johnny finds him, Ashley will murder Rocky.

Alvin tells Rocky that he is ashamed of him and tells Rocky that he made all of his money honestly, he inherited it! But it is Johnny's duty to protect Rocky. When Johnny tells Rocky that he is going to call in the police, Rocky tells Johnny that Ashley might even be in the house now, as he does not know all of his guests. Rocky only knows that Ashley is between thirty-five and forty and Johnny must find him. Johnny does not like this case because of Rockwell.

At dinner Rocky is a good host, and Johnny does not spot anyone suspicious. After dinner Rocky tells Johnny that Ashley must be there, and Johnny must stay with him.

They go down to the billiards room to play pool. None of the players call themselves Ashley. One of the players, Mr. Gibson mentions a "massa" shot, and he seems to recognize Johnny's name. Gibson tells Johnny that he runs a brokerage business in San Francisco.

Johnny talks to Mr. Sam Edwards, who looks familiar and excuses himself to get a drink. Gibson invites Johnny to have lunch with him the next time he is in San Francisco. They can go to the Cliff House.

Johnny tries to sink the eight ball and manages to rip the cover of the table. Johnny tells them that the play is over for Gibson, but that is not his name. Johnny tells the group that Gibson had talked about making a "massa" shot, and only the British call it that. Americans call it a "masse" shot.

Only and actor could make that slip. Johnny tells him that his real slip was calling the restaurant "Cliff House", not "Cliffhouse". Ashley pulls a gun to shoot Rocky and Johnny slugs him with a pool cue. "Hmm. Not as rusty as I thought!"

"You know something? Dear old Alvin Peabody Cartwright furnished the high powered legal talent that got Ashley off with nothing more than deportation. And needless to say, Cartwright is really through with Rockwell, as it would be. Expense account, aw forget it. Alvin P. handed me a check big enough for three expense accounts.

Notes:
- A masse shot is one where the cue ball is struck in such a fashion as to move in a circular path, around a blocking ball.
- Sam Edwards plays a character with his own name — typical Jack Johnstone.
- The announcer is Hugh Douglas.

Producer:	Jack Johnstone	Writer:	Jack Johnstone
Cast:	G. Stanley Jones. Howard McNear, Chester Stratton, Marvin Miller, Sam Edwards		

• ❖ •

Show: **The Real Smokey Matter**
Show Date: **9/18/1960**
Company: **Philadelphia Mutual Liability & Casualty Insurance Company**
Agent: **Harry Branson**
Exp. Acct: **$621.00**

Synopsis: Harry Branson calls Johnny and reminds him how he had convinced Harry to sell a policy to Smokey Sullivan. Harry is not sure if something has happened.

Johnny goes to Philadelphia, Pennsylvania where Harry tells Johnny that he did not say that anything was wrong, after all Smokey is a criminal. Johnny reminds Harry about all the cases Smokey has helped him with.

Harry shows Johnny a newspaper with the headline "Toy Factory Burned, work of Smokey Sullivan". The article relates how Smokey's body was found in the ashes, and was identified by a ring. Harry has tried to find Smokey but he has not been able to find him. Harry tells Johnny that he must find the real Smokey.

Johnny goes to the police and meets with Capt. Fletcher who takes Johnny to the morgue where he sees Smokey's ring. Fletcher tells Johnny that by naming a suspect he has put the others off guard. He named Smokey as a suspect because his name would be acceptable as a suspect. Fletcher tells Johnny to find Smokey.

Johnny searches for Smokey and calls Marty Ross, a newspaper reporter and plants a story. Johnny rents a car and calls the police with the license number. Johnny calls Marty and then goes out and almost runs down a policeman, and Marty sees it and reports it.

Johnny is put in jail and Capt. Fletcher comes to see him, but Johnny will not tell him why he did what he did.

Three days later Johnny goes before the judge who tells Johnny that his car was a deadly weapon and of the reporter who saw the accident.

Johnny is told by the judge that Smokey Sullivan came to help and went to the scene of the fire and recognized the work of a crony called "The Twin", who wore the same type of ring that Smokey had.

The judge tells Johnny that the newspaper article had worried Smokey. The judge orders Conroy to remove the handcuffs and Smokey enters the courtroom, and the judge fines Johnny $15 and tells him that the next time he has a case, please, please do not scare one of our patrolmen out of his wits.

Notes:
- This is an AFTRS program that contains a story about the census.
- The announcer is John Wald.
- In the script on file in the KNX Collection in the Thousand Oaks Library, Bob Bailey congratulates station KNX on their 40th anniversary.

Producer:	Jack Johnstone	Writer:	Jack Johnstone
Cast:	Harry Bartell, Stacy Harris, Vic Perrin, Lou Merrill, Tom Hanley, Bill James		

◆ ❖ ◆

Show: The Five Down Matter
Show Date: 9/25/1960
Company: Every one
Agent:
Exp. Acct: $0.00

Synopsis: Betty Lewis calls Johnny and comments about the concert that afternoon at Memorial Hall. "Let's make a day of it and have lunch, take a walk in the park, go to the concert, go somewhere and get married and have dinner together and find something to do this evening" offers Betty. "Sure, why not Let me put on my best bib and tucker and — whoa. Somewhere along the line I heard something about marriage. You know how I feel, but this job of mine..." complains Johnny. Betty hangs up dejectedly. "Dollar, you dope" remarks Johnny.

The phone rings again but it is not Betty, it is Pat McCracken and he has an assignment and is coming right over. The phone rings again and it is George Reed, and he has an emergency regarding Alvin Peabody Cartwright. Johnny tells George that he is sorry, but he has a personal matter to attend to. "More important than murder?" asks George.

Three calls in five minutes all requesting my services. Johnny starts to call Betty when Harry Branson calls, and he needs Johnny for a case. Johnny tells him he will call him back.

The phone rings again and Earle Poorman is on the line. Earle wants Johnny to come down, and Johnny tells him he will call back. The phone rings again and Buster Favor is on the line. Buster tells Johnny that since he is going to Los Angeles, he will drive over and meet him. The phone rings again and Alvin Peabody Cartwright is on the phone. Alvin tells Johnny that it is vital that he see him at his summer place in Beverly Hills. This time it is more serious, and Alvin cannot talk to Johnny about it on the phone. There is nothing more important Alvin implores.

Johnny muses that all of them require Johnny to be on the west coast. Johnny calls back all of the callers, but there is no answer. Johnny cabs to the airport and gets a call at the gate. Louis De Marsac is calling and he must see Johnny, but Johnny tells him that he cannot talk now. As Johnny runs onto the plane Luis tells Johnny that he will see him.

In New York, Johnny runs into Randy Singer who needs him to handle a case on the west coast. Randy tells Johnny that he will beat him there on a jet flight, but Johnny says that they are all full. Johnny wires everyone on a stopover in Chicago. In Los Angeles, California Johnny runs into Smokey Sullivan, who has a car for him. Smokey tells Johnny that it is awful about Alvin, you will never believe it.

Johnny and Smokey drive to the Cartwright house. Johnny knocks on Alvin's door and Alvin answers and tells him that he did not think Johnny would make it, what with all the bodies in the library. Bodies!

Johnny goes to the library with his gun drawn. Inside the floor is strewn with the bodies of six people. Huh? Wait a minute.

Among the bodies are Pat and George, and Johnny asks if he should put them out of their misery. Everyone gets up and congratulates Johnny. Alvin takes Johnny's gun from him, and it goes off!

Pat McCracken tells Johnny that this gathering marks the end of 5 years of Johnny's series of investigations for a pretty good line up of insurance companies. So, Happy Anniversary! It is also five solid years of the broadcasts of these cases on CBS.

You have performed a great service throughout this country to the insurance companies, no question about it. Your broadcasting has helped to expose a lot of crookedness, fraud, that sort of thing. And has saved the insurance companies a lot of money. And that means it has saved the people, their clients, the people who listen to your program every week. It saved them a lot of money too. Incidentally these CBS shows of yours have provided a lot of entertainment, a lot of pleasure to millions. In other words, Johnny, a lot of people think mighty well of you. And with very good reason.

Pat has made a list of the people most involved in his cases, and Alvin demanded the right to give this party to show you how much we love and appreciate you. Johnny is flabbergasted, and almost breaks up, especially when Betty walks in, promising not to make Johnny marry him, not yet anyway. Alvin tells Johnny that he can have anything he wants, and Johnny only asks to hold on to the friendship of people like them.

"Oh, mighty wonderful people, all them, some others too, I mean behind the scenes in the job of bringing you these radio reports week after week. The associate directors on the show Kenny Hodge, Bob Shue. The announcer Johnny Wald. A mighty wonderful technical crew Bob Chadwick, Bill James, Tom Hanley, and I mean Jack Johnstone our producer and director who, he is the guy who makes it...what was that Jack? Okay. Give them a lot of credit, huh. Because believe me, they deserve it."

Notes:
- **This program contains commercials for Pepsi and Ex-Lax.**
- **This is a fifth anniversary show, five years of the Bob Bailey run.**

- The announcer is John Wald.
- This program contains a special news bulletin from WROW in Schenectady that details the IUE Local 301 decision not to strike against General Electric. There was also a vote at the KAPL (the Knolls Atomic Power Laboratory) in Niskayuna and West Milton that was just the opposite. Negotiations will continue this week.
- After the program there is also a commercial for Utica Club beer.

Producer: Jack Johnstone   Writer: Jack Johnstone
Cast: Virginia Gregg, Lawrence Dobkin, G. Stanley Jones, Harry Bartell, Vic Perrin, John Dehner, Howard McNear, Marvin Miller, Forrest Lewis, Herb Vigran

♦ ❖ ♦

Show: **The Stope of Death Matter**
Show Date: **10/2/1960**
Company: **Tri-Western Life Insurance Company**
Agent: **Hal Barker**
Exp. Acct: **$248.75**

Synopsis: Hal Barker calls Johnny from Reno, Nevada. Hal wants Johnny to come out. A client, Walter Bisbee has died in a mining accident in Virginia City, but Hal does not think it was an accident. Hal is convinced that Walter Bisbee was murdered, and he knows who did it and why. Come on out and get the details.

Johnny flies to Los Angeles and then to Reno, Nevada. Hal meets Johnny and drives him to Virginia City, Nevada, the largest of the old mining towns of the Comstock Lode.

Hal tells Johnny that due to modern mining methods, Bisbee and his partners are pretty well off. Bill Hargrave was his partner and they have a partnership policy for $35,000, double indemnity. The accident happened in the old Catterwall #2 mine.

Walter was exploring a stope in the mine while Bill had gone to Carson City for supplies. When he returned, Bill said he discovered that the stope ceiling had collapsed. Hal had talked to a state geologist who knew the mine, and he told him that there was no way that the mine should have collapsed, unless someone helped it. That is the kind of bad luck Bisbee and Hargrave have been having lately, and the insurance would have come in handy. And, the geologist found signs of a charge of nitro.

The police are not holding Hargrave because without Bisbee's body, there is no proof that he is dead. Hargrave has witnesses that he was in Carson City. When they arrive at the mine, Hargrave is waving at something. Hal and Johnny go to the mine where Hargrave tells them that he had gone down there and found Bisbee. But he was murdered!

Johnny recounts how Hargrave had been the prime suspect, and how he had rigged a hoist over an air shaft and lowered himself into the mine to find Bisbee's body. Hargrave is upset that his partner had been killed over a new find.

Johnny agrees to go down with the sheriff to recover the body. Hargrave tells them that Bisbee would have wanted to be buried in the mine, and all the gold in the world cannot change that.

Hargrave recounts how they worked together to recover gold from a number of mines. Without his partner, Hargrave says he is finished and does not want to see another mine. Hargrave tells the sheriff to leave Bisbee there and bury him in the mine.

Johnny enters the mine with the sheriff. Johnny notes that the marks on Bisbee's face indicate he was knocked down and kicked to death with a hob nail boot. They note the right-foot mark of the man who kicked him. The sheriff notes that Bisbee is too big to get through the air shaft, so he will have to stay down there.

Johnny notes that there are marks from a new pair of boots and Johnny wonders if Bisbee was killed and then the mine was blasted. Johnny thinks a timer might have been used to set off the explosion while Bill was in town. The sheriff is convinced that Bill did not kill Walter, but Johnny is not convinced.

Johnny drives to Bill's shack with Hal, and Johnny wonders if they had had a falling out, what with separate quarters. Johnny tells Hal to bring the sheriff back to Bill's place.

Johnny has an idea and tells Hal to have the sheriff take a good look at the footprint in the mine. Bill is not home, so Johnny opens the door with a pocketknife and looks for a pair of shoes and something else.

On the wall is an old lever action .30-30 rifle commonly found in the west. Johnny takes the gun down and puts it on the bed just as Bill comes back. Johnny tells him that he is looking at the habits of a murdered man, and his partner.

Johnny asks what kind of timer Bill used. Too bad the stope did not fill up completely. You found a way in, and you told us that Walter had been killed.

Johnny tells Bill of the lone footprint and the new boot marks. The one footprint is where you stood on your right foot and kicked him with your left. And now I find a rifle with a shiny spot on the right-hand side of the stock caused by a left-handed man. Bill grabs the rifle and tells Johnny that he killed Walter. Johnny tells him that he had unloaded the gun, and when Bill checks the gun Johnny slugs him. "Phew, I guess I really should have thought to take the shells out of that thing."

"So maybe there were dozens of left-handed men around Virginia City, and who knows maybe there were some right-handed men who kick with their left foot. Bill just didn't happen to think of that when he confessed to killing him."

Notes:
- This program contains a commercial from CBS about the need for election campaign contributions, and a commercial for Ex-Lax.
- This program is probably one of the most commonly misspelled titles. It is usually called *The Stroke of Death* rather than *The Stope of Death*. A stope is defined as a step-like excavation caused by the removal of ore. Incidentally, the term stope is also used in *The Deep Down Matter*.
- The announcer is John Wald.

Producer:	Jack Johnstone	Writer:	Jack Johnstone
Cast:	Hershel Bernardi, Russell Thorson, Forrest Lewis		

♦ ❖ ♦

Show:	The Recompense Matter
Show Date:	10/9/1960
Company:	Tri-Sate Life & Casualty Company
Agent:	Don Boomhauer
Exp. Acct:	$0.00

Synopsis: Don Boomhauer calls Johnny from Sarasota. Don tells Johnny that Earle Poorman has moved to California bag-and-baggage, so Don is still running the office. Don does not have a real problem, but a client, Bill Trasker the fishing guide, is dying. The insurance is negligible, only $2,500. Bill is in a coma and keeps asking for Johnny when he wakes up. He keeps trying to give a clue to a murder. Johnny is on his way.

Johnny flies to Sarasota, Florida where Don meets him at the airport and drives towards Sarasota. According to Doc Crutcher, nothing short of a miracle will cure Bill. The insurance will be enough to bury Bill and pay his bills. Bill was asking for Johnny and was very vague and only mentioned Gerald or Gerry. Doc Crutcher is waiting for Johnny at Bill's shack.

At the shack, Johnny learns that Doc has given Bill the last of seven doses of a new miracle drug. Inside Bill is awake and glad to see Johnny. Bill tells Johnny that it is too late now. Bill tells Johnny to tell the police that he did it, and he mentions Gerald Thornley and then tells Johnny that he did it again.

Bill passes out, but Doc tells Johnny that Bill seems to be stronger. Doc calls for an ambulance and Don agrees, so they can investigate the confession murder and try Bill for it.

Johnny puts Bill in Don's car and drives him to the hospital. Later Don tells Johnny that something is wrong in wanting to cure Bill so that he can be investigated for murder. Don wants Johnny to investigate what Bill said, and Johnny tells him he will try. Later Doc calls and tells them to keep their fingers crossed.

Barney Phillips calls and Johnny asks if he knows Gerald Thornley, and that they will investigate what Bill had told them. Phillips tells Johnny that Bill was the nicest man you could ever meet. He was always doing things for others since he got there seven years ago, even though he did not have much. Johnny tells Don that he wants no part of this, but Don convinces him to continue.

Johnny borrows a car and drives to Bill's shack to search for Bill's past. All of Bill's clothes have New York labels. Johnny drives to the airport in Tampa and wires Ripley Keener, a friend on the New York Times and then flies to New York City.

Rip picks up Johnny at the airport and tells him that he had written a story on Thornley. He was a crooked promoter who disappeared seven years ago. The police are convinced that he was murdered. Rip tells Johnny to nail the old guy for murder.

Rip tells Johnny that Thornley made millions and took money from poor people and left them hungry. Every deal was legal at the time, but he caused a lot of real estate laws to be rewritten. The feature that Rip wrote was about how he had left enough money to pay back all the people he had stolen from.

Johnny tells Rip he may get a Pulitzer Prize yet. Johnny calls Randy Singer and then goes to his office and gets a set of fingerprints for Thornley. Johnny has a hunch as he goes back to Tampa.

Johnny goes to the hospital where Bill is improving. Johnny takes Bill's fingerprints, and then Bill tells Johnny his story. At police headquarters, a technician compares the prints, and they are identical, Bill Trasker is Gerald Thornley.

Johnny tells the chief that the dirty real estate tactics did not bother Bill until he came down with kidney problems. Then Thornley realized that he would die one of the most hated men in the world. Giving back the money was not enough, so he arranged his own disappearance to make it look like murder so he could get away and do good for people.

Johnny tells Lt. Phillips that Bill had said "no murder", and that he "did not do it". Now we know what he did. Johnny tells Phillips that Thornley is legally dead, so it is Bill Trasker who is in the hospital.

"After sticking around for a few days to make sure that old Bill's recovery would be complete, well I changed my mind about giving Rip Keener the material for a feature, let him wonder about it. Expense account total, including the trip back to Hartford, $200 and uh, no Don, forget it, just forget it."

Notes:
- This is an AFRTS program that contains a story about Cyrus W. Field, who laid the first Atlantic cable, and a story about the 14th amendment.
- The announcer is John Wald.

Producer:	Jack Johnstone	Writer:	Jack Johnstone
Cast:	Russell Thorson, Bartlett Robinson, Parley Baer, Barney Phillips, Richard Crenna, Herb Vigran		

♦ ❖ ♦

Show: **The Twins of Tahoe Matter**
Show Date: **10/16/1960**
Company: **International Life & Casualty Insurance Company**
Agent: **Michael J. Kendry**
Exp. Acct: **$416.00**

Synopsis: Michael J. Kendry calls Johnny from Lake Tahoe. He is at the Seven Pines Lodge in Al Tahoe. Johnny comments on the great fishing in the lake, and Kendry tells Johnny that fishing is just what he might be doing, fishing for the body of Marvin W. Smedley. Huh?

Johnny flies to San Francisco and rents a car to drive to Lake Tahoe, Nevada along Route 50, which goes through a series of old mining towns. Johnny comments on the beauty of Lake Tahoe and its clear blue waters dotted with boats and bathers. Johnny also comments on the bawdy gambling places on the Nevada side of the lake.

At the Seven Pines Lodge, Johnny meets Kendry. Johnny gets a room next to Kendry and goes to talk to him in his cabin. Johnny is told that Smedley was a wealthy client. Johnny had passed a small stone house on the way in, and that is where Smedley lived with a housekeeper, Mrs. Turner, and twin nephews.

Mrs. Turner woke up this morning to the sound of a shot. She went to see if the twins had heard it but they were not there. She remembered that Tracy had said he would be out gambling all night, and Alfred was at a house party at the upper end of the lake. She did not want to awaken old Mr. Smedley, so she decided it was a backfire and went to bed.

In the morning, she found the library a mess, and the safe opened. She told the police that Smedley used to get up at night and count his money in there. He did not trust the banks and kept all his money in the safe. The police were called and they found a set of footprints going down to the lake and signs of a body being dragged to the lake. Kendry is sure that it was one of the twins, as they had been mooching off Smedley for years. Both of the boys are in jail, but they have airtight alibis.

Johnny examines the walkway down to the lake and talks to Sgt. Bill Corter. The footprints were made from new shoes, but both of the boys dressed alike to cover up for each other. They were always mischief-makers and always swore that it was the other when they got into trouble.

The police never knew which one to arrest and the boys always threatened to sue for false arrest. The uncle would always end up paying a fine to get the boys out of jail. Corter tells Johnny that they have found the shoes, in the boy's shared closet.

Johnny talks to May Turner, the housekeeper who is very upset. She tells Johnny that she knew something like this would happen. Everyone knew Smedley kept all his money in the safe. Johnny tells Corter that anyone could be a suspect. Mrs. Turner tells Johnny that she had warned Smedley about the boys, now one of them has gone and killed him.

Johnny goes to the jail to talk to the twins, and they impress Johnny as high-spirited kids who are bored. They tell Johnny that it was good that their uncle died, as he had a lung condition and would not live too much longer.

The boys tell Johnny that their uncle had toiled as a prospector, and did not want them to work, and told them that he was leaving them his insurance. One of them asks Johnny if he has proof that their uncle was killed. Alfred tells Johnny to look at the old prospectors who came back for handouts if he wants suspects.

Johnny goes to a local casino, and the manager tells Johnny that one of the twins was there all night at the craps table. He watches them so they do not pull tricks on the dealers, but he does not know which one was there. Johnny goes to the house where the party was held, and a girl tells Johnny that the party broke up around nine this morning, and one of the twins was there all night.

Both of the twins have alibis that are hard to break, but one of them must have killed their uncle, but something one of them said gives Johnny a hunch.

Johnny calls Smedley's lawyer, Mr. Kenneth McMannis. Johnny visits him and asks one question about the will that gives Johnny a fresh start.

Johnny calls Sgt. Corter and he tells Johnny that they have found the body about one hundred fifty feet out and hung up on a rock in twenty feet of water. There is a bullet hole in his head, but they will never find the gun. Johnny tells him that he is going to play a little bluff.

Back at the house Mrs. Turner is told that Smedley is in the morgue. Johnny tells her that he has spoken with the lawyer, and that all the insurance goes to the twins. Johnny tells her that the rest of the estate goes to her, for her service. That was her motive.

Johnny tells her that the gun and the body were found in the lake and asks Mrs. Turner to give him a set of her fingerprints. She tells Johnny that half of her life she took care of him and he gave her nothing. She hated the boys but no one could have put it on them. He gave them all his money, so there was nothing left for her. "What's left for you now, Mrs. Turner?"

"Oh sure, from here on in it's up to the courts, and no doubt the whole estate will go to the twins. You know something? I hate this kind of a case. It leaves a bad taste in my mouth."

Notes:
- This program contains commercials for reducing crime and delinquency by taking the family to religious services, CBS where stars shine during the daytime, and have been named by their celestial forebears. Those named are Arthur Godfrey, Art Linkletter, Bing Crosby, Rose Mary Clooney, Gary Moore and Durward Kirby. You won't find them in your book of the planets and stars. But no compendium of show business luminaries would be complete without them. Monday through Friday, your radio set is your personal telescope on this star-studded display, on your CBS Radio station, and a commercial for Ex-lax.
- Tom Hanley and Bill James are credited in the cast, but the script lists Gus Bayz instead of Tom James.
- The announcer is John Wald.

Producer:	Jack Johnstone	Writer:	Jack Johnstone
Cast:	Virginia Gregg, Jeanne Tatum, Paul Dubov, Forrest Lewis, Sam Edwards, Herb Ellis, Tom Hanley, Bill James		

◆ ❖ ◆

Show: The Unworthy Kin Matter
Show Date: 10/23/1960
Company: Tri Western Life Insurance
Agent: Frank Harmon
Exp. Acct: $500.00

Synopsis: Frank Harmon calls Johnny and asks where he has been. Jack Price in Corpus Christi has been trying to get hold of Johnny for several days. Jack has a big problem, and now it looks like Johnny has to prevent a murder.

Johnny is ready for a rest after the last case, but a job is a job. Johnny cabs to Frank's office where Frank is waiting for Jean Unworthy to arrive.

Johnny is told that five years ago, Eric Bean killed a prominent businessman in Ypsilanti, Michigan. Johnny remembers that it was a senseless murder because the victim did not give Bean a few dollars. Johnny was in on the case and was there during the trial when Bean promised he would get out and kill everyone involved in sending him to jail.

Frank tells Johnny that Bean has escaped, and over the past five days Bean has killed four of the people he promised to kill. The police have no idea where he is, or when he will hit next. Another victim is Albert Unworthy, who lives in Corpus Christi, and is insured for half a million dollars.

Frank tells Johnny that the whole case has been dumped in his lap. Jean is demanding that Johnny be made a bodyguard to her father. Johnny realizes that by putting two people together, Bean can finish off his threats. Besides Johnny has to go to New York in the morning.

Johnny does not want to be a bodyguard and turns the job down, until a beautiful Jean Unworthy enters the room. Boing! Johnny is totally taken by Jean and can only say "wow!" Johnny tells Jean that he must be in New York tomorrow, but that is no problem because she has an appointment in New York tomorrow too. They can leave tonight and stay at the Pierre and have a wonderful time.

Johnny flies to New York City and promises himself to behave and gets a room at the Gotham Hotel. Dinner was over fifty bucks and the clubs were $130. The next day Johnny sees a newspaper and calls Frank Harmon to complain about the story of Johnny going to Corpus Christi. Frank tells Johnny that it was his idea to flush out Eric Bean.

Johnny flies to Corpus Christi, Texas and would almost be ready to marry Jean if she asked. Doug Johnstone meets Johnny in the airport, and the story is all over the papers. Doug knows Jean's father and wants Johnny to put Jean in a cab so they can talk. Jean agrees and takes a cab home.

In his office, Doug tells Johnny that Mr. Unworthy is loaded, in spite of Jean's efforts to spend it. There are rumblings that her father is getting ready to cut her off. The phone rings and Jean is on the phone and tells Johnny that Eric is in the house. There are two shots and Jean cries "You killed him!".

Johnny rushes to the house and finds Mr. Unworthy dead, with three bullet holes in his temple. Jean tells Johnny that it was terrible and she is very upset. She tells Johnny that Mr. Unworthy had been so nice to her from the day he adopted her.

She was alone when the man came in. He was short and heavyset with thick curly hair. The description is that of Eric Bean. She tells Johnny that she has never seen Bean before. He came in and knocked her down and shot her father. Doug calls the police and the family doctor.

After getting a statement, the doctor gives Jean a sedative. Before going out Jean tells Johnny that now he is in danger. Johnny and Doug go back to his office. Johnny uses the phone to call the police in Ypsilanti and talks to Sgt. Brauer.

Brauer tells Johnny that Bean has set a pattern of killing people in the area. Johnny tells Doug about how her father had gotten upset about her spending, and the too perfect description of Bean. Johnny realizes that he heard two shots on the phone, but there were three in the body.

Johnny borrows a car and goes to Jean's house. Johnny tells Jean that he has found the murderer and wants to know what she did with the gun. She tells Johnny that it is in a fishpond under the library window. "Not a chance for me?" she asks. "Not a chance" replies Johnny.

"And I learned about women from her. Following Eric Bean's pattern, the police in Michigan were able to pick him up in less than two weeks, before he could kill again."

Notes:
- This program includes a station identification for WROW in Albany, New York at the beginning and end.
- This program contains commercials for Pepsi, *Art Linkletter's House Party* and Ex-Lax.
- The announcer is John Wald.

Producer:	Jack Johnstone Writer: Jack Johnstone
Cast:	Virginia Gregg, Richard Crenna, Frank Gerstle, Russell Thorson, Stacy Harris, James McCallion, Bill James, Gus Bayz

◆ ❖ ◆

Show:	**The What Goes Matter**
Show Date:	**10/30/1960**
Company:	**Tri-State Life & Casualty Insurance Company**
Agent:	**Earle Poorman**
Exp. Acct:	**$368.50**

Synopsis: Earle Poorman calls Johnny and one of Earle's important clients is in trouble, but he does not know who, what, when, where or why. Earle wants Johnny to come on down. "Okay baby, you're paying for it."

Johnny flies to Los Angeles, California on a jet in a little over five hours. At the terminal, Johnny bumps into a man in the walkway. He apologizes and recognizes Johnny and wants to talk. He falls against Johnny again and tells Johnny that he will talk later and walks away.

Earle meets Johnny and he tells Earle that he was jostled and checks to make sure he still has his wallet. Earle tells Johnny that he loves it here and lives on Bundy Drive.

Earle tells Johnny that he got a phone call from a client who has a policy for a third of a million. Earle gives Johnny a cigarette and tells him that the man had told Earle to send for Johnny or they would lose him. Johnny tells Earle that this case makes no sense, then again there was the man in the airport. Earle asks Johnny "What goes?"

Johnny describes Earle and Mike's new house in Westwood, and the good company of the Poormans. Johnny wonders if Earle made up the whole thing. Maybe the man who bumped Johnny was the man, but why did he shy away when he saw Earle. Mike suggests that maybe the man was out to get a client and wanted to get rid of Johnny.

The phone rings, and the caller asks for Johnny. The caller asks if he really is Johnny Dollar and he admits being the man who bumped into Johnny at the airport, and who had called Earle. The caller mentions a connection with something, and when he bumped into Johnny, haven't you looked in your (click).

Johnny tells Earle that the caller was the man from the airport, and the phone sounded like the wires were cut. Johnny goes to get his cigarettes from his topcoat, but Earle gives him one of his. Johnny wonders if the phone line was cut.

Johnny and Earle decide to go to the office and look through the files. Johnny grabs his coat and they leave. The files are searched and the list of large policies comes to a dozen names that have to be called.

Johnny muses that he should have realized he had been carrying the clue all the way from the airport, and if he had stopped bumming cigarettes. Yeah, figure that one out.

Johnny calls the Branfords and Earle tells Johnny that they are in Florida. The last name on the list is Bernard Sealegger. "Barney the Bum", "Barney the Butcher", alias "Sealegs Brown" and a bunch of other names exclaims Earle. Earle tells Johnny that Barney is wanted by the police for narcotics running. If he is the man, let him get bumped off! The policy is only six months old, and Earle decides that they must find him.

Johnny calls Lt. Jim Spaulding of the Los Angeles police. Spaulding tells Johnny that Barney had tried to call him as well, because he is helping the police. Earle reaches for a cigarette in Johnny's coat and finds a card with an address on Bundy Drive, not too far from where Earle lives. So, Barney had slipped the card into his pocket when he bumped into Johnny at the airport.

Johnny takes Earle's car and drives to the house and knocks at the door. Johnny notices a utility service box and when he goes to look at it, a gun gets put into his back. The man takes Johnny's gun and hits Johnny when he gets smart with him. He takes Johnny to a window to see what Johnny will get after the stoolie is dead.

In the window is a small air conditioner pumping air into the room with a gas bottle attached. The room is being filled with gas while Barney sleeps. Johnny struggles with the man and the gun goes off. The man starts to shoot Johnny with his own gun when Spaulding arrives.

"Yeah, Barney was still alive, but barely, which is more than you can say for his would-be assassin. One of the lieutenant's bullets had caught him square in the head. So, that is that."

Notes:
- This program includes a station identification for WROW in Albany, New York at the beginning and the end.
- This program contains commercials for Sylvania Blue Dot flash bulbs to

- be used at Halloween, US Savings bonds and the various savings plans, and Ex-Lax.
- Bundy was the maiden name of Jack Johnstone's wife.
- The announcer is John Wald.

Producer:	Jack Johnstone	Writer:	Jack Johnstone
Cast:	Virginia Gregg, Vic Perrin, Forrest Lewis, Frank Gerstle, Chester Stratton		

◆ ❖ ◆

Show:	**The Super Salesman Matter**
Show Date:	**11/6/1960**
Company:	**Universal Adjustment Bureau**
Agent:	**Pat McCracken**
Exp. Acct:	**$189.95**

Synopsis: Pat McCracken calls Johnny, who answers "Greetings master". Pat can only tell Johnny that the Rochemonte necklace is missing. The necklace is insured for $321,400, and Johnny is on his way!

Johnny cabs to Pat's office where he tells Johnny that the necklace was part of a collection of crown jewels. Mrs. Rochemonte, who is a wealthy widow living in Hartford, Connecticut bought the necklace. She puts the necklace in a bank vault whenever she travels, otherwise she keeps the necklace in a safe in her home, to which she is the only one with the combination, and no one has broken into it.

A couple days ago, she gave the necklace to a jeweler, Clayton Parker, to have it cleaned. Parker called on her in the middle of the night, barged in on her and gave her the necklace and told her it was paste. She then gave it to Wilson Brothers who told her that Parker was right.

Pat tells Johnny about a similar case in 1956 in Chicago, another in 1959 in Philadelphia, and in each case the jeweler who discovered the switch meets the description of Parker. His shop has not been searched for legal reasons.

Pat tells Johnny that Parker's shop does not have a burglar alarm nor one on the safe, and there is a dark alley in the rear. Pat is not asking Johnny to do anything illegal mind you. But, if someone unknown to us were to find the necklace in the shop muses Pat. "What did you say your name was?" asks Johnny. "I didn't. And yours?" asks Pat. "What's it to you." responds Johnny. "Okay?" "Okay."

Johnny gives $100 to a friend named "Fingers", and that night Johnny gets into Parker's shop where he searches the store and finds nothing while Fingers opens the safe. Fingers leaves, and as Johnny exits the window he is slugged while the assailant calls for the police.

Johnny wakes up and leaves before the police arrive and cabs home. The next day Johnny is ready to call Pat and drop the case but decides to think about the case. There are only two people who could have substituted the fake jewels, Mrs. Rochemonte or Parker. Johnny decides to go to Parker's home to search there.

Johnny gets a wild idea and gets some business cards printed and buys a tank style vacuum cleaner and an old suitcase. Johnny drives to the Parker house and knocks at the door, posing as a door-to-door salesman.

Mrs. Gloria Parker answers and Johnny tells her he is responding to a coupon she sent in, and gives her his card, "James Dakin, Sales Engineer". Gloria comments on Johnny's job selling and Johnny tells Gloria that she is much more attractive than other women he meets at the door. She tells Johnny that she did not send in a coupon, and Johnny tells her he is only there for the free demonstration.

Johnny tells her that he will clean the whole house for her as things have been tough this week. Gloria relents and lets Johnny in. Johnny unpacks and starts cleaning the house, regretting he did not read the instructions first. Johnny leaves the study for last.

Gloria leaves to go fix some drinks and Johnny runs for the desk. In the third drawer of the desk Johnny finds the Rochemonte necklace. The phone on the desk rings and Johnny closes the drawer. Gloria comes back into the study with a gun instead of the drinks.

Gloria tells Johnny that he should have been smarter. Her husband had just called, and he had recognized Johnny. Clayton did not call the police because he did not want them poking around.

Johnny tells her that he has proof that her husband has stolen the necklace, but she sees that the desk is still locked, and tells Johnny he does not. Clayton comes in and Johnny tells him that he was welcomed into the house by Gloria.

Johnny tells him to call in the police, and he tells Johnny that he does not want them involved. Clayton admits to exchanging the jewels and opens the desk, but the jewels are gone. Johnny is searched but he does not have the necklace.

Clayton searches the house and makes Johnny strip to his shorts. The police come in with Pat McCracken and Clayton is shot. Pat tells Johnny the he was worried because Johnny did not call in, and he had seen Parker rush from his office, so it was obvious. "Do you want to see the necklace, somewhere inside this vacuum cleaner I didn't sell?"

"Parker is dead. His wife yammered all over the place in hopes of getting off easy. Optimist. So, that's that. And don't forget my commission on over $320,000."

Notes:
- This program contains commercials for the dangers of forest fires caused by careless fires, and the accuracy of CBS news.
- Cast Information from the KNX Collection at the Thousand Oaks Library.
- The announcer is John Wald.

Producer: Jack Johnstone   Writer: Jack Johnstone
Cast: Lawrence Dobkin, Russell Thorson, Virginia Gregg

Show:	**The Bad One Matter**
Show Date:	**11/13/1960**
Company:	**Mono Guarantee Insurance Company**
Agent:	**Culpepper Walker**
Exp. Acct:	**$231.20**

Synopsis: Pat McCracken calls and asks Johnny how old he is. "Just exactly thirty, uh, why?" asks Johnny. Pat tells Johnny that he is young enough to remember how he felt when he was a young man. Pat wonders if Johnny ever got into any real trouble, and Johnny tells him that he was no mama's boy. If Johnny had a police-record, he would be just right for this case. Pat wants Johnny to go out and see Culpepper Walker in Little Rock. He is having problems with a kid, just a kid. And be sure to take along a pair of brass knuckles, a length of chain and maybe a switchblade knife. That kind, "a real bad one".

Johnny flies to Little Rock, Arkansas and arrives at 8:50 p.m. and Johnny comments on the changes in Little Rock since it was founded in 1772 and the surrounding countryside of well-tended farms.

Johnny meets with Walker the next morning and he tells Johnny all about Pete Maguire, who lives in an area outside of town called Milltown. Pete is eighteen or nineteen and works in a cotton mill. He is the only one who knows who killed Mr. Ambrose Briarly who was insured for $50,000.

Briarly was driving with the payroll for a cotton mill. He had some car trouble, and it was dark before he got back on the road. His car was run off the road and someone took the $17,000 payroll. The skid marks on the road show just how it happened.

The Maguire boy was caught running away from the scene by the police chief. The chief talked to Maguire and got nothing. The partners of the cotton mill are the ones who insisted that Johnny be brought out to investigate.

Johnny rents a car and drives to Milltown. The police chief tells Johnny that he was there just after it happened. The bank had told him about Briarly's car trouble and he decided to make sure that the money got to the mill OK. When he got to the car, he saw another car driving away, and Pete trying to get his motorcycle started.

The chief grabbed Pete, who told him he should have chased the other car. The chief tells Johnny that you could still see the tracks on the rainy road where the other car had shoved Briarly's car off the road. He could not read the tracks of the car, but he could read the marks from Pete's motorcycle.

The doc came along and Mr. Briarly said over and over that" you saw it, you tell 'em boy who did it." before he died. Pete is a no-good kid and had been a troublemaker all his life. He is nothing but trouble. He is a cop hater, just like his old man who I had to kill one night in a robbery. The kid needs to go to the pen.

The public defender, Percy Van Ashworthy Tetwiler got the judge to release Pete, but the chief will get him if he runs out. The chief tells Johnny that he will not retire with that kid running loose, him with no more money than when he started by walking a beat.

Johnny visits Percy Van Ashworthy "Ted" Tetwiler who tells Johnny that Pete has had the odds against him since he was born. He was a stupid little runt and the other kids bullied him and left him to get caught for their mischief. The chief never let up on him either, so he hates the cops. Ted got him released hoping he would open up to him.

Ted sees Pete coming in and Johnny asks Ted to help him. Johnny asks Ted to tell Pete that Johnny is a troublemaker he is trying to get out of town. Pete comes in and Johnny puts on an act for Pete, who wants to talk.

Pete tells Ted that the police are following him and he knows that they are trying to trick him. Ted asks Pete to tell him what he knows, but Pete keeps quiet. Pete leaves and Johnny follows him.

Johnny asks if Pete wants to learn how to shake a tail from an expert, and Johnny asks Pete if he can help him learn the ropes around town. Pete agrees to meet Johnny on seven-mile road at a railroad crossing. Johnny is to walk down the gully to a tool shack by the railroad.

Johnny is tailed by the police and meets Pete an hour later. Inside the shack Pete tells Johnny, "the big eye", that he knows who he is, and Johnny tells him that the insurance company paid him to come, not the law. Pete admires Johnny and figures he can help him.

Pete tells Johnny that the chief runs the town. Pete only thinks he knows who killed Briarly. The only car he saw was a police car coming from the direction of the mill. Pete tells Johnny that the chief is trying to trick him so he will run away and the chief can kill him.

Johnny remembers how the chief had Ted release him and how the chief had to retire with no money and how the payroll would help out. Sure!

Johnny smells kerosene and then the locked door starts burning. Johnny pulls the pins from the inside hinges, and the chief is outside. He tells Johnny that he saw the shack on fire, but Johnny tells him he set it on fire to cover up the killing of Briarly. The chief shoots at Pete and Johnny slugs him. Johnny gets the chief to agree to sign a confession.

"Yeah, pretty smart using that poor ignorant kid as a means to keep any suspicion away from himself. But, believe me, not smart enough."

Notes:
- This program includes a station identification for WROW in Albany, New York at the end.
- The announcer is John Wald.

Producer:	Jack Johnstone	**Writer:**	Jack Johnstone
Cast:	Lawrence Dobkin, James McCallion, Forrest Lewis, Russell Thorson, Sam Edwards		

Show:	**The Double Deal Matter**
Show Date:	**11/20/1960**
Company:	**Philadelphia Mutual Liability & Casualty Company**
Agent:	**Harry Branson**
Exp. Acct:	**$2,044.45**

Synopsis: The opening of this program is missing.

Johnny travels to Philadelphia, Pennsylvania and to the Eastern Trust offices on Walnut Street. Ted Plainer tells Johnny that the case is about Michael Jonathan O'Banyon, known as "Mickey the Hood".

He was an old rumrunner and gunrunner and who knows what else back in the twenties. After being released on parole, Mickey opened a small drug import company, and Bruce Terwilliger the previous agent sold him half a million coverage on his business and a quarter million on his life. The beneficiary is Mary "Toodles" Baker, a cheap stripper. Ted wants to take him off the books but the company will not cancel the policies without proof.

Johnny tells Ted that it is a police matter, but Ted tells Johnny that the police cannot find anything on him. Ted is sure that something is going on, but Johnny does not want to try to frame Mickey. Call me when he does something illegal. Ted gets a phone call and the caller wants to talk to Johnny.

On the phone is Harry Branson from Philadelphia Mutual Liability & Casualty Company. Something terrible has happened, and he must see John right away. The Canary diamonds have been stolen again. Johnny tells Ted that Harry will pay him a lot of money for his case. Wouldn't it be nice if I could tie these two cases together? But fat chance.

Johnny goes to see Harry who tells him that the Canary diamonds have been stolen. When Johnny brought the diamonds back from Paris they got so much publicity that a client, Mrs. Arthur Pierpont Galloway just had to buy them. She bought them and insured them with Harry for $515,000.

She got a call from a magazine that wanted to take pictures of the diamonds there in her home. She thought the maid and chauffeur would be enough protection, but when the man came he tricked her into being alone with him and he walked off with the diamonds. The description is somewhat confused and the police think that they might know who the man was. Lt. Bernard Barry is in charge of the case, and Johnny wants to go see the police first. Harry is flustered that Johnny is acting so cool, but Johnny is just thinking of his commission.

Johnny goes to see his friend Lt. Barry who tells him that the description is of a man who was wearing enough makeup for a whole chorus line. The chauffeur noticed that the man was trying to cover up a scar on his face by his left eye. Johnny thinks it might be "Mickey the Hood", and the police agree and have been tailing him, but they have found nothing, and he has an alibi.

Johnny remembers that with his importing business he must ship things out, but Barry tells him that all his shipments are being searched. Johnny remembers that the diamonds were previously smuggled out in cans of fruit. The diamonds are so unique that he would have to get them out of the country. Johnny has no idea how he can trip up Mickey.

Johnny goes to the O'Banyon Drug Imports store and only Mickey is there. Johnny poses as "Mr. Russell", a storeowner from the south looking for exotic drugs and medicines. Johnny tells him that he had seen his ad in the phone book.

A woman walks in that Mickey recognizes as Mrs. Peterson. He has the nerve pills for her, and they are free. She hopes that she can swallow the huge pills, and Mickey tells her to chew them and only take one a day. She thanks him and promises to send a postcard from Hong Kong.

Johnny asks if Mickey is always so nice to his customers. Mickey recognizes his voice from the radio, Johnny Dollar! Mickey should have realized it when Johnny mentioned a non-existent ad in the phone book. Mickey tells Johnny that he had nothing to do with diamonds and no one can prove it. So, leave me alone, or else.

Johnny starts to add things up in the store and remembers Mickey's oriental contacts, having met Mrs. Peterson in a travel office, and the large bottle of pills he had made up. Would he be there to collect the remaining pills when she got to Hong Kong? Mickey tells Johnny he is smart enough to steal the diamonds, but he did not do it. Johnny realizes he should have followed Mrs. Peterson.

Johnny calls all the travel companies in Philadelphia until he finds the one that arranged Mrs. Peterson's trip, and they tell Johnny that she is in the Belleview Stratford hotel. Johnny goes to the hotel and tells Mrs. Peterson that he needs the pills she got from the store. She gets upset and Johnny tells her to take her pills as he gets his credentials out.

Johnny empties the bottle and Mrs. Peterson bites into a pill and then spits out a diamond into his hand. What a beautiful stunt! Johnny asks Mrs. Peterson how she would like a couple thousand dollars of extra spending money on the trip? All she has to do is go to the police and explain where she got the pills.

"Proof? It was all Lt. Berry needed. The Canary diamonds are home again, and that will save Philly Mutual from having to pay off a big claim. And Eastern Trust and Insurance has plenty of reasons to drop O'Banyon as a client. After all, he ought to be out of circulation for a long, long time."

Notes:
- The Canary diamonds were mentioned twice, once in *The Canned Canary Matter*, and here in *The Double Deal Matter*.
- This program contains commercials for vacuum cleaned Commander cigarettes, Sylvania Blue Dot flashbulbs to be used at Thanksgiving and Ex-Lax.
- The announcer is John Wald.

Producer: Jack Johnstone   Writer: Jack Johnstone
Cast: Virginia Gregg, Chester Stratton, Harry Bartell,
             Barney Phillips, Paul Frees

Show:	**The Empty Threat Matter**
Show Date:	**11/27/1960**
Company:	**Floyds of England**
Agent:	**George Reed**
Exp. Acct:	**$2,561.00**

Synopsis: George Reed calls, and Johnny asks how dear old Floyds of England is these days. George tells Johnny that if he read the Wall Street Journal he would see that the leading insurance companies are doing quite well and Floyds is among the leaders. Johnny suggests that George has gotten a big fat raise and wants to take Johnny out for dinner tonight. George tells Johnny that he will get more than a free dinner out of this one. George has an unusual problem. George knows that Johnny does not like acting as a bodyguard, but this case is different. Come on over to my office.

Johnny cabs to George's office where George tells him that Charles Stockerly is a retired attorney. He has no regular address. He was highly successful, married and adopted two kids and lived the good life. His wife died two years ago, and he has a worthless hateful son to bother him. Stockerly has a lot of insurance, which is why he called George about the threats on his life. The threats are real, which is why he has been running away. Right now, he is in Tahiti, in the town of Papeete. Johnny does not want this job, but will take it on, because all his life he has dreamed of seeing Tahiti.

Johnny flies to New York and then to Fiji and then to Viti Levu. Then Johnny flies to Suva, a tropical paradise with attractive people. Then another flight to Papeete, Tahiti. It is an ideal place to get away from things, and Johnny can really relax there. Johnny finds Mr. Stockerly in a shack near the hotel, or rather what was left of him.

In the beach-front shack, Johnny meets Dr. Dentley. Mr. Stockerly looks as though he had been beaten. The doctor tells Johnny that Stockerly was collecting flowers on a nearby mountain and had been followed. Stockerly thinks that he was shoved by someone and fell sixty feet through the brush. Stockerly would have left the island if he were not sedated and lives in a constant state of fear.

Johnny decides to spend the night in the cabin to guard Stockerly. Johnny tells the doctor about his job, and the doctor arranges to have some food brought to Johnny. That night every sound wakes Johnny up. At five thirty, Stockerly wakes up and tells Johnny that they must leave.

On the flight, Stockerly tells Johnny that the death of his wife really upset him and he would have lost his mind, had it not been for his daughter Joyce. His son Andrew had been given too much and has never done a day's work in his life. He also does not like his sister. Joyce supports herself and is happily married.

Stockerly tells Johnny that the threats must have come from Harry Linker, a man he had sent to prison. Linker called him and threatened him before a trip to Europe, and in Paris he called again and Stockerly was almost run down by an American car. In London, Stockerly was almost murdered. In Jakarta, more threats and a poisonous reptile was found in his trunk, and scorpions in a briefcase in Stockholm. Stockerly had run and run, but Linker keeps following him.

Johnny tries to explain it as coincidence and promises to stay awake and protect him. Sure, it was coincidence when they were almost hit by a baggage truck in San Francisco.

In Hartford, Johnny puts Stockerly in his apartment. Stockerly has pulled down the shades, and when Johnny raises one of them, a bullet breaks the window. Another bullet enters the room, and Johnny thinks Stockerly might have a point.

Johnny digs a slug out of the wall and calls Dr. Bill Peters and tells him to come to the apartment, with a gun. Bill arrives, quiets Stockerly's nerves and agrees to stick around. Bill is sure that Stockerly will kill himself if the threats go much farther.

Johnny goes to police headquarters and they tell Johnny that Linker has changed and is running a hardware store. Johnny goes to the store and Linker convinces Johnny that he is sincere.

Johnny calls on Stockerly's daughter, and she is upset about the situation and wants to bring her father there. Johnny gets a call and Bill Peters tells Johnny that he got a phone call and Stockerly took it. He got white as a sheet and started yelling, "No, no, you will never get me!" and lunged for the window. Bill gave him a shot and he is OK now. Suicide! What's the matter with me!

Johnny goes to George Reed's office and looks at the policy, where Joyce is the sole beneficiary, and Andrew is specifically omitted irrevocably. And there is a suicide clause. So maybe Andrew could not get any of the money, but if Stockerly killed himself, neither would Joyce! And Andrew would love that. Maybe the attempts are a long campaign to drive Stockerly out of his mind.

Johnny drives to Andrew's home and notices all the travel stickers on his luggage. He tells Johnny that no one can prove he tried to kill his foster father. Johnny is about to take the law into his own hands when Andrew pulls a gun.

When Johnny tells him that he wants the gun so he can compare it with the slugs he pulled from his wall, Andrew says "That was your apartment? But you drove him over there in a car. You left him there, and I thought..."

Johnny tells Andrew that he left Stockerly alone just long enough to park his car. Johnny takes the gun from Andrew and slugs him.

"All I hope is that they lock that bird up for the rest of his life. And that somehow Joyce and her husband can bring the poor old man back to normal."

Notes:
- This program contains commercials for safe driving, and two for Ex-lax.
- Bob Bailey previews the next week's show with "Next week a story of real intrigue, plus a couple of the most intriguing characters I ever met."
- John Wald ends with the normal "Be sure to join us next week, same time and station for another exciting story of Yours Truly, Johnny Dollar." Too bad neither of them would be on the next broadcast, as the show was moved to New York with a new cast and crew after this program.

Producer: Jack Johnstone Writer: Jack Johnstone
Cast: Virginia Gregg, G. Stanley Jones, Ben Wright, Ralph Moody, Harry Bartell, Carleton G. Young

Bob Readick

Bob Readick (1925-1985) became the fifth actor to play Johnny Dollar after CBS radio moved the production of radio programs to New York.

Bob was an established motion picture, radio, stage and television actor, and he came from a family of actors — his father, Frank Readick, played *The Shadow* (before Orson Wells), in addition to many other radio roles. Bob appeared in 3 films, and over 85 radio programs, including his stint as Johnny Dollar. Other than some basic biographical information, very little is known about him.

Bob Readick was a capable actor, and portrayed a softer Johnny Dollar, similar to that of John Lund. Many give Bob short shrift because he followed Bob Bailey, but Bob Readick was a solid actor, and his portrayal is a good one. Bob died in 1985.

In October of 2017, I visited the Thousand Oaks Library in Thousand Oaks, California to review newly discovered scripts in the Pacific Pioneer Broadcasters collection. During this visit, I was able to document 7 new stories (5 new Bob Readick stories, one new Mandel Kramer story and a story that was written for broadcast after the end of the series.)

These new stories helped to clear up stories which were previously classified as "Missing", identify stories which were mistitled and correct the dates for a number of programs in the December, 1960 to January 1961 timeframe. The details are in the Canonical Johnny Dollar section.

The following are the Bob Readick programs.

Show:	**The Urned Income Matter**
Show Date:	**12/4/1960**
Company:	**Northeast Indemnity**
Agent:	**Toby Tetrick**
Exp. Acct:	**$418.15**

Synopsis: Toby Tetrick calls, and Johnny is glad to hear from Toby. Glad because he likes the large fees Toby's company passes out on his cases, and he can use one right now, he is running a little short. Toby tells Johnny that the case is a robbery, $5,000 in cash. Johnny is worried about the commission he would get on 5Gs. Toby tells Johnny that the case just happened in Hartford, so grab a cab and come on over.

Johnny cabs to Toby's office because he could use some extra dough. Toby tells Johnny that he should have had him go straight to Mercy Hospital. The client is Phillip Standish, who lives alone at the Ashley Arms Apartments.

Last night someone broke in, beat him and took the $5,000. He thought he had the money concealed well — it was on the wardrobe in his bedroom — that is, the urn was on his wardrobe. It was a brass funeral urn and he kept his money in it. It was heavy and had a tricky lock on the top.

Standish has an interest in an import business in New York that gets goods from the Orient. His policy covers losses up to $5,000, and he wants Johnny on the job. Toby urges Johnny to go easy on the expense account, but Johnny tells him that "Oh, but who knows. Pursuit may take him to the furthest corners of the earth…".

Johnny goes to Mercy Hospital and meets Standish, who does not want the police involved — only Johnny. He wants Johnny to run the man down, because he knows who the man was. He does not want the police involved because it would bring out something from his past — 15 years ago he went to prison for forgery.

His cellmate was Thomas Slade, and Johnny recognizes the name. Standish does not remember what Slade was in for, but he remembers talking about places to hide stolen goods, and Slade suggested the funeral urn — a place where even experienced crooks would never look. So that is where he had hidden what money he has. Standish does not trust banks because of what he did.

Standish tells Johnny that there is more than $5,000 in the urn, and if it is returned, he will pay Johnny more than the insurance company will. Standish is sure that only Slade knew where he kept his money, and that Slade has kept track of him.

Standish tells Johnny that Slade lives in Los Angeles, and gives Johnny the address, 1308 Pandora Avenue, an area that Johnny knows well. Standish is sure that Slade is going back to LA and is sure that Slade will not be able to open the urn, and will not trust anyone else either. He will feel that the money is safe.

Johnny cabs to police headquarters and asks Sgt. Jimmy Wormser if he has a flyer on Tommy Slade. Jimmy has one on his desk, the boys in LA wanted him to know that Tommy was headed their way. The police watched him, but he did not do anything except for a visit to the Department of Health to get a permit to carry someone's remains back to California.

Johnny is told that Tommy is going to New York to catch the Starlighter Express for LA. If Johnny hurries, he can catch the train in New York. Johnny is sure that he and Tommy Slade have crossed paths before. Johnny cabs to the airport for a plane to New York and gets a roomette on the train. Johnny tips a porter to find out if Slade is on the train — and there is a man named Slade on the train.

Johnny has a cocktail in the observation car, and then has dinner with a stranger — Tommy Slade! Tommy introduces himself, and Johnny gives him the name Harry Walker. When asked his destination, Johnny tells Slade that he is not sure that he is going all the way to the coast. Tommy goes back to his roomette, and Johnny must bide his time or figure out a way to get him out of his roomette to search it.

Johnny has drinks with a pretty little blond who must leave to go take care of her children. Johnny goes out onto the observation deck on a beautiful evening. Johnny dozes off and wakes up when something is thrown over his head and something knocks him out. Tommy tells Johnny that now he is going over the side.

Johnny wakes up in a roomette looking at the face of a stranger who turns out to be one Dr. Springer. Doc Springer tells Johnny that no damage was done, but his head will hurt for a while.

Doc Springer tells Johnny that a conductor came onto the observation deck, and a man told him that Johnny had fallen from his chair and then walked away. Johnny asks if the conductor knew who the man was, but the conductor does not know. So, Johnny rests for five minutes and is ready to settle with Tommy.

Johnny finds Slade's room and the door is open, the room is empty, and the urn is on the table. Johnny sees where the urn had been picked at, but it has not been opened. Slade appears and tells Johnny that he thought Johnny would try that and pulls a gun with a silencer on him. Johnny slams the roomette door closed and dodges bullets from Slade's gun. Johnny breaks open the window and climbs out of the moving train.

Johnny takes a car, train and plane back to his apartment in Hartford. After cleaning up, Johnny goes to the hospital, makes a phone call to the police, and goes to Standish's room.

Standish is glad to see Johnny and the urn. Johnny tells him that he had a slight accident with the urn. A wheel on the Pullman car almost cut the urn in two. The money did not fall out, but it did jar loose the false bottom.

Johnny tells Standish that he is making a fortune in one of the foulest, filthiest rackets in the world. Johnny tells Standish that he remembers what Slade went up for, and that he had turned to Slade's caper when he got out.

Johnny asks if he was holding out on Slade, and that is why Slade came after him, for the two kilos, two pounds of pure uncut stuff worth $8,000 — $10,000 wholesale. But once carefully cut, it would be worth over a million for that much heroin. Johnny calls him a "dirty rotten son" just as the police come into the room.

"Interesting side light on the case, I saw in the afternoon papers that the railroad company didn't look too kindly on Tommy Slade's little act. I mean when he was caught standing there blasting away at the lock on the door of his roomette. Come to think of it, I better tip the Federal boys to his having gone back to his old racket. Expense account total $418.15, and no padding on this one."

Notes:
- This is an AFRTS program that lacks all but the AFRTS identification at the end.
- This program is called either *The Earned Income Matter* or *The Urned Income Matter*. Given Jack Johnstone's proclivity for wordplay, I have opted for the latter.
- Ralph Camargo is Phillip Standish, Ralph Bell is Tom Slade, William Mason is Roby Tetrick, Jack Grimes is the police sergeant, Bill Smith is the doctor, Sam Raskyn is the steward.
- The address "1308 Pandora Avenue" was used in three Johnny Dollar programs, *The Harried Heiress Matter*, *The Shadow of a Doubt Matter* and *The Urned Income Matter*. I have been told that the address was Jack Johnstone's home.
- $10,000 in 1960 dollars is worth over $82,000 in 2017.
- This is the first of the New York run, and Bob Readick's first program.
- Music Direction is by Ethel Huber.
- The Announcer is Art Hannes.

Producer: Bruno Zirato, Jr.   Writer: Jack Johnstone
Cast: Ralph Camargo, Ralph Bell, William Mason, Sam Raskyn, Jack Grimes, Bill Smith

◆ ❖ ◆

Show: **The Wrong Ending Matter**
Show Date: **12/11/1960**
Company: **Eastern Allied Casualty Insurance Company**
Agent: **Tommy Hines**
Exp. Acct: **$100.00**

Synopsis: Johnny gets a call from Tommy Hines of the Eastern Allied Casualty Insurance Company in New York City. Tommy wants Johnny to investigate the death of Alice Drummond, the wife of mystery writer Drake Drummond. Drummond has called and asked for Johnny Dollar to work on the case. Her death could be suicide or murder. Her insurance policy was for $21,000 and does not pay in the event of a suicide.

Alice Drummond was confined to a wheelchair from an accident at the chemical plant where she had worked. On the day she died her husband had left for a business trip. Johnny asks if anyone saw him leave, and Tommy tells him that a neighbor saw him leave.

When Drummond came home he flagged down a police officer who found her dead. The police say that Alice was poisoned and that she committed suicide, but Drummond says that she was murdered and will give a reward two-to-three times the insurance value to whoever can find the killer. When Tommy tells Johnny that Drummond lives at 1533 Birchbrook Road in Bronxville, Johnny tells him that he knows people who live on the same street.

Johnny goes to Bronxville, New York to meet his police contact Lt. Ralph Teeter. Teeter tells Johnny that Alice died within a couple of hours of her husband leaving town. He tells Johnny that Alice had died from an exotic insecticide that she had access to when she was working at the chemical plant. Also, he mentions that the apartment where she died was completely locked from the inside!

Johnny goes to meet Drake Drummond, and he tells Johnny that his wife was deeply religious and would not have committed suicide. Drummond also tells Johnny that a neighbor, Mr. Chatsworth, saw Alice alive as Drake was walking to the station to catch the train for his trip. Drummond tells Johnny that when he got home, officer Griggs noticed Drummond and saw that he couldn't get into the apartment. They broke in and found Alice dead. Drummond recognized the danger of the poison and they left the apartment. After Drummond leaves, Johnny tells Teeter that he believes that Alice was murdered.

Johnny and Teeter talk to the neighbor, Mr. Chatsworth, who tells them that Alice Drummond was the most cheerful girl he had ever known. He also mentions that he heard her throw the door bolt when Drummond left and that Drummond had checked that the garage door was locked.

Things seem just a little too pat for Johnny. Drummond conveniently has witnesses who saw him leave on his trip while his wife was still alive. Drummond had told Teeter that it took 20 minutes to walk to the train and 40 minutes to return that evening, that there was a prowl car outside when he arrived home, and that the officer helped him discover his wife's body.

Johnny searches the apartment, which contains a cabinet full of guns and fishing tackle. In the kitchen Johnny finds a clue, a piece of knotted fishing line, that convinces him that Drummond murdered his wife.

Johnny tells Drummond that he tied the fishing line to the bag of poison that he had placed on a kitchen shelf and ran the fishing line through a slit in the kitchen window sashes. He was able to pull the deadly bag off the shelf from outside his apartment knowing the paper bag would burst when it hit the floor. He was able to pull out all of the fishing line except the small knotted piece that Johnny found.

Also, he knew the schedule of the police patrol, so he waited outside until the car approached then called the officer when he could not open the door.

Drummond confesses and says, "My...story kinda had the wrong ending... didn't it?"

"Yeah, his story has the wrong ending...for him. I uh, I'm kinda glad I'm on my end of the job, solving crimes rather than cooking them up. Expense Account total, including incidentals and a trip back to Hartford, call it $100. Yours Truly, Johnny Dollar"

Notes:
- This program is typically called *The Locked Room Murder Matter*. However, the title on the script is *The Wrong Ending Matter*.
- The *Wisconsin State Journal* for 12/11/1960 provides the following program description: "6:10 p.m.   Johnny Dollar (WKOW): 'Locked Room Murder.'"
- The December 11, 1960 issue of *The Washington Post*, on page G6, gives this description of the program: "Johnny must cope with the mystery writer's favorite problem, a 'Locked Room Murder'. He is asked to determine whether a crippled young housewife committed suicide."
- Birchbrook Road in Bronxville is also mentioned in *The Wayward Heiress Matter* and *The Deadly Crystal Matter*.
- The program information was provided by Stewart Wright from a script on file at the Thousand Oaks Library.
- The script notes that Bob Bailey is playing Johnny Dollar.

Producer: Bruno Zirato, Jr.   Writer: Jack Johnstone
Cast: Unknown

♦ ❖ ♦

Show: **The Wayward Kilocycles Matter**
Show Date: **12/18/1960**
Company: **Tri-State Life & Casualty Company**
Agent: **Earle Poorman**
Exp. Acct: **$400.00**

Synopsis: Earle Poorman calls Johnny from Los Angeles, and the weather is wonderful. But Earle is having a problem with all the small claims. Earle wants Johnny to come out and put a stop to a bunch of armed robberies.

Johnny flies to Los Angeles, California and arrives the next day. Johnny cabs to Earle's office where he learns that the robberies have taken place in Lamosa Beach, a new development in the area, which has a nice shopping mall a half-mile long. The robberies seem to have been done by the same man as the description matches.

The jobs are pulled in the morning when the owners are all alone. The robber also carries an army .45, and his timing seems to be perfect. There have been seven robberies in the past week. Earle wants Johnny to act fast, as the robber may move on.

Johnny borrows Earle's car and drives to the coffee shop on Lamosa Beach. Johnny notes that Lamosa Beach is an exclusive community and the mall has a number of upscale shops.

At "The Coffee Nook", Mrs. Webster tells Johnny that the robber took $135 from her, and that she wishes that there was a bank around as she has to keep too much money in the store. The police drive up and go to the nearby radio and television store where another robbery has just taken place. Johnny hangs around the edge of the crowd and after the police leave he talks to the storeowner, Mr. Marx.

Marx wonders how the robber knew that he was alone and wants to close the store. Marx tries to sell Johnny a television with a remote-control unit and gives a demo to Johnny. While they are talking the television changes channels all by itself. Marx notes that the last time it did that was just before the robbery.

Johnny tells Marx who he is and Marx repeats that the remote-control system acted the same way just before he and Mrs. Webster were robbed, and maybe three days ago when the previous store was robbed. Johnny wonders if the remote control explains how the robber knew that Marx was alone.

Johnny is told that some types of sound waves activate the remote using 44.6 to 56 kilocycles. Johnny now knows that the robber has a pal who knows when storeowners are alone and coordinates with the robber via a radio. Johnny figures he can find the accomplice if he can find a direction finder.

The police arrive to investigate another robbery — two in one day again. Johnny calls Bob McKenny in North Hollywood, a radio ham known as W6BFG. Bob used to handle the engineering on Johnny's programs and Bob tells Johnny that all the robber would need is a small receiver. Bob agrees to bring down a direction finder and will be there first thing in the morning.

Johnny drives back to Earle's and then meets Bob in the morning. A direction finder is set up and they wait. Johnny explains how the remote works, but Bob tells him that the remote puts out sound waves, not radio waves, so his theory is not correct. Bob gets an idea about sympathetic resonance and thinks that the sender is somewhere along the main street.

Johnny learns that on top of the shop there is a small apartment, and Bob sees and antenna on the roof. Marx tells Johnny and Bob that he has two boarders and one of them, Willard Thorson never seems to leave. Johnny is sure that from the tower, Willard can see everything. The other boarder, Harry Williams leaves early and comes in late at night. Bob is sure that the antenna is the cause of the interruption. Johnny has an idea, and they sit down to watch TV.

Three days later the TV acts erratically and Bob discovers that the signal comes from upstairs. Johnny hears the voice of Thorson tell Harry that the coast is clear in the jewelry store down the street.

Bob goes upstairs to grab Willard while Johnny runs down the alley to Beckham's Jewelry store with his .38 ready for action. Johnny stops Harry, and his knuckles are still sore from where Harry ran into his fist.

"Yes, I guess there is nothing like modern electronics as an aide to crime, and as an aide to catching a crook. Two of them in this case."

"Next week, a crook, a firebug, unwittingly solves a case for me, and hands me a Christmas present to boot."

Notes:

- The *Wisconsin State Journal* for 12/18/1960 provides the following program

description: "6:10 p.m.   Johnny Dollar (WKOW): tracking holdup men by radio."
- The next week teaser in this program fits the next case *The Art for My Sake Matter.*
- Bob McKenny figured in *The Missing Missile Matter* and *The Vociferous Dolphin Matter.*
- Leon Janney is Mr. Marx, Les Damon is Earle Poorman, Bill Sterling is Bob McKenny, Athena Lorde is Mrs. Webster.

Producer:	Bruno Zirato, Jr. Writer: Jack Johnstone
Cast:	Leon Janney, Les Damon, Bill Sterling, Athena Lorde

♦ ❖ ♦

Show:	**The Art for My Sake Matter**
Show Date:	**12/25/1960**
Company:	**Masters Insurance and Trust Company**
Agent:	**Tim Bradley**
Exp. Acct:	**$0.00**

Synopsis: Johnny gets a call on Christmas morning from his old friend and reformed arsonist Smokey Sullivan. Smokey wants Johnny to come to his apartment in Elmira, New York. Smokey has spotted a known firebug, Larry Logan aka Larry the Torch. He tells Johnny that Larry usually goes to work in a hurry, so Johnny better get to Elmira fast.

Johnny arrives in Elmira, New York on Christmas day, gets a room at the Mark Twain Hotel and goes to see Smokey. Smokey shows him newspaper clippings of some of the fires that Laurence Logan, aka "Larry the Torch", aka Charlie "Paraffin" Briscomb, aka Louis Elf, and even "Smokey" Logan had set.

Smokey tells Johnny that he now drives a street sweeper for the City of Elmira and saw Larry when he was driving the big machine. Smokey also mentions that Larry carries a gun and that Larry recognized him and he was going into the office of Masters Insurance.

Johnny goes to the home of Tim Bradley, the local agent for Masters Insurance and Trust Company. Johnny shows Tim several pictures of Larry Logan. Tim tells Johnny that Larry has a policy with Masters Insurance, but not on a building. Logan has a policy on an Antonio Breenocellis painting called "The Madonna" that is worth $7,400.

Johnny contacts local art expert Malcolm Godfrey, and he tells Johnny that a Breenocellis painting isn't worth that amount. There is one that has been sitting in Minnie Gilbert's pawn shop for years, and she only wants $35 for it.

Johnny goes to the pawn shop to see the painting but it is not there — she sold it to Larry Logan that very day. As he is leaving the pawn shop, local art dealer/collector Harrison Barclay shows up and he wants to buy the painting.

Johnny is able to find out where Logan is living, and he talks to the landlord of Logan's rooming house. Johnny tries to get into Logan's room to look at the Breenocellis painting but the Landlord rebuffs Johnny.

A short time later, Johnny isn't concentrating as he is driving and nearly hits Smokey who is on the way to a fire that he believes that Logan might have set. When they get to the site of the fire, it is at Logan's rooming house. Johnny manages to save the damaged painting, and Smokey realizes that the fire wasn't set, it was simply an accident.

Logan shows up and admits that he was planning to scam the insurance with a worthless painting, but since he never filed a claim, charges can't be filed. Logan gives Johnny the painting.

Minnie and Barclay show up, and apparently the damaged painting isn't worthless. It is now apparent that Breenocellis painted over a real masterpiece, a Barrone. Johnny sells the painting to Barclay for $31,000 and gives Smokey a substantial portion of the money.

In the end of the dramatic portion of the show Johnny says, "Yeow-zah! Merry Christmas to me! And a big hunk of the thirty-one thousand we settled for goes to Smokey Sullivan. Expense account total? Forget it. And to you folks who listen to these reports of mine on the air...from the bottom of my heart... Merry Christmas."

Notes:
- Most catalogs list this program as *The Christmas Present Matter*, but the title on the script is *The Art for My Sake Matter.*
- The Wisconsin State Journal for 12/25/1960 provides this program description: "6:10 p.m. (WKOW): Johnny Dollar receive[sic] unexpected Christmas gift."
- *The Washington Post* for December 25, 1960, on page E11, provides this program description: "Johnny spends Christmas Day trying to locate a professional arsonist who planned to collect $7,400 in insurance on an ancient painting. He also hoped to become the owner of the painting."
- The program information was provided by Stewart Wright from a script on file at the Thousand Oaks Library.
- The script notes that Bob Bailey is playing Johnny Dollar.
- Mark Twain is buried in the Woodland Cemetery in Elmira, New York. The cemetery is mentioned in the story.

Producer: Bruno Zirato, Jr.   Writer: Jack Johnstone
Cast: Unknown

♦ ❖ ♦

Show: **The True Love Matter**
Show Date: 1/1/1961
Company: **Eastern Trust & Insurance Company**
Agent: **Harvey Mclean**
Exp. Acct: **$190.40**

Synopsis: Johnny gets a phone call from Monica Merrill in Miami. She says she got his phone number from Harvey McLean of Eastern Trust and Insurance Company. Monica wants Johnny to come to Miami. Johnny calls Harvey to verify that Monica had contacted Harvey (Johnny doesn't like Harvey or working for him). Harvey tells Johnny to come down to Miami, and that Monica is even better looking that she sounds.

Johnny flies to Miami, Florida and goes to see Harvey. He tells Johnny that Monica is the manager of a store that had jewels stolen, and they were insured for $170,000. Johnny finds out from Harvey that the owners of the jewelry store that Monica manages are also the primary stockholders of the insurance company that Harvey works for — Eastern Trust and Insurance Company. Johnny also finds out that the thefts have not been reported to the police.

Johnny goes to the jewelry store, which is on the wrong end of Collins Avenue, but Monica isn't there. Johnny believes he has seen the clerk before. He gets the clerk to write down Monica's address on one of his business cards, so he can get the clerk's fingerprints. Johnny leaves and then gets his police contact, Sgt. Kramer, to send the prints to the FBI for identification.

Johnny finally meets Monica and she is gorgeous. Monica is sure that the thefts, a single stone at a time, are an inside job. She tells Johnny that there are only three employees — two women and Henry Barker. Johnny is suspicious that Monica and Harvey seem overly concerned about each other and might be working some kind of scam.

Sgt. Kramer Contacts Johnny and tells him that the clerk at the jewelry store is Harry Harkin, an ex-con who was one of the cleverest safecrackers in the business and also a fast man with a gun.

Johnny stakes out the jewelry store at night. He lets Harvey know what he is doing and gives Harvey a gun he has loaded personally. Harvey follows Johnny's orders and walks by the store several times each night.

On the second night of the stakeout, Harkin is waiting for Johnny. He tells Johnny that he recognized him the first time he came into the shop. Harkin tells Johnny that Monica wanted him to check the shop at night and gave him a gun and a set of store keys. He gives Johnny the gun and Harvey tells him that Monica knows about his record. He also tells Johnny that he has gone straight. Johnny brings the clerk into his plan and Harkin leaves the store.

Later, shortly after one of Harvey's nightly rounds, Harkin returns and opens the door and supposedly shoots Johnny. Harvey immediately shows and shoots Harkin. Then Monica shows up and tells Harvey that their plan has worked and that Harkin and Dollar are dead. In their euphoria, the two lovers discuss success of the criminal scheme and how Harkin was the fall guy and Johnny was their pigeon.

Johnny gets up and Harvey tries to shoot him, but Johnny had loaded his gun with blanks. Dollar slugs Harvey. Harkin gets up, he has in deed gone straight.

At the end of the dramatic portion of the script Bob Bailey wishes the audience, "...and may 1961 be the greatest year ever for all of you!"

Notes:
- **Most catalogs list this program as *The Missing Jewels Matter*, but the title on the script is *The True Love Matter*.**

- *The Wisconsin State Journal* for 1/1/1961 provides the following program description: "6:10 Johnny Dollar (WKOW): solves missing jewels case."
- *The Washington Post* for January 1, 1961 provides the following program description: "An insurance man is romantically involved with a woman who manages a jewelry shop. He makes the mistake of asking Johnny to investigate the mysterious disappearance of valuable jewelry."
- The program information was provided by Stewart Wright from a script on file at the Thousand Oaks Library.
- The script notes that Bob Bailey is playing Johnny Dollar.

Producer: Bruno Zirato, Jr.   Writer: Jack Johnstone
Cast: Unknown

• ❖ •

Show: **The Big Date Matter**
Show Date: **1/8/1961**
Company: **Tri-State Life & Casualty insurance Company**
Agent: **Don Boomhauer**
Exp. Acct: **$20.00**

Synopsis: Don Boomhauer calls Johnny, but Johnny wants to duck whatever Don has for him. Don pleads for only five minutes with Johnny. Don does not want Johnny to take on a case, but if he will come down he can keep Don from getting involved in something serious, like spending a few years in a federal prison. Don tells Johnny to come down to Sarasota, and he relents. But he is sure it is a gag, it has to be. And yet, coming from Don Boomhauer...

Johnny flies from Miami to Sarasota, Florida and goes to Don's office. Johnny tells Don he only came to Sarasota to delay his return to snowy Hartford. Don mentions the jewelry robbery Johnny had just been working on, and Johnny tells him he almost got his head shot off and wants to relax.

Don tells Johnny that all he wants Johnny to do is to verify some figures, and Johnny notes he only likes to verify one type of figures, those on a pretty girl. Don gives Johnny a list of the money he has been paid, and Don tells him to sign it so that the Bureau of Internal Revenue will not send him up the river.

His accounts had been messed up and the tax man just wants proof that Don actually paid Johnny the money. Johnny is about to sign the paper when shots ring out. Don tells Johnny to duck but Johnny looks out the window and goes outside to investigate.

Johnny notices a backfiring car with a pretty blond sitting in it. As a crowd gathers Don tells Johnny that she might be a good date for a wing-ding Johnny is going to be taken to that night out on Bird Key.

As Johnny gets to the car, all the merchants on Main Street are on the sidewalk watching the car to see what will happen. The girl cannot get the car to stop so Johnny gets her to pull the hood release so he can open the hood, but it is stuck. A police sergeant arrives and asks what is going on. Johnny explains what is going on, and the sergeant tells Johnny to stop all the noise.

Finally, the car stops backfiring and the girl thanks Johnny and drives away. The sergeant accuses Johnny of causing the car to make the noise and threatens to arrest him for disturbing the peace.

Johnny goes in to talk to Don and tells him that the girl is a living doll. Johnny is thinking and bets Don that the girl dances like a dream. Johnny signs the statement (legibly too, Don notes) and wishes he had noted the license on the car and is sure that no one knows who the girl is but Johnny will find her. Johnny has an idea and asks to borrow Don's car.

Just as Johnny is ready to leave, the police arrive at a jewelry store across the street and the sergeant comes in to arrest Johnny. He tells Johnny that he knows that Johnny and the girl were causing a disturbance so that his confederate could rob the jewelry store across the street. Don is told that $60,000-$70,000 was stolen, and Don realizes that he insures most of it.

The sergeant is ready to take Johnny downtown until Don tells him who Johnny is: Johnny Dollar, the insurance investigator and friend of the lieutenant who comes down there now and then. Johnny shows him his ID and Johnny asks Don if he is on expense account. As Johnny leaves the sergeant tells him that Lt. Phillips will have to identify him, as Johnny is his only suspect.

Johnny takes Don's car and goes to the agency that sells the type car the girl was driving, but she has not been there. Johnny checks every car agency in town and finds nothing. Johnny drives aimlessly and hopes Don can explain to the police so that they will not follow him and cramp his style.

Johnny finds himself way out on Bee Ridge Road and turns around on a dirt road, only to see the car he had been looking for stalled up ahead. Johnny drives to the car and the girl recognizes Johnny. She tells Johnny that the car just stopped and she needs somebody to fix it. The hood is open and Johnny looks into the car as he tells the girl that he was out looking for her. Johnny tells her his name and she acts as if she recognizes his name.

Johnny replaces an ignition wire and spots a device used to make the car backfire, just like the Chicago gangsters used to do to hide gun shots. Johnny hears a noise in the car and goes to investigate and finds a man named Jim with a .38 in the back seat. Johnny spots the loot in a bag and Jim tells Johnny to turn around so he can be nice to him and shoot him in the back of the head.

A car drives up the road and the girl, Sally, recognizes it as a police car. Jim is distracted and Johnny slugs him just as the police sergeant walks up and asks the girl if she is OK. Johnny thanks him for tailing him and Johnny tells the officer he had asked Sally for a date but suggests that she have a date with him instead, say at headquarters.

"So, thanks to sheer luck and clean living of course, I'll pick up a commission on the recovery of all that jewelry."

"Next week, a fishing trip with a real friendly crowd of people one of whom is a killer."

Notes:
- **Existing catalogs typically place this program at the end of the Readick**

programs, but the recent discovery of *the True Love Matter* script clearly places this program in January of 1961. In the story, Johnny is escaping the cold of a Connecticut winter in Miami and is called to go to Sarasota, which fits the story.
- The *Wisconsin State Journal* for 1/8/1961 provides the following program description "6:10 p.m.   Johnny Dollar (WKOW): involved in jewel thieves' getaway."
- There are two versions of this program available, one is a network version with the first minute missing and after the program, a public service announcement for mental health that offers the publication "How to Deal with Mental Problems" and Dallas Townsend gives a promo for his new CBS program *The Sound Story*. The other is an AFRTS program that contains a story about Rev. Eugene Wood and his services to German POWs, and a story about military uniforms.
- Madeline Sherwood is Sally, Robert Dryden is the sergeant, Carl Frank is Don, Larry Haines is Jim, Larry Robinson is the car dealer.
- Art Hannes is the announcer.
- Musical supervision is by Ethel Huber.

Producer:	Bruno Zirato, Jr. Writer: Jack Johnstone
Cast:	Madeline Sherwood, Robert Dryden, Carl Frank, Larry Haines, Larry Robinson

◆ ❖ ◆

Show:	**The Very Fishy Matter**
Show Date:	**1/15/1961**
Company:	**Greater Southwest Insurance Company**
Agent:	**Theodore Jarvis**
Exp. Acct:	**$245.50**

Synopsis: Theodore Jarvis calls from Las Vegas and asks about the weather in Hartford. The weather is nice and warm in Nevada, can you fly on out? Johnny agrees to come if he can be guaranteed time to drop a fishing line at either Lake Mead or Lake Mohave Resort. That is exactly what Jarvis wants Johnny to do, among other things, like escorting a very lovely and wealthy young lady. And the expense account is virtually unlimited. Johnny is on his way!

Johnny senses that there is something fishy with this case. Johnny flies to Las Vegas and cabs to Ted Jarvis' office, about the only place in Vegas without a slot machine, besides the offices and churches. Ted tells Johnny that this case is about the Lisa Birdwell fortune. Jarvis wants Johnny to go fishing with Lisa at Lake Mohave.

Lisa used to be a schoolteacher in Salt Lake City and considered becoming a Mormon. When her father died, he left her $10,000-$12,000 and she decided to have a little fling. When she came to Vegas she discovered the roulette wheel and won over $400,000 and stopped gambling. Lisa bought a small ranch and brought her foster brother Tony to manage the ranch. Now she is just enjoying life by cruising around on her 52-foot yacht. Ted is afraid that if anything happens to Lisa, Tony will get all the money. Get down to the lake as Tony has already arranged for Lisa to be murdered.

Ted is sure that Tony has planned the murder because when he called the ranch last night, he accidentally got connected to a phone call in which Tony promised someone $10,000 to kill Lisa. Ted tells Johnny that he gasped and Tony hung up. Ted is sure that someone on the boat is going to kill her. Ted called Lisa, who pooh-poohed the idea.

She is fishing with a crowd that includes: Jim Furee, a dealer in town with a bad reputation, Sadie Reese, a b-girl to put it kindly, Clara Hinkley a visiting school teacher Lisa picked up somewhere, Charles Schroder, an elder in the Mormon church, and Paul Holder, who runs the boat for her. One of these people is going to kill her.

Johnny rents a car and drives to Lake Mohave Resort and meets with Ham Pratt. Ham tells Johnny that Lisa left about an hour ago, and that the boat will not be hard to miss. They were probably headed for the Big Basin area. All of the guests arrived last night at the same time, except for Paul who runs the boat. Johnny asks for a boat, fishing gear and a string of big fish.

Johnny takes the boat up the lake, finds the yacht and fakes running out of gas beside Lisa's boat. Johnny comes on board, and after she sees the string of fish Johnny has, she invites him to stay as long as he likes. Johnny spends the day and shows Paul where to take the boat to catch fish. Johnny is invited to stay with them and he accepts so that he can survey the guests.

Paul holder is a friendly young man. Jim Furee is tall, dark and suave who would kill his own mother for a prize. Sadie Reese is happy as long as Jim is there to bait her hook. Clara Hinkley fished alone because of her shrill voice and incessant talking. Charles Schroder spent most of his time talking to Lisa from the Book of Mormon. Johnny joins them and the conversation ends.

Johnny offers cigarettes and both Charles and Lisa accept. Lisa tells Johnny that she has had an uneasy feeling all day and is afraid and wants Johnny to look after her. After a fish dinner, everyone goes to bed.

Later Johnny switches cabins with Lisa and puts a rolled-up blanket in her bed. Johnny goes on deck to wait and falls asleep. Later there are shots, and Johnny runs to Lisa's cabin where everyone is gathered.

The dummy is discovered and Charles is glad that Lisa is OK. Jim notes that Johnny's boat is missing and Johnny tells them that he used the boat just to get on board. Paul is told to make coffee and they talk.

Johnny tells the group why he is there and that one of the group is a phony. Johnny tells them that his boat had been cut loose to mislead the others. Jim is told that he is a gambler and a likely suspect because he has a prison record, and there is nothing phony about Sadie or Clara. Johnny tells Paul that he is not the phony either.

Johnny points to Charles as the phony and Charles pulls a gun and tells them that there is a bullet in it for each of them. Paul breaks a pitcher on Charles' head and Johnny gets the gun away from him. Johnny tells Lisa that Charles claimed to be an elder in the Mormon Church, and that he had accepted a cigarette earlier that day. But Mormons do not smoke or drink coffee.

"Well, he talked all right, plenty. And of course, he implicated Lisa's foster brother Tony. So now it is all up to the courts.

"Next week, well believe it or not, I go to jail. Fact! And I don't mean just to pay someone a little call. No, I was thrown into the clink, and for what I have to admit is plenty good reason. And then, believe this or not, I engineer a highly unsuccessful jailbreak which means in the end that luck was with me. Because if the break had succeeded, I wouldn't be around to tell you about it."

Notes:
- There is new jazzier music during the program now, with the same theme at the beginning and the end.
- The *Wisconsin State Journal* for 1/15/1961 provides the following program description: "6:10 p.m.   Johnny Dollar (WKOW): asked to protect beautiful and wealthy woman."
- The *Washington Post* for January 15, 1961, on page G6, provides the following description of the program: "Johnny is asked to protect a beautiful and wealthy young woman while she takes a fishing trip."
- Once again, a future Johnny Dollar, Mandel Kramer, is in this program.
- This program contains commercials for the Radio Free Europe Fund, and the *Arthur Godfrey Time* show with the Kirby Stone Four, Dick Harmon and singer King Ling.
- There is a post-program commercial for the "Lucky Block Number Call" on KRLD, Dallas, Texas.
- Mandel Kramer is Ted, Teri Keane is Lisa, Jim Boles is Ham, Danny Ocko is Charles, Bill Mason is Paul, Joan Lorring is Sadie, Robert Dryden is Jim.
- Musical supervision is by Ethel Huber.
- The announcer is Art Hannes.

Producer:	Bruno Zirato, Jr.	Writer: Jack Johnstone
Cast:	Mandel Kramer, Teri Keane, Jim Boles, Danny Ocko, Bill Mason, Joan Lorring, Robert Dryden	

◆ ❖ ◆

Show: **The Short Term Matter**
Show Date: **1/22/1961**
Company: **New Jersey State Mutual Life Insurance Company**
Agent: **Bill Tilton**
Exp. Acct: **$82.80**

Synopsis: Bill Tilton calls and Johnny is terrible and Johnny asks Bill if he wants to buy a pair of skis. Johnny is terrible because of the North Slope over on Chickapee Mountain in New Hampshire. Johnny tells Bill that he and Doc Hubble were skiing when his chair broke loose and he fell on his back. The doc is making him wear a corset, a sacro-lumbar support, and Johnny can hardly breathe. Bill tells Johnny that he will find someone else, even though it is Larry

Moody that he has a line on. "Fingers Moody", the safe operator? Johnny tells Bill that he will not let anyone else have a crack at him — ohhhhhhh!!

Johnny moves slowly with the corset but feels better with the prospect of getting Moody. Johnny flies to Patterson, New Jersey to meet with Bill, who chastises Johnny for trying to be superman and tells Johnny that he will not handle the case.

Bill relents and tells Johnny that Moody pulled a job 4 years ago in Chicago. Johnny recalls how he had followed every false lead Moody left until a state trooper picked him up. Bill tells Johnny that night before last $33,000 was taken from a store in Patterson, and Bill is sure that it was Moody because of the modus operandi, three witnesses, and a trail of $5 bills leading to an alley.

Bill gets a call from the police and they tell him that Moody has been picked up in Pemberton, New Jersey but the money was not with him. Bill tells Johnny to find the $33,000.

Johnny walks to police headquarters and meets with Lt. Walter Ivin who gives Johnny directions to Pemberton. Johnny is told that Pemberton will not let Moody loose until they get him for running down a citizen with his car. Ivin is sure that Moody will not get out on bail, so they have all the time in the world. Johnny asks about the jail and is told that it is adequate. Johnny notes that he has a little stunt that, if it works, might lead them to the money.

Lt. Ivin remembers the Merryman case in Chicago and is sure that Moody will tell them nothing about the money. Ivin asks about the stunt, but Johnny tells him that he would not let Johnny get away with it. (Ohhh, this darn corset!)

Johnny goes back to Bill's office, empties his pockets and leaves his cashmere jacket. Johnny borrows Bill's car and tells Bill he will see him in jail. Johnny buys an extra key to the car and some other things. In Pemberton, Johnny looks for a police officer and fakes an accident by running into him.

Johnny is thrown into a cell with Moody. Johnny tells him that they will not keep Johnny in that jail, as he will break out. "Alone?" asks Moody. "That depends.", Johnny tells Moody.

Johnny tells Moody that for a price, he will take Moody with him. Johnny tells Moody that the man he hit has died and Moody gets anxious and begs Johnny to take him for $5,000, no $10,000 and then half of the money, then $20,000. Johnny tells Moody that in the corset he has some hacksaw blades and an extra key. Pretty smart, eh?

After midnight Johnny and Moody cut their way out and drive to New Lisbon. Along the railroad tracks Johnny is told to stop at a tool shed. Moody goes to the shed and Johnny watches him get a sack and return with the money and a gun. Johnny is told to "get out of the car, Mr. Johnny Dollar!"

Moody tells Johnny that he knows that Johnny had chased him all over the country four years earlier, and that he recognized Johnny's voice. When Moody aims to shoot Johnny tells him that a car is approaching without it's lights, and that means the police, and Moody runs away shooting.

"You know something? That was a police car. It had been following us all the way from the jail in Pemberton. And the only reason they let us break out was because Bill Tilton, reading my mind I guess, had called the chief of police and told them who I was. And the chief figured out why I had gotten myself locked up and what I was up to. He and his boys nabbed Larry Moody with no trouble at all. The moral of the story? Don't ever underestimate the ability of a small-town cop. Oh, I uh beg your pardon, police officer."

"Next week, another locked room mystery. See if you can figure it out."

Notes:
- This program contains commercials for Done's Pills for back aches, and Commander cigarettes.
- The script in the Thousand Oaks Library notes that the alternate title for this program is *The Dollar Put in Jail Matter.*
- The *Wisconsin State Journal* for 1/22/1961 provides the following program description: "6:10 p.m.   Johnny Dollar(WKOW): thrown in jail wearing steel corset."
- Musical supervision is by Ethel Huber.
- The announcer is Art Hannes.
- Robert Dryden is Bill, Santos Ortega is Larry, Lawson Zerbe is Lt. Ivin, Jack Grimes is the officer.

Producer:	Bruno Zirato, Jr.	Writer: Jack Johnstone
Cast:	Robert Dryden, Santos Ortega, Lawson Zerbe, Jack Grimes	

♦ ❖ ♦

Show:	**The Death by Jet Matter**
Show Date:	1/29/1961
Company:	Continental Insurance Company
Agent:	Fred Briscoe
Exp. Acct:	$70.00

Synopsis: Fred Briscoe calls from Boston and Johnny asks Fred why no one ever calls from somewhere nice and warm. Fred tells Johnny that he has an insurance problem that is making him hot. Come on up to Boston and come prepared. You usually carry a gun, don't you?

Johnny drives to Boston, Massachusetts and meets with Fred. Over Lunch at the Union Oyster House Fred tells Johnny that he is expecting Henry R. Girson, who is probably trying to get a free lunch. Girson is very wealthy but lives in a ramshackle apartment and is hated by everyone because he got rich by taking advantage of others. Lately he has just been counting his money that he is trying to keep from a niece and two nephews, who are poor and could use the money. Jerry and Paul had studied for the ministry, but are just drifters now and live in Syracuse, New York just waiting for Girson to die. Nancy Trimmer lives in Boston and works at a supermarket.

Girson arrives and asks Johnny if he can keep his relatives from killing him. Girson sits down and wants lunch. His policy is for $47,000 double indemnity and he would commit suicide to keep his relatives from collecting. Johnny notes that the suicide clause would prevent payment, which means that the premiums would have been paid for nothing all these years. After lunch Girson wants to take Johnny to his place where he is safe. Johnny wonders why Girson can wander all over town to get to the restaurant, but only feels safe in his apartment.

Johnny drives Girson to the apartment in a horrible part of town near the railroad tracks. Girson tells Johnny that he is well off and probably has a couple of million, but there is no need to waste it. Girson tells Johnny that one of his relatives is going to kill him.

Girson shows Johnny a series of notes with biblical quotations. One is from Philippians 2:12, "Work out your own salvation". Another note has a passage from Isaiah 38:1, "Set thine house in order". Another has Revelations 2:10, "Be thou faithful unto death". Another has Romans 6:23 "The wages of sin is death".

Girson tells Johnny that the notes came in the mail from Syracuse. Girson tells Johnny that he let his relatives starve a little and is not giving them anything. He has to leave his money to the family because he does not want to give it to charity. The quotations are threats to Girson who remembers that the boys had studied to be ministers. Johnny decides to call on Nancy Trimmer first, to see what she knows about her cousins.

Johnny drives to Nancy's apartment and Nancy thinks that Johnny is from the parole board and she tells him that she is playing her new job straight. Johnny tells her that he is with her uncle's insurance company, and she tells Johnny that she does not want any insurance but will be glad to take any part of her uncle's money she can get.

Johnny asks her about her cousins, but she knows nothing about them. All they ever told her was to improve her mind. She shows Johnny a stack of paperbacks she has been reading to improve herself and tells Johnny to leave.

Johnny calls Fred to update him and arranges to fly to Syracuse. Johnny tells Fred that Girson will be safe in his apartment but notes he never should have hung up the phone and flown to Syracuse, or to have left Girson alone.

Johnny flies to Syracuse and cabs to the apartment of the boys. Paul is home and does not know where Jerry is. Johnny tells him of the insurance, but he does not want the money, as he and Jerry are going to continue with their studies. Uncle Henry's money is tainted, and they do not want it. Paul tells Johnny that Jerry had left just after Fred Briscoe had called to say that Johnny was coming.

The phone rings, and Fred tells Johnny that it is all over — Girson is dead. As Fred tells Johnny that Girson committed suicide, Jerry comes in. Both of the boys tell Johnny that they do not want the money.

Johnny calls Fred again and is told that Girson committed suicide by turning on the gas in his bedroom. Also, all the windows and doors were locked. Fred tells Johnny that Nancy had been there to beg for some money and left after he had given her some. Johnny tells Fred that he is sure that Nancy killed Girson.

Johnny flies back to Boston and Fred meets him at the airport. Johnny and Fred go to Nancy's apartment and invite themselves in. Johnny shows Fred a mystery magazine that Jack Johnstone, who dramatizes his cases, writes for occasionally. Johnny finds a story called "Death by Jet".

Johnny tells Fred that Nancy did not know that he was a special investigator, so Johnny's talk about the money she would get reminded her about the story. She figured this was the answer, so why waste time. Nancy rips up the magazine as Johnny explains that the jets refer to gas jets.

He tells Fred that Nancy had gotten into the basement and turned off the gas line to the apartment and then went to see Girson. When he was not looking, she opened the valve on the heater, and then went downstairs and turned the gas back on when Girson was asleep.

Johnny tells Fred that Nancy probably did not even wipe her prints off the valve, but Nancy tells him that "she wiped them off real good". Call the police Fred.

"So, it looks as though the boys will get the old man's fortune whether they want it or not, and his insurance. You can build a lot of fine churches with money like that. Expense account total, oh call it 70 bucks."

"Next week, proof that a man's best laid plans can really go awry."

Notes:
- This program contains commercials for CBS news and their expanded coverage, and for Commander cigarettes.
- The script in the Thousand Oaks Library has *The Death by Jet Matter* as the title for this program, but Bob Readick gives *The Paperback Mystery Matter* as the name of the case.
- The *Wisconsin State Journal* for 1/29/1961 provides the following program description: "6:10 p.m.- Johnny Dollar (WKOW): investigates murder of Boston man."
- Edgar Stehli is Mr. Girson, Ralph Camargo is Fred Briscoe, Teri Keane is Nancy Trimmer, John Thomas is Paul, Richard Holland is Jerry.
- Musical supervision is by Ethel Huber.
- The announcer is Art Hannes.

Producer:	Bruno Zirato, Jr.	Writer: Jack Johnstone
Cast:	Edgar Stehli, Ralph Camargo, Teri Keane, John Thomas, Richard Holland	

♦ ❖ ♦

Show: **The Planner Matter**
Show Date: **2/5/1961**
Company: **Masters Insurance & Trust Company**
Agent: **Fred Larker**
Exp. Acct: **$15.95**

Synopsis: Fred Larker from Masters Insurance calls, and Johnny moans that "times are tough — there is not much money flowing in". Fred has a case for Johnny but there is no expense account, only a large fee.

As Johnny notes (as he is getting his .38) that his past few jobs have not paid well when he receives a telephone call from his old friend Smokey Sullivan who is at Bradley Field on his way to new job in Boston. They make arrangements to meet later at Johnny's apartment.

After Smokey's call, Fred Larker from Masters Insurance and Trust calls Johnny. Larker is afraid that a policy holder, Harrison Otway Parkford (who is loaded), might be murdered by his nephew, Chester Pearson. Parkford has been receiving anonymous threatening letters. Larker has a premonition that an attempt on Parkford's life might be made very soon. Fred tells Johnny that Parkford lives at 15424 North Elm with his nephew Chester. Johnny notes that Parkford lives not too far from Betty Lewis.

Fred tells Johnny that Chester is the same age he is. The Parkfords had been receiving threatening letters, but no one knows the source as they arrived in various manners and from various places. Chester only found out when there was a barrage of notes. They went to the police and demanded protection, but they only watched for a while.

Johnny goes directly to Parkford's home in Hartford and the police are already there. The police tell Johnny that Parkford has been murdered by a hit on the head with a "heavy blunt instrument", and there is a pipe next to the deceased. Chester Pearson supposedly shot and killed the murderer before he could escape. Witnesses Bill James and Mary Hanley, corroborate Chester's story. The police tell Johnny not to touch anything until Doc Bayless arrives.

Johnny searches the killer and finds a note in the killer's pocket. He copies down the information, but it doesn't make any sense. Doc Bayless arrives and yells at Johnny about getting in the way. And yes, he will do an autopsy (although the cause of death is obvious) — it is the law — and he will call Johnny.

Over dinner in his apartment, Johnny and Smokey discuss the case. As they talk, Johnny shows the note to Smokey. The note only has "545", "win", "r hall", "2 dr left". They figure out that the note was a plan with instructions for the murder. Smokey mentions that there was a contract killer called "The Planner" who used such notes on his hits. He is on the lam in Chicago and is a hired killer.

Johnny goes to the police and tries to convince them that a professional killer was employed to kill Parkford, but Chester tells Johnny that it was Parkford's birthday and they were planning a party. Chester tells Johnny that Parkford was born at 5:45 p.m. and was usually asleep in front of the television by 3:00. Mrs. Tetley had stopped by with some jam and then Chester had gone to pick up Tom and Mary Hanley and then Bill James. They stopped for drinks and arrived at 5:45 and yelled "Happy Birthday" at the front door. Chester then came in and saw the man and shot him.

Johnny mentions cui bono (who benefits) and makes a call to Fred Larker who confirms that Chester is the beneficiary of Parkford's policy and that Chester had made trips to Boston and New York.

Johnny checks Parkford's house and finds a fireplace poker with some of the old man's hairs on it. His theory is that Chester had killed Parkford before the killer struck the old man with the pipe. He used "The Planner" as the fall guy to divert attention from himself. The medical examiner, Dr. Bayless, now agrees with Johnny that the poker was the murder weapon. Under interrogation Chester breaks down and confesses.

"Sure, too easy...make sure the old man was murdered...then make sure by someone else, somebody with a record for such things who could take the blame...then knock him off and be a hero. Nice idea, huh? But only if it works. Expense account total, including a cab ride back to my apartment, $15.95. Yours Truly, Johnny Dollar."

Notes:
- Two people mentioned in the script are Tom Hanley and Bill James, Hollywood sound effects artists who often worked on the series. The Hanley character doesn't appear in the episode, but the James character does.
- The program information was provided by Stewart Wright from a script on file at the Thousand Oaks Library.
- The *Wisconsin State Journal* for 1/29/1961 provides the following program description:" 6:10 p. m.   Johnny Dollar (WKOW): brutal murder investigated."
- There is no "next week" teaser available.

Producer:	Bruno Zirato, Jr. Writer: Jack Johnstone
Cast:	Unknown

• ❖ •

Show:	**The Who's Who Matter**
Show Date:	**2/12/1961**
Company:	**Western Indemnity Company and Greater Southwest Insurance Company**
Agent:	**Ted Beckham**
Exp. Acct:	**$306.25**

Synopsis: Johnny is called by a man who had trouble getting Johnny's number and finally had to call Pat McCracken at the Universal Adjustment Bureau. He thought Johnny was going to drop by and pick up his check for his services on that oil refinery case he handled last week. The caller is Ted Beckham in Fort Worth, and he has okayed Johnny's expenses for the investigation. Johnny tells him that the only case he handled last week was in Hartford, and the week before he was in Little Rock, Arkansas, and the week before that he was also in Hartford and before that in Los Angeles. Ted gets angry and tells Johnny that he is not Johnny Dollar, but an imposter who is impersonating Johnny Dollar.

Johnny is upset by the phone call accusing him of impersonating himself. The phone rings again and Pat McCracken asks if Beckham has called? Pat tells Johnny that Beckham heads up a new company, but Pat wants Johnny to go to Dallas, Texas and look into an arson case for Al Pinker at Greater Southwest. Johnny tells Pat that he will handle both cases, he will kill two birds with one stone.

Johnny flies to Fort Worth, Texas and cabs to the Western Indemnity office. Johnny bullies his way into Beckham's office and shows him his credentials. Beckham admits that he is Johnny Dollar. Beckham tells Johnny that another young man had done some investigations for him and said that he was Johnny Dollar.

He did a good job for Beckham, but the size of expense accounts made him suspicious. Beckham called about the expense account because the other Johnny Dollar had agreed to come in to pick up the check. After talking to Johnny in Hartford, Beckham was suspicious because of the amount of the check.

Al Pinker comes to the office and greets Johnny. Al tells Johnny that he has a real problem with the Geary Brothers Department Store fire. Beckham tells Al that he also has a policy on that building, and the other Johnny Dollar is investigating the fire. Johnny tells Al that he is there to run down two people, a fire bug and a guy named Johnny Dollar.

Al and Johnny drive to Dallas, Texas and Johnny updates him on the double. Al describes the fire, which Johnny does not think is too complicated a matter for the police, but agrees to look into it for Al.

Johnny gets a room at the Statler Hilton and drives to the department store to look around. Johnny sees that the fire was on the second floor of the building and hears a voice cry out "Who's there" and then shots are fired. Suddenly the scene is silent and then the voice tells Johnny to give up and there are more shots.

Johnny tries to move to another spot and ends up falling through the floor. When Johnny wakes up he is on the floor and his gun and his ID are gone. The police arrive and slug Johnny so he will not shoot anymore.

Johnny wakes up in police headquarters with a police guard. The guard is sent to look at the papers that were just brought in from the scene and the sergeant tells Johnny that the other investigator found the clues to pin the arson on Jerry Springer, a professional torch man. Just when their investigator was going to come in and report, you show up and try to shoot him.

The sergeant tells Johnny that the other man is named Johnny dollar. The first policeman brings in Johnny's real ID and the police are confused. Johnny decides to run the other man down for the police.

Johnny drives to the Western Indemnity office in Ft. Worth and picks the lock to get in. Johnny sees the envelope addressed to Johnny Dollar and the check on the desk. The door opens and the secretary enters and tells someone that she wondered when he was going to get there.

She turns on the light and sees Johnny sitting at the desk as she reaches to give the other Johnny his check. Johnny tells him that he should have taken a better look last night and the impostor pulls a gun. He tells Johnny that he is going to leave and Johnny asks him how long he was going to try and get away with his act by solving crimes he had set up?

The impostor tells Johnny and the secretary to get into a closet when Beckham arrives causing a distraction allowing Johnny to slug the impostor. Beckham tells Johnny that he suspected the man as soon as he got the expense account. He knew all about Johnny, but the expense report was so small Beckham knew the first man could not be Johnny Dollar!

"Okay then Mr. Beckham, on the strength of that last remark, I will not expect you to question this expense account."

"Next week, a fireman, the dangerous kind, that carefully sets fires instead of putting them out."

Notes:
- The *Wisconsin State Journal* for 1/29/1961 provides the following program description: "6:10 p.m. Johnny Dollar (WKOW): perplexed with double mystery."
- The *Washington Post* for February 12, 1961, on page G6, provides the following program description: "Johnny charges into a mystery which begins with a case of arson and includes the unknown identity of a young insurance investigator."
- This program contains commercials for heart month in February and the drive for research funds, Commander cigarettes and a post-program pitch for lowering accident rates on the highways.
- Ethel Huber does the musical supervision.
- Ian Martin is Ted, Bill Sterling is Al, Lawson Zerbe is Pat, Bill Lipton is the officer, Rosemary Rice is Carol, Roger De Koven is the sergeant, Leon Janney is the man.
- The announcer is Art Hannes

Producer: Bruno Zirato, Jr.   Writer: Jack Johnstone
Cast: Ian Martin, Bill Sterling, Lawson Zerbe, Bill Lipton, Rosemary Rice, Roger De Koven, Leon Janney

◆ ❖ ◆

Show: The Wayward Fireman Matter
Show Date: 2/19/1961
Company: Masters Insurance & Trust Company
Agent: Harrison Hadley
Exp. Acct: $227.00

Synopsis: Harrison Hadley calls Johnny from Buffalo and his problem is two fires. One occurred yesterday and one is still burning. Harrison will arrange for a room at the Statler for Johnny. So far, the total insurance coverage is $400,000. "Then you can afford my expense account for two" Johnny tells him. "I don't understand" answers Hadley. "You will when you see me" replies Johnny.

Johnny is sure that a lot of people think that most crimes are solved by a lot of Sherlock Holmes type deduction, or by the equally mysterious scientific razzmatazz that goes on inside some of the fabulous crime labs. But most of Johnny's crimes are solved by hard work, and information from stoolies.

Johnny calls Smokey Sullivan, who is working in Syracuse, but is on vacation. His new job is working for the city as a special consultant for the arson squad. Smokey is sure that all the firebugs have left town since he got there. Johnny tells Smokey to go to Buffalo and wait for him at the Statler.

Johnny flies to Buffalo, New York and is met at the airport by Harry Hadley. Harry tells Johnny that the police are sure that the first fire at a small department store was arson, and that the owner has had problems paying his bills. That fire was worth $200,000.

The second fire was at the Strath Rubber Company warehouse. The owner is named Morley and has been having financial troubles. The police are sure that the same method was used in both fires, but they do not know how they were set.

Johnny is sure that his friend will know. Johnny and Harry go to his hotel room and hear a window close. Inside they find Smokey unconscious on the floor.

Johnny gets a bottle of brandy for Smokey, who is badly beaten. Smokey comes to and tells Johnny that he does not want a doctor. Smokey tells Johnny that he was beaten by "Bottles" Burton who uses chemicals to set fires. He is a bad one and a pyromaniac since he was a kid.

They put Burton into an institution and let him shovel coal into the furnace to try and cure him, but he is still sick. He does not set fires for money, only for himself. Smokey tells Johnny that Bottles always sets three fires on three days in a row. Smokey is sure that Bottles knows Johnny is in town as he was surprised to see Smokey in the room when he came there.

Harry tells Johnny that he did call the police, and Johnny surmises that if a reporter was there, Burton must know that Johnny is in town. But Smokey tells Johnny that Burton thinks Johnny is dead. Smokey is sure that Burton will not set the fire tonight.

Smokey tells Johnny that Burton always gets a job around the fire, like as a fireman or at a powerhouse or a blast furnace, somewhere where there is fire. Johnny tells Harry to get the word out to the press that Smokey is dead and his body is in the morgue, but Smokey will stay in the hotel.

Johnny cabs to police headquarters to get a mug shot of Burton and then checks all the fire houses until he finds one where a fireman named Charlie Smith works or used to. He seems to have disappeared a couple days earlier. He was a good man and always seemed to enjoy his work.

Johnny returns to the hotel and moves Smokey to an adjoining room. Smokey tells Johnny that Burton may go nuts waiting for Johnny to leave town, and Johnny has an idea.

Johnny goes to radio station WBEN and talks to Bill Peters, the program manager who had made the announcement that Johnny was in town. Johnny is sure that Burton keeps tabs via the news broadcasts, so Johnny writes an article for the newscaster Jack Ogilvy to read.

Back in his room Johnny listens to the broadcast as Jack reports that Johnny Dollar is leaving the case due to the death of his colleague Smokey Sullivan. "Dollar has checked out. But is he afraid of the pyromaniac killer?"

Smokey comes out and tells Johnny he is fine and then collapses. "Oh fine" moans Johnny as he carries Smokey back to bed. Later there is a knock at the door announcing a telegram, but Burton is there when Johnny opens the door.

Burton pushes his way in with a gun and makes Johnny sit facing away from him. Burton is going to kill Johnny so that he can set another fire. Burton take's Johnny's gun and knows he has to kill him. Smokey comes in and breaks a chair over Burton's head and collapses again.

"Well, it is up to the courts, naturally. And this time I'm betting there will be no parole for Burton, ever. Not only because of the fires, but the murder attempt on Smokey. And come to think of it, on me! As for the insurance money that will have to be paid out. Well, you can't win 'em all. Expense account total, including room and board and Smokey's expenses, plus a little gratuity and to cover his doctor bills, $227 even."

"Next week, another locked room mystery. It's called The Two Tired Matter. Remember that title, and join us, won't you?"

Notes:
- This program contains commercials for the heart fund and the need for money for research, and Commander cigarettes.
- Nat Polen is Smokey, Bill Smith is Harrison, Bernard Grant is Burton, George Petrie is George Peters, Robert Dryden is the chief, Jack Ogilvie of WBEN played himself.
- Musical supervision is by Ethel Huber.
- The announcer is Art Hannes.

Producer:	Bruno Zirato, Jr. Writer: Jack Johnstone
Cast:	Nat Polen, Bill Smith, George Petrie, Bernard Grant, Robert Dryden, Jack Ogilvie

◆ ❖ ◆

Show:	**The Two Tired Matter**
Show Date:	**2/26/1961**
Company:	**World Wide Mutual**
Agent:	**Les Walters**
Exp. Acct:	**$4.90**

Synopsis: Les Walters calls and tells Johnny to drive to Treeman Pharmaceuticals, which is located in a small industrial center south of Manchester. The owner, Walter Treeman is dead. He had a $68,000 straight-life policy. Les does not want to pay the beneficiary, Claire Treeman, if the death was a suicide.

Johnny notes that there are two ways of spelling "two". Johnny buys gas and drives to Treeman Pharmaceuticals where he meets deputy sheriff Danny Howard. Danny tells Johnny that the family doctor has been called, and that he knows why Treeman died. Claire Treeman comes in and she knows who Johnny is, and is sure that her father did not kill himself as it would cancel the insurance. Agnes, the secretary to Mr. Treeman agrees that it would. Barton Wilder enters the room and tells Agnes to shut up.

Agnes tells Johnny that she is the personal secretary to Mr. Treeman, but she is the only one who can run the business now that Mr. Treeman is gone. She is sure it was suicide and will tell Johnny why later.

Barton Wilder is in charge of operations, and Mr. Treeman wanted him to take over the operations, but that he had given the company to his daughter Claire — he had plans for her. He wanted her to marry Bruce Simmons of the Hartford Simmons.

Johnny and Danny go to look at the body and meet Dr. Harmon who tells Johnny that this is a puzzling case. He knows the others in the case and agrees it might be murder. The circumstances say murder is impossible, but under certain circumstances it could be suicide.

Johnny and Dr. Harmon look at the body, which is contorted, the skin color is odd, and there are capillary blotches in the eyes that point to panocygen, a poison that makes cyanide look harmless.

The office was sealed as Mr. Treeman was scared of drafts. Only a small amount of the poison would kill Treeman and the ventilation system would remove all traces. Dr. Harmon notes that Danny had broken a window to get in and noted the symptoms.

Johnny meets with Agnes Grant and she wants to tell Johnny what happened. She tells him that she came in early to work undisturbed. She tells Johnny that Mr. Treeman was sick of the way things had been going and was going to Miami.

He did not want to spend the money to fly, so Agnes suggested he drive. Barton Wilder had agreed to give Mr. Treeman two tires for his car.

Johnny goes to the office and sees two mounted tires there. Barton tells Johnny that Treeman told him to leave the tires in the office. Also, Bruce Simmons had come in and given Treeman $100 for expenses.

Agnes tells Johnny that Treeman had come in at 7:30 and locked the office door. His last words were "I'm going, Agnes. I may never see you again." At noon she knocked on the door and got no answer.

Danny tells Johnny that he came by the office to pass the time of day — after all it is cold outside! He found Agnes pounding on the door and went to see what was going on and saw what had happened. He had everyone leave as Dr. Harmon was sure that poison was used. Danny had looked thru the office and found nothing.

Agnes tells Johnny that Claire had brought Treeman's luggage to the office at 8:30, and Johnny starts to wonder if some sort of gas capsule was used. Agnes tells Johnny that Barton brought the tires at 9:00 and had knocked on the door and Treeman let him in. Agnes is sure it was suicide, but she is the only one.

Claire talks to Johnny and tells him that her father was worried about the business and that she suggested that he take a vacation. Her father had tried to run her life, and now she can marry who ever she pleases. Now Johnny must decide if it was murder or suicide.

Johnny searches the office and finds that the office was sealed, there was nothing to hold the poison and that Danny had broken the window to let any gas out. Doc Harmon confirms that Treeman could not have swallowed a container after smelling the gas.

Johnny wonders if the plant could be the source of the poison. Danny thinks that Wilder could marry Claire and improve the business — he killed Treeman to get him out of the way, but he cannot prove it.

Johnny thinks that Bruce Simmons had a motive — his family is broke and marrying Claire would give him money.

Danny decides to sit on the tires rather than the corpse and notices that one of the tires had no air in it. Johnny yells at Danny to get up! The answer has been in front of them the whole time!

The gas was inside the tires. Doc examines the tires and finds a toothpick in the valve stem. Johnny tells Danny to get Barton and put him in cuffs.

"Yeah, plenty of the deadly gas remained in that tire — only Barton could have put it in there and arranged for the slow release in the tightly-closed office to kill Mr. Treeman when he was alone in side. Now, it's up to the courts. Expense Account total, $4.90 for a tank of gas. Yours Truly, Johnny Dollar."

Notes:
- The program information was provided by Stewart Wright from a script on file at the Thousand Oaks Library.
- The *Wisconsin State Journal* for 1/29/1961 provides the following program description: "6:10 p.m.   Johnny Dollar (WKOW): poisonous gas kills man in locked room."
- *The Washington Post* for February 26, 1962, on page G6, provides the following program description: "The owner of a pharmaceutical plant is found dead after exposure to poisonous gas {sic} Johnny learns the victim's firm was doing poorly and at least four persons will benefit from the death."
- The script folder for this program in the Thousand Oaks Library contains 2 promotional messages and a teaser that were to be played the week before this program.
PROMO #1:
" Johnny Dollar here...I hope you make sure to catch my program on Sunday. It's another of those locked room mysteries. And who knows, maybe you can find the solution before I do. Try it, huh? That's Sunday, here on this station. Yours Truly, Johnny Dollar."
PROMO #2:
Suicide or murder? Both of 'em are possible, I mean in the insurance investigation I tackle on my program a bit later on. As usual, I'll be right here on this station that brings you all the top shows on radio. So, stick around, will ya? Yours Truly, Johnny Dollar."
TEASER #1:
Next week another locked room mystery. It's called the *Two Tired Matter*...remember that and join us, won't you? Yours Truly, Johnny Dollar."

Producer: Bruno Zirato, Jr.   Writer: Jack Johnstone
Cast: Unknown

♦ ❖ ♦

Show: **The Touch-Up Matter**
Show Date: 3/5/1961
Company: **Star Mutual Insurance Company**
Agent: **Terry Holmes**
Exp. Acct: **$0.00**
Synopsis: Terry Holmes calls Johnny at 2 a.m. from a party and needs Johnny to come over right away to the Chadwick residence on Weathersfield Avenue.

No one has been murdered, but the company will murder him if they have to pay the claims on the biggest jewel robbery ever pulled in Hartford. Terry wants Johnny to come out.

Johnny dresses and drives to the Hartford, Connecticut residence of Bruno Chadwick, a local showplace mansion. In the library, Terry tells Johnny what has happened.

The party was for the Chadwick's fortieth anniversary and the guests are most of the local wealthy people of Hartford including Mr. and Mrs. Lloyd Augustus Brownfield, the Fritz Melchior's, the Lawrence Comstock's, Kenneth Gordon Hodge, Mary Ann Hooper and a bunch more.

A Mr. Thompson B. Thompson barged in to the party and said he was up from New York and wanted to discuss a business deal with Mr. Chadwick. He was young and handsome, so Mrs. Chadwick told him to stay, and he became the life of the party and the old women all tried to occupy his time while he cased the jewelry the ladies were wearing.

They were in the music room listening to Mrs. Jackson Lee Kenworthy Price squawk out an encore of "Sweet Mystery of Life" when the lights went out. Mrs. Chadwick screamed about her necklace, and then all the other women screamed about theirs, and when the lights came on, two million worth of jewels and Mr. Thompson were gone.

Lt. McQuaid walks in and tells Johnny that they have sent a police officer to the motel where Thompson was staying. He was registered there, but his car had Connecticut plates. Officer Conroy calls from the motor court and reports that the car was stolen as Thompson drives in.

McQuaid shows Johnny a snapshot of Thompson taken with one of those new instant cameras and tells him that Thompson did not object to having his photo taken at all. Officer Conroy calls back and he is sure that Thompson is there as he sees a shadow moving in his room. Officer Conroy is told not to disturb Thompson unless he tries to leave. McQuaid and Johnny leave for "an easy kill".

At the Pearson Motor Court, they meet officer Conroy and go to unit 7. Lt. McQuaid knocks at the door and gets no answer. They break in the door to find no one there. Johnny notices a pinwheel device on the lamp that is making the shadows on the window shade. Officer Conroy finds an open window and gets a chewing out from McQuaid.

Johnny finds all the missing jewelry lying on the floor under a table. Officer Conroy is sure that Thompson knew the police were there, so he left the jewels and ran. McQuaid tells Officer Conroy his stupidity paid off, and Johnny tells Officer Conroy that he left his squad car parked right where Thompson could see it when he came back.

Back at the Chadwick Mansion, everyone was happy to get the jewels back, and Terry is relieved that he will not have to pay the claims. Everyone thanks Johnny for finding the jewels so quickly and he tells them that it was the police who did the work. Terry and Johnny talk about how Thompson will need to be captured.

Johnny notes how Thompson seemed to use makeup to make himself look younger and how he made sure that everyone knew where he was staying and wonders why he went back to the motel. That all adds up to a hunch. Johnny borrows the jewelry to play his hunch.

Next morning Johnny takes the jewels to a jeweler named Caldwell who tells Johnny that they are beautiful, but paste, imitations. Johnny knows now that no one would suspect anything until the jewels were cleaned, so Thompson had all the time in the world to disappear quietly.

Lt. McQuaid walks in and Johnny gives him all the jewels but Mrs. Chadwick's — Johnny will return that one personally. Johnny leaves telling Caldwell to give McQuaid the good news about the jewels. Johnny is amazed at how neatly things fell into place.

Johnny returns Mrs. Chadwick's necklace and Johnny asks to borrow the instant camera. Johnny also asks where the jewelry is cleaned and Mrs. Chadwick tells him she uses Rickter's, as they would trust no one else. All the ladies use Rickter's.

Johnny goes to Mr. Rickter who takes Johnny to the back room where the jewels are cleaned and mounted. Johnny takes a number of pictures, supposedly for a magazine story, and stops at the bench of a lean middle-aged man who is Ernest, a new employee, but their best stone setter.

Johnny is told that Ernest is leaving for a new job in Philadelphia next week. Johnny asks to take a photo of Ernest standing up straight. Johnny asks Mr. Rickter to have the photo retouched. When Rickter says "of course, Mr. Dollar" Ernest knows who Johnny is. When Mr. Rickter tells Ernest that he does not look well, he tells Rickter that Mr. Dollar knows why.

Johnny tells Ernest that he would get the jewels in for cleaning and make copies of them. Last night he stole the real jewels and left the copies in the motel room for the police to find. Ernest tells Johnny that, as they say in the movies, he will go along quietly.

"The gems he had stolen, we picked them up in his apartment and then took them along to police headquarters. It's funny. Lt. McQuaid even forgot to bawl me out for keeping that first picture of Ernest. Expense account total, what expense account? But believe me, I want a nice fee out of this one!"

"Next week, what might have been a pleasant trip across the country if it weren't for a killer gunning for me."

Notes:
- The announcer is Wally King.
- Musical supervision is by Ethel Huber.
- Jack Johnstone loved to recycle names. Named in this episode are: Augustus Brownfield who was a character in *The Canned Canary Matter*, Fred/Fritz Melchior who was the agent in *The Hair Raising Matter* and *The Mystery Gal Matter* and a character in *The Deadly Chain Matter*, Lawrence Comstock was a character in *The LaMarr Matter*, Kenny Hodge is noted as an associate director of the program in *The Five Down Matter*, and

Mary Ann Hooper is the name of a character in *The Harried Heiress Matter* and worked for CBS. The name Chadwick appears in numerous contexts both as characters and crew.

Producer: Bruno Zirato, Jr.   Writer: Jack Johnstone
Cast: Jim Stevens, Carl Frank, Lawson Zerbe, Bill Lipton, Elsbeth Eric, Jean Gillespie, Guy Repp, Raymond Edward Johnson, Luis Van Rooten, Robert Dryden

♦ ❖ ♦

Show: **The Morning After Matter**
Show Date: **3/12/1961**
Company: **Amalgamated Life Association**
Agent: **Timothy Handley**
Exp. Acct: **$0.00**

Synopsis: Timothy Handley calls and needs Johnny's services. Johnny tells him he is heading out to go fishing in South Carolina. Handley tells Johnny that he is waiting for him at 500 Fifth Avenue. Goodbye.

Johnny is ready for a vacation at the Arundel Plantation near Georgetown, South Carolina. Johnny flies to New York City and goes to Penn Station to catch his train to South Carolina. Sucker that he is, Johnny takes a cab to Handley's office where Handley tells Johnny that Mrs. Brownberg should be there soon. She had insisted that Johnny be brought into the case. "Brownberg? Hmm."

Johnny is told that she is the wife of Thaddeus Brownberg who flew his own plane and disappeared seven years ago after he lost his fortune on Wall Street. Brownberg lost his memory just before he left, and his plane was found in the Alleghenies. The insurance payment of over $600,000 has been held up.

Mrs. Lita Spencer Brownberg comes in and barks at Johnny to "sit down and let me tell you something. You must find my husband, and you must find him before this Wednesday." Johnny is told that on Wednesday there is a hearing, and if he does not come back, he will be declared dead. She could really use the money, because when he disappeared there was less than $100,000 in the joint bank account, and she has had to scrape and scrimp ever since.

Johnny tells her that things will not be so bad if he is declared dead, and she gets indignant. She tells Johnny it was the cold-blooded insurance company that ordered the hearing. Handley tries to weasel his way out by saying that there is no hope because the police have not been able to find him.

Mrs. Brownberg knows all about Johnny and the miraculous way he solves his cases and she gives him a picture of Thad. "Now you have to find him" she snarls and storms out of the office. Handley implores Johnny to do something. Johnny looks at the picture and wonders.

Johnny tells Handley that he is not sure about the picture, but thinks the face looks familiar. Johnny leaves to go to the police 18th precinct and talk to his friend Randy Singer. Johnny asks their artist Billy Cross to copy the picture and make it up with over 50 different hairstyles and beards. Johnny thinks one with a beard looks familiar. Later that night Billy tells Johnny to give up like everyone else.

Johnny rushes to Mrs. Brownberg's penthouse apartment at midnight and listens to her yammer on about poor old Thad. She is sure that he would not kill himself. He loved to fish and would just take off and go. Suddenly Johnny sees a mounted fish and knows just where it came from. Johnny calls Handley and tells him he is going fishing!

The lunker bass could have only come from one place. Johnny flies to Los Angeles and on to Las Vegas where he rents a car and drives to Lake Mohave Resort.

Johnny talks to Ham Pratt and shows him a picture of a man with a beard. Ham recognizes the man as Ted Bennom, who has been fishing here for 6-7 years. Ham does not seem to know much about his past, but Bennom hangs out at Cottonwood Cove up the lake. Johnny and Ham drive up the lake in Ham's boat to Cottonwood Cove.

At the cove Johnny spots Ted Bennom and calls him Mr. Brownberg. Ted knows who Johnny is and tells him he has been expecting him to show up sooner or later. Over drinks they talk, and Johnny likes him. Ted stubbornly maintains his identity until Johnny asks for fingerprints.

Ted tells Johnny that he knew Thaddeus Brownberg and that he never suffered from amnesia, and that he lost most of his fortune deliberately. He could make money but his wife's extravagance kept demanding more and more. She only wanted his money.

Ted gets Johnny another drink and tells him that the wife only wanted him to be there so he could build up another fortune for her to go through, and he finally realized this and that she did not love him.

He realized he could be free of her and the nerve-wracking fight to make money for her by disappearing and providing for her. After the hearing tomorrow, Thad will not exist. He will be free and she will be well off. "Don't you see Mr. Dollar?" Johnny suddenly feels woozy and tries to fight the drugs in the drink but loses.

Johnny wakes up to the smell of coffee. Johnny tells Ted that he knows all about the woman but he has to get him back. Ted tells Johnny that it is Thursday, and that Thaddeus Brownberg is dead.

Ted suggests that they go out on the lake and talk. Johnny has a better idea. "Let's go out on the lake and fish, Mr. Bennom!"

"And so, we fished, and it was great, all three days of it. Right? Wrong? I don't know. Who is to judge? As for the expense account, forget it."

"Next week, a case involving a prize fight in which the only prize to be won is death."

Notes:
- This program contains two commercials, the first is Dennis James for All-Bran cereal, the second is for Commander cigarettes.

- Gertrude Warner is Lita, Carl Frank is Thaddeus, Robert Dryden is Timothy, Bill Sterling is Billy, Jim Boles is Ham.
- Art Hannes is the announcer.
- Musical supervision is by Ethel Huber.

Producer: Bruno Zirato, Jr.   Writer: Jack Johnstone
Cast: Gertrude Warner, Carl Frank, Robert Dryden, Bill Sterling, Jim Boles

◆ ❖ ◆

Show: **The Ring of Death Matter**
Show Date: **3/19/1961**
Company: **Surety Mutual Insurance Company**
Agent: **Don Pinkley**
Exp. Acct: **$389.00**

Synopsis: Don Pinkley calls Johnny from New Orleans, and he has a small problem as long as Johnny knows a little about boxing. Johnny remembers winning $20 from Tom on a boxer named Touchy Tarantino, a fighter with a future. "Not any more Johnny" Don tells Johnny. It is suicide or murder. Fly on down and I'll tell you.

Johnny flies to New Orleans, Louisiana, gets a room at the Roosevelt Hotel and explores the town, "The most interesting city in the country" it's called.

The next morning Johnny meets with Don, who tells Johnny that Tony Tarantino is insured for $25,000, and was a promising fighter, with a nice wife named Angie. He has done well physically, but has a crooked promoter named Raul Martinez.

Recently in Los Angeles Tony fell out of the ring, and Raul left him flat. Now Martinez has another fight for Tony, but a doctor in Los Angeles told Tony that one blow to the left side of his head would kill him. The fight is tomorrow in Mexico, but Don does not know where. But Johnny will try to find out.

Johnny calls his friend Johnny Ortez at police headquarters and finds out where Tony was taken from a stoolie named Miguel Andrati. For $50 Johnny gets the name of a small town in Mexico, withheld for diplomatic reasons.

Johnny flies to Brownsville, Texas and cabs to the small town in Mexico. Johnny sees the posters for the fight between Tony and Pancho Gutierrez. Johnny finds Tony's wife in a hotel, she had discovered where Tony was and wants Johnny to save her husband.

She tells Johnny that Raul has Tony tied up in the coliseum, and Tony will believe everything Raul says. Johnny is sure that there is no way that Tony can beat Pancho. Angie tells Johnny that the odds are on Tony for the fight, and Johnny realizes that Raul's money is on Pancho.

A man named Jose enters the room and tells Angie that she had better sit or he will kill her. Jose tells Johnny that he had better forget about this matter if he wants to live. Jose slugs Johnny to keep him quiet.

Johnny wakes up on top of a rubbish heap in Brownsville, minus his gun. Johnny cabs back to the town and goes to the coliseum and Tony's dressing room. Johnny meets a punch-drunk Tony who is convinced he is OK, because Raul says he is.

Tony tells Johnny that he is going to take a dive in the fourth round, but Johnny suggests that it is not like Tony to do that. Tony tells Johnny that this fight will be enough for him to make some money and make a new start.

Tony had gone back to Raul after the Los Angeles fight because he had run out of money and had told Raul that he had to help him. That is why he is there. Johnny asks if Tony knows for sure if the fight is fixed. Johnny tells Tony that he is being set up for a sucker, but Tony does not believe him. Johnny tells Tony that Angie is there and will be in the arena tonight. Tony is worried because she will know it if he takes a dive.

Jose meets Johnny in the hallway and tries to slug Johnny again, but Johnny gets the best of him and locks him in a closet. Johnny overhears Raul talking to Tony, and Raul tells Tony that if Johnny comes back he will be shot, just like Pancho will kill Tony if he does not take the dive.

Johnny rushes to the police and talks to the chief, but the name of Martinez elicits only a shrug, and eventually gets Johnny kicked out of the office. Johnny realizes that Martinez must have the town under his thumb.

Johnny goes back to see Angie and is told that she has left with Jose. Johnny searches the town but cannot find her. Johnny buys a ticket for the fight and spots Angie in the back of the arena. Johnny goes to her but Raul puts a gun in Johnny's side and they watch the fight.

The fight starts and Tony starts to tire quickly, and by the fourth Pancho is trying to set Tony up, but Tony lasts out the round. Pancho constantly tries to hit the left side of Tony's head, but Tony fends him off.

In the sixth round Tony manages to nail Pancho with a right uppercut and knocks Pancho out. The crowd goes wild, but Johnny senses the gun moving as Raul aims it at Tony. Johnny swings at Raul and the gun goes off in Raul's face.

"Yes, Martinez was dead, and of course, the police moved in. And when they realized that he was definitely, finally out of the way, I'm sure they all breathed a deep sincere sigh of relief. And believe it or not, Angie and Tony and I had a formal escort back to the border that was fit for royalty. Expense account total, including all the incidentals I could think of, $389 even."

"Next week, a trip to South Jersey and a murder to stop a murder."

Notes:
- This program contains two commercials, the first is Dennis James for All-Bran cereal, the second is for Commander cigarettes.
- Robert Dryden is Touchy, Joan Lorring is Angie, Ralph Camargo is Martinez, Mandel Kramer is Don, Danny Ocko is Jose.
- Art Hannes is the announcer.
- Musical supervision is by Ethel Huber.
- This is a remake with variations of *The Squared Circle Matter*, broadcast on 12/30/1956.

Producer: Bruno Zirato, Jr.   Writer: Jack Johnstone

Cast: Robert Dryden, Joan Lorring, Ralph Camargo, Mandel Kramer, Danny Ocko

• ❖ •

Show: The Informer Matter
Show Date: 3/26/1961
Company: Philadelphia Mutual Liability & Casualty Insurance
Agent: Harry Branson
Exp. Acct: $115.20

Synopsis: Johnny gets a call from a very hesitant man named Fred Ackerlloyd, and Fred is calling about a murder. His name is or was Phil Bernesconi. The police know about it, but they do not know who did it, but he does. He tells Johnny that telling who committed the murder would be like signing his own death warrant. Johnny notes how informers play a big part in solving of crimes, and this caller was one of those. But Johnny did not keep him on long enough to make him tell what he knew.

Johnny calls Pat McCracken and Pat tells him he will have to call all the companies they cover. The name was Phillip, or Phil Bernesconi, and the caller says he was murdered? Johnny tells Pat that the caller was named Fred Ackerlloyd, and had told Johnny what he had told Pat, and hung up. Johnny had tried the local directories and the operator but could not find a number for anyone named Ackerlloyd. Pat tells Johnny to forget it, but Johnny has a hunch.

Johnny remembers seeing a stack of phone directories in Pat's office and arranges to come in and look at them. Johnny cabs to Pat's office and looks through the phonebooks. Pat picks up a phonebook from Vineland, New Jersey his hometown, and discovers the name of Fred Ackerlloyd in it at 2424 E. Elmer Street.

Johnny rushes off to Philadelphia and wonders if Pat is right. Johnny rents a car and drives to Vineland, New Jersey, gets a room in the hotel and starts to look for Mr. Ackerlloyd. The clerk at the desk gives Johnny a telegram from Pat that tells Johnny he was right. "It was murder. You are on expense account."

Johnny is told to contact Harry Branson at Philadelphia Mutual. Johnny asks the desk clerk if he knew Bernesconi, and Johnny is told that the clerk is not a bit surprised that he was murdered. He kept to himself, but no one could figure out how he could retire, as he was in his mid-fifties. Then they learned that he had been in the rackets and had not done well by his friends.

Johnny makes a phone call to Harry Branson who, in spite of several interruptions by Johnny, tells John to "come right down and go to Vineland, New Jersey as Phillip Bernesconi, insured for $30,000, has been murdered. The police thought it was an accident, which would have made it $60,000, but the chief tells me...what did you say?"

Johnny tells Harry he is in Vineland. Johnny asks who the beneficiary is, and Harry tells him it is Harvey Renzolli, the chief of police. Johnny tells Harry that he does not want to see him yet as Renzolli had promised Bernesconi protection from his old gangster pals.

Johnny drives to the Ackerlloyd house on Elmer Street where he meets an old man who is the landlord. Johnny knocks and a tall young man with black hair and a hat opens the door. Johnny asks for Ackerlloyd and is invited in. After confirming who Johnny is, the man tells Johnny that they will have to kill him the same way they will kill Ackerlloyd.

Johnny draws his gun, a shot is fired, and Johnny is hit and knocked unconscious by the man. The man calls for Lucy to tell the landlord the shots were a backfire while he goes to get Ackerlloyd and then they can leave town.

Lucy tells the landlord that the noise was a backfire, and that the other man had left out the back door. Lucy gets rid of the man, and Johnny manages to grab her, even with a gunshot to his ribs.

Johnny turns out all the lights and Lucy tells Johnny she is not part of the gang. Tony killed Bernesconi because the gang found out he was going straight and hanging out with cops. Fred Ackerlloyd was a friend of Phil's from the old days and had come down to warn Phil.

Johnny rips Lucy's skirt and ties her up with it. Johnny watches Tony bring Ackerlloyd in and throw him on the floor. Tony turns on the lights and Johnny fights with Tony. Johnny goes down because of his wounds and Tony starts to shoot Johnny when the police enter, there is gunfire and Tony is hit.

The chief comes in and tells Johnny to stay still as he does not look too good. The chief tells Johnny that Ackerlloyd used to be the bookkeeper for a mob in Philadelphia. When he came here and started hanging around with Phil, who was going straight, the chief had been keeping an eye on him.

When Phil was killed the chief knew Ackerlloyd was innocent but would not talk. The chief knew who Johnny is because Harry Branson had called. The landlord had called the chief and told him something funny was going on. The landlord comes in, sees what is going on, and faints. Johnny suggests they let him rest for a while.

"I understand that Tony recovered well enough to be tried and convicted in Bernesconi's murder. Lucy, his girlfriend gave enough evidence against the mob in Philly to enable the police there to round them up. Where she is now, I don't know. Like Fred Ackerlloyd, she moved away, a long way away. Expense account total, including the services of a doctor, for the bullet crease in my side, $115.20. And believe me, I'll welcome a big fat fee on this one."

"Next week, my job is to protect a wanted criminal from, believe it or not, a policeman."

Notes:
- This program contains a commercial with Dennis James for All-Bran cereal, one for Commander cigarettes and one for Buick Specials that placed first and second in the class "C" US Auto Club Economy run.
- Johnny is shot for the 11th time.
- William Redfield is Tony, Lawson Zerbe is Pat, Ralph Bell is Fred, Teri Keane is Lucy, Bill Lipton is the clerk, Larry Haines is the chief.
- Art Hannes is the announcer.

- Musical supervision is by Ethel Huber.

Producer:	Bruno Zirato, Jr. Writer: Jack Johnstone
Cast:	William Redfield, Lawson Zerbe, Ralph Bell, Teri Keane, Bill Lipton, Larry Haines

♦ ❖ ♦

Show:	The Two's a Crowd Matter
Show Date:	4/2/1961
Company:	Worldwide Mutual Insurance Company
Agent:	Paul Ferris
Exp. Acct:	$379.50

Synopsis: Paul Ferris calls Johnny from New York. Johnny has not spoken with Paul since the affair with Tony Valentine, who made a lot of noise about getting Johnny before Johnny could get him. Paul tells Johnny that Valentine has escaped with a man named Sandy Rhinehart. They pulled a red-light robbery the other night and killed the driver of the car, a man named Barton Osborne. Johnny is sure that Valentine is not a killer, but Paul tells Johnny that Osborne was a policyholder with coverage of $75,000 and the heirs want the company to investigate. Paul wants Johnny to investigate because he knows Valentine's habits.

Johnny recounts to Paul how Valentine was not a killer but would pose as a highway patrol car to stop drivers at night and rob them with a pistol. Paul tells Johnny that Randy Singer thinks that Rhinehart pulled the trigger.

Johnny flies to New York City and cabs to the 18th precinct. Johnny talks to Randy about Valentine, and Randy tells Johnny that they want Rhinehart. They have found the gun used in the robbery, and Rhinehart's prints are all over it.

Also, a man matching Tony's description was seen boarding a plane to Oklahoma City hours after the robbery. The airline clerk identified Valentine from a picture. Officer Conroy enters and gives Randy a message.

Johnny reminds Randy that Valentine was supposed to go to Overton, Oklahoma, as that is where Johnny thinks Valentine's money is stashed. Randy reads the message which is about Sgt. Mike Thomasson, who is the nephew of Osborne, and who does not know that Rhinehart is the killer. Thomasson has taken a vacation and gone to Oklahoma to follow the lead on Valentine. Thomasson is a crack shot and is really mad over the murder. Randy is sure that he will kill Valentine. Randy tells Johnny to go out and save Valentine's life.

Johnny thinks that all Randy has to do is call the Oklahoma City police and have them pick up Valentine, that is if he stays on in Oklahoma City. If Tony has gone to Overton and Thomasson finds him, no one will ever see Valentine again.

Johnny cabs to the airport and flies to Oklahoma City, Oklahoma. Johnny recounts how Oklahoma City had been the center of the rush for free prairie land, but which has now grown to a city of over 300,000 people and is filled with sky scrapers and businesses.

Johnny rents a car and drives to the police, and talks to a police captain, but they have not seen Valentine. They did talk to Randy and they know about Thomasson, who has searched the city for two days but found nothing in his unofficial investigation. Thomasson had come in and told the police he had some other leads he was following out of town. Johnny asks for directions to Overton and the captain tells Johnny that there is not much in Overton except for an old abandoned oil well called "Bleeding Heart #1". Johnny is sure that he bleeding heart refers to Tony Valentine, and that he has stashed some of his loot there.

Johnny leaves and drives north to Overton. After crossing the empty prairie, Johnny spots a railroad shack. Inside the shack an old man is sleeping. Johnny goes in, wakes up the man, and shows him the picture of Tony Valentine.

The man saw Tony around sundown going to the old oil well. The man has not seen anyone else. Johnny tells the man to watch out for anyone else who might come asking questions, for he is a killer. He might have credentials for the New York police, but do not believe him. Johnny starts to leave but a man blocks his way.

Johnny is sure that the man is Mike Thomasson, who does not know who Johnny is. Johnny notices a bad, mad look on his face. Johnny edges towards the desk, which has a lamp on it, but Thomasson comes in and recognizes that Johnny is not Valentine. He shows the old man the picture, and the man tells Thomasson that he is a killer. Johnny calls him by name and he gets edgy allowing Johnny to knock over the lamp and dive for him. Thomasson fires and Johnny fights with him and overpowers him.

Johnny drives to the oil well and parks his car. Johnny walks to the oil well and he can see Valentine inside a shack collecting money from under the floor. Johnny kicks in the door and Valentine recognizes him.

Johnny tells Tony that he knows that Rhinehart killed Osborne. Tony is relieved but wants to take his money and skip the country. Johnny tells him he can go back with Johnny, or he can leave him for Thomasson, who thinks that Tony killed his uncle.

Thomasson's car drives up and Tony wants Johnny to shoot him, but Johnny does not want to be a cop killer. Thomasson calls for Tony to come out and Johnny breaks a lantern and sets the shack on fire. Johnny tells Tony to show himself in the door as Johnny goes out the back.

Johnny dives out the window and circles around to tackle Thomasson and knock him out. Tony gives Johnny a gun and thinks they better head back to New York before Thomasson wakes up.

"Funny, I never did think to find out if Mike Thomasson kept his job on the force after that little episode. Tony of course is back in the pen finishing out a somewhat extended term."

"Next week, strange vengeance for an even stranger crime."

Notes:
- This program contains two commercials, the first is Dennis James for Kellogg's All-Bran cereal. The second is for Commander cigarettes.

- Bill Lipton is Tony, Larry Haines is Randy, Roger De Koven is Mike, Robert Cole is the old man, Mandel Kramer is the police captain, Joseph Julien is Paul.
- Art Hannes is the announcer.
- Musical supervision is by Ethel Huber.

Producer: Bruno Zirato, Jr.   Writer: Jack Johnstone
Cast: Bill Lipton, Larry Haines, Roger De Koven, Robert Cole, Mandel Kramer, Joseph Julian

♦ ❖ ♦

Show: **The Wrong Sign Matter**
Show Date: 4/9/1961
Company: **Tri-Mutual Insurance Company**
Agent: **Harley Tilson**
Exp. Acct: **$129.30**

Synopsis: Harvey Tilton calls Johnny from Uniontown, Pennsylvania. He wants to make sure that a policy for $1.2 million is not paid to the wrong person. Can Johnny take the case? "Sure can."

Johnny flies to Pittsburgh and rents a car to drive to Uniontown, where Harvey's office is in the same building as CBS station WNBS. Johnny talks to the staff and Bill Freese tells Johnny that Mrs. John Stacy Minert's death might not have been from natural causes.

Bill tells Johnny that her new secretary Danny Pringle was the only person who could have known about Mrs. Minert's affairs. Bill is sure that Pringle forced Mrs. Minert to change her will and leave everything to him, or he will eat his shirt. Bill has no proof, but why else would a young man tie up with an old skin-flint like her. And Pringle is not one of those "lah-dee-dah" male secretary types either, if you know what I mean.

She was so tight-fisted that her niece Dora Minert had to play housekeeper and nurse for her at no pay so Mrs. Minert could save a few dollars. In the new will, everything goes to Danny rather than Dora and Bill thinks Danny killed Mrs. Minert for the money. Bill has nothing against Danny, it is just wrong for Danny to get away with it.

Johnny meets with Harvey and he tells Johnny that Pringle had plenty of reasons for Mrs. Minert to die and made no bones about it. Dr. Hugo Bessum examined the body and said that Mrs. Minert died of natural causes and Bill knows about the doctor's report. But Bill is in love with Dora Minert in spite of the fact she was going to inherit a million bucks or so, or because of it. Harvey wonders if Johnny thinks that Bill killed Mrs. Minert to marry Dora and get the money. However, the doctor had said death was by natural causes.

Johnny tells Harvey that Bill had just as much reason to want Mrs. Minert out of the way as Danny did, unless he knew that she had changed the beneficiary. Harvey tells Johnny that no one knew about the change until she died. The policy states that the beneficiary is the heir of her estate as specified in the will, and Mrs. Minor typed the will herself. Harvey had the will checked out with the company attorneys, and it was legal, but this new will does not make sense.

Dora had found the new will in a safety deposit box after her aunt died. Dora was so upset that she brought it to Harvey, who wanted to tell her to burn it up. No, Danny will get the money that should go to Dora. Harvey has a photostat of both wills, and the typing is pretty bad on both, including a number of repeated errors.

Johnny wonders why Pringle had not typed the will for her since she was leaving everything to him. Harvey shows Johnny that the signature of the witnesses, Marjorie and John Durkin, match exactly on both copies of the will. Marjorie did some cleaning for Mrs. Minert, and both of the Durkins died a month or so ago in a hit-and-run accident. Johnny notes that they died only a few days after the new will was made. Hit and run, huh?

Johnny starts to wonder about the typing. Johnny wonders if Dora liked Danny, but Harvey tells him that she hates Danny. Also, Dora is not upset about her aunt's death as her aunt had worked Dora too hard. Johnny is sure that there is something fishy going on, so Johnny has three people to work on.

Johnny talks to the police who tell Johnny to talk to Dr. Bessum. The doctor tells Johnny that his autopsy was far from routine after he heard about the new will, but the result was the same, natural causes.

Johnny drives to the Minert house on Bailey Avenue and Dora, a tall good-looking blonde, is there. She tells Johnny that she is cleaning up the house and looking into rooms she had never been in before, including Danny's room. Dora had hoped that there would be some recompense for all her hard work.

Danny is out for the moment, but he will be back to make sure that Dora does not take anything of his. Dora shows Johnny a key ring with keys to every room in the house. Mrs. Minert kept it tied to her. Dora tells Johnny that she had a key to the safety deposit box because Mrs. Minor did not trust Danny.

Dora had to go into the box to get the stock certificates and other papers, and that is where she found the new will. The old will was kept in the house in a file, and Pringle got it out to show the police. Johnny notices a typewriter, but it is Danny's. Dora wants to leave Danny's room before he comes in and finds her there. Dora wonders why her aunt wrote a new will when she found out she was going to die.

Danny comes in to tell her that she has no business in his room. Danny demands that Johnny leave until Johnny shows him his credentials. Suddenly Danny is most hospitable.

Danny tells Johnny he took the job to get what he could out of the old girl and that he had thought that Mrs. Minert was richer than she was. He has a certain charm for people like her, and that he has charmed other women in the past. But Mrs. Minert decided to leave everything to him because he had a lot of charm. He was going to leave, but during her last illness he relented and repented, and Mrs. Minert appreciated the change.

Johnny asks if anyone else could have used the typewriter, and Danny tells Johnny that Mrs. Minert used it, but no one else. Johnny points out the similarities between the two wills, including the signatures that match exactly.

Johnny tells him that it is impossible to anyone to sign his or her name exactly the same way twice and gives Danny a piece of paper for him to sign. Johnny tells Danny that he made the new will, traced the signatures and then killed the Durkins so they would not talk.

Danny, with a gun in his hand, admits everything that Johnny has accused him of. Johnny tells Danny he did not come alone and tells Danny that the police came with him. Danny turns to look and Johnny slugs him. When Dora asks where the police are, Johnny tells her "it's the oldest gag in the world Dora, but amateurs still fall for it."

"On the strength of his statement to us, well, I hope they do pin the murders of the Durkins on him. As for that second will, it can't be genuine simply because of those two sets of absolutely identical signatures."

"Next week, a storybook murder that suddenly comes true."

Notes:
- This program contains a single commercial for Commander cigarettes. After the program there is a commercial for Arthur Godfrey, and one for Columbia's stereo phonograph and record library on sale at Music House in Haddenfield, New Jersey.
- Bob Readick welcomes WKAT in Miami to the network, but the second time he uses the call letters he calls it WKAP.
- Lawson Zerbe is Harvey, Robert Dryden is Pringle, Joan Lorring is Dora, Larry Haines is Bill.
- Art Hannes is the announcer.
- Musical supervision is by Ethel Huber.

Producer: Bruno Zirato, Jr.   Writer: Jack Johnstone
Cast: Lawson Zerbe, Robert Dryden, Joan Lorring, Larry Haines

♦ ❖ ♦

Show: **The Captain's Table Matter**
Show Date: 4/16/1961
Company: **Greater Southwest Insurance Company**
Agent: **Barton H.B. Hollister**
Exp. Acct: $438.00

Synopsis: Barton H.B. Hollister calls (Oh not Hollister in Phoenix, Arizona.) That's right. (Oh, here we go again.) What was that? (Nothing, nothing at all, just go right ahead). Hollister wants Johnny to come to Phoenix to defend the life of a client, Henry Kirkum. Johnny tells Hollister that he has never liked, does not now like, and never will like these bodyguard assignments. Johnny tells Hollister to call the Phoenix police. Hollister tells Johnny that the client does not live in Phoenix, and that Johnny will be paid handsomely for his efforts. Suddenly Johnny is interested. Johnny wants to talk about how much he will be paid, but Hollister hangs up. "Okay friend, just wait until you see my expense account."

Johnny recounts how he had so far avoided assignments from Hollister, who is an egotistical, finicky, penny-pinching, stuffed-shirt who always demanded rather than asked. Johnny notes $4.00 for a cab, no let's start this off right, $6.00 for a cab to the airport and plane fare to Phoenix, Arizona. Johnny arrives early in the morning and cabs to Hollister's office where he yells at Johnny for not being there earlier. Johnny is too late, as Kirkum has been found dead.

Kirkum, who was insured for $70,000, has been murdered, or committed suicide. The police think it was murder. The only suspect they are holding is the beneficiary, Walter Pinkley. Walter is also a policyholder, so if he did commit the murder, Hollister is stuck with two policies.

Hollister wants Johnny to rent a car and drive to the small town of Tuttle, 30 miles northeast of here. The police in Tuttle is Alfred Appleby. Then go to the Yucca Flower Rest Home, where Pinkley and Kirkum lived. The rest home is for people with lung problems.

Johnny insists on talking about the fees in the case, and Hollister tells Johnny that if he can prove suicide, Johnny will get $1,000, oh, OK, $1,500. But will get nothing if it was murder. Johnny insists on $2,000 in either case and wins the argument.

Johnny rents a car and drives to Tuttle, Arizona and stops at the city hall. In the jail, he meets Walter Pinkley who thinks the murder of Henry was awful. The chief picked on Walter because he had told everyone at the captain's table that he was going to visit with Henry because he was his friend. Henry appreciated Walter's abilities as a composer and shows Johnny a musical score for a concerto.

Walter tells Johnny that it was nice of Henry to leave him the money so that he now can buy a piano and compose. Walter tells Johnny that Henry had been worried about something lately. He and Henry had talked for hours, but Henry seemed depressed.

Walter left around ten when Henry told him he had to write an important letter for someone who was coming to visit. Walter tells Johnny that they found Henry on the floor with a pistol the next morning, but Henry would never commit suicide. Walter is happy that the jail is so quiet, so he can work on his music. Johnny is sure that Walter is not a killer in his book.

Johnny drives to the rest home, which has an office and a number of cabins. Chief Appleby meets Johnny at the door and tells Johnny that he has the case all sewed up. The chief thinks it was Pinkley because he has proof. The scene was made to look like suicide, and the gun had no prints on it, but only Pinkley was in to see Kirkum. What Pinkley did not know is that Kirkum had written a letter to Johnny.

Appleby gives Johnny the letter that says "Dear Mr. Johnny Dollar, honored sir. There is within this place one who would avenge himself upon my life. Nor have I been remiss in my endeavor to assuage the passion that manifestly provoked his wish for my demise. But alas, I had made it only too clear I could no longer abide his ridiculous concettos. And so, because of my resentment over his stupid concettos he seeks revenge. And lest he seek to destroy me ere you come to afford me protection, I tell you now his name is, but hark there is a knock upon my door. I shall finish this anon."

Johnny learns that Kirkum was an old ham actor but he and Appleby disagree over the word "concetto", with the chief thinking it referred to Pinkley's concertos. This is all the proof that Appleby needs and is sure that Kirkum wrote it before Pinkley came in.

Johnny remembers the reference to the others at the captain's table. Johnny is told that they all eat their meals together every day and have for years. The other members of the group are an old lady named Sarah Sanderson, a man who calls himself "Captain" Howard, and an old man named David Hesher. Johnny asks the chief to get them together so he can talk to them.

Johnny gets a dictionary and looks up a word and then goes to meet the others. Mrs. Sanderson just cried, and Hesher's mind was going and he was no help at all. But Captain Eustis Howard tells Johnny that he has used his mind to solve more complicated cases than this. Howard is convinced that Pinkley is the killer, and that he could have written the so-called music Pinkley wrote in a week.

Johnny reminds the chief that Kirkum had changed the beneficiary of the policy recently. Appleby tells Johnny that the previous beneficiary had been the whole group. Johnny notes that the others were cut off in the change, and the letter that was left on the desk, where Pinkley could have seen it. Johnny is convinced that the killer misread the letter the same way he and the chief did, and left it there, thinking it blamed Pinkley.

Johnny shows the chief that the dictionary defines "concetto" as an old Italian word for conceit. Add them up and the old conceited Captain was cut off along with a couple of others who did not care. He did not like the snub it implied any more than being turned down by Pinkley over the music. He made the killing look like a suicide so no one would get the money.

When he found the letter, he was sure he could get both Kirkum and Pinkley, so he wiped the prints off the gun. Howard admits he killed Kirkum but is surprised that the chief would take him in like some common person, and for a very small mistake.

"Oh Mr. Barton H. B. Hollister, you better shed a bit of your conceit and pay me not only the fee you promised, but an expense account total, including the trip back to Hartford, and believe me all the incidentals I could possibly cook up, a total of $438 even."

"Next week, the fog closing in over a dark abandoned pier in San Diego. A killer on the loose."

Notes:
- The preview in this program indicates that the next program should be *The Simple Simon Matter*, but with no dated scripts it is impossible to tell.
- Edgar Stehli is Walter, Richard Dendrick is Barton, John Griggs is Eustis, Jim Boles is the chief.
- Art Hannes is the announcer.

- Musical supervision is by Ethel Huber.

Producer: Bruno Zirato, Jr.   Writer: Jack Johnstone
Cast: Edgar Stehli, Richard Dendrick, John Griggs, Jim Boles

◆ ❖ ◆

Show: **The Latrodectus Matter**
Show Date: **4/23/1961**
Company: **Philadelphia Mutual Liability & Casualty Insurance**
Agent: **Harry Branson**
Exp. Acct: **$111.35**

Synopsis: Harry Branson calls John and he is as confused as usual. Harry has a client, Eustis Royal Pennybank. Johnny recognizes the name as that of a bug chaser or butterfly collector who made the magazines a year or so back. Harry corrects Johnny in that Pennybank is one of the greatest entomological researchers in the country today. Pennybank has told Harry that he is being threatened. Harry wants Johnny to fly down so he can meet Pennybank in his office.

Johnny flies to Philadelphia, Pennsylvania and cabs to Harry's office where he meets Dr. Pennybank, an old man with sharp piercing green eyes. Pennybank tells Johnny that his work has always been of value to the scientific world. In his home are priceless records from his research in toxicology.

He alone had determined that the south Jersey cattle killing a few years ago was done with the venom of the Agkistrodon moccasin, he proved that the killers used the deadly venom of the copperhead snake to kill the cattle. Only he was able to differentiate it from the venom of the Agkistrodon piscivorus, the water moccasin.

He has decided to study and classify the various Arachnida, a profuse class of the order Araneae, a small part of the insect world. He has records in his home that are of international importance in these troubled times, but someone has tried to steal them from him, usually at night.

He will turn the records over to the authorities only after he has finished his research. He cannot have copies made, as that would run the risk that they would be leaked out, and he needs the papers for his research. Pennybank has, for his protection, isolated a group of the genus latrodectus. Pennybank tells Johnny to come to his home in Kenwood tonight, and leaves to make a speech to the Academy of Science whether they like it or not. He is in danger, and he must see Johnny tonight.

Johnny wonders if Pennybank is an old crackpot, but Harry tells Johnny that there is a $50,000 policy with several scientific organizations and his niece, Clara Benson, as the beneficiary. Johnny parks his bags at the Belleview Stratford and rents a car.

Johnny drives to Dr. Pennyback's around three p.m. and hears a door slam in the back. As Johnny knocks he hears a car pull away and finds the door unlocked. Johnny goes in and finds Pennybank dead on the floor.

Pennybank is dead with two bullets in the chest, and the car Johnny had seen was a dark green compact model. Johnny looks at the laboratory, which is full of all sorts of live insects, complete with their food in a refrigerator. On an empty cage, Johnny spots the words latrodectus, Black Widow.

Johnny hears footsteps approaching and Johnny jumps the man as he enters the door. Johnny realizes the man is a police officer and shows him his ID. Johnny then shows him the body of Pennybank. The officer tells Johnny his work is done and slugs Johnny and takes him into town, where Johnny's ID is checked and officer Fallon apologizes.

The lab crew examines the house and takes the body for an autopsy. The initial report names the cause of death as a .25 Colt. The police could find only a few things belonging to the niece in the house.

Johnny notes how a belt loop had been torn, like if a key chain had been torn off, but no keys were found. The cleaning woman has been in the hospital for several weeks and was fed up with the old man. Johnny thinks about the term latrodectus and gets a hunch.

Johnny visits the beautiful niece, Clara Benson in her apartment, and she is upset about her uncle and has no idea who could have killed him. He was peculiar, but he was doing no harm.

Clara tells Johnny that men had come and offered money for his reports, but Clara does not know who they were. Johnny asks about her car, which is an old beat-up model, and she is upset that Johnny would suspect her. She tells Johnny that her husband had died recently from a hit-and-run driver and is so alone now.

Johnny wonders: cui bono, who benefits. No one but the beautiful black haired young widow. And what about the papers in the safe? And the missing keys? And what about using latrodectus for protection?

Johnny looks for used car dealers in the area and finds the dealer that sold her the old car earlier that day in trade for a new green compact. Johnny drives back to the apartment but Clara is gone.

Johnny drives to Pennyback's home and sees a light on inside. Johnny climbs in through a window and looks for the source of a light. In the kitchen Johnny sees a doorway to the cellar and hears keys trying to open a lock. Johnny hears a scream and runs down to find Clara covered with Black Widow spiders.

"But by the time I could reach her side and beat them away she had fallen unconscious. She had been struck by tens, by scores of them. On her hands, on her arms, struck down by the beautiful deadly protectors of that safe, latrodectus, Black Widows.

Clara died within minutes before I could possibly get help. And the papers she had killed her uncle to obtain: nothing. Nothing but the confused scribblings of a demented old man. Expense account total, including the trip back to Hartford, $111.35."

"Next week, one of the toughest gangs I ever had to deal with, a gang of kids. A rat-pack."

Notes:
- **Art Hannes is the announcer.**

- Musical supervision is by Ethel Huber.
- This program contains commercials with Dennis James for Kellogg's All-Bran, and Arthur Godfrey for a cancer life savings facts booklet and the need to make contributions to the cancer fund.
- The copperhead (Agkistrodon contortrix) is misidentified as Agkistrodon moccasin, but the water moccasin is correctly identified as Agkistrodon piscivorus.

Producer:	Bruno Zirato, Jr. Writer: Jack Johnstone
Cast:	Lawson Zerbe, Elaine Rost, Robert Dryden, Ralph Bell, Jack Grimes

◆ ❖ ◆

Show:	The Rat Pack Matter
Show Date:	4/30/1961
Company:	Eternity Mutual Insurance Company
Agent:	George Franklin
Exp. Acct:	$0.00

Synopsis: The opening to this program is missing.

Johnny tells George that only 700 more dollars and Johnny can tool around the countryside in a brand-new fancy sports car that will run him slightly over $10,000, "so if you want me to come to Corpus Christi, you will have to guarantee me that amount". George tells Johnny that his car sounds like the little hunk of iron he keeps stashed in his garage, the Franzetti. George loves it, now that he has gotten used to it. Come on down and drive mine, and if you clear up this case, the car is yours for as long as you like, and maybe he can dig up a little extra for Johnny, say $700.

Johnny flies to Corpus Christi and George meets Johnny at the airport, but the Franzetti is safe in his garage until after Johnny cleans up the case. George has rented a new compact car for Johnny to drive to Summit Hill, Texas, a nice well-to-do residential area inhabited by retired oil people.

George has been writing checks to settle claims for malicious mischief to cars. Most have been hot-rodded in the country and abandoned. Johnny tells George that it sounds like the work of kids, and George agrees. It is the work of a rat-pack. The police force is only one man and a couple of half-witted deputies. Even the police have had a car stolen. When the state police come in, everything settles down. That is why Johnny will not get the Franzetti.

Johnny buys a blank book with "Official Business — Federal Population Survey" embossed on it and drives to Summit Hill where he interviews a number of families.

At a gas station Johnny is told that the owner has a gun and would use it. Chief Foster cannot do anything, and the kids always seem to know when the police are around. They hot wire the cars and use Halloween costumes to disguise themselves. The man tells Johnny not to go there tonight but go in the daylight.

Johnny goes to visit the Briarleys and is let in, as Mrs. Briarley knows Johnny is taking a survey, but Mr. Briarley is carrying a shotgun. Their son Frank is out on a date and Mrs. Briarley is unsure about having bought a new car with all those awful things being done. They wish something could be done, and Johnny tells them that there is a local informant in town who tips off the kids. Johnny tells them that there are no places for the kids to get together and blow off steam.

Mrs. Briarley tells Johnny that the parents provide for that by giving their children everything they want. But they do not give the kids cars, as they do not want to spoil them. Their son Frankie is twenty-two and does not work because he does not have to. Johnny starts to yell at them but hears a noise outside.

Johnny pulls his gun and goes outside and yells at the kids just as they drive off with the new car. Johnny tries to blow out a tire by shooting at the car. After five shots, someone puts a switchblade in his back and tells him not to turn around.

The knife is pulled along Johnny's neck and he feels blood. "Jean" is told to take his gun, and Johnny sees heavy gloves, torn jeans and a mask on the figure of a girl. Johnny calls the boy a tough guy, and the boy tells him to turn around to see his face. Johnny turns slowly and knocks the knife from the boy's hand but is knocked out with his own gun.

Johnny wakes up on the Briarley's couch with the taste of bourbon in his mouth. They tell Johnny that they had found him after the chief called to tell them that their new car had been wrecked. They searched him and know who he is. Mr. Briarley tells Johnny that he has thought about what Johnny had told him.

Frankie comes in and asks about the missing car. Frank is introduced to Johnny, and he knows who Johnny is. He tells Johnny that he and his girl had taken a bus to a dance. Johnny hopes he is not involved with the kids. Frankie plays innocent but tells Johnny that if he finds out who the gang is, maybe Johnny can help.

They cannot leave because their parents will not let them do anything. Mrs. Briarley gets upset but Johnny tells her to let Frankie work things out for himself. Frankie tells Johnny that he knows who the kids are. Johnny wants to know who they are, but Frankie tells Johnny they would not think much of him if he did.

These cases of mine usually have big fat dramatic endings, and the devil with any kind of a message, well not so this time. I honestly do not know if I did the right thing or not on this one. Too much faith in the younger generation, well maybe I have.

But the next evening there at the home of the Briarleys there was a meeting of the parents, of all the wealthy, doting indulgent parents of all the kids in their late teens and early twenties. I tore into those parents, and by the time I finished there were plenty of red faces among them. Incidentally, out of the corner of my eye, I thought I saw the face of a teenager in the shadows outside one of the windows.

What I said to those people in laying down the law to them, well I honestly do not remember exactly. But it must have given them a jolt. And if they carry out their plans there won't be a kid in that town with an idle moment on his hands. But their activities, their projects will be their own, with as little parental advice and guidance as possible.

Then the following night, thanks to a tip-off by young Frank, without the knowledge of his parents, I barged into a meeting of the kids, seven or eight of them. As I might have expected, they were there in their foolish masks and makeup knowing that I would be among them. And if you think I had been rough on their parents, but again, by the time I had finished with them...

Johnny tells the kids that they will go to jail if they continue with their activities. They take off their masks, and one tells Johnny he will get a job to repay the damage he has done.

"Well I sure hope I did the right thing by simply leaving it the way it stood, and yet, what else could I have done, have them all locked up for something that was only partly their doing. Try to make them into criminals, I don't think so. Incidentally because of a call to get right back to Hartford, I never did drive George Franklin's Franzetti. But I did get that $700 fee, and that will help me buy one of my own. Expense account total, including...oh, what am I talking about, this one is on the cuff."

"Next week, a doll, a purple doll and all that goes with it."

Notes:
- Musical supervision is by Ethel Huber.
- Dan MacDonald is the announcer.
- William Redfield is George, Gertrude Warner is Mrs. Briarley, Phil Meader is Frank, Jack Grimes is the kid, Roger De Koven is the gas station attendant, Robert Dryden is Mr. Briarley.
- The Franzetti is a fictitious automobile. But the early 1960's was the age of the sports car, with the Corvette, the Jaguar XKE and a host of other European imports. The $10,000+ price tag is over $82,000 in 2017 dollars.
- The next story in the Johnny Dollar canon is *The Purple Doll Matter* broadcast on 5/7/1961. While the program is missing, a program listing from the *Tampa Bay Times* gives this overview: "Freelance insurance investigator Johnny Dollar becomes involved with a beautiful girl when he is called in on *The Purple Doll Matter*. The girl, Sandra Kellogg, tells Johnny that she fears her wealthy uncle is in danger from an ex-gangster hired as a handyman on his isolated estate. She leads Dollar to her uncle's home where they arrive too late to save his life. Later, police find the handyman dying of a gunshot. Johnny then attempts to beat Sandra to her own home, but the explosion of a booby trap wired to her front door brings a third casualty and the solution of the case."
- The *Tampa Bay* article above is dated 4/16/61, two weeks before the date of the program. This information is provided by Dr. Joe Webb.

Producer: Bruno Zirato, Jr.   Writer: Jack Johnstone

Cast:	William Redfield, Gertrude Warner, Phil Meader, Jack Grimes, Roger De Koven, Robert Dryden

♦ ❖ ♦

Show:	**The Simple Simon Matter**
Show Date:	5/21/1961
Company:	Tri-Western Life Insurance Company
Agent:	Frank Francis
Exp. Acct:	$450.00

Synopsis: Frank Francis calls Johnny from Los Angeles, and wants Johnny to get there before noon, or it will be too late. He will meet Johnny at the airport. Johnny has to find out if the recent death of a policyholder was an accident, suicide or murder.

Johnny flies to Los Angeles, California and the flight arrives early. Frank meets Johnny and takes him to his office. He tells Johnny that he will get a phone call at noon for Johnny. On the way in, Frank tells Johnny that Gerald Raymond Hilton is on the books as an accident or suicide. His wife is the beneficiary of the $16,000 policy, with double indemnity for accidental death.

The accident happened on a side road near Newhall, where Gerry lost control on a curve and went into a canyon and died. Frank is sure that it was not an accident. The police found that Hilton had stopped or been stopped.

The phone call Frank is expecting makes him feel otherwise. The investigation found that the car had been driven over the edge of the road. Gerry had been having financial troubles, and his wife is sick but working in a factory. Frank thinks that it was suicide made to look like an accident.

Hilton had a shady reputation, and only the policy to leave the wife and a three-year-old son who needs an operation. Frank has known the wife for years, and Gerry deserved to have a police record. The caller told Frank to get ready to pay off the policy, and that he would only give his information to Johnny Dollar.

In the office, the call comes in and Johnny answers. The operator has a person-to-person call from San Diego. A voice tells Johnny that Gerry Hilton was not an accident or a suicide, and the voice knows who did it. Johnny is told to meet him on the Pescadero Pier in San Diego at 11:00 p.m., and no tricks. The voice tells Johnny that maybe he will recognize him and hangs up.

Frank wants the money to go to the family, and Johnny thinks he recognizes the voice, so Johnny is going to go.

Johnny rents a car and visits Gerry's widow, Marjorie. The apartment is small and Tommy is on a cot, very sick. Johnny learns that a free clinic will do the intestinal operation. She tells Johnny that Gerry would never commit suicide and he had tried to get her out of the shabby apartment. They got married last year, and Tommy is not their child. Gerry was sure that something was going to turn up soon. He was better than Tommy's father, Allie Parson.

Johnny recognizes the name as Alfred H. Parson, and the "H" stands for heroin. The police have been looking for him for five years. He came to see Marjorie a couple weeks ago, and Gerry threw him out. Alfred was always good at smooth talk. Johnny gives her $50 in case Tommy needs something. Johnny is puzzled by Marjorie, and the way she talked — like a movie gun moll.

Johnny drives to San Diego and finds the Pescadero pier, which has no ships and only an old warehouse. Johnny catches a couple movies and dinner while he waits. At eleven Johnny goes to the pier, which is shrouded in fog.

Johnny is stopped by a voice that tells Johnny to hide behind a box. Johnny recognizes voice as Simon "Simple Simon" Hacker. Johnny had chased him once and had to let him go. Simon knows where Allie Parson is, and knows that Johnny will protect him. He tells Johnny that the police in Newhall know that Gerry was dead before he went over the cliff. Allie killed Gerry so he could get his girl back.

Johnny gives Simon $100 and just as he is about to talk, Simon is shot several times. Three shots are aimed at Johnny, so he dives into the water and swims under the pier and back to his car.

Johnny goes to the harbor police and tells them about Simon. So maybe Allie is making a play for Marjorie, and she would be a push over for Allie.

Johnny drives back to her apartment at 4 a.m. and there is a light on. Johnny spots her bags packed, and she tells Johnny she is taking Tommy to the hospital. Johnny tells her that she knew where Allie and Gerry got their money, and there were probably three or four husbands before Allie. "There were only two", she blurts out.

Johnny tells her that Allie killed Gerry because he was afraid Gerry would tell the police where Allie was, and Allie killed Simon because Marjorie had called and told Allie where Johnny was going. Marjorie calls for Allie, and Parson comes out with a gun.

Allie takes Johnny's gun and prepares to shoot him with a silenced gun. Marjorie tries to close the door and the police come in with Simon and shots are fired. The police tell Johnny that Simon had told the police what was happening and brought them to Marjorie's apartment.

Johnny talks to Simon who is not doing too well. Simon tells Johnny that he wanted to go straight but waited too long. But he tried. Johnny notes he tried but waited too long, as Simon dies.

"Marjorie and the boy, I don't know. I kinda felt sorry for the poor kid Tommy. But her, I can't help wondering if she even deserves a break. Expense account total, including a trip back to Hartford, call it $450 even."

"Next week, a most ingenious method of blackmail."

Notes:
- This program contains a commercial about the Eisenhower commission on American goals. CBS feels that this is an important document.
- Johnny notes that he is traveling with only one bag   a glorified briefcase that contains everything he owns.
- Jackson Beck is Frank Francis, Elizabeth Lawrence is Marjorie, Mason Adams is Simon, Bernard Grant is Allie, Maurice Tarplin is the police lieutenant.

- Art Hannes is the announcer.
- Musical supervision is by Ethel Huber.

Producer: Bruno Zirato, Jr.   Writer: Jack Johnstone
Cast: Jackson Beck, Elizabeth Lawrence, Mason Adams, Bernard Grant, Maurice Tarplin

♦ ❖ ♦

Show: **The Lone Wolf Matter**
Show Date: 5/28/1961
Company: State Unity Life Insurance Company
Agent: Harvey Wakeman
Exp. Acct: $88.40

Synopsis: Harvey Wakeman calls Johnny from New York, and he has a problem, or rather his client Thomas Rayburn Morgan does. He is a stockbroker over in Newark. Morgan called Harvey and he needs Johnny Dollar, and no one else. Harvey gives Johnny the address and tells Johnny that he will call Morgan and tell him Johnny is on the way over. Harvey has no idea what the problem is, and Johnny wants to beg off a blind assignment. Harvey tells Johnny that he has told Morgan that a man like Johnny comes expensive and will require a big fee. Fee? I'm on my way.

Johnny flies to Newark, New Jersey and cabs to Morgan's office on Commerce Street. Morgan tells Johnny that he is the only one who can help Morgan, especially in the area of confidentiality. Morgan has not talked to the local authorities or the police in Philadelphia, where the letter came from. Morgan tells Johnny the matter could cause complete and utter ruin for him and his family. Morgan makes Johnny promise that he will keep the details quiet.

The letter is addressed to "Thomas, or rather Danny Fairland", and continues on how the writer has followed Morgan's business ever since the time they worked together on an investment scheme some years ago. The writer has fallen on hard times and is sure that Morgan would be more than happy to help him out, as he has never revealed the details of their enterprise to anyone.

The writer wants Morgan to withdraw $10,000 from the bank and he will contact him later on where to deliver the money. The writer has completely written out the details of their scheme and has given it to a friend. If anything happens, the friend will give it to the newspapers. The signature is "HBW".

Morgan tells Johnny that the writer is Henry B. Wolf, and the crime is a stock swindle that Morgan was involved in many years ago. Morgan was young and gullible, and he thought he could get enough money to start his business. Morgan had kept a list of those he had defrauded and has anonymously paid them back with interest. Morgan asks Johnny what he can do, and Johnny tells him "that is a good question."

Johnny is convinced that Morgan is telling the truth, but how to find Wolf? Morgan has withdrawn the money and is waiting for the call. If it were not for his family, Morgan is not sure what he could do. Johnny tells him that all you can do is pay Wolf off, but he will constantly need money.

Johnny asks Morgan to have his secretary buy him some magazines as Johnny is going to stay in the office until Wolf calls. Johnny spends three days reading in Morgan's office, going to lunch with him and spending his nights with Morgan at his home, posing as an old school friend.

On the third day, the call comes in and Wolf tells Morgan he has no choice but to lend him the money he needs. Wolf tells Morgan that if he calls in the police, Morgan's old transgressions will be released to the papers. Wolf laughs when Morgan asks how he can be sure that Wolf will not come back asking for more money.

Wolf has called Morgan's wife and told her that he is going to have dinner with him tonight and then Wolf gives Morgan the instructions. After hearing what Wolf wants, Johnny tells Morgan he is leaving and tells Morgan to meet Wolf in Monroe Park and give him the money. "See you someday" he tells an abashed Morgan.

Johnny makes a phone call and then has drinks and dinner with an old friend, retired Judge Amos Ordway, who has been around a long time and has a good memory.

The judge remembers the swindle and was a lawyer at the time and a few of his clients were bilked. Johnny is told that those who were repaid may not have a claim in the courts. The laws were not as strict then and the operation could have been construed as legal. If the less guilty one of them has lived a good life, there might not be a problem.

Johnny tells the judge he knows who Danny Fairland is, but the judge plays ignorant. The judge does tell Johnny that if he needs a good broker to go see Thomas Morgan.

Later that night Johnny goes to a local park, roughs up a park guard and takes a key, after making a $5 deposit to the guard's pocket. Johnny waits in the park maintenance shed with the unconscious guard. At eleven Johnny hears footsteps of a man pacing. Johnny opens the shack door as another man walks up.

Henry has met Morgan and tells him he had to make sure that Morgan was alone. He laughs and tells Morgan he might just do this again. Morgan is told to leave and Wolf waits for him to go.

A man who has overheard the blackmail conversation approaches Wolf. He wants the money and the envelope so he can do the same thing. Wolf tells the man that there is no envelope, and it was only a bluff.

Suddenly Johnny tells him who he is. Johnny tells Wolf that he is a lone wolf. And even if he tries to tell anyone about his past, he would only embarrass himself. No one would believe him if he tried to claim that Danny Fairland was someone else.

Johnny tells Wolf that if he tells what he knows, he will go to jail for the blackmail, not for a swindle everyone has forgotten. Any tales of the past would not make the papers, as Johnny knows a judge.

Turn him in? Take the chance that he might be able to hurt Thomas Morgan? Or let him go with the full knowledge that I could prove a charge of blackmail against him? What would you have done? Oh? Well that's just exactly what I did. Expense account total, including incidentals, $88.40."

"Next week, a raging blizzard in the middle of May, and the pure white snow carries the mark of death."

Notes:
- This program contains a commercial for CBS news, which goes all over the world to bring the most up to date events. Also, it is National Hospital Week.
- Santos Ortega is Wolf, Sam Gray is Morgan, William Redfield is Harvey, Robert Dryden is the Judge.
- Art Hannes is the announcer.
- Musical supervision is by Ethel Huber.

Producer: Bruno Zirato, Jr.   Writer: Jack Johnstone
Cast: Santos Ortega, Sam Gray, William Redfield, Robert Dryden

◆ ❖ ◆

Show: **The Yaak Mystery Matter**
Show Date: **6/4/1961**
Company: **Four State Mutual Insurance Company**
Agent: **Steve Yokum**
Exp. Acct: **$207.75**

Synopsis: Steve Yokum calls Johnny from Kalispell, Montana. Steve wants Johnny to fly out about his client John Turner Whiticum, who is insured for $500,000 double indemnity. It looks like the company will be out a million if it has happened. Steve does not know if Whiticum is dead or not, but Johnny has to find out.

Johnny buys the paper and checks the weather for Montana and flies to Kalispell, Montana where Steve meets him with a jeep. Steve tells Johnny that he is going up to the town of Yaak, Montana, up in the real snow country.

Steve tells Johnny that Whiticum made his money in lumber and retired after his wife died. He and his daughter Valerie and her husband Lou Larson have gone up to Shorty Bessum's camp to do some hunting. Steve has heard from Shorty, and Whiticum and the kids are out in the woods hunting.

After lunch Johnny and Steve drive through a wet snowfall on the way to Yaak. Steve tells Johnny that the hunting is good in that area. After buying gas in Yaak, they drive on to Shorty's camp. In the cabin, Kate Bessum gives them coffee with rum to warm them up.

Shorty tells Johnny that he told them not to go out, but Whiticum did not listen. Shorty thinks Whiticum was trying to make his son-in-law into a real man. After the snow storm, Shorty and others started looking for them, but could not find anything. Shorty hears a horse and they go outside.

Lou Larson is on the horse and they take him off and into the cabin. Larson is still alive and Johnny wonders how he survived. Later that night Larson tells Johnny that the others are dead.

It was somewhere on the south side of Lost Horse Mountain. They made camp when the snow started. It was in an area near a deep crevice. Kate calls the area Dead Man's Hole, a death trap. Lou was sent to find wood, and his horse followed him. He heard a loud sound and looked back to see snow and rocks falling down. It was an avalanche.

Johnny tells them to put Lou to bed in Mr. Whiticum's room, and Johnny asks Shorty how far it is to the area. Shorty tells Johnny it is only a couple hours if you know where to go. Shorty tells Johnny that no one has ever come out of the chasm and that it does not take much the start an avalanche in that area.

Johnny looks through Lou's room and in a suit case he finds a topographic map of the area around Lost Horse Mountain, and a book about the legends of the area. Next morning Johnny wants to look at Dead Man's Hole before it washes out in the spring floods.

Shorty and Johnny leave and head into the woods as a storm starts to blow in. Johnny wants to get into the chasm before the storm hits, but it breaks before he gets there.

While waiting for the storm to ease, Johnny uses binoculars and spots the bodies on the side of the chasm. Johnny rigs a line to go down and get the bodies, because Johnny saw bullet holes in their heads through the binoculars.

While Johnny is trying to get a line on the bodies bullets start to hit the area and trigger another avalanche. Shorty pulls Johnny up and tells him that he saw the rocks shot away.

Johnny tells Shorty about the book that Lou had brought, and that Lou had killed Whiticum and his daughter for the money. Whiticum did not like Lou, so by killing them he would get all the money. Larson only married the daughter to get at the money.

While Johnny is wondering if Lou is around and armed, Lou comes up with the rifle to kill them. Lou tells them that he was just wandering around, and that he really had spent the previous night in the hay shed with his horse. Lou tells Shorty and Johnny to back up into the chasm, and Johnny tells Lou to look behind him, but he does not take the bait. Just as Lou is going to shoot, Steve shoots him. Steve had decided to follow Lou and almost lost him.

"So, the laws of succession take over, and somebody else gets the insurance, and the old man's estate. And as for Lou Larson, well even hanging is too good for that kind. Expense account total, including the trip home, $207.75."

"Next week, The Stock in Trade Matter, and the stock I'm talking about is just exactly that — stock."

Notes:
- Bob Readick makes an announcement for National Radio Month: "The CBS Radio network and this station are both very much a part of National Radio Month. But the figures show that you the listener are just as much a part of the celebration. You take part every month of every year with your purchases of new radio sets. Today there is an all-time record number of radio sets in use. Today there are more listeners than ever. And the number one network for the best sound around is of course, CBS Radio."

- Robert Dryden is Shorty, Bill Lipton is Steve, Athena Lorde is Kate, Allan Manson is Lou.
- Kalispell is in the northwest corner of Montana, and Yaak is almost on the Canadian and Idaho borders.
- I have changed the name of this episode, which is usually listed as "Yak", to correspond to the actual name of the location.
- Art Hannes is the announcer.
- Musical supervision is by Ethel Huber.

Producer: Bruno Zirato, Jr.   Writer: Jack Johnstone
Cast: Robert Dryden, Bill Lipton, Athena Lorde, Allan Manson

◆ ❖ ◆

Show: **The Stock in Trade Matter**
Show Date: 6/11/1961
Company: Worldwide Mutual Insurance Company
Agent: Ripley Teeter
Exp. Acct: $325.00

Synopsis: Ripley Teeter calls from Memphis, the finest town on earth. Rip has trouble in Summerville. The trouble is murder.

Johnny flies to Memphis, Tennessee and meets with Rip, who tells the secretary Mary Belle to get a rental car for Johnny. Rip tells Johnny that the deceased is Valney Beauregard Exum. Early this morning his housekeeper found him with his head broken in, and there were no prints on the heavy poker that was used. That is why Johnny was called.

The area is rich in plantations and the Exum money came from cotton. He is living in the plantation house, but the land has all been sold off. Valney somehow managed to keep up the payments on his insurance policy for $35,000, but Rip does not know where his money came from. After the war a lot of the families had to sell off their land and made investments. "You mean the Civil War, Rip?" "I said THE WAR, didn't I?" as Rip laughs.

Rip thinks that Valney got his money from his kinfolk, a niece and a couple of nephews who are also the beneficiaries. There is Clara Belle Otway Exum who lives in town. A nephew also named Valney Beauregard Exum lives in Corpus Christi, Texas. The other nephew is Culpepper Van Buren Oglethorpe who lives in Summerville and works in a real estate office. Rip is sure that neither of them would kill Exum, as they are a fine old southern family.

Valney had no enemies and no real friends. Dolly Cato did the day work cleaning for Valney. The insurance is only $10,000 apiece and the plantation is only worth $10,000. Johnny thinks he better go see the place.

Johnny drives to Summerville, Tennessee and goes to meet Clara Belle Exum in the five-and-dime store where she works. Clara is glad that her uncle is dead. With the money from the insurance she can pay her bills and buy some new things. She tells Johnny that Mrs. Cato probably has more money than Valney did. She worked for Valney out of pity. Clara tells Johnny that she does not know where Valney's money came from. Clara Belle did not know anything.

Johnny drives to the Exum home, which is a wreck with missing columns, broken windows and peeling paint. Johnny meets Sgt. Aiken at the door and gets a look at the crime scene.

Valney was found sprawled on the desk with a tin box in front of him. Johnny is told there were no prints on the box. Aiken thinks that Valney let someone in and was killed late last night. Anyone he would let in at night must have been a friend. Aiken does not know where Valney got his money, but he would cash a check once in a while.

Johnny finds a piece of paper in the hinge and it looks like parchment used for insurance policies, and Johnny wonders if that is where his money came from. Sgt. Aiken tells Johnny that Culpepper Oglethorpe is not doing anything and is stupid enough to kill his kinfolk for money. Aiken tells Johnny that Culpepper did not kill Valney, because he is in jail.

Johnny has no clues he could put his fingers on. Aiken tells Johnny that the other nephew lives in Texas. Aiken had called the nephew and he told Aiken that he could not make it back and would pay for a funeral. Johnny thinks that the other Valney is his only hope and is ready to fly to Corpus Christi.

Johnny has to admit that sheer luck helped him solve this case. It came in the form of a stack of letters in the mailbox, one with a well-known name, Intrastate Telephone Company. Johnny rips the letter open before Sgt. Aiken can stop him, and it contains a dividend check for $250, dividends on 500 shares worth over $40,000. Johnny knows because he owns some of the stock.

Johnny flies to Corpus Christi, Texas and gets a room at the Robert Driscoll. The next day Johnny talks to his friend Wayne Stockseth who tells Johnny that he does have a client named Exum who has a small account. Valney had called Wayne to tell him he had some Intrastate Telephone shares to sell. Just then Valney walks in and sits at Wayne's desk with Johnny watching from the next desk.

As Valney signs the certificates he tells Wayne he wants cash as he has to take a business trip. Johnny tells Wayne to call the police, as the signatures are forgeries. He is Valney Beauregard Exum, but the certificates were stolen from his uncle, who has the same name, when he was murdered. Johnny is sure he can prove it with the pieces of paper that were left in the tin box. Valney tries to run, but Johnny stops him.

"What Exum didn't know of course, was that Wayne, who had done a lot of investigating before handing over all that money, in spite of the way he had carried a small account with the firm, set things up for the murder and robbery. Expense account total, including a trip back to Memphis and then back to Hartford, call it $325 even."

"Next week, one of the cleverest rackets in jewelry that I ever saw. Over a million-dollar's worth."

Notes:
- **Art Hannes is the announcer.**
- **Musical supervision is by Ethel Huber.**

Producer: Bruno Zirato, Jr.   Writer: Jack Johnstone
Cast: Joan Lorring, Mandel Kramer, Ralph Bell, Robert Dryden, Wendell Holmes

Mandel Kramer

Mandel Kramer (1916–1989) became the sixth and final actor to play Johnny Dollar.

Mandel Kramer was an established New York actor with a long radio and television record.

Mandel Kramer was a very personable Johnny Dollar. As the program tried to adapt to the hip nature of the 1960's, Johnny tried to move with it. The Johnny Dollar of Mandel Kramer was a personable ladies man who was also able to get the job done.

Mandel continued as Johnny Dollar until September 30, 1962 when the "Golden Age of Radio" ended. Mandel died in 1989.

The following are the Mandel Kramer Johnny Dollar programs.

♦ ❖ ♦

Show: The Low Tide Matter
Show Date: 6/25/1961
Company: Tri-Mutual Insurance Company, Ltd
Agent: Frederick Bennom
Exp. Acct: $0.00

Synopsis: Frederick Bennom calls Johnny and has an important matter for him. Bennom usually uses investigators from his own company, but none of them is a fisherman. Bennom understands from the radio broadcasts that Johnny is a very good fisherman. Bennom wants Johnny to meet him at 3:30 to discuss the case.

Johnny notes he would not select Tri-Mutual as a company to work for, as they are notoriously stingy. But mention fishing and Johnny is gone. At 3:30 exactly Johnny is brought into the office and tells Bennom that he will have to pay Johnny's expenses, and a fee or a commission on the amount of the insurance involved. Bennom corrects Johnny and tells him that the commission will be on the amount of money saved. Bennom finally agrees to the larger of the fee or the commission.

Bennom tells Johnny that the Foster Machine Tool Company has a partnership policy for $500,000. He is worried about Charles Foster, who asked if the policy could be cancelled. Business has not been good, and Foster suspects his partner, Michael Brady, of being responsible for the down turn. Brady would not cancel the policy and told Foster that he needed a vacation. Bennom has tried to contact them, but they have gone fishing. Bennom wonders if Brady is right, and that Brady knows that the only way to get the business is to get Foster out of the way. Brady has refused to tell anyone, including their wives, where he has gone fishing with Foster. Johnny has no idea what his first move will be.

Johnny calls on Mrs. Foster who is worried sick about her husband. After talking, Johnny suspects that Bennom might be right. Johnny calls on Mrs. Kathy Brady, who is a living doll, and is not worried about her husband. They are living high on the hog, and she has been partying while Mike is away. Mike will come back, he always does. He has gone fishing at Lake Mead, Lake Mohave and in Maine too.

She senses that Johnny is worried about Mr. Foster, and assured Johnny that sort of thing could not happen again. Johnny asks what she means, and she tells Johnny that Mike had another partner a couple years ago. They went hunting in Canada, and some fool shot his partner and almost killed Mike. He was so upset he sold the business.

Kathy really wants Johnny to come to one of her parties, but Johnny tells her he has to go a long, long way away. Johnny realizes how well Mike could use the money and how much of a gold mine the machine tool company is. And what about that hunting accident?

Johnny is ready to have a drink and cook a steak when he has a brainstorm and calls Ham Pratt at Lake Mohave Resort. Johnny asks Ham if he has seen Charles Foster, and Ham tells Johnny that the police, the sheriff and the coroner seem to think that Charles Foster has been in some sort of accident.

Johnny grabs a flight to Las Vegas and rents a car for the drive to Lake Mohave. At the resort, Ham tells Johnny that the authorities have asked Brady to hang around. Ham tells Johnny that Foster and Brady had not been getting along, and they went fishing separately on Monday.

Foster went up to the Big Basin and Brady went down by the dam. The wind came up and everyone came in but Foster. After the wind died down, they went looking for Foster but all they found was the boat, beached up by the big island, and the body has not been found.

The sheriff calls and tells Ham that Brady can leave, but Johnny tells him not to relay the message. Johnny asks for a boat and makes a phone call to the weather bureau to get the direction of the winds during the storm. Johnny explores all the shoreline along the Arizona side of the lake north and east of the island. In a cove called the "rock pile" Johnny finds a body in fifteen feet of water, with a foot tangled in an anchor line. Johnny dives for the body and, after dark Johnny brings the body of Charles Foster back to the dock.

Johnny does not want Ham to call the police yet, as they have no proof that Foster was killed. Johnny wants a way to get Brady to show his hand and gets an idea.

The next morning Ham eats breakfast with Brady and tells him it is the least he can do, what with all he has gone through. Ham tells Brady that he had been expecting someone else to join him when Johnny comes in and is introduced as Johnny Harris. Brady thinks he recognizes Johnny's voice, but Ham tells him that "Mr. Dollar" is one of their best fishermen.

Johnny tells Brady that he is going to go to the rock pile today and invites him to come along. Brady asks Ham why he introduced Johnny as "Mr. Harris" and then called him "Mr. Dollar", but Ham nervously tells Johnny that the dam level is going to be lowered today, so the rock pile will be exposed. Ham tells Brady that the water might go down by twenty feet, and Brady tells them he is going out to do some things.

Johnny tells him that he wants to go to the rock pile and move the body of the man he murdered and hide it somewhere else. Mike tells "Mr. Johnny Dollar" that he cannot deny that, nor can Johnny deny who he is.

Brady pulls a gun and tells Johnny it is too bad Johnny caught up with him. Johnny tells Brady that there is no way he can get off a shot before Johnny draws his gun. Johnny outdraws Brady and shoots him. Ham tells Johnny that he had a lot of nerve, but Johnny tells Ham he was scared to death. "I guess I'll never qualify for a part on Gunsmoke."

"Needless to say, Ham's talk about dropping the level of Lake Mohave by a full twenty feet was all a bluff, but it worked. Expense account total, including the trip back to Hartford, well Mr. Bennom, I'll just forget that, in view of my nice fat commission on that half-million-dollar policy."

"Next week, somebody takes a crack at the perfect crime, and with pretty amazing results."

Notes:
- This program contains commercials for Mentholatum Deep Heat Rub and Alpine cigarettes.
- Santos Ortega is Bennom, Teri Keane is Kathy, Bernard Grant is Brady, Robert Dryden is Ham.
- This is the first program with Mandel Kramer as Johnny Dollar.
- Art Hannes is the announcer.
- Musical supervision is by Ethel Huber.

Producer: Bruno Zirato, Jr. **Writer:** Jack Johnstone
Cast: Santos Ortega, Teri Keane, Bernard Grant, Robert Dryden

◆ ❖ ◆

Show: The Imperfect Crime Matter
Show Date: 7/2/1961
Company: State Unity Life Insurance Company
Agent: Lou Little
Exp. Acct: $0.00

Synopsis: Lou Little calls, and Johnny is glad to hear from him. Johnny tells Lou that his wealthy clients have not been cooperating to give Johnny some business. He has a crazy writer on his hands right now. Johnny tells him that the only writer he knows is Johnstone, the man who puts his stories on the air. "Is he normal?" asks Lou. Johnny replies that "he is a bit of a nut about fishing." Lou tells Johnny that all writers are crazy about something, and this author is a nut on murder, and writes nothing else. Can you think of anyone better qualified to plan a perfect crime? Lou thinks that Johnny better come over so they can talk about it. Johnny agrees.

Johnny drives to Lou's Hartford, Connecticut office where Lou tells Johnny that he should really want to be a body guard to Mrs. Porter, the wife of G. Stanley Porter. Johnny recognizes the name and really likes Porter's books and the way he can take a simple plot and develop it into a real story. Mrs. Porter is coming over to talk to Johnny about her problem.

Lou had sold them each a $750,000 policy with double indemnity, and now they are not getting along. Mrs. Porter arrives and Johnny's eyes light up at Denise Porter, about 26 with a figure to die for, and an apprehensive look in her eyes. Denise tells Johnny that her husband has been really good to her, but it seems insincere lately. "Like a last meal", suggests Lou.

Denise tells Johnny that her husband has been married four other times, and she just found out about them. Each of the other wives had died. All he thinks about is planning the perfect crime, and after each of the wives died he wrote a book about the murder of a woman. Johnny thinks it would be ridiculous to write about killing a wife, and then collecting the insurance.

She wants to know what her husband is writing, but he keeps himself locked up at night while he writes. Denise asks Johnny to protect her, and Johnny tells Denise he will get back to her in a couple days.

Johnny goes home to think this case over, and wonders about an author who writes crimes, and who thinks he could get away with it. Johnny decides to take the case, but not to tell Denise, primarily because of the plane ticket to New York that had fallen from Denise's purse in Lou's office.

Johnny calls Randy Singer in New York and then drives to the Porter home. Inside Johnny sees an impressive house after being met at the door by Mr. Porter. He follows Johnny's radio shows and describes Johnny as six feet, 160 pounds (on the nose, Johnny notes), with dark hair and gray eyes and built like a steel spring. Johnny asks for his wife, and Porter tells Johnny that his wife has probably been talking to the insurance company, but he has all the insurance he can use.

Johnny tells him that for policies like theirs, they like to keep in touch. Porter tells Johnny that he likes to surround himself with beautiful things, like Denise.

But writing is his life, and he gets ideas from everyone he meets. Even his former wives, whom he loved dearly, gave him ideas that he wrote down so he will not forget.

Denise had nursed him back from an illness, and he cannot think of losing her. Denise is in New York with some girlfriends and will not be home until after the theater. Porter asks Johnny to come upstairs so he can talk. Johnny is surprised when Porter walks up the stairs with a cane, as he is totally blind.

In the study, Johnny finds a complete apartment, but all Porter can talk about is plots for his books. After drinks Porter fixes a steak dinner for them. Porter washes the dishes and tells Johnny that he always eats upstairs when Denise is away. But late at night he loves to go down stairs to raid the big refrigerator after he puts his typewriter away. Johnny tells him that he would love to raid it with him for two or three nights, but only if no one knows that he is there.

Johnny goes to move his car and thinks from experiences that he might have a hunch. Johnny calls Randy and he tells Johnny that a man met Denise at the plane, and they made a stop at a machine tool supplier before going to some clubs.

Johnny is sure that he was called in as a cover-up for the police, to convince Johnny to convince the police that, when it was all over, Mr. G. Stanley Porter had slipped up. That he had forgotten the trap he had set and that he had fallen into it himself. That's what it would look like all right.

Back with Porter, they are talking, and there is noise at the front door. Porter tells Johnny that it is Denise coming in. Johnny hides in the kitchenette when Denise comes in.

She tells Porter that she and the girls liked the play, and that she has left some milk and chocolate cake in the refrigerator for his late-night snack. Johnny comes out and tells Porter that it was a silly little game he had played with his wife.

Porter tells Johnny that he will show him his latest manuscript later, but he has not written the ending yet. Johnny asks if there is a character like Porter in it, but he will not tell Johnny. Porter suggests going down for the cake, but Johnny tells him a snooze would be better.

After Porter falls asleep, Johnny goes down stairs slowly and finds several dozen ball bearings that Denise and her boyfriend had bought. Had Porter stepped on them, he would have crashed to the bottom. Denise could then have collected the ball bearings and no one would have thought anything except that a blind man had missed a step and fallen. There would be no marks or signs of being pushed.

Johnny collects the ball bearings and is met on the top step by Porter, whose ears have told him everything. Porter tells Johnny that he has provided an ending to the book, and that he has known all about Denise and her boyfriend for a long time. Johnny tells him that he knew Porter would not be the one to do the plotting. Porter asks for the balls, so he can give them to Denise. His will be a lonely life after that.

"I left him then, and walked out to my car, drove home to my apartment, poured myself a good stiff drink, and have been quietly sitting here writing out this report. Whatever may have happened when he faced her with the evidence of her attempt to murder him is none of my affair. The expense account, forget it."

"Next week, I start out to collect a small debt, but instead I collect a bullet."

Notes:
- This program contains a commercial for Mentholatum Deep Heat Rub.
- Allan Manson is Lou, Evelyn Juster is Denise, Raymond Edward Johnson is Porter, Eugene Francis is Randy.
- Art Hannes is the announcer.
- Musical supervision is by Ethel Huber.
- The director for this program is Ed Oates.

Producer: Bruno Zirato, Jr.   Writer: Jack Johnstone
Cast: Allan Manson, Evelyn Juster, Raymond Edward Johnson, Eugene Francis

• ❖ •

Show: **The Well of Trouble Matter**
Show Date: 7/9/1961
Company: State Unity Life Insurance Company
Agent: Lou Little
Exp. Acct: $0.00

Synopsis: Lou Little calls, and Johnny tells him it must be a mistake. He had to wait for two years to get an assignment from Lou, now it's two in two weeks! Lou has a problem getting rid of $1,000 and tells Johnny to come over and get it.

Johnny cabs to Lou's office where Lou gives Johnny a check for $1,000. The check is from G. Stanley Porter, who insisted that Johnny take the money for his last case.

Johnny notices a big stack of money on Lou's desk, and Lou tells Johnny it totals $2,388.24. Lou got it from Jeremy L. Withers, who mails him the cash for his insurance premiums every year. Johnny tells Lou about Durango Laramie Dalhart, who lived in Bum Spung, Oklahoma, and would bring in the premiums cash, in person, totaling nearly $4,000 a year.

Johnny recounts to Lou how Durango had once washed his money and looks at a bill in the stack and asks for the location of Mr. Withers. Johnny calls the police and gets some interesting information.

Johnny buys gas and drives to Granby and then to Millbury Corners. Johnny finds the shabby Withers place in a weed-grown lot. Johnny knocks on the door and introduces himself. Withers unchains and unbolts the door and Johnny tells him he wants to talk about his insurance premiums. Johnny tells Withers that some of the new $20 bills are hot and wants to know where he got the money.

Johnny asks Withers about the money and tells him that it is not counterfeit, but it is plenty hot. Johnny asks why Withers locks himself in and he tells Johnny it is to protect himself from nosy people like Johnny.

Johnny tells Withers that the money is from a bank robbery over in Millville where over $20,000 in new twenties was taken. Johnny remembers the serial numbers because he had worked on the case and had to memorize a series of sequential serial numbers. Withers tells Johnny that it was just part of his money he gets from a pension. Johnny asks how he can pay the insurance premium on a pension.

Withers tells Johnny that he had saved his money and bought insurance. After his wife died and he retired, he continued to buy insurance for his daughter to get when he dies. He tells Johnny that he was a flagman for the railroad. Johnny asks if Withers would like to talk to a judge and he tells Johnny that he had a stepson named Bernard.

Johnny recognizes him as "Barney the Bum" who was killed in a failed bank robbery after the Millville job. Withers tells Johnny that Bernard was no good and deserved what he got. Withers tells Johnny that he kept his money out of the bank, and under the floor but he has used up all his money, now he is using Bernard's money. He did not turn Barney in because he was looking out for himself.

Withers tells Johnny that Bernard's partner had killed the bank guard, and that is why he locks himself in. The killer is Jerry McNear, and he has not told the police because the police would want to know where the money is. McNear has not killed him, because if he does, he will not get the money.

There is a noise outside, but Withers tells Johnny that it is only a shutter. Withers tries to work a deal with Johnny for lenience with the police and finally tells him about the Hacker Farm up the road. At the back of the house there is a well, and in the well shaft there is a shelf, and that is where the money is. Jerry McNear comes in and thanks Withers for telling him where the money is and shoots him. Johnny knocks out a lamp, but McNear laughs and shoots at Johnny three times.

Johnny realizes that he does not have his gun. The first shot puts a crease in Johnny's hair and the others miss when he rolls under the table.

After McNear leaves, Johnny goes to his car and drives up the road to find the Hacker farm while following McNear with his lights out. McNear turns into a farm where the lights are on in the house, but Johnny continues up the road to the real farm.

Johnny parks and locates the well. Johnny secures the rope and bucket and climbs down the well. Johnny finds a hole big enough to crawl into and finds two suitcases with the bank money in them. Johnny then hears McNear, who tells Johnny that he stopped so he could follow Johnny.

Johnny tries to bluff about a gun and puts his jacket and hat on a suitcase. McNear lights a match and shoots the suitcase. Johnny cries out and drops the suitcase into the well. McNear climbs down the well and when he comes along side of the shelf, Johnny slugs him and he falls into the water.

"All he could do when he recovered from the shock of his fall, was stand there in the water at the bottom of the well, knee-deep in the money from the suitcase I'd thrown down there, cursing me as I climbed out and pulled the bucket out of his reach. He was still there when I brought back a couple of the state police. Expense account total, why bother with it when I'll collect such a nice commission on the loot I recovered. Not bad you know. I mean for one night's work."

"Next week, one of the most valuable violins in the world that inspires a man to murder."

Notes:
- This program contains commercials for Mentholatum Deep Heat Rub, 7-Up, Tender Leaf Iced Tea and Alpine cigarettes.
- Parker Fennelly is Withers, Leon Janney is McNear, Allan Manson is Lou.
- Johnny is shot for the 12th time.
- Art Hannes is the announcer.
- Musical supervision is by Ethel Huber.

Producer: Bruno Zirato, Jr. Writer: Jack Johnstone
Cast: Parker Fennelly, Leon Janney, Allan Manson

♦ ❖ ♦

Show: **The Fiddle Faddle Matter**
Show Date: 7/16/1961
Company: **Tri-State Life & Casualty Insurance Company**
Agent: **Earle Poorman**
Exp. Acct: **$681.80**

Synopsis: Earle Poorman calls Johnny, but this time from Florida. Earle and Mike have moved back to Sarasota and have taken over the Tri-State office again. Earle asks Johnny how his musical ear is, and Johnny tells Earle he can tell the difference between a fiddle and a bass drum. Earle tells Johnny that may be good enough, so come on down.

Johnny flies down to Earle's office and greets Don Boomhauer who tells Johnny that Earle probably wanted Johnny to come down just to go fishing or convince him to move to Florida. Don tells Johnny that this is really an unimportant case.

Joseph R. Tetrick retired from the oil and gas business and has an air-conditioned vault built into his house to keep his collection of fiddles in, but he does not know a hemisemidemiquaver from a g-string. The collection has a couple of Strads and an Amati and a Guarneri.

It seems a Mr. Bisiach in Italy has made a collection of musical instruments, and one in particular is called the Canary, and it is insured for $10,000. The Bisiach was taken to a fiddle maker, Antonio Depolito, for a checkup and this morning the place was broken into and the fiddle was gone.

Two hours ago, Tetrick called and told Earle that he had the answer to the whole thing. Johnny is about to call Earle when he comes into the office. Earle is very glum, and tells Johnny that Tetrick must have known who took the fiddle, as he was dead when Earle got there.

So far, the investigation has showed nothing to tell who killed Tetrick. Johnny borrows a car from Don and goes to the shop of Depolito. There were some cheap violins in the window and Depolito was working on a re-varnishing job on a violin.

Johnny tells Depolito who he is, and Depolito tells him it was awful what had happened. The violin was beautiful and sang like a bird. Oh, if only his son...

Depolito was working on the Bisiach last night and had locked the shop and drawn the shades. He fell asleep and woke up when someone was in the shop. The man hit him, and he was out until morning when the police came.

Johnny looks at a window with the glass cut out, but it is an amateur job. Johnny asks where a Bisiach could be purchased, and Johnny is told that a fine violin is like a fine jewel. Earle comes in and tells Johnny that the only place where a Bisiach could be purchased is from the Wurlitzer Collection in Chicago. Johnny thinks that the violin is the key to Tetrick's murder and asks Earle to drive him to the airport.

Johnny flies to Chicago and spends the night in the Blackstone Hotel. The next morning Johnny talks to an expert at the Wurlitzer collection, and they will put out an alert. Johnny is told that no artist will use it, because of its unique color. Johnny is told that Emil Victor, the previous owner, will be heartbroken. Victor sold it because of an accident that injured his hand and left him blind. Johnny suddenly remembers a name and has a hunch, and asks for the address of Emil Victor, and a list of concert bookings for the whole country.

Johnny makes several calls to Earle and learns that the man Johnny is looking for had been in Sarasota on the night in question, and where he will be playing next.

Johnny cabs to the flat of Emil Victor and tells him of his suspicions and what he plans to do with his help. Victor cannot believe that the young musician could do that to his own father. Johnny tells him that Depolito had told Johnny that the shades were drawn when he was working, but he could see the police in the window the next morning. Johnny remembers that the scratches on the glass in the window were on the inside.

Also, Johnny remembers that Depolito was a master at refinishing violins and remembers that Depolito had mentioned that his own boy would never have a violin like that. Johnny tells Emil that he is going to help find the violin, and they hurry to catch a plane to El Paso, Texas.

Johnny and Emil get into the concert for Antonio Depolito, who was playing a reddish-brown violin. Emil is sure that the violin is the Canary by its sound, like a father knows his son. The varnish had changed the tone, but it is still the Bisiach.

Johnny gets the police and goes to the dressing room. Johnny faces Antonio with the facts he knows, and he reacts violently. After Emil tells him what he knows, Antonio confesses to stealing the violin with his father's help, and to the murder of Tetrick.

Tetrick had called Antonio to tell him of his suspicions, and when Tetrick started to call Earle, Antonio killed him. Antonio tells Johnny that Tetrick deserved to die for keeping the Canary in a vault, but knows his talents are wasted as an audience will never hear his skills again. Johnny reassures Antonio that where he is going, he will have a captive audience.

"So, from here on out it is up to the courts. And that means for his father too. You know, I wonder if the Tetrick estate will put those priceless fiddles in that collection into the hands of musicians where they could be used and appreciated. I hope so." The expense account includes a couple of days fishing with Earle Poorman."

"Next week, *The Old Fashioned Murder Matter* — as if there was anything new fashioned about it."

Notes:
- This program contains commercials for the Kingston Trio for Seven-up, Alpine cigarettes and Mentholatum Deep Heat Rub.
- Santos Ortega is Depolito, Leon Janney is Emile, Richard Holland is Tony, Frank Behrens is Don, Sam Gray is Earl, Bill Lipton is the violinist.
- A hemisemidemiquaver is a 64th note.
- Leandro Bisiach made musical instruments in the late 19th early 20th century.
- Antonio Stradivari was born in 1644, worked in Cremona, Italy until his death in 1737.
- Andrea Amati (1525-1611) is known as the founder of the great Cremona school of violin making.
- Guarneri is a family of 16-17th century violin makers from Cremona, Italy.
- Art Hannes is the announcer.
- Musical supervision is by Ethel Huber.

Producer: Bruno Zirato, Jr. Writer: Jack Johnstone
Cast: Santos Ortega, Leon Janney, Richard Holland, Frank Behrens, Sam Gray, Bill Lipton

◆ ❖ ◆

Show: **The Old Fashioned Murder Matter**
Show Date: 7/23/1961
Company: State Unity Life
Agent: Herbert Lynn
Exp. Acct: $347.85

Synopsis: Herbert Lynn calls and promises Johnny a generous fee in addition to his expenses. Lynn is worried about a murder that has not yet been committed but will probably be attempted. Lynn hopes Johnny can forestall any attempts.

Johnny flies to Denver, Colorado, gets a room at the Brown Palace hotel and meets with Herbert Lynn the next morning in his office at Mile High Center. Lynn tells Johnny to rent a car, as the client lives in Green Mountain Falls, Colorado, not too far from Colorado Springs and Manitou Springs. Johnny remembers a fishing trip with Ray Smischny (it's easier to say than to spell) at his Lucky 4 ranch.

Lynn's client is Howard Hartsell, who is 73 and was quite wealthy at one time which explains his insurance policy for a quarter of a million dollars. Lynn is certain that someone wants to kill Hartsell, most likely one of his three beneficiaries, maybe two of them.

Clara Johnson, 45, a niece who teaches school in Colorado Springs and is as mean, selfish and grasping an old maid as Lynn has ever seen. She was mad when she found out that she was not the only beneficiary of the policy. In response to Johnny's question, Lynn tells him that Clara teaches chemistry.

Bonnie, another niece who is young, good looking and smart, and is married to a plumber named Harry Briggs, and they also live in Colorado Springs.

Tony Johnson is Hartsell's nephew and lives in Manitou Springs. Tony inherited a great deal of money from his own family and went through it in less than a year. He is now working as a bartender at a cheap saloon. Lynn describes him as a lazy, no good wastrel.

Lynn is sure that Tony is the likely culprit — Lynn has an instinct about such things. Lynn thinks that Clara would be next, and Bonnie would not be capable of thinking about murder. Johnny laughs, because detective stories tell him that he should suspect Bonnie because she is above suspicion.

Johnny is told that there have been several attempts to kill Hartsell, twice by the same car in front of his house. A small caliber bullet was fired through his living room window, narrowly missing him, and there was a mysterious fire at his home while Hartsell was confined to his bed.

Lynn tells Johnny that Hartsell's health has not been good lately. His family doctor, Dr. Easterday (it should be Yesterday, as he should have stopped practicing long ago.) is the only one that Hartsell will trust and is living with him now. Hartsell is recovering from a liver ailment, but Lynn thinks that Hartsell was poisoned, but no one has been there to visit since the doctor moved in. Lynn wants Johnny to find out who is after Hartsell, and bring him to justice, it has to be a "him" — Tony Johnson. If Lynn is right, whoever is planning to kill Hartsell will get Johnny also.

Johnny rents a car and laments not being able to stop at the U. S. Mint to see if they are handing out samples.

Johnny stops to see Clara first, and it is a short visit. Clara tells Johnny that it was indecent that Howard would include those others in his estate. With all that money, she could give up teaching and enjoy herself. Bonnie has a husband to support her, and Tony is just a saloonkeeper. If only he would die before she is too old. Johnny almost tricks her into admitting she would like to kill the old man.

Johnny then goes to meet Bonnie at her husband's plumbing shop. She tells Johnny that he is cute for a private eye — no derby or cigar. She and Harry are concerned about uncle Howard and would like to be able to take care of him, but he would not allow it. She will be glad to get the money — at the proper time.

Johnny does not like Tony when he meets him, or the bouncer standing near him. Tony offers to cut Johnny in on the insurance if he can get rid of uncle Howard. Johnny leaves and gets into his car to drive to Hartsell's when he hears a familiar sound — a bomb! Johnny escapes just as the car explodes.

Johnny rents another car and drives to Green Mountain Falls to meet Hartsell and Dr. Easterday.

Dr. Easterday meets Johnny at the door and tells him that he is too late — Howard Hartsell has just died. Easterday tells Johnny that Hartsell died of a severe case of toxic jaundice. Johnny gets an idea, and remembers Dr. Ed Wilson, who treated him for an infected finger when he was there last.

Johnny calls Ed, and learns that arsenic, even in minute amounts, can cause a type of poisoning that can lead to toxic jaundice. Johnny asks Ed if an old doctor could be fooled but Ed is noncommittal. Johnny demands an autopsy over Dr. Easterday's objections.

The autopsy result was death from arsenic poisoning. Now Johnny has to find out who gave it to him and how it was delivered over a long period of time. Dr. Easterday tells Johnny that he has lived there since Hartsell started to worry that someone was trying to get him. Dr. Easterday has allowed no one into the house, has purchased all the food, cooked it and ate it with Hartsell. The only time Hartsell was alone was when he was in his private bathroom.

Clara never visited and Tony only came once to deliver a bottle of whiskey. Hartsell had taken some for a while, but Dr. Easterday stopped that, and also finished up the bottle. Bonnie was not allowed in, nor was her husband when he came to fix the plumbing two months ago. Johnny remembers that he was told that there was a fire in the posterior of the house, something only a doctor or a nurse (who would know about arsenic) would say.

Johnny remembers that Bonnie had said posterior, so she must have been a nurse, and her husband is a plumber. Johnny and Dr. Easterday search the house and find a container half full of arsenic attached to the waterline to the second floor.

"Funny, it wasn't the sweet gentle Bonnie who finally broke down and confessed that little plot, but her husband, the plumber who had rigged the device, who had also rigged my car for that explosion. So, once more it is up to the courts. My only regret is that worthless Tony and that selfish Clara will share that nice hunk of insurance."

Notes:
- This is an AFRTS program with only the AFRTS identification at the end.
- Leora Thatcher is Clara, Lawson Zerbe is Dr. Easterday, Patsy Campbell is Bonnie, John Seymour is Herbert Lynn, Richard Holland is Tony, William Lipton is Dr. Wilson.
- The $250,000 policy would be worth over $2 million in 2017 dollars.
- Music Supervision is by Ethel Huber.
- Allan Burns is the announcer.

Producer: Bruno Zirato, Jr.   Writer: Jack Johnstone
Cast: Leora Thatcher, Lawson Zerbe, Patsy Campbell, John Seymour, Richard Holland, Bill Lipton

Show:	The Chuckanut Matter
Show Date:	7/30/1961
Company:	Western Maritime & Life Insurance Company
Agent:	Lucien Peterson
Exp. Acct:	$391.18

Synopsis: Lucien Peterson calls Johnny from Seattle. He is doing fine but has had to settle a number of large claims lately, and the home office does not like him. Right now, Luke does not want to pay off on Mrs. Myra Brittingham. She is not dead, yet. Luke has a hunch and thinks that if he told the police, they would laugh at him. Luke wants Johnny to come out and see if her husband Mark would try it.

Johnny flies to Seattle and arrives late at night and stays at the Benjamin Franklin Hotel. The next morning Johnny goes to visit Lucien who tells Johnny he will get him a rental car so he can drive to Chuckanut, Washington, just this side of Bellingham.

The Brittinghams live on Pallioop Lane, a rugged road that winds up the mountain and is treacherous if the road is wet. Both of the Brittinghams are insured for $500,000 and each is the beneficiary of the other.

Mark is about thirty-five and a playboy and sportsman living first on money his father gave him, and now on the insurance left him by his last wife. Myra is wife number four. Luke is sure that Mark married her because she had an incurable disease, but modern science found a cure for it.

Johnny asks if the former wife died from an incurable disease and is told that is what the police and the courts decided, but Luke is sure Mark helped the old biddy on her way. Luke has no evidence, and they have not been getting along lately. Myra is older than Mark and loves to spend his money before he can. Johnny is supposed to scare the truth out of Mark. Luke tells Johnny to go on the pretense of buying the property, and then let it slip out who he is.

Johnny drives up to Chuckanut and the road up the mountain was anything but a road. On a tight turn, Johnny almost hits a police car, and a new compact car that has crashed on the road. Johnny stops and meets Sgt. Bill Foreman who knows who Johnny is, and wonders how he found out so quickly that one of the Brittinghams is in the car. Johnny looks into the car to see Mark Brittingham.

Sgt. Foreman tells Johnny that Myra had called the police. She was alone, and while sitting on the porch she saw a car coming up the road. She did not want any prowlers and called the police. She screamed over the phone that there had been an explosion and Foreman came right over. Johnny asks Foreman if she had recognized the car and is told that the sun would have been in Myra's eyes and to Mark's back.

Foreman had warned Mark about how he drove up the road, but he had been a racing driver and took Foreman up one day, and Mark could handle a car.

Foreman mentions Hartford Homer Ransom, the sudden death detective. He reconstructs traffic accidents and lives near there. Johnny asks Foreman to call Ransom and suddenly Johnny notices that Mark looks like he had thrown his arm up in front of him. Foreman thinks it was a reflex, but Johnny thinks a professional driver would have slumped down. He must have put his arm up while he was in the curve. Johnny tells Foreman to get an autopsy started and then goes to see Myra.

The home on the mountain is new, modern and expensive. Mrs. Brittingham is forty but does not look it. Johnny introduces himself and tells her who he is.

On the porch, Myra asks if it was Mark, and tells Johnny that she had warned him and knew he would kill himself. She is not sad, as it settles things. She tells Johnny that she married Mark for his money, while he had it. She hates the small house and fought with Mark over money. Mark should have gotten a job, but he just sulked.

One night he was laughing to himself and told her that it would be nice for her if he would die. He had been taking long trips lately and left her alone. Myra tells Johnny that she wants to get as far away as possible. Johnny wonders why she painted herself so darkly, and what about the alarm when she saw the car?

The next morning Johnny meets with Sgt. Foreman, Dr. Bascom the coroner, and Mr. Ransom, who knows more about inertia, matter and motion and reaction times than anyone Johnny knows.

Ransom does not understand why the right arm was up and is sure Mark must have done it while on the curve. Johnny wonders about a bird or animal in the road, but that is discounted. The car was OK, and there was nothing wrong found in Mark's autopsy. Dr. Bascom had given Mark a physical only two weeks ago.

The only conclusion is suicide, but Ransom cannot agree because the tire tracks were erratic and the right arm shielding his eyes from the sun. Johnny has an idea that it was the sun and asks for time to play a hunch that Mark was murdered.

Johnny asks Sgt. Foreman to bring Myra to the office on some pretext. When Johnny calls, Foreman is to drive her home. Johnny tells Foreman that when he is on the curve where Mark died, take it very slowly with one foot on the brake.

Johnny goes to the house and searches it and finds a lot of mirrors. Johnny is looking for a signaling mirror with a whole in the middle and finds it hidden in a book on the porch. Johnny calls Foreman and Johnny aims the mirror at the car while it is on the curve. Foreman is able to stop the car and waits for Johnny to come down.

Foreman tells Johnny that Myra has not said a word since he raised his arm and stopped the car. Myra asks Johnny how he knew she killed Mark? Johnny tells her he didn't. He had a hunch, and it seems to have paid off.

"$500,000? That's a nice round figure, a lot of money. Don't they ever learn that millions aren't enough to murder for? Expense account total, call it a nice round figure, like uh, say $391.18."

"Next week I'll be back with another exciting adventure that will really surprise you."

Notes:
- This program contains a commercial for Big Brothers and Big Brother Week, and a post-program safe driving tip from Kelly Maddox about what a flashing red light means.
- Joan Ellison is Myra Brittingham, Robert Dryden is Sgt. Bill Foreman, Richard Kendrick is Luke Peterson, Bernard Landrow is Homer Ransom and Ivor Francis is Dr. Bascom.
- Music Supervision is by Ethel Huber.
- Art Hannes is the announcer.

Producer:	Bruno Zirato, Jr.	Writer: Jack Johnstone
Cast:	Joan Ellison, Robert Dryden, Richard Kendrick, Bernard Lenrow, Ivor Francis	

♦ ❖ ♦

Show:	The Philadelphia Miss Matter
Show Date:	8/6/1961
Company:	Amalgamated Life Association
Agent:	George Caldwell
Exp. Acct:	$485.75

Synopsis: George Caldwell calls Johnny from Meridian, Mississippi. George understands that Johnny has a top security clearance, and Johnny confirms that. George has a client who has asked for Johnny to be brought in. The client is Dr. Emit Melcher, who owns the Melcher Labs, and does a lot of work for the government. George does not know what the problem is, but it is top secret.

Johnny flies to Meridian with two stopovers and arrives around seven p.m. Johnny takes a cab to the Amalgamated office, and the cabby asks Johnny to repeat his destination, and then tells him that he drove Johnny around New York City once.

The driver is Bernie Yorkin, and he remembers the tip that Johnny gave him. Bernie asks what the case is, and Johnny tells him he does not know. Bernie promises to keep an eye on Johnny.

George Caldwell is in the office and he tells Johnny that he had called the labs, and Mr. Melcher is out of town. But his secretary, Miss Mona Little Wolf is waiting for Johnny. Mona is a Philadelphia girl, and part Indian.

Johnny cabs to the lab with Bernie again. Bernie tells Johnny that there are a lot of government secrets at the lab, so call Bernie if you need him.

Johnny meets Mona, and the trip was worth it. Johnny and Mona hit it off immediately, and Johnny learns that she is part Indian, and Mona asks if Johnny's last name isn't Big Wolf? Mona tells Johnny that she is the secretary but knows nothing about what Melcher is working on.

Mona tells Johnny that she is going on vacation tomorrow, and with Melcher out of town, they decide to spend a pleasant evening in Meridian. Bernie is still waiting and takes Johnny and Mona into town.

At 3:00 a.m. Johnny and Mona close down the last club and look for a cab.

Mona tells Johnny that she had better get away on her vacation when a cab drives up. The driver forces Mona into the cab and hits Johnny.

Johnny wakes up in his hotel with Bernie pouring bourbon into him. Bernie tells Johnny that he found him passed out on the sidewalk while he was driving. Johnny grabs the phone and makes a call to Mona's apartment, but there is no answer. Bernie remembers seeing a car drive away, not a cab.

There is a knock at the door and Bernie opens it and a man forces his way into Johnny's room. The man is Dr. Melcher. Johnny asks Bernie to look around for Mona with his buddies, and he leaves.

Dr. Melcher tells Johnny that it is too late, that the classified materials have been stolen. Melcher tells Johnny that he has found that the vault where a formula has been stored has been broken into and the product has been stolen. Unless it is found within two days it will be too late.

What Dr. Melcher tells Johnny is classified, but it concerns an experimental fuel. The fuel Melcher is working on is very powerful and very unstable. If it is not cared for carefully it could explode, and knowledge of it would be worth millions. The sample that was stolen is incomplete and must be handled carefully.

Johnny is told that only Caldwell knew Johnny was coming, but Johnny remembers that Caldwell had phoned Mona, and since she knew what was happening, she had to act fast. The club last night was really a rendezvous with the goon that hit Johnny. Bernie calls and tells Johnny that Mona took a bus to Philadelphia, and Johnny hangs up and heads for the airport.

Johnny flies to Philadelphia, Pennsylvania and calls the bus line and asks them to check on all passengers coming there. Johnny meets with Lt. Harry Langley of the police, but a day later the police have found nothing. Harry tells Johnny that the bus line has no record of a woman buying a ticket to Philadelphia.

Harry tells Johnny that Philadelphia only had 200 people in it when he was born, but that was in Indiana. Johnny realizes that he has the wrong city and asks for an atlas. Johnny finds a third Philadelphia just north of Meridian.

Johnny flies back to Meridian, rents a car and drives north to Neshoba County, the heart of the Indian country where Mona could hide easily. At an old farmhouse outside of Philadelphia, Johnny finds Bernie asleep in his cab. Johnny wakes Bernie and he tells Johnny that he had found out that Mona and Willie Picktooth are inside the house. Bernie has been waiting for a day, and that has been too long, what with them shooting at Bernie.

Mona starts shooting and Johnny warns her about the danger of the fuel. She tells Johnny that it is worth a fortune, and they will be able to get out after dark, after all, they are Indians. Suddenly the house explodes several times.

"Any comments on this case? Why bother." notes a saddened Johnny.

Notes:
- This is an AFRTS program and contains a story about the activities of Rev. Eugene Wood, a story on democracy and opportunity.

- Mason Adams is Bernie, Arthur Kohl is Melcher, Rita Lloyd is Mona, Martin Blaine is Harry.
- Stuart Metz is the announcer.
- Musical supervision is by Ethel Huber.

Producer:	Bruno Zirato, Jr. Writer: Jack Johnstone
Cast:	Mason Adams, Arthur Kohl, Rita Lloyd, Martin Blaine

◆ ❖ ◆

Show:	**The Perilous Padre Matter**
Show Date:	8/13/1961
Company:	Tri-Western Life Insurance Company
Agent:	Jack Price
Exp. Acct:	$485.00

Synopsis: Jack Price calls Johnny, but he does not have an insurance problem. He asks if Johnny has heard of the Padre Island treasure, and Johnny has not, but he knows of the island. Jack tells Johnny that the island is over 115 miles long, so it will be hard to find the old Spanish ship, and all the doubloons. Jack wants Johnny to come down and hunt for treasure, among other things

Johnny flies to Corpus Christi, Texas and cabs to the Robert Driscoll hotel and gets a room. Johnny walks to Jack's office and feels a gun in his back and is told to walk straight ahead or he will get shot. Johnny tells the man to consider his wife and thirteen children but is told his sob story will get him nowhere. The man tells Johnny that they do not like the eastern hoods coming into town. Try anything in Corpus, and you will become the corpus.

Johnny laughs at the joke that Doug Johnstone was playing on him and tells Doug that his brother Jack will never put it in the script. Doug asks Johnny how he found out so soon and Johnny asks about what. Doug tells Johnny that Jack Price is a good friend, and his wife had called this morning to find out what had happened to Jack.

Doug was told that Johnny had been called, so he wondered if Jack and Johnny had gone out there last night, but that did not make sense. Doug takes Johnny to get some equipment and get out to Padre Island.

Doug takes Johnny to get a beach buggy, an old jeep with huge tires on it, from Obie O'Brien. Doug tells a curious Obie that Johnny is wild about fishing, and they will pick up the fishing tackle later. At Doug's house, they get some extra gas, some shovels and an old Winchester .30-30.

On the way to the island Doug tells Johnny about the history of the Spanish treasure fleet of 1553. They left from Vera Cruz, Mexico with a cargo of gold. Three ships were lost in a storm, and some got through to the east. Several ships tried for Tampico, south of here, but thirteen ships came aground on Padre Island. A salvage fleet recovered most of the wrecks and took the gold away. A client of Jack's, Jose Pinetta, found a chart in an old chest that shows the location of a ship.

Doug notices a car abandoned on the road but continues driving. The chart gave locations for finding the ship, but the markers are hard to find now. Before the Civil War, a man found a chest full of jewels and buried it, and then lost the location. Jose has only told Jack about the chart.

Jose has bought a lot of sophisticated search gear and had agreed to pick up Jack yesterday. Jose was unsure of one of his suppliers, Tony Larker. When Jose did not show up, Jack got worried and went looking for Tony but could not find him. Jack then told Doug and went looking for Jose.

Johnny spots Jack's Model A beach buggy in the dunes and they head for it. Suddenly there are shots and they hide behind the jeep. Johnny is sure that Jack and Jose are not shooting at them, so it must be Larker.

Bullets hit the tires and Johnny gets a shovel to dig in and wait for dark, and to make a plan of action for nightfall. A thunderstorm blows in and they separate and head for Larker. Johnny is about to reach the car, when it drives off.

Doug spots Jack and Jose in the dunes. Jack has a head wound and Jose is dead. Jack tells Johnny that Jose had found the treasure and was going to get Jack when his car broke down. Larker followed them, so Jack and Jose decided to dig in the dunes to distract him. Larker came up on them and shot both of them.

Suddenly Larker is back and tells them to drop their guns. Larker tells Johnny that he will shoot them and force Jack to tell him where the treasure is. Larker starts to fire when Johnny calls "Obie".

Obie O'Brien hits Larker and Johnny gets his gun. Obie tells them they should have let him come with them, and that he had a hard time following them. Now the only thing he has to show for it is soaked clothes and sore knuckles.

"Treasure? I am afraid the secret of its location there on Padre island died with Jose Pinetta. Unless of course, someone happens to find out where Jose hid the chart. But you can bet your bottom dollar that there will be plenty of people looking for it. Maybe even Jack Price and Obie O'Brien. As for Doug, he says he has had enough of it."

"Next week, one of the dirtiest rackets I've ever had to deal with, to say nothing of the man behind it."

Notes:
- This program contains commercials with the Kingston Trio for Seven-up, Ipana toothpaste, instant Tender Leaf Iced Tea, and Mentholatum Deep Heat Rub.
- Luis Van Rooten is Doug, Larry Haines is Tony, Maurice Tarplin is Price, Lawson Zerbe is Obie.
- The announcer is Stuart Metz.
- Musical supervision is by Ethel Huber.

Producer: Bruno Zirato, Jr. Writer: Jack Johnstone
Cast: Luis Van Rooten, Larry Haines, Maurice Tarplin, Lawson Zerbe

Show:	**The Wrong Doctor Matter**
Show Date:	8/20/1961
Company:	**Tri-Western Life Insurance Company**
Agent:	**Jack Price**
Exp. Acct:	**$532.40**

Synopsis: Jack Price calls Johnny and tells him to come on back to Corpus Christi. Jack tells Johnny their adventure on Padre Islands had taught them all a lesson. Jack asks Johnny if he would like to take on another case? Johnny says sure, as long as the fees are big and Jack does not check the expense account too carefully. Jack thought he was talking to that fine, generous, self-sacrificing, do-it-for-nothing gentleman named Johnny Dollar. Seriously, Jack wants Johnny to come down on an international incident.

A client is involved with narcotics, and the case could be dangerous. Johnny tells Jack, that whenever he is called in on a case that is a lead-pipe cinch, he usually gets shot at. So, this one that looks big and dangerous, maybe this one will be a lead-pipe cinch. Johnny will come down first thing tomorrow.

Johnny takes a midnight flight to Corpus Christi, Texas and cabs to the Robert Driscoll for breakfast and a shower. Jack calls and tells Johnny that he is at the office and the case is hotter than he thought. The client, Julio Olivera had worked on the shrimp boats. One of them started carrying heroin, and the judge gave Julio three years just for being on board. He is out of jail now and is clean. Consuelo Diaz, his girlfriend, tells Jack that, well come on to the office.

Johnny picks up his .38 lemon squeezer and his hat to take with him. There is a knock at the door and a voice tells Johnny that it is room service. Johnny opens the door and a man enters with a silenced gun and tells him to get on the floor. Johnny tries for the gun and is hit. Johnny is on the floor when the maid walks in. The man tells the maid that his friend hurt himself and tells her to get the doctor. The man tells an unconscious Johnny that when the doctor gets there he will be dead.

Johnny plays it smart and goes to the floor. When the maid leaves, Johnny kicks the man and knocks his gun away. Johnny gets into a real fight and takes a number of hits. The man puts Johnny in a squeeze-hold and there is a knock on the door. Johnny yells to break down the door and the maid enters with the hotel detective. The man is hiding behind the door and he shoots the detective and leaves.

Johnny wakes up to see Jack Price with a bottle of brandy. Jack tells Johnny that the welcoming committee was Diego Hernandez. Jack did not think that Hernandez would find out about Johnny. Hernandez was the skipper on the boat Julio was on and was never caught.

Consuelo had called Jack because she found out the Hernandez was in town, and the police know it now. Hernandez had come to town to get Julio, whose testimony put the finger on the drug racket. Hernandez had visited Consuelo trying to get information.

Jack realizes that she probably told Hernandez that Johnny was coming. Julio is out of town and does not know about Hernandez. Johnny tries to get dressed and tells Jack to leave a note for the police.

Johnny and Jack go to Consuelo's house in the country and the front door is wide open and the house smells of cordite. Hernandez had gotten there and done his job too well. Julio was dead and Consuelo was barely alive.

Jack calls the police and Johnny tries to help Consuelo. She finally tells Johnny that it is no use now with Julio gone. Consuelo tells Johnny that Hernandez did the shooting. Hernandez wanted Julio to go back into business again. Johnny asks Consuelo to tell him where Hernandez went and she says "Doctor" and then "Doctor Velasquez" and dies. Johnny tells Jack that she did not make much sense, but then again, maybe she did.

Johnny spends the next 15 hours working with Sgt. Ortiz to find a doctor named Velasquez in any city in Texas. Johnny is frustrated at not finding the doctor, and realizes the answer was right under his nose. Fifty miles below the border is the town of Doctor Velasquez!

Ortiz tells Johnny that it will take a long time to get the proper authorization, but Johnny tells him he will go on his own. Johnny wants to beat Hernandez to the city and tells Ortiz that what he is going to do is none of his business. Johnny wonders where he could get a light plane, and Ortiz suggests they take a ride.

Johnny rents a plane and flies to the town of Doctor Velasquez, Mexico using a highway map for navigation. The town is a group of ramshackle buildings in the desert. Johnny manages to land the plane and taxis onto the road into town to block any cars coming in.

Johnny hides as a car comes and Johnny recognizes Hernandez as the driver. Johnny calls him down and Hernandez tells Johnny that he will kill him. Johnny takes his gun for a souvenir and tells him to put his hands behind his back.

Hernandez pulls a gun from his sleeve and Johnny shoots him. "Why don't I ever learn to frisk these punks before I tell them to lower their hands? Next time I might not be so lucky."

"It was well after dark when I finally got us back to Corpus Christi, and I had quite a time landing in the small private field from which I had borrowed the plane. Ortiz, of course, denied any knowledge of the whole thing, but I noticed the landing lights were on and waiting for me. And also, by pure coincidence, a young fellow from the narcotics squad just happened to be there to meet me. Nor did he suggest that I might have picked up my prisoner anywhere but this side of the border. Just the same Jackson, maybe it would not hurt to keep this report under wraps for a while."

"Next week, one murder, three suspects and each of them with plenty of reason, plenty of opportunity."

Notes:
- **This program contains commercials with the Kingston Trio for Seven-up, and Mentholatum Deep Heat Rub.**

- Ralph Camargo is Diego, Robert Dryden is the sergeant, Nellie Sonnenberg is Consuelo, Lawson Zerbe is the voice, Maurice Tarplin is Price, Hilda Haines is the maid.
- The announcer is Stuart Metz.
- Musical supervision is by Ethel Huber.

Producer: Bruno Zirato, Jr.   Writer: Jack Johnstone
Cast: Ralph Camargo, Robert Dryden, Nellie Sonnenberg, Lawson Zerbe, Maurice Tarplin, Hilda Haines

♦ ❖ ♦

Show: **The Too Many Crooks Matter**
Show Date: **8/27/1961**
Company: **Mono Guarantee Insurance Company**
Agent: **Freddie Friedkin**
Exp. Acct: **$250.00**

Synopsis: Freddie Friedkin calls and wants Johnny to do him a favor. Ever hear of Mrs. Ambrose Winifred Van Turkle? She is an old fuss-budget and lives over at 1227 South Terone. They have just under a million dollars on her jewelry. "You're kidding. My regular commission on a million dollars! I'll take the case."

Johnny muses that "Too many cooks spoil the broth, but too many crooks can mess up an insurance investigation".

Johnny drives to see Freddie Friedkin who meets him on the street. Freddie tells Johnny that Mrs. Van Turkle is an important client, and keeps her jewelry in her home in Hartford, Connecticut. Nothing has happened to her, but it has to Freddie.

Today is the servant's day off, so Freddie had promised to drive Mrs. Van Turkle into the office to look at her policies. But the vice president has called a meeting and Freddie dare not leave. So, Freddie told Mrs. Van Turkle that Johnny would drive her into the office. Mrs. Van Turkle knows all about Johnny and listens to his program every week. She will be waiting for Johnny to pick her up. Johnny agrees to do the task, not as a favor to Freddie, but to see the female that has put a scare into "Fearless Freddie Friedkin".

Johnny drives to the Van Turkle house, a huge brownstone with a large yard. Johnny drives into the portcullis and toots the horn and waits. Johnny gets out of his car to get Mrs. Van Turkle and is slugged. Johnny recognizes Willie McPeak, a second story man with a record as long as your arm as the man who slugged him.

Johnny staggers into the house and finds Mrs. Van Turkle unconscious in the drawing room. Johnny phones Dr. Blakey and tells him what has happened. Mrs. Van Turkle is a patient of his, and he agrees to come right away.

Johnny calls Sgt. Harry Simmons, who promises to send someone over right away. Johnny decides to look around the house and finds the safe in the library broken open and emptied. On the floor is a diamond that had been dislodged from its setting.

Johnny pockets the stone and calls Freddie to ask how much her jewelry is insured for. Johnny tells him to send her a check, if she stays alive.

Johnny goes to visit Sgt. Simmons who tells Johnny that an old friend just left town an hour ago, a strong-arm man named Willie McPeak. The police just put him on a train to New York. Johnny tells Simmons that Willie is also a burglar and is the man he saw in Van Turkle's house and who hit him. Simmons agrees to call the New York police and have them grab McPeak. Johnny thinks that he can find Willie faster than the police.

Johnny flies to New York and cabs to the 18th precinct to see Randy Singer. First, Johnny makes five calls to old friends who are willing to give him information, for money that is, and then talks to Randy. Johnny tells Randy what has happened and Randy tells him that a lot of fake diamonds are floating around the city. The police have tried to catch who is fencing the goods but have been unsuccessful so far. Randy thinks that an intermediary is involved. Everyone is complaining to Randy, and now Johnny wants something.

While Johnny talks to Randy, he is rubbing the diamond he found on the glass top of Randy's desk. Johnny tells Randy about McPeak and Randy tells Johnny that McPeak has tried a number of rackets but is only successful at burglary. Johnny tells Randy that McPeak has stolen almost a million dollars in jewels.

Johnny gets a phone call from "Spotty", who tells Johnny that McPeak was just seen going into apartment 2-A at 718 East 49th with a briefcase. Johnny takes a cab to the building and pushes all the buttons but 2-A to get into the building.

Johnny finally slips the lock on the front door and goes to apartment 2-A where he hears voices arguing. A voice is about to tell Willie something about the stones, but Willie pulls a gun and shoots the other person in the room. Johnny breaks in and gets the drop on Willie. Johnny checks the other man who is dead. Johnny opens Willie's brief case and discovers {garbled}.

Johnny calls Randy and tells him what has happened. Randy tells Johnny that there is a guy living there named Horace Petersley who deals in hot jewelry, and Johnny tells Randy that he lived there, Willie just shot him. Johnny tells Randy to send another man over, as he is coming to the office with Willie McPeak and the Van Turkle jewels.

Johnny asks Randy to call the gemologist Fritz Melchior and have him come to Randy's office. Johnny cabs to Randy's office and Melchior is there and waiting. Johnny gives him the Van Turkle jewels and tells him to get to work. Randy wants to book Willie as Conroy is tired of holding his gun on him. Johnny believes that if he is right, Willie might want to use the gun on himself.

Johnny reminds Randy that he had been rubbing the jewels on the glass, but not scratching it. When Petersley told Willie that the deal was off and gave the paste back to Willie, Johnny suddenly remembered that the diamond had not scratched the glass.

Johnny realizes that there are too many crooks involved in this case, including a little old lady who figured on collecting a million dollars on her fake jewels.

Mr. Melchior confirms that the jewels are fakes. Melchior uses several tests to prove his point that the jewels are just glass.

Willie gets really upset and tells them that he stole the jewels and killed a man to make a deal with him. "I've been robbed!" Willie yells as he is taken down to be booked. Randy hates to admit that Johnny has done a good day's work.

"As for the phony jewels, well (old Mrs. Van Turkle has completely recovered from the beating by the way) they are fakes. The real gems she always keeps in the vault in the bank. The paste she had there in the wall safe was for casual wear."

Notes:
- This program contains commercials for No-Doz, Newport Menthol cigarettes, and Sinclair Dino gasoline.
- This program contains a aircheck for KRLD in Dallas, Texas and a Public Service Announcement about safe driving from Kelly Maddox.
- Walter Otto is credited for the sound patterns.
- This program is extremely noisy and some of the details might not be correct, especially the names.
- The announcer is Art Hannes.
- Musical supervision is by Ethel Huber.

Producer:	Fred Hendrickson	Writer:	Jack Johnstone
Cast:	Court Benson, Sam Gray, Jackson Beck, Bill Smith, James Stevens, Tom Gorman, Maurice Tarplin		

• ❖ •

Show:	**The Shifty Looker Matter**
Show Date:	9/3/1961
Company:	Floyds of England
Agent:	Geoffrey Reed
Exp. Acct:	$4.40

Synopsis: Geoffrey Reed calls Johnny from Floyds. He is George's younger brother and has taken over here because George has been transferred to the head office. Johnny recounts the cases that George had Johnny working on. Geoffrey tells Johnny that George had told him that if Geoff had any problems of and unusual nature, he could call on Johnny for assistance. (uh oh) This policy was written by George himself (I shudder) and is for $100,000 on the return of a child. The term of the policy forbids bringing in the police. Johnny wants to call in the FBI, but Geoff tells him he cannot. Geoffrey wants Johnny to come over and read the policy and meet the father, that will change his mind.

Johnny buys gas and drives to Geoffrey's office. Geoffrey looks like his brother but is decidedly British and always makes his point by the longest possible route.

Geoffrey starts by telling Johnny that he will be keeping an eye on Johnny's expense accounts, as they get out of hand on occasion. Geoffrey also tells

Johnny that he understands the nature of George's policies. Johnny is told to read the policy on Steven Looker and his seven-year-old daughter Cynthia. Johnny thinks he knows the name but cannot remember from where.

Mr. Looker is retired and lives in the Wakefield Towers in Hartford, Connecticut. Mr. Looker had been out late the previous evening and Cynthia was alone. When he returned this morning, she was gone. A tape-recorded ransom message was left on his telephone demanding $100,000, the exact amount of the policy.

Johnny reads the policy, which is written to insure her specifically against kidnapping. The terms are for payment in unmarked bills up to $100,000, and no law enforcement or the press are to be brought into the case until Mr. Looker has attempted payment or gets the child back. Johnny tells Geoff that the policy is illegal.

Geoff tells Johnny that he is being brought in because he is not one of the groups excluded in the policy. The policy was issued just after Cynthia was born which was just shortly after the Bealer kidnapping and the abduction and murder of the Hammerthwait child. The ransom is supposed to be paid tonight and Mr. Looker is coming to pick up the money. The secretary Sarah announces Mr. Looker and Johnny stays, acting as the employee who picked up the money.

Johnny seems to recognize Looker, who complains that Johnny being there was a breach of policy. Looker knows all about kidnappings, and what happens if you do not do what they say. Cynthia is all he has, and no one will take her away.

Johnny asks for proof that Cynthia was kidnapped. Looker gives the tape to Geoff to play for this "doubting Thompson". Johnny asks why he records his phone conversations and Looker tells Johnny that he used to work in electronics and tape recordings. After his wife died, he hooked up a tape recorder to record messages. It will also record calls when Looker answers if he chooses to.

Johnny tells Looker that the only reason an individual would need a recorder is if he expects to be threatened and wants a record of it for the police. Suppose he had contacts with people of questionable reputations?

Geoff plays the tape, which tells Looker that they have Cynthia and to leave them 100G's in unmarked bills. They will let Looker see her before he gives them the money. Looker stops the tape when the caller tells him to "put the money in a paper bag at 11:00 and bring it to…" Johnny tells Looker that the tape must be left as evidence, but he takes it with him. Looker tells Geoff that he will call from his apartment when he gets Cynthia back. Johnny knows that the apartment has a switchboard, so there will be a record of the call as evidence.

Johnny tries to follow Looker and loses him after five minutes. Johnny remembers where he knows the name and goes to the library to look up Steve "Shifty" Looker in the newspaper files.

Johnny finds a story from September of 1954, about the breakup of the Maroni mob in Chicago. Everyone got off without a prison term. Shifty had used a clever elaborate radio hookup to jam the police radios whenever the gang was pulling a job. Shifty got off by turning states evidence, but Maroni got a seven-year stretch and swore he would get even. Maroni was also involved in kidnapping. Johnny calls the police and asks about "Stinky" Maroni. The police agree to check on it for Johnny.

Johnny goes to see the police but there is no word yet. The police lieutenant accuses Johnny of knowing that one of Maroni's henchmen, Steven Looker, is living in Harford now. He has been here for seven years and has been behaving. The worst thing Maroni could do would be to harm the girl, as Looker has no money.

The police are about to put a watch on Looker when officer Conroy brings a teletype message in. The message tells Johnny that Maroni does not get out of the pen for another two weeks. Johnny realizes he has been blind and runs out. Was it Maroni's upcoming release, or something Looker had planned all along? How would a kidnapper expect Looker to come up with the money unless he knew about the insurance policy? But the policy was a secret and the demands were for the exact amount of the policy. Looker must have known who Johnny was? Johnny decides to go to Looker's apartment.

Johnny knocks at the door, tells Looker it is special delivery, and when the door is opened he sees Looker's bags packed. Johnny opens the bags and asks why the money is packed in the bag. Shifty pulls a gun and tells Johnny he was waiting for him. Looker starts to shoot Johnny when the police arrive. The lieutenant tells Johnny that he had put a tail on Johnny when he left headquarters, and Johnny did not even notice. "You must be slipping."

"Well, let's see now. Expense account total is exactly $4.40? Okay, Geoffrey, it's perfectly all right, as long as you don't forget my commission on just exactly 100,000 clams. Not bad for a single day's work. I'll take it anytime."

"Next week, one of the cleverest, most diabolical weapons for murder I've ever seen."

Notes:
- This program contains a commercial for Mentholatum Deep Heat Rub.
- Court Benson is Reed, Roger DeKoven is Looker, Carl Frank is the Lieutenant, Allan Manson is the voice on the tape, Guy Repp is Conroy, Barbara Cassar is Sarah.
- The announcer is Art Hannes.
- Musical supervision is by Ethel Huber.

Producer: Bruno Zirato, Jr.   Writer: Jack Johnstone
Cast: Court Benson, Roger De Koven, Carl Frank, Allan Manson, Guy Repp, Barbara Cassar

Show:	The All Wet Matter
Show Date:	9/10/1961
Company:	State Unity Life Insurance Company
Agent:	Lawrence Penworthy Thurston
Exp. Acct:	$300.00

Synopsis: Lawrence Penworthy Thurston calls. He is the local representative of the State Unity Life Insurance Company in Cayce, South Carolina. He wants Johnny to make sure he visits all the sights in South Carolina while he is there in Columbia. Can you come right away? One of their most important clients is sure that someone wants to kill her.

Johnny flies to Columbia and cabs to the DeSoto Hotel. The next morning Johnny visits the State Unity office on State Street, which is close to station WCAY that carries Johnny's cases. Thurston is a nice old southern gentleman who offers Johnny a cigar.

The client is Mrs. Melanie Ramsey Pembrooke who comes from one of the oldest families in the area. The Ramsey side of the family has the money in the family, and Mrs. Pembrooke lives in Ramseyville, South Carolina. Thurston is sure that someone is trying to kill her because of the package she received yesterday.

Thurston called Johnny because Ramseyville does not have a police department. Mrs. Pembrooke told Thurston that the package had an "infernal machine" in it. Johnny clarifies that to mean a bomb.

Johnny rents a car and drives to Ramseyville, which is not very big. Mrs. Pembrooke, who is in her late forties, meets Johnny at the door of her home. She tells Johnny that her husband Peter is away, he is a salesman who sells machine tools, but is not very good at it. Her husband is eleven years younger than she is and is no way near as wealthy as she is. He had gone to Minneapolis, Milwaukee and Duluth on his last trip and should be home any time.

She received the badly wrapped package yesterday. She shook the package and noticed a ticking sound inside it. She threw the package out the window and into a fishpond. When she went out to look at it later, it had fallen apart.

Mrs. Pembrooke shows Johnny the contents and Johnny describes it as a crude time bomb and tells her that throwing it into the fishpond broke the wiring and ruined the detonating device.

She tells Johnny that the package was meant for her and that the package was mailed from Chicago. When Johnny notes that Chicago could have been a stopover on her husband's trip she is sure that her husband is not involved. Johnny notes that any fingerprints were long gone.

Johnny checks the hotel in Duluth, and Peter had left to come home. Johnny wonders if someone mailed the package from Chicago for him. Mrs. Pembrooke is positive that her husband would not do such a thing as he is too good hearted and not to suspect him. Johnny tells her that she is not to tell her husband about the bomb until Johnny has had a chance to talk to him.

Johnny visits station WCAY and speaks with Bill Barrett of the news bureau. Johnny asks Bill about any fine plantation homes in the area, and Bill tells Johnny about the Ramsey place. Mrs. Pembrooke, the last of the Ramsey line, owns it.

Bill tells Johnny that Pete Pembrooke was smart and married into money, that is if she does not catch him. Bill calls Pete a Romeo who married for the money. Bill tells Johnny that Melanie is a really shrewd person, manners notwithstanding and that she seems to be the only person in the area who is not wise to Pete's playing around. Johnny is told that she would throw Pete out if she ever caught him.

Johnny receives a call from Mrs. Pembrooke, who tells Johnny that her husband just came home. Johnny goes to the Pembrooke home, where Pete has been in the bath for an hour. Mrs. Pembrooke and Johnny go up to the bathroom and find the door locked. Johnny breaks down the door and they find Pete dead in the bathtub.

Dr. Eustis Culpepper is called and declares the cause of death a heart attack. He asks Johnny if the radio above the tub was on when Johnny got there, and Johnny tells him no. Too bad, as Pete had a history of heart problems. Dr. Culpepper tells Johnny he can make preparations for the body, but Johnny has a better idea. Johnny calls the police and thinks about the package mailed from Chicago. Johnny ponders about Pete mailing the package or having it mailed. "Have it mailed?"

Johnny has an idea and finds a pile of pulp magazines in the living room and finds what he is looking for. "Surprise your friends with mail from all over the world, signed and sent by you. For only fifty cents plus regular postage we'll mail your letter, your package from anywhere in the United States." And the address of the re-mailing outfit, Chicago, Illinois of course. Johnny could call the company to find out who paid to have the package sent, but goes back upstairs to poke around.

The police arrive and join Johnny after talking with the doctor. Johnny wonders about what the autopsy will reveal, if anything. Johnny shows the officer that the door was locked from the outside and uses the hem of his handkerchief to show how it could be done. Johnny is sure that someone came in, killed Peter and then locked the door.

Johnny shows the officer the radio on the shelf above the tub and tells him that a radio should never be anywhere near water. Johnny shows how the cord is unplugged, like someone pulled it from the wall to keep from shocking themselves after using it as a murder weapon. Johnny shows him how the radio is wet inside and the switch is still on. Bad heart or good, he didn't have a chance.

Johnny tells the officer that the only other person in the house murdered him after she found out he was playing around, and only married her for her money. And that was too much for the fine old family pride. The phony "infernal machine" was a cover to keep her from being suspected.

Mrs. Pembrooke comes in with a gun to shoot Johnny and the police officer, but the officer hits her and gets the gun away from her. "And to think that I, a gentleman sir, would ever strike a woman that way!" Johnny tells him not to worry about it, he will get over it.

"So, from here on in it's up to the courts. It's not to be broadcast, but a tidy hunk of this expense account went to that officer who so fortunately for a moment forgot to be a gentleman. You'll notice I haven't given his name."

"Next week, a wild old man, living in, believe it or not, an ancient castle, that is complete with chamber of horrors."

Notes:
- This program contains a commercial about the new Net Alert news system in use for important news bulletins, and for the United Campaign.
- There is some evidence that the broadcast date for this program is actually 10/1/1961. There is a *Suspense* program called *No Hiding Place* in circulation dated 10/1/1961 that has the next week teaser from this program at the beginning of the file. There is no way to accurately determine the date.
- Toni Darnay as Melanie, Lawson Zerbe is Thurston, Dan Ocko is Dr. Culpepper, Cliff Carpenter is the policeman.
- The announcer is Art Hannes.
- Musical supervision is by Ethel Huber.

Producer: Bruno Zirato, Jr.   Writer: Jack Johnstone
Cast: Toni Darnay, Lawson Zerbe, Dan Ocko, Cliff Carpenter

♦ ❖ ♦

Show: **The Buyer and the Cellar Matter**
Show Date: 9/17/1961
Company: Worldwide Mutual Insurance Company
Agent: Don Reagle
Exp. Acct: $477.30

Synopsis: Don Reagle calls and tells Johnny that he has been moved from Chicago to San Francisco. Johnny has some fine memories of San Francisco, fine memories of fat fees. "Is this going to be another one?" Johnny wonders. Don tells Johnny that Harvey Layman is missing and insured for $250,000. Johnny is on his way.

Johnny flies to San Francisco, California and cabs to the Huntington Hotel on Nob Hill. The next morning Johnny visits Don in his office near station KCBS, which carries his reports for CBS and helped him solve an arson case once.

Don tells Johnny not to unpack his bags. Harvey Layman has disappeared, and his wife is the beneficiary. They have not really been getting along lately, but he has a good business, and would be worth more money later on. His wife is not domineering, she is overpowering! While Layman is working, she is spending on herself. Layman is stubborn and will not give up hope for her changing her ways.

Layman is a commission buyer of antiques and left a week ago for Beverly Hills to see a man, but he never came back. Layman is extremely punctual and would not just up and change his schedule.

Don has checked the hotels, and there is no sign of him. Layman went to see John Arthur Whittington Maynard, who has told Don that Layman never showed up. Maynard was a movie producer thirty-years ago and made a number of big-money horror films. Layman was a buyer of unusual things, and Johnny remembers that Maynard had an old movie castle set moved to his property to use as a home. Johnny gets the description of Layman and is told that the wife has promised to send a picture.

Johnny drives to the Layman house in Marin County. Johnny notes that the house was definitely decorated by a woman, for a woman. Johnny is convinced after talking to Doris Layman, that he either left to get away from her or she did him in.

Mrs. Layman tells Johnny that she would not dirty her hands by murdering Harvey, he is worth more alive than dead. She refuses to believe that he would run off. The police, those "big talking, do nothing men", have accomplished nothing, and the movie-struck police in Beverly Hills are just as bad.

Mrs. Laymen tells Johnny that Harvey had called her from Maynard's home. He always calls, she insists on it, and Harvey always obeys. She had forgotten to tell that to the police, but they should have known. Harvey had gone there to collect $10,000. Doris tells Johnny that Maynard had told Harvey he should feel honored to have helped decorate the place and threatened Harvey. Doris told Harvey to go down there and collect the money or else. Doris tells Johnny to leave and forget about the case.

From his hotel, Johnny calls an old friend, Sgt. Brady at the Beverly Hills Police Department. Brady tells Johnny that there was a phone call made to a Marin County number from Maynard's house. Brady thinks Maynard might have called Layman, but Johnny tells him that Maynard did not know Layman was coming. The police know Maynard, and he is a nut. The police have searched the place and found nothing. Brady tells Johnny that if Maynard ever did kill anyone, he would invite the police over to show the body to them.

Johnny flies to Los Angeles, rents a car and drives to Beverly Hills and to police headquarters. Sgt. Brady is out so Johnny drives up to the Maynard house up in the mountains. Johnny gets that wee small voice in his brain that says "watch it Dollar, you may be getting into more than you bargained for. So, watch it Dollar. Watch it."

Johnny describes the house, once a movie set, as a medieval castle. The drawbridge is lowered as Johnny approaches and Johnny sees Maynard standing there, a short, fat unkempt man resembling Quasimodo. Maynard invites Johnny into the castle. When Johnny tells Maynard he is an investigator, he starts to throw Johnny out mistaking him for a salesman.

Johnny tells him he is there about Harvey Layman. Maynard takes Johnny in to show him all the things his dear friend Layman had bought for him. Johnny is sure that most of the things in the house deserved to be in a museum, and especially the things in the basement torture chamber. Maynard tells Johnny that he was the master of murder, mayhem and torture.

Johnny is taken to the wine cellar, which is full of dusty wine bottles that have been there for twenty-nine years, according to Maynard. Maynard tells Johnny that he has not seen Layman for over a year. Maynard also tells Johnny that he never drinks the wine in the cellar.

Maynard holds a bottle up to the light for Johnny, and Johnny sees what Maynard really means. Johnny tells Maynard that everything just looks real, that most of the house is just imitation. Johnny tells Maynard that the dust and cobwebs even fooled the police.

Johnny tells him that the dust is just fuller's earth. Johnny would have been fooled if Maynard had not picked up the wine and held it up to the light. Maynard protests when Johnny starts to investigate a pile of bottles and pulls a gun. Johnny remembers a movie where Maynard had a man buried under bottles of wine, and Maynard tells Johnny that Harvey Layman is buried there, and Johnny will join him.

Maynard is about to shoot when Sgt. Brady comes in. Maynard fires and Brady shoots him. Johnny is glad he left word at headquarters for Brady to join him. Johnny tells him that the bottle of sherry, which was supposed to have been there for twenty-nine years did not have any sediment in it. The age dust and cobwebs were all fake. Johnny tells Brady that he just took a wild guess.

"Needless to say, wild as the whole thing may seem, they found Layman's body buried there in the caller."

"Next week, Savannah Georgia, after one of the cleverest crooks I've ever had to tangle with."

Notes:
- This program contains commercials for Dupont Zerex antifreeze and for the United Fund drive.
- Fuller's Earth was also mentioned in *The Mei-Ling Buddah Matter.*
- Leon Janney is Maynard, Gertrude Warner is Doris, William Redfield is Brady, Carl Frank is Don.
- The next show should be *The Clever Crook Matter*, but it is not available.
- The announcer is Art Hannes.
- Musical supervision is by Ethel Huber.

Producer: Bruno Zirato, Jr.   Writer: Jack Johnstone
Cast: Leon Janney, Gertrude Warner, William Redfield, Carl Frank

♦ ❖ ♦

Show: The Double-Barreled Matter
Show Date: 10/1/1961
Company: Mono Guarantee Insurance Company
Agent: Phil Easterday
Exp. Acct: $760.00

Synopsis: Phil Easterday calls Johnny from San Diego, and Johnny tells him it has been a long time. Phil wants Johnny to come out to sunny California. The problem is a series of burglaries against the same couple. But exactly nothing has been taken in any of them. Phil will meet Johnny at the airport.

Johnny flies to Los Angeles and then on to San Diego, California landing around noon. Johnny notes that San Diego is the oldest settlement in California and has the perfect climate that Los Angeles brags about. Johnny likes it there.

Phil meets Johnny and tells him that whether anything is taken or not, burglary is breaking and entering with the intent to commit a felony. Mr. Charles Hastings Warner and Mrs. Trudy Warner's apartment has been broken into seven times in the past two months. Phil does not know what Hastings does for a living, but he has several policies worth over a million. The burglaries were never reported to the police. Phil's wife plays bridge with Mrs. Warner who told her, and she told Phil who called Mrs. Warner who did not want to report them because noting was stolen, but she is worried. Johnny thinks the whole thing is suspicious.

Johnny gets the address and decides not to tell the Warner's he is coming. Johnny rents a car and drives to the apartment, which is a cottage behind a local hotel, and very well furnished. Mrs. Warner is in her mid-twenties and very dignified and well-appointed with diamond earrings. Johnny senses a blue blood, but the nasal twang and poor grammar in her voice says otherwise.

Johnny uses the old foot-in-the-door trick to get in the door to talk to her about the burglaries. She tells Johnny that she should not have talked to that insurance man's wife. Trudy wonders what would have happened if she were to have come home and found somebody in the apartment with a gun.

All of the burglaries have taken place after Charlie has come home and they have gone out at night, as they do a lot of night clubbing. Whoever did it was very thorough, and Charlie told her not to worry about it as it was probably some psychopath. Charlie is so cool and casual about everything.

Over a drink, Trudy tells Johnny that Charlie is not employed, at least since she married him, and does not know what he did before that. Trudy tells Johnny that Charlie tells her his money comes from the stock market. Charlie is out hunting near El Centro, and he goes almost every week. Charlie is hunting for doves, or pigeons or whatever. Charlie stays at the Blue Bird motor court and he left this morning.

After a second short drink (just to keep her company, believe me) Johnny leaves and starts making calls to stock brokerages, and no one has ever heard of Warner. Johnny calls an old friend, Pete Fuller on the Chicago Sun Times and Pete tells Johnny all about "Chicky" Warner. Johnny gets the rundown, and realizes he is involved in one of the most important and dangerous cases in his career.

Johnny decides to act fast and follow a hunch based on Warner's character. Johnny buys a collection of sporting clothes and a 12-gauge double-barreled shotgun and three boxes of shells with #9 bird shot, and a hunting license. Johnny ages his new clothes by driving his car over them and then drives to El Centro and gets a room at the Blue Bird motor court.

In the bar, Johnny meets Warner, a man of 50. Johnny strikes up a conversation and hopes Warner can tell Johnny where to go to find doves. Warner tells

Johnny that he can tell him where to find so many doves he will call them pigeons. Johnny asks if he can tag along, and Warner agrees.

There will be two of you, as he is going with some other guy named Al Milford. It is good to have some witnesses along to make sure Warner does not go over his limit. Warner tells Johnny that he can watch Milford to make sure he does not blow Warner's head off by mistake. "When a man has a gun on him, you never know. Remember that."

Very early the next morning, the three men take off for Calexico and then off on a dirt road that winds very close to Mexico. Johnny does not like Milford, who is very shifty. Warner places Johnny and Milford together, and when the sun comes up Johnny has more action than he can handle.

Johnny notices that Warner was only shooting one shot at a time, and Milford was not shooting at all after the first big flurry. Johnny edges towards Warner and finds Milford lying in the brush aiming at Warner with a .38. Milford aims the .38 at Johnny and shows Johnny his credentials. He knows who Johnny is, and Al tells Johnny that he is with the narcotics squad.

They know how Warner gets the pure uncut heroin across the border. He picks it up from a contact on these hunting trips and always has a witness with him. Johnny surmises that the Feds had searched Warner's apartment, but Al cannot confirm that. No one has ever found the dope on him and Al has to find out how he brings it in.

Warner walks up and tells Al he will never find out and shoots him in the arm with a shotgun slug. Warner tells Johnny to toss him the .38 or he will get the other barrel, but Johnny takes his time.

Johnny tells Warner that he wants the other barrel and walks towards him, complementing him on the hiding place for the dope. "Only one shot at a time is what gave you away" Johnny tells him. Johnny tells Warner that if he shoots, the hammer will fall on the white stuff it is loaded with. Warner tries to bribe Johnny, but the only deal he will make is to slug Warner. Johnny tells Al that, as a reward for his cleverness, Warner can carry him back to the car.

"That one shotgun barrel loaded with heroin, sure it was only a guess, but thank heavens it was the right one. You know, for a second there I was afraid he might have a shell in it."

"Next week, one of the rottenest rackets in the world, but a story with a real twist at the end."

Notes:
- This program contains a commercial for Mentholatum Deep Heating Rub.
- Santos Ortega is Warner, Elizabeth Lawrence is Trudy, Court Benson is Easterday, Carl Frank is Al, Robert Dryden is Pete.
- Most catalogs list the next program as *One of the Rottenest Rackets Matter*, but I do not believe that a program by that name exists (See *VII. The Canonical Johnny Dollar* for more on this.). But the next program, *The Medium Rare Matter* agrees with the next week tag in this story.
- The announcer is Art Hannes

- Musical supervision is by Ethel Huber

Producer: Bruno Zirato, Jr.   Writer: Jack Johnstone
Cast: Santos Ortega, Elizabeth Lawrence, Court Benson, Carl Frank, Robert Dryden

♦ ❖ ♦

Show: **The Medium Rare Matter**
Show Date: 10/8/1961
Company: **Tri-Western Life Insurance Company**
Agent: **Jack Price**
Exp. Acct: **$465.30**

Synopsis: "I am thy father's spirit, Doom'd for a certain term to walk the night." (Well good for you replies Johnny.) "And for the day confined to fast in fires till the foul crimes done in my days of nature are burnt and purged away." (Bravo, Mr. Shakespeare!) Johnny asks Jack Price why the long quote from act one of Hamlet. Jack asks Johnny if he believes in ghosts. A lot of innocent people in Corpus are beginning to, because of a psychic medium that has moved in on them. He has been holding séances and doing the clairvoyance bit. Johnny asks if the medium is rare, medium or, maybe well done? Jack asks Johnny to come down and help him save the company's money.

Johnny flies to Corpus Christi, Texas and gets a room at the Robert Driscoll Hotel. Later, Johnny asks Jack if the police have looked into this phony. They have, but there is no proof.

The man operates outside the city limits, and uses the name Udi Vishnu, but Jack thinks that the Hindu accent is tinted with Brooklynese. Udi does not charge for his act but relies on contributions. He is operating out beyond the Ranch 66 roadhouse, in an old abandoned theater called the Temple of the Living Truth.

Every night the place is packed with the people who think he is a new prophet, and the floor is covered with their contributions that include insurance policies that have been cashed in. People are coming from all over the area and are staying at a hotel that Vishnu owns nearby.

Jack thinks he is committing murder because in the past two weeks two clients have been murdered. Johnny suggests that he go out and to see the show, and Jack gives him a reserved seat ticket for the show.

Johnny rents a car and drives to the temple, where only those with reserved seats are admitted. Inside Johnny sees a bare stage with a reading platform. Most of the audience looks like poor folks, the most likely to be taken in.

At 8:27 the organ music starts and then Udi Vishnu glides onto the stage at 8:30. Johnny notes an almost hypnotic stare in his eyes. Udi starts with a statement about his powers and urges the audience to join him in possessing the super natural powers within them.

Udi calls on seat number H-41, and a woman tells Johnny that the number is her seat number. Vishnu sees a vision of a farm in Oklahoma near El Reno, and a small girl named Martha Winters and a dog she was not supposed to have that she named Skipper. Vishnu sees her school and the teacher, Miss Albright, who helped Martha decide not to run away. Martha believes in Vishnu, as does the crowd for two more hours. Johnny talks with the people after the program, but none had told anyone anything that Vishnu knew about them.

Later, Jack tells Johnny that he has to find out how Vishnu gets all of the information about the people. Even Houdini or Thurston or Blackstone would have to take a backseat to this punk. Suddenly, Johnny has an idea about the reserved seats.

Johnny remembers that a magician had set out to expose the phony mediums in all the big cities, but Vishnu only plays to the small towns who would never have heard of the other magician. Johnny tells Jack to get two tickets for tonight's show and get the county authorities and the newspapers there as well. Johnny is going to prove that the mystic is a mistake.

Johnny spends several hours to get the answer to a key question, the amount of the phone bill of the mystic's hotel. Johnny visits the hotel and looks at the register, which shows two critical things, the home address and the ticket number of each person.

Johnny goes back to town and runs up $120 in very necessary phone calls. Jack has the tickets and they go to the show with a number of county authorities and members of the national press.

The program begins as usual and within an hour Udi has the audience in his grasp. Finally, Vishnu calls on one of the numbers Johnny had compiled. Vishnu calls the number L-13. Vishnu starts to tell a man what he knows, but Johnny jumps up and takes over. Johnny tells the man that he was there last night and has the same powers as Vishnu.

Johnny tells seat L-13 that he knows all about him by using the same sort of trickery Vishnu uses. His name is Martin Mefford, and he lives in Cotton Valley, Louisiana, and his car license number is CFU160, and he is a plumber's helper. The man agrees and Vishnu tells the crowd not to believe Johnny.

Johnny continues and tells Mefford that he walks with a limp because he broke his leg when he was six and Tommy Parkins shoved him from a tree. Miss Bruster in the first grade promised him a book if he stopped chewing his nails and Mefford agrees. Johnny calls out seat number C-41 and repeats the same sort of thing as Vishnu protests.

"By the time I got through telling those people things even Vishnu had not found out about them, and some of it was pretty personal, they fairly tore the place apart. Then when Udi dragged a gun from under his robes to protect himself and pulled off a couple of shots, then the police moved in.

As for the radio and newspaper story that followed, well believe me that Udi Vishnu, whose real name turned out to be Bernie Bildrick, will not try that trick again, even if he does get out of the pen."

Jack asks Johnny how he got all the information, and Johnny tells him he used the same trick that the magician in New York had used. He would call the ticket agent at the hotel and get the names and addresses of a guest who had bought a ticket to the show. All Johnny had to do was look at the register.

Johnny got on the phone and called the police chief and the mayor of the town and then called a few other people to get the information. So, that's that.

"Whether they can pin the two murders on him that Jack told me about remains to be seen, that's up to the authorities and is out of my hands now."

"Next week, a nice quiet little town in south Jersey that doesn't stay that way for long."

Notes:
- There are several plays on the title of a previous story, *The Medium, Well Done Matter* in this story.
- Maurice Tarplin is Jack, Dan Ocko is Udi, Evelyn Juster is the first woman, Bill Lipton is Mefford, Toni Darney is the second woman. Also heard were Guy Repp and Sam Raskyn.
- The quote from Hamlet Act I is spoken by the ghost character.
- The announcer is Art Hannes.
- Musical supervision is by Ethel Huber.

Producer:	Bruno Zirato, Jr.	Writer:	Jack Johnstone
Cast:	Maurice Tarplin, Dan Ocko, Evelyn Juster, Bill Lipton, Toni Darnay, Guy Repp, Sam Raskyn		

♦ ❖ ♦

Show:	**The Three for One Matter**
Show Date:	**10/22/1961**
Company:	**International Life & Casualty Insurance Company**
Agent:	**Christian Albeck**
Exp. Acct:	**$81.50**

Synopsis: Christian Albeck calls Johnny from Boston and he has a bit of a problem. He wants Johnny to come up and Johnny agrees if he will pay his expenses, commission and maybe a little fee. Christian tells Johnny that there is a $250,000 policy involved, and Johnny is on his way.

Johnny flies to Boston, Massachusetts and cabs to Christian's office, not too far from station WEEI which broadcasts Johnny's reports. Christian is a sharp individual, who Johnny feels is often one step ahead of him. Johnny suggests that Christian spring for lunch at the Union Oyster House, and he agrees. He also tells Johnny that he will need a rental car to drive up to Center Harbor, New Hampshire near Lake Winnipesaukee where Johnny handled another case.

Over lunch Johnny is told that he is to find out what happened to John Stuart Kirkman, who lives on Red Hill Road. Kirkman is retired and is worth a lot of money. Kirkman left the house after dinner last night and has not come back. Johnny tells Chris that if he had told Johnny of his suspicions on the last case, it would have saved the company a lot of money.

Chris tells Johnny that the beneficiary of the policy is the wife Mona, and she will get half a million if it was an accident. Chris tells Johnny that there are three people who might be worth looking into.

The first is Charles D. Hockaway, a junior partner in Kirkman's firm. Hockaway had borrowed a lot of money from Kirkman and has not paid it back. It was almost $100,000 and Kirkman was going to take legal action, and Hockaway is worried and resentful because Kirkman did not really need the money. Hockaway has recently rented a cabin in Center Harbor.

The second person is Mildred Armstrong, Kirkman's first wife. The divorce was generous, but he did not add to the settlement when Kirkman started making money and she swore she would get him. She too has moved to Center Harbor.

Third is Tony Benson who lives across the lake. He is an irresponsible bum and is just no good. Tony is a dental assistant with the local dentist. He was in love with Mona, or rather her fortune, but Kirkman married her and used her fortune to enlarge his. Tony will stop at nothing to get even with Kirkman.

Johnny rents a car and drives to Center Harbor. Johnny checks in at the Garnet Inn and gets a visit from police chief Mike Sharp. The chief tells Johnny that he has just found Kirkman, or rather his body.

Johnny and Sharp drive to the spot where Kirkman slid off the road. Johnny spots the tire tracks and Sharp tells Johnny that Kirkman lost control and went over the edge of the cliff. Doc Higbee, the coroner, is inspecting the body and Johnny notes that there were no skid marks on the road. Johnny wonders if Kirkman was dead before he went over.

Doc Higbee tells Johnny that the only mark on Kirkman is the one on his head that killed him when the car rolled over. Doc is irritated that Johnny would question him, until he finds out just who Johnny is. Doc listens to Johnny's cases on WGAN in Portland and WEEI in Boston. Doc Higbee decides to do an autopsy and Sharp tells Johnny that there are three people he wants to keep in the area. They are the same three Johnny is interested in. Johnny requests that a mechanic look at the car while Sharp rounds up the suspects.

Johnny goes to clean up for dinner and finds Tony Benson in his room. He saw the note Johnny had left for chief Sharp and decided to wait for Johnny in his room. Better breaking and entering than murder. Tony tells Johnny that he did not have a grudge against Kirkman but did against Mona. Tony knows he will get a fair deal from Johnny.

Johnny asks him why he thinks it was murder rather than an accident and Tony tries to back pedal saying that the police will try to pin anything on him.

Johnny gets a call from Mildred Armstrong who must see Johnny right away. She is not the one who murdered or, um, had Kirkman murdered. Johnny asks her why she thinks it is murder. She is glad when Johnny tells her it looks like an accident. Johnny tells her to come to the hotel.

There is a knock at the door, and it is Charles Hockaway. Johnny surmises that Charles came to tell Johnny that he did not murder Kirkman. Johnny again asks why Charles thinks it was murder? Charlie tells Johnny that Kirkman and he were not on good terms, but he did not do it. Chief Sharp shows up with Mildred, and all three suspects are in the room with Johnny.

Johnny goes into the hallway and the chief tells Johnny that Kirkman did die in an accident. Also, Frank Marshall the mechanic can find nothing wrong with the car. There was no fluid in the brake line, but that was caused by a tiny hole in the brake line, maybe it was a defective piece of tubing. Johnny tells Sharp to keep an eye on the suspects while he goes to look at the car.

At the garage, Frank tells Johnny that if the brake lines were tampered with he would have seen it because of the mud in the undercarriage. Frank tells Johnny that the hole in the brake line is smaller than his smallest drill bit, which is 1/128th of an inch, and the hole is smaller than that. Johnny inspects the brake line and under a magnifying glass Johnny sees that it was drilled, but not by a drill bit, which leaves a burr. There is no burr on the hole.

Back at the hotel Johnny asks Tony if he is a dental assistant. Johnny tells Tony he should be more careful with the drills he borrows from the office and uses to drill holes in brake lines. Johnny tells him he forgot to clean off the bits of copper off the drill after he used it. Tony tells Johnny he is pretty smart. "No, just smart enough" Johnny replies.

"So once again it's up to the courts. And how about the switch on this one. I mean the logical suspect being the logical suspect for once?"

"Next week, one of the cleverest ways to work a racket that ever tripped up a crook."

Notes:
- This program contains only a single commercial for Dupont Zerex Antifreeze.
- Leora Thatcher is Mildred, William Mason is Tony, Robert Donley is Chris, Robert Dryden is the chief, Reynold Osborne is Charles, Arthur Kohl is the doctor, Bill Lipton is Frank.
- Johnny references another case in Cold Harbor, *The Winnipesaukee Wonder Matter.*
- The announcer is Art Hannes
- Musical supervision is by Ethel Huber

Producer: Bruno Zirato, Jr.   Writer: Jack Johnstone
Cast: Leora Thatcher, William Mason, Bob Donnelly, Robert Dryden, Reynold Osborne, Arthur Kohl, Bill Lipton

♦ ❖ ♦

Show: **The Bee or Not to Bee Matter**
Show Date: **10/29/1961**
Company: **Universal Adjustment Bureau**
Agent: **Pat Fuller**
Exp. Acct: **$471.00**

Synopsis: Pat Fuller calls Johnny from the Universal Adjustment Bureau. Pat Fuller tells Johnny that Pat McCracken has retired at age 50 with a real nice pension from the company. Pat tells Johnny he may have to cover the whole country on this thing. It is one of the simplest and oldest rackets and the hardest to catch up on. Come on over and let's talk.

Johnny cabs to Pat's office and finds Pat to be a sharp operator, just like his predecessor. Pat tells Johnny that the Universal Adjustment Bureau only handles the larger claims for the companies that they cover. Pat has uncovered thirteen claims ranging from $250 to $4,000. The racket is false injury. Johnny recalls handling a similar case on the west coast some time ago.

The reported injuries were falls in a hotel. A couple registers and makes the hotel aware that they have important business out of town the next day. The wife manages to fall in the lobby and the man yells for the manager. When he gets there the manager is threatened with a suit of $100,000, but the managers usually settle for cash. This couple is smart as the woman usually slips on a spot of oil or grease. Also, a doctor is called in for a quick examination and agrees it was an accident.

Thirteen cases in less than four months. Pat is sure that the same couple is pulling the stunts but they do not use the same names or appearances. Pat has a picture taken of a model in the lobby of a hotel, and they happen to be in the background. The home address is always the same, 21st Street and Fairmont Avenue in Philadelphia. Johnny recognizes the address as the Eastern Penitentiary.

Johnny tells Pat that sending the pictures to all the hotels would accomplish nothing. Johnny thinks that they have to be caught in the act. Pat shows Johnny a list of where they have hit, and Pat cannot see a pattern. Johnny has a hunch and borrows the photo and the list of cases.

Johnny flies to Philadelphia, Pennsylvania and goes to the penitentiary. One of the assistant wardens recognizes the man as Harry Bain, who got out last year after serving a term for burglary, and had a record a mile long. He pulled jobs all over the country and would always hire a lawyer before each job to have an alibi. He was only convicted after he was caught with the goods in his possession. The warden cannot figure out how a woman could recover from the injuries in so short a time.

Johnny gets a list of the places where Harry pulled jobs before he was caught, and the list matches Johnny's list of hotel jobs. All of the cities are places where Harry had contacts with a lawyer. But there are three new names: Little Rock, Duluth and New Orleans. Johnny bets that Bain will hit one of these cities. Johnny receives a call from Pat Fuller. They have hit again in Little Rock. So, where does Johnny go?

Johnny goes to the Belleview Stratford Hotel, and rings up $181.40 calling the managers of all of the larger hotels in both New Orleans and Duluth. Johnny buys an armload of reading materials and after three days he finally gets a call.

Mr. Devereaux in New Orleans calls and tells him that there is a couple named Chatsworth from Philadelphia, and they gave 21st and Fairmont as their address. Johnny tells him to hang on to them and he will get there as soon as he can.

Johnny flies to New Orleans, Louisiana and arrives early in the morning. Johnny cabs to the Hotel de Phillipe and meets with the manager, who cannot believe that the Chatsworths are those nasty people and refuses to let Johnny into their rooms. The Chatsworths come through the lobby and Johnny hopes Devereaux will not tip them off.

They start toward the café and Johnny bribes a bellboy for the room number of the Chatsworth suite. Johnny and the Bellboy dicker over the use of his uniform, and Johnny must resort to "other" tactics. Johnny ties him up in the linen closet and goes up to the Chatsworth suite where he searches the bags. In one bag Johnny finds something you will never believe.

Johnny hears the lock and hides under the bed. Chatsworth comes in and tells a bellboy to call the manager and the doctor. He opens the bag and takes a bottle out and puts it on her leg. Already the ankle is swelling. Later the doctor demands a hospital visit.

Chatsworth tells the manager he will sue for $50,000. Chatsworth relents and will settle for $10,000 and tells the manager that their lawyer Franky Tobello will see to it. Devereaux wants to pay the doctor's bill and will give Chatsworth $1,000 to avoid any publicity. Chatsworth wants a decent offer and Devereaux settles on $2,000 cash.

"The price they settled on? Two thousand bucks cash, immediately. But as Devereaux, the poor excited sucker, was about to go down stairs and get it, I crawled out from my uncomfortable spot under the bed. And you know something? Henry Bain and the woman gave up without a struggle when they found out who I was, and what I was doing there. And the manager, when I pulled the little glass jar out of their suit case and showed him how they made their phony accidents look so real, real enough to fool a doctor, well believe it or not the shock was too much for him and he almost fainted. So, that was that. And the expense account total comes to $471. Wait a minute. I forgot to tell you about the trick. Their little trick for making the ankle swell up and look like the worst sprain on record? Well you see that jar, the one that Bain had opened and then clapped against her ankle contained exactly three nasty little yellow jackets. Bees. Yes, clever."

"Next week, one of the nicest killers I've ever met."

Notes:
- This program contains commercials for Dupont Zerex Antifreeze, and for the efforts of the religious charities abroad.
- John Thomas is Pat, Ivor Francis is the manager, Robert Dryden is Bain, Gertrude Warner is Mrs. Chatsworth, Bob Donnelly is the warden.
- This the first appearance of Pat Fuller, who replaced Pat McCracken when he retired after 25 years.
- This story is very similar to the un-broadcast story called *The Key to Crime Matter   Pat Fuller Version*, including Pat Fuller.
- There is a little confusion at the end over the names. Harry Bain used the name Henry Chatsworth, but at the end Johnny calls him Henry Bain.
- The announcer is Art Hannes.
- Musical supervision is by Ethel Huber.

Producer:	Bruno Zirato, Jr. Writer: Jack Johnstone
Cast:	John Thomas, Ivor Francis, Robert Dryden, Gertrude Warner, Bob Donnelly

♦ ❖ ♦

Show:	**The Monticello Mystery Matter**
Show Date:	11/5/1961
Company:	**Inter-Allied Insurance Company**
Agent:	**Henry Foreman**
Exp. Acct:	**$71.70**

Synopsis: Henry Foreman calls Johnny from Port Jarvis, New York. Johnny tells Henry that he is really fortunate to have the Delaware River and the Neversink so close by. Johnny tells Henry that the Neversink is his favorite trout stream. Henry wants Johnny to do work on a case for the wife of an important client, Mr. Rudolph Teckler who lives near Monticello, when they are not in the city. Henry has no idea what the problem is and Teckler had asked that Johnny come up if he has the free time, which could be a couple days or weeks. Teckler told Henry that the case is very important to Johnny, and Teckler would pay the expenses. Johnny is on his way.

Johnny flies to New York and rents a car for the drive to Port Jarvis. Johnny meets with Foreman who still does not know what Teckler's problem is. Mrs. Teckler has a sizeable policy and is the widow of Horace Rathbone Mellinger, of the steel and oil fortune.

Johnny drives to Monticello, New York and on to Bethel and to a spot near Swan Lake and Kenoza Lake. A steel fence surrounds the estate but the gate is unlocked. Johnny goes in to find a delightful two-story log cabin surrounded by huge trees and a 20-acre lake that is full of lunker bass.

Johnny meets Rudy Teckler who is also a fisherman. Johnny suggests that they go fishing but remembers that he is there on business and it is out of season. Rudy tells Johnny that this is a private lake and he can tell the game warden to go away if he shows up. He and his wife have invited Johnny to come here, but not on business. Johnny realizes that this is too good to be true. When Johnny meets Mrs. Teckler that little bell in the back of his head that has saved his life rings out loud and clear. Mrs. Teckler was a short, sweet, pert and pretty woman with a lovely complexion who is almost sixty.

Nancy tells Johnny that they love the place, which belonged to her late husband who used it for a hunting lodge. Rudy tells Nancy that she works too hard when they come up there, and next year they will bring the servants. "Next year?" she asks. Rudy does not like hunting so he put in the lake and stocked it with fish.

She remembers that Johnny likes fishing, and decided to invite him, as she is an old fan of his radio program. Bringing Johnny there was much better than inviting him to a party in New York. Nancy tells Johnny to go fishing, and he better bring back some fish. Johnny recalls that Nancy is short, sweet, pert and pretty — and adds smart. Johnny wonders what her real reason for him being there is.

Johnny and Rudy go fishing, but before they can start to fish a storm blows in. Rudy tells Johnny that the rain will ruin the fishing and they head to the dock during a downpour.

After cocktails and dinner, Johnny starts to worry as he has sensed a tension between Rudy and Nancy. Rudy gets a little too liberal with the highballs and Johnny tries to talk to him after Nancy retires. Rudy tells Johnny that he does not have a thing to worry about as long as he can drown his sorrows.

Johnny helps Rudy to his room and puts him to bed. Johnny sleeps soundly and just after sunup Rudy pounds on Johnny's door. Something has happened to Nancy!

Rudy tells Johnny that Nancy has disappeared. Her bed has been slept in, but she is not there. The only thing missing are her nightgown, robe and slippers. There is no sign of her anywhere.

Johnny dresses, and Rudy hopes she is all right. Rudy tells Johnny that last night he had gotten the feeling that she was worried about something, but he does not know what. Johnny searches the estate and does not find Nancy.

Johnny asks Rudy if there are problems because of the difference in their ages or over money, but Rudy insists that there are none. Johnny goes to mix a couple drinks and notices the lack of a hangover in Rudy.

Johnny and Nancy had been drinking Scotch so Johnny checks the bourbon Rudy had been drinking from and discovers that it held only weak tea. Johnny wonders if Nancy was the sorrow he had to drown because she was wise that he married her for her money. And was Nancy the one who was afraid? But where is the body?

Johnny decides to check the obvious place. Johnny tells Rudy that he is going to play a hunch and goes to the dam at the foot of the lake and removes the top planks in the spillway. Rudy comes out and Johnny tells him he is going to lower the lake to find where Rudy put the body after he killed Nancy last night.

Rudy tells Johnny he will show him the place, but now all the insurance and the whole estate will be his, without her there to dole it out to him. There is plenty for both of them, they will be rich! Johnny suggests that Rudy tell that to a judge.

"Any comments? Why bother, I hate this kind of case, but it does happen."

"Next week, the everglades of Florida, and believe me there are spots in there that can be pretty dangerous."

Notes:
- This program contains commercials for the expanded CBS news coverage, and for CBS where you will find Arthur Godfrey, Art Linkletter, Gary Moore, Bing Crosby and Rosemary Clooney, guaranteed entertainment at the star's address.
- **William Redfield is Rudy, Adele Ronson is Nancy, Reynold Osborne is Henry.**
- **The announcer is Art Hannes.**

- Musical supervision is by Ethel Huber.

Producer: Bruno Zirato, Jr.   Writer: Jack Johnstone
Cast: William Redfield, Adele Ronson, Reynold Osborne

♦ ❖ ♦

Show: **The Wrong One Matter**
Show Date: 11/12/1961
Company: **Tri-State Life & Casualty Insurance Company**
Agent: **Earle Poorman**
Exp. Acct: $0.00

Synopsis: Earle Poorman, a welcome voice calls Johnny from warm, sunny Florida. Earle tells Johnny that the fishing is red hot, and Earle wants Johnny to come down about a broken ankle. Earle has one, and he wants Johnny to come down and handle a client for him that lives down the road. Johnny tells Earle that something is fishy about this case, but Johnny relents and agrees to come down.

Johnny flies to Sarasota, Florida and cabs to Earle's office where he finds Earle with a cast on his ankle. Johnny offers to autograph the cast, but Earle demurs. Earle wants Johnny to run the boat for him so he can get his mind off matters.

Earle shows Johnny a letter mailed yesterday that is written on wrapping paper. The letter, which is written in poor grammar, tells Earle that "if the company does not want to pay off the policy real quick they should come there, because his pal is away gatoring and cannot help him". The letter is from Emmett Dennery. The policy is for $2,000, and Waldo Blake is the beneficiary. Dennery is no mental giant, but he is still a client. This letter is why Johnny is here.

Earle knows nothing about the client other than Dennery and Blake live in the Everglades and hunt and trap for a living. Johnny is the one who will go visit Emmett, so that he and Earle can go fishing. Earle tells Johnny that despite the tone of the letter, Dennery has nothing to fear but the game warden.

Earle shows Johnny a map that was pinned on the policy that shows where Emmett lives. Earle tells Johnny that he will do all right, in spite of Johnny's concerns. Johnny recounts how in his last trip to the Everglades he had the services of a guide named Ben Osceola.

Johnny takes Earle home and goes out to look for the road on the map, which is near the location of his previous case. Johnny drives up to a small shack where a man is standing with a .30-30 in his arms. Johnny reminds Ben of who he is, and Ben welcomes him. Johnny tells Ben who he is looking for, and Ben tells Johnny that Dennery is not his friend.

He and the man called Lefty do not obey the law and take game they should not take from Seminole lands. The Seminole stay away from the men, as they are taboo. Ben last saw Dennery when he was a child and tells Johnny that Dennery and Lefty look like twins. Ben will not take Johnny to the place where Dennery lives but allows Johnny to take his airboat. Johnny gives Ben $20 for the boat and tells Johnny that it is too bad he cannot go with him, as Johnny must be very careful.

Johnny drives the airboat into the swamps and notes the large amount of animal life. Johnny reaches an island with and old shack surrounded by racks of drying hides.

Johnny heads for the cabin and opens the door to find a dead body on a bed inside the dank gloomy interior of the filthy shack. Johnny can see that the man has been dead for several days. Johnny is about to cover the body with a rag when a voice tells him to stay put or he will shoot Johnny.

Johnny spots a high-powered old-fashioned rifle aimed at this head and held by an old man dressed in ragged clothes. The man's eyes remind Johnny of a maddened snake. The man takes Johnny's gun, "a real purdy one" and accuses Johnny of killing the man on the bed and sits Johnny down on the floor.

The man accuses Johnny of killing Emmett Dennery, and Johnny tells him that if he is Waldo Blake, he will get the insurance Emmett had. Johnny reaches into his pocket to show Waldo the money and Waldo grabs Johnny's wallet to count the money in it. Johnny grabs the rifle and throws Waldo to the floor.

Johnny tells Waldo that it is good that Emmett probably died of natural causes. Johnny tells the man that he could not pass up the opportunity to get back the money he had paid on premiums. Johnny knew something was wrong because the letter was only mailed yesterday, and the body had been dead for several days.

Johnny tells him that he had written the letter to get the money when it really was Lefty Blake who had died. When the man tells Johnny that he cannot prove that the body is Waldo, Johnny shows how the laces on the boots were tied with a left-handed bow knot, something a right-handed man would not do. Emmett admits to Johnny that after paying all those years only to have Waldo go first, it was the only thing he could have done. Johnny reminds him that he could have cashed in the policy and gotten most of his money back. Johnny tells Emmett that it is up to the company to determine what will happen to him.

"So, there you are Earle. Like I said to the old rascal, it is up to the company now. As for the total on my expense account, well let's wait until I can tote up the cost of all the fishing we are going to do. Okay?"

"Next week, a fishing guide who turns out to be a guide to murder."

Notes:
- This program contains a commercial for Pat Summerall and *Sports Time* on CBS every day but Sunday.
- Mandel Kramer welcomes CBS radio station WNEB in Worchester, Massachusetts.
- Martin Blaine is Earle, Bill Lipton is Ben, Jim Boles is Emmett.
- The previous cases mentioned are *The Wayward Moth Matter* and *The Salkoff Sequel Matter*, which concerned the research of a rocket scientist, and how Johnny assisted in the launch of the Explorer 1 rocket in 1958.
- The announcer is Art Hannes.

- Musical supervision is by Ethel Huber.
- The director is Edward Oates.

Producer: Bruno Zirato, Jr.   Writer: Jack Johnstone
Cast: Martin Blaine, Bill Lipton, Jim Boles

◆ ❖ ◆

Show: **The Guide to Murder Matter**
Show Date: **11/19/1961**
Company: **Tri-State Life & Casualty Insurance Company**
Agent: **Earle Poorman**
Exp. Acct: **$85.00**

Synopsis: Johnny answers the phone at Earle Poorman's home and accuses Earle of running off to the office when they were supposed to go fishing. Earle reminds Johnny of the article in the Herald Tribune about him being there, and Johnny reminds him that the evening paper and WSPB mentioned it too. Earle tells Johnny that all the publicity has every fishing guide in the area bidding to take Johnny out fishing, and Earle is looking over the offers. The winner is Captain Barney Beale, who is a good captain and a client of Earle's. Earle tells Johnny to come pick him up and crosses his heart and hopes to die that there is no insurance matter for Johnny to look into. But if he tries to get me involved in another mess...

Johnny buys gas for Earle's car and drives to his office. Johnny and Earle drive to Captain Beale's boat at Lemon Bay, Florida and Johnny describes Beale as a capable captain, formerly from New England. Barney tells Johnny that he learned to fish off Cape Cod, and what he learned there serves him well here.

Johnny spends the day fishing and is exhausted by midafternoon from catching fish after fish. After picking out some fish to take home, Barney complements Earle on his new car, which is a lot fancier than the old 1922 Maxwell he drove down from New England and has in the garage. Johnny asks to see the car and Barney takes Johnny to the garage and unlocks the door. In the garage is the Maxwell with a dead man in the seat.

Johnny determines that the man had died from carbon monoxide poisoning, that the ignition switch was on, and the gas tank was empty. Johnny finds no marks on the body, and Barney does not know who the man is. Barney comments on the nice clothes and the full head of hair on the man.

Barney tells Johnny that he used the car a week ago last Saturday and bought a full tank of gas for it. The garage has been locked ever since, and only Barney has the key. Barney notices a latch on a window is open, but the opening is full of spider webs. Barney leaves to call the coroner and Earle hobbles in.

The coroner, Dr. Hill, tells Johnny that the man has been dead for a day or two. The cause is carbon monoxide poisoning and he is sure that it was a suicide. Johnny tries to ask for an autopsy, but the coroner leaves to arrange for the body to be picked up.

Johnny takes another look around and checks out the window. One of the panes was brand new, and glass shards are on the floor. Johnny moistens a shard and uses it to take fingerprints of the corpse.

Earle and Johnny leave after Barney refuses to take any money from Earle. Earle notes that Barney was very casual about finding the body, and Johnny mentions how the suicide did not leave any note, which they typically do.

After leaving Earle at home, Johnny takes the glass to the police and sees Lt. Barney Phillips, who had helped him on other cases. Johnny asks for the prints to be analyzed by the FBI and goes fishing.

Two days later Lt. Phillips calls Johnny to tell him that the suicide had a record. His name was Maury Spencer, and he operated in New England selling fishing boats. He would steal a boat, fix it up and sell it to some sucker. Phillips shows Johnny a list of aliases that includes "Baldy" Spangler.

In a picture the man looks a little like the corpse and has a bald spot. Johnny tells him it must have been plastic surgery, and even Barney Beale noted the full head of hair. Johnny leaves to prove that the suicide was a murder.

Johnny visits the coroner to look at the body. Johnny pulls on the hair and it comes off, it was a small toupee. Under the toupee is a hole that Johnny guesses is from a gaff like a fishing guide would have used. Dr. Hill tells Johnny that the wound would not have killed him, so he could have been put in the car to make it look like a suicide. Johnny asks the coroner to follow him to Lemon Bay to see Captain Beale.

On the way, Johnny tells Earle that Barney lives in a shack, has a boat held together by baling wire, and does not spend a cent he does not have to, and yet he gave away a fishing trip. And there was a repaired window in the garage to hold the fumes from the car.

At the marina, Barney tells Johnny that he should not have tried to fool a smart man like Johnny, and that his conscious has been bothering him. He thought having Johnny around was a good way to keep suspicion off himself.

He killed Baldy because of all the people he had hurt Down East and got off scot-free every time. When he came down to Florida and suggested that Barney help him, someone had to stop him to keep him from hurting all the kind people here.

"I don't know. Who am I to judge? But I hope they handle the old fellow as gently as possible in spite of what he did and must pay for."

"Next week, a city held at bay by a single man with a timebomb."

Notes:
- This program has a single commercial about how CBS is proud to bring such stars as Bing Crosby and Rosemary Clooney, Art Linkletter, Gary Moore and Durward Kirby and *Arthur Godfrey Time*.
- Ivor Francis is Barney, Ian Martin is Earle, Lawson Zerbe is Dr. Hill, Jim Boles is Lt. Phillips.
- The car is a Maxwell, and not one reference to Jack Benny!

- This same murder method was used in *The Hair Raising Matter*, broadcast on 11/30/1958.
- The announcer is Art Hannes.
- Musical supervision is by Ethel Huber.

Producer: Bruno Zirato, Jr.   Writer: Jack Johnstone
Cast: Ivor Francis, Ian Martin, Lawson Zerbe, Jim Boles

♦ ❖ ♦

Show: **The Mad Bomber Matter**
Show Date: **11/26/1961**
Company: **Greater Southwest Insurance Company**
Agent: **Hank Parnell**
Exp. Acct: **$350.00**

Synopsis: Hank Parnell calls Johnny from Muddy Gap, Wyoming. Hank is the owner, editor, reporter and everything else for the local paper "The Weekly Tribune". He is also the local agent for the Greater Southwest Insurance Company. Hank wants Johnny to hightail it out on expense account. There is no insurance business yet, but if Johnny cannot give him a hand, Greater Southwest will not have an office, agent or a town. Hank wants Johnny to keep Muddy Gap from being blown off the map.

Johnny travels by plane, train and car to Muddy Gap. Johnny describes how Muddy Gap is in the heart of the old Indian country, and in oil country. The town's principle business is oil storage and huge storage tanks surround the town.

Johnny meets with Hank, who tells Johnny that he is also the mayor and acting police chief. Hank asks Johnny what he thinks would happen if one of the oil tanks were to explode? He is sure that it will happen unless Johnny can stop Billy Benbow.

Billy was born here and is a real troublemaker. During the last war, Hank and his father used the paper to get Billy drafted, but Billy swore he would get back at the town. While in the Army Billy worked with explosives and every blast he set off was for someone in the town, starting with the draft board. At the end of the war Billy went completely off-base and started blowing things up and ended up in a hospital. Billy has escaped from the hospital, and Hank received a phone call the other day warning him that he has not forgotten.

Hank is sure that Billy is coming back to get even and is just waiting for a chance to blow up the town. Hank has printed nothing in the paper so as to not alarm the residents. Hank tells Johnny that the state police will be glad to help, after Billy has done something. Hank tells Johnny that the phone has rung every day at noon, and the line was empty when he picked up the receiver. Johnny tells Hank that he needs more evidence.

The phone rings, and Johnny picks up the extension. A voice tells Hank "I better prove that I haven't forgotten." The caller confirms that he is Billy Benbow and there is an explosion in the back of the office.

Johnny crawls out from under the desk and sees that the press room is totally destroyed. Johnny tells Hank that he is sure that Billy only wants to put the paper out of business, but where is Billy?

Johnny finds a timing device that was used to set off the blast. Pete Branson comes in and smells dynamite, but Hank tells him it was only a can of benzene he used to clean the type. Pete, along with Tony Battan are the whole police department.

Pete gets the crowd out of the way and Johnny asks Hank about Pete's face. Hank tells Johnny that it was marred when he was dragged by a horse. Johnny is not sure that the excuse about the benzene was wise, as they do not know if Billy is finished yet. Hank tells Johnny that everyone on the draft board is dead except for Grampa Wheedon. "Oh, Lord that old house of his!" Hank tells Johnny that the house is down by the terminal, and if it were blown up, it would set off the whole town.

Johnny calls the operator and asks her where the call earlier came from. The operator tells Johnny that he sounds just like that Johnny Dollar on the radio, and the townspeople would really like to know that. She tells Johnny that the call came from the only phone booth in the town, outside the drug store.

The phone rings again and Billy tells Johnny that the big one is coming later, maybe tonight. Hank wants to evacuate the town, but Johnny tells him that it is too late. Johnny is sure that Billy has been here for weeks and asks Hank to let him handle things his own way.

Johnny wants Hank to call the deputies and have them all follow his orders exactly. Johnny is sure that his hunch is right.

When Tony arrives first, Johnny tells Hank and Tony what he wants them to do, and they cannot believe him, but agree to say nothing to anyone, even Pete.

When Pete arrives, Hank and Tony leave and Johnny asks Pete for his gun and starts to go to see Grandpa Wheedon. Johnny tells Pete that he thinks that the mad bomber will hit Grandpa next. Pete asks Johnny what kind of a man he could be, and Johnny asks him how he knows it is a man?

Pete does not seem to like it when Johnny mentions a madman and bets they will find nothing. Pete tells Johnny that he has not been on the force too long and has been working on ranches lately doing odd jobs. Johnny mentions that his hands are kind of soft and he immediately knew the smell of dynamite when he came into the office earlier.

Johnny tells him that the scars on his face are from an explosion, and he is sure that no one would recognize him, "would they Billy?"

Pete pulls another gun and tells Johnny to reach. Billy knew he would have trouble with Johnny, because he is not dumb like the others. He is going to kill Johnny and then go to his place and set the timer on another bomb. The bomb will be planted out by the tank farm by Grandpa Wheedon's. He will set the timer so that he will have enough time to get out of town in Johnny's car.

Hank comes in with the bomb he found in Pete's room. Pete threatens Hank, and Tony warns Pete that he will get him if he shoots Hank. While Pete is distracted, Johnny slugs him. "Wow-ee, that's a mighty good left you have there, Dollar!" Johnny tells Hank that Pete was right, Hank is kind of stupid for carrying the bomb so Pete could shoot at it. "Oh, my gosh!" exclaims Hank.

"Remarks, why bother on this one."

"Next week, a beautiful girl, a handful of coins, and a mysterious disappearance."

Notes:
- This program contains a commercial about the noise of older cars and the better engineering of today's cars. Smoother cars increase the need control speed. Take care and get there.
- Court Benson is Hank, Lawson Zerbe is Pete, Cliff Carpenter is Billy, Barbara Cassar is the operator.
- Muddy Gap, Wyoming is north of Rawlings.
- The announcer is Art Hannes.
- Musical supervision is by Ethel Huber.

Producer:	Bruno Zirato, Jr. Writer: Jack Johnstone
Cast:	Court Benson, Lawson Zerbe, Cliff Carpenter, Barbara Cassar

◆ ❖ ◆

Show:	**The Cinder Elmer Matter**
Show Date:	**12/3/1961**
Company:	**Worldwide Mutual Insurance Company**
Agent:	**Charlie Warren**
Exp. Acct:	**$377.80**

Synopsis: Charlie Warren calls Johnny from warm sunny southern California and he can just imagine how Johnny is doing with all the cold and snow in New England. Johnny reminds him of the beauty he is missing: the clean crisp invigorating air, the sparkle of the sun on sleet covered branches, the sound of sleigh bells, rolling fields drifted high with pure white snow. Charlie adds all the mud and slush Johnny has to plow through. Charlie asks Johnny if he can come out to California to enjoy the beauties of the area, if he can keep his expense account under control. Johnny will arrange to take a propeller driven plane so he can get some sleep and will meet Charlie in the morning.

Johnny flies to Los Angeles and is not able to sleep on the flight. Johnny's seatmate is a cute little brunette who needs help with her vacation plans. At the airport, a tall young man who plays right tackle for the Los Angeles Rams meets the girl, and Johnny's plans go out the door with them.

Charlie meets Johnny and gives him the keys to the rental car, complete with snow chains. Johnny is to head out past San Bernardino for Crestline, California. Johnny can get directions to the Hillcrest Lodge in Crestline. Charlie wishes he could go with Johnny, what with all the snow and skiing, but all Johnny wants is some sleep.

The case is about the disappearance of Bartley Harmon. Harmon and his wife Nora and his business partner Elmer Wrightson went up to the lodge for a few days. The "poor little shrimp" has disappeared.

Harmon and Wrightson are both only five feet three and one hundred fifteen pounds and look like twins. But Nora is five feet eleven, blond and built like an Olympic champion. Wow!

Barley went off for a walk and has just disappeared. The sheriff's office has been notified, and they have not been able to find anything, and they know what they are doing. The policy is $200,000 double indemnity, and Harmon has a bad heart. The business will go to the partner and the insurance goes to Nora. Johnny wonders how Nora and Wrightson get along, and Charlie tells him that Nora is beautiful, rich and a lot younger than Wrightson. Johnny figures he better get up there quick.

Johnny drives through San Bernardino and the heat really gets to him because of the lack of sleep. At 4,000 feet Johnny has to stop to put on chains and is invigorated. At the lodge, Roy Turner of the sheriff's office meets Johnny and tells him that he does not like the situation.

There is no love triangle as Wrightson is the same kind of "homely, pedantic, facts-and-figures little shrimp" that her husband was, and she is tired of that type. Nora is much younger and more athletic, and she makes the most of what she has. She always brings too many clothes, including a trunk full of shoes. She likes the lodge and Bartley and Wrightson come to keep an eye on each other.

The hills and cabins in the area have been searched. Harmon headed over to "Old Ironsides", a mountain with a steep cliff-like face on it. Roy gets a phone call and Harmon's body has been found.

Johnny and Roy go to the airport and fly to the area in a helicopter. On the snow above the tree line they spot the body. The chopper lands and Johnny and Roy get out to look at the body. Roy tells Johnny that Harmon believed in a legend about a cave full of gold and came up to look for it every year. Johnny thinks that it was heart failure, until they spot two things: another set of smaller footprints and a cigarette butt with lipstick on it.

Roy is sure that Nora is guilty, and her alibi of being shopping at Lake Arrowhead is not so sound now. Johnny is unsure though. Wrightson was supposedly asleep in his room all afternoon.

Roy tells a deputy to have the lipstick analyzed when he and Johnny take the body in. Johnny wants to go along but opts not to.

In San Bernardino, Doc Hanley tells Johnny that the lipstick is quite unusual. A deputy takes Johnny back to the lodge, and Johnny bribes a bellboy to take a lipstick from Nora's room. Johnny takes it back to Doc Hanley and he confirms that it is the same type.

The autopsy shows that Harmon was beaten to death, and death was so sudden that the blood stopped circulating before bruises could form. Hanley tells Johnny that Nora had the motive and the ability, but Johnny wonders why she would leave so many obvious clues. Johnny leaves to keep Roy from arresting the wrong person.

In his room, Johnny meets with Roy who tells Johnny that Harmon was followed up the mountain, and every time Harmon stopped, she stopped and smoked a cigarette and left the butt in the snow. Roy tells Johnny that he found a pair of snow boots in Nora's room that matched the prints in the snow. Johnny realizes that the important clue here is the cigarette butt. Johnny asks Roy if he left any butts on the trail, and Johnny tells Roy that the position of the butts is important.

On the trail, Roy takes Johnny to the first location and Johnny shows him that the butt was not crushed out, and only placed on the snow. If it was lit, it would have melted some of the snow, but it didn't. The butts were put out somewhere else and left here to incriminate Nora Harmon. So, it has to be Elmer Wrightson, the only other person with a motive.

Roy wants to look to see if Elmer has snow boots just like Nora, but Johnny feels that, with a trunk full of shoes she probably has several pairs. So, Elmer might have borrowed a pair, and Johnny suggests they try the old Cinderella trick, only they will call it the Cinder Elmer trick, and have him try on a pair of Nora's boots.

"Her snow boots fit him all right. And little old Cinder Elmer, the dumb jerk, should have known better. He should have made us come up with some really concrete evidence. But luckily for us, Elmer just broke down and confessed to the whole bit. So, once again it is up to the courts."

"Next week, one of the cleverest coverups for a firebug I've ever seen. And believe me, I've seen plenty."

Notes:
- This program contains a commercial about the high volume of holiday mail, and the need to mail early and often, and to use postal zone numbers.
- At the end of the program there is a public service announcement for Welcome Wagon by WROW in Albany, New York.
- Cliff Carpenter is Roy, Eugene Francis is Charlie, Robert Dryden is Hanley, Jim Stevens is the pilot.
- Musical supervision is by Ethel Huber.
- The announcer is Stuart Metz.

Producer:	Bruno Zirato, Jr.	Writer: Jack Johnstone
Cast:	Cliff Carpenter, Eugene Francis, Robert Dryden, Jim Stevens	

♦ ❖ ♦

Show: The Phony Phone Matter
Show Date: 12/17/1961
Company: Trinity Mutual Insurance Company
Agent: Bert Helfer
Exp. Acct: $0.00

Synopsis: Bert Helfer calls and wishes Johnny a Merry Christmas. Johnny tells Bert he is not taking on any cases until after the holidays. Bert asks Johnny to come over to his office, but the answer is no. Bert tells Johnny that he only wants to give him his money for the San Francisco job he did a few weeks ago. "Are you sure that's all?" asks Johnny.

Johnny checks out with his call service and goes to see Bert, who is alone in the office. Bert finishes up a call so that no one will bother him while he is in Florida. Bert gives Johnny his expenses in cash, as the banks are closed and he knows Johnny will need the money for shopping. Bert gives Johnny a message from his call service to call Exmont 3-5770 immediately.

Johnny does not recognize the number, but Bert knows the number, and it belongs to Harvey L. Hallet, who owns Hallet Industries in Hartford, Connecticut. Bert shows Johnny the Hallet buildings from his window and relates that they have a lot of insurance on the plant. There have been a number of burglaries lately, and Bert does not trust Hallet. Bert tells Johnny that he had given Johnny's number to Hallet, and Johnny decides he will call Hallet back. Johnny relates how a phone call can be used to cover up a crime and based on Bert's mistrust, Johnny wants to call Hallet.

Johnny calls Hallet's number and reaches Mary Hallet who tells Johnny that Mr. Hallet is leaving for New York. Hallet takes the phone and wants to talk to Johnny about some burglaries next week and hangs up the phone. Suddenly there is an explosion outside and a building has just blown up, the Hallet Industries building.

Johnny cabs to the building to find it fully involved in flames. Johnny finds police Lt. Jimmy Harmon who tells Johnny that he is there to investigate the burglaries at Hallet's plant. Harmon tells Johnny that he has gotten nowhere and feels that Hallet did not want him to find out anything and gave him too much cooperation. Hallet was always underfoot and getting in the way. Harmon tells Johnny that he does not trust Hallet, and that he suspects arson, and the arson squad is already working on the building.

Mr. Hallet arrives and tells Johnny that he heard the explosion from his home, and Johnny tells Harmon that he can corroborate the fact that Hallet was on the phone with him. Johnny mentions insurance, but Hallet tells him that the money cannot make up for the business. Hallet tells Johnny that the color of the smoke and the smell are odd. There were solvents stored in the back room, but it was always locked. Hallet wonders if the night watchman was injured.

Harmon comes back to confirm that arson was involved. Also, he thinks that the watchman, Ben Matthews, saw who did it and knew the person. The door had a dead-latch lock on it, and Ben's key is in the inside of the lock, so he let someone in he recognized. Harmon knew Ben, and he never would let anyone in he was not supposed to, but if his boss asked him to open it...but Hallet will not have to testify because there is a bullet in Ben's head.

Johnny asks about the device used to start the fire, and Harmon tells him that there was no device, only a wick was used. Johnny tells Harmon that Hallet was at home, where Johnny talked to him on the phone.

Johnny calls Jonathan Buckley who verifies that Hallet's money is in his bank. After Johnny mentions arson and the murder of the watchman, Jonathan can only tell Johnny that Hallet's financial condition is pretty bad. Harmon tells Johnny that he has checked over all of Hallet's employees, and can vouch for all of them, Hallet is the only one he does not know about.

Johnny calls New York and talks to his pal Randy Singer of the New York Police. Randy asks Johnny what kind of a jam he needs to get Johnny out of in New York. Johnny asks Randy if the name Harvey Hallet means anything, and Randy tells Johnny that Hallet is really "Paraffin Peterson", who has been chased out of New York, along with his girlfriend Mary. Peterson only uses a paraffin wick to start fires. But how to prove that Hallet started the fire when he was on the phone with Johnny?

Johnny wonders if Hallet Electronics might have a product to help in this situation. Johnny and Harmon go to Hallet's home where he is just returning. Johnny notices a tape device on the table that Mary had left there. Harmon runs the tape back and plays it.

On the tape is the conversation that Hallet had with Johnny. So, the message was prerecorded. And his wife played it when Johnny called. Then his wife called Hallet at the plant and told him to go ahead. "Any comment Mr. Hallet?"

"Expense account total, forget it. I'd rather take this time to wish all of you, where ever you are, a Merry Christmas."

"Next week, well next week there won't be any case. But I think you will want to be here anyway. Next week at this time, you'll be hearing our annual Christmas Eve *Sing with Bing*. We'll be back two weeks from now. Merry Christmas from Yours Truly, Johnny Dollar."

Notes:
- There are two versions of this program. The Network version contains a commercial message about the families abroad who are suffering from hunger and can benefit from CARE packages.
- The AFRTS version contains a story about the benefits of democracy and a story about the US Navy and the USS Providence that stopped in Vera Cruz to help the local people with blood deposits.
- This program title was used twice, once on 5/8/1960, and again on 12/24/1961, but the storylines are different.
- Pat Canel is the announcer.
- Musical supervision is by Ethel Huber.

Producer: Bruno Zirato, Jr.   Writer: Jack Johnstone
Cast: Jackson Beck, Michael Kane, William Redfield, Teri Keane, Eugene Francis, David Kern

♦ ❖ ♦

Show: **The One Too Many Matter**
Show Date: 12/31/1961
Company: **Eastern Liability & Trust Insurance Company**
Agent: **Hal Kemper**
Exp. Acct: **$4.80**

Synopsis: Hal Kemper calls Johnny and wishes him a happy New Year. Hal asks if Johnny has any plans for New Year's Eve. Johnny tells Hal that he will greet 1962 with other plans that include getting a good night's sleep. Hal asks

Johnny to come to his house and talk to Dr. Begley, the famous heart doctor about a patient, Mrs. Nancy Cunningham, who is an important client of Hal's. Johnny asks to wait until after New Year's Eve, but Hal tells Johnny that if he waits, Mrs. Cunningham might not live to see 1962.

Johnny drives to Hal's house in Hartford, Connecticut through an obstacle course of crazy drivers. Johnny meets Dr. Begley who tells Johnny that Mrs. Cunningham lives in a small house that she can take care of, given her heart condition. Today he learned something that will want to make Johnny go right over there.

Tonight, two persons, Donald Kingman and Walter Baird, the nephews of Mrs. Cunningham, will visit. The nephews are heirs to her estate and considerable insurance. Dr. Begley has arranged for Johnny to stay there as long as the two nephews are there. Dr. Begley is sure that one of the nephews is there to murder her.

Mrs. Cunningham had called Hal and wants to change the beneficiary of the estate to a charity. The nephews will be there before they are cut out of the will. The only time they have been there before was for money, but now they are "good-hearted Joes".

Johnny learns that on Donald's last visit, gunshots broke a window just missing Mrs. Cunningham, but Donald reported it and made the police investigate. The police said the bullets were strays fired in the woods, but Dr. Begley remembered that Donald was a good rifle shot. That evening the heat was on low but went off. And Dr. Begley found a cotter pin in the mechanism that jammed the thermostat, and she could have frozen to death. Dr. Begley is sure that the boys were there to get to her before the will is changed. Johnny agrees to go see Mrs. Cunningham.

Johnny drives to Mrs. Cunningham's house, where Don Kingman opens the door and invites Johnny in and introduces him to Walt. Johnny talks to the nephews, who have fixed up a nice party with catered food and a portable bar. Walt fixes drinks (scotch and soda for Johnny) and Don is surprised that Aunt Nancy knows Johnny. The boys admit that it is time they paid more attention to their aunt, after all she has done for them.

The clock chimes nine, and Walt leaves to drive to a liquor store to buy some champagne. Don asks Johnny how long he has known Nancy when there is the sound of an automobile accident outside. Don tells Johnny that they knew Nancy was going to cut them off, and that is one reason they decided to be nice. She told them today that she was leaving them in the will after all.

Don starts acting woozy, drops his glass and collapses on the floor. Johnny starts to feel the same way, and he falls to the floor. When Johnny wakes up a policeman is slapping him. Sgt. Rogan gives Johnny a drink of brandy and asks what he knows about what has happened. Rogan tells Johnny that Mrs. Cunningham is dead in the bedroom with a bullet in her.

Rogan tells Johnny that a .22 bullet is in Mrs. Cunningham's head. An officer was investigating a crash, heard the shot and radioed for Rogan to investigate. Rogan broke in and found them. Johnny tells Rogan about the drinks, and Rogan tells Johnny that there is sediment in his and Don's glass. Also, an envelope of penorphene was found under the bar. Walter's glass had some in it also but Walter had left before drinking any.

Johnny tells Rogan about Walter pouring the drinks and leaving on an errand to the liquor store. The time is now ten forty, so Rogan needs to find Walter. The phone rings, and Rogan takes the call. Rogan asks Johnny what time Walter left, and Johnny tells him it was at nine. Rogan tells Johnny that the accident down the street involved Walter Baird, who is in the hospital. Rogan tells Johnny that the door was locked when he got there, so who killed Mrs. Cunningham?

Johnny wonders if Dr. Begley was the killer because he found out that she was not leaving the money to a hospital or a charity. Rogan wonders if Johnny had anything to do with the killing, but Johnny tells him not to kid about that. Rogan wonders if the doctor would know about the penorphene, but Johnny tells him that anyone could get the drug, and the only ones who would benefit were Walter and Don.

Johnny has an idea and notes Don's glass on the table. Johnny is sure that Donald killed Mrs. Cunningham and then drank from his drink. All of the glasses had the drug, but it was Walter who suggested going out before Don would have had to tell him to go out, before he could have touched his drink. By leaving, Walter was the obvious suspect, except for the accident, which Don could not foresee.

Don had gotten up to stiffen his drink, but it was really to pour a new one without the drug. When Johnny started to go out, Don faked his collapse, got up and killed Mrs. Cunningham, came back and put the drugs in his drink and went out with an alibi that Johnny would have to corroborate.

Johnny tells Rogan that the glass is on the table now, but earlier when he faked the collapse, Donald dropped his glass and it rolled on the floor. Only Don could have put the glass on the table. Satisfied?

"When he came to, and we told him how he had worked it, how he had made the mistake of setting the glass back on the table, told him that we made a paraffin test of his hand to prove our point, well Don not only confessed, he showed us where he had hidden the gun."

"Next week, I'll be back with another case for you, but for now, I would like to wish all of you the very best of the new year."

Notes:
- This program contains a commercial about the Cotton Bowl between the Mississippi Rebels and the Texas Longhorns, a CBS special. The man to stop is Jimmy Saxton.
- Mandel Kramer wishes everyone the very best of New Years.
- Lawson Zerbe is Begley, Allan Manson is Don, Nat Polen is Hal, Robert Dryden is Rogan, Doug Parkhurst is Walter, Ethel Everett is Nancy.
- Art Hannes is the announcer.
- Musical supervision is by Ethel Huber.

Producer:	Bruno Zirato, Jr. Writer: Jack Johnstone
Cast:	Lawson Zerbe, Allan Manson, Nat Polen, Robert Dryden, Doug Parkhurst, Ethel Everett

♦ ❖ ♦

Show:	**The Hot Chocolates Matter**
Show Date:	1/7/1962
Company:	Tri-Eastern Indemnity Associates
Agent:	Harvey Weller
Exp. Acct:	$49.35

Synopsis: Harvey Weller calls, and Johnny knows why he is calling. Johnny has heard on the radio that $100,000 in diamonds was stolen from MacDilby's jewelry store. Harvey wants Johnny to work on the case, but Johnny asks if he has thought about how much Johnny's commission will be. As Harvey starts to calculate it, Johnny tells him he is on his way.

Johnny flies to New York City and cabs to MacDilby's House of Jewels on Madison near 57th street. In the store, Johnny meets Randy Singer who wants to know how Johnny found out so quickly. "Never underestimate the power of radio" Johnny tells him.

Mr. MacDilby is introduced to Johnny, and he knows all about Johnny and his fine work. So far, the loss is $104,218.51, approximately. There was one witness, but Mr. MacDuggan the night watchman is in the hospital. There was no sign of forced entry, so MacDuggan must have let the thief in. Miss Tavish, who always opens the store in the morning, discovered the robbery.

So far, the only missing employee is Daniel Fairling, the cleaning boy. Mr. MacDilby tells Johnny that the safe was not opened and the jewels were in the display cases because the store was open late last evening. Johnny decides to visit MacDuggan in Belleview Hospital.

Johnny cabs to the hospital and sees officer Rogan trying to get the attention of the nurse. Rogan had been trying to get her attention because MacDuggan was conscious again. Johnny arranges to watch MacDuggan while Rogan goes to call Randy. MacDuggan tells Johnny to "Ask Fairling. Ask Danny Fairling" and goes out again.

Johnny runs to the phone and runs into Rogan who tells him Randy is on the way. Johnny looks up Danny Fairling in the phone book and cabs to his apartment. Johnny finds the apartment house door open and goes up to apartment 3-B.

A neighbor tells Johnny that Danny and his wife have split up. She thinks that they are going to make up because a delivery boy just delivered a box of chocolates to her. The neighbor tells Johnny to knock again and then there is an explosion. Johnny breaks down the door to find that the box of chocolates had contained a bomb. Mrs. Fairling is dead, and Johnny asks the neighbor to stay until the police arrive.

Johnny calls Randy's office and learns that MacDuggan has died. Johnny tells Randy what MacDuggan had said about Danny Fairling, and Randy tells Johnny to get over to his office.

Johnny cabs to the 18th precinct, and in Randy's office he is told that they have discovered that Danny had a record, and that Danny was picked up earlier that morning. Danny's wife had told the police where to find him.

Johnny tells Randy about the bomb and asks to talk to Danny. Randy asks Danny about the jewelry and Danny tells Johnny that they cannot prove that he took the jewels. Danny tells Johnny that he was late this morning and left when he saw the crowd. Johnny asks if he knows anything about the robbery and offers Danny legal assistance if he can help them.

After briefing Randy, Johnny asks Randy not to tell Danny about his wife or to tell the other precinct that they have Danny in custody until he can check on some things. Johnny is not convinced that they are holding the right man. He has a better idea, but he does not like it.

Johnny goes to talk to MacDilby and the loss is just as he had estimated. Randy tells MacDilby that they suspect Danny because of his record. Johnny asks to look around the store and Miss Tavish gladly offers to show him around.

Johnny wants to follow up on his idea and finds what he is looking for in a cleaning closet, a box of chocolates. Miss Tavish tells Johnny that Danny loves chocolate, especially the French ones he cannot afford.

Johnny goes to the candy shop and learns that a box of chocolates was delivered to the Fairling apartment that morning. A man bought them last evening and came back an hour later to ask that the box be delivered today. The customer was a well-dressed Scottish gentleman.

Johnny talks to Danny and tells him that he suspects MacDilby because the store was not broken into. MacDuggan knew who was at the door and let him in.

Johnny tells Danny that he got to work early and saw what MacDilby had done and threatened to blackmail him, because MacDilby had told Danny to stay home that morning. Johnny tells Danny that MacDilby had promised to give him a share of the money and offered him legal help, but MacDilby had other plans for Danny.

When Johnny asks Danny about his wife, Danny tells Johnny that he had walked out on her for a couple days, but was going back to her, because he loves her. Johnny asks if Danny likes French chocolates and tells Danny that MacDilby did not know that he had moved out. MacDilby thought that Danny would be there in the apartment, so he sent a box of chocolates with a bomb in it. Danny is upset when he learns that his wife is dead and tells Johnny that if the law does not kill MacDilby, he will.

"Don't worry, the law will take care of MacDilby. And Danny, his term will be a short one because of his testimony, and my testimony. Expense account total, including the ride back to Hartford, $49.35, and uh, don't forget the commission."

"Next week, high adventure in the colorful romantic gold rush country that can also be very deadly."

Notes:
- This program contains commercials for No-Doz, Kent cigarettes, and regular priced Sinclair Dino gasoline that performs like premium.

- Eugene Simes does the music supervision, and the music is heavy with bongo drums and jazzy sounds.
- Walter Otto is mentioned for the sound patterns, and Mike Shoskus for technical supervision.
- Art Hannes is the announcer.

Producer:	Fred Hendrickson Writer: Jack Johnstone
Cast:	Jackson Beck, Sam Gray, Gilbert Mack, Bill Lipton, Guy Repp, Betty Garde, Ivor Francis, Vicki Vola

◆ ❖ ◆

Show:	**The Terrible Torch Matter**
Show Date:	**1/21/1962**
Company:	**New Jersey Fire & Casualty Insurance Company**
Agent:	**Fred Larkin**
Exp. Acct:	**$1,500.00**

Synopsis: Fred Larkin calls from Trenton and gets Johnny out of bed. There is trouble in the town of Woodbine where Johnny handled a case several years ago. Johnny remembers something about a mattress factory that billed its clients more than they actually paid for the mattresses. Fred remembers that he covered the business for more insurance than necessary and really lost on that one. The trouble this time is a couple of fires. Fred asks Johnny to come on down so he can tell him all about it. Fred tells Johnny that if he can help end what he thinks is going on, he can count on his expenses and a nice big fat commission. "Freddy, you speak the language I love to hear. I'm on my way."

Johnny flies to Philadelphia, rents a car and drives to Trenton, New Jersey using the same route George Washington did. Fred takes Johnny to Hildebrechts Restaurant for lunch and tells him that he thinks that the fires were arson, and there will be more of them. The area around Woodbine is mainly farm area, but there are a number of factories in the town. The two fires occurred just outside of town.

A promoter has opened up an industrial area. Fred agrees with Johnny that it is a bad area for the development as there is no high-rent area for the factories in town to get out of. The development is slowly going broke, and there have been two fires so far. When someone gets away with it, fire can be a catchy idea.

The first fire was a week ago, and the last was yesterday. There are eleven factories in the development. However, eight of them are owned by people who are related to each other. Johnny tells Fred he is going to call in some help, Smokey Sullivan.

Fred is surprised when Johnny tells him that Smokey was one of the best arsonists in the business and got away with a lot of fires but has gone legitimate now. Smokey knows all about firebugs and has been a real help to Johnny. Right now, he is a consultant for the arson squad in Boston. Johnny asks about a bank, and Fred tells him that there is a loan office there that cashes checks. Johnny tells Fred he will use it for getting information.

Johnny arranges with Smokey to come to Trenton. Over dinner Johnny convinces Smokey that the area would be a great place for a firebug, especially if the owners got the arsonist from where they came from. Johnny wants Smokey to find out if the fires were arson.

The next morning Smokey and Johnny leave for Woodbine, New Jersey where Smokey goes to investigate the fires and Johnny talks to the one-man loan office. Johnny tells the owner, Mr. Hanley M. Becker that he wants to know the financial condition on all eleven factories in the development.

Becker tells Johnny that the financial information is confidential and there are only nine companies out there now. Becker starts to stutter when he tells Johnny that the insurance company had better pay off the claims, so that he can collect the loans he has made out there.

Johnny tells Becker that he thinks that arson is involved, and if so, there will be no payoff, which really flusters Becker. Becker tells Johnny that the loans were to pay off the properties and build housing for the workers that no longer work there. Only the warehouses are of any value now. Johnny tells Becker that if the remaining plants burn and arson is involved, he will get nothing. Suddenly Becker is more than willing to tell Johnny anything.

Johnny goes to wait for Smokey and by 2 p.m. Smokey is not back. At five o'clock Smokey is still not back, so Johnny goes back to the loan office to see Becker. Johnny asks Becker where the new-comers came from, and the answer is Patterson. Johnny remembers some arson jobs there and thinks that Smokey has found something. Johnny mentions that Smokey has his car and Becker loans Johnny his.

Johnny wonders about Becker and drives to the factory area. The area is empty and overgrown with weeds. Johnny spots his car by a windowless warehouse and stops there. Johnny goes in and finds Smokey unconscious on the floor.

Smokey is still alive and Johnny drives him to the motel where Dr. Rosenberg brings Smokey around. Smokey tells Johnny that it was Pete Larrison from Patterson. He must have thought that Smokey was trying to muscle into his territory. Smokey tells Johnny that Pete is going to fire the warehouse tonight. Smokey tries to tell Johnny about the others as he runs out the door to go to the warehouse.

Johnny goes to the warehouse and smells the strong odor of gasoline. Johnny turns on the lights to find Pete Larrison there with a gun. Walter is there behind Johnny and takes his gun.

Pete shows Johnny the arrangements for the fire, which will look like spontaneous combustion. Johnny sees strips of heavy felt soaked in gasoline leading to stacks of upholstered material and cardboard cartons. Pete sets the fuse by the door and tells Johnny that the police will suspect him.

Johnny tells Pete that Smokey is still alive, but Pete tells Johnny that no one would believe Smokey because Pete has a perfect alibi. He and Walter will be playing pinochle with Hanley Becker when the fire starts. Becker does not know about the fires, only the owners who have hired Pete know what is going to happen.

Walter starts to take the gas cans out and Johnny swings around, grabs a can and throws it at Pete as he rolls out the door. Pete shoots several times and the factory goes up like a bomb.

"Me? I guess I was OK. The blast rolled me a hundred yards or so across that sandy ground, and I came to only a couple of minutes later. Walter, who was blown up against the side of my car, ended up with a concussion. As for Pete, well I don't think I need to tell you. And that's it Freddy. The company can prosecute the factory owners any way it sees fit. Expense account total, including a chunk for Smokey, and damage to the rental car and the trip home, call it $1,500 even."

"Next week, the biggest blunder that I've ever made."

Notes:
- This program contains a commercial for YMCA week.
- This case makes a reference to *The Smoky Sleeper Matter*, but that case took place in Vineland, New Jersey not Woodbine.
- Leon Janney is Hanley, Sam Gray is Fred, Mason Adams is Pete, Larry Haines is Smokey, James Demetrie is Walter.
- Art Hannes is the announcer.
- Musical supervision is by Ethel Huber.

Producer:	Bruno Zirato, Jr. Writer: Jack Johnstone
Cast:	Leon Janney, Sam Gray, Mason Adams, Larry Haines, James Demetrie

◆ ❖ ◆

Show:	**The Can't be so Matter**
Show Date:	**1/28/1962**
Company:	**Worldwide Mutual Insurance Company**
Agent:	**Les Walters**
Exp. Acct:	**$0.00**

Synopsis: Mary, the operator at the Worldwide Mutual office calls Johnny. She has a call that Johnny thinks is from Les Walters. After Johnny addresses Les as "a big bum", the voice on the phone turns out to be Jonathan Harmon. Johnny was expecting Les to call about going to a hockey game to celebrate a recent birthday, if Les can get away from his wife that is. Jonathan tells Johnny it is too bad about Les' wife and tells Johnny that William Willoby was found dead this morning from "lead poisoning". Jonathan tells Johnny to go on out there and find out what happened. "I wonder what he meant about Les and his wife?"

Johnny cabs to the Hartford, Connecticut address of Willoby at 19525 East Maple Street and in Apartment 5-B Johnny meets Sgt. Bravo. Bravo had called the insurance company and had been watching Willoby since he moved there. They thought he might be involved in narcotics but had left here to get away from some debts. He came back with a lot of money recently and the police were suspicious.

Bravo tells Johnny that someone Willoby knew must have killed him. One of the glasses on a table had smudged prints, and Willoby was shot by a .45. When Johnny mentions Les Walters, Bravo tells Johnny that he had seen Les' wife Connie having lunch with Willoby in a cozy bar on Route 44. Johnny remembers that Willoby had made a play for Connie before she married Les. Johnny wonders if Les found out about it and killed Willoby.

Johnny cabs to the Worldwide Mutual office where Jonathan tells Johnny that Walters had not come in that day and had not called in. Jonathan tells Johnny that he was concerned that there was some worry between Les and his wife.

Johnny leaves to check with the switchboard operator and she tells Johnny that Les had not called in today. Johnny tells her to call him if Les were to call, and not to tell Les that Johnny was looking for him.

Johnny goes to see Connie Walters, and she wishes him a happy birthday. Johnny asks Connie if Les owns a gun, and she mentions that Johnny is the big gun collector. Connie tells Johnny that Les has been trying to find something to give Johnny to thank him for solving an embezzlement case that got him promoted. Johnny asks where Les is, and she does not know where he is.

Johnny asks Connie about Willoby and she tells Johnny that he had a crush on her once. She went to lunch with him once last week after seeing Willoby at a gas station, but that was all. Connie tells Johnny that Les did not know about the date.

The phone rings and the operator at Worldwide is calling. Les had called earlier and said he would not be in today or tomorrow. He called collect from EQuity 3-0114, which is over in Waterbury.

Johnny calls the Equity number, hoping he is wrong. The number is for Berghoff's Gun Shop. Johnny asks Berghoff if Les Walters had bought a gun lately, and he tells Johnny that Les had bought a gun this morning — a .45.

Johnny still cannot believe the circumstantial evidence that points to Les Walters, his failure to check in, the slip-up on the date for the hockey game, Connie seeing Willoby, and her being so evasive about where Les was. But did Connie know about Willoby? But what is Johnny to do?

Johnny calls Sgt. Bravo and he tells Johnny that progress has been made, and he will call Johnny when they make an arrest.

Back at Connie's place she asks Johnny why he is acting so strangely. The doorbell rings and Les is there. In the foyer, he tells Connie he got it at the gun shop while she is trying to keep him quiet. Les tells her he finally got it — a genuine single-action Army Colt .45. Connie tells Les that Johnny is there and the phone rings.

Les goes in to tell Johnny he spoiled the big surprise and tosses the gun at a not-too-happy Johnny. Les tells Johnny that he bought the gun as a surprise for Johnny's birthday. Connie tells Johnny that Sgt. Bravo is on the line.

Bravo tells Johnny that the prints led the police straight to Shorty Scarpone, who confessed to the whole thing. A relieved Johnny hangs up and joins Les and Connie. He can finally tell them that not a thing is wrong with him now.

"I can only tell you this, I was never so glad to be wrong in my life. And I mean all wrong about a case. Expense account total? What expense account?"

"Next week, a talisman, a good luck charm that proved to be anything but."

Notes:
- This program contains a commercial for Junior Achievement.
- There is a post-program commercial for Durward Kirby's favorite program, the *Gary Moore Program*, a WROW station identification and a Welcome Wagon announcement.
- Mason Adams is Bravo, Margaret Draper is Connie, Arthur Kohl is Harmon, Pat Hosley is the operator, Casey Allen is Les, Sam Gray is Berghoff.
- Art Hannes is the announcer.
- Musical supervision is by Ethel Huber.

Producer: Bruno Zirato, Jr.   Writer: Jack Johnstone
Cast: Arthur Kohl, Casey Allen, Margaret Draper, Mason Adams, Pat Hosley, Sam Gray

♦ ❖ ♦

Show: **The Nugget of Truth Matter**
Show Date: 2/4/1962
Company: Union States Casualty Insurance Company
Agent: Ted Newberry
Exp. Acct: $20.00

Synopsis: Ted Newberry calls, and Johnny congratulates him on getting engaged to Mary Ann Hooper. Ted tells Johnny that the announcement in the papers was just a bit of skullduggery by Mary Ann's mother, and now she will not talk to her mother or Ted. Johnny reminds Ted that when he does fall, the world will hear it. Ted tells Johnny that the only woman for him is Pandora Peters, the most beautiful girl he has ever met. When she did come to visit Ted, all she wanted was to find out how to talk to Johnny! Ted has set up a date for Johnny at 2:30, in his office.

Johnny shaves and showers, puts on a new tie, and cabs to Ted's Hartford, Connecticut office, arriving at 2:18. Ted tells Johnny that he forgot to tell Johnny that Pandora is married.

She is married to Phillip Truesdale Peers, a nice family, but with not too much money. Phil has invented some electronic gadget and is using his wife's money to get started. Both have $100,000 policies with each other as the beneficiaries. Johnny is curious, but Ted tells him that Phillip does not need Pandora dead to get her money.

Pandora arrives and she is as lovely as Ted described her. Johnny can only stare at her, and she is worth staring at, but there was something there, a coldness that did not belong. Pandora has a serious problem and tells Johnny that someone is threatening to kill her.

Pandora drops her car keys, and Johnny notices that the key chain has a golden skull on it. Pandora tells him that it was carved from a single nugget found by her grandfather in Alaska. It is her good luck talisman.

Pandora started getting notes in the mailbox about two months ago, just after Phil got the final patent on his invention, a little battery kind of thing. Pandora was not too enthusiastic at first, but she told Phil to go ahead when the notes started.

The first one started with a quotation, "What profiteth a man if he gain the whole world but suffer the loss of his own soul" and it added that it was sinful for one man to profit from the device, and it should be given to the world. Phil laughed at it, and the police thought it came from a religious fanatic. More notes came with increasing levels of threats they thought were for Phil.

Yesterday another note came addressed to Pandora and she shows a copy of it to Johnny. The note says, "Blind foolish woman, it is you who are guilty because of your money and that device of the devil. It is you who must die. And very soon."

The police have the originals of the notes, and now Pandora is frightened. Pandora wants Johnny to find out who is behind the notes. Pandora has some errands to run and will then go home to fix dinner. Johnny tells her to continue her plans while he talks to the police. Johnny thinks that there is something very fishy about this deal.

Johnny cabs to his apartment to get his car, which promptly breaks down on him. Johnny drives to police headquarters after the carburetor is fixed and talks to Sgt. Bill Budd who has been on the case from the beginning. Sgt. Budd tells Johnny that they had put a tail on Phil and looked at all the kooks but found nothing.

Sgt. Budd tells Johnny that the Peters have some problems and she has some money and he thinks that Pandora was writing the notes to scare Phil out of spending her money. That would explain how the notes got past the police. Johnny suggests that maybe Phil was writing the notes to scare her, so that he could kill her and get all her money.

Phil Peters comes in all hysterical and tells Sgt. Budd and Johnny that it has finally happened and it is terrible. Officer Conroy tells Budd and Johnny that he was the one who found the body. Pandora has been murdered.

Phil tells them that Pandora has been murdered, and they should have taken the letters seriously. Budd gives Phil a slug of brandy to calm him down.

Officer Conroy tells them that he was on patrol and investigated a call about a car blocking the road. When he got there, he found no one in the car, and the motor running. Conroy looked around and found the body by a nearby pond. Conroy turned off the engine and called homicide. Lt. Briggs and Doc Campbell got there and Conroy left. Conroy is sure that the weapon is in the pond. Conroy then drove to the Peters home to tell Mr. Peters what had happened, and he insisted in being brought to headquarters.

The phone rings, and Conroy tells Lt. Briggs he will be right back because he has the Peter's car keys. Johnny looks at them and discovers the answer to the whole thing. Johnny asks for Phil's keys and he gives them to Johnny. The key chain has a golden skull on it, for good luck. Johnny tells Phil that it is not good luck for him, as his keys are the ones Pandora had when Johnny talked to her earlier.

That means that Phil had to be with her, and that he killed her. Phil tells them he had to kill her to get the money for his invention, and Budd calls for someone to record the confession.

"So, with that full confession, complete with signature, there will be no problem. He did it, he'll pay for it. Expense account total, and that may as well include the work on my car, do you think you can afford all of twenty bucks?"

"Next week, the most unlikely crook I've met in a long, long time."

Notes:
- The first commercial break is about the efforts of CBS News to break in to space and expand their coverage.
- Mary Ann Hooper was a script secretary for Jack Johnstone in Hollywood
- Rita Lloyd is Pandora, Jim Stevens is Ted, Don MacLaughlin is Bill, Court Benson is Phil, Bill Lipton is Conroy.
- Art Hannes is the announcer.
- Musical supervision is by Ethel Huber

Producer:	Bruno Zirato, Jr.	Writer: Jack Johnstone
Cast:	Rita Lloyd, Jim Stevens, Don MacLaughlin, Court Benson, Bill Lipton	

◆ ❖ ◆

Show:	**The Do It Yourself Matter**
Show Date:	2/11/1962
Company:	**Greater Southwest Insurance Company**
Agent:	**Royal B. Harkins**
Exp. Acct:	**$833.70**

Synopsis: Royal B. Harkins calls Johnny from Los Angeles and tells Johnny that one of their offices in the Simi Valley is having a problem with fires. Roy is sure that a firebug is at work, and they are willing to pay Johnny's expenses. When Johnny mentions his usual fee, Roy starts to get upset, and when Johnny mentions a commission if money is saved, Roy is ready to call off the case, but relents.

Johnny flies to Los Angeles, California and arrives just after noon. Johnny cabs to Royal Harkins' office, where Roy is hesitant about Johnny's unknown fees. Johnny reminds Roy that he has saved them a lot of money on his other assignments.

Roy tells Johnny of the Bel Aire and Topanga Canyon fires the previous year, where 450 homes were destroyed and Greater Southwest insured many of them. Roy had decided to make up for the losses by selling more and more insurance.

There is a great deal of development in the Simi Valley and Roy has established an autonomous office in Moorpark, California, just north of Thousand Oaks.

The office has full authority to settle all claims, as that is the best way to compete with the bigger companies.

A young man, Harry Walterson, took their course and passed, and has sold more insurance in three months than Roy has sold in three years. The premiums have been rolling in, but there have been nine fires in less than six weeks. The losses were high, but Walterson has been able to sell even more insurance. The premiums are not covering the losses though.

The police and fire departments are good, but they cannot keep up with the development of homes and have not found anything to prove arson. With all the brush-covered hills, the new homes are at risk. Johnny wonders if the new home owners are setting the fires, and Roy tells Johnny he has to find out.

Johnny rents a car and drives to Moorpark and the office of Harry Walterson. Johnny asks Harry about the homeowners setting the fires and Harry tells Johnny, in between numerous phone calls, that the homes are new and the homeowners want to stay. The policies do not cover everything, and homeowners would not want to risk losing everything in a fire.

Harry tells Johnny that the first fire was probably caused by sunlight refracted through some glass bottles, even though the owner, Mr. Orloff, did not like all of the development in the area. And the other fires started at night.

Harry tells Johnny that the fires always start on windy nights, which occur often here. Harry offers to take Johnny to dinner and buzzes the receptionist who tells Harry that he has a number of calls, so Johnny prepares to drive back to Los Angeles.

Johnny buys some dinner and finds a county fire chief at home, but he cannot help Johnny. The chief tells Johnny that it only takes one cigarette to start these fires, and with more people coming in, the new people do not know how to handle the brushy country. The chief gets a call, and another fire is burning.

Johnny and the chief drive to the fire to find a new house burnt to the ground. The owner had no idea how the fire started, and Johnny is sure that he did not set it. Johnny inspects the ruins for hours and finds nothing. The chief tells Johnny that a cigarette probably started the fire.

Harry arrives and tells Johnny that he heard about the fire from a neighbor. Harry tells Johnny that he had gone to Hollywood to see a movie and found out about the fire when he came back. Harry tells the chief that old Timothy Handler was the one who told him about the fire and the chief remembers that Timothy was there before the fire department got there.

Johnny gets a motel room and goes to Harry's office the next morning where Harry pays off the previous night's fire and collects more and more insurance applications. Harry tells Johnny that the people are scared, but he checks to make sure that the owners do not over-insure.

Johnny tells Harry he has to fly back to Hartford, but Johnny gets a motel room for the week and calls Pat Fuller at the Universal Adjustment Bureau for information on fire claims. Pat calls back and tells Johnny that Greater Southwest is the only company in the Simi Valley that is paying off on house fires, nine or ten in a row. Johnny tells Pat that he does not like what he thinks.

Johnny gets two more rental cars and an old truck, some old clothes and several fire extinguishers. Johnny starts a tailing job because of the Latin phrase he remembers from school, "cui bono", who benefits? And how benefits?

The one big beneficiary was not the homeowners, but the man who collected the commissions on all the policies. After a week of trailing Harry 24-hours a day, Johnny finally gets a windy moonlit night and follows Harry to a new home where Harry lights the brush to start another fire.

Johnny uses a fire extinguisher to put out the fire and gives one to Harry to use. Harry asks Johnny how he knew, and Johnny tells Harry it was by remembering his Latin.

"He didn't have a leg to stand on, he knew it. And he confessed to the whole dirty rotten business. For my money, they can lock him up for life, because if there is one thing I can't take, it's a crooked insurance man. I'm glad they are few and far between. Expense account total, including car mileage and the trip back to Hartford, $833.70."

"Next week I'll be back with another exciting story."

Notes:
- Royal Harkins was the agent for Greater Southwest in *The Big H Matter* and *The Frantic Fisherman Matter*.
- This program contains a commercial about mental illness   America's number one illness.
- Herb Duncan is Harry, Raymond Edward Johnson is Royal, Joseph Julian is the chief, John Thomas is Pat.
- Bill Gillian is the announcer.
- Musical supervision is by Ethel Huber.

Producer:	Bruno Zirato, Jr. Writer: Jack Johnstone
Cast:	Herb Duncan, Raymond Edward Johnson, Joseph Julian, John Thomas

◆ ❖ ◆

Show:	**The Takes a Crook Matter**
Show Date:	**2/18/1962**
Company:	**Worldwide Mutual Insurance Company**
Agent:	**Les Walters**
Exp. Acct:	**$0.00**

Synopsis: A man calls Johnny to ask if he remembers a case Johnny was accidentally involved in four weeks, three days, thirteen hours ago, in the course if which he saved a man's life. Johnny recognizes the caller as Hal Leonard of the Federal Bureau, who is OK now. Hal thanks Johnny for walking in and saving his life. Johnny asks how Hal has recovered from his amnesia. Johnny tells him he was in the print shop because he thought Becker was fencing loot from a burglary, but Hal reminds Johnny that he found out what Hal had been tracking Becker for. Hal tells Johnny that he is now eligible for a nice long prison term. The crime is possession of evidence. Hal reminds Johnny that he was packing up the burglary evidence into his car, evidence that was really evidence in Hal's case. Hal tells Johnny he will fly up and relieve Johnny of the evidence.

Johnny recalls how he had forgotten all about the evidence in his car, which he had not used in four weeks.

Les Walters calls, and he wants to see Johnny about the Morre Madonna, a picture painted by Marcel Morre that is worth a couple hundred thousand. It was in an exhibition at the Manhart Gallery in Hartford, Connecticut. Johnny tells Les that he cannot imagine why anyone would pay $200,000 for that impressionistic atrocity. Les tells Johnny that Worldwide insured it, and it has disappeared.

Johnny tells Les that he must wait for a Federal man to come up, and Les is happy that Johnny has finally been caught! Johnny will be able to start on the case later that night, but he will come over for an update.

Johnny decides to drive his car to verify that the evidence is still there, or better yet to remove it from the car. Johnny outlines the layout of the garage as he opens the quick-lift door. Johnny opens the trunk and the garage door closes, and Johnny is slugged.

Johnny wakes up in the garage and opens the door to find the car trunk empty. Johnny passes out and then tries to get up to his apartment, holding something in his hand. Johnny bumps into Hal Leonard in the hallway.

Hal takes Johnny up to his apartment where Johnny tells him what happened. Johnny gives Hal the keys to the garage and his car, and Hal leaves. The phone interrupts Johnny, and Les Walters is wondering what happened to Johnny. Les tells Johnny to go see Thaddeus Brittingham, who lives in the Selfridge, a swanky apartment house in Hartford.

Johnny cabs to a rooming house to see "Little Willie", a stool pigeon that has an uncanny knowledge of art and art thieves. Willie tells Johnny that, for $100, he has been waiting for Johnny to visit him so that he can tell Johnny all about the Madonna.

Willie tells Johnny that a man had been watching the Madonna, and finally took the painting home to copy it. Johnny had better act fast because the man probably has a buyer for it. For $150, Willie tells Johnny that the man is Charlie Starkey, who is out of the pen again. He is living at 324 South Crocus.

Johnny arranges to mail $150 in cash to Willie and cabs to the address on Crocus, but Charlie has left in a big hurry, leaving all his clothes and paints. Mrs. Botz the landlady shows Johnny the money that Charlie paid her with and Johnny grabs it only to discover that it is counterfeit.

Johnny searches the room and finds the Madonna. Johnny stashes the painting in his apartment and remembers that he had grabbed a part of the attacker and has a receipt with the name of Harvey Twiller on it. It was a receipt for an apartment at the Selfridge.

Johnny cabs to the Selfridge and the doorman knows that Mr. Brittingham is expecting Johnny, but Mr. Twiller is not. Johnny convinces the doorman to let him in and Johnny goes to apartment 5-A to find Scotty Bagney, not Mr. Twiller. Scotty is out of the pen now and is holding a gun on Johnny.

Scotty invites Johnny in, and asks him to drop his gun, and Johnny obliges. Scotty tells Johnny that he had been trailing Johnny after hearing about the job in Becker's print shop. Scotty is about to shoot Johnny when Hal Leonard walks in and tells Johnny that he had found Scotty's prints on his garage door. Scotty tells Johnny and Hal that he does not have the stuff, as he used it to make a purchase.

Johnny tells Scotty and Hal that the purchase was a copy of the Morre Madonna. Johnny tells Scotty that Starkey was a master copyist and a good fence that could sell to the rich who would buy such things. Scotty did not know that Starkey would steal the paintings and copy them, give the sucker the copy and skip town, while letting the original be discovered or even returned.

Johnny tells Scotty that the original is in his apartment. Hal wants the counterfeit money he was looking for, and Johnny starts to search Scotty when there is a knock at the door. Charlie Bagney comes in ranting that Scotty gave him counterfeit money and Hal arrests Charlie. Johnny describes the whole affair as a quadruple play, Dollar-to-Scotty-to-Charlie-to-Hal.

"It's kind of a complicated mess, I know, but the painting is back to its owner, the counterfeit money is recovered, I'm in the clear with Uncle Sam, and all is well. Expense account total, well why not just pay me the commission on that lovely Madonna."

"Next week, a couple of sweet little old men, real characters, especially one of them — the killer."

Notes:
- There is no "it" in the title of this program when Mandel Kramer introduces it as *The Takes a Crook Matter.* The script calls this program *The Takes a Crook Matter.*
- The music on this program is decidedly jazzier.
- The first commercial break is for adventure in the form of joining the Peace Corps.
- Martin Blaine is Hal, Ralph Bell is Scotty, Jack Grimes is Les, Leora Thatcher is the landlady, Bill Kramer is Willie, Guy Repp is the doorman, Luis Van Rooten is Charlie.
- Art Hannes is the announcer.
- Musical supervision is by Ethel Huber.

Producer: Bruno Zirato, Jr. Writer: Jack Johnstone
Cast: Martin Blaine, Ralph Bell, Jack Grimes, Leora Thatcher, Bill Kramer, Guy Repp, Luis Van Rooten

Show:	**The Mixed Blessing Matter**
Show Date:	2/25/1962
Company:	**Worldwide Mutual Insurance Company**
Agent:	**Charlie Warren**
Exp. Acct:	**$497.40**

Synopsis: Charlie Warren calls from Los Angeles and Johnny calls him a bum and yells at him for assigning him to a case high in the mountains where he nearly froze his ears off. Charlie tells Johnny that he has an assignment for Johnny in the Mohave Desert, out near Lake Mohave. Johnny tells Charlie he will grab all of his fishing tackle and head right out, but Charlie tells Johnny to bring a .38 also. Charlie will meet Johnny at the airport and give him the whole story.

Johnny flies to Los Angeles and Charlie meets him there. Over cocktails Charlie tells Johnny that he was only kidding about bringing a gun along. Charlie has called Ham Pratt and arranged for Johnny to have a boat and all the necessities for the next day.

When Charlie mentions that the fishing is better in the afternoon, Johnny gets suspicious. Charlie tells Johnny that he has to pick up some money from Jake Kessler over in Kingman. The money is $40,000 to pay off a retirement policy. After making the delivery, Charlie tells Johnny that he can spend the rest of the week fishing, on expense account. Johnny knows that there is only one problem with this assignment, it sounds too easy.

Johnny describes Jake Kessler as he goes to meet him. Jake has made a fool of himself and took a dare and tried to ride a horse and ended up breaking an ankle and dislocating a knee. The injuries are why Jake needed to call someone to pay Barney Blessing.

The policy was originally set up to pay Barney a monthly income, but now Barney wants the money all at once. Jake wonders if the company is suspicious just like he is. Jake tells Johnny that Barney Blessing was a gunman for the mobs and moved here only last year with his dog Ricky and a man named Harry Higbee.

Harry was called "The Twin" and was the reason why Barney never got caught. Whenever Barney went out to do a job, Harry was planted somewhere as an alibi. Harry came west with Barney to blackmail him. Barney must have read the fine print and has demanded to be paid "in hand".

Jake has never met Barney or Harry, and no one has seen either of them for a year. Johnny asks Jake why he sent for Johnny, and Jake tells him that he has a nose for trouble, and Barney told Jake that if he showed up without the money, well um.

Johnny gets the money and directions to Barney's ranch, along with the necessary paperwork. Johnny wants to borrow the policy to copy it, but Jake has already done that for Johnny.

Johnny drives to Hackberry, Arizona and then on to the Cottonwood Mountains. The ranch is a tidy little farm with a lot of greenery and beef cattle. An old man meets Johnny with a high-powered rifle and tells Johnny to leave.

When Johnny mentions the insurance money, the attitude changes. Barney recognizes who Johnny is, and Johnny tells Barney that Jake is laid up so he brought the money. Johnny asks Barney to sign the papers and compares it to the signature on the policy.

Johnny asks about Higbee "The Twin" and Barney tells Johnny that he paid Harry off and threw him out. Johnny asks about the dog, Ricky, and Barney tells Johnny that he died, and is buried outside. Johnny tells Barney he saw the mound of earth and wants to see what is under it.

Barney gets anxious and waves the rifle at Johnny. Johnny pulls his gun and shoots the rifle out of Barney's hands. Johnny tells Barney to dig up the mound of earth.

Barney digs up the grave and finds the remains of Ricky, but Johnny wants him to dig some more, but Barney hesitates. Johnny tells Barney that he is really Harry Higbee and had killed Barney when Harry found out that Barney was taking the money in cash so he could get out of the country, and away from Harry.

Johnny tells Harry he decided to claim the money, and that Barney's fingerprints are on file, and they will match the body. Harry admits that Barney is under the dog.

Jake admits that it was just a hunch and did not know how to prove it. Johnny tells him to hang on to that nose of his.

"Doggone it, because of a call from Hartford I again had to miss out on the fishing. But I am going to keep on trying, you can depend on that. Expense account total, including mileage on the rental car and the trip home, $497.40."

"Next week, a case that could be marked Top Secret that blows wide open in more ways than one."

Notes:
- This program contains a commercial for saving for college education and the need to support your college.
- Luis Van Rooten is Harry, Cliff Carpenter is Jake, Maurice Tarplin is Charlie.
- Art Hannes is the announcer.
- Musical supervision is by Ethel Huber.

Producer:	Bruno Zirato, Jr. Writer: Jack Johnstone
Cast:	Luis Van Rooten, Cliff Carpenter, Maurice Tarplin

◆ ❖ ◆

Show:	**The Top Secret Matter**
Show Date:	3/4/1962
Company:	**Surety Mutual Insurance Company**
Agent:	**Len Walker**
Exp. Acct:	**$993.70**

Synopsis: Len Walker calls Johnny from San Francisco. Len tells Johnny that three little explosions have cost him over a million dollars apiece. The explosions were caused by rocket fuel at the Bascom Development Company. Len tells Johnny to come on out, maybe Johnny can be sent aloft on their next blowup. Len tells Johnny that if he can get to the bottom of this, they will pay Johnny enough to fly high and wide and handsome for a long time to come. Johnny will catch the first plane.

Johnny flies to San Francisco, California via New York City. In New York Johnny meets his old friend George Langley, who is only going as far as Chicago. He is a vice president of a big chemical company, so Johnny wants to pick his brain.

George tells Johnny that he is trying to turn down a rocket fuel contract. George asks Johnny if he still has a top security clearance, and Johnny shows him his credentials from the OSI, CIA, and the CIC.

George tells Johnny that a new solid rocket fuel is about to hit the market. It was developed by sheer luck by an East German scientist at their plant. The scientist came for a nondescript job, developed the formula, and turned it over lock, stock and barrel. The fuel puts them light years ahead of the competition. Johnny asks George about Bascom, and he tells Johnny that he has never heard of them. Johnny is left to talk to George about fishing for the rest of the flight.

Johnny lands in San Francisco and cabs to Len's office near station KCBS. Len tells Johnny to get dinner and prepare to drive to the Bascom site tomorrow. Bascom is located south of San Francisco, near Big Sur on a hidden dirt road. The three explosions resulted in three deaths, which is the major cause of the losses. Bascom was the beneficiary, along with the families. Len tells Johnny to ask Bascom about the particulars.

The next day, after a good night's sleep at the Huntington Hotel, Johnny drives down beautiful Highway 1 along the coast. At Point Sur Johnny finds the road and arrives at what looks like summer cottages with an armed guard. Johnny passes a building and is immediately caught in an explosion.

Johnny almost gets past the explosion but the rental car is turned over. Johnny is taken out of the car to Horace Bascom's office, where Johnny is held at gunpoint until he tells Bascom who he is. Bascom tells Johnny that he is very fortunate and could have ended up on the rocks below the plant. Bascom is not upset about the explosion, as others more knowledgeable will look into it.

Bascom tells Johnny that they are working on a revolutionary semi-liquid rocket fuel, a powerful gelatinous propellant. Bascom is sure that they will succeed, and he will be on top of the industry with sole ownership of the secret. Johnny goes out to look at the ruined building with Bascom and Dr. Welcome, but nothing is found.

Johnny speaks with Dr. Welcome later, and he tells Johnny that the chemicals are unstable, but they take all the necessary precautions, and each of the men who died was alone in the labs when the explosions occurred. Welcome tells Johnny that they are very close to finding the formula, even in light of the salary cuts, and that an East German named Hans Kellerhaus gave the idea of the fuels to Bascom. Bascom comes in, and he reports finding nothing. Johnny tells Bascom that he has to go back to San Francisco for the evening, so Bascom loans Johnny his car.

Johnny drives south, finds a phone and makes a series of calls that blow the case wide open. First, Johnny calls George Langley in Chicago, and then he calls Hans Kellerhaus, who left Bascom to work at a larger, more established company.

Johnny is talking to the gas station owner when one of the tires explodes and the car goes over the side of the road onto the rocks. Johnny gives the station owner $100 to borrow his car and then drives back to Bascom's plant.

Johnny slips the lock in Bascom's office and searches it until he finds a hidden switch with wires running to Building 1. Bascom comes into his office and Johnny asks him "why" the reason for the explosions.

Johnny tells Bascom about the explosion that happened because he knew Johnny was coming, the switch in his office, and Bascom's help in combing the ruins that only misdirected Johnny away from the detonator.

Also, there was the salary cutbacks for needed money, and the statement that he alone would have the secret of the fuel. Bascom tells Johnny that he had gone to Europe "on vacation" but was really there to contact Kellerhaus.

Bascom got Kellerhaus into the country and he agreed that Bascom was to have complete control of his discoveries. Kellerhaus found out what Bascom was doing and decided to leave after signing over everything to Bascom. But Kellerhaus had not finished the fuel. The only way he could continue was to cash in on the insurance.

Johnny asks Bascom to leave with him, but Bascom tells Johnny he will not leave, as he has a loaded .38 in his open desk drawer. Johnny convinces him that it would not make any difference, and they leave.

"It's almost unbelievable, I mean the length to which some people will go to promote their own selfish interests at the sacrifice of others. Don't they know that somehow, sometime, there has to be a showdown? Expense account total, including repair charges on the rental car and the trip back to Hartford, $993.70."

"Next week, a tale of the problems, at least one of the problems that goes with the owning of a gold mine."

Notes:
- Melville Ruick is Bascom, Court Benson is Dr. Welcome, Frank Campanella is George, William Mason is the gas station attendant.
- Art Hannes is the announcer.
- Musical supervision is by Ethel Huber.

Producer: Bruno Zirato, Jr.   Writer: Jack Johnstone
Cast: Melville Ruick, Court Benson, Frank Campanella, William Mason

Show:	**The Golden Dream Matter**
Show Date:	3/11/1962
Company:	Greater Southwest Insurance Company
Agent:	Jake Kessler
Exp. Acct:	$451.80

Synopsis: Jake Kessler of Worldwide Mutual in Kingman, Arizona calls Johnny. Jake has a problem with a Greater Southwest client. Jake has retired and the two companies want him to keep an eye on their offices for them. The problem is a client who was insured by the San Francisco office. The client is a mining engineer, and he has disappeared. Johnny tells Jake he will grab his fishing rod and come out for some great bass fishing while he tries to help Jake.

Johnny flies to Las Vegas and rents a car the next day, and then drives across the desert and the Hoover Dam to Kingman, Arizona. Jake tells Johnny he might have a chance to get some fishing done, as the one person who can help Johnny find Myron Kingsley is Ham Pratt. The old mine, the Golden Dream is very close to the Lake Mohave Resort.

It seems that a man named Marty Spiller has been selling stock in the mine, mostly to people in the east who could not afford to check on the mine. One stockholder got suspicious and hired Kingsley to look around. It has been several days since Ham has seen Kingsley in his room.

The phone rings and Ham is calling for Johnny. Ham tells Johnny that he came for nothing, as they just found Kingsley's body at the bottom of a mineshaft.

Johnny drives to Lake Mohave Resort and goes out to the mine with Ham. Ham has been carrying a gun since he thinks that Kingsley might not have fallen into the mineshaft, being an experienced engineer and all that. Ham tells Johnny that the people in the area do not like Marty Spiller.

After a very rough jeep ride across the desert, Johnny and Ham arrive at the mine at sunset. Ham tells Johnny that they stopped working the mine back in the late thirties. Spiller came along four years ago and has done just enough to keep his rights by re-washing the tailings, which is mostly worthless rock. Spiller has not taken any gold from the mine, but he is selling stock in it though.

At the mine, Ham tells Johnny that when Kingsley arrived, Spiller supposedly left for California. In the mineshaft, Johnny spots Kingsley's body about a hundred feet below in the water. Johnny convinces Ham to lower him down on a rope to retrieve the body.

On the way down, Johnny notes small tunnels leading off the shaft. Near the bottom, Johnny tells Ham that there is a big shaft at the bottom. Johnny yells and there is no response from Ham, except for some falling rocks. Then there are gun shots aimed at Johnny as the rope slips and Johnny falls into the water.

Johnny notes that he cheated when the ropes slacked and threw a rock into the water from the tunnel entrance. After the gunshots, huge boulders were rolled into the water.

A voice yells at Johnny, who remains quiet as several more boulders crash into the water. Johnny struggles up the tunnel to get to the main shaft of the mine and the surface. Johnny reaches the surface in the growing darkness and slowly edges towards the jeep where he spots a man tying another one to a 10 by 10 timber. Johnny quietly crawls across the desert as he stalks Spiller. Johnny rushes across an open spot only to have Ham tell Johnny that he is OK. Ham tells Johnny that Spiller had hit him with a gun, and when Ham came to, he tied up Spiller and decided to go down after Johnny. When Johnny asks how Ham was certain that he was alive, Ham tells Johnny that "if a lousy punk like Spiller could kill off a man like you, well this I gotta see." "I hope you never do", replies Johnny.

"We brought up Kingsley's body the next morning. The bullet that had killed Kingsley before he had been dropped into the mineshaft had come from Spiller's gun. A simple ballistics test proved that conclusively. So again, it is up to the courts. Expense account total, $451.80."

"Next week, well as you listen to it, just remember that old saying — Ike and Mike they look alike."

Notes:
- This program contains a commercial for the payroll savings plan to buy US Savings Bonds.
- Warren Sweeney is the announcer.
- Musical supervision is by Ethel Huber.

Producer:	Bruno Zirato, Jr. Writer: Jack Johnstone
Cast:	Cliff Carpenter, Robert Dryden, Sam Raskyn

♦ ❖ ♦

Show:	**The Ike and Mike Matter**
Show Date:	3/18/1962
Company:	**Tri-Western Life Insurance Company**
Agent:	**Jack Price**
Exp. Acct:	**$0.00**

Synopsis: A voice asks Johnny if he wants to hop aboard the next plane for the mighty sovereign state of Texas. Jack Price tells Johnny that there is no way Johnny can save Jack any money on this case. Johnny can come down, but only on a bare minimum expense account with no service fees or commission. Johnny asks Jack if he thinks Johnny would accept such and assignment from Jack of all people, and Jack tells him yes, he would. Johnny tells Jack that he is right!

Johnny flies to Corpus Christi, Texas and takes the airport limousine to the Robert Driscoll hotel where he gets a room, not a suite mind you, just a room. Jack meets Johnny in his room and Johnny wants to order drinks, but Jack tells him not to, as it is too late for Johnny to do what Jack wanted him to do. Also, it is too late to cancel the policy because of what happened after Jack called Johnny.

Jack tells Johnny that the policy was for $25,000 straight life, with double indemnity. Jack asks Johnny if he remembers a character named Lou Livercum. Johnny remembers that "Little Louie" Livercum was a slippery stock promoter Johnny had chased all over the country a couple years ago, only to have a slick lawyer get him off.

Jack tells Johnny that a new man in the office sold a policy to Isaac Prelinger, who was known as "Smarty Ike" in the local pool halls. He had no visible means of support and was just a smart fast-talking bum from San Antonio. Jack was checking the policy and discovered that Livercum was the beneficiary. Jack realized that something was wrong and Johnny suggests that Livercum fronted the money for the policy and planned to have Ike killed to get the money. Jack tells Johnny that Livercum's last address was in Oregon. So that is why Jack called Johnny so he could look into the policy to see if Jack could cancel it.

Jack tells Johnny that the shack Ike lived in burnt to the ground just a few hours ago. Jack identified the body based on the policy medical information and is sure that it was Ike Prelinger that died. Jack tells Johnny that the arson squad called the death accidental and typical: Ike got drunk and fell on the bed with a lighted cigarette and the shack went up.

Johnny rents a car and drives to Jack's office to read the policy and the physical details about Ike. Johnny calls Pete Frawley of the arson squad at home and arranges to meet Pete at the morgue to look at Ike's body.

Pete tells Johnny that there were no prints, and the ID was made from general physical characteristics. The autopsy proved that the body was Ike's. Pete tells Johnny that there were a flock of empty liquor bottles around, and Pete had been able to isolate the ashes from the cigarette in Ike's hand.

Johnny tells Pete he suspects someone wanted to kill Ike and used the fire as a cover up. Pete tells Johnny he had thought the same thing, but the autopsy proved that Ike was not injured or poisoned before the fire, and that there was smoke in Ike's lungs.

Johnny suggests that maybe someone smothered him enough to knock him unconscious, but Pete tells him he needs evidence to prove that. Johnny tells Pete about the beneficiary angle, and Johnny thinks he better fly out to Oregon.

On a hunch, Johnny drives to Jerry Deke's pool room and Jerry convinces Johnny that his hunch is right. Deke tells Johnny that Ike made his money playing pool and was a very consistent player. Deke tells Johnny that Ike never used liquor. Deke had given Ike some once, and Ike told him that liquor was nothing but poison.

Johnny calls Jack and tells him what he has learned, and that he is sure that murder was involved and is flying out to Oregon. Johnny reminds Jack of the old saying, "Ike and Mike, they look alike", and tells Jack to meet him in his office.

In Jack's office Johnny reviews the application and calls Pete Frawley to tell him that he is sure that murder was involved because Ike did not drink. Johnny wants a further autopsy to look for a fracture on the first metatarsal on the right foot. Johnny tells him that if they do not find the fracture, to call missing persons in San Antonio with a complete description of Ike. They might be looking for somebody who looks like Ike. If they are not, call every other town in Texas until he gets a match.

Johnny flies to Eugene, Oregon via Houston, Los Angeles, and Portland and arrives the next morning. Johnny cabs to Lou's house and asks the cab to wait.

Livercum was the same suave, slippery character Johnny remembers. Lou has heard about Ike's death, and has filed a claim. Lou tells Johnny that they worked together once, but Johnny asks if they are still working together. Lou tells Johnny that his neighbors can prove he has been home all week, and that Johnny cannot prove that Lou was involved in Ike getting killed.

Johnny makes a call to Pete and learns that the body did not have a broken bone. It was a dead ringer for Prelinger. Pete had called San Antonio, and they have a missing man named Mike Ringler.

Johnny tells Pete that when Ike learned he had a double, he moved to Corpus, called Lou Livercum and set up the scheme to split the $50,000. Johnny tells Pete he will stay there until Ike shows up.

A man enters with a gun and tells Johnny to hang up. Lou tells Ike who Johnny is and Ike prepares to shoot Johnny. The cabby comes in asking for Johnny, and in the confusion Johnny slugs Ike. Johnny has the cabby help him take Lou and Ike to police headquarters.

"Yup, it was good hunting. Not only because Ike will have to pay for the murder of Mike Ringler, but more important to me, because Lou Livercum is finally ending up where he belongs, behind bars. Expense account total? Oh, why don't you figure it up Jackson. And don't forget my commission on the insurance that won't have to be paid out."

"Next week, only the shadow of a doubt locks up a case for me."

Notes:
- This program contains a commercial about the folks who drop in to visit every day, Arthur Godfrey, Gary Moore, Bing Crosby and Rose Mary Clooney, CBS Radio's stars.
- William Redfield is Pete, Maurice Tarplin is Jack, Reynold Osborne is Louie, Lawson Zerbe is Deke, Ralph Bell is Ike, Bill Lipton is the Cabby.
- The announcer is Bill Gillian.
- Musical supervision is by Ethel Huber.

Producer: Bruno Zirato, Jr.   Writer: Jack Johnstone
Cast: William Redfield, Maurice Tarplin, Reynold Osborne, Lawson Zerbe, Ralph Bell, Bill Lipton

Show:	**The Shadow of a Doubt Matter**
Show Date:	3/25/1962
Company:	Western Indemnity Company
Agent:	Ted Orloff
Exp. Acct:	$450.00

Synopsis: Ted Orloff calls Johnny from Los Angeles. Ted wants Johnny to come out to see Barney Garrison, who owns a small bottling plant. Barney told Ted that someone has embezzled $170,000 from the till. Johnny will be right out.

Johnny flies to Los Angeles and Ted meets Johnny at the airport. While Ted complains about the California drivers, he tells Johnny that Barney owns a bottling plant that handles all types of drinks. Barney Garrison got the money to set up the plant somehow and Ralph Betterly is the vice president and handles the bookkeeping.

It is a partnership, but they are really opposites. Betterly is a quiet neat little man and has a nice home on Pandora Avenue in Westwood. Barney is a big well-fed backslapping salesman type. He is a bachelor and thinks he is a lady's man and has a new home in Palm Springs. Barney called yesterday to say he had been going over the books and discovered the missing money. Barney is waiting for Johnny in Palm Springs, California. Barney has arranged for Johnny and Ted to take his private plane to Palm Springs.

Johnny and Ted fly on Barney's private twin-engine Beech and in Palm Springs Johnny notices some long thin clouds that turn out to be skywriting for "Poppola", Barney's new product. Ted tells Johnny that today is the announcement of the product. Barney arrives and tells Ted that he has discovered that Betterly has taken the money.

Barney takes Johnny and Ted to his new home and shows them around. Johnny describes a big neon sign with a clock in it advertising "Now is the time to drink Poppola". The sign is for a photo shoot planned for the next day. Barney shows Johnny some instant photos of himself in front of the sign at 10:05 a.m. and one of the skywriting.

Johnny forces Barney to talk about the theft, and Barney tells Johnny that Ralph is not a full partner and only gets a quarter of the profits, which have been pretty low because of the startup costs of Poppola. Also, Ralph has a lot of hospital bills and his wife died just a few days earlier. Barney is sure that Ralph is the only one who could have stolen the money, as Ralph is the only other man with the combination to the safe, and who knew that the money was in the safe.

Barney tells Johnny he needs a lot of cash to pay off the Mexican boys who, uh...Barney tells Johnny that a secret ingredient does not cross the border legally, and that is why he needs the cash.

Johnny gets angry and asks Ted if he knew about the smuggling, which he did not. Also, Barney tells Johnny that he had not told the police, and Johnny tells him that if the police found out, they would put him out of business. Barney tells Johnny that he is too smart to get caught. Johnny wants to leave and Ted wants to cancel the policies, but Barney tells Ted that he still owes him the money.

Johnny rents a car for the drive back to Los Angeles so he can follow a hunch. When Johnny gets to 1308 Pandora Ave., the police are there and they tell Johnny that Garrison had called them. They broke in the door and found Betterly dead of suicide. Lt. Harvey May tells Johnny that if Betterly had shot himself, there should be powder burns.

The doctor thinks Betterly was shot from a distance and died between 9:30 and 11:30, but no one in the area heard anything. May tells Johnny that Garrison had proof he had been in Palm Springs since yesterday, but Johnny is almost sure he can prove otherwise. Johnny asks May to call the Palm Springs police, but to give Johnny time to get there first.

Johnny drives to Palm Springs alone, not quite as sure as he thought he was, but the facts added up. Garrison needed money to support his life style. Also, the call to the police to insure the body would be found and establish a time of death set to remove suspicion from Barney. Johnny knew he would be called on to support Barney's alibi.

At Barney's house, there is a party in progress and Barney invites Johnny in. Barney tells Johnny that he had called Ralph to see how he was. Johnny tells Barney that he had tried to plant the idea of suicide with Johnny earlier.

In Barney's office Johnny tells him that he tried hard to plant an alibi with Johnny. Johnny asks Barney if he is pretending that he does not know that Ralph is dead, and Barney acts shocked and tells Johnny "suicide, too bad." Johnny tells Barney that Ralph was murdered, and that Barney did it and knows when it happened. Barney asks when Ralph died but Johnny does not answer.

Barney shows Johnny the photo of the clock taken at 10:05 with the sky writing in the background. Johnny looks at the picture and Barney tells Johnny that the picture had to be taken today, because of the skywriting.

Johnny tells Barney that the pool in the picture runs north to south, and Barney faced south in the picture. But the shadows in the picture indicate that the picture was taken in the afternoon, shortly before Johnny arrived. Barney pulls his gun, complete with silencer, but a police sergeant walks in and Johnny tells Barney to give the gun to him.

"Once again it is up to the courts, but when the West Los Angeles police run down the $170,000, where ever Garrison put it, and I am sure they will, he won't have a leg to stand on. Expense account total, call it $450."

"Next week, like a lot of other people, I open the trout season, but in a way, I don't suggest you try."

Notes:
- This program contains a commercial about the program *Dimension of a Woman's World* with Betty Furness heard three times a day on CBS.
- This program has a post-program promotion for *Red Barber's Sports-a-Rama* program and for the Welcome Wagon.
- The address "1308 Pandora Avenue" was used in three Johnny Dollar

programs, *The Harried Heiress Matter, The Shadow of a Doubt Matter* and *The Urned Income Matter*. I have been told that the address was Jack Johnstone's home.
- Robert Dryden is Barney, Bernard Grant is Lt. May, James Stevens is Ted, Eugene Francis is the police sergeant, Jocelyn Summers is the girl.
- Pat Canel is the announcer.
- Musical supervision is by Ethel Huber.

Producer: Bruno Zirato, Jr.   Writer: Jack Johnstone
Cast: Robert Dryden, Bernard Grant, James Stevens,
            Eugene Francis, Jocelyn Summers

♦ ❖ ♦

Show: **The Blue Rock Matter**
Show Date: **4/1/1962**
Company: **State Unity Life Insurance Company**
Agent: **Phil Taylor**
Exp. Acct: **$200.00**

Synopsis: Phil Taylor calls Johnny from New York and tells Johnny that he is slowly going mad. Johnny tells him that he is ready to open the trout season by dropping flies in front of ravenous rainbows. Johnny tells Phil he is going to a private stream not far from Hartford, but Phil tells Johnny that he is going to go fishing on the Esopus River, just outside of Mount Tremper, New York. Johnny knows the stream well, and Phil tells Johnny that they will pay his expense account. Johnny is on the way.

Johnny packs his trout fishing gear, including a pair of long johns, and flies to New York and goes to Phil's office. Phil tells Johnny that he does not have the time to go fishing, besides the man that Phil wants Johnny to watch knows Phil. The man is Thomas Gerald Aspenwald, a man who would stop at nothing to get at the Emory Archibald fortune. Johnny thought that Archibald, the stockbroker was dead, but Phil tells him that he will be dead soon of an incurable disease.

Tom Aspenwald was married to Nancy Archibald, and Nancy's five-year-old son Barry is the last of the family. Barry's father died about the time he was born. Originally Archibald had left half of the estate to Tom, and half to Nancy. But the new will leaves the whole estate to Nancy and the boy, unless the boy dies before the old man does, in which case Tom gets the money.

Phil has learned that Tom is taking the boy away for a few days. Phil has made reservations for Johnny at the home of Mr. and Mrs. Fritz Hornblock, who have a home near a big pool. Johnny tells Phil he knows all about the Blue Rock pool, which is a very dangerous place to be and a great place to fake an accident. Tom Aspenwald and Barry are the only other guests at the Hornblock place. Johnny is ready to drive up.

Johnny spends the night and then buys a fishing license and rents a car for the drive to Mt. Trempler and arrives as the weather turns cold and windy. At the Hornblock house, Fritz insists on carrying Johnny's baggage to his room.

Fritz offers Johnny a drink of schnapps, but Johnny tells him he has a bottle of scotch he carries in case of snakebite. As Fritz finishes his drink, Tom Aspenwald arrives and is introduced. Tom tells Johnny that he brought his stepson to teach him to fish.

Fritz tells Johnny that Barry has gone to town with "Mama", who promised to buy him some rock candy. Barry loves the candy, even though it makes him sick, like it did last time Tom was there. Fritz promises to take care of Barry.

Johnny asks Tom about his plans and Fritz tells them that the big hole below the bridge will have no one fishing there, but Fritz will not let Tom take Barry there as it is too dangerous. Maybe he can take Barry later in the day. Johnny suggests that they hit the hole first thing in the morning, but Tom tends to waffle. Johnny tells Tom that he should take Barry later in the day after he has caught his limit.

Tom leaves to get some dry flies he forgot, but Fritz tells Johnny that Tom brought along every fly ever made. Johnny tells Fritz that Tom should know that dry flies are not appropriate for this time of the year. Wet flies, streamers or nymphs would be more appropriate, and Fritz tells Johnny that he has some worms ready for them.

Mama returns with Barry and Johnny talks to him and learns he really is not too fond of his stepfather. Barry was clutching a bag of blue rock candy, but Johnny is vaguely reminded of something else. Johnny is told that Barry really loves the blue candies, and he would rather play with the farm animals than fish. Johnny is sure that Aspenwald will get rid of the boy in the river, but it turns out to be a fatal mistake.

Aspenwald wears a new fishing jacket at dinner with a bulging pocket and is in a better mood. Barry asks if he bought some more "rocks" and Tom tells him that he has had too many.

Fritz makes plans to go to town in the morning, and Mama must take some butter to a neighbor so Barry will be alone for a few minutes to play with the chickens. Johnny tells Tom that Fritz has given him a secret weapon to use the next morning.

At dawn the temperature is in the 20's, but after a hearty breakfast Johnny and Tom go fishing. Johnny notices a coating of ice on the rocks and the missing bulge in Tom's jacket pocket. Johnny manages to catch his first trout using one of Fritz's secret weapons, a fat worm.

Tom tells Johnny that he knows who he is and pushes Johnny off a slippery rock into the water. Johnny manages to hold on to Tom's leg and pulls him in. After they both get out Tom admits he brought the boy up here to kill him. Tom tells Johnny that he goofed by telling Tom how old Barry was before he met him, so he made other arrangements.

Johnny notices a blue-green stain on the jacket and recognizes that it is blue vitriol, or copper sulfate that Tom had bought in Kingston. The copper sulfate looks just like the candy Barry loves and Tom had left it for Barry to eat. Johnny slugs Tom and runs to the farmhouse to find Barry.

"The big dramatic ending, I'm sorry. Not this time. Thanks to the fact that

Mrs. Hornblock had changed her mind and had taken Barry along on her morning errand. By the time they got back, I'd cleaned up every chunk of the blue vitriol that Aspenwald had planted, mostly around the chicken coop. So, the only casualty: Aspenwald who had nearly frozen to death in his wet clothes on the frozen ground where I had knocked him out. And he was a very docile prisoner when I handed him in at the Kingston hoosegow. Expense account total, including a little extra for the Hornblocks, oh, call it $200 even"

"Next week, a lesson in how to crack a safe, and I'm perfectly serious about that."

Notes:
- This program contains a commercial for Newport filter cigarettes.
- Blue vitriol is a blue, crystalline hydrous solution of copper sulfate used in insecticides, germicides, and hair dyes and in the processing of leather and textiles.
- The Esopus is a famous trout stream in eastern New York state.
- William Mason is Tom Aspenwald, Karl Weber is Phil Taylor, Luis Van Rooten is Fritz, Bryna Raeburn is Mrs. Hornblock, Sarah Fussell is Barry.
- Art Hannes is the announcer.
- Musical supervision is by Ethel Huber.

Producer:	Bruno Zirato, Jr. Writer: Jack Johnstone
Cast:	Bryna Raeburn, Karl Weber, Luis Van Rooten, Sarah Fussell, William Mason

♦ ❖ ♦

Show:	**The Ivy Emerald Matter**
Show Date:	4/8/1962
Company:	**Surety Mutual Insurance, Ltd.**
Agent:	**Bob Baker**
Exp. Acct:	**$0.00**

Synopsis: Bob Baker calls Johnny from Boston. Johnny hopes there is a big fat commission on this call. Bob asks Johnny if he has ever heard of the Ivy Emerald, the biggest green emerald in the world, but Johnny is only interested in the folding green stuff. Bob tells Johnny that the emerald has been stolen, and Johnny must find it before it is cut up. The emerald is insured for $625,000, so Johnny is on his way.

Johnny flies to Boston, Massachusetts and meets with Bob Baker in his office. Bob tells Johnny the client is Mrs. Oscar B. Sterlingwaite, Emily Sterlingwaite, a rich old widow. The emerald is called the Ivy Emerald because of the mounting, which looks like an ivy plant. The emerald was placed in the safe last night, but this morning it was missing. Also, the safe was opened the old-fashioned way, with the dial.

Normally the jewelry was in a vault, but it was in the safe with the paste copies of her real diamond because she had just worn it. The fact the paste diamonds were not taken means that the thief was an expert. No one else knows the combination to the safe that has an oil-dampened movement made by the Darlington Safe Company in Boston. Bob knows Mr. Darlington and tries to convince Johnny that he is honest.

Johnny rents a car and drives to the Sterlingwaite home on Beacon Hill. The uniformed butler shows Johnny in to Mrs. Sterlingwaite, who shows Johnny the safe, which is hidden behind a removable panel. Harry Darlington had installed it just for her when he was dating her many years earlier. The dial is oversized because of her eyes, as she does not see very well.

No one knows about the safe except Hendricks the butler, but he has been with her for forty years. But only she knows the combination. Johnny learns that Arnold Bixby, the former chauffeur left about a month ago, and Emily gives Johnny a picture of him. Johnny wonders at the picture and is sure that he has seen the man before.

Johnny tells Emily that he can open the safe for her. Johnny tells her to open the safe while he goes out and closes the big double doors. Johnny waits outside and goes in when Emily has opened and then closed the safe. Johnny then opens the safe with the combination.

Johnny tells Emily that there is a crack in the doors that allowed him to watch her turn the large combination dial at arms-length to open the safe. Johnny is sure that others could have watched also. Johnny is sure that Arnold is still in the area and has an idea.

Johnny thinks there are three possibilities: Mrs. Sterlingwaite, but she is not the type. Then there is the ex-chauffeur who was familiar to Johnny, but only vaguely. Third was Darlington.

After Johnny meets with Darlington, there is no doubt that he is innocent. Darling is truly upset at the loss of Mrs. Sterlingwaite's jewels, as he has let her down. Johnny tells him that Emily would love to have him there to comfort her, and suggests he call her. Johnny shows Darlington the picture of Arnold, and he tells Johnny that the man was employed in the plant under the name of Roger Gove.

Roger was a truck driver and loader, but Darlington fired him when he found Roger in his office one night. Darlington confirms that his safe has a record of combinations for all safes he sold, and Johnny is convinced that is how Roger got the combination, but Darlington tells Johnny that the safe was locked.

Johnny next takes the case in the right direction by contacting an old friend, an ex-con who knows the underworld, Smokey Sullivan. Smokey is still working with the Boston fire department and he tells Johnny that he does not know where the emerald is, or who took it, but he does have a lead.

Smokey tells Johnny that five blocks away there is a man who is a fence and gem cutter from Chicago named Fritz Bildow. Smokey tells Johnny that Fritz has a shop where he makes cheap jewels for the kids. Johnny shows Smokey the picture of the chauffeur, and he tells Johnny that the man is Manny Breed, a jewel thief.

Johnny figures out the plot and Smokey tells Johnny that he had spotted a pile of trash outside the shop and had started watching Bildow thinking he was going to burn the place. Smokey had called Lt. Tommy Winkler to check up on

Bildow, and at three this morning Smokey had seen Bildow working on a big gold setting, like an ivy leaf.

Johnny and Smokey rush to the shop located in an alley. Manny gets the drop on Johnny and Smokey, and tells them that Bildow had recognized Smokey, and that is why he is ready for anything. Manny knocks on the door and takes Johnny and Smokey inside, where Johnny spots the stone.

Manny gets Johnny's gun and is about to close the door and shoot Johnny when Lt. Winkler rushes in and shoots Manny. Tommy had come to follow up on the arson angle from Smokey, and Johnny tells him he has helped recover the Ivy Emerald.

"So, the emerald's back, and all's right with the world. Just one thing though, my commission on this one is to be split three ways. A third to Smokey, and a third to Tommy Winkler. As for the expense account, well if you pay that commission promptly, you can forget it."

"Next week, proof the hard way about how wrong one can sometimes be."

Notes:
- This program contains a commercial for Newport Menthol cigarettes.
- Abby Lewis is Emily, Lawson Zerbe is Darlington, Joseph Julian is Smokey, William Griffis is Bob, Jack Grimes is Breed, Sam Gray is Fritz, William Mason is Winkler.
- Warren Sweeney is the announcer.
- Musical supervision is by Ethel Huber.

Producer: Bruno Zirato, Jr.   Writer: Jack Johnstone
Cast: Abby Lewis, Lawson Zerbe, Joseph Julian, William Griffis, Jack Grimes, Sam Gray, William Mason

♦ ❖ ♦

Show: **The Wrong Idea Matter**
Show Date: **4/15/1962**
Company: **Eternity Mutual Insurance Company**
Agent: **Tim Harrington**
Exp. Acct: **$229.57**

Synopsis: A voice tells Johnny that he is not going to like this. Tim Harrington from Knoxville, Tennessee tells Johnny that Alpheus Brannigan, the kid who Johnny got sent up for embezzlement based on a tip from his pretty wife, had sworn he would get even with Johnny and his wife. Alfie got out of prison a couple weeks ago on good behavior. Tim thinks they were suckers, and his wife is a client. Tim has tried to find her but she has disappeared, so Johnny is on his way.

Johnny flies to Knoxville, Tennessee and takes a limousine to Tim's office. Tim tells Johnny that the policy on Marylyn Brannigan is only $7,500 and her brother Charlie is the beneficiary. Johnny tells Tim he should not worry about the courtroom threats to get even, as Johnny has heard too many of them. Tim is sure that Alfie was not kidding. Marylyn has not seen Alfie, because he would not let her see him, and would not answer her letters. She called Tim and asked for advice and Tim told her to call the police. Sgt. Piper of the police called the other day and told Tim that Marylyn has disappeared. Tim tells Johnny that he had better watch out for himself too.

Johnny goes to see Sgt. Piper, who is a big florid man who chews a cigar. Sgt. Piper tells Johnny that he has found no signs of Marylyn or Alfie. Marylyn had her own car and is an accountant. The license on the car was ULL166, and an APB has not been put out, because she is not guilty of any crime.

Johnny yells at Sgt. Piper that Alfie did nothing until the police dropped their guard, and then he acted. Johnny is sure that Alfie has gotten to Marylyn and taken her away. Johnny grabs the phone to call the state police and the FBI but Sgt. Piper relents and issues an ABP and apologizes to Johnny for not acting sooner. Johnny tells Sgt. Piper to call him at the Andrew Johnson Hotel.

After dinner at the Rathskeller, Johnny gets a room at the hotel, and is called by Sgt. Piper. He has located Marylyn at 21270 South Peachtree Street in Jefferson City. Sgt. Piper has not told the police to keep an eye on her, so Johnny rents a car and drives to the address in Jefferson City where Johnny finds Marylyn's car is outside.

Johnny gets in to find a scared Marylyn Brannigan. She had not heard from Alfie for three years, wondering what he meant in the courtroom. She tells Johnny that Alfie never changed his mind about what he said.

She tells Johnny that she had to tell Johnny about where Alfie was, and that the money he embezzled was for a holiday present for her. They had only been married a few weeks but she really loves him. Because Alfie would not see her or answer her letters, she is not sure of what to do.

Johnny tells her that the police should be there, but they are not. She has no phone so Johnny goes out to a filling station to call the police and tells her to keep the door locked. Marylyn kisses Johnny on the cheek as he leaves. Outside Alfie stops Johnny in the dark and slugs him.

Johnny wakes up in his car to the slaps of a police officer and a whiff of smelling salts. The police tell Johnny that Sgt. Piper had called them about Marylyn, and they went out to check the address. There was no one in the house when they got there, and they had seen a car drive away. The police give Johnny his wallet and he tells them to go back to headquarters and spread the word.

Johnny makes a difficult drive back to Knoxville and visits Sgt. Piper and then goes back to his room to get some sleep. Alfie and Marylyn meet Johnny in his room. She tells Johnny that Alfie came back to her. Alfie had seen Johnny at the cottage and assumed that he was there to take her away. Marylyn is so happy about all the things he had done for her.

Alfie tells Johnny that it was the least he could do for her. He had to prove that he was worthy of her. He was serious about what he said in court, about how he would show everyone and make up for the crazy thing he did. He has worked hard and studied to improve himself. When he got out he went to see her brother Charlie, who had liked him. Now he has a steady job and a place to live far away from all the bad memories. Now they can start again, the right way.

Johnny tells Alfie that if he wants to keep things right, to hold his temper, even when he sees his wife kissing another man. Johnny is glad to have a case end on a happy note for once as they help him to his bed.

"Well, you know something? Sure, those two are even younger than they realized, but I think that maybe those kids will do all right. I hope so. Anyway, expense account total, including a doctor who came to make sure I was all in one piece, hotel, mileage on the car and the trip back to Hartford, $229.57."

"Next week, the most clever device for covering up a murder I have ever seen."

Notes:
- This program contains commercials for Winston Burdette, Arthur Godfrey and many more of the exclusive stars of CBS Radio and for Newport Menthol cigarettes.
- Jimsey Sommers is Marylyn, Lawson Zerbe is Piper, Richard Holland is Alfie, Herb Duncan is Tim, Bill Lipton is the policeman.
- Art Hannes is the announcer.
- Musical supervision is by Ethel Huber.

Producer: Bruno Zirato, Jr.   Writer: Jack Johnstone
Cast: Jimsey Sommers, Lawson Zerbe, Richard Holland, Herb Duncan, Bill Lipton

◆ ❖ ◆

Show: **The Skidmore Matter**
Show Date: 4/22/1962
Company: Tri-Western Life Insurance Company
Agent: Jack Price
Exp. Acct: $276.28

Synopsis: Jack Price calls and Johnny tells Jack that he is one of the few people in the country who tack on an extra fee to his expense reports. Jack tells Johnny that this time he does not need any extra fees. Doug Johnstone has a problem and has suffered a considerable loss already. So, if Johnny will not come down without the lure of an extra fee to help an old friend, Jack will find someone else. Johnny is on the way and Jack will meet Johnny at the airport.

Johnny flies to Corpus Christi and Jack meets Johnny with a rental car. Jack tells Johnny that he is going to Skidmore, and that Doug is running a retirement home. Doug has done well in the stock market and other investments related to the oil business, but he has been losing heavy equipment from a warehouse in Skidmore, and Jack has to pay for all the stolen equipment. There is a guard now, but there is no police department in Skidmore. The watchman is Joe Hernandez.

Johnny drives to Skidmore, Texas and at the warehouse Johnny is met by a small man about 4 feet 10, and 100 pounds. As Johnny approaches, the man pulls a huge old revolver and waves it in Johnny's face.

Johnny tells him who he is, and Joe knows who "Juanito Dollar" is, "the famous, what you say, investigate". Joe is expecting Johnny and introduces himself as Jose el Guerro de Santiago MacPherson Julio Hernandez. The McPherson is a most honorable ancestor.

Joe tells Johnny that Mr. Price will not lose anymore equipment, so Johnny can go home now. Nothing has disappeared since Joe started working, except for a skip loader. Joe tells Johnny that no one will bother him now because of his .45 caliber pistola and proves it by shooting out a window in Johnny's rental car. Johnny is not so sure.

Joe introduces Johnny to his wife Carmilla and then shows Johnny the warehouse with the equipment waiting to be sold. Johnny sees tractors, bulldozers, graders, power shovels, skip loaders and spare parts.

The last robbery was just after the wedding of Joe's 32nd cousin Fernando. Joe had thrown a party there, and Johnny tells Joe he must have been boiled to the ears to sleep while all the equipment was stolen.

Joe's cousin, Fernando Ortiz, had recommended him to Doug Johnstone. Ortiz operates heavy equipment and repairs it in his shop in Tres Rios, Three Rivers. Johnny tells Joe he is going to see Doug Johnstone and tells Joe to pack his bags.

Johnny meets with Doug, but Doug did not even know that he and Ortiz were related. Doug has just found out that Ortiz owns a piece of an equipment repair shop. Ortiz had done some jobs for Doug doing earth moving. Johnny tells Doug to replace Joe with someone smarter. Doug tells Johnny that Ortiz is coming that evening asking for more work, even though Doug has told him there is none. Johnny arranges to be there later. Johnny drives to Skidmore to check up on Joe.

Johnny gets a room at the Robert Driscoll hotel and has dinner. Johnny goes to meet with Doug and Ortiz, who really is a sharp character. Doug tells Ortiz that there is no more work at the rest home and Ortiz is insistent that he be called if there is any more work. Johnny is concerned that Ortiz was not surprised to see Johnny at the meeting, and that he was stalling for time during the meeting, which lasted from 8:30 to 9:00.

Doug gets a call from Jack Price who tells Johnny that Joe has been murdered, and Jack will meet Johnny to go to Skidmore. Joe was murdered at 8:25 according to Joe's wife, and Johnny is sure that Ortiz did it.

Johnny finds the warehouse crawling with state police, and meets an old friend, Sgt. Billy Roscoe, who is in charge. Roscoe tells Johnny that someone used Joe's clothes to muffle the shot from Joe's .45, and that any prints on the gun had been wiped off. Carmilla had not seen anyone but Johnny and Fernando there all day.

Carmilla had told an officer that Ortiz had been there just before supper to give Joe some wine, but he did not want it and chased Ortiz away. Joe went to the warehouse, and Carmilla got a call from Ortiz at exactly 8:25. The time is right because Ortiz asked Carmilla what time it was. He told her to get Joe to the phone, so she went to the shed and was opening the sliding doors when she heard a loud noise. Doug notes that Ortiz had been at his office at 8:30.

Carmilla went in and found the body and called the police. The police do not know if Ortiz was on the phone when she got back. Johnny thinks that Ortiz had talked to Joe about Johnny and knew Joe was supposed to be in the warehouse. Johnny is sure that he made the call so Carmilla would find the body when he was in Doug's office in Corpus.

When Sgt. Roscoe mentions that Carmilla heard a loud bang when she opened the door, Johnny has an idea. Johnny realizes that she should have heard a muffled thump, not a loud bang.

Jack notices a burn mark on the door and the smell of iodine. Johnny tells them that Ortiz killed Joe earlier in the evening, came to Corpus and called Carmilla who set off the noise when she opened the door. Johnny tells them that the answer is like the old schoolboy chemistry trick to make stink bombs with carbon disulfide.

This one was nitrogen iodide. It was made into a paste and spread on the door, and when it was disturbed it exploded to make Ortiz's alibi. Johnny asks Sgt. Roscoe to take a sample for analysis.

"That's really all there is to the case. It was nitrogen iodide all right. And the run down on Fernando Ortiz brought out the fact that he had been quite a prankster in his high school days. But you know what gave me a big surprise? The way he made a full confession after I told him exactly how he had set up his alibi. Expense account total, $276.28."

"Next week, one of the most beautiful spots on earth that really shouldn't be the site for a murder."

Notes:
- This program contains commercials for the Peace Corp and for Newport Menthol cigarettes.
- The newly discovered script for this program gives an alternate title of *The Jose el Guerro de Santiago MacPherson Julio Hernandez Matter.*
- Joseph Cabibbo is noted for the sound patterns.
- Santos Ortega is Jose, Maurice Tarplin is Jack, Richard Keith is Doug, Ralph Camargo is Ortiz. Also heard were Bill Lipton and Sam Raskyn.
- Gaylord Avery is the announcer.
- Musical supervision is by Ethel Huber.

Producer:	Bruno Zirato, Jr.	Writer: Jack Johnstone
Cast:	Santos Ortega, Maurice Tarplin, Richard Keith,	
	Ralph Camargo, Bill Lipton, Sam Raskyn	

♦ ❖ ♦

Show: The Grand Canyon Matter
Show Date: 4/29/1962
Company: Northeast Indemnity Associates
Agent: Bill Walker
Exp. Acct: $550.00

Synopsis: Bill Walker calls from New York and asks Johnny if he has ever seen the Grand Canyon. Johnny replies that he has always wanted to, but not at this time of the year. Bill tells him the canyon is always beautiful, especially when some is paying him to look at it. Bill asks if the name Orloff means anything, and Johnny mentions Ted Orloff in Los Angeles. Bill means Kristie Orloff, well, come on down and I'll give you the whole story.

Johnny flies to New York City and cabs to Bill's office at 5th avenue and 42nd street. Bill has made reservations for Johnny at the Waldorf, and Johnny has tickets to Phoenix in the morning. Bill tells Johnny that tonight, cocktails, dinner and a show are on him.

Bill tells Johnny that most people have never heard of Kristie Orloff and reminds Johnny of a summit meeting in 1957 that took place in Apalachin, New York between all the crime bosses. Kristie was there as one of the small fish.

Bill is sure that Kristie has the Oterez necklace that belonged to a countess. It was sold to Winkler and Winkler and has been quietly stolen. Bill has the insurance on the necklace for just under a million. Johnny remembers that the necklace could have been broken up and sold very easily.

Bill is working with Randy Singer at the 18th precinct, and Randy is sure that Kristie has the necklace. Randy suggested that Bill call for Johnny. Johnny asks why he is going to the Grand Canyon, and Bill tells him to get the details from Randy. And remember Kristie's background if you meet him.

Johnny goes to Randy's office and talks with him after some good-natured jesting. Randy tells Johnny that they have nabbed the men who actually took the necklace: Izzy Frambless and Opie Norton. Both Izzy and Opie told the police that the rocks had been given to Kristie Orloff, but the police could not find any trace of the jewels when they searched Orloff's apartment. Kristie is a great passer of hot goods and has contacts on the west coast.

The Los Angeles police are watching the contacts, and Johnny is on his way to the Grand Canyon because that is where Orloff is. Randy has an officer watching Orloff on the train as far as Chicago, but after that Orloff is alone until he gets to the Grand Canyon.

Johnny questions the information from the stoolies but Randy is sure that Orloff is going to the canyon. Johnny gets a description of Orloff, who looks like a sweet old man.

Johnny spends a pleasant evening with Billy Walker and buys a camera for the trip. Johnny flies to Phoenix and rents a car for the drive to the Grand Canyon, Arizona. Johnny is hard pressed to describe the vast beauty of the canyon and the Colorado River.

Johnny gets a room at the El Tovar hotel and gets a phone call from Randy. Randy tells Johnny that Orloff will arrive the next day by train, and that the Los Angeles police have advised Randy that Ricky Fortino, a big-time criminal who is into all sorts of rackets, is going to the canyon also. Randy wonders why the criminals always travel by train when they could fly. Randy tells Johnny to be careful.

Johnny wanders outside after dinner to view the canyon by moonlight. Johnny puts his camera on a post to get a picture and climbs over the railing to set the camera. Johnny is hit by a boot and feels himself falling, falling into the darkness.

When Johnny wakes up he is tangled in a bush over the trail, 20 feet below the handrail. Johnny realizes that Ricky Fortino is there and has recognized him and might suspect why Johnny is there. Johnny does not know what Fortino looks like, so Johnny figures Fortino will stay away from Johnny, thinking that Johnny knows him.

At breakfast Johnny looks over the guests and does not find any one suspicious. When Orloff arrives, Johnny follows him and watches his room. Johnny goes on a bus trip with Orloff, and they turn out to be active shutterbugs.

Kristie notes that Johnny likes to take pictures and Johnny, using the name Jerry Glenn, notes he has used two rolls of film just on the bus trip. Kristie asks about the mule trip the next morning and Johnny agrees to accompany him the next day, and to join him for dinner that night.

Johnny realizes that the hiding place for the necklace is in the one thing Orloff kept with him at all times except meals. Johnny notes that Orloff had taken over 60 pictures without changing the film.

Johnny calls Randy and arranges for him to call Orloff later. Johnny watches the room until dinner during which Orloff gets a phone call from New York. Johnny goes to Orloff's room and searches for the camera and finds the necklace inside. Johnny takes the necklace and pockets it.

When Johnny hears footsteps, he exits out an open window. Johnny watches Orloff give a small wiry man the camera, but the necklace is gone! Ricky pulls a gun and accuses Orloff of pulling a dodge on "Big Hugo" and gets ready to shoot Orloff.

"With one quick movement from somewhere under his coat Orloff pulled a gun and got off a shot and so did Fortino. And then, by the time it was over, the two of them lay on the floor, both very dead. Come to think of it, there is an extra dividend on this case, Fortino's mention of "Big Hugo", whoever he is. So now the police know of another big-shot to gun for. Expense account total, including a couple extra days there at Grand Canyon, call if $550 even."

"Next week, I'll be back with another exciting adventure."

Notes:
- This program contains a commercial for a Rexall 1-cent sale.
- Sound patterns are by Joseph Cabibbo.
- Eugene Francis is Randy, Casey Allen is Bill, Arthur Kohl is Kristie, Ralph Bell is Ricky, Guy Repp is the guide, Sam Raskyn is the hotel clerk.
- Art Hannes is the announcer.
- Musical supervision is by Ethel Huber.

Producer: Bruno Zirato, Jr.   Writer: Jack Johnstone
Cast: Eugene Francis, Casey Allen, Arthur Kohl, Ralph Bell, Guy Repp, Sam Raskyn

Show:	**The Burma Red Matter**
Show Date:	**5/6/1962**
Company:	**Mono Guarantee Insurance Company**
Agent:	**Jimmy Bartell**
Exp. Acct:	**$0.00**

Synopsis: Jimmy Bartell from Mono Guarantee calls and tells Johnny that it is high time he answered the phone. Jimmy has been trying to reach Johnny for four weeks. When Johnny asks if he tried his call service, Jimmy had forgotten about that. Johnny recounts to Jimmy that he has been in Grand Canyon, then Corpus Christi, then Knoxville and then Boston over the past four weeks.

Jimmy tells Johnny that he has been up to his neck in trouble and beating his brain out while Johnny has been out gallivanting. Jimmy tells Johnny that the problem is the Burma Red and it is insured for half a million. Johnny has to get it back before they have to pay out. Johnny wants to know what it is before he starts gallivanting around looking for it. Jimmy tells Johnny to come on over and get the details.

Johnny cabs to the office of Jimmy Bartell, who specializes in property insurance and fine art works. Jimmy tells Johnny that the Burma Red may not even be in the country now. It was brought into the country by a countess a couple years ago as part of a collection and written up in all the picture magazines. It was part of the Buckingham collection in England and bought by Winkler and Winkler.

Johnny thinks that this case is just like the case of the Ivy Emerald he just finished. The stone is a single un-mounted ruby that was sold to Mrs. Harvey Laraman Brittingham who lives in Hartford. It was stolen from the safe a few weeks ago, and Jimmy needs Johnny to get the stone back.

The prime suspect in the case is Oscar Mayfield, but the police have not been able to pin anything on him and he is back in New York. Jimmy is sure that Oscar got away with it, and Johnny agrees. Johnny tells Jimmy that Oscar promised him that if he ever tried to interfere with him again, he would see to it that Johnny had a very nice funeral.

Johnny cabs to the Hartford, Connecticut police headquarters where he talks to Sgt. Hollie Holcomb, who does not provide any encouraging information. He tells Johnny that all the hallmarks on the safe were Oscars', but they could not prove anything because of his alibi and his lawyer. They have contacted Randy Singer in New York, and Sgt. Holcomb suggests that Johnny go visit him.

Johnny gets all of the details on the case, and the all unconfirmed evidence points to Oscar Mayfield, but Oscar had an unshakeable alibi.

Johnny calls Randy who is surprised that Johnny has just found out about the robbery. Randy has kept an eye on Oscar, but they have found nothing. Johnny and Randy are both sure that Oscar has passed the stone on to someone else. Randy is sure that the stone is either on its way out of the country or being cut up into smaller stones, but they cannot find it.

Randy has heard "unofficially" that an officer rolled Oscar in an alley and found nothing. Randy knows that the stone is not in Oscar's apartment, but Johnny reminds him how he found the Oterez necklace that Randy's boys overlooked in a camera. Johnny gets the address for Oscar, but Randy tells Johnny that he will not be there when Johnny gets there as Mayfield is leaving for Mexico City this afternoon.

Johnny decides to play a trick to get Oscar to stick around. Johnny remembers from a previous run-in with Oscar, that he used a fence named Hugo. Johnny decides to wire Oscar "Urgent, that before you make any deal, you call me immediately at Plaza 3-9970. Signed Hugo".

Johnny then flies to New York and cabs to 614 E. 49th street. The doorman balks at telling Johnny Mr. Mayfield's apartment number until Johnny tells him that he is an investigator. Johnny shows him his credentials and gets the apartment number 7-G. Johnny goes in and knocks and then opens the unlocked door to find and empty apartment with bags in the bedroom. Oscar comes from behind a door and puts a gun into Johnny's back and takes his gun. Oscar reminds Johnny of his promise to Johnny and tells him that the apartment is sound proof.

Oscar tells Johnny that he was expecting him, but he does not have the stone, because it has been successfully dealt with. He knew the telegram was a fake and tried the phone number eight times until the phone company told him that the number is used for testing and always has a busy signal. Oscar waited for Johnny until the doorman called him.

Randy walks in and takes the guns from Oscar. Randy tells Johnny he is off duty and just stopped by for a visit. Oscar tells Randy he will not find the ruby, and Randy tells Oscar he will book him for the little show he just put on.

There is a knock at the door and Johnny answers it. There is a delivery boy at the door and Johnny poses as Oscar. The boy is Rosy Gilliam, and he has a package from Hugo. Rosy wants a receipt and is expecting a fin or a tenner from Oscar. Johnny opens the package and learns that Hugo meets Rosy whenever he needs him to make deliveries.

Inside the package is a pile of money. Johnny asks how to spell Hugo's last name and the boy tells Johnny "I should know how to spell Hemperschlag?" Randy takes Rosy into custody and promises to protect him. Johnny is sure that the money is payment for the ruby. Oscar, knowing he is beaten, grudgingly gives Johnny the address for Hugo.

"Mr. Hugo Hemperschlag believe it or not, turned out to be a gem setter for the famous jewelry house of Winkler and Winkler, where he couldn't help but know about all the important stuff brought into this country, and with the know-how to break it up, after he had arranged to have it stolen. Expense account total, in view of the commission I'll get on this one, forget it."

"Next week, I'll be back with a rather unusual story."

Notes:
- This program is interrupted for a special announcement: "To the parents of school-boy patrol members who were taking the Washington trip, the

busses with the patrol will arrive at the Durham Union bus station at 7:15-7:30. Parents are urged to use the Sears parking lot."
- This program contains commercials for DuPont Dacron clothes and suits for men and for Kent cigarettes with the micronite filter.
- Sound patterns are by Joseph Cabibbo.
- Paul McGrath is Oscar, Al Hodge is Randy, Ivor Francis is Jimmy, Jack Grimes is Rosy, Santos Ortega is Holcomb, Mercer McLeod is the doorman.
- Roger Foster is the announcer.
- Musical supervision is by Ethel Huber.
- Interestingly, in *The Too Many Crooks Matter*, Johnny goes to another fence on E. 49th Street, that time at #718.
- There is a station identification for WDNC in Durham-Raleigh at the end of the program.

Producer: Bruno Zirato, Jr.   Writer: Jack Johnstone
Cast: Paul McGrath, Al Hodge, Ivor Francis, Jack Grimes, Santos Ortega, Mercer McLeod

♦ ❖ ♦

Show: **The Lust for Gold Matter**
Show Date: **5/13/1962**
Company: **Universal Adjustment Bureau**
Agent: **Pat Fuller**
Exp. Acct: **$0.00**

Synopsis: Johnny gets a call from Pat Fuller. Johnny tells Pat that he doesn't want another assignment right now, he has been going too hard lately. He is tired and needs to get away for a few days. Pat tells Johnny that he only called to read a cable or a telegram, whatever it is from Emmett Gowan. Johnny tells Pat that Emmett knows more about fishing than anyone and that he is a pal of Johnny's. The cable says "This spot is the closest thing to heaven a fisherman could possibly find. Sailfish, dolphin, amber jacks, snappers, bonefish tarpon, just about anything you could think of. If you don't come down here and be my guest, and right away, I'll never forgive you. I mean it, this is really urgent. Signed Emmett Gowan." Johnny thinks the cable is for Pat, but Pat tells Johnny it is addressed to YOU!

Johnny cabs to Pat's office and Pat confirms the invitation from Emmett Gowan to spend some time fishing off the island of Cozumel, Mexico. The trip will be on the expense account because Pat wants Johnny to fly over to Mexico City after a few days of fishing to look into a missing client, Juano Anzana. The wife wants someone to look into the matter, so Pat wants Johnny to look into it.

Johnny cabs home, packs and starts the long flight to Cozumel, via New York, New Orleans and Merida, Yucatan. Once in Cozumel, Yucatan Johnny gets a room at the Cabana el Caribe, where Emmett Gowan meets Johnny.

Johnny tells Emmett that he is really tired, but Emmett tells Johnny that a few days fishing will fix that. Johnny tells Emmett that he cannot understand why the Universal Adjustment Bureau is footing the bill for the trip. Emmett mentions Juano Anzana but is evasive about giving Johnny any information except about fishing. So, Johnny goes fishing.

Johnny relates that the fishing that afternoon was almost good enough to be a lie. In a lagoon, off of a mangrove island Johnny catches a large tarpon, and then a big snook, then a moon-eyed snapper, then a large barracuda, followed by three more tarpons. At the end of the day Johnny is bushed and has forgotten all about the insurance investigation business.

The next day Johnny and Emmett go across the bay to a fishing camp Emmett runs near Matanceros, where a Spanish Galleon sank. A number of treasure hunters have worked it over, including Juano Anzana, but Anzana has found another shipwreck, the *Pinaña*. That is where Johnny and Emmett are heading to use their scuba gear to explore the ship.

Emmett tells Johnny that Juano discovered the ship, then he was brought there by Emmett to do some spear fishing. Emmett tells Johnny that Juano is the most disagreeable man Emmett has ever met and would not trust him. Juano found something but would not say anything about it, but his eyes told Emmett that he found something.

Emmett tells Johnny that, in retirement, he is very content, and does not want to get involved in more money that would ruin his paradise. He was afraid he might find something. Emmett was called by Juano's wife stating he had not come back, and then Pat Fuller called, so that is why Johnny is here. Johnny asks if Juano would dive alone, and Emmett tells him that where treasure is involved, anything is possible, and any man can be dangerous.

Johnny and Emmett arrive at the wreck and secure the boat on the beach. Johnny and Emmett don their scuba gear and see that another boat has been there. Emmett calls for Anzana, and then goes to the boat to take a look. The boat was well hidden, but Juano was not there.

Johnny dives down onto the clear, clean warm water to look for Anzana. Johnny notes how clean and clear the water is and how he is surrounded by all types of fish, including a large shark. Johnny easily finds the *Pinaña*, but so was finding the body of a man.

Johnny notes that the body on the wreck was a Mexican, with a bullet hole in the back of his head. Johnny is able to read a name on the dog tags of a bracelet: Juano Anzana.

Johnny notes that Emmett's boat has moved so Johnny surfaces and sees a very unfamiliar face. The man tells Johnny to get in his boat and helps Johnny in. The man tells Johnny that he will join the man in the water, the man who came after his treasure, the treasure that he discovered first.

Johnny tries to find out what is going on, but the man starts to shoot Johnny, but Johnny capsizes the boat and surfaces to find Emmett in the water subduing the man. After getting the man to the beach Emmett tells Johnny that the man is Anzana, who had been maddened by the treasure.

Johnny is sure that Anzana killed the man and put his bracelet on the body so that he could just disappear when he found the treasure. That way he would be free and have the treasure. Emmett tells Johnny that he knew the hidden boat was Anzana's, and there were no bubbles.

So, he hid his boat and dived to hide his presence. Emmett heard what was going on, so he kind of helped Johnny capsize the boat. Emmett suggests they take Anzana back to the police, and Johnny agrees.

"You know, the ironic part of it all is that there wasn't one single dollar's worth of treasure in the wreck of the *Pinaña*. So, he had murdered for nothing, and now of course will have to pay for it. Expense account total, after four more days of absolutely fabulous fishing...aw, wait a minute. This one is on the house."

"Next week, the two-step matter. That means two steps to murder."

Notes:
- This program contains commercials for clothes made from Dacron by DuPont, and for Kent cigarettes.
- Walter Otto and Don Creed provide the sound patterns.
- Robert Dryden is Emmett, Ralph Camargo is Anzana, Lawson Zerbe is Pat.
- Musical supervision is by Ethel Huber.
- The announcer is Warren Sweeney.
- Emmett Gowan is a character in *The Froward Fisherman Matter*.
- There are two versions of this program. At the end of one version is a CBS spot about driving safely. At the end of the other version is a Welcome Wagon commercial from WROW in Albany.
- *Suspense* is next with the episode *Hide and Seek*.

Producer:	Bruno Zirato, Jr. Writer: Jack Johnstone
Cast:	Robert Dryden, Ralph Camargo, Lawson Zerbe

♦ ❖ ♦

Show:	**The Two Steps to Murder Matter**
Show Date:	**5/20/1962**
Company:	**Western Maritime & Life Insurance Company**
Agent:	**Pete Brenneman**
Exp. Acct:	**$511.80**

Synopsis: Pete Brenneman calls Johnny from Las Vegas. Pete is checking the schedules so that Johnny can get there for breakfast. Pete has a client named Harvey Skillman with a straight life policy for $62,000 and Harvey has been poisoned. Johnny is on his way.

Johnny flies to Las Vegas, Nevada via Los Angeles and arrives for an early breakfast. Pete takes Johnny to the Silver Dollar Café for breakfast where Johnny notes a little old lady playing a slot machine at that early hour.

Pete tells Johnny that the police are convinced that Johnny came out here for nothing. The police doctor told Pete that the poison was penorphene alcolaid. The doc found some in a coffee cup and the police found the sugar bowl laced with it. Johnny notes that the poison tastes terrible, and Pete tells Johnny that Harvey was almost addicted to coffee. Johnny is sure that no one would have drunk the coffee with the poison in it, so it must have been taken deliberately but Pete is sure that Harvey did not commit suicide. Pete is sure about Harvey and wants to tell Johnny why, if he will only listen.

Pete tells Johnny that Harvey, who was 31 when he hit it lucky at the craps table and ran a five-spot up to $44,000. He quit his job to help his sister Mary who is a nurse, and who came down with a crippling bone disease last year. Harvey used all his money and savings to take Mary to the Mayo Clinic and to a doctor back east. Now she will be cured in a year or so. However, Harvey ran low on money and came back to try and win some more to help Mary but lost everything except his insurance.

Pete gave Harvey a job and all his best prospects and Harvey was able to save some money. But Lippy Lorenzo, who used to work for Al Capone and retired here, lowered the boom. Harvey told Pete that Lippy had something on Harvey and could blackmail him for everything he has, but Harvey did not tell Pete what it was. Harvey told Pete that he had paid his debts to society but had to settle things with Lippy.

Harvey decided to settle things with a deck of cards — double or nothing for the $10,000 that Harvey had. Harvey went through with it and won, and Lippy paid off. The police thought Lippy had gotten to Harvey, but the poison convinced the police doctor that it was suicide.

Johnny realizes that if it were proved or declared suicide, Mary would get nothing, which is not what Harvey wanted. Pete had seen Harvey in his apartment just before he died. Pete was going to take Harvey to the airport, and the apartment door was open when he got there. They drank some coffee, and Harvey was OK until he put the poison-laced sugar in his coffee. Johnny wants to go to Pete's office to make a phone call.

Johnny notes that a professional must know a lot about one thing, but Johnny must know a little about a lot of things, and most importantly, what pro knows the most about what things.

Johnny calls Dr. Les Crutcher in Sarasota because Les had studied rare and exotic plants and herbs, the kind of drugs used by witch doctors in the jungles. Les reminds Johnny of the foul medicine he made Johnny take the last time he visited.

Johnny asks about the glass of herbal tea Les gave Johnny to deaden the taste of the medicine for hours. The tea was a secret of Les' taken from a member of the milkweed plant family, gymnema sylvestre. Les refers Johnny to Dr. Raymond Anthony Corberly at U.C.L.A. and tells Johnny that he came across the plant doing medical work for the Chicago police.

A wayward doctor who worked for Al Capone would brew it up for a murderer who would give the tea to a victim, and then administer a rank poison. The tea disables the ability to taste sweet and bitter things. The doctor was Willie somebody.

Johnny flies to Los Angeles to see Dr. Corberly who gives Johnny a sample of the plant and Johnny wonders about using the dried leaves as tea.

Johnny flies back to Vegas, drives to police headquarters, and then goes to the ranch of Lippy Lorenzo. Lippy invites Johnny in and tells Johnny that he is retired.

In a nearby vase is a dried up gymnema sylvestre plant. Johnny tells Lippy that he made Harvey a cup of coffee laced with the plant to numb his mouth so that he could not taste the sugar he was going to lace with the poison. Lippy pulls a gun with a silencer on it.

Johnny calls for the police, but Lippy thinks it is a gag, until the police come in and take his gun. Johnny calls the police doctor to tell him how to fill out the death certificate on Harvey.

"So, it's just the way you want it Pete. The company will have to pay the insurance to Mary Skillman, $62,000. Expense account total, $511.80."

"Next week, one of the most clever devices for murder I ever saw."

Notes:
- This program contains a commercial break for Douglas Edwards, Dimension in England, Rose Mary Clooney and Peter Kalischer from Moscow, Art Linkletter and other CBS Radio programs, and one for Kent cigarettes.
- Joseph Cabibbo does the sound patterns on this program.
- Jim Stevens is Pete, John Griggs is Les, Bill Smith is Dr. Corberly, Lawson Zerbe is Lippy, Bill Lipton is the police sergeant.
- Musical supervision is by Ethel Huber.
- The announcer is Art Hannes.
- Gymnema sylvestre is a member of the milkweed family and is native to the tropical regions of India. It is called the "sugar destroyer" because the leaves effectively block sweet tastes in the mouth when chewed.

| Producer: | Bruno Zirato, Jr. | Writer: Jack Johnstone |
| Cast: | Jim Stevens, John Griggs, Bill Smith, Lawson Zerbe, Bill Lipton | |

◆ ❖ ◆

Show:	The Zip Matter
Show Date:	5/27/1962
Company:	Western Maritime & Life Insurance Company
Agent:	Pete Brenneman
Exp. Acct:	$200.00

Synopsis: Johnny gets a call from a man who knew that Johnny would still be here in Vegas. Pete Brenneman has tracked Johnny down to the Stardust because the airlines did not have a reservation for him, so he started calling the big hotels. Pete has a little problem, "unless you don't care about a little extra fee on this trip, why don't you come over here to the office and let me tell you all about it?" "Okay, why not."

Johnny cabs to Pete's office, glad for the opportunity to get a better look at Las Vegas, Nevada, where everywhere there is a slot machine or a casino. Johnny notes the variety of people who come there to gamble.

Pete shows Johnny a picture of Willard Rayfield Swift attached to a policy. Johnny cannot remember seeing Swift, but Pete tells Johnny that Swifty is a compulsive gambler who hangs out at the Stardust. He is only 31, and his father left him a lot of money, doled out in weekly allotments of $300. Swifty has gambled away his money and is in debt, but the lenders do not know that the money will stop coming soon. They also do not know about a policy on his uncle, Fred Payton, who died the other day leaving a policy for $120,000 to be divided up three ways.

A third goes to a niece Doreen Janice Clayford, a real good-looking girl who's married to a fellow with a feed store. A third also goes to a nephew Kenneth Kermer who is about 40 and runs a ranch north of here. The $40,000 share Swifty will get is just about what Swifty owes. If one of the beneficiaries dies, the remainder will split the money 50-50. Johnny notes that it is worth it to them if one dies.

Pete tells Johnny that Swifty and Kenneth have always had bad blood between them. Ken would not go far enough to kill anyone, but Swifty would. Pete is sure that if Johnny has not seen Swifty at the casino, he is up to something.

Pete tells Johnny that Shorty Callahan has been breathing down Swifty's neck for the $40,000 he is owed, and people who try to cheat Shorty end up dead. Pete tells Johnny to protect Ken Kermer from Swifty, as no one would complain if Swifty were killed by Shorty, or one of his boys.

Pete gets a call from Doreen Clayford who tells Pete that she met Swifty who was on his way to see Ken. Swifty had been drinking, and she is going to follow him, even though he told her not to. Doreen tells Pete to get the police and hangs up.

Pete and Johnny drive to Glendale after stopping at Doreen's house. On the way, Johnny and Pete spot a storm coming over the mountains and drive even faster. The storm slows Johnny and Pete when it catches them, and they must avoid mudslides and boulders on the road.

Pete turns off onto the side road as Johnny wonders about whether Ken or Doreen might be planning something. Pete tells Johnny that Ken might, but not Doreen. At the ranch, Johnny spots Doreen's car, with her standing at the door waving.

Doreen tells them that Swifty got there ahead of her and that the door was open when she got there. She heard shouting and a shot from within a tool shop and went to investigate, but the door was locked. Johnny breaks in the door and inside they find a man on the floor unconscious, and the other dead.

Johnny determines that the dead man is Ken Kermer, who had been shot with a .38 that went through him and landed on the floor. Pete and Doreen work on Swifty while Johnny investigates the scene.

Swifty wakes up and tells Doreen and Johnny that he came here to see if Ken would let him have some money. Ken would not let Swifty in out of the rain, but when Doreen arrived he took Swifty into the shop and locked the door. They had a big argument and Ken hit him when he turned his back on Ken. The next thing Swifty knew, Doreen was trying to wake him up. Swifty is sure that Doreen must have killed Ken.

Doreen wonders how she could have locked the door on the outside from the inside and gotten out the keyhole. Doreen accuses Swifty of killing Ken and throwing the gun out the window. Swifty is sure that Shorty must have done it after he was knocked out, but Shorty got the wrong man.

Pete is sure that Swifty is right about Shorty because the glass was broken from the outside in, but Johnny tells him that a bullet would not break the glass. Johnny thinks that Swifty shot Ken for the insurance money, but Swifty asks Johnny where the gun is, after all he was outside looking for it.

Johnny wonders how Swifty knew Johnny was looking for the gun, when he was supposed to be unconscious? Swifty points to the fresh mud on Johnny's feet for his reason.

Johnny accuses Swifty of lying about Ken seeing Doreen's car and that he hit himself, but Swifty again asks where the gun is. Swifty tells Johnny that maybe he swallowed the gun, or maybe it was a .38 caliber zip gun.

Johnny muses about the zip gun angle and is sure that Swifty did it as he just told Johnny how he did it. The shop is full of enough pipe to make a zip gun. Johnny mentions that the bullet on the floor does not have any rifling. While Pete holds Johnny's gun on Swifty, Johnny searches for a piece of pipe big enough for a .38 slug. Swifty agrees to cooperate as maybe a judge or a jury will...so Swifty points to a short piece of pipe on the workbench with the hammer beside it.

"So once again it's up to the courts and I'm sure Swifty will go up for life, at the least. Expense account total, including the trip back to Hartford, call it $200 even."

"Next week, the fastest jailing of a murder suspect you ever saw. Me!"

Notes:
- This program opens with "From Hollywood..." and the unmistakable voice of Dan Cubberly. This opening must have been edited in at some point.
- This program contains commercials for No-Doz and for Newport menthol cigarettes.
- Jim Stevens is Pete, Leon Janney is Swifty, Rita Lloyd is Doreen.
- Sound patterns are by Joseph Cabibbo.
- Musical supervision is by Ethel Huber.
- The announcer is Art Hannes.

Producer: Bruno Zirato, Jr.   Writer: Jack Johnstone
Cast: Jim Stevens, Leon Janney, Rita Lloyd

• ❖ •

Show: **The Wayward Gun Matter**
Show Date: **6/3/1962**
Company: **Amalgamated Life Associates**
Agent: **Adolph Dorfman**
Exp. Acct: **$0.00**

Synopsis: Adolph Dorfman calls Johnny and tells him that he has been trying to reach Johnny for days. Johnny tries to explain that he was in Las Vegas on a case. Dorfman tells Johnny to get over to his office right away because he wants to know what is happening on the Clete Martin case. Johnny tells him that he has not solved the case yet and tells Dorfman that he has one possible clue yet to checkout. Dorfman is also upset that Johnny has sent in an incomplete expense report, but Johnny tells him that Dorfman demanded that Johnny send in a report every Friday, whether the case was complete or not! Johnny will be glad to explain the expenses when the case is over, but Dorfman demands that Johnny come to his office and explain the report face-to-face.

Johnny explains that Dorfman has always been, and always will be a short tempered, crotchety old maid, and nothing but trouble on a case. Johnny cabs to Dorfman's office and fights over the various items on the expense report.

Johnny tells Dorfman that he is waiting for a call from New York, where their top ballistics expert will have information for Johnny that will solve the case. Dorfman has one other item to discuss but Johnny accuses him of just stalling.

Dorfman stalls Johnny with inane chatter about Las Vegas. He tells Johnny that Alfred W. Berriman, the contractor and client, was shot last night. Police Sgt. Anset arrives and thanks Dorfman for catching Johnny for him. Anset wants Johnny's great big .38, but when Johnny says that he does not have it on him, Anset tells Johnny that they have his gun at headquarters, and they are holding Johnny on suspicion of murder.

Johnny really cannot repeat his reaction to being nailed by Dorfman and Sgt. Anset. Johnny demands his rights to a phone call and tells Dorfman he is using his phone, "and don't be surprised if you pay through the nose for the phone call".

Johnny calls Randy Singer, who has no word for him yet and promises to call Johnny right back. Johnny tries to explain to Anset who he is, but Anset knows all about Johnny, and is just doing what Lt. Bartley told him to do.

At Hartford, Connecticut police headquarters Johnny accuses Lt. Harry Bartley of pulling a boner by having him arrested and mentions a reporter outside the jail who is probably calling his paper right now. Bartley tells Johnny that he has been stalling on the Martin case, and had gone out of town, all very suspicious. Also, there was the micro-photo of the bullet that Johnny would not explain.

When Berriman, who was bidding on a project in Lakewood County got shot, Bartley wondered if there was a connection. Johnny tells Bartley that he has held out certain information because of the rotten political situation in Lakewood. Bartley knows who Johnny is talking about, and Johnny tells him that the politician could make it very hot for anyone who gets in his way. Johnny tells Bartley that there was no way Berriman or Martin could have underbid the inside competition if they had kept alive.

Johnny had gone to visit the politician and had noticed a collection of guns, that included a gun just like the make, model and finish Johnny carries. Johnny created a diversion and switched guns so he could have the politician's gun checked by ballistics experts in New York. If it matches the gun used in the murders, Bartley will have his murderer, and Lakewood County will be clean.

Bartley is suspicious despite Johnny's story and has Sgt. Anset lock Johnny up. Bartley tells Anset that he will take care of the booking paperwork.

Johnny is visited by Bartley and he tells Johnny that the newspapers, cigarettes, coffee and reporters were brought in for Johnny. Johnny is upset about his reputation, and for Bartley letting a murder run around free. Johnny asks Bartley to let him take a special phone call when it comes in. Bartley gets an urgent phone call and leaves.

Officer Handley takes Johnny to Bartley's office where he welcomes Johnny. He tells Johnny of the call from Randy Singer, who is also an old friend. Randy told Bartley that the report proves the politician's gun did kill Berriman and Martin, so Johnny is a hero again.

Johnny tells him that his reputation is ruined after being booked for suspicion of murder. "Booked? You know, I must have forgotten to." Bartley tells Johnny with a grin. Bartley decided to throw the politician off course by publicizing that the police had arrested the murderer. They picked up the politician in Hartford and told him about the gun switch, and he became so confused that he broke down and made a full confession.

Johnny is worried about the newspaper articles but is told that the afternoon papers will have a story giving Johnny full credit for the whole case. The only hero is Johnny Dollar because he laid the groundwork and deserves all the credit.

"After this, I think I better keep my tricks to myself. Well now, wait a minute, how can I when every case I handle gets broadcast all over the country? Yeah, I guess I just can't win. Expense account total? Well all I want now is one big fat apology from meddling old Adolph Dorfman at Amalgamated Life for having trapped me into that night in jail."

"Next week, San Francisco, and a ship, a most unusual ship."

Notes:
- This program contains commercials for Newport cigarettes and for Sinclair gasoline.
- This program contains a post-program commercial for Welcome Wagon in Albany on WROW.
- Robert Dryden is Adolph, Ralph Bell is Anset, Martin Blaine is Bartley, Nat Polen is Hanley.
- Sound patterns are by Joseph Cabibbo.
- Musical supervision is by Ethel Huber.
- The announcer is Art Hannes.

Producer: Fred Hendrickson   Writer: Jack Johnstone
Cast: Robert Dryden, Ralph Bell, Martin Blaine, Nat Polen

Show:	The Wayward Clipper Matter
Show Date:	6/10/1962
Company:	Western Maritime & Life Insurance Company
Agent:	Hartfield Wormser
Exp. Acct:	$900.00

Synopsis: Johnny is called by Hartfield Wormser in San Francisco. He is reading a report of a case in Las Vegas, and Hartfield is sure that Johnny Dollar is the man he needs. The problem is piracy, and he will expect Johnny in the morning.

Johnny cabs to the airport and flies to San Francisco where he has lunch at The Grotto with Hartfield. Wormser points out a big boat rigged for salmon trolling. The *Brownie Boy*, an 85-foot tuna clipper was docked next to it. The owner is Gus Brownfield, and the *Brownie Boy* was newly insured for more than $100,000. It was stopping for fuel and repairs as well as an increase in the insurance. It left early in the morning for a checkout cruise, but it had too much fuel on it. The Coast Guard has searched for the boat and cannot find it.

Johnny asks about the issue of piracy and Wormser tells him that it is possible that someone stopped her, refueled her and took her. An inspector looked at the boat and it has too much power for a tuna boat. Wormser has a friend with a boat that will do 20-knots. He met the *Brownie Boy* out at Four Fathom Bank and the *Brownie Boy* passed him like he was standing still.

Johnny points out that tuna clippers are built for range not speed and is curious that a boat out of L.A. went to Seattle for engine inspections and to San Francisco for insurance. Johnny remembers a shrimp boat in the Gulf of Mexico that was taking just enough shrimp to be legal and he is sure that the *Brownie Boy* is not in the tuna business. Wormser muses that maybe their business is narcotics, like heroine.

Johnny goes to the Huntington Hotel on Nob Hill and makes a phone call to Lt. Terry Martin at the Coast Guard. Martin will let Johnny know if the *Brownie Boy* is found. Johnny then calls an old friend in Chinatown named Lee Chin Singh.

Lee tells Johnny that he had been suspicious of the *Brownie Boy* and had made inquiries, so he is glad that Johnny has called, especially since Johnny has been generous in paying for his services in the past. After some haggling, Johnny agrees to give Lee $400 plus $100 if the information leads to recovery.

Lee tells Johnny that there are rumors of large quantities of illicit substances entering the city from unusual channels. There are two men involved with Brownfield, and one was on the vessel when it left and the other was driving a panel truck. One of the men is Tony Calarafino, a Chicago mobster. The other is named Vokolovsky. Johnny goes back to Wormser and arranges to rent a fast two-seat airplane.

Johnny notes how whole nations are being ruined by being fed dope from pushers feeding school children, the future leaders of the countries. Johnny is sure the flag-waving boys across the Atlantic are plotting to overthrow the country and Vokolovsky is involved. Johnny is sure that the fuel issue is a red herring as it allowed the *Brownie Boy* to get further out to sea to rendezvous with a boat to get the "stuff" back to a port where it was not expected.

Johnny travels to Santa Barbara and meets with Chief Petty Officer Parley Warren. Johnny infers that he is only interested in the insurance angle, but Warren knows about Johnny and asks why the *Brownie Boy* would come to Santa Barbara. Johnny suggests that it is just a hunch.

Warren tells Johnny that the Coast Guard has found the boat, which had run out of gas, and is towing it to port. Warren is surprised that San Francisco let the boat leave with only Brownfield on board. Johnny tells him that he will meet the *Brownie Boy* when it docks.

Johnny expenses a crowbar and a chisel and goes to meet the boat. When the boat arrives Johnny notes that it is only given a cursory inspection. After Gus Brownfield leaves, Johnny goes on board and finds nothing. As he is about to leave he hears a noise in the galley where he finds a man coming out from behind a panel.

Johnny hits the man, who turns out to be Tony Calarafino — he was left behind to watch over a million-dollar cargo of uncut heroine. As Johnny is tying up Tony, Gus and Vokolovsky come in and Gus tells Johnny to stay put. Gus tells Vokolovsky that Johnny has discovered the stuff and that a call he got from Lee Singh was correct and that Vokolovsky owes Singh $500. Gus tells Vokolovsky to get a pin from the boat's railing. They can hide Johnny where Tony was and then dump him at sea.

Johnny tries to tell Gus that he will not get away with his plan as Vokolovsky will double-cross him.

[First Ending]

Gus is about to hit Johnny when CPO Warren enters the galley and tells Gus to go on deck. Warren tells Johnny that the Coast Guard had been watching him and Johnny tells him that he hoped they would.

[Alternative Ending]

As Gus and Vokolovsky cast off, Johnny tells Gus that he was smart to get the Coast Guard to escort him into port. Gus tells Vokolovsky to head for Los Angeles and to get some sinkers to tie to Johnny so that they can throw him overboard.

Gus spots a Coast Guard boat and tries to outrun it. Johnny breaks the boat's thrusters and Vokolovsky tries to shoot Johnny but is shot by the Coast Guard. Gus is also shot, and Johnny tells the Coast Guard about the cargo.

"By the time the courts, yeah maybe Uncle Sam himself, gets through with these lads (Vokolovsky, Gus and Tony), come to think of it, who knows, maybe the company will end up owning a real nice tuna clipper. So, expense account total, including all the extras I could think of, call it $900 even. And if you're wondering about Lee Chin, sure I'll give him that extra $100 — I may need him again some time. And he's really handy as long as I am wise to him. Yours Truly, Johnny Dollar."

Notes:

- Most catalogs list this program as *The Tuna Clipper Matter*, but the title on the script is *The Wayward Clipper Matter*.

- There are two endings for this story as noted above.
- Story details from the Pacific Pioneer Broadcasters collection at the Thousand Oaks Library.

Producer: Fred Hendrickson Writer: Jack Johnstone
Cast: Unknown

◆ ❖ ◆

Show: **The All Too Easy Matter**
Show Date: 6/17/1962
Company: Western Indemnity Company
Agent: Ted Orloff
Exp. Acct: $491.34

Synopsis: Ted Orloff calls Johnny, and he has a problem with fires. Ted is sure that the fires are arson, but someone has to prove he is right. "Can you make it?".

Johnny flies to Los Angeles, California and arrives at noon. Johnny cabs to Ted's office and runs into him at the front door. They jump into Ted's car and rush to the scene of another fire, the sixth. The building is old and uninhabited, and Ted is sure that the fire bug will set fifteen more fires before he is finished. Ted has contacted the arson squad and they agree the fires were arson, but they refuse to grab the guy who is doing it. Ted tells Johnny that he knows who the arsonist is just as the walls of the building collapse.

Over a drink, Ted tells Johnny about Alpheus Brockway Broxton, a widower 82-years old who the doctor says has a heart condition and will only live a few more years. But he does not look like he is sick. He is a playboy in spades but has had to slow down after his last wife died. He is now living a simple life and his step-daughter has married and is the beneficiary of his estate.

Broxton is not rolling in money, but he does have a lot of property in the poorer sections of LA. The taxes are getting higher and higher each year and Broxton still has insurance on the properties. So now he is burning down the properties and collecting the insurance from Ted. Johnny wonders that the answer is too obvious, too easy.

In the office, Johnny gets a list of the unburned properties and Broxton's address. Ted reminds Johnny about the phrase "cui bono", and Ted cannot think of anyone else who would benefit. The police feel that the arsonist is someone other than poor little Mr. Broxton.

Johnny wonders about Broxton's age, and Ted suggests that he might have hired a professional, so Johnny decides to assist Ted with the case. Ted gets a call from Fred Klein, the Fire Commissioner who tells Ted that there is another fire. When Ted tells him that he has hired Johnny, Fred talks to Johnny and they agree to meet.

Johnny rents a car and drives to see Fred Klein. Fred tells Johnny that he is not upset at Ted's feelings about the department, because most people turn around when they get results. Fred tells Johnny that they originally thought Ted was right until they looked into the fires. Fred tells Johnny that he should talk to Broxton, and he will agree that a man with a heart condition could not set the fires.

Also, a pro did not set the fires because they do not follow a pattern, and pros always follow a pattern. The department has a file on all the pros, and Fred is convinced that an amateur is setting the fires because there is a different method used on each fire. Fred tells Johnny to talk to Broxton, and then they will compare notes. Fred tells Johnny that he has only eleven men, and Johnny can spend more time on a fire than any of his men can.

Johnny drives to Mr. Broxton's, and Johnny is sure he did not set the fire, and the excitement would kill him. Broxton was content with his life and not interested in making more money to give to his stepdaughter who had assured Broxton they were doing fine. As Johnny drives away convinced that Broxton is innocent, he thinks about his own phrase "cui bono" and the insurance policy. Johnny decides to follow up on the policy angle.

Johnny calls Broxton and asks for an address. Johnny buys an imitation leather portfolio with gold lettering on it that says "Federal Housing and Occupation Survey".

Johnny drives to Sherman Oaks and a poorly kept house. While Johnny paces the room, the woman tells Johnny that she is Lois Claytor and her husband is Ben. Lois tells Johnny that she is a typist for Aerojet and her husband is in the import business and has an office in the back room. Ben left for Mexico the previous day on business. She describes the equipment Ben imports and shows Johnny a brochure.

Johnny starts to inspect the office, but it is locked. Johnny questions that the house belongs to a successful businessman, especially when he spots a repossession notice for the television.

After a cursory inspection of the house Johnny leaves and makes two phone calls. One is to a company in East Los Angeles, one of the companies that Ben sells to. They tell Johnny that Ben has only been a pain to them, what with his phony deals in Mexico. The other is a call to an air conditioner company yields the same results.

Johnny visits the state employment office and learns that Claytor has had a dozen jobs in the past five years and stayed on each long enough to get fired and collect unemployment and some disability insurance. Tie that in to the fact Broxton did not have long to live and it all adds up.

Johnny calls Fred Klein and updates him and goes back to the house where he tells Lois that he did not finish the survey the last time and tells her he will have to break into the office.

In the room, Johnny finds long strips of paraffin tape, candles, cans of solvent, gasoline, even a couple of crude timing devices made to set off a blaze. He'd been right. Ben Claytor was behind the fires to add every possible dollar to the old man's bank account before he died and left it to Lois. And there was all the evidence he could need.

Suddenly Ben is there with a gun and tells Johnny not to move. Lois takes Johnny's gun as Ben tells Johnny he made a mistake by giving Lois his real name. Ben was going to clean out the room, but now he has no choice but to kill Johnny.

Lois tells Ben she put up with the fires but she will not let him kill Johnny. Ben tries to take the gun from Lois and Johnny slugs Ben just as Fred Klein comes in. Johnny tells him that Ben and Lois Clayton are done playing with fire.

"Not a very pretty one, I know. And I hope the shock of it all isn't too much for poor old Mr. Broxton. Expense account total, including the trip home, $491.34."

"Next week, two good men, two beautiful girls and one not so beautiful motive for murder."

Notes:
- The title on this script is *The All Too Easy Matter* (or *The Too Much Arson Around Matter*).
- This program contains commercials for No-Doz, Newport cigarettes, and Sinclair gasoline.
- Musical supervision is by Ethel Huber.
- The announcer is Art Hannes.
- The cast credits have been edited from this program.

Producer:	Fred Hendrickson	Writer: Jack Johnstone
Cast:	Unknown	

◆ ❖ ◆

Show:	**The Hood of Death Matter**
Show Date:	**6/24/1962**
Company:	**Four State Insurance Company**
Agent:	**Luther Pennyroyal**
Exp. Acct:	**$200.00**

Synopsis: Ol' cousin Luther Pennyroyal in Nashville calls Johnny, and Luther has a problem with Henry Sweetwater and his accident policy. Luther thinks that the accident he had was on purpose, and Mr. Sweetwater is trying to take them. Johnny is on his way.

Johnny flies to Nashville, Tennessee and the plane passes over the tower of station WLAC. Johnny cabs into the Andrew Jackson Hotel, and then cabs to Luther's office.

Lou tells Johnny that the client is an old crook by the name of Henry Sweetwater who made a lot of money with a lot of snide property deals. Lou tells Johnny that he should not have written the policy because of the special clauses in it. Henry claims a car hit him and Doc Caroway has looked at him and does not think the claim is legitimate either.

Lou and Johnny drive to the town of Laverne, where Henry lives with a pretty young wife Billy Mae. Lou thinks Billy married Henry for his money. Lou tells Johnny that he could have married Billy Mae if she did not say she loved Henry. When Lou's car starts making noise he pulls over and Johnny pulls a bomb from the engine compartment just before it explodes.

Lou is shaken up, and tells Johnny that he is sure Henry found out Lou is investigating. Lou tells Johnny that Henry says he laid on the road until Billy Mae came back from shopping in Nashville. Henry is claiming shock and disability and everything else on top of the broken arm. Lou tells Johnny that Dr. Caroway knew Henry and used to be an osteopath. When Henry told Lou that he never heard the car coming, Lou was sure that he was faking it.

Johnny and Lou look at Henry's house from the road and notice smoke coming from the chimney. Just as Lou tells Johnny that Henry always has a fire going, the house explodes. Johnny describes the explosion and sees Henry tottering out of the door and collapse.

Johnny rushes to him and Doc Caroway arrives and Henry is put to bed. Johnny inspects the house and finds evidence of dynamite in the fireplace. Lou is sure that Henry staged the blast. Johnny is sure that someone is out to get Henry.

Doc Caroway tells Johnny that he has given Henry a mild sedative, on account of his heart condition. Johnny notes that Henry had been locked inside the house, as he had checked the locks. Doc tells Johnny that only Billy Mae and Patty have keys to the door but Henry usually kept the doors open hoping folks would come over and keep him company.

When Lou suggests that Henry himself threw the dynamite in the fire, Johnny thinks maybe he did. Johnny muses about an old trick used by the forty-niners, and goes to inspect the woodpile where he finds a number of logs filled with dynamite, but who did it?

Billy Mae arrives and she was the first suspect until Johnny sees the way she tends for her husband. She tells Johnny that she has called her sister because Patty has done nursing work. She tells Johnny that she is glad that Henry and Doc Caroway have let bygones be bygones but does not explain. Billy asks Johnny if he can stay around for a while after Patty gets there.

Patty arrives and is cool and calculating in the way she cares for Henry. Patty tells Johnny that she would not weep if Henry died, but that will not keep her from caring for him. Patty tells Johnny that Henry thinks Patty ran him down because he thinks she would do anything to get his money and be free to marry Lou Pennyroyal. They would have gotten married if they had any money, and Lou wants to go back to college and study botany. When Johnny mentions motive, Patty gets defensive. Patty tells Johnny that Doc felt Henry had cheated him once, and he probably did.

Johnny borrows Patty's car and drives back to Nashville. Johnny drives to Lou's apartment, slips the lock and searches it, and finds nothing other than a plant that was all too familiar. Johnny finds a Dr. Bradley who is willing to drive back to Laverne with him. Johnny explains the situation and the possible effects on Henry's heart.

When they arrive, Johnny spots Lou and Doc Caroway's cars. Patty tells Johnny that Henry has had a heart attack. Johnny runs upstairs and tells Dr. Bradley that if he has an antidote for aconite poisoning to use it. Dr. Bradley asks if he means aconitum napellus, the monks hood plant and should have recognized the symptoms.

Downstairs, Johnny tells Billy that Henry will recover. Billy relates that Patty went to her room after the police came and picked up Lou. Billy asks how Johnny knew, and he tells her that he had found the monkshood plant in Lou's room, and when Henry had all the right symptoms it turned out to be aconite poisoning. Johnny tells her that he had put the bomb in his own car and had called Johnny in to cover for him. Now he will have plenty of time to think it over.

"So, here's another one for the courts. I hope they throw the book at Lou. A crooked insurance man is the lowest order of operator in this racket of mine. Thank goodness, they come few and far between. Expense account total, including incidentals, let's make it $200 even."

"Next week, a story based on the impossible that is scientific fact."

Notes:
- This program contains commercials for No-Doz, Kent cigarettes, and Sinclair gasoline.
- After this program there is a commercial for Cartwright Ford in Troy, New York, a weather forecast and a WROW station identification.
- Musical supervision is by Ethel Huber.
- The announcer is Art Hannes.
- Monkshood (Aconitum napellus) is described as one of the most poisonous plants of European flora. Pliny describes it as "plant arsenic". Alkaloids are responsible for its poisonous effect. The main alkaloid is aconitine, which acts as a stimulant that paralyzes the nervous system.

Producer: Fred Hendrickson   Writer: Jack Johnstone
Cast: Herb Duncan, Bill Adams, Madeline Sherwood, Vicki Vola, Jackson Beck

◆ ❖ ◆

Show: **The Vociferous Dolphin Matter**
Show Date: **7/1/1962**
Company: **Trinity Mutual Insurance Company**
Agent: **Will Burnett**
Exp. Acct: **$531.80**

Synopsis: A very perky voice asks if Johnny has been out to sunny southern California lately. Will Burnett needs Johnny's help because of a couple of fish, two mammals Petey and Sue, who are dolphins. Johnny asks if Will has issued a life insurance policy on a couple of dolphins, and Will tells him that an important client wants a policy issued. Will is in favor of it, but the whole fishy deal needs looking into. Johnny thinks Will is nuts. "Dolphins? Well if you are willing to pay the freight, OK. I'll see you sometime tomorrow."

Johnny flies to Los Angeles and Will meets Johnny in the airport with a rental car. Will has a client waiting and cannot go with Johnny to Shelter Point, just north of San Diego. Professor Doctor Yuriantha Euridisee Eswell has her private oceanarium there. She is an eccentric, a non-conformist, an oddball, who once held down chairs of zoology and ichthyology at two important colleges and is an important client. This policy is important if the dolphins can do what she thinks they can, which is un-curl that lip based on scientific knowledge.

Johnny drives south and runs into a coastal fog. Just as Johnny reaches Shelter Point a bullet whizzes past his head. Johnny eases towards the marksman in the fog and finds a woman holding the rifle.

Johnny tells her who he is, and she is Penelope Wyman, and tells Johnny that she was aiming at some sharks and the bullet must have ricocheted. She asks Johnny if he came here because he was worried about Aunt Yuri too? She tells Johnny that he should be worried.

Penny tells Johnny that she was going swimming but saw a lot of sharks around the pier. She admits that she had the rifle there because of the experiments Aunt Yuri does with the dolphins. Her Aunt is using her money to prove that the dolphins can talk. Penny thinks that someone is trying to stop her and that there have been a number of near accidents lately. She still insists on doing everything herself in spite of the fact she could afford help. She works all alone except for Penny and Carl Petermill, who handles the recording equipment and was Penny's fiancé.

Aunt Yuri comes in with Carl and tells Johnny she is making progress. She tells Johnny that she wants insurance on her children Petey and Sue. Johnny goes to the large tank and watches the dolphins put on a great show while Carl fools with some electronic equipment. Yuri tells Johnny that they are her children and are completely obedient. Yuri is going to demonstrate that they can talk.

Carl holds a mike while Sue is called to the edge of the pool. Yuri tells her to talk to her, and the dolphin emits a series of high-pitched squeals. Yuri tells Johnny that the tape recorders record the sounds made by the dolphins, at ultra-high speed, sounds that the human ear cannot hear properly. Carl puts the tape on another machine that plays the tape back at a lower speed that makes it understandable. Carl plays the tape and Yuri hears a garbled "mother", but Johnny hears a much different word, "murder".

As soon as Johnny questions the words, he is ordered to leave. As he drives past the house, Penny tells Johnny she is going shopping, and Johnny offers to take Penny to dinner at the El Cortez.

Johnny phones Will with an update, gets a room and waits for Penny. During dinner Penny tells Johnny that she should not have left her aunt alone. She tells Johnny that she broke off the engagement with Carl because of his lack of formal education and his past working as a barker for a freak show, which is what he hopes to do again.

Penny tells Johnny that she will get her aunt's money when she dies, except for the dolphins, which go to Carl. Johnny and Penny do the night club thing, and he sends her home at 4 a.m. An hour later Penny calls to tell Johnny that Aunt Yuri is dead.

Johnny rushes to Shelter Point to find Penny waiting for him at the cut off. She tells Johnny that Carl had been off for the night, and she takes Johnny to the tank where Johnny finds the body floating in the tank, with the dolphins protecting her.

Carl runs up and accuses Penny of hitting Yuri on the head and pushing her into the pool to get the money. He tells Johnny that he can prove it with the dolphins that can talk and will tell him who killed Yuri.

Carl rigs up a tape and asks one of the dolphins "who killed Yuri". The voice on the tape says, "Me see murder. Me see Penelope kill." Johnny sends Carl to La Jolla to get the police, and he leaves.

Johnny has been thinking about a man that knows every electronic trick, Bob McKenny an engineer with CBS. Johnny takes the tape and Penny to see Bob at his home.

Bob experiments for hours and eventually gets the tape to play at its original speed, and the tape plays the voice of Carl faking the voice of the dolphins. Penny tells Johnny that Carl was going to get the aquarium and the dolphins, and Johnny is sure that he was afraid that Yuri would find out about the electronic tricks, so he killed her to preserve his sideshow and the life he wanted. "But instead, he has booked himself a one-night stand, and its blackout is permanent."

"Thanks to Carl, the police and he were still there at Shelter Point waiting for us. Expense account total, including hotel and the trip home, $531.80."

"Next week, the calm blue beautiful waters of the Pacific almost hide the work of a team of killers."

Notes:
- This program contains commercials for No-Doz, for Kent cigarettes, and for Sinclair gasoline.
- Bob McKenny was also in two other programs: *The Missing Missile Matter* and *The Wayward Kilocycles Matter.*
- Musical supervision is by Ethel Huber.
- The announcer is Art Hannes.

Producer:	Fred Hendrickson Writer: Jack Johnstone
Cast:	Larry Robinson, Ethel Everett, Joan Lazer, Bill Lipton, Ben Yafee

◆ ❖ ◆

Show:	**The Rilldo Matter**
Show Date:	7/8/1962
Company:	**Trinity Mutual Insurance Company**
Agent:	**Will Burnett**
Exp. Acct:	**$250.00**

Synopsis: Will Burnett calls Johnny and is glad that he is still there in San Diego. Will tells Johnny that he cannot leave until he gets a sample of the famous fishing there in San Diego, California. Ted Pflueger knows more about fishing the coast than anyone else, so when he heard that Johnny was here, he called Will who arranged for Johnny to go fishing with Ted. "You fixed me up on the expense account? Just fishing?" Johnny asks. Oh, there is one thing Johnny can ask Ted about, Bernard W. Bessom, who is an appliance dealer and a client. Johnny is to ask Ted about Bessom. Ask him if he thinks Bessom is still alive.

Johnny buys gas and drives to Ted Pflueger's place on Emerald Bay. Pflueger is a gruff individual with a heart of gold. They load up Johnny's car with tackle and drive north to Balboa harbor. Johnny is sure he is getting a runaround as he talks to Ted about fishing.

In Lonestar Beach, Ted points to a large building, Bessom and Associates, the big appliance house. At a red light, Johnny points out a gorgeous doll sitting in a convertible outside of the Bessom building. Johnny describes it as the face you see on every beautiful girl from the neck up. The girl asks Johnny what time it is, and Johnny gives the time as 2:50. When Johnny asks if there is anything else she wants, she tells Johnny that he needs to know something: the light has changed! Johnny tells Ted that a girl that pretty should be involved in every one of his cases.

Ted tells Johnny that Bernie Bessom is a real fine fellow, but his partners, Tony and Joe Rilldo are sharpies. They made their money running liquor during prohibition. Ted is sure that they would do anything to get Bernie's part of the business away from him. Ted called Bernie this morning to come fishing and he has not been able to reach him at home or the office. Nor did he show for a poker game last night. But Ted wants to go fishing even though he is afraid of what else might be out there.

Johnny and Ted arrive in Balboa and prepare to take off in Ted's 21-foot boat that is full of tackle. After a final tackle box is hefted aboard, the deckhand Manuel is surprised that Ted is going out after coming in so late last night. Ted tells Johnny to wait until the tide goes out, and he will see what is going on.

Johnny and Ted fish off the lee side of San Clemente Island until dusk when Ted starts back. Ted has been waiting for the tide to go all the way down. He tells Johnny that last night he saw a boat drifting, and what the people were doing. He is sure that the boat was the Rilldo brother's and that Bernie was with them.

Johnny rigs up a set of small grappling hooks on a heavy line, and at a large bed of kelp they start to drag around the kelp bed. Ted searches the water as they search for a body. Finally, they snag something and bring up a piece of Bernie's jacket.

Johnny strips to his shorts and dives in to recover the badly beaten lead-weighted body of Bernie Bessom. The body is brought on board, and Ted tells Johnny that he knew the boat belonged to the Rilldo brothers, and he saw what they were throwing overboard. Johnny is sure that the Rilldo brothers will deny everything.

A large boat approaches with its spotlight on Ted's boat. Johnny reaches for a .22 Ted keeps on the boat as the larger craft slowly bears down on them. Johnny and Ted are sitting ducks as the boat approaches.

The boat slows and the girl Johnny had seen earlier calls to them, but the boat does not belong to the Rilldos. She is Molly Boyle and had seen their lights. She asks if they have any spare gas and Ted throws her a line. Johnny goes on board and offers to pour the gas as he introduces himself.

She in turn introduces her boyfriends, Tony and Joe Rilldo. Tony tells Johnny to drop his gun and Molly tells Joe it would be easy since she used her own boat. Tony tells Ted he will be in trouble if he meddles with him. They do not know anything about Bessom, but Ted tells them what they have done.

Tony tells Johnny that he does not have a case on him but will when he shoots Ted for meddling. As the seas pick up and the boat starts to rock, Tony starts to shoot Ted. Ted pulls Joe overboard and Johnny goes after Tony and the gun. Johnny pulls Ted back on board and they pull a waterlogged Joe onto the boat.

Johnny gets another gun from Molly, who tries to tell Johnny that she had nothing to do with the Rilldos, as she is a nice girl. She tells Johnny that she can be good to Johnny and that he has to help her.

"Well, it's up to the authorities now. And I don't really think they will have any trouble putting those three where they belong. The real reward for all that? A couple of days of really great fishing, thanks to Ted Pflueger. Expense account total, with only the fare back to Hartford, call it $250 even."

"Next week, a case I call the weather or not matter."

Notes:
- This program contains commercials for No-Doz, for Kent cigarettes, and for Sinclair gasoline.
- Musical supervision is by Ethel Huber.
- The announcer is Art Hannes.

Producer: Fred Hendrickson   Writer: Jack Johnstone
Cast: John Gibson, Hetty Galen, Larry Robinson, Marty Green, Ralph Camargo, Marty Myers

♦ ❖ ♦

Show: The Weather or Not Matter
Show Date: 7/15/1962
Company: Tri-State Life & Casualty Insurance Company
Agent: Earle Poorman
Exp. Acct: $247.92

Synopsis: Earle Poorman calls and Johnny asks how things are in Los Angeles. Earle tells Johnny he is back in Sarasota, but they are thinking about moving back to California. Earle asks Johnny to come down and investigate a murder that has not happened yet, but if Earle can read the signs, there is one in the making.

Johnny flies to Sarasota, Florida, rents a car and drives to the office Earle shares with Don Boomhauer. Over a lunch of shrimp cooked in beer at the Plaza Hotel, Earle tells Johnny about the case.

The client is T. Rockway Mayfield, a crazy character who made a pile of money in New England. He retired here and spends his time sunning himself with a jug beside him, shooting at sea gulls with an air pistol and never hitting them. He also throws large parties with lots of pretty girls.

He told Earle he came here to get away from his stepchildren Betty and

Frank Merriton. He had been supporting the kids while his wife was alive but when she died, he left them flat until he dies. Tomorrow is Mayfield's birthday, and the kids are coming. Earle thinks they are coming to murder him. On the drive to Mayfield's home Earle tells Johnny to keep an eye on Mayfield. And, Earle might even take Johnny fishing afterwards.

Earle drives up to a huge mansion that is guarded by a high wall. The house is concrete and stucco with aluminum and glass surrounded by a large patio complete with a bar and bartender. Johnny is introduced and Mayfield makes a bad joke about dollars and cents.

Mayfield has been listening to Johnny on the radio for years and orders the bartender to bring Johnny a scotch and soda, a gin and tonic for Earl, and a cognac with root beer and a piece of mint for himself. Mayfield invites Earle and Johnny to his party the next day. Mayfield tells Johnny that the girls always come to get at his money, but they won't succeed until he dies. Mayfield tells Johnny that his stepchildren are arriving the next day and Johnny volunteers to pick them up.

Mayfield shows Johnny his pride and joy — a complete weather station with all the necessary tools. Mayfield tells Johnny he cannot plan a party if he does not know what the weather will be. Mayfield asks Johnny how good a shot he is, and for an hour Johnny and Mayfield feed the birds and shoot at them with an air pistol. Mayfield dismisses Earle and Johnny and goes to make his weather report for the party.

Johnny gets his rental car and goes to talk to an old friend, Sgt. Phil Phillips at police headquarters. Phillips tells Johnny if the kids are what Mayfield describes, he needs protection while they are here. Phillips tells Johnny that Mayfield has told the police not to show up. If they do he will throw them out, stop the party and get the people down on them. Johnny tells Phillips to keep a prowl car near the wall, just in case. Johnny is concerned that the case seems like a waste of time, yet…yeah.

The next day Johnny kills time by hitting some golf balls, going to the Jungle Garden, the Ringling Circus Museum and stopping in at station WSPB to talk to the boys.

Johnny picks up Betty and Frank. Betty is beautiful with a head on her shoulders. Frank is a weak, wishy-washy, well-spoken nothing, with a capitol "N" who tells Betty that it is ridiculous for Mayfield to make him sweat and toil when he has all that money that he does not know what to do with.

Betty tells Frank that daddy will be furious when he finds out Frank does not have a job and is chiseling off his friends. He is sure that daddy will give him money and has a sob story that would melt the heart of a statue, so do not interfere. Betty tells Johnny that she loves parties and asks Johnny to dance with her now and then. At the house, Mayfield takes the kids into the library and Johnny goes swimming until dinner.

At the party there is a bevy of pretty girls, and Johnny dances with Betty and makes plans to meet her back up north. Around 11:00 the lights go out and Mayfield tells Johnny that it is a gag and that he has a timer on the lights.

Johnny goes to look for the switch box with Betty just as the lights go out again and there are three shots from near the weather station. The lights go on again and Johnny and Mayfield discover that Frank is dead from a couple of .38s in the chest. Sgt. Phillips and his men scale the wall and do a complete investigation but cannot find the gun.

Johnny has a hunch and kicks himself for not having wised up before. It was Mayfield who had been telling everyone about the kids. And that crazy drink yesterday that Johnny had noticed did not have a drop of liquor in it, and probably the same thing tonight. So, Mayfield is sober as a judge.

And the gun, the answer is in the weather station, which had a weather balloon large enough to carry a gun out over the Gulf of Mexico, never to be seen again.

Johnny tells Mayfield to come with the police to get a paraffin test of his shooting hand, and he admits that he killed Frank. Sgt. Phillips has to admit that using a weather balloon was really clever. "Was it?" Johnny asks.

"So, the Mayfield fortune will go to Betty, and I can't think of a more deserving girl, or come to think of it, a prettier one. Expense account total, including the trip back to Hartford, $247.92."

"Next week, a complex and unusual story with a twist that will surprise you, I think as much as it surprised me."

Notes:
- This program contains commercials for Pepsi, No-Doz, Kent cigarettes and Sinclair gasoline.
- Musical supervision is by Ethel Huber.
- The announcer is Art Hannes.

Producer: Fred Hendrickson   Writer: Jack Johnstone
Cast: Ian Martin, Bill Kramer, Joe Hardy, Ivor Francis, Constance Simons, Karen McCrary

♦ ❖ ♦

Show: The Skimpy Matter
Show Date: 7/22/1962
Company: Mono Guarantee Insurance Company
Agent: Danny Nixon
Exp. Acct: $10.80

Synopsis: Danny Nixon calls Johnny and asks if he remembers Amos Crutchfield. Johnny remembers that he is the former city attorney who retired in a blaze of glory after he clamped a lid on the policy rackets. Danny tells Johnny that Amos also had Skimpy Dingle sent up four years ago, and Johnny remembers him. The parole board has released Skimpy for good behavior, and Danny reminds Johnny of the threats Skimpy made to Johnny and Crutchfield. Crutchfield is sure Skimpy was serious, and Danny agrees with him. Danny also has a new policy on Crutchfield's life for $75,000.

Johnny buys gas and drives to the Hartford, Connecticut Parole Office where a very cute parole officer tells Johnny that Skimpy has not reported in yet, and they have no address for him. Johnny is told that Skimpy's brother, Percy Dingle, is the one who convinced the parole board to release Skimpy. Percy is a psychologist who has kept Skimpy out of jail a number of times and can be very convincing.

Johnny gets Percy's address and leaves. Johnny goes to see Crutchfield and notices a new compact car out front. Johnny realizes he should have taken a better look at it as he rings the doorbell and hears shots ring out inside. Johnny breaks in the door to find Crutchfield on the floor.

Crutchfield is still alive and Johnny notices how the assailant had come in and left through an open window. Johnny puts Crutchfield on the couch and hears a car pull away. Johnny calls for a doctor and the police.

Doctor Franklin Edwards arrives and patches Crutchfield up, noting that one bullet came very close to his heart. Johnny tells the doctor to stay until the police arrive and he leaves. As Johnny drives back to Hartford, a car driven by Skimpy hits him. Skimpy gets out and shoots at Johnny four times, but only one bullet grazes his arm.

Johnny drives home to fix his arm and is about to make a call when Percival Dingle knocks at the door. Johnny drags him in with his gun drawn, and Percy tells Johnny that Skimpy was right, Johnny is a killer. Percy tells Johnny that he wants to talk rationally, so Johnny sits down and holsters his gun.

Percy tries to convince Johnny that he needs to have some sympathy for Peter. Percy tells Johnny that Peter has been in trouble because of a lack of education and guidance, but Peter had rebelled against authority. Peter feels that Johnny and Crutchfield have been persecuting him and are the only ones who can help him.

Percy tells Johnny that he knows Peters mind and that the last incarceration was a fulcrum that provided the lever to convince Peter of the error of his ways. His release from prison is proof that Peter has reformed. Percy tells Johnny that he can provide help to Peter.

Percy feels that Crutchfield is a doddering old fool who only convinced the judge to give Peter an unjust sentence. Johnny tells Percy that the judge should have given Skimpy thirty years. Johnny tells Percy he is full of impractical theories, and Johnny has seen more of Skimpy's kind than Percy ever will.

The more he thinks about it, the more he is convinced that Skimpy is rotten all the way through, and that Skimpy got out because of Percy's smart pitch to the parole board, and that Percy is all wrong. Percy is sure that they can work things out. Johnny tells him that it is a plot to get Johnny close to Skimpy, so he can shoot Johnny the way he shot Crutchfield.

Percy is shocked that Peter has tried to kill a man so Johnny shows Percy the wound on his arm. Percy is sure that Peter has to see that Johnny is on his side. Percy knows where Peter is and will let Johnny see him, if he agrees to talk to him. Johnny agrees to go see him only to turn him over to the police. Percy tells Johnny that he will go to Peter and tell him that Johnny will talk to him, and if the reaction is proper, Percy will call Johnny.

Johnny takes a nap and orders some food from a nearby restaurant. The phone rings, and Percy arranges for Johnny to meet Peter in room 4 in a rooming house at 1217 North Chalma and thanks Johnny. Johnny drives to the decrepit old boarding house and sees Skimpy pacing thoughtfully in the room. Johnny goes in and knocks. Skimpy opens the door and Johnny kicks it in.

Skimpy tells Johnny to put his gun away, as his brother has convinced him to talk to Johnny. He admits he was wrong about trying to kill Johnny and hopes Mr. Crutchfield will be OK. He could not believe Johnny would help him. Johnny tells him he is there to take him to the police, and that his brother is living in a dream.

Peter agrees that his brother was stupid, stupid enough to get Johnny here where he cannot miss. Skimpy pulls a gun and shoots once and misses but Johnny fires and hits him. As Johnny reaches for Skimpy's gun on the floor, Skimpy pulls another one and tells Johnny it is aimed at the back of his head.

There is a shot and footsteps as Percy comes in and Johnny tells him he had seen him outside and hoped that Percy would pull the trigger when he saw what Peter was doing. When Percy asks if he killed Peter, Johnny tells him that, "just like your brother, you are a pretty lousy shot."

"Skimpy, and without his brother's support anymore, he will be lucky if he ever gets out of the pen. Percy? Well I hope he never forgets his lesson in practical psychology. Expense account total — $10.80?"

"Next week, a very bad case of not knowing enough about your friends."

Notes:
- This program contains commercials for No-Doz, Newport cigarettes, and for Sinclair gasoline.
- Walter Otto does the sound patterns.
- Michael Schoskis does the technical direction.
- Stuart Metz is the announcer.
- Musical supervision is by Ethel Huber.
- Johnny is shot for the 13th time.

Producer:	Fred Hendrickson Writer: Jack Johnstone
Cast:	Rosemary Rice, Larry Haines, Jack Arthur, Melville Ruick, William Redfield

◆ ❖ ◆

Show:	The Four's a Crowd Matter
Show Date:	7/29/1962
Company:	Star Mutual Insurance Company
Agent:	Dennis Taylor
Exp. Acct:	$400.00

Synopsis: Dennis Taylor calls Johnny from Colorado Springs. An important client, Melvin Lockerty is spending the summer at a nearby guest ranch. Lockerty is having guests for the week, but he believes that one of his guests is going to try to murder him. Johnny is on his way.

Johnny flies to Denver, Colorado the home of station KLZ, and takes a ferry plane to Colorado Springs where Dennis Taylor meets Johnny and loans him his car while Johnny is in town. Dennis tells Johnny that one of the relatives coming to see Lockerty is going to kill him.

The visitors are the children of Lockerty's brother Henry, so Johnny better get to the "No Name Ranch" as quickly as possible. Dennis tells Johnny that Lockerty had hornswoggled his brother out of some mining property just as the properties were beginning to pay off. Dennis is sure that Lockerty is a crook and was the cause of his brother killing himself. Dennis boils the case down to dollars and cents and does not care what happens to Lockerty.

Johnny describes the ranch and his room, which has a view of Pikes Peak. Lockerty visits Johnny and does not want the relatives to know why Johnny is there. He invited them to the ranch to try and make peace with them. Johnny is told that Henry made a promise to him to get even with Lockerty for the stolen money. Lockerty tells Johnny that he has been getting letters threatening his life.

Johnny is surprised that any of the guests he sees could kill anyone. Johnny watches the relatives unload their car. The driver is about 26, tall blond and beautiful. Another, a couple years younger is a brunette, a real doll with a mischievous sparkle in her eye. The third is a very naturally beautiful girl, in spite of the horn-rimmed glasses, plain dress and hair tied in a bun.

Johnny goes out and Kitty Lockerty introduces herself, thinking that Johnny is the manager. Teckla and Marion Lockerty introduce themselves to Johnny, who takes their bags to their cabins and then watches as the girls go to see Lockerty. Johnny hears a lot of yelling and then the girls leave without speaking to each other.

Later Lockerty tells Johnny that he told them that he knew that one of them was going to kill him because Harry made one of his daughters promise to kill him. Lockerty tells Johnny that Teckla is all concerned with herself and Katherine, Kitty, is a hot-tempered little lynx, while Marion is quiet and smart, but remember that still waters run deep. Johnny arranges for the girls to go to a barn dance that night and Lockerty tells Johnny he will be sleeping with a gun.

Johnny sashays to the barn dance and manages to take each of the girls outside for a quiet walk.

Teckla tells Johnny that Lockerty has a silly notion that they are going to kill him. She tells Johnny about her father and that she would kill Lockerty if her father had asked her to. Johnny agrees to meet her later and seals the deal with a kiss.

Johnny then talks to Kitty who tells him that she wishes someone would kill Melvin. Kitty is really chilly and wants Johnny to warm her up, just as Marion calls for Johnny.

Marion has a walk with Johnny and tells him that she knows who Johnny is, and that he is there to protect Uncle Melvin. She tells Johnny that they came up to the ranch to humor Lockerty. Besides, would a secretary like Kitty or a softy like Teckla or herself, an old-maid schoolteacher, kill Uncle Melvin?

After the dance, Kitty and Teckla go to town with some boys and Marion goes to her cabin. Johnny visits Lockerty, who is going to stay up all night reading. Johnny agrees to stay until the girls are back when a shot comes through the window and kills Lockerty.

Everyone at the ranch rushes to Lockerty's cabin, Kitty and Teckla show up with their boyfriends and Marion shows up in her bathrobe. Johnny asks Kitty and Teckla why they got there so quickly, and Kitty tells him that they and their boyfriends had gone to town for a beer and were just coming back, and Pete Mackenzie tells Johnny she is right.

Kitty tells Johnny that she saw Marion's light go on just as they were driving up. Marion tells Johnny that she could not sleep and was going to make some cocoa and read when she heard the shot. Johnny wonders who else could have a motive, as everyone seems to have an alibi.

Johnny makes a call to Colorado Springs and the only other man who would want Lockerty dead, but Dennis Taylor is at home. The sheriff arrives and convinces Johnny that if the murder weapon were in a murky pond, there would be no fingerprints if it were ever found.

Johnny gets a hunch and is sure that since one of the girls recognized him, she would also need and airtight alibi. Johnny remembers that she had told Johnny why the others had come and had tried to defend them, but she was in her cabin when it happened and had just turned on her light.

Johnny remembers about the timing devices people use to turn on their lights and buys one. That night Johnny sits on the porch and talks to the girls and asks them to look at the clock and then to look at his cabin. Johnny asks them to tell him exactly what time he gets to his cabin and turns on the lights.

Johnny leaves and later the girls see his lights go on and look at the clock. Johnny comes from around the corner and tells them that he had used an automatic switch, the same way Marion did to turn on his lights. Marion tells Johnny that Lockerty did not deserve to live, but Johnny tells her that nobody deserves to be murdered.

"Expense account total, including the trip home, call it $400 even."

"Next week, a case with a real switch to the finish."

Notes:
- The name of the dead brother seems to change from Henry to Harry halfway through the story.
- This program contains commercials for Newport cigarettes and Sinclair gasoline.
- Walter Otto does the sound patterns.
- Michael Schoskis does the technical direction.
- Musical supervision is by Ethel Huber.
- The announcer is Art Hannes.

Producer: Fred Hendrickson   Writer: Jack Johnstone

Cast:	Bill Smith, Constance Simons, Edgar Stehli, Freddy Chandler, Hetty Galen, Reynold Osborne

♦ ❖ ♦

Show:	**The Case of Trouble Matter**
Show Date:	8/5/1962
Company:	Mid-States Industrial Insurance Company
Agent:	Tom Bartley
Exp. Acct:	$256.10

Synopsis: Tom Bartley calls Johnny from Des Moines. The Case Paper Products Company is being blown off the maps. There have been fires and explosions in their warehouses, and they have cost Tom $125,000. If there are any more, or if the main plant is hit...Johnny agrees to fly out as soon as possible.

Johnny flies to Des Moines, Iowa and circles the tower of station KRNT. Johnny rents a car and goes to Tom Bartley's office where the secretary greets Johnny with a "Yes Mr. Case?". Johnny corrects her and is told that Tom has gone to Indianola where Tom wants Johnny to meet him. Johnny will know where to find Tom.

Johnny drives to Indianola and finds a thick pall of smoke that once was the Case Paper Products Company building. Tom finds Johnny and shows him the results of fire number three that will cost them $50-60 thousand. Tom is sure that the fire is arson, and so are the owners, Albert and Ed Case.

Tom tells Johnny that the fires have all started with an explosion, which makes Johnny sure that an arsonist with a pattern is at work. Tom takes Johnny to his home for drinks and dinner with his wife Millie.

As soon as Millie sees Johnny, she calls him "Ed", and Tom remarks that Johnny does look a little like Ed Case and Tom tells Johnny that Millie used to be a singer. Tom tells Johnny that Albert runs the business, and Ed only takes the profits, as he is the black sheep of the family. Albert Case is supposed to drop by after he returns from the site of the last fire.

Tom tells Johnny that business has not been good but disagrees that Albert would ever burn his own buildings. There is a call from Albert and he tells Tom that the fires were set, and he has proof. He tells them not to come over and the phone goes dead. Johnny, Millie and Tom rush to the home of Albert Case and spot him sitting at a desk and talking on the phone. Johnny breaks in the door and they find Albert dead, shot through the forehead.

Tom calls the police and Johnny searches the home. The police arrive and a young police officer asks if Johnny is related to Mr. Case. The policeman finds a bullet hole in the window and tells them to leave.

Johnny tells Tom that the bullet came from inside the house and was fired by someone Albert knew or let into the house, which is why the phone went dead. Tom tells Johnny that Albert was not married, and that Ed will inherit the business. Ed lives in Grinnell, just beyond Colfax, and both of the towns have warehouses in them.

Johnny gets his car and drives to Colfax. Johnny stops at a fire at a Case

Paper Products warehouse. Johnny stumbles over an old man sobbing over the loss of the warehouse. He had told Albert that it would happen as soon as the car came prowling around. The car was a big white Peratti convertible and Albert said he knew who was setting them. As soon as Johnny stands him up the man thinks that Johnny is the man and shoots at him. Johnny takes the man's gun and drives off.

Johnny visits the police in Grinnell and talks to Lt. Cal Golden who calls Johnny Mr. Case. Golden finally realizes that Johnny is not Ed, and Johnny tells Golden he thinks Ed Case is the firebug, and the man who killed Albert. Golden agrees to put out an APB and gives Johnny the address of Ed Case.

Johnny goes there but Ed is not home, so Johnny calls on the woman next door and she mistakes Johnny for Ed Case. The woman gives Johnny a description of a "blond hussy with green eyes and an olive complexion" from Des Moines that is always visiting Ed Case.

Johnny rushes off when he realizes that the description of a petite blond with green eyes matches the description of Millie Bartley. Johnny calls Tom and learns that Millie has gone out. She was talking to Bernice, with whom she used to dance, and left.

Johnny goes back to Ed's house, slips the backdoor lock and leaves the door open. Inside, Johnny is stopped by a gun in his back and a voice that tells Ed Case he is trying to stall over the $5,000 just before he slugs Johnny.

Johnny wakes up after nightfall when the all-too-familiar petite figure of a woman enters the house. She tells Eddie that it must have been Louie getting even because Eddie did not pay him for setting the last fire. She tells Eddie that she saw him kill Albert from outside the house. She tells Eddie that he had to kill Albert.

When Johnny calls her Millie, and turns on the light, she realizes that Johnny is not Ed and Johnny realizes that she is not Millie but Bernice. Eddie comes in and Bernice takes Johnny's gun. Ed tells them he heard everything.

Ed tries to think of a plan to kill both Johnny and Bernice. Ed takes Johnny's gun to shoot him when there is a knock at the door. Ed slaps Bernice and shoots her, giving Johnny the chance to hit Ed.

Millie is at the door, and Johnny tells her not to go into the room, as Ed has killed Bernice. Millie tells Johnny that she came alone to see if she could help Bernice, and Johnny tells her to call Tom and tell him what has happened.

"I guess it's pretty obvious what will happen to Ed Case. Now it's two murders against him. As for the insurance and the estate, Iowa Law will have to take care of that. Expense account total, including the trip home, $256.10."

"Next week, a story with a twist that will surprise you as much as it did me."

Notes:
- This program contains commercials for Newport cigarettes and Sinclair gasoline.
- Sound Patterns are by Walter Otto.
- Technical direction by Fred Cusick.

- The announcer is Stuart Metz.
- Musical supervision is by Ethel Huber.
- This story was done as *The Burning Carr Matter*, broadcast on 12/9/1956. The location and business and names are changed, but the plot is the same.
- Grinnell is due east of Des Moines.
- At the end of the program there is a promotion for Lowell Thomas, a WDNC station identification and a commercial for Stanback Cold remedy.

Producer: Fred Hendrickson   Writer: Jack Johnstone
Cast: John Seymour, Abby Lewis, Teri Keane, Edgar Stehli, Jack Grimes, Jim Stevens, Gilbert Mack

◆ ❖ ◆

Show: **The Oldest Gag Matter**
Show Date: **8/12/1962**
Company: **Star Mutual Insurance Company**
Agent: **Larry Spangler**
Exp. Acct: **$0.00**

Synopsis: Larry Spangler calls Johnny from Hartford, Connecticut. Larry has never met Johnny, as he has only been there a year. Larry asks if the name Briscum means anything, and Johnny replies that Lloyd Briscum runs some sort of factory out on the edge of town. Larry tells Johnny that Briscum is an important client and he would like Johnny to come with him to the factory. The business partner has called Larry and told him that Briscum is dead. His housekeeper found him a few minutes ago with a bullet in his head. Since Johnny's apartment is on the way, he will pick him up on the way to the Briscum house.

Johnny describes Larry as a new-age Madison Avenue insurance man with a gray suit, shined shoes and crisp haircut and eager to set the world on fire. Larry has a few ideas as to who killed Briscum but will wait to see what the police say.

John Barber, the business partner, supposedly called the police. Larry leaves all sorts of clues and hints about things that were supposed to have happened.

Larry tells Johnny that Trudy the ward is above suspicion, as Larry is a good friend of hers. Mike Briscum is the adopted son, who lived off of Briscum. Johnny remembers seeing Mike's name in the paper after a fight at a club. The beneficiaries of the insurance are Mike, who gets one third, and Trudy, who gets two thirds, and the business goes to Barber.

At the house, Sgt. Danny Gilbert, a "too sure" police officer, is in charge. Gilbert takes Johnny in to see the body with an old, battered .38 in the right hand. Johnny sees the powder burns and no sign of a struggle. Gilbert thinks it happened last night and is sure that Briscum committed suicide, but Johnny is not sure.

Gilbert tells Johnny that business had not been good, and Briscum has had Mike and Trudy living off of him. Johnny doubts suicide based on what Larry told him. The lab crew can find nothing to prove anything but suicide, but

Johnny is sure that Briscum had someone help him pull the trigger. Johnny asks Gilbert for the results of the autopsy and goes to talk to the family.

Trudy is sure that her father would not commit suicide. She moved away because Briscum was a tyrant and would not even allow her fiancé into the house. Trudy is not upset, and she confirms that with the money she will be free to do as she chooses, which could make her a suspect.

Mr. Barber is sure that Briscum did not commit suicide, and that he was not worried about the business. The business was not doing well because of his old-fashioned practices. Barber is free now to make the necessary profitable changes to the factory, which makes him a suspect.

Mike is not sorry about Briscum's death as he was not family, and he wished at times he could have helped him on his way to get the insurance money. Johnny tells Mike that there will be no money if it was suicide. Mike tells Johnny that killing himself was against what Briscum believed in. Mike can see anyone in the house killing Briscum and even suggests making a play for Trudy as they are not really related. But he could never get Trudy away from Larry Spangler.

After the body is removed Sgt. Gilbert lets the beneficiaries leave. As Barber leaves to go to the plant Johnny suggests that he can go now to make the changes he wants, and Mike gets a ride with him so he can go to town and tie one on. Larry starts to take Trudy home and leaves his car with Johnny to take home.

Trudy asks Johnny if he thinks it was suicide and tells him that the insurance is nothing compared to the rest of the estate and she will be satisfied without it. Johnny tells her that it really seems to be adding up to be suicide, which will make Larry happy because the company will not have to pay off. Johnny drives Larry's car and thinks about something Larry had said about the route to the office.

Johnny goes to the morgue where Dr. Frandler tells Johnny that it was suicide, and there was only a light bruise on the forehead. Johnny tells a confused doctor that he is sure that Briscum was hit on the forehead and shot where he was hit. Johnny is sure that someone put the gun into Briscum's hand and pulled the trigger while he was unconscious.

Johnny also tells Dr. Frandler that his apartment was not close to the route between Larry's office and Briscum's house. It was just an excuse and the suggestions were to cover up the murder if it was not done well enough.

Calling Johnny in is the oldest gag in the world, a cover up to take suspicion from Larry, and after all, he had the motive. Johnny realizes that if he tears into Larry, he can get the evidence he needs.

Johnny goes to see Larry and tells him that his lack of experience tripped him up and that he left latent prints on the gun, on Briscum's hand and the arm of the chair he sat in. Larry tells Johnny that prints are impossible because he wore a pair of cotton gloves. Oops! Johnny tells him that only the rankest amateur would let himself get tripped up like that.

"And only the rottenest kind of insurance man would have tried a thing like that. Thank heaven there are not very many of them. Expense account total, wait a minute, of course, there isn't any! And you know what? I'm glad there

isn't. This kind I wouldn't want to collect on any way."
"Next week, do you remember who the Lorelei were? Look it up, hmm? Then join us."

Notes:
- This program contains a commercial with the Kingston Trio for Seven Up, and for Mentholatum Deep Heating Rub and Instant Tender Leaf Iced Tea.
- William Mason is Larry, Charita Bauer is Trudy, Raymond Edward Johnson is Barber, Ivor Francis is Doc, Ralph Bell is Danny.
- The announcer is Art Hannes.
- Musical supervision is by Ethel Huber.

Producer: Bruno Zirato, Jr.   Writer: Jack Johnstone
Cast: William Mason, Charita Bauer, Raymond Edward Johnson, Ivor Francis, Ralph Bell

♦ ❖ ♦

Show: The Lorelei Matter
Show Date: 8/19/1962
Company: Star Mutual Insurance Company
Agent: Ed Williams
Exp. Acct: $0.00

Synopsis: Johnny is called and asked if he is "that" insurance investigator. When Johnny tells the caller that he is a free-lance investigator, the man wants the Johnny Dollar who works for the Star Mutual Insurance Company. Johnny tells the caller he works on assignment, so he tells Johnny to get an assignment and get over here right away. Johnny tells the caller he does not know who he is or where he lives, so the caller stumbles and identifies himself as Timothy Jerrad, and tells Johnny to rush over to his apartment. Jerrad tells Johnny to check with the insurance company after he gets there and mentions a murder, but it has not occurred yet. If Johnny does not hurry he will have Johnny fired.

While running errands downtown, Johnny stops and sees Ed Williams in the Star Mutual building. Johnny asks Ed about Jerrad, and Ed tells Johnny that even with the life policy of 2 million, Jerrad is still a crackpot.

"All-or-Nothing Jerrad" was a clever stock manipulator and used to be loaded, but five or six wives have taken care of most of the money. His present wife is young and pretty but sensible. She is Lorelei Lambert, an artist from Quebec who spends a lot of time out of town painting.

Johnny tells Ed about the phone call, and Ed tells Johnny that Jerrad has a persecution complex. Ed tells Johnny that Lorelei is the beneficiary, but she is not the type to murder anyone, as Jerrad has taken very good care of her. Ed tells Johnny to go over and keep Jerrad happy, so he will not lose the great big premiums.

Johnny goes to the old-fashioned Fleur de Lei apartments in Hartford, Connecticut where two doormen tell Johnny that he is expected. Johnny walks up to suite 3-A and knocks and the most beautiful girl Johnny has ever seen tells Johnny not to bang on the door as she stands there with a purse and attaché case in one hand and a suitcase in the other. Mid-twenties, petite, brown eyes and hair, umm, umm!

She introduces herself as Mrs. Jerrad and Johnny tells her who he is. She has been up on Cape Ann painting seascapes and came back today rather than next week because of Timothy. She hands Johnny her bags and opens the door. When Johnny mentions that she is lovely, she tells Johnny that she would slap his face if he did not know she was married. Johnny tells her that Jerrad wants to see him. Inside she calls for Timothy and searches the apartment.

In the bedroom she finds Timothy in bed, dead. Johnny notes only one solid blow behind the ear by someone who sneaked up and struck once. Lorelei sobs and Johnny calls the police.

Johnny calls the doorman up, but he has seen no one come into the building that day except Johnny. Johnny asks about new tenants, and Mr. Bascome is the newest one, he came here in 1937.

The police arrive with the doctor and Sgt. Barney Foster and Johnny go over the apartment and find nothing. Foster tells Johnny to get Lorelei out of the apartment for a few days. He tells Johnny that the killer must have been somebody Jerrad knew, so he is going to start running down everyone the Jerrads have known for the past five years.

Foster tells Johnny that he could be the suspect because of the attractive young wife, but Johnny makes light of it. Foster is going to seal the apartment and let no one in, but Johnny makes sure he can get back in. Foster tells Johnny not to act on any crazy hunches, but to call him if anything comes up. Promise?

Johnny arranges with Betty Lewis to stay at the Statler hotel with Lorelei. Johnny gets that silly feeling that a hunch is brewing as two days go by with no word from anyone. Finally, on the third day he goes back with Lorelei to help the hunch materialize. Lorelei tells Johnny what a good person Betty is and almost breaks down.

In the apartment, Lorelei tells Johnny about Cape Ann and wants to take her clothes out of the apartment, but Johnny says no. Johnny comments on her name Lorelei and the legendary sirens that enticed men to their deaths. She shows Johnny her sketches and Johnny recognizes the scenes. She tells Johnny that she had never been to the cape before but will go again.

Johnny tells her that she won't. Johnny tells her that she is a destroyer of men as she was the one person who would benefit from her husband's death, and the one person who could get in with her own key in the back door, without being seen by the doormen.

Johnny suspects that she overheard Jerrad talking to Johnny on the phone and decided to use him as an alibi and left by the back door again. When she insists that Johnny helped her with her luggage, Johnny reminds her that she was not carrying the portfolio full of the sketches she had made. She had to have been in the apartment.

Lorelei tells Johnny that she did kill her husband because he was an egotistical, self-centered, crazy old man. She killed him because of the money with which she can enjoy life and invites Johnny to join her. "Nice Try Lorelei, but not this time."

"Oh, why do they do it? Why don't they learn? Don't they know it won't work? That sooner or later they are bound to be found out? And why a lovely little thing like Lorelei? Lorelei, destroyer of men. Expense account total, who wants it. Who wants anything out of a case like this?"

Notes:
- This is an AFRTS program that contains a two-part story on the benefits of a democratic society.
- Rita Lloyd is Lorelei, Sam Gray is Barney, Herb Duncan is Ed, Arthur Kohl is Jerrad, Guy Repp is the doorman.
- Musical supervision is by Ethel Huber.
- Art Hannes is the announcer.
- The Lorelei is a large rock on the Rhine River in Germany. The river is difficult to navigate, and the many wrecks there gave rise to the legend of a siren like creature that lured mariners to their deaths.

Producer:	Bruno Zirato, Jr.	Writer: Jack Johnstone
Cast:	Rita Lloyd, Sam Gray, Herb Duncan, Arthur Kohl, Guy Repp	

• ❖ •

Show:	**The Gold Rush Matter**
Show Date:	8/26/1962
Company:	**Greater Southwest Insurance Company**
Agent:	Jake Walton
Exp. Acct:	$700.00

Synopsis: Paul Keller calls Johnny to welcome him to San Francisco and to tell him not to unpack, but to hop over to Virginia City, Nevada. Contact Jake Walton about the new gold rush going on now. This one has all the same old problems, including a couple of murders.

Johnny flies to Reno where he rents a car for the drive to Virginia City. Johnny describes the old Virginia City and the Comstock Lode. Johnny asks an old man for directions to Jake's office and is told that he is not there. Johnny is told not to go there, as Jake and the sheriff are out at the Scarlet Queen mine. Johnny asks if his car can make the trip, and the man tells him he better get a horse.

Johnny is directed to Jake Beckley's stable, but Johnny is warned not to go to the mine as there has been another killing, and there will be more. The man tells Johnny that there will be more dynamite accidents like the one that blinded him.

Johnny rents a horse and rides up the Six Mile Canyon trail. At the top of a ridge Johnny sees a body being taken from the mine just as a bullet whizzes by his head.

Johnny takes cover and circles around a boulder when a girl with a rifle tells

Johnny to drop his little lemon squeezer. Johnny is held at gunpoint while the girl calls for Jake. Jake walks up and tells Leona that he will make sure that Johnny will not try any tricks and slugs him.

Just as Jake throws the punch Johnny rolls out of the way, grabs Jake's arm and gets him on the ground. Johnny grabs for the girl's leg and pulls her down and gets the rifle.

Jake gives Johnny his gun and identifies himself as Jake Walton, just the man Johnny has been looking for. Jake and Leona had been at the mine because of the accident. When Johnny tells them who he is, Jake tells Leona that he is the man Jake has been waiting for. Leona tells Johnny that they thought he was the one causing all the problems.

Jake tells Johnny that this was the second killing, and that someone is using dynamite at the wrong time and place. Leona tells Johnny that her Uncle Dave was blown out of the mine and blinded. Johnny realizes that Dave was the man he met in town. Leona asks Johnny who he was shooting at, and he tells her "just a couple of rattlesnakes". Leona tells Johnny that she almost shot Johnny when she heard the shots.

Johnny, Jake and Leona go to the mine, located on the edge of the Comstock Lode. Jake tells Johnny that the mine will not pay off, and Leona tells them that Dave should own the mine, but a crooked lawyer fixed it so that Ski Lambert owns the mine. Jake thinks that the lawyer might have been right. Dave had been working in the mine until the accident.

Jake tells Johnny that the mine re-openings are caused by a government rise in the price of gold. All three go into the mine and Johnny catches Leona as she "trips" at the bottom of a ladder, and Johnny tells her he hopes she had fallen on purpose.

At the end of the mine is an area shored up with 12-by-12 timbers and the acrid smell of dynamite. Jake tells Johnny that this is the site there the dynamite went off and killed two people. Johnny asks for the lantern and it breaks as Jake hands it to Johnny, forcing them to climb out in darkness.

Back outside the mine, Jake drives Johnny and Leona to town via a shortcut as Leona starts laying plans for a dinner with Johnny. Johnny asks to borrow Jake's jeep to investigate a little idea he has.

Johnny wants to go investigate who had shot at him and a second tunnel to the mine mentioned by Jake, and the shortcut, which could have allowed someone from town to get there and shoot at him. But who?

After dinner and apple pie with Jake and Leona, Johnny takes the jeep and a lantern and drives out of town, hearing gunshots on the way. At the mine, Johnny finds the hidden second tunnel under some roofing materials. Johnny goes into the mine and looks at the shoring in the tunnel where he finds a hidden door to the second tunnel.

Johnny hears someone coming and plants the lantern as a decoy and starts to climb the ladder when a blast goes off. After the blast, Johnny hears Leona ask if the blast got him and Dave is not sure. Leona and the old man — all Johnny needs to know!

In a saloon in town Johnny meets Jake and asks him to get a rope and a gun. As Jake drives, Johnny tells Jake what happened at the mine.

Johnny knocks at Leona's door, and she is very surprised to see him. Johnny goes in to meet a very nervous uncle Dave, who recognizes Johnny by his voice. While Leona fixes a drink, Dave talks to Johnny and slowly moves his hand towards a table drawer while Johnny slowly draws his .38.

Johnny tells Dave that he went to the mine because of Dave's blindness, blindness that was an act because he had told Johnny what kind of car he was driving. Johnny tells Dave that he told everyone he was blind to back up the story that he was dynamited, and that he has been causing the explosions to get the mine back.

Johnny tells Dave that his next victim would have been Ski Lambert, the owner. Leona comes in with her rifle and Jake comes in with his rifle and shoots Leona in the hand.

"I do not know if Leona was actually involved in the murders in the mine or not. I hope not, because she was a doll. Then, sometimes, they are the most dangerous kinds. Anyhow, it will be up to the courts again to figure it out. Expense account total, including the way back to Hartford, call it $700 even."

Notes:
- This program contains commercials for No-Doz, Kent cigarettes and Sinclair Dino gasoline.
- Gene Simes does the musical supervision.
- Walter Otto does the sound patterns.
- Michael Schoskis does the technical direction.
- The announcer is Stuart Metz.

Producer: Fred Hendrickson   Writer: Jack Johnstone
Cast: Cliff Oland, Reynold Osborne, Teri Keane, Leon Janney, Rosemary Rice, Sam Raskyn

♦ ❖ ♦

Show: **The Doninger Doninger Matter**
Show Date: **9/2/1962**
Company: **New Jersey State Mutual Life Insurance Company**
Agent: **Maurice Parkely**
Exp. Acct: **$155.70**

Synopsis: Maurice Parkely calls Johnny and tells him that things are bad. He has $40,000 worth of troubles and Johnny suggests that Maurice just mail him a check. Maurice tells Johnny that a check is not involved, it is all cash, so Johnny will fly down and pick it up. But there is a hitch. The policy beneficiary is Walter P. Doninger, and they cannot find him. Johnny mentions his commission on the $40,000 and Maurice tells Johnny to come down, and they will talk about it.

Johnny flies to Trenton, New Jersey and cabs to Maury's office. Johnny and Maury head out for lunch at Hildebrechts where Johnny fills up on soft-shelled crabs.

The client is Walter P. Doninger VII. Walter the VII is the last of the line, now that his sister has died and left him the $40,000 "cash in hand" as the policy reads. The money must be paid in cash within 10 days of the death, which is less than a week from now. If they cannot find Walter, the company will have to pay an additional thousand every week or fraction thereof.

Johnny wonders if Doninger is trying to dodge the company to get more money, and Maury thinks it is a possibility. The policy has had eight addresses for Doninger, and he is not at the last address. Maury has not considered a pattern to the moves.

Back in the office, Maury tells Johnny that the addresses start in Trenton, then Atlantic City, Bloomfield, Cranford, Dumont, East Rutherford, Franklin, Gibbstown and Highbridge. Johnny realizes that they go in alphabetical order, so the next town should start with an "I".

Johnny checks an atlas and finds almost a dozen New Jersey towns starting with "I". Maury suggests writing to the towns, but Johnny has a better pattern. Johnny bets Maury that if he cannot find Walter P. Doninger VII in Interlaken, Johnny will work for free. If he is there, Maury will add an additional thousand, and he agrees. Johnny tells Maury that the answer is in the atlas.

Johnny explains that the cities are ordered in descending order of population, so Walter is going up the alphabet and down in population with each move. Johnny is sure he will find Doninger in Interlaken.

Johnny rents a car and drives to Interlaken, New Jersey. Johnny ends up at the New York and Long Branch Railroad station and asks for directions to city hall. A man tells Johnny that he recognizes Johnny's voice. He is Bill McGrogan and knows everyone in town and is willing to help Johnny for a small fee that Johnny can expense.

Johnny tells Bill that he is looking for Walter Doninger. Bill is suddenly quiet and tells Johnny that for $50 he will deliver Walt, after all, Walt is loaded. Bill tells Johnny to get a room at the Larchmont Hotel and he will get Doninger there tonight. Johnny asks if it would not be easier to just tell him where Walter is, but Bill tells Johnny that Walt moves around too much. Johnny gives Bill $25 and promises the rest when Bill delivers Doninger.

Johnny visits the police department and Sgt. Holloway tells Johnny that he will try to find Doninger, but he does get around a lot. After he heard his sister died, Doninger has lived in about three different rooming houses. Johnny has dinner and calls Maury.

There is a knock on the door and Johnny opens it to find a man with a gun and silencer. The man tells Johnny that he expected to see Johnny on his case, but not this fast. He is Walter "Scrappy" Doninger. Scrappy tells Johnny he is not going to take any chances and is going to kill Johnny.

Scrappy tells Johnny that he pulled a heist up in Hartford, and the goods were insured, so he knew Johnny would be assigned to the case. But he does not know how Johnny found him so soon. Scrappy tells Johnny that Bill McGrogan set Johnny up for $100.

There is another knock at the door that allows Johnny to slug Scrappy. Johnny asks who it is, and it is Walter P. Doninger VII. Johnny lets him in and

Walter shows Johnny his identification and Walter also admits that he was stalling for time to get more money.

Maury calls to tell Johnny that Tri-State Insurance in Hartford wants him to work on a big jewelry job, and the crook has the same name as the man Johnny is looking for. Plus, there is a $10,000 reward out for him.

Johnny tells Maury that he has his man right there. Johnny asks Maury to call Tri-State and tell them their job is done, and to mail the reward to Johnny. "I am up to HERE in Doningers!"

"So, for once I got real lucky. Now you can see why I've called this report The Doninger Doninger Matter. Expense account total, including the trip home with Scrappy Doninger in tow, $155.70, plus commission of course. Plus, the extra $1,000 on Walter VII. Oh, and I couldn't find Bill McGrogan again, so he will never get that other $25, maybe just a jail term someday for the kind of company that he keeps."

Notes:
- This program contains commercials for No-Doz and Kent cigarettes.
- There are a variety of spellings for the name of this story. The script in the Thousand Oak Library is *The Doninger Doninger Matter.*
- Walter Otto does the sound patterns.
- Eugene Simes does the music supervision.
- Mike Schoskis does the technical supervision.
- Art Hannes is the announcer.

Producer:	Fred Hendrickson Writer: Jack Johnstone
Cast:	Jack Arthur, Jack Grimes, Ian Martin, Santos Ortega, Melville Ruick, Neil Fitzgerald

♦ ❖ ♦

Show:	**The Four C's Matter**
Show Date:	**9/9/1962**
Company:	**Greater Southwest Insurance Company**
Agent:	**Royal J. Harkins**
Exp. Acct:	**$401.23**

Synopsis: Royal J. Harkins calls Johnny from Los Angeles and tells Johnny that if he flies to New York now, he can get there by 4 a.m. to be in Royal's office at 9 a.m. sharp. Johnny tells Roy that he is busy, but Roy is not to be deterred. There is a conspiracy here to commit murder!

Johnny calls Betty Lewis to cancel a date, and she offers to drive him to the airport. As Johnny rushes to catch a flight to Los Angeles, California, Betty tells him to look up an old school mate, Doris Crutten, who is planning to go to Europe this fall.

Johnny arrives at 8:30 as the plane circles station KNX. Roy meets Johnny and he has a rental car for him. The name of the client is Harvey Crutten, of Three C's Imports: Crutten, Carding and Callenger. Harvey is the senior partner and he lives on Mulholland Drive and is insured for $250,000, double indemnity.

The beneficiary is Doris Crutten but the business will pass to the partners.

Royal shows Johnny a newspaper with two articles. One is about Wilbur Carding threatening Harvey Crutten, the other is about Earl R. J. Callenger threatening Harvey Crutten. Roy tells Johnny that both partners threatened Crutten because he is bad for their business. Carding hates him because he will not sell out before the business goes bust, and Callenger hates him because Crutten is a playboy and has gone after his wife. Roy is paged and takes the call. His office tells him that Harvey Crutten is dead.

Roy tells Johnny that Harvey was killed while driving his Minerva-Pechini sports car. The police told Doris that he lost control on Dead Man's Curve and crashed 300 feet to the bottom of the canyon. Harvey was not a wild driver in spite of the car. Roy is sure that he was murdered and driven off the road.

Johnny drives to Mulholland Drive and the Crutten home. Johnny reaches Dead Man's Curve just as the car is being lifted out. Johnny goes to the car and meets an old friend, Sgt. Mike Conroy. Conroy is sure that the car was in perfect condition, as Mike knows where Crutten lives, and he could not back out of the driveway without brakes. Conroy estimates that the car was doing 90 when it went over and he thinks the accident was suicide. Conroy tells Johnny that Doris is a real dish, but she works like a handyman and drives an old jalopy.

Johnny drives to the modest Crutten house that is immaculate. In the garage, Johnny spots a 1938 automobile. Doris comes into the garage and tells Johnny that she rebuilt it herself. Johnny introduces himself, and Doris tells Johnny she is a fan of his.

While Doris installs a sink, she tells Johnny that fixing things is her hobby. When Johnny mentions that Doris is not upset about the death of her husband, she tells Johnny that she had been waiting for him to die since she married him.

Doris tells Johnny that she stayed married to Crutten to get his money and his insurance. Doris tells Johnny that she was at a poker game with some girls and got home at 1:00 a.m. to find Harvey's car gone. She had no idea where Harvey was going and asks if Johnny had met Earl Callenger's wife Moira. She tells Johnny that if either Carding or Callenger got to Harvey, she can only say "thanks, or sorry if you like."

Johnny leaves to call Sgt. Conroy who tells Johnny that the doctors found nothing in the autopsy. Johnny arranges to see the car and then drives to the headquarters of the Three C's Importers.

Earl Callenger is glad Crutten is gone so Moira his wife can come back to her senses. He blames himself for letting Moira be influenced by Crutten. Earl tells Johnny that he and Carding and three salesmen were on a train coming from San Francisco when the accident happened, and the police will confirm that.

Wilbur Carding and the salesmen give Johnny the same story, but Johnny is stuck with a motive for the killing. Johnny asks about the Three C's name and realizes that there is a fourth "C" and leaves. This is no hunch, as Johnny remembers what Betty had said about her friend Doris going to Europe this fall, alone.

Johnny drives to police headquarters and Sgt. Conroy shows him the special metric tools in a tool kit in the trunk of the car. Johnny notices that one tool is missing, the wrench that bleeds the brake lines. Johnny thinks he knows where the wrench is.

Back at the Crutten home Johnny goes to the garage and searches for the missing metric wrench. Doris walks in and tells Johnny that she expected to find him back at the garage. She admits that she used the special wrench to fix the car's brakes.

Johnny tells her that she loosened the bleeder valve so that the brake would be useless when Harvey got to Dead Man's Curve. She had waited so long for someone else to do it and they didn't, so she had to do it herself. "I shouldn't have, I guess." "No Doris, you shouldn't have."

"So once again, it's up to the courts. I suppose if she hadn't done it somebody else would, like her, in the mistaken belief that he could have gotten away with it. Expense account total, including mileage on the rental job and the trip home, $401.23."

Notes:
- This program contains commercials for No-Doz, Kent cigarettes, and Sinclair Dino gasoline.
- Musical supervision is by Ethel Huber.
- Walter Otto does the sound patterns.
- Technical supervision is by Fred Turner.
- Art Hannes is the announcer.

Producer:	Fred Hendrickson Writer: Jack Johnstone
Cast:	Grace Matthews, Mercer McLeod, Frank Milano, Walter Kinsella, Vivian Smolen, Robert Dryden, Joseph Boland, Barbara Wipple, Larry Robinson

♦ ❖ ♦

Show:	**The No Matter Matter**
Show Date:	**9/16/1962**
Company:	**Eastern Liability and Trust**
Agent:	**Raymond Tillerton**
Exp. Acct:	**$0.00**

Synopsis: Raymond Tillerton calls Johnny around 11 p.m. and wants Johnny to come to his apartment immediately. There is no matter to investigate, but he has to see Johnny immediately and hangs up.

Johnny does not know Tillerton, but Eastern Liability was an old and generous client, so Johnny dresses and drives to the Kearnsley Arms Apartments in Hartford, Connecticut. At the end of a dingy hallway Johnny rings at 4-A but gets no answer.

Johnny opens the door to find a dead girl sitting by a window with an ugly hole in her blouse. Johnny goes to the bedroom to use the phone and a man tells Johnny he should not have come and slugs him. Around dawn, Johnny wakes up and calls the police and faints.

Johnny wakes up again and washes his face when the police arrive. Johnny tells the officer there has been a murder and points to the dead girl, but she is gone. Johnny explains what happened and the officer asks what really happened, as there is no evidence of a woman ever being there. The officer asks about the absence of cordite smell and asks Johnny what is really going on. Johnny talks to the building super who tells him that Tillerton rents apartment 4-A.

Johnny drives to a drugstore and then to the offices of Tillerton. Johnny tells Tillerton who he is, but Tillerton denies calling Johnny, he was in New Haven last night visiting his mother on her birthday. Johnny tells him something is very wrong. Johnny is sure that Tillerton's voice was the one on the phone and in the apartment.

Johnny takes a train to New Haven, Connecticut and cabs to the home of Tillerton's mother. Mrs. Tillerton invites Johnny in and tells him it was nice to have one of her sons there for her 87th birthday. Raymond is in insurance and is doing very well. She tells Johnny that he stayed until after supper, but Johnny notes that would still allow time for him to get back to Hartford and call him.

As Johnny hails a cab, Johnny sees a car drive up, and the driver is a dead ringer for the dead girl in the apartment, except she is a blond. She tells Johnny that she is Clara, an old friend of the family. When Johnny tells her who he is, she is glad to meet him, as she has something very important to talk to Johnny about.

She suggests that they go to Danny's Bar, and talk over a drink. In the very dark bar there is one lone customer and no bartender. Johnny asks how Clara just happened to show up when he was leaving, but Clara does not know what Johnny is talking about. Johnny asks about the blouse with the phony bullet hole, but Clara is confused.

Johnny tells her that her hair is probably a wig, and she pulls a .25 automatic on Johnny. Clara calls for Tilly, and the man at the bar comes over and slugs Johnny. When Johnny wakes up a policeman is slapping him.

He had gone through Johnny's pockets and knows who he is. He had heard a shot from across the street and came over, because Danny's is supposed to be closed. He was suspected to be partners with that guy Tillerton. Tilly, the guy they will nab for pushing drugs around here.

Johnny leaves and goes back to Hartford. Johnny goes back to the apartment and Tillerton is there. He is glad to see Johnny because of the things Johnny had said earlier, and because of a call from the building super saying that the police had been there.

Johnny tells him about visiting his mother and Tillerton tells Johnny that he had visited someone else that evening and had spent the night in a hotel. Johnny tells Tillerton he came back to Hartford and set up the phony murder scene with the brunette who is mixed up in the narcotics racket with him.

Johnny tells him about the trip to New Haven. Tillerton can only repeat the name Warren, his twin brother called "Tilly". Johnny mentions that Tillerton's mother had told him that Warren was dead, but Ray tells Johnny that he had gone to see Warren once more to plead with him to straighten his life out.

He tells Johnny that to his mother, Warren is dead. That way she can reject him the way her religion, her beliefs, and her heart tell her she must reject him. Ray has tried to help him, but Warren is mad about the money their mother will leave to him and not to Warren. Ray swears that what he has said is true, but Johnny is confused about what has happened.

Ray tells Johnny that the act was a plot to make it look like Ray had killed the girl so that his mother would cut him off. Then Warren would be happy, because he had told Ray that if he were out of the will, Ray would be too. He would get Ray involved in a scandal somehow. Johnny realizes that he was called so that the police would not be there and they could work out their plot.

Warren comes into Ray's apartment with Clara and tells them Johnny is right. Ray tries to reason with Warren, but Warren tells them that they have the guns, including Johnny's gun they got in New Haven. Warren tells Johnny that he will kill Ray with Johnny's gun and Johnny with Clara's gun, but only Johnny and Ray's prints will be on the guns.

Clara gets anxious for Warren to shoot and Johnny rushes her. Warren turns and shoots Clara and Johnny then slugs Warren. Well, this time she really is dead.

Ray tells Johnny he took an awful chance rushing Clara, and Johnny tells him "I have never seen a girl who was really fast on the trigger, and I hope I never do."

"You know something else? The part I am really grateful about is that one more dope peddler is out of business and Warren is. You can be sure of that. Expense account total, $11.45, so forget it."

"Next week, a heist, but with one of the most unusual twists in many a day."

Notes:
- This program contains a single commercial for Sinclair Dino gasoline.
- Ethel Huber does the music.
- Sound patterns are by Walter Otto.
- Mike Schoskis does the technical supervision.
- Art Hannes is the announcer.

Producer:	Fred Hendrickson	Writer: Jack Johnstone
Cast:	Richard Keith, Guy Repp, Arthur Kohl, Ethel Everett, Evelyn Juster, Bill Lipton, Constance Simons	

Show:	The Deadly Crystal Matter
Show Date:	9/23/1962
Company:	World Mutual Insurance Company
Agent:	Les Walters
Exp. Acct:	$100.00

Synopsis: Les Walters calls and he is ready to blow a gasket. Les has $300,000 in troubles and will pick Johnny up at his apartment. Les tells him only to think about his commission on $300,000!

Johnny is picked up by Les and taken to the airport to go to New York. Les has just come back from Bronxville, New York, where Mrs. Gurney Dalrymple Weatherwell lives at 1263 Birchbrook Road.

Today is the servant's day off, and she wears $300,000 in jewels at all times to remind herself of when she was poor. She only takes the jewels off when she takes a bath. She left the jewels on a dressing table and they were gone when she was finished. The police were not called and Les only knows what he has told Johnny. She wants Johnny, and only Johnny, to handle the case.

As Johnny is given a list of the items, Les almost hits a car with a good-looking girl in it. The most valuable piece is a 23-carat ruby pendant. Johnny asks when the items were taken, and Les tells him that she took a bath — two weeks ago today and has just notified Les.

Johnny flies to New York and sitting next to him is the girl Les almost hit. She is Lynn Peters and not friendly.

Johnny drives to Bronxville where Mrs. Weatherwell tells Johnny that her jewels were taken while she was "taking her tub". There was no sign of forced entry, and the servants are above suspicion.

The doorbell rings, and Lynn Peters gives Johnny a package from Charley. The package contains the jewels. Johnny helps close the latch as Mrs. Weatherwell puts on the ruby when he would rather follow Lynn. Johnny is told the case is closed and the door is shut on his back. Johnny is sure that something fishy is going on and that Mrs. Weatherwell will give him no more information. So, there is only the girl to go on.

Johnny drives into town to see Randy Singer, who does not recognize the name. Johnny looks at the mug books for ten hours and fifteen minutes. Suddenly Johnny finds the right picture, with the name Ruth Balachay. Randy knows Ruth as "The Quick Dip", a former pick pocket who is clean now.

Johnny gets the address and cabs to 2120 W. 94th Street. Ruth opens the door and recognizes Johnny and slams the door in his face. Johnny cases the apartment for three days and finally calls Les to ask who the insurance beneficiary is. The answer is Charles Weatherwell, a stepson who lives in New York and who will get the insurance immediately upon Mrs. Weatherwell's death, half a million's worth.

Les tells Johnny that as soon as she dies, Charles will be pounding on his door demanding the money. Mrs. Weatherwell hates Charles but he is her only heir. Les also tells Johnny that Mrs. Weatherwell is ready to die. The doctor is there and he cannot figure what is causing her anemia.

Johnny goes to the apartment and asks for Charlie, who comes out with a gun and a hypo. Lynn rolls up Johnny's sleeve so that Charlie can give him a shot that will put him out for about five days. He did not study chemistry for nothing.

Johnny gets the shot in his muscles and Charlie tells Lynn that by the time Johnny wakes up, they will have the money and the ruby and be in Europe.

Johnny notes that the best action sometimes is to play possum, but Johnny is worried about the injection. Johnny sterilizes his pocketknife with a match and makes an X shaped cut over the needle mark and squeezes for dear life. Johnny is giddy but does not pass out.

Johnny gets a drink at a bar and has a doctor work on his arm. Johnny drives back to Bronxville and is met at the door by Dr. Harmon Brierley. Johnny asks if Mrs. Weatherwell is wearing the ruby pendant.

Johnny is sure that the ruby has been switched with something else. On her chest is a pinkish mark that causes the doctors to treat Mrs. Weatherwell for one of the most fiendish poisons ever known.

Thirty-six hours later doctors Brierley, Radford and Wilson are sure Mrs. Weatherwell will recover. The doctors ask Johnny why he suspected the poison potassium peradichromate, which caused the red corpuscles to deteriorate. Johnny tells them that earlier that year a young student had made some jewelry from various crystals he had made in the lab. There was a furor in the press because some of the crystals that looked like jewels were actually poisons that would bring about the exact symptoms of Mrs. Weatherwell.

Johnny tells them that when he said he had the ruby, he must have substituted a deadly crystal for the real jewel. When the doctors ask if Johnny knows the name of the man, he tells them "I certainly do." Mrs. Weatherwell does recover. Johnny goes home and, after calling Les, gets some sleep and goes back to Les' office the next morning.

The next day Les tells Johnny that the article about Mrs. Weatherwell dying was published, and a retraction will be printed the next day. So, Johnny is waiting for Charlie to arrive. The intercom buzzes, and Charlie comes in and is somewhat speechless when he sees Johnny.

Charlie asks how Johnny got there, and Les tells Charlie that he had a call from his stepmother and can return it if he wishes. When Charlie tells Les that she is dead, Les mentions the erroneous article in the paper. Charlie tells them that it is true, it has to be, and Johnny asks if it is true because he poisoned her. He tells them that it is a trick and pulls a gun and fires. Johnny slugs Charlie and takes his gun.

"Lynn Peters, nee Ruth Balachay, had made the mistake of waiting for Charlie outside in a car. So, she'll have her day in court too. And the original ruby, the real one, we found it sewed into the lining of Charlie's coat. Expense account total, well just for kicks, why don't we call it 100 bucks."

"Next week, I want all of you to be sure and listen, you may be sorry if you miss it. I call it the Case of the Tip-off Matter."

Notes:

- Birchbrook Road in Bronxville is also mentioned in *The Wayward Heiress Matter* and *The Wrong Ending Matter.*
- Next week's program is the last in the series, and along with *Suspense* which would end the same day, mark the end of daily radio drama.
- The only commercial is for Sinclair Dino gasoline.
- Ethel Huber does the music.
- Sound patterns are by Walter Otto.
- Technical supervision is by Larry Solow.
- Art Hannes is the announcer.

Producer: Fred Hendrickson   Writer: Jack Johnstone
Cast: Carl Frank, Olive Deering, Elsbeth Eric, Sam Gray, Casey Allen, Dean Carlson, Renee Santoni

◆ ❖ ◆

Show: The Tip-Off Matter
Show Date: 9/30/1962
Company: Northeast Indemnity Association
Agent: George Hardy
Exp. Acct: $349.40

Synopsis: George Hardy calls Johnny and asks him to write down "130-07-05-83". "Got it!" Johnny is told that he wants to see you at the state prison. If it is who George thinks it is, Johnny will be going to the commission over $100,000.

Johnny buys gas for his car and drives to the state prison in Wethersfield, Connecticut where the father of our country once planned the historic battle of Yorktown. In other words, George Washington slept there. Johnny is taken to the hospital ward to see a thirty-year old man who looks like he was 100. The man is Turner McGackie, up for safe cracking.

Mac tells Johnny that he is supposed to get out, but instead he is lying there dying. He sent for Johnny to stop a killing. Mac tells Johnny that the money from his last job was never recovered. He tells Johnny that he is the only investigator he respects.

He hated Johnny's guts until the warden told him what Johnny had done for his kid brother Tommy, getting him into a foster home and getting him a good education. Johnny tells Mac that his brother just graduated from high school with honors. Mac is thankful that Johnny led his brother to believe that he was killed, so he would have nothing to live down. Mac tells Johnny to listen as he explains where the money from the robbery is.

Mac tells Johnny about Joe Perelli, an old friend who is posing as a fisherman, and living in Mac's old cottage where there is a safe in the basement to which Joe knows only half the combination. The other half was given to Danny Russelloff who is in the pen with Mac.

Mac would not have given Danny the combination if he had known what Johnny had done for Tommy. Mac is sure that Danny will kill Joe. Mac agrees to give Johnny the combination so that he can have the money and save Joe's life.

Mac also tells Johnny that Danny is being released today, so Johnny has to act fast. As Mac tries to give the combination to Johnny, he dies. The warden tells Johnny that Danny has been released, and good riddance.

Johnny rents a charter plane and flies south and lands on a beach near Cutchogue where Johnny walks to a gas station and rents a car. Johnny gets directions to Joe's place and is told that if no one answers to go in, as Joe is probably drunk.

Johnny gets to Mike Perelli's place and a drunken voice tells him to come in, and Johnny sees that Joe has a gun and takes a shot at Johnny. Johnny takes the gun from him and Mike calls Johnny "Danny", thinking he is Russelloff. Johnny tells Perelli that he came to get the money in the safe. He tells Johnny that the money belongs to Mac, and Johnny tells him that Mac is dead.

Joe realizes that Johnny is an insurance dick. Johnny tells him he is there to get the money and save his life. He promised Mac to save Perelli's life, and he tells Joe that Danny has the other half of the combination. Johnny is sure that Danny would take the money and kill Perelli. Johnny tells Perelli that if he does not want Johnny's help Johnny will send him to prison if Danny does not kill him. Johnny tells Perelli he is moving in to wait for Danny.

Johnny goes to the gas station and gives the gas station attendant $100 to use his car and make some calls. Johnny calls George and tells him what is going on. George tells Johnny that maybe Danny is playing smart and reporting to his parole officer. Johnny is sure that Danny will act quickly.

Johnny asks George to get Pete Larkin, a detective to watch for Danny. Johnny will check back with George each day. Johnny goes back and verifies that the safe is still there. Joe tells Johnny his part of the combination.

Johnny hears a car approaching and turns off the lights. Joe tells Johnny that it is Danny and gets anxious, so Johnny slugs him. Johnny waits for the man to come to the house and Johnny swings open the door to find Jimmy, the gas station attendant.

Jimmy gives Johnny the key to the trunk and tells him that he thinks Johnny is "the most". Johnny tells Jimmy that if anyone knew that Johnny Dollar was there, Johnny Dollar might end up real dead. Understand? Jimmy understands and leaves.

Johnny waits for three days and calls George from the gas station every day only to learn that Danny is sitting tight in Hartford. On the fourth day George tells Johnny that Danny got away from Pete Larkin and they do not know where he is.

Jimmy tells Johnny that a car went down the road and came back. Johnny gives him a sawbuck and goes back to Perelli's but changes his mind and goes down a side road to an old fishing camp where he sees Danny's car and footprints leading to Perelli's.

Johnny crawls to the cabin and hears nothing. Johnny looks in to see Mike Perelli dead on the floor. Joe had not told Danny the combination so Danny will have to blow the safe. As soon as the safe blows, Johnny rushes in and tells Danny to freeze. Danny waves a bottle of nitro at Johnny and throws it.

"I had heard of such things, but never thought them possible. But, so help me, when I picked myself up on the edge of the wreckage of that cottage, most of my clothes were blown completely off. And yet by some miracle I suffered no more than a couple of bruises and a slight headache. As for Danny, well let's not go into that. He's paid for all his crimes. Expense account total $349.40. And don't forget my commission, in spite of the fact that a lot of bits and pieces of the money had to be pasted back together."

Notes:
- This program contains a commercial for Sinclair Dino Gasoline.
- The music supervision is by Ethel Huber.
- Sound patterns are by Walter Otto.
- Half way through the program, Joe Perelli becomes Mike Perelli.
- The cast listings for this program have been sliced onto the end of most copies of *The Winsome Widow Matter*.

Producer: Fred Hendrickson   Writer: Jack Johnstone
Cast: Jackson Beck, Joseph Julian, Jack Grimes, Bob Maxwell, Peter Fernandez

♦ ❖ ♦

With the ending of this program, the era of uninterrupted, regularly scheduled daily radio drama, commonly called the Golden Age of Radio ended, and radio changed forever.

OR DID IT?

While researching recent discoveries at the Thousand Oaks Library, researcher Stewart Wright discovered two Yours Truly, Johnny Dollar scripts written by Jack Johnstone that were never broadcast. Both of the programs are titled *The Key to Crime Matter*, and have a handwritten date of 10/7/1962 — the week after the series ended. These programs are cataloged below.

♦ ❖ ♦

Show: The Key to Crime Matter — Pat Fuller Version
Show Date: 10/7/1962
Company: Universal Adjustment Bureau
Agent: Pat Fuller
Exp. Acct: $572.89

Synopsis: Pat Fuller of the Universal Adjustment Bureau has Johnny investigate a string of burglaries involving money, furs, jewelry, watches, and such, taken from hotel rooms in Philadelphia. Loss claims totaling $4,871 have been filed with 5 different insurance companies.

Two weeks later there were 7 thefts in Cleveland and claims filed with 5 different insurance companies with a total loss of about $3,000. Every week since then, there have been similar groups of thefts in several cities including Chicago, Milwaukee, St. Louis, Memphis, New Orleans, Mobile, Tallahassee, Jacksonville, Atlanta, Charlotte, Washington, Baltimore, and Atlantic City. The most recent thefts occurred in Trenton. Pat thinks one man is behind the thefts. There have been no signs that any of the hotel rooms have been broken into.

Pat and Johnny agree that the next target is probably New York City. Johnny thinks he knows how the rooms are being broken into. Johnny visits each city and hotel and checks the registers. He finds similar hand writing for several different names and found that the man checks into the hotels at least a day before any of the burglaries occurred.

Johnny goes to New York City and checks with a clerk at the Commodore Hotel who has an incredible memory for names and faces of guests who have stayed at the Commodore, and when they stayed there. He helps Johnny go through the guest registration cards and quickly finds a hand writing match: a Mr. Charles Hathaway Halsey. The clerk is able to give a complete description of the man, but Mr. Halsey checked out that morning.

Johnny wants to stay in the suite Halsey had, but it is already occupied. Johnny wants it anyway. He knows how the thief is getting into the room. He will lie in wait for the thief in the suite. After two days, the phone rings and Johnny doesn't answer it, he is sure it is the thief checking to see if the guests are out. Johnny turns out the lights and waits in hiding.

A few minutes later he hears the door being unlocked, and the thief enters and begins to go through the room and luggage looking for valuables. All the while the thief is talking to himself. Johnny has planted a surprise in his luggage: a large rat trap which triggers and break several of the thief's fingers.

An armed Johnny Dollar comes out of hiding and confronts the man. The thief is surprised that Johnny doesn't recognize him. He is Charles Everhurst aka "Light-Fingered Charlie". His plan was simple: get one of the best rooms in a hotel, make a duplicate key, check out, and return a day or two later and steal the current guest's valuables.

Notes:
- This is the "Pat Fuller" version of this story.

Producer:	Unknown	Writer: Jack Johnstone
Cast:	Unknown	

♦ ❖ ♦

Show: **The Key to Crime Matter — Philadelphia Version**
Show Date: **10/7/1962**
Company: **Universal Adjustment Bureau**
Agent: **Pat Fuller**
Exp. Acct: **$742.89**

Synopsis: In the space of a few minutes Johnny gets calls from three Philadelphia based insurance contacts: Harry Branson (Philadelphia Mutual Liability and Casualty Insurance Company), Lester Larkin (Eastern Trust and Insurance Company), and Murdo Phillips (Trinity Mutual Insurance Company). All three call Johnny to investigate hotel burglaries.

Johnny is at the Hartford airport getting ready to catch a plane for Philadelphia when he is intercepted by Pat Fuller of the Universal Adjustment Bureau.

(From here this version is the same as the "Pat Fuller" version.)

Pat Fuller of the Universal Adjustment Bureau has Johnny investigate a string of burglaries involving money, furs, jewelry, watches, and such, taken from hotel rooms in Philadelphia. Loss claims totaling $4,871 have been filed with 5 different insurance companies.

Two weeks later there were 7 thefts in Cleveland and claims filed with 5 different insurance companies with a total loss of about $3,000. Every week since then, there have been similar groups of thefts in several cities including Chicago, Milwaukee, St. Louis, Memphis, New Orleans, Mobile, Tallahassee, Jacksonville, Atlanta, Charlotte, Washington, Baltimore, and Atlantic City. The most recent thefts occurred in Trenton. Pat thinks one man is behind the thefts. There have been no signs that any of the hotel rooms have been broken into.

Pat and Johnny agree that the next target is probably New York City. Johnny thinks he knows how the rooms are being broken into. Johnny visits each city and hotel and checks the registers. He finds similar hand writing for several different names and found that the man checks into the hotels at least a day before any of the burglaries occurred.

Johnny goes to New York City and checks with a clerk at the Commodore Hotel who has an incredible memory for names and faces of guests who have stayed at the Commodore, and when they stayed there. He helps Johnny go through the guest registration cards and quickly finds a hand writing match: a Mr. Charles Hathaway Halsey. The clerk is able to give a complete description of the man, but Mr. Halsey checked out that morning.

Johnny wants to stay in the suite Halsey had, but it is already occupied. Johnny wants it anyway. He knows how the thief is getting into the room. He will lie in wait for the thief in the suite. After two days, the phone rings and Johnny doesn't answer it, he is sure it is the thief checking to see if the guests are out. Johnny turns out the lights and waits in hiding.

A few minutes later he hears the door being unlocked, and the thief enters and begins to go through the room and luggage looking for valuables. All the while the thief is talking to himself. Johnny has planted a surprise in his luggage: a large rat trap which triggers and break several of the thief's fingers.

An armed Johnny Dollar comes out of hiding and confronts the man. The thief is surprised that Johnny doesn't recognize him. He is Charles Everhurst aka "Light-Fingered Charlie". His plan was simple: get one of the best rooms in a hotel, make a duplicate key, check out, and return a day or two later and steal the current guest's valuables.

Notes:
- This is the "Philadelphia" version of this story.

Producer: Unknown   Writer: Jack Johnstone
Cast: Unknown

The Audition Programs

The catalog of Yours Truly, Johnny Dollar contains five audition programs for the starring role. The program chosen changed for each of the actors, although the title was the same for several.

The audition actors include one regular Johnny Dollar (John Lund) as well as two major stars (Gerald Mohr and Dick Powell) who auditioned for the part and opted to accept other shows.

There is an audition of a Bob Bailey program, *The Ellen Dear Matter*, but this is not an audition for actors, it is an audition for potential sponsors. Stewart Wright has provided the contents of the sponsor advertisements for this audition.

The following are the audition programs for Yours Truly, Johnny Dollar.

◆ ❖ ◆

Dick Powell:
Show: Milford Brooks III
Show Date: 12/7/1948
Company: East Coast Underwriters
Agent: Austin Farnsworth
Exp. Acct: $1,182.23

Synopsis: Mr. Brooks is trying to jump out of the window at the insurance company. He wants to kill himself (there is no suicide clause) to get the 2 million from the policy because he cannot get a $500,000 loan to give to Harold Hatcher — a known gangster.

To keep Perry out of trouble, Johnny goes to New York City with Perry to visit "Butter" — a girlfriend. While Johnny "entertains" Butter, Perry disappears. After an hour-long search Johnny calls Lt. Fisher at missing persons and reports Perry missing.

The police report finding Perry's top coat and ID on the 125th Street ferry, and a matchbook with "HH" on the cover.

At Hatcher's club, bar girl Janelle points Johnny to Harold's office. After a short talk, the police show up. Janelle spills the beans about a personal note Hatcher has for Perry's debt to him. The personal note is found in one of Hatcher's suits.

Then Johnny follows Janelle to a garage apartment where Perry is. Then Hatcher shows up. It seems Janelle was putting Perry up to faking the suicide and framing Hatcher and running away with her. After a fight and the police, Perry is in the hospital and makes a full statement of insurance fraud.

Notes:
- Audition only, Powell never did the series.
- Powell notes "He can pad an expense account with the best of them".
- His suit size 42, shirt size is 15 1/2 x 33 and a hat size of 7 3/8 except after a case when it is 7 1/2.
- $1 tips to taxi and for a shoeshine.
- Perry has a crew haircut.
- $18 for brandy to calm Perry down.
- Perry gives three cheers for dear old Eli as they drive past Yale.
- Johnny tells Butter he found Perry in a box of Cracker Jacks dressed in a Brooks Brothers suit.
- Bourbon and soda is the drink at Butter's.
- Johnny starts to sing *Slow Boat to China*.
- Powell stammers several times, once over "East Coast".
- Expense Account includes a $318 bracelet for Butter.
- Next week "Special Investigation Singapore!"
- Music Supervision by Dick Aurant.

Producer: Anton M. Leader   Writer: Paul Dudley, Gil Doud
Cast: Dick Powell, William Conrad, Daws Butler, Joseph Kearns, Clarke Gordon, Mary Shipp, Ed Max, Betty Lou Gerson

◆ ❖ ◆

John Lund:
Show: The Trans-Pacific Matter — Part A
Show Date: 11/24/1952
Company: Corinthian Liability & Risk
Agent: Al Harper
Exp. Acct:

Synopsis: Al Harper at Corinthian has a job for Johnny, but he won't like it. However, the commission will be big. The policy is for $200,000 and Johnny will have to travel to Hong Kong, and Johnny is not scared yet. The policyholders are people they have had trouble with before. "Remember the Trans-Pacific Import Export outfit?" "Yeah, I sent flowers to the widow." This is their Hong Kong outfit. Johnny is scared, but he will take a crack at it.

Johnny finds Hong Kong a city of difficulties with shortages in everything. The city is full of immigrants as Johnny makes his way to the American Consulate. A secretary tells Johnny that life is very difficult in Hong Kong and asks if life is like this in America.

Mr. Grover meets with Johnny, who tells him why he is here. Grover remembers the company run by Will Meadow that was burned to the ground last month. Grover has met Meadow and realizes Johnny is there because he suspects fraud. Johnny tells him of the similar fire in Shanghai where Trans-Pacific made a lot of money. Johnny asks for introductions to the fire department and police and Grover tells him that he will do what he can.

Grover comments on the elections and asks for his hotel. Johnny tells him he does not have a room, and Grover tells him to talk to Miss Vedras his secretary as her father runs a hotel and might have a room. Grover asks about the case in Shanghai, and Johnny tells him that the investigator was killed before he could build a case. The death was blamed on war conditions. Miss Vedras arranges for a room and the room looks out over an alley with few amenities.

That night Johnny is visited by Miss Vedras who tells Johnny that Mr. Harrison of the fire control office will see him the next day. Vedras asks why Johnny is here and tells him that he has been followed. Johnny looks out and spots the man in the shadows, and Vedras tells him that she recognizes the man.

Johnny asks her about the music outside his room, and Miss Vedras tells him that it is a love song. She knows many Americans and wants to marry one who will take her from China, as there is no good here. She thinks that Americans are very impatient people, yet they live better than the Chinese do.

Johnny is disturbed by the pleading in Vedras' eyes, the sounds and smells of the restless crowded city, and the watcher on the street. Johnny is concerned because everyone is a potential assassin.

Next morning a different man follows Johnny to the office of Mr. Harrison, who was not able to meet with Johnny.

Johnny goes to visit William Meadow and tells him who he is. Meadow asks them what is wrong with the insurance company, and Johnny tells him that this case is too similar to the previous one, and Meadow tells Johnny that careless people die every day in Hong Kong. Johnny tells him he came to get a reaction, and Meadow is on the defensive and having him followed, so Meadow must have a reason and is afraid of Johnny.

Meadow tells Johnny that Corinthian means nothing, and the company is going to pay. Johnny has a platform to build a suspicion on and a veiled threat about the other agent who had been killed. Johnny is sure that Meadow is telling him that this is his town, and people who get in his way can get hurt. A real nice situation. Johnny goes back to his hotel and watches the window that night.

Notes:
- John Lund can be seen in the Universal International picture, *Just Across the Street.*
- Music is by Eddie Dunstedter.
- Dan Cubberly is the announcer.

Producer: Jaime del Valle   Writer: E. Jack Neuman
Cast: John Lund, Joseph Kearns, Lillian Buyeff, Robert Griffin, William Johnstone

Show:	**The Trans-Pacific Matter — Part B**
Show Date:	11/28/1952
Company:	**Corinthian Liability & Risk**
Agent:	**Al Harper**
Exp. Acct:	$4,515.00

Synopsis: Mr. Grover at the consulate calls and tells him that Superintendent Clyde of the police is upset at Johnny's attitude and Grover told him he had talked to Johnny and told him to be careful. Johnny tells Grover that he had been cautious and has just scalped the thug Meadow had following him. Johnny is going after Meadow next and tells Grover that the claim is no good, Miss Vedras was killed in his room for no reason. Johnny agrees to come over and talk.

After five days Johnny rents a 1935 Packard and has difficulty driving in the crowded streets, but the horn worked wonderfully.

In Grover's office Johnny tells him that he had forced the man with the gun to tell him that Meadow had hired him. Grover asks if his actions are for the insurance company or for Miss Vedras. Johnny tells him he came to know Miss Vedras very well, and she was there in his room and he talked to her. She was there each night until she was killed waiting for Johnny to come back. Johnny complains that he cannot get the police to do anything, and Johnny tells him he has to go after Meadow.

Johnny drives to Meadow's house and the houseboy tells Johnny that Meadow is not there and that he will be back next week. Johnny forces the houseboy to tell Johnny that Meadow is in Kowloon, but after a little convincing, Johnny is told that Meadow is in Repulse Bay, on the other side of the island where he has a cottage. The houseboy dials the number and Johnny hears Meadow's voice. Johnny calls the police superintendent and tells him that Meadow is going to confess and tells him to have his men there in an hour.

Johnny gets to the cottage as the police arrive. Clyde tells Johnny that they are there to make sure that nothing unnecessary happens and will arrest Johnny if he does anything illegal, as his case is mostly circumstantial. Clyde is very cautious and tells Johnny to make his play. Clyde tells Johnny that he has checked on him, and he has a very good reputation in the states.

Johnny walks to the cottage and tells Meadow that he knows that he is still alive and that he had killed the girl. Johnny wants him to make a statement and tells him he had gotten a statement from the punk.

Johnny is invited in and shot at. Johnny returns fire and Meadow is shot and falls down the stairs. Meadow tells Johnny that he hit him in the arm but it should have been his stomach. Meadow refuses to make a statement and dies. The police arrive and tell Johnny to have his arm looked at.

"Expense account item 15, $43 even for medical fees and hospital charges. I don't suppose it could be called hewing to the niceties of jurisprudence since Meadow was dead and he refused before dying to speak or write his confession. But there were two police carloads of expert witnesses who took the fact that he had opened fire as acceptable admission of guilt for the crimes accused. The same thing cleared me legally on the grounds of self-defense. I'd hoped it would clear my minds, but it hasn't. Luisa Vedras is still there. I guess she always will be. Nothing good came out of this assignment except saving your company some money it didn't know it had."

Notes:
- John Lund can be seen in the Universal International picture, *Just Across the Street*.
- Music is by Eddie Dunstedter.
- Dan Cubberly is the announcer.

Producer: Jaime del Valle Writer: E. Jack Neuman
Cast: John Lund, Joseph Kearns, Lillian Buyeff, Robert Griffin, William Johnstone

Gerald Mohr:
Show: **The Trans-Pacific Matter — Part 1**
Show Date: **8/29/1955**
Company: **Corinthian Liability & Risk**
Agent: **Al Harper**
Exp. Acct: **$0.00**

Synopsis: Al Harper at Corinthian has a job for Johnny, but he won't like it. However, the commission will be big. The policy is for $200,000 and Johnny will have to travel to Hong Kong, and Johnny is not scared yet. The policyholders are people they have had trouble with before. "Remember the Trans-Pacific Import Export outfit?" "Yeah, I sent flowers to the widow." Johnny is scared, but he will take a crack at it.

Johnny flies to Hong Kong and finds it a city with simplicity with shortages in everything. The city is full of immigrants as Johnny makes his way to the American Consulate.

A secretary tells Johnny that life is very difficult in Hong Kong and asks if life is like this in America. Mr. Grover meets with Johnny, who tells him why he is here. Grover remembers the company run by Will Meadows that was burned to the ground last month. Grover has met Meadows and realizes Johnny is there because he suspects fraud. Johnny tells him of the similar fire in Shanghai where Trans-Pacific made a lot of money. Johnny asks for introductions to the fire department and police and Grover tells him that he will do what he can.

Grover comments on the elections and asks for his hotel. Johnny tells him he does not have a room, and Grover tells him to talk to Miss Vedras his secretary as her father runs a hotel and might have a room. Grover asks about the case in Shanghai, and Johnny tells him that the investigator was killed before he could build a case. The death was blamed on war conditions.

Miss Vedras arranges a room for Johnny that looks out over an alley with few amenities. That night Johnny is visited by Miss Vedras, and she tells Johnny that

Mr. Harrison of the fire control office will see him the next day. Vedras asks why Johnny is here and tells Johnny he has been followed. Johnny looks out and spots the man in the shadows, and Vedras tells him that she recognizes the man.

Johnny asks her about the music outside his room, and she tells him that it is a love song. She knows many Americans and wants to marry one who will take her from China, as there is no good here. She thinks that Americans are very impatient people, yet they live better than the Chinese do.

Johnny is disturbed by the pleading in Vedras' eyes, the sounds and smells of the restless crowded city, and the watcher on the street. Johnny is concerned because everyone is a potential assassin.

Next morning a different man follows Johnny to the office of Mr. Harrison, who was not able to meet with Johnny.

Johnny goes to visit William Meadows and tells him who he is. Meadows asks them what is wrong with the insurance company, and Johnny tells him that this case is too similar to the previous one, and Meadows tells Johnny that careless people die every day in Hong Kong.

Johnny tells him he came to get a reaction, and Meadows is on the defensive and having him followed, so Meadows must have a reason and is afraid of Johnny. Meadows tells Johnny that Corinthian means nothing, and the company is going to pay.

Johnny has a platform to build a suspicion on and a veiled threat about the other agent who had been killed. Johnny is sure that Meadows is telling him that this is his town, and people who get in his way can get hurt. A real nice situation. Johnny goes back to his hotel and watches the window that night.

"Tomorrow night, a complicated lesson on how to get shot at by your best friend and like it."

Notes:
- This audition used the music used in the Bob Bailey series.
- George Walsh is the announcer.

Producer: Jack Johnstone   Writer: E. Jack Neuman, Gil Doud
Cast: Gerald Mohr, Lillian Buyeff, Will Wright, Tony Barrett, Harry Bartell, Ben Wright

◆ ❖ ◆

Show: **The Trans-Pacific Matter — Part 2**
Show Date: **8/29/1955**
Company: **Corinthian Liability & Risk**
Agent: **Al Harper**
Exp. Acct: **$4,515.00**

Synopsis: Superintendent Clyde calls, and Johnny tells him he has a bird in his room that is ready to sing. He just scalped the two-bit thug William Meadows had on him and Meadows is next. Clyde warns Johnny that he will be arrested if he does anything illegal. Johnny tells Clyde to send a wagon for the thug, as he has a knife and a gun and tried to kill Johnny. Clyde will send someone over.

After five days Johnny reports additional expenses. Johnny is working over the thug in his room when Inspector Clyde arrives and takes the thug's gun. Clyde knows the man as Pen Lu. Johnny tells Clyde that he got his information about Meadows by duress and gets very angry at Clyde's inaction. Clyde tells Johnny that his evidence against Meadows is only circumstantial. Clyde tells Johnny that he has checked on Johnny and discovered that Johnny has an enviable reputation in the states, but the case is complex and must be investigated cautiously. He will question the man and tell Johnny what he learns. Clyde warns Johnny not to do anything rash or he will be arrested.

Johnny rents a 1935 Packard and has difficulty driving in the crowded streets, but the horn worked beautifully. Johnny drives to Meadows' house and the houseboy tells Johnny that Meadows is not there and that he will be back next week. Johnny forces the houseboy to tell Johnny that Meadows is in Kowloon, but after a little more convincing, Johnny is told that Meadows is in Repulse Bay, on the other side of the island where he has a cottage. The houseboy dials the number and Johnny hears Meadows' voice.

Johnny gets to the cottage as the police arrive. Clyde tells Johnny that they are there because the houseboy had called and told them what Johnny had done to him.

Clyde tells Johnny that he is hot-headed and impetuous, but he was right about Pen Lu who admitted he had been hired by Meadows to kill Johnny. His gun was checked and found to be the one that killed Luisa Vedras but Clyde does not know why Meadows had Vedras killed.

Johnny tells him that Pen Lu thought that Vedras was Johnny. He tells Clyde that he had gotten to know Vedras and that this is a bad job for his nerves. Johnny tells him that she came there each night until she was killed waiting for Johnny to come back. Clyde asks if Johnny is there to get Meadows for the company or for Luisa, and Johnny tells him that Luisa was a lovely girl. Clyde tells Johnny to make his play.

Johnny walks to the cottage and tells Meadows that he knows that he is still alive and that he had killed the girl. Johnny wants him to make a statement and tells him he had gotten a statement from the punk sent to kill him.

Johnny is invited in and shot at. Johnny returns fire and Meadows is shot and falls down the stairs. Meadows tells Johnny that he knew he would not take him. Johnny tells him he is hit in the arm, and Meadows says it should have been his stomach. Meadows refuses to make a statement and dies. The police come up to the cottage and tell Johnny to have his arm looked at.

"Expense account item 16, $43 even for medical fees and hospital charges. I don't suppose it could be called hewing to the niceties of jurisprudence since Meadows was dead and he refused before dying to speak or write his confession. But there were two police carloads of expert witnesses who took the fact that he had opened fire as acceptable admission of guilt. The same thing cleared me legally on the grounds of self-defense. I had hoped it would clear my mind, but it hasn't. Luisa Vedras is still there. I guess she always will be."

"Monday night, the story of a ship, the Molly K. Destination: Davy Jones' locker. Join us, won't you?"

Notes:
- Audition Program
- George Walsh is the announcer.

Producer: Jack Johnstone Writer: E. Jack Neuman, Gil Doud
Cast: Lillian Buyeff, Will Wright, Tony Barrett, Harry Bartell, Ben Wright

♦ ❖ ♦

Researcher Stewart Wright has documented that in September, 1955, there was an audition for a new Johnny Dollar, and a number of actors auditioned for the role. The actors included Paul Dubov (*Jeff Regan, Investigator* and *The Adventures of Frank Race*), Larry Thor (*Broadway Is My Beat*), Jack Moyles (*A Man Named Jordan, O'Hara*, and *Rocky Jordan*), and Bob Bailey (*Let George Do It*). Other actors such as Tony Barrett, Vic Perrin, Barney Phillips, Hy Averback, and Frank Gerstle had solid radio experience. There was another non-radio actor who auditioned: Chuck Connors. But the winner was Bob Bailey.

The script is simply called *Lead Audition* and takes place in Hong Kong. All of the dialog is between the Lead (Johnny) and Louisa, played by Lillian Buyeff. It probably would be the end of a script.

The following information is provided by Stewart Wright and Jeanette Berard:

♦ ❖ ♦

Show: Lead Audition
Show Date: 9/13/1955
Synopsis: Johnny is in Hong Kong at a cheap hotel, and Louisa shows up to ask why he is here. Johnny asks her about the death of Harry Bartell. She deflects him and says he should go back to America.

Johnny reminisces about how much he dreamed about her, but he wants no roots, and must live alone. She asks how he could let her think he loves her.

Johnny confronts her for having killed Harry and taken his ring. She denies it. Johnny pulls the ring off her hand. They tussle for her purse, in which he finds a .25 Colt. He tells Louisa to "Get up. Get out. Dirty, little, yellow rat!"

Cast: Lillian Buyeff, Bob Bailey

For many years it was thought that the script identified as an audition using *The Ellen Dear Matter* was an audition for Bob Bailey. However, Stewart Wright has uncovered a document in the Thousand Oaks Library that details the contents of *The Ellen Dear Matter — Audition* script. The audition was not for actors — it was for sponsors. The details are below.

The Audition Programs

♦ ❖ ♦

Show: The Ellen Dear Matter
Show Date: 1/6/1957
Company: Western Maritime & Property
Agent: Arthur Arthur
Exp. Acct: $453.95

Synopsis: The following information is taken from a CBS Radio memo dated January 29, 1957, written by Jack Johnstone. The memo outlines the cast and commercials for an audition of sponsors, and is transcribed as written:

Cast:
Bob Bailey	Johnny Dollar
Pat	Lawrence Dobson
P. A.	Virginia Gregg
VI	Virginia Gregg
ART	Harry Bartell
JAC	Jay Novello
COR	Jack Edwards
THOR	Barney Phillips
BURR	John Dehner

ANNCR: From Hollywood it's time now for

SOUND: PHONE RING...UP

JOHNNY: Johnny Dollar

PAT: Pat McCracken Johnny, Universal Adjustment Bureau

JOHNNY: Oh, hi, Pat. What's on your mind?

PAT The sleek, lovely, Ellen Dear.

JOHNNY: On the strength of that description I'll take her!

PAT: And she's loaded with three hundred, twenty-five thousand dollars' worth of jewelry.

JOHNNY: Hey, that girl needs a bodyguard. Sleek, lovely...

PAT: Only she isn't a girl Johnny. She's a boat.

JOHNNY: I've lost my enthusiasm. What's the matter with the old tub?

PAT:	That's what I want you to find out... For a slight consideration, of course.
JOHNNY:	(BEAT) Okay, Pat, I'll be right over
MUSIC:	MT AND UNDER (JD A-1)
ANNCR:	Bob Bailey in the exciting adventures of the man with the action-packed expense account — America's fabulous freelance insurance investigator...
JOHNNY:	Yours Truly, Johnny Dollar.
MUSIC:	JD A-1
CUBBERLY:	**FIRST COMMERCIAL** (LIVE) (SUNSWEET 16 R 20) Are you one of those cup-of-coffee-and run folks who just won't take time for breakfast? Well, the best thing I can say to you is...don't. Don't fool yourself that way. Breakfast is the most important meal of the day, according to every authority I have ever run across. You can go without a midday meal perhaps, but go without breakfast and you're tired before you start. Best start for breakfast is a dish of delicious SUNSWEET prunes. Especially in the winter when you need extra energy to protect yourself and your family from winter cold and winter ills. There's more energy in SUNSWEET prunes... more blood-building iron... more of such important vitamins as A, B2, and Niacin... than any other fruit. You'll love the taste of SUNSWEET prunes, too. They're fully-ripened in California sunshine...ripened until they're packed with natural sweetness and full rich prune-plum flavor. And they're packed in foil-wrapped boxes to protect all the flavor and goodness until you open the box in your own home kitchen. No other fruit can take the place of prunes on your table... SUNSWEET prunes, the prunes packed in California by the growers themselves.
MUSIC:	JD B-1
CUBBERLY:	**SECOND COMMERCIAL** (ET) (BON AMI "A") We'll continue with Johnny Dollar in a moment.
SOUND:	APPROACHING JET, BUILDING UNDER ANNOUNCER
ANNCR:	Now — shortcut cleaning...with Jet Bon Ami!

SOUND:	(JET UP FULL...UNDER AND OUT)
JINGLE:	Froth...SHH...WSSH-WSSH...Dirt's off! (ASCENDING SLIDE WHISTLE) Spray on lacy froth... Then wipe with a cloth...WSSH-WSSH...WSSH-WSSH And the dirt's all off. (ASCENDING SLIDE WHISTLE IN THREE SEPARATE SHORT TOOTS) Get Jet Bon Ami, new Jet Bon Ami... Push the button, spray it on, then you wipe it dry. Sparkles, glistens, my oh my! Cleans windows, mirrors Jet Bon Ami ... Porcelain, tile, Jet Bon Ami... Makes everything glisten, listen, listen, listen, Get ready, get set, get Jet Bon Ami!
ANNCR:	Today there is a short-cut way to clean windows... painted wood work... porcelain...tile! Use the sensational new white froth cleaner...Jet Bon Ami! Just spray a lazy white froth... wipe with a dry cloth... the dirt's off thanks to Jet Bon Ami. A little bit cleans better than a lot.
VOICE:	Listen, Pet...get Jet Bon Ami!
CUBBERLY:	And now, back to Johnny Dollar
MUSIC: 37-5?	
CUBBERLY	**THIRD COMMERCIAL** (LIVE) (SWIFT & CO BROWN 'N' SERVE SAUSAGE) We'll return for the third act of Johnny Dollar in a moment. Which comes **first** when it's breakfast time at your house?... the sausages or the eggs? Well, if you'd discovered SWIFT'S PREMIUM BROWN 'N' SERVE SAUSAGES, that becomes a difficult question to answer and here's why — listen" (SOUND of SAUSAGE SIZZLING UP THEN UNDER FOR:) What you hear is both eggs and SWIFT'S PREMIUM BROWNS 'N' SERVE SAUSAGES frying deliciously. They've been in the pan just **three minutes**, and **both** eggs and sausages are cooked through and through — ready to eat. (FRYING SOUND OUT)

	So you see, when you're having eggs with quick-fixing SWIFT'S PREMIUM BROWN 'N' SERVE SAUSAGES, it's bound to be a tie — they're both ready to serve in **three minutes flat!** Yet with all this modern speed, SWIFT hasn't forgotten wonderful, old-fashioned **flavor.** And another thing... since these sausages are fully cooked, the size you **buy** is the size you **serve.** There's practically **no** shrinkage! You try package of SWIFT'S PREMIUM BROWN 'N' SERVE SAUSAGES. From Swift — to serve your family better.
MUSIC:	(J.D. A-1??)
COUBBERLY:	**FOURTH COMMERCIAL** (ET) (CHEF-BOY-AR-DEE) Johnny Dollar will return in a moment.
ANNCR:	Say, the next time you plan a party how about making it a pizza party? A spicy pizza pie bubbling with tiny sauce and mellow cheese is a quick trick to make your party a success. And when you use Chef Boy Ar Dee pizza pie mix your pizza takes no time at all, it's that easy. Each gay yellow carton of Chef Boy Ar Dee pizza pie mix contains all the ingredients, the flour mix for a flaky crust, the to raise it, the rich pizza sauce, even the Italian style cheese. So how about it? The next time you plan a party how about making it a pizza party with Chef Boy Ar Dee pizza pie mix.
SINGER	Oh, tay pizza motte bella what a tasty pizza pie Boy Ar dee's the chef that treats you to the real Italian style Boy Ar Dee pizza pie, By Chef Boy Ar dee. Chef Boy Ar Dee. Chef Boy Ar Dee.
MUSIC:	IN AND UNDER (VIDEO MOODS 1013-A-1
CUBBERLY:	**FIFTH COMMERCIAL** (LIVE) (RENUZIT HOME PRODUCTS) We'll continue with Johnny Dollar after this message. Can you spell Renuzit? R — E — N — U — Z — I — T. Don't know what we do at our house without Renuzit Home Dry Cleaner! it's always ready and waiting, at a moment' [sic] notice, to spruce up our furniture upholstery and rugs and keep their original colors looking like new! It's been doing just that for three years, too. But it's also great fo [sic] other non-washable fabrics -- wool, silks, or rayon! Try Renuzit Home Dry Cleaner yourself! Notice what an efficient job it

	does. And notice, too, how it leaves absolutely no offensive odor whatever. No wonder this wonderful Renuzit Cleaner carries the Good Housekeeping Seal of Approval. No wonder so many homes wouldn't be without it. So reach for the quart, half gallon, gallon or two-gallon can of Renuzit at your favorite grocery, department, variety or hardware store. You'll love Renuzit.
MUSIC:	IN AND UNDER– J. D. TEN A–9
	SIXTH COMMERCIAL (ET — TRACK 1)
ANNCR	Our star will return in just a moment
VOICES	Why don't you
(SINGING)	Livvvvv modern! Livvvvv modern! Live, live, live modern! Change to L & M!
ANNCR:	Only with L & M can you enjoy the **full exciting flavor** — of today's finest tobaccos through the **modem miracle** of the **L & M Miracle Tip.** Through the pure-white Miracle Tip — L & M tastes **richer** — smokes **cleaner** — draws **easie** [sic]. No other cigarette — plain or filter — gives you all the flavor you want — the rich and exciting flavor you get only from L & M. So light up — Free up — let your taste come alive. **Live modem!** Smoke an L & M!
VOICES:	Make today your Big Red Letter Day
(SINGING:	And start to live the modern way Live! Live! Live modern! Get L & M today!
ANNCR:	Now here is our star tell you about next week's story
JOHNNY:	Next week a prizefighter who could only win by losing… because his life depended on it. Join us, won't you? Yours Truly Johnny Dollar
MUSIC:	J.D. B–5
ANNCR:	Yours Truly, Johnny Dollar, starring Bob Bailey, originates in Hollywood. It is produced and directed by Jack Johnstone

who also wrote tonight's story. Heard in our cast were: Virginia Gregg, Lawrence Dobkin, Harry Bartell, Jay Novello, Jack Edwards, Barney Phillips and John Dehner. Musical supervision is by Amarigo Marino. Be sure to join us next week, same time and station, for another exciting story of Yours Truly, Johnny Dollar. Dan Cubberly speaking.

MUSIC: UP TO FILL

Notes:
- The announcer is Dan Cubberly.
- Musical supervision is by Amerigo Marino.
- This memorandum was provided by Stewart Wright.
- The information in this memo is unique, as it provides the cost of the cast members. For this half-hour audition, Jack Johnstone was paid $175 ($1,520 in 2007 dollars), Amerigo Marino was paid $50 ($435 in 2007 dollars), and the cast members were paid "scale", which was noted on the memo as $63.20 ($550 in 2007 dollars).
- The various musical and sound effect notations are shown as they appear in the original document.

Producer: Jack Johnstone Writer: Jack Johnstone
Cast: Virginia Gregg, Lawrence Dobkin, Harry Bartell, Jay Novello, Jack Edwards, Barney Phillips, John Dehner

VI: So, Who Was the Best Johnny Dollar?

Invariably, this question always seems to come up in any discussion of Yours Truly, Johnny Dollar. And for the most part, the answer is pretty much decided.

Most serious discussions will always put Bob Bailey at the top of the "Best" category for the character, and rightly so. Bob was a veteran radio actor who was able to take a character that had grown dull and predictable and infuse life into it. When Bob was angry, you knew he was angry. When his heart was ready to melt, you melted with him. Bob was the consummate actor playing a part that was, in a sense, written for him.

For the role of second place, most assign Mandel Kramer to that position. Mandel was an excellent radio voice and was able to continue to bring life and credibility to the character. However, when I sit down to listen to Johnny Dollar, more often than not, I will listen to my favorite number two: Charles Russell.

Many will dismiss Charlie for the very reason that I enjoy listening to him. He was sarcastic, irreverent, droll, and somewhat lecherous. Hardly a sentence goes by without some sort of offhanded remark, some of which I feel are very witty. These qualities seem, for some Freudian reason perhaps, to appeal to me, and I enjoy them. Charlie was a good actor and portrayed a character who was in his infancy. Everyone built his character portrayals on Charlie, knowingly or otherwise. Given that many of the writers who wrote for Charlie also wrote for other Johnny Dollars, the personality would have to come through.

The rest of the Johnny Dollars: Edmond O'Brien, John Lund, Bob Readick, while accomplished actors, all claim third place in the race for the best Johnny.

In reality though, for the programs to have continued to hold a place in the hearts of the old-time radio audience some forty to fifty years after the actors walked up to the microphone and intoned "Johnny Dollar" to the sound of a ringing phone, they had to have some sort of staying power. There had to be some magic there.

So, in the final analysis, maybe the best Johnny Dollar should be the one that you are listening to at the moment.

VII: Reports

After reviewing over seven hundred Yours Truly Johnny Dollar programs, each in the form of an expense report, it would be a shame not to include a series of reports here.

EXPENSES BY ACTOR

Each Johnny Dollar program included the various expenses incurred during the investigation and ended with an expense account total. Each of the stories outlined in the above sections includes the total expenses, if available.

Because these expenses were incurred during a different century than the one in which this book was written, the totals may not necessarily make sense. So, for each of the actors who portrayed Johnny Dollar, I have listed the total expenses obtained from the various programs. That total is then converted to current (2017) dollars using information available from the Federal Reserve Bank of Minneapolis web site.

When you look at the total expenses incurred, the numbers can be misleading. For example, Bob Bailey expensed over $136,000 ($1,000,000 adjusted) in six years, but what these figures do not tell is how much was earned in the way of fees and commissions, which could have been considerable.

Actor	Actual Expenses	Expenses Adjusted for Inflation
Bob Bailey	$136,992.75	$1,161,648.74
Charles Russell	$39,777.68	$408,025.80
Dick Powell	$1,182.23	$9,016.34
Edmond O'Brien	$72,432.90	$711,681.56
Gerald Mohr	$4,515.00	$41,157.26
John Lund	$43,289.50	$395,016.79
Mandel Kramer	$19,696.45	$159695.27
Bob Readick	$4,714.45	$38,594.93
Grand Total	**$320,285.77**	**$2,915,820.36**

Employers and Agents

Over the run of the program, Johnny Dollar worked for a number of insurance companies, and a few individuals. The table below lists each of the employers and the cases assigned by them. Also included are the agents (if known) and the expenses for the cases.

Actor Key

CR = Charles Russell   EO = Edmond O'Brien
JL = John Lund   BB = Bob Bailey
BR = Bob Readick   MK = Mandel Kramer
GM = Gerald Mohr   DP = Dick Powell

Company/Program	Agent	Actor	Expenses
Alliance Bonding Company			
The Calgary Matter	Mr. Matthews	EO	$1,180.00
Company Total:			**$1,180.00**
Allied Adjustment Bureau			
The Lancer Jewelry Matter	Pat Corbett	JL	$70.25
The Underwood Matter	Red Eagan	JL	$491.50
The Rochester Theft Matter		JL	$155.42
Company Total:			**$717.17**
Allied Casualty & Insurance Company			
The Macormack Matter	Ed Barth	BB	$265.91
Company Total:			**$265.91**
All-States Insurance Company			
The Baltimore Matter	Don Freed	JL	$294.60
Company Total:			**$294.60**
Amalgamated Life Associates			
The Crystal Lake Matter	Tom Wilkins	BB	$423.00
The Wayward Gun Matter	Adolph Dorfman	MK	$0.00
Company Total:			**$423.00**
Amalgamated Life Association			
The Jimmy Carter Matter	Waldo Bottomly	BB	$117.00
The Negligent Nephew Matter	Leonard Tillson	BB	$10.50
The Morning After Matter	Timothy Handley	BR	$0.00
The Philadelphia Miss Matter	George Caldwell	MK	$485.75
Company Total:			**$613.25**

Company/Program	Agent	Actor	Expenses
Ambassador Life & Casualty Insurance Company			
Bodyguard to Anne Connelly	Franklin Haley	CR	$845.30
	Company Total:		$845.30
Amercon Northern Trust Company			
The Matter of Reasonable Doubt	Ben Guardley	BB	$596.45
	Company Total:		$596.45
American Continental Insurance Company			
The Diamond Protector Matter	Robert Ferry	CR	$1,142.89
	Company Total:		$1,142.89
American Continental Life Insurance			
The Robert Perry Case	Mr. Gordon	CR	$1,263.00
Bodyguard to the Late Robert W. Perry	Mr. Gordon	EO	$463.00
	Company Total:		$1,726.00
American Federated Life Insurance Company			
Haiti Adventure Matter	Harvard Huntington	CR	$424.70
	Company Total:		$424.70
American Pioneer Life Insurance			
The Case of Barton Drake	W. K. Green	CR	$1,482.63
	Company Total:		$1,482.63
American Volunteer Liability Insurance Company			
Dr. Otto Schmedlich	Homer Shally	CR	$1,211.69
	Company Total:		$1,211.69
Apex & Great Northern Bonding Company			
The Missing Chinese Stripper Matter	Phineas Perch	CR	$611.44
	Company Total:		$611.44
Associated Insurance Companies of New England			
The Henry J. Unger Matter	Calvin Porter	EO	$50.39
	Company Total:		$50.39
Assured Equity & Trust Company			
The Meek Memorial Matter	Max Green	BB	$98.30
	Company Total:		$98.30

Company/Program	Agent	Actor	Expenses
Athena Life & Casualty Company			
The Maynard Collins Matter	Ed Grimm	EO	$310.00
Company Total:			$310.00
Atlas Indemnity Insurance Company			
The Independent Diamond Traders Matter	Eric Carlson	JL	$64.20
Company Total:			$64.20
Baltimore Liability & Trust			
The Emily Braddock Matter	Frank Preston	JL	$738.32
Company Total:			$738.32
Bay State Bonding & Liability Company			
The Village Scene	Doug Strand	EO	$68.30
Company Total:			$68.30
Britannia Insurance Company			
The Paul Barberis Matter	Ad Meyers	EO	$160.30
Company Total:			$160.30
Britannia Life Insurance Company			
The Howard Caldwell Matter	Mr. Nathan	EO	$1,050.00
The David Rockey Matter		EO	$840.75
The Jarvis Wilder Matter		EO	$540.00
The Soderbury, Maine Matter		EO	$84.90
The Morgan Fry Matter		EO	$136.65
Company Total:			$2,652.30
Britannia Underwriters Association			
The Circus Animal Show Matter		CR	$152.70
Company Total:			$152.70
Britiannia Casualty & Life			
The Man Who Wrote Himself to Death		EO	$635.24
Company Total:			$635.24
Camden Life & Fidelity Company, Ltd.			
The Berlin Matter	Dave Hopkins	JL	$693.03
Company Total:			$693.03

Company/Program	Agent	Actor	Expenses
City of New Bedford Police Department			
The New Bedford Morgue Matter		EO	$213.30
Company Total:			$213.30
Clayson Mutual Assurance Company			
The Harold Trandem Matter	Jack Barton	EO	$736.82
Company Total:			$736.82
Columbia Accident & Life Insurance Company			
The Chicago Fraud Matter	Niles Hartley	JL	$219.77
Company Total:			$219.77
Columbia All-Risk Insurance Company			
The Woodward Manila Matter	Ralph Weaden	EO	$3,940.00
The Emil Lovett Matter		EO	$93.45
The Month-End Raid Matter		EO	$396.50
The Fair-Way Matter	Sam Harris	EO	$0.00
The Protection Matter	Phillip Martin	EO	$101.92
The Janet Abbe Matter	Bob Rudd	EO	$2,796.00
The Birdy Baskerville Matter	Phillip Martin	EO	$137.27
The Youngstown Credit Group Matter		EO	$195.20
The Alma Scott Matter		EO	$572.00
The Birdy Baskerville Matter	Phillip Martin	JL	$137.27
The Emil Carter Matter		JL	$572.00
The Shayne Bombing Matter		JL	$123.70
The Nancy Shaw Matter	Phillip Martin	JL	$604.65
The Nelson Matter	Phillip Martin	JL	$301.01
The Lester Matson Matter	Phillip James	JL	$154.50
The William Post Matter	Ray Kemper	JL	$87.05
The Alfred Chambers Matter	Phillip Martin	JL	$114.05
The Fair-Way Matter	Sam Harris	JL	$25.95
The Woodward Manila Matter	Ralph Weadon	JL	$2,611.80
Company Total:			$12,964.32
Commonwealth Mutual Assurance Company			
The Dan Frank Matter	Jim Bates	JL	$194.90
Company Total:			$194.90
Concourse Mutual Life Insurance Company			
The Jones Matter	George Dean	JL	$418.40
Company Total:			$418.40

Company/Program	Agent	Actor	Expenses
Consolidated Indemnity Company			
The Road-Test Matter	Mr. King	JL	$217.40
	Company Total:		**$217.40**
Constant Sun Trading Company			
The Expiring Nickels and the Egyptian Jackpot		CR	$5,350.40
	Company Total:		**$5,350.40**
Continental Adjustment Bureau			
The Lester James Matter	Ed Talbot	JL	$151.22
The Forbes Matter	Mr. Turner	BB	$363.51
	Company Total:		**$514.73**
Continental Assurance Company			
The Felicity Feline Matter	Henry Parker	BB	$407.20
	Company Total:		**$407.20**
Continental Fire & Casualty Company			
The Upjohn Matter	Matt Brandon	JL	$293.65
	Company Total:		**$293.65**
Continental Insurance & Trust Company			
The DeSalles Matter	Hillary Fuchs	BB	$416.00
The Froward Fisherman Matter	Clark Thorness	BB	$181.00
The Wayward River Matter	Lee Harkins	BB	$100.00
The Wayward Killer Matter	Paul Hemple	BB	$315.17
The Telltale Tracks Matter		BB	$0.00
The Life at Steak Matter	Bill Ferguson	BB	$0.00
The Deadly Chain Matter	Bill Ferguson	BB	$27.35
The Mystery Gal Matter	Fred Melchior	BB	$0.00
The Back to the Back Matter	Ed Barrenger	BB	$25.80
	Company Total:		**$1,065.32**
Continental Insurance Company			
The Loss of Memory Matter	Les Crutcher	BB	$95.00
The Village of Virtue Matter	Ben Orloff	BB	$100.00
The Virtuous Mobster Matter	Ben Orloff	BB	$174.00
The Fatal Filet Matter		BB	$0.00
The Deep Down Matter		BB	$131.50
The Paperback Mystery Matter	Fred Briscoe	BR	$70.00
	Company Total:		**$570.50**

Company/Program	Agent	Actor	Expenses
Corinthian All-Risk Insurance Company			
The Adolph Schoman Matter	Harold Warner	EO	$150.80
The Monopoly Matter	Mr. Brandt	EO	$63.80
The Byron Hayes Matter		EO	$180.80
The Arthur Boldrick Matter		EO	$77.30
The Cumberland Theft Matter		EO	$834.75
The Amelia Harwell Matter	George Parker	EO	$122.35
The Monopoly Matter	Mr. Brandt	JL	$62.20
The Arthur Boldrick Matter		JL	$77.30
	Company Total:		$1,569.30
Corinthian Insurance Company			
The Radioactive Gold Matter	Ed Trask	JL	$165.45
The Hamilton Payroll Matter	Bill Fedderson	JL	$417.65
	Company Total:		$583.10
Corinthian Liability & Bonding Company			
Out of the Fire, Into the Frying Pan		CR	$1,463.00
	Company Total:		$1,463.00
Corinthian Liability & Risk			
The Trans-Pacific Import Export Company, South China Branch	Al Harper	EO	$3,544.00
The Trans-Pacific Matter	Al Harper	JL	$4,515.00
The Trans-Pacific Matter	Al Harper	GM	$4,515.00
	Company Total:		$12,574.00
Corinthian Life & Liability Insurance Company			
The Richard Splain Matter	Bruce Harvard	EO	$375.00
	Company Total:		$375.00
Corinthian Life Insurance Company			
The Able Tackett Matter		EO	$4,077.80
The Joan Sebastian Matter	Mr. Semplin	EO	$356.75
The Jeanne Maxwell Matter	Mr. Semplin	JL	$266.85
The Jeanne Maxwell Matter	Mr. Semplin	JL	$265.85
	Company Total:		$4,967.25
Cosmopolitan All-Risk Insurance Company			
The Hartford Alliance Matter	Barton Keefe	EO	$180.00
	Company Total:		$180.00

Company/Program	Agent	Actor	Expenses
Cosmopolitan Bonding & Insurance Corporation			
The Brisbane Fraud Matter		JL	$286.20
	Company Total:		$286.20
County Court, Kings County			
The Rudy Valentine Matter		EO	$10.85
The Rudy Valentine Matter		JL	$10.85
	Company Total:		$21.70
Delaware Mutual Life Insurance Company			
The Walter Patterson Matter	Mr. Elgin	JL	$610.13
	Company Total:		$610.13
Delta Liability			
The Fathom-Five Matter	Ralph Steedler	BB	$684.95
	Company Total:		$684.95
Dr. Ludwig Goya			
The Edith Maxwell Matter		EO	$0.00
	Company Total:		$0.00
East Coast Underwriters			
Milford Brooks III	Austin Farnsworth	DP	$1,182.23
The Parakoff Policy		CR	$1,230.20
The Virginia Beach Matter	Carl Brewster	EO	$855.75
	Company Total:		$3,268.18
East Coast Underwriters Association of America			
The Sidney Rykoff Matter	Edward Holey	EO	$982.28
	Company Total:		$982.28
Eastern Allied Casualty Insurance Company			
The Squared Circle Matter	Paul Kendrick	BB	$491.20
The Wrong Ending Matter	Tommy Hines	BR	$100.00
	Company Total:		$591.20
Eastern Casualty & Trust Company			
The Callicles Matter	Dave Blaine	BB	$1,100.59
	Company Total:		$1,100.59

Company/Program	Agent	Actor	Expenses
Eastern Fire & Casualty Company			
The Magnolia And Honeysuckle Matter	Gil Randall	JL	$176.45
Company Total:			**$176.45**
Eastern Indemnity & Fire Company			
The Punctilious Firebug Matter	Jeff Connors	JL	$309.25
Company Total:			**$309.25**
Eastern Indemnity & Insurance Company			
The King's Necklace Matter	Marty Fenton	JL	$348.60
The Milk and Honey Matter	Mr. Mitchell	JL	$1,480.20
The Uncut Canary Matter	Mr. Harrison	JL	$373.85
The Classified Killer Matter	Ted Albright	JL	$191.15
The Bilked Baroness Matter	Ben Turner	JL	$50.45
The Paterson Transport Matter	Tom Benson	JL	$184.45
The Jan Breugel Matter	Tom Leslie	JL	$135.85
The Carboniferous Dolomite Matter	Bill Wesley	JL	$2,074.05
Company Total:			**$4,838.60**
Eastern Indemnity Insurance Company			
The Undried Fiddle Back Matter	Tom Harrison	JL	$480.30
The Sulphur and Brimstone Matter	Philip Martin	JL	$585.60
Company Total:			**$1,065.90**
Eastern Insurance Company			
The Firebug Hunter Matter	Arnold Whelan	CR	$410.00
Company Total:			**$410.00**
Eastern Liability & Trust			
The No Matter Matter	Raymond Tilotton	MK	$0.00
Company Total:			**$0.00**
Eastern Liability & Trust Company			
The Pearling Matter	Morton Scotman	BB	$714.35
The Hollywood Mystery Matter	Hal Spidle	BB	$0.00
The Only One Butt Matter	Fred Wakely	BB	$25.55
The Man Who Waits Matter	Ted Bessem	BB	$0.00
Company Total:			**$739.90**
Eastern Liability & Trust Insurance Company			
The One Too Many Matter	Hal Kemper	MK	$4.80
Company Total:			**$4.80**

Company/Program	Agent	Actor	Expenses
Eastern Life & Trust Company			
The Thelma Ibsen Matter	Milton DeFranco	JL	$84.15
Company Total:			$84.15
Eastern Maritime & Insurance Company			
The Aromatic Cicatrix Matter	James Harrington	JL	$196.10
Company Total:			$196.10
Eastern Seaboard Casualty Insurance Company			
The Plantagent Matter		BB	$702.13
Company Total:			$702.13
Eastern Trust & Insurance Company			
The Eleven O'Clock Matter		BB	$21.40
The Basking Ridge Matter	Stuart Smith	BB	$29.55
The Hapless Ham Matter		BB	$100.00
The True Love Matter	Harvey Mclean	BR	$190.40
Company Total:			$341.35
Eastern Trust Insurance Company			
The Broderick Matter	Robert Steele	BB	$1,132.14
Company Total:			$1,132.14
Empire Insurance, Limited			
The Draminski Matter	Bill Gardner	JL	$348.40
Company Total:			$348.40
Employee Cooperative Group Insurance Company			
The Syndicate Matter	Wilbur Runion	JL	$236.04
Company Total:			$236.04
Estate of E. P. Watkins			
The Happy Family Matter	Pat McCraken	BB	$73.00
Company Total:			$73.00
Eternity Mutual Insurance Company			
The Confidential Matter	Mort Parkinson	BB	$912.61
The Rat Pack Matter	George Franklin	BR	$0.00
The Wrong Idea Matter	Tim Harrington	MK	$229.57
Company Total:			$1,142.18

Company/Program	Agent	Actor	Expenses
Federal Insurance & Claims Adjusters			
The Costain Matter		JL	$227.50
	Company Total:		$227.50
Federal Life Insurance Company			
The Sarah Dearing Matter	Ed Gross	JL	$372.25
	Company Total:		$372.25
Federal Underwriters Inc.			
The Dameron Matter		JL	$551.10
	Company Total:		$551.10
Financial Surety Company			
The Weldon Bragg Matter	Jim Waldo	EO	$65.80
The Stanley Springs Matter	Ed Best	EO	$0.00
The Hatchet House Theft Matter		EO	$1,182.75
	Company Total:		$1,248.55
Fine Arts Securers			
The Stolen Portrait of the Duke of Massen	Frederick Kimble	CR	$1,563.40
	Company Total:		$1,563.40
Floyds of England			
The Missing Mouse Matter	George Reed	BB	$38.20
The Mad Hatter Matter	George Reed	BB	$870.40
The Ming Toy Murphy Matter	George Reed	BB	$225.70
The Michael Meany Mirage Matter	George Reed	BB	$420.10
The Funny Money Matter	George Reed	BB	$171.25
The J. P. D. Matter	George Reed	BB	$204.80
The Silver Belle Matter	George Reed	BB	$317.10
The Hope to Die Matter	George Reed	BB	$0.00
The Boron 112 Matter	George Reed	BB	$2,431.00
The Durango Laramie Matter	George Reed	BB	$1,460.00
The Doting Dowager Matter	George Reed	BB	$17.80
The Blue Madonna Matter	George Reed	BB	$620.00
The Fairweather Friend Matter	George Reed	BB	$203.50
The Cautious Celibate Matter	George Reed	BB	$1,053.45
The Twin Trouble Matter	George Reed	BB	$0.00
The Night in Paris Matter	George Reed	BB	$5,878.00
The Embarcadero Matter	George Reed	BB	$1,174.00
The Missing Missile Matter	George Reed	BB	$0.00
The Wrong Man Matter	George Reed	BB	$1.00

Company/Program	Agent	Actor	Expenses
The Nuclear Goof Matter	George Reed	BB	$0.00
The Alvin's Alfred Matter	George Reed	BB	$0.00
The Collector's Matter	George Reed	BB	$371.20
The Twisted Twin Matter	George Reed	BB	$196.55
The Killer Kin Matter	George Reed	BB	$0.00
The Too Much Money Matter	George Reed	BB	$0.00
The Empty Threat Matter	George Reed	BB	$2,561.00
The Shifty Looker Matter	Geoffrey Reed	MK	$4.40
Company Total:			$18,219.45

Four State Fire & Casualty Insurance Company

The Fire in Paradise Matter	Fred Hanley	BB	$241.28
Company Total:			$241.28

Four State Fire Insurance Corporation

The Bennet Matter	Andrew Cord	BB	$1,140.37
Company Total:			$1,140.37

Four State Insurance Company

The Todd Matter	Don Freed	BB	$1,095.00
The Evaporated Clue Matter	Henry Bascome	BB	$574.00
The Hood of Death Matter	Luther Pennyroyal	MK	$200.00
Company Total:			$1,869.00

Four State Mutual Insurance Company

The Peerless Fire Matter	Henry Willowby	BB	$14.46
The Price of Fame Matter		BB	$2,341.00
The Bolt Out of The Blue Matter	Harry McQueen	BB	$171.50
The Yaak Mystery Matter	Steve Yokum	BR	$207.75
Company Total:			$2,734.71

Global Casualty

The Picture Postcard Matter	Tom Wilkins	BB	$1,723.00
Company Total:			$1,723.00

Grand East All-Risk Insurance Company

The Adam Kegg Matter	Al Begney	EO	$230.40
The Sidney Mann Matter	Dave Robinson	EO	$188.00
Company Total:			$418.40

Grand East Life & Liability Insurance Company

The Arrowcraft Matter	Millard Snell	EO	$940.20
Company Total:			$940.20

VII: Reports

Company/Program	Agent	Actor	Expenses
Great Chesapeake Fidelity Insurance Guarantee			
The Big Red Schoolhouse	Paul McGraw	EO	$3,227.00
	Company Total:		**$3,227.00**
Great Columbian Life Insurance Company			
Death Takes a Working Day	Harry Del Hubbel	CR	$823.00
Death Takes a Working Day		EO	$823.00
	Company Total:		**$1,646.00**
Great Corinthian Life Insurance Company			
The Archeologist		EO	$456.90
Alec Jefferson, The Youthful Millionaire	Bob Douglas	EO	$711.00
	Company Total:		**$1,167.90**
Great East Insurance Company			
The Singapore Arson Matter		JL	$2,112.00
	Company Total:		**$2,112.00**
Great Eastern Fidelity & Life Insurance Company			
The San Antonio Matter	Ed Quigley	JL	$573.49
	Company Total:		**$573.49**
Great Eastern Fire & Casualty			
The Elliot Champion Matter	Don Vickers	JL	$516.54
	Company Total:		**$516.54**
Great Eastern Insurance Company			
The Port-O-Call Matter	Bob Redden	EO	$450.60
The Lloyd Hammerly Matter		EO	$2,350.00
The Willard South Matter	Lou Creager	EO	$373.00
The Neal Breer Matter		EO	$556.70
The Douglas Taylor Matter	Mr. Nibley	EO	$181.20
	Company Total:		**$3,911.50**
Great Eastern Life Insurance Company			
The Nora Falkner Matter	Jim Morris	EO	$1,120.40
The George Farmer Matter	Mr. Mitchell	EO	$33.65
The Baxter Matter	Luther Bishop	EO	$324.10
The Allen Saxton Matter	Stanley Mitchell	JL	$119.93
The Nathan Gayles Matter	Mr. Bishop	JL	$235.00
The Nathan Swing Matter	Mr. Mitchell	JL	$435.05
	Company Total:		**$2,268.13**

Company/Program	Agent	Actor	Expenses
Great Industrial Assurance Corporation			
The Dead First-Helpers	Bill Hudson	EO	$520.25
	Company Total:		**$520.25**
Great Northern Bonding & Surety			
The Lillis Bond Matter		EO	$308.90
	Company Total:		**$308.90**
Great Plains Guaranty Company			
The Open Town Matter	Ralph Kearns	BB	$516.20
	Company Total:		**$516.20**
Greater Southwest Insurance & Liability Company			
The Midas Touch Matter	Jake Kessler	BB	$978.35
The Mohave Red Matter	Jake Kessler	BB	$0.00
The Mohave Red Sequel Matter	Jake Kessler	BB	$307.00
	Company Total:		**$1,285.35**
Greater Southwest Insurance Company			
The Allanmee Matter	Fred Brinkley	BB	$341.10
The Frisco Fire Matter		BB	$923.91
The Winsome Widow Matter	Herb Shilling	BB	$250.00
The Big H Matter	Royal J. Harkins	BB	$447.45
The Frantic Fisherman Matter	Roy Harkins	BB	$650.85
The Will and a Way Matter	Jake Kessler	BB	$3,280.00
The Redrock Matter	Jake Kessler	BB	$496.25
The Very Fishy Matter	Theodore Jarvis	BR	$245.50
The Captain's Table Matter	Barton H.B.	BR	$438.00
The Mad Bomber Matter	Hank Parnell	MK	$350.00
The Do It Yourself Matter	Royal B.	MK	$833.70
The Golden Dream Matter	Jake Kessler	MK	$451.80
The Gold Rush Matter	Jake Walton	MK	$700.00
The Four C's Matter	Royal J. Harkin	MK	$401.23
	Company Total:		**$9,809.79**
Greater Southwest Life Insurance Company			
The Sidewinder Matter	Jake Kessler	BB	$345.40
	Company Total:		**$345.40**
Guarantee Transport Insurance Company			
The Flight Six Matter	Pete Cardley	BB	$608.10
	Company Total:		**$608.10**

Company/Program	Agent	Actor	Expenses
Hartford Police			
The Glen English Matter		EO	$0.00
	Company Total:		$0.00
Hartford Police Bunko Squad			
The Henry Page Matter		EO	$53.00
	Company Total:		$53.00
Hartford Police Department			
The Mickey McQueen Matter		EO	$0.00
The Mickey McQueen Matter		EO	$0.00
	Company Total:		$0.00
Hemispheric Insurance Company			
The Kay Bellamy Matter	Bert Welch	JL	$135.40
	Company Total:		$135.40
Hemispheric Life Insurance Company			
The Enoch Arden Matter	Henry Grant	JL	$1,879.80
	Company Total:		$1,879.80
Highworthy Insurance Underwriters Association			
The Case of the Hundred Thousand Dollar Legs	Harvey Anthony	CR	$948.76
	Company Total:		$948.76
Honesty Life Insurance Underwriters			
Milford Brooks III	Austin Farnsworth	CR	$1,182.23
	Company Total:		$1,182.23
Industrial Insurers Incorporated			
The Department Store Swindle Matter	Eban Stevens	CR	$511.50
	Company Total:		$511.50
Inter-Allied Insurance Company			
The Blooming Blossom Matter	Paul Brannon	BB	$61.55
The Monticello Mystery Matter	Henry Foreman	MK	$71.70
	Company Total:		$133.25

Company/Program	Agent	Actor	Expenses
Inter-Allied Life Insurance Company			
The Curse of Kamashek Matter	Jimmy Sayer	BB	$985.00
The Killer's List Matter	Pat Cummings	BB	$146.50
	Company Total:		$1,131.50
Intercoastal Maritime & Life			
The Marley K Matter	Byron Kay	BB	$81.00
	Company Total:		$81.00
Inter-Coastal Maritime & Life Insurance Company			
The Meg's Palace Matter	Byron Kay	BB	$221.60
The Charmona Matter	Byron Kaye	BB	$103.80
The Silver Queen Matter	Byron Kaye	BB	$58.35
	Company Total:		$383.75
Inter-Commercial Insurance Companies of America			
The Caligio Diamond Matter	Henry Glacen	EO	$65.34
	Company Total:		$65.34
Intercontinental Bonding & Indemnity			
The Gino Gambona Matter	Roger Stern	JL	$112.07
	Company Total:		$112.07
Intercontinental Indemnity & Bonding Company			
The Cuban Jewel Matter	Roger Stern	EO	$708.83
	Company Total:		$708.83
Intercontinental Indemnity & Bonding Corporation			
The Jonathan Bellows Matter	Roger Stern	JL	$208.60
The James Forbes Matter	Roger Stern	JL	$148.48
	Company Total:		$357.08
Intercontinental Marine Insurance Company			
The Fishing Boat Affair		CR	$1,264.28
The SS Malay Trader		EO	$0.00
	Company Total:		$1,264.28
International Casualty & Life Insurance Company			
The Harried Heiress Matter	Bert Larkin	BB	$7,604.25
	Company Total:		$7,604.25

Company/Program	Agent	Actor	Expenses
International Insurance & Bonding Company			
The Voodoo Matter	Nelson Price	JL	$461.40
	Company Total:		$461.40
International Insurance Corporation			
The Madison Matter	Paul Dupree	JL	$525.39
	Company Total:		$525.39
International Life & Casualty Company			
The Winnipesaukee Wonder Matter	Christian Albeck	BB	$0.00
	Company Total:		$0.00
International Life & Casualty Insurance Company			
The Phony Phone Matter	Art Ingles	BB	$1.35
The Twins of Tahoe Matter	Michael J. Kendry	BB	$416.00
The Three for One Matter	Christian Albeck	MK	$81.50
	Company Total:		$498.85
Keystone Mutual Assurance Company			
The Ben Bryson Matter	Ed Murphy	JL	$823.82
	Company Total:		$823.82
King Hart			
Murder Ain't Minor		CR	$0.00
	Company Total:		$0.00
Lakeside Life & Casualty Insurance Company			
The Indestructible Mike Matter	Peter Branson	BB	$1,126.50
	Company Total:		$1,126.50
Lloyds Underwriters Association			
The Racehorse Piledriver Matter		CR	$1,449.22
	Company Total:		$1,449.22
Marigold Police Department			
The Marigold Matter	Walt Younger	JL	$4.00
	Company Total:		$4.00
Marine & Maritime Casualty, Ltd.			
The Molly K Matter	Dave Borger	BB	$547.60
	Company Total:		$547.60

Company/Program	Agent	Actor	Expenses
Masters Insurance & Trust Company			
The Poor Little Rich Girl Matter	Bert Major	BB	$317.75
The Diamond Dilemma Matter	Bert Majors	BB	$284.30
The Ugly Pattern Matter	Barry Winters	BB	$101.00
The Curley Waters Matter		BB	$0.00
The Date with Death Matter	Bert Wells	BB	$47.00
The Double Exposure Matter	Frederick	BB	$17.20
The Art for My Sake Matter	Tim Bradley	BR	$0.00
The Planner Matter	Fred Larker	BR	$15.95
The Wayward Fireman Matter	Harrison Hadley	BR	$227.00
	Company Total:		**$1,010.20**
Maurie Strand Bail Bond			
The Tom Hickman Matter	Maurie Strand	EO	$2,204.06
	Company Total:		**$2,204.06**
Max Krause Bail Bond & Insurance Agency			
Witness, Witness, Who's Got the Witness	Max Krause	CR	$500.71
	Company Total:		**$500.71**
Mid-Eastern Indemnity Corporation			
The Templeton Matter	Lud Barlow	BB	$413.28
The P.O. Matter	Harry McQueen	BB	$397.70
	Company Total:		**$810.98**
Mid-Eastern Life & Casualty Company			
The Mary Grace Matter	Ben Perrin	BB	$0.00
	Company Total:		**$0.00**
Mid-States Industrial Insurance Company			
The Primrose Matter	Brad Taylor	BB	$914.15
The Case of Trouble Matter	Tom Bartley	MK	$256.10
	Company Total:		**$1,170.25**
Miss Melanie Carter			
The Melanie Carter Matter		CR	$0.00
	Company Total:		**$0.00**
Monarch Life Insurance Company			
The Barbara James Matter	Frank Garber	EO	$344.59
	Company Total:		**$344.59**

Company/Program	Agent	Actor	Expenses
Mono-Guarantee Insurance Company			
The Silver Blue Matter	Ralph Dean	BB	$541.25
The Delectable Damsel Matter	Ralph Single	BB	$230.00
The Rhymer Collection Matter	Fred Porter	BB	$35.50
The Bad One Matter	Culpepper	BB	$231.20
Too Many Crooks Matter	Freddie Freidkin	MK	$250.00
The Double-Barreled Matter	Phil Easterday	MK	$760.00
The Burma Red Matter	Jimmy Bartell	MK	$0.00
The Skimpy Matter	Danny Nixon	MK	$10.80
	Company Total:		**$2,058.75**
Mutual Liability Company			
The Eighty-Five Little Minks	Ed Bonner	EO	$384.16
	Company Total:		**$384.16**
National All-Risk Insurance Company			
The Blackmail Matter	Phillip Shaw	JL	$22.68
The Bishop Blackmail Matter	Phillip Shaw	JL	$46.35
The Black Doll Matter	Phillip Shaw	JL	$467.60
	Company Total:		**$536.63**
National Fidelity Life Insurance Company			
The Gravedigger's Spades		EO	$763.90
	Company Total:		**$763.90**
National Life & Casualty Insurance Company			
The Isabelle James Matter	Don Maynard	JL	$335.04
The Oscar Clark Matter	Don Maynard	JL	$168.59
The Philip Morey Matter	Don Maynard	JL	$99.38
	Company Total:		**$603.01**
National Marine Indemnity			
The Hollywood Matter	Abe Sandstrom	BB	$618.45
	Company Total:		**$618.45**
National Medical & Hospitalization Insurance Company			
The Bobby Foster Matter	Walter Jackson	JL	$196.96
	Company Total:		**$196.96**
National Surety & Life Insurance Company			
How Much Bourbon Can Flow Under the Bridgework?		CR	$2,603.00
	Company Total:		**$2,603.00**

Company/Program	Agent	Actor	Expenses
National Underwriters			
The Latourette Matter		JL	$219.50
	Company Total:		$219.50
National Underwriters Association			
The Long Shot Matter	Jim Darryl	BB	$490.80
	Company Total:		$490.80
New Britain Insurance Company			
The Valentine Matter	Roy Vickers	BB	$1,290.38
	Company Total:		$1,290.38
New Britain Mutual Insurance Company			
The Wayward Heiress Matter	Al Turner	BB	$10.00
The Paradise Lost Matter	Al Turner	BB	$50.00
	Company Total:		$60.00
New England Mutual Trust & Casualty			
The New Cambridge Matter	Dave Taylor	JL	$125.00
	Company Total:		$125.00
New Jersey Fire & Casualty Insurance Company			
The Smoky Sleeper Matter	Fred Larkin	BB	$130.49
The Terrible Torch Matter	Fred Larkin	MK	$1,500.00
	Company Total:		$1,630.49
New Jersey State Mutual Life Insurance Company			
The Heatherstone Players	MatterGarrett	BB	$51.25
The Short Term Matter	Bill Tilton	BR	$82.80
The Doninger Doninger Matter	Maurice Parkely	MK	$155.70
	Company Total:		$289.75
New York Mutual			
The James Clayton Matter	Chet Graham	JL	$56.35
	Company Total:		$56.35
New York Police Department			
The Jane Doe Matter		EO	$0.00
	Company Total:		$0.00
Northeast Fidelity & Bonding			
The Alvin Summers Matter	Fred Wilkins	BB	$923.00
	Company Total:		$923.00

Company/Program	Agent	Actor	Expenses
Northeast Indemnity			
The Urned Income Matter	Toby Tetrick	BR	$418.15
	Company Total:		$418.15
Northeast Indemnity Affiliates			
The Big Scoop Matter	Joe McNab	BB	$187.40
	Company Total:		$187.40
Northeast Indemnity Associates			
The Imperfect Alibi Matter	Joe McNab	BB	$192.40
The Grand Canyon Matter	Bill Walker	MK	$550.00
	Company Total:		$742.40
Northeast Indemnity Association			
The Tip-Off Matter	George Hardy	MK	$349.40
	Company Total:		$349.40
Northeastern Fidelity & Bonding Company			
The Two Faced Matter	Nick Walters	BB	$9.80
	Company Total:		$9.80
Northeastern Indemnity Association			
The Wayward Money Matter	Fred Norwood	BB	$104.70
	Company Total:		$104.70
Northwest Indemnity Alliance			
The Amy Bradshaw Matter	George Atkins	BB	$185.20
The Crater Lake Matter	Peter Wilkerson	BB	$495.60
	Company Total:		$680.80
Northwest Surety Company			
The Lonely Hearts Matter	Dave Elwood	BB	$416.40
The Midnite Sun Matter	Bill Chadwick	BB	$600.00
	Company Total:		$1,016.40
Nutmeg State Casualty & Bonding Company			
Murder Is a Merry-Go-Round		CR	$692.18
	Company Total:		$692.18
Nutmeg State Liability Underwriters			
Who Took the Taxis for a Ride?		CR	$1,100.00
	Company Total:		$1,100.00

Company/Program	Agent	Actor	Expenses
NYPD Homicide			
The Lucky Costa Matter		EO	$0.00
Company Total:			$0.00
Old Caledonia Insurance Company			
The Skull Canyon Mine	Oscar Wheaton	CR	$947.99
Company Total:			$947.99
Old Caledonia Security Insurance Company			
How I Turned a Luxury Liner Into a Battleship		CR	$2,747.27
Company Total:			$2,747.27
Oriental West Cargo Bonding Company			
The Slow Boat From China	Mr. Fundy	CR	$1,407.00
Company Total:			$1,407.00
Paramount Insurance Adjusters			
The Henderson Matter	Tim Connors	BB	$802.50
The Denver Disbursal Matter	Perry Jaimerson	BB	$391.80
Company Total:			$1,194.30
Philadelphia Mutual Liability & Casualty Company			
The Ricardo Amerigo Matter	Harry Branson	BB	$182.65
The Laird Douglas Douglas of Heatherscote Matter	Harry Branson	BB	$1,113.40
The Wayward Widow Matter	Harry Branson	BB	$365.50
The Casque of Death Matter	Harry Branson	BB	$101.20
The Double Deal Matter	Harry Branson	BB	$2,044.45
Company Total:			$3,807.20
Philadelphia Mutual Liability & Casualty Insurance Company			
The Ingenuous Jeweler Matter	Harry Branson	BB	$181.00
The Larson Arson Matter	Harry Branson	BB	$79.75
The Real Smokey Matter	Harry Branson	BB	$621.00
The Informer Matter	Harry Branson	BR	$115.20
The Latrodectus Matter	Harry Branson	BR	$111.35
Company Total:			$1,108.30
Philadelphia Mutual Life & Casualty Insurance			
The Monoxide Mystery Matter	Clarke Bender	BB	$74.65
Company Total:			$74.65

Company/Program	Agent	Actor	Expenses
Philadelphia Mutual Life & Casualty Insurance Company			
The Clever Chemist Matter	Harry Branson	BB	$84.35
	Company Total:		$84.35
Piedmont Mutual Life Insurance Company			
Pearl Carrasa	Bob Case	EO	$712.55
	Company Total:		$712.55
Plymouth Insurance Company			
The Blackburn Matter	Bob Hall	EO	$345.75
The Vivian Fair Matter		EO	$150.00
The Virginia Towne Matter		EO	$0.00
The Millard Ward Matter	Willard Dunhill	EO	$419.95
The Hannibal Murphy Matter		EO	$734.40
The Paul Gorrell Matter	George Post	JL	$369.80
	Company Total:		$2,019.90
Plymouth Life Insurance Company			
The Rum Barrel Matter		EO	$43.55
	Company Total:		$43.55
Plymouth Mutual Insurance Company			
The Beauregard Matter	Dave Brace	JL	$203.40
	Company Total:		$203.40
Premier Life & Casualty Company			
Here Comes the Death of the Party		CR	$1,434.67
	Company Total:		$1,434.67
Providential Assurance Company			
The Moonshine Murder Matter	Clark Tracy	BB	$340.00
The Melancholy Memory Matter	Bert McGraw	BB	$579.12
The Mason-Dixon Mismatch Matter	Bert McGraw	BB	$319.00
The Dixon Murder Matter	Bert McGraw	BB	$968.20
The Confederate Coinage Matter	Bert McGraw	BB	$405.10
The Hand of Providential Matter	Ernest L. Whiteman	BB	$0.00
The Moonshine Matter	Clark Tracy	BB	$340.00
The Deadly Swamp Matter	Charles K. Sinclair	BB	$161.60
	Company Total:		$3,113.02
Providential Fire & Marine			
The Royal Street Matter	C. D. Binford	BB	$517.20
	Company Total:		$517.20

Company/Program	Agent	Actor	Expenses
Providential Life & Casualty			
The Golden Touch Matter	Steve Kilmer	BB	$240.00
Company Total:			$240.00
Providential Life & Casualty Insurance Company			
The Shankar Diamond Matter	Steve Kilmer	BB	$50.00
Company Total:			$50.00
Providential Property Insurance Company			
The Canned Canary Matter	Jack Price	BB	$1,121.00
Company Total:			$1,121.00
Richard Porter			
The Shepherd Matter	Richard Porter	BB	$485.00
Company Total:			$485.00
Samuel Ruben & Associates			
The Salt City Matter	Samuel Ruben	BB	$3,262.00
Company Total:			$3,262.00
Seaboard Mutual Life Insurance Company			
The Great Bannock Race Matter	Bill Blake	JL	$1,207.90
Company Total:			$1,207.90
Seven Seas Maritime Underwriters Association			
The Island of Tin-Yutan	Enos McCartle	CR	$3,286.44
Company Total:			$3,286.44
Shipper's Indemnity			
The Story of The Ten-O-Eight	Harry Poulden	EO	$312.00
Company Total:			$312.00
Sierra All-Risk			
The Jackie Cleaver Matter	Carl Mason	EO	$280.00
Company Total:			$280.00
Special Program			
The Five Down Matter		BB	$0.00
Company Total:			$0.00

Company/Program	Agent	Actor	Expenses
Star Mutual Insurance Company			
The Shady Lane Matter	Pete Carlson	BB	$186.60
The Sick Chick Matter		BB	$0.00
The Hair Raising Matter	Fritz Melchior	BB	$47.50
The Touch-Up Matter	Terry Holmes	BR	$0.00
The Four's A Crowd Matter	Dennis Taylor	MK	$400.00
The Oldest Gag Matter	Larry Spangler	MK	$0.00
The Lorelei Matter	Ed Williams	MK	$0.00
	Company Total:		**$634.10**
State Unity Life			
The Silent Queen Matter	Vic Carson	BB	$436.25
The Old Fashioned Murder Matter	Herbert Lynn	MK	$347.85
	Company Total:		**$784.10**
State Unity Life Insurance Company			
The Ghost to Ghost Matter	Oscar M. Trimley	BB	$31.50
The Lone Wolf Matter	Harvey Wakeman	BR	$88.40
The Imperfect Crime Matter	Lou Little	MK	$0.00
The Well of Trouble Matter	Lou Little	MK	$0.00
The All Wet Matter	Lawrence P. Thurston	MK	$300.00
The Blue Rock Matter	Phil Taylor	MK	$200.00
	Company Total:		**$619.90**
Strool Bail Bond			
The Jack Madigan Matter	Manny Strool	EO	$2,720.00
	Company Total:		**$2,720.00**
Surety Mutual & Trust Company			
The Cronin Matter	Joe Parker	BB	$263.30
The Suntan Oil Matter	Dave Lawler	BB	$474.84
	Company Total:		**$738.14**
Surety Mutual Insurance Company			
The Ring of Death Matter	Don Pinkley	BR	$389.00
The Top Secret Matter	Len Walker	MK	$993.70
	Company Total:		**$1,382.70**
Surety Mutual Insurance, Ltd.			
The Cui Bono Matter	Don Hancock	BB	$382.65
The Saturday Night Matter	Peter H. Fillmore	BB	$301.01
The Ivy Emerald Matter	Bob Baker	MK	$0.00
	Company Total:		**$683.66**

Company/Program	Agent	Actor	Expenses
Surety Mutual Ltd.			
The Blinker Matter	Fred Wills	BB	$434.50
	Company Total:		$434.50
Swanson Industrial Insurance Corporation			
The Belo-Horizonte Railroad	George Donnelly	EO	$1,492.54
	Company Total:		$1,492.54
Transworld Fidelity Company			
The Lorko Diamonds Matter	Ben Tyler	BB	$1,214.60
	Company Total:		$1,214.60
Treasury Department, Bureau of Narcotics			
The London Matter	Mark Nelson	EO	$1,580.20
	Company Total:		$1,580.20
Tri Western Life Insurance			
The Unworthy Kin Matter	Frank Harmon	BB	$500.00
	Company Total:		$500.00
Tri-Eastern Indemnity Associates			
The Star of Capetown Matter	Joe McNab	BB	$1,283.60
The Hot Chocolates Matter	Harvey Weller	MK	$49.35
	Company Total:		$1,332.95
Tri-Mutual Insurance Company			
The Wrong Sign Matter	Harley Tilson	BR	$129.30
	Company Total:		$129.30
Tri-Mutual Insurance Company, Ltd			
The Hapless Hunter Matter	Jerry Holland	BB	$13.13
The Low Tide Matter	Frederick Bennom	MK	$0.00
	Company Total:		$13.13
Tri-Mutual Insurance Ltd.			
The Nick Shurn Matter	Don Wilkins	BB	$486.20
	Company Total:		$486.20

Company/Program	Agent	Actor	Expenses
Trinity Mutual Insurance Company			
The One Most Wanted Matter	Bob Tank	BB	$3,995.00
The Phony Phone Matter	Bert Helfer	MK	$0.00
The Vociferous Dolphin Matter	Will Burnett	MK	$531.80
The Rilldo Matter	Will Burnett	MK	$250.00
	Company Total:		**$4,776.80**
Trinity Mutual Insurance Company, Ltd.			
The Caylin Matter	Walt Albright	BB	$596.85
	Company Total:		**$596.85**
Tri-State Assurance Company, Ltd			
The Piney Corners Matter	Bob Crale	JL	$120.70
	Company Total:		**$120.70**
Tri-State Guaranty Company			
The Kranesburg Matter	Bob Lauder	BB	$409.10
	Company Total:		**$409.10**
Tri-State Insurance Company			
The Yankee Pride Matter	Carl Bush	EO	$2,686.00
The Queen Anne Pistols Matter	William Carter	EO	$365.35
The Yankee Pride Matter	Carl Bush	EO	$2,686.00
	Company Total:		**$5,737.35**
Tri-State Insurance Group			
The Edward French Matter		EO	$2,739.50
The Alonzo Chapman Matter		EO	$672.08
The Leland Case Matter		EO	$496.13
The Tolhurst Theft Matter	Jim Madison	EO	$77.60
	Company Total:		**$3,985.31**
Tri-State Insurance Underwriters			
The McClain Matter	Don Taylor	BB	$768.60
	Company Total:		**$768.60**
Tri-State Life & Casualty Company			
The Blood River Matter		EO	$740.00
The Parley Barron Matter	Earle Poorman	BB	$421.50
The Three Sisters Matter	Earle Poorman	BB	$351.20
The Eastern Western Matter	Earle Poorman	BB	$207.00
The Double Trouble Matter	Earle Poorman	BB	$178.70
The Clouded Crystal Matter	Earle Poorman	BB	$168.50

Company/Program	Agent	Actor	Expenses
The Net of Circumstance Matter	Earle Poorman	BB	$151.50
The False Alarm Matter	Earle Poorman	BB	$161.00
The Recompense Matter	Don Boomhauer	BB	$0.00
The Wayward Kilocycles Matter	Earle Poorman	BR	$400.00
	Company Total:		$2,779.40

Tri-State Life & Casualty Insurance Company

Company/Program	Agent	Actor	Expenses
The Search for Michelle Marsh		CR	$786.00
The Burning Carr Matter	Earle Poorman	BB	$385.26
The Kirby Will Matter	Danny Newcum	BB	$331.25
The Wayward Moth Matter	Earle Poorman	BB	$204.00
The Salkoff Sequel Matter	Earle Poorman	BB	$0.00
The Lucky 4 Matter	Earle Poorman	BB	$224.95
The Gruesome Spectacle Matter	Ed Barrett	BB	$148.00
The Bayou Body Matter	Earle Poorman	BB	$168.65
The Fancy Bridgework Matter	Earle Poorman	BB	$200.00
The Deadly Debt Matter	Don Boomhauer	BB	$200.00
The What Goes Matter	Earle Poorman	BB	$368.50
The Big Date Matter	Don Boomhauer	BR	$20.00
The Fiddle Faddle Matter	Earle Poorman	MK	$681.80
The Wrong One Matter	Earle Poorman	MK	$0.00
The Guide to Murder Matter	Earle Poorman	MK	$85.00
The Weather or Not Matter	Earle Poorman	MK	$247.92
	Company Total:		$4,051.33

Tri-State Life Insurance Company

Company/Program	Agent	Actor	Expenses
The Earl Chadwick Matter	Leland Scarf	EO	$1,575.00
	Company Total:		$1,575.00

Tri-Western Indemnity Company

Company/Program	Agent	Actor	Expenses
The Wayward Truck Matter	Ted Orloff	BB	$501.05
	Company Total:		$501.05

Tri-Western Life & Casualty Company

Company/Program	Agent	Actor	Expenses
The Glacier Ghost Matter	Walter Bascomb	BB	$431.60
The Impossible Murder Matter	Walt Bascomb	BB	$516.25
	Company Total:		$947.85

Tri-Western Life & Casualty Insurance Company

Company/Program	Agent	Actor	Expenses
The Bum Steer Matter	Hal Verski	BB	$0.00
	Company Total:		$0.00

Company/Program	Agent	Actor	Expenses
Tri-Western Life Insurance Company			
The Hired Homicide Matter		BB	$0.00
The Unholy Two Matter	Jack Price	BB	$287.20
The Stope of Death Matter	Hal Barker	BB	$248.75
The Simple Simon Matter	Frank Francis	BR	$450.00
The Perilous Padre Matter	Jack Price	MK	$485.00
The Wrong Doctor Matter	Jack Price	MK	$532.40
The Medium Rare Matter	Jack Price	MK	$465.30
The Ike And Mike Matter	Jack Price	MK	$0.00
The Skidmore Matter	Jack Price	MK	$276.28
	Company Total:		**$2,744.93**
Tri-Western Property & Casualty Insurance Company			
The Doubtful Dairy Matter	Peter Hardy	BB	$418.00
	Company Total:		**$418.00**
Twin State Insurance Company			
The Starlet Matter	Ken Ralston	JL	$366.05
	Company Total:		**$366.05**
Union States Casualty Company			
The Laughing Matter	Ed Renzer	BB	$791.55
	Company Total:		**$791.55**
Union States Casualty Insurance Company			
The Nugget of Truth Matter	Ted Newberry	MK	$20.00
	Company Total:		**$20.00**
United Adjustment Bureau			
The Clinton Matter	Al Davies	BB	$2,385.03
	Company Total:		**$2,385.03**
Universal Adjusters			
The Oklahoma Red Matter	Frank Ahern	JL	$286.45
	Company Total:		**$286.45**
Universal Adjustment Bureau			
The Chesapeake Fraud Matter	Pat Kelleher	BB	$1,124.98
The Lansing Fraud Matter	Jim Carter	BB	$1,121.13
The Duke Red Matter	Niles Pearson	BB	$802.65
The Jolly Roger Fraud Matter	Pat McCracken	BB	$523.23
The LaMarr Matter	Pat McCracken	BB	$0.00
The Medium, Well Done Matter	Pat McCracken	BB	$892.90

Company/Program	Agent	Actor	Expenses
The Tears of Night Matter	Pat McCracken	BB	$405.16
The Sea Legs Matter	Pat McCracken	BB	$841.95
The Phantom Chase Matter	Pat McCracken	BB	$1,723.00
The Rasmusson Matter		BB	$1,965.00
The Yours Truly Matter	Pat McCracken	BB	$528.00
The Killer's Brand Matter	Pat McCracken	BB	$528.00
The Ideal Vacation Matter	Pat McCracken	BB	$115.25
The Model Picture Matter	Pat McCracken	BB	$103.00
The Shy Beneficiary Matter	Pat McCracken	BB	$410.00
The Sunny Dream Matter	Pat McCracken	BB	$12.00
The Carmen Kringle Matter	Pat McCracken	BB	$0.00
The Latin Lovely Matter	Pat McCracken	BB	$0.00
The Time and Tide Matter	Pat McCracken	BB	$403.50
The Wayward Trout Matter	Pat McCracken	BB	$815.00
The Rolling Stone Matter	Pat McCracken	BB	$146.00
The Limping Liability Matter	Pat McCracken	BB	$1,020.20
The Johnson Payroll Matter	Pat McCracken	BB	$526.50
The Missing Matter Matter	Pat McCracken	BB	$0.00
The Close Shave Matter	Pat McCracken	BB	$383.20
The Perilous Parley Matter	Pat McCracken	BB	$8.00
The Deadly Doubt Matter	Pat McCracken	BB	$41.00
The Love Shorn Matter	Pat McCracken	BB	$377.00
The Lake Mead Mystery Matter	Pat McCracken	BB	$196.45
The Wayward Sculptor Matter	Pat McCracken	BB	$26.15
The Really Gone Matter	Pat McCracken	BB	$401.05
The Backfire That Backfired Matter	Pat McCracken	BB	$450.00
The Little Man Who Was There Matter	Pat McCracken	BB	$12.34
The Buffalo Matter	Pat McCracken	BB	$0.00
The Further Buffalo Matter	Pat McCracken	BB	$1,800.00
The Double Identity Matter	Pat McCracken	BB	$20.00
The Sudden Wealth Matter	Pat McCracken	BB	$38.25
The Red Mystery Matter	Pat McCracken	BB	$0.00
The Burning Desire Matter	Pat McCracken	BB	$874.20
The Merry Go Round Matter	Pat McCracken	BB	$0.00
The Look Before the Leap Matter	Pat McCracken	BB	$9,571.00
The Wholly Unexpected Matter	Pat McCracken	BB	$0.00
The Magnanimous Matter	Pat McCracken	BB	$0.00
The Super Salesman Matter	Pat McCracken	BB	$189.95
The Bee or Not to Bee Matter	Pat Fuller	MK	$471.00
The Lust for Gold Matter	Pat Fuller	MK	$0.00
The Key to Crime Matter	Pat Fuller	MK	$742.89
The Key to Crime Matter	Pat Fuller	MK	$572.89
	Company Total:		**$30,012.82**

Company/Program	Agent	Actor	Expenses
Universal Bonding & Indemnity Company			
The Barton Baker Matter	Charlie Maxwell	JL	$604.15
	Company Total:		$604.15
Washingtonian Insurance Company			
The Montevideo Matter	Bill Brandon	EO	$1,650.00
The Marie Meadows Matter	Bill Brandon	EO	$110.40
The Montevideo Matter	Bill Brandon	EO	$1,650.00
	Company Total:		$3,410.40
Washingtonian Life Insurance Company			
The Celia Woodstock Matter	Sam Miller	EO	$73.60
The Malcolm Wish, M.D. Matter		EO	$577.40
The Horace Lockhart Matter		EO	$583.85
The Merrill Kent Matter	Mr. Lavery	EO	$378.40
The Celia Woodstock Matter	Mr. Miller	JL	$73.60
The Harpooned Angler Matter	Phillip Martin	JL	$1,043.90
The Terrified Taun Matter	Tom Benson	JL	$2,296.45
The Frustrated Phoenix Matter	Mr. Bradley	JL	$153.50
The Temperamental Tote Board Matter	Ben Gordon	JL	$354.95
The Sarah Martin Matter	Ed Reynolds	JL	$318.05
	Company Total:		$5,853.70
West Coast Underwriters			
The Little Man Who Wasn't All There	Bradford L. Coates	CR	$942.08
	Company Total:		$942.08
Western Indemnity Company			
The Flask of Death Matter	Paul Peters	BB	$431.00
The Shadow of a Doubt Matter	Ted Orloff	MK	$450.00
The All Too Easy Matter	Ted Orloff	MK	$491.34
	Company Total:		$1,372.34
Western Indemnity Company, Greater Southwest Insurance Company, Universal Adjustment Bureau			
The Who's Who Matter	Ted Beckham	BR	$306.25
	Company Total:		$306.25
Western Life & Trust Company			
The Markham Matter	Ed Porter	BB	$968.20
	Company Total:		$968.20

Company/Program	Agent	Actor	Expenses
Western Life & Trust Insurance Company			
The Alkali Mike Matter	Bill Kemper	BB	$525.00
The Fatal Switch Matter	Art Bascomb	BB	$386.21
	Company Total:		**$911.21**
Western Maritime & Life Insurance Company			
The Chuckanut Matter	Lucien Peterson	MK	$391.18
The Two Steps to Murder Matter	Pete Brenneman	MK	$511.80
The Zip Matter	Pete Brenneman	MK	$200.00
The Wayward Clipper Matter	Hartfield Wormser	MK	$900.00
	Company Total:		**$2,002.98**
Western Maritime & Property			
The Ellen Dear Matter	Arthur Arthur	BB	$453.95
The Ellen Dear Matter – Audition	Arthur Arthur	BB	$453.95
	Company Total:		**$907.90**
Western Maritime & Property Insurance Company			
The Malibu Mystery Matter	Peter Hanley	BB	$101.50
The Wayward Diamonds Matter	Peter Hanley	BB	$218.00
The Baldero Matter	Arthur Arthur	BB	$0.00
	Company Total:		**$319.50**
World Insurance & Indemnity Company			
The Stanley Price Matter	Hanley Conrad	JL	$113.40
The Amita Buddha Matter	Hanley Conrad	JL	$527.15
The Howard Arnold Matter	Hanley Conrad	JL	$123.66
	Company Total:		**$764.21**
World Mutual Insurance Company			
The Deadly Crystal Matter	Les Walters	MK	$100.00
	Company Total:		**$100.00**
World Wide Mutual			
The Two Tired Matter	Les Walters	BR	$4.90
	Company Total:		**$4.90**
Worldwide Maritime & Insurance Company			
The Hampton Line Matter	Jack Loring	JL	$158.55
	Company Total:		**$158.55**

Company/Program	Agent	Actor	Expenses
Worldwide Mutual Insurance Company			
The Alder Matter	Vic Kelly	BB	$833.14
The Carson Arson Matter	Jim Paris	BB	$56.90
The Noxious Needle Matter	Waldo R. Westbury	BB	$61.20
The Mei-Ling Buddah Matter	Marty Bruce	BB	$300.00
The Lost By a Hair Matter	Fred Starkey	BB	$162.70
The Leumas Matter	Les Walters	BB	$89.50
The Two's A Crowd Matter	Paul Ferris	BR	$379.50
The Stock in Trade Matter	Rip Teeter	BR	$325.00
The Buyer and The Cellar Matter	Don Reagle	MK	$477.30
The Cinder Elmer Matter	Charlie Warren	MK	$377.80
The Can't Be So Matter	Les Walters	MK	$0.00
The Takes a Crook Matter	Les Walters	MK	$0.00
The Mixed Blessing Matter	Charlie Warren	MK	$497.40
	Company Total:		**$3,560.44**

Total Expenses   **$320,285.77**

Recycled Programs

In the years between 1949 and 1962, a number of Yours Truly, Johnny Dollar programs were "recycled". Among the programs in the YTJD canon, a number of programs were repeated, some were repeated and renamed, and some were imported or exported from/to other programs.

Based on the information taken from the programs in this document, and based on research done by Stewart Wright, the following tables list the various programs and how there were recycled.

Repeated Programs

The following programs were repeated as written:

Program Name	Dates Repeated	Writer
Death Takes a Working Day	8/14/1949 2/3/1950	Paul Dudley, Gil Doud
Milford Brooks III	12/7/1948 3/25/1949	Paul Dudley, Gil Doud
The Birdy Baskerville Matter	11/10/1951 3/10/1953	Blake Edwards
The Celia Woodstock Matter	3/3/1951 1/12/1954	Gil Doud
The Fair-Way Matter	7/11/1951 1/5/1954	Gil Doud
The Monopoly Matter	2/3/1951 12/1/1953	Gil Doud
The Rudy Valentine Matter	12/30/1950 12/22/1953	Gil Doud
The Woodward Manila Matter	11/25/1950 6/29/1954	Gil Doud
The Yankee Pride Matter	10/14/1950 7/9/1952[1] 8/27/1952	Gil Doud

Program Name	Dates Repeated	Writer
The Montevideo Matter	12/23/1950 7/23/1952[2] 9/3/1952	Gil Doud

Notes:
1. Scheduled but preempted
2. Scheduled but preempted

Modified and Repeated Programs

A number of programs were repeated but modified in the process. Some were only title and character changes, some were expansions of the story, and there are several stories that were combined to form a new story.

In the data that follows, the programs are listed in date order by the original program name, date and writer.

Program Name	Program Date	Writer
Witness, Witness, Who's Got the Witness	10/22/1949	Paul Dudley, Gil Doud
The Jack Madigan Matter	10/21/1950	Paul Dudley, Gil Doud
The Tom Hickman Matter	8/13/1952	Gil Doud

Program Name	Program Date	Writer
Bodyguard to Anne Connelly	12/3/1949	Paul Dudley, Gil Doud
The Virginia Beach Matter	8/31/1950	Gil Doud

Program Name	Program Date	Writer
Haiti Adventure Matter	12/17/1949	Paul Dudley, Gil Doud
The Port-au-Prince Matter	5/30/1950	Gil Doud, David Ellis

Program Name	Program Date	Writer
The Robert Perry Case	3/4/1949	Paul Dudley, Gil Doud
Bodyguard to the Late Robert W. Perry	3/3/1950	Paul Dudley, Gil Doud

Program Name	Program Date	Writer
The Big Red Schoolhouse	4/4/1950	E. Jack Neuman, John Michael Hayes
The Clinton Matter (5-part program) (See Imported/Exported section below.)	3/12/1956 3/16/1956	John Dawson

Program Name	Program Date	Writer
The Adam Kegg Matter	11/11/1950	Gil Doud
The Sidney Mann Matter	8/6/1952	Gil Doud

Program Name	Program Date	Writer
The Adolph Schoman Matter	1/6/1951	Gil Doud
The Amelia Harwell Matter	7/2/1952	Gil Doud

Program Name	Program Date	Writer
The Emily Braddock Matter	5/19/1953	E. Jack Neuman
The Thelma Ibsen Matter	1/09/1953	E. Jack Neuman
The Broderick Matter	11/14/1955	John Dawson
(5-part program)	11/18/1955	

Program Name	Program Date	Writer
The Brisbane Fraud Matter	5/26/1953	E. Jack Neuman
The Callicles Matter	4/30/1956	John Dawson
(5-part program)	5/04/1956	

Program Name	Program Date	Writer
The Walter Patterson Matter	12/26/1952	E. Jack Neuman
The Chesapeake Fraud Matter	10/17/1955	John Dawson
(5-part program)	10/21/1955	

Program Name	Program Date	Writer
The Ben Bryson Matter	12/29/1953	Les Crutchfield
The Confidential Matter	9/14/1956	Les Crutchfield
(5-part program)	9/10/1956	

Program Name	Program Date	Writer
The Oklahoma Red Matter	6/09/1953	E. Jack Neuman
The Duke Red Matter	1/23/1956	John Dawson
(5-part program)	1/27/1956	

Program Name	Program Date	Writer
The Eighty-Five Little Minks	3/14/1950	E. Jack Neuman, John Michael Hayes
The Templeton Matter	2/10/1957	John Dawson

Program Name	Program Date	Writer
The Alma Scott Matter	12/29/1951	Gil Doud
The Emil Carter Matter	6/16/1953	Gil Doud

Program Name	Program Date	Writer
The Lester James Matter	3/31/1953	E. Jack Neuman
The Forbes Matter.	12/26/1955	John Dawson
(5-part program)	12/30/1955	

Program Name	Program Date	Writer
The Underwood Matter	2/27/1953	E. Jack Neuman
The Henderson Matter	11/28/1955	John Dawson
(5-part program)	12/2/1955	

Program Name	Program Date	Writer
The Joan Sebastian Matter	10/28/1950	Gil Doud
The Jeanne Maxwell Matter	3/06/1953	Gil Doud
The Jeanne Maxwell Matter	7/20/1954	Gil Doud

Program Name	Program Date	Writer
The Beauregard Matter	1/26/1954	Les Crutchfield
The Kranesburg Matter	8/24/1956	Les Crutchfield
(6-part program)	8/31/1956	

Program Name	Program Date	Writer
The Dan Frank Matter	5/4/1954	Les Crutchfield
The Open Town Matter	7/23/1956	Les Crutchfield
(5-part program)	7/27/1956	

Program Name	Program Date	Writer
The New Cambridge Matter	12/19/1952	E. Jack Neuman
The Plantagent Matter	3/5/1956	John Dawson
(5-part program)	3/9/1956	
(See Imported/Exported section below).		

Program Name	Program Date	Writer
The Piney Corners Matter	3/23/1954	Les Crutchfield
The Shady Lane Matter	7/9/1956	Les Crutchfield
(5-part program)	7/13/1956	

Program Name	Program Date	Writer
The James Clayton Matter	12/5/1952	E. Jack Neuman
The Shepherd Matter	4/16/1956	John Dawson
(5-part program)	4/20/1956	

Program Name	Program Date	Writer
The Douglas Taylor Matter	10/06/1951	Gil Doud
The Singapore Arson Matter	11/28/1952	Gil Doud

Program Name	Program Date	Writer
The Baltimore Matter	1/02/1953	E. Jack Neuman
The Rochester Theft Matter	5/12/1953	E. Jack Neuman
The Todd Matter	1/09/1956	John Dawson
(5-part program)	1/13/1956	

Program Name	Program Date	Writer
The San Antonio Matter	4/28/1953	E. Jack Neuman
The Valentine Matter	10/31/1955	John Dawson
(5-part program)	11/4/1955	

(See Imported/Exported section below).

Program Name	Program Date	Writer
The Trans-Pacific Import Export Company, South China Branch	8/24/1950	Gil Doud, David Ellis
The Trans-Pacific Matter (John Lund Audition)	11/24/1952 11/28/1952	E. Jack Neuman
The Trans-Pacific Matter (Gerald Mohr Audition)	8/29/1955	E. Jack Neuman, Gil Doud

These programs are virtually the same, with modified details and storyline elements. The 8/24/1950 program was used as an audition for John Lund (11/24 and 11/28/1952) and Gerald Mohr (8/29/1955).

Imported/Exported Programs

Several programs started life as episodes of other programs or were used on other programs.

Program Name	Program Date	Writer
The Queen Anne Pistols and the Dealer on King George Road (The Voyage of the Scarlet Queen)	2/18/1948	Gil Doud
The Queen Anne Pistols Matter	11/4/1950	Gil Doud

The first iteration of this program was the Scarlet Queen episode, which was adapted and used as a Johnny Dollar episode.

Program Name	Program Date	Writer
The Prodigal Daughter (Jeff Regan)	7/17/1948	E. Jack Neuman
The Pearling Matter (5-part program)	6/18/1956 6/22/1956	John Dawson

The Jeff Regan program was expanded and used as a 5-part episode in 1956.

Program Name	Program Date	Writer
The Lonesome Lady (Jeff Regan)	7/24/1948	E. Jack Neuman
The Chicago Fraud Matter	2/6/1953	E. Jack Neuman
The Lansing Fraud Matter (5-part program)	12/12/1955 12/16/1955	John Dawson

The Jeff Regan program was modified to become *The Chicago Fraud Matter*, which was further expanded to become the 5-part program *The Landing Fraud Matter*. These programs have the same storyline, but the names and locations are different.

Program Name	Program Date	Writer
The Story of the Lost Lady (Jeff Regan)	10/16/1948	E. Jack Neuman & Larry Roman
The Lady from Brazil (Jeff Regan)	10/19/1949	E. Jack Neuman
They've Got More Than Coffee in Brazil (Jeff Regan)	6/18/1950	E. Jack Neuman
The Madison Matter	4/14/1953	E. Jack Neuman
The McClain Matter (5-part program)	2/10/1956 2/6/1956	John Dawson

This program series is the one of the longest-lived programs in this import/export series of programs. These programs have the same storyline elements, but the names and location are different.

Program Name	Program Date	Writer
The Story of the Man Who Liked Mountains (Jeff Regan)	8/7/1948	E. Jack Neuman
The Fall Guy (Rocky Jordan)	5/1/1949	E. Jack Neuman
The Salt City Matter (5-part program)	4/2/1956 4/6/1956	John Dawson

The Rocky Jordan program (edited by Gomer Cool & Larry Roman) was adapted to become the Jeff Regan program, which was expanded and used as a 5-part Johnny Dollar story.

Program Name	Program Date	Writer
The Story of the Diamond Quartet (Jeff Regan)	8/14/1948	E. Jack Neuman
The Tears of Night Caper (The Adventures of Sam Spade)	7/24/1949	Bob Talman Gil Doud
The Tears of Night Matter (5-part program)	5/21/1956 5/25/1956	John Dawson

This program started out as a Jeff Regan episode, was adaped and used as a Sam Spade episode, and ended up as a 5-part Johnny Dollar story.

Program Name	Program Date	Writer
The Man Who Came Back (Jeff Regan)	8/21/1948	E. Jack Neuman
The Champion Caper (The Adventures of Sam Spade)	8/07/1949	E. Jack Neuman
The Elliot Champion Matter	12/12/1952	E. Jack Neuman
The Upjohn Matter	9/19/1954	E. Jack Neuman
The Bennet Matter (5-part program)	2/19/1956 2/24/1956	John Dawson

This program series is the one of the longest-lived programs in this import/export series of programs. It started as a Jeff Regan story, then as a Sam Spade story, and then was used as two separate Johnny Dollar episodes which were then merged together to create the 5-part Johnny Dollar story.

Program Name	Program Date	Writer
The Lady with No Name (Jeff Regan)	9/25/1948	E. Jack Neuman
The Lady in Distress (Richard Diamond, Private Detective)	5/23/1951	E. Jack Neuman, John Michael Hayes
The New Cambridge Matter	12/19/1952	E. Jack Neuman
The Plantagent Matter (5-part program)	3/5/1956 3/9/1956	John Dawson

The Richard Diamond program has a number of story elements that would later be included in *The New Cambridge Matter* and *The Plantagent Matter*.

Program Name	Program Date	Writer
The Big Red Schoolhouse	4/4/1950	E. Jack Neuman, John Michael Hayes
The Civic Pride Caper (The Adventures of Sam Spade)	4/13/1951	John Michael Hayes
The Clinton Matter (5-part program)	3/12/1956 3/16/1956	John Dawson

The Big Red School House is different in that it was originally a Johnny Dollar story which was then exported to Sam Spade and the imported back into the 5-part Johnny Dollar story.

Program Name	Program Date	Writer
The Hatpin Murder (Richard Diamond)	9/27/1950 8/16/1953	Blake Edwards
The Baxter Matter	1/12/1952	Blake Edwards

The story was first done as an episode of Richard Diamond, then exported to Johnny Dollar and then used again as a Richard Diamond story.

Program Name	Program Date	Writer
Little Chiva	3/23/1951	Blake Edwards
(Richard Diamond, Private Detective)		
The Voodoo Matter	8/04/1953	Blake Edwards

The story was first done as an episode of Richard Diamond, then exported to Johnny Dollar.

Program Name	Program Date	Writer
The Fur-Flaunting Floozy	9/26/1951	E. Jack Neuman
(The Line-Up)		
The Baltimore Matter	1/02/1953	E. Jack Neuman
The Rochester Theft Matter	5/12/1953	
The Todd Matter	1/09/1956	John Dawson
(5-part program)	1/13/1956	

The *Line-Up* program and *The Baltimore Matter* and *The Rochester Theft Matter* all share common story elements which were consolidated in *The Todd Matter*.

Program Name	Program Date	Writer
The Man in the Church	10/12/1949	E. Jack Neuman
(Jeff Regan)		
Big John McMasters	3/4/1951	E. Jack Neuman
(Night Beat)		John Michael Hayes
The San Antonio Matter	4/28/1953	E. Jack Neuman
The Valentine Matter	10/31/1955	John Dawson
	11/4/1955	

The *Night Beat* program (which was a salute to the member of the press, was adapted into *The San Antonio Matter*, and then expanded into *The Valentine Matter*.

Program Name	Program Date	Writer
The Curse of Kamashek Matter	9/3/1956	Jack Johnstone
(5-part program)	9/6/1956	
The Curse of Kamoshek Matter	4/22/1962	Jonathan Bundy
(Suspense)		

This is the only Jack Johnstone program used on the Johnny Dollar series that was exported to another program. In this instance, Jack Johnstone (using his pseudonym Jonathan Bundy) rewrote one of his programs for *Suspense*.

VIII: The Canonical Johnny Dollar List

For this edition, I have included a table of the "known" episodes of Yours Truly, Johnny Dollar. I have included this information because, based on recent research, the established list of programs has changed.

For this second edition, I have relied on the Old Time Radio Researchers (OTRR) collection of mp3 programs, version 2. This collection includes all the known digital programs and has the most complete versions of the programs. I have also included program information uncovered during my research at the Thousand Oaks Library.

But there is a need to also recognize the sources of the recordings, for without them, we would have nothing. I asked OTR collector Dr. Joe Webb about where the recordings came from. His answer is that many of the recordings came from:

- Studio production transcriptions
- Network line recordings
- AFRS & AFRTS transcriptions

The Armed Forces Radio Service (AFRS) and the Armed Forces Radio and Television Service (AFRTS) were the networks provided by the military to entertain servicemen and women all over the world. The civilian networks, such as CBS and NBC, would send transcription disks to the military networks for them to air. I remember listening to the AFN when I was stationed in Germany, many years ago, and Suspense, Gunsmoke and other programs were part of the programming schedule. Unfortunately, I never heard Johnny Dollar while I was there. No doubt that many programs were recorded by servicemen and have entered the OTR community along with programs taken from transcription disks.

Because the programs from the AFRS and AFRTS play such an important role as a source of programs, I have created a list of those programs with an AFRTS identifier in the index.

Additionally, airchecks made by hobbyists and others, usually from taped recordings of broadcast programs, such as those from WROW (11 programs) provide another source of programs. The programs identified as coming from WBBM (5 programs) were most probably done by WBBM.

The pre-5-part and the 5-part programs are mainly from CBS recordings with occasional AFRS transcriptions.

Around 1957, when tape recorders became available, is when the home recordings really start to play a big role in things.

Without these various efforts, we would not have any list, let alone one that is mostly complete.

The biggest change to the canon of programs in this edition is the addition of 6 Bob Readick programs.

In 2014, the Thousand Oaks Library found a collection of scripts provided by the Pacific Pioneer Broadcasters (PPB). In this collection were copies of known scripts performed by Bob Bailey, Bob Readick and Mandel Kramer. But in this collection, there were six scripts that, on face value, were unknown:

- *The Wrong Ending Matter*
- *The Art for My Sake Matter*
- *The True Love Matter*
- *The Death by Jet Matter*
- *The Planner Matter*
- *The Two Tired Matter*

Additionally, a script for *The Wayward Clipper Matter* (commonly cataloged as *The Tuna Clipper Matter*) was in the PPB files and has been added to the Mandel Kramer programs.

The question then became, where do these programs fit into the program canon? After visiting the Thousand Oaks Library and reading these new scripts, some clarity was found.

However, to figure out exactly where these programs fit into the canon required analyzing the "next week" teasers in the programs and researching various newspaper databases for hints about the various program contents. These research efforts have established that:

- The last Bob Bailey program was on 11/27/1960.

The next series of programs should be:

- *The Urned/Earned Income Matter* on 12/4/1960.
- *The Wayward Kilocycles Matter* on 12/18/1960.
- *The Art for My Sake Matter* (sometimes called *The Christmas Present Matter*) on 12/25/1960.
- *The True Love Matter* on 1/1/1961.
- *The Big Date Matter* (typically placed at the end of the Readick programs) on 1/8/1961.
- *The Very Fishy Matter* on 1/15/1961
- *The Short Term Matter* (also listed as *The Dollar Put in Jail Matter*, a separate program, in other lists) on 1/22/1961
- *The Death by Jet Matter* (also called *The Paperback Mystery Matter* in other lists) on 1/29/1961

- *The Planner Matter* on 2/5/1961
- *The Who's Who Matter* on 2/12/1961
- *The Wayward Fireman Matter* on 2/19/1961
- *The Two Tired Matter* on 2/26/1961

By looking at the details of these programs, the "next week" teasers show a logical progression from one program to the next. However, the addition of these new programs does create a problem — there are now too many programs.

There are three hard dates into which the programs in the Bob Readick and Mandel Kramer series must fit:

- 12/4/1959 is the date of the first Bob Readick program.
- 12/17/1961 is the date of a Mandel Kramer program preceding a known preemption by the network for a Bing Crosby special.
- 9/30/1962 is the date of the last Yours Truly, Johnny Dollar program.

Given these constraints, there are 95 calendar weeks between 12/4/1959 and 9/30/1962. But the addition of the new programs listed above bring the total of programs in the specified timeframe to 96 programs. So, what to do?

A careful analysis of the "next week" teasers, an analysis of all the program titles shows that there is one program — *One of the Rottenest Rackets Matter* which was supposedly broadcast on 10/1/1961 — that does not seem to fit into the catalog. This program does not fit because:

- Firstly, every Jack Johnstone script begins with "The" — this one does not.
- Secondly, the next week tag for the previous program *The Double-barreled Matter* states "Next week, one of the rottenest rackets in the world, but a story with a real twist at the end."
- Thirdly, the way the Johnny discovers the personal information fits the "twist" at the end.

So, by deleting this program from the list, and adjusting the dates of the following programs by one week, all of the programs match what we know about the dates in the newspapers and the next week teasers.

Does the above mean that the broadcast dates provided here are all accurate? Unfortunately, no; definitive information from unshakable primary sources is sometimes lacking, especially for some of the Readick and Kramer programs. I am convinced that the vast majority of the programs listed in the canonical tables are accurate based on all of the information available, but there are nagging doubts about a handful of the Readick/Kramer programs.

For example, the following programs logically follow each other based on the "next week" teasers at the end of the programs:

Broadcast Date	Program Title	Next Week Teaser
3/5/1961	The Touch-Up Matter	Next week, what might have been a pleasant trip across the country if it weren't for a killer gunning for me.
3/12/1961	The Morning After Matter	Next week, a case involving a prize fight in which the only prize to be won is death.
3/19/1961	The Ring of Death Matter	Next week, a trip to South Jersey and a murder to stop a murder.
3/26/1961	The Informer Matter	Next week, my job is to protect a wanted criminal from, believe it or not, a policeman.
4/2/1961	The Two's A Crowd Matter	Strange vengence for an even stranger crime.
4/9/1961	The Wrong Sign Matter	Next week, a storybook murder that suddenly comes true.
4/16/1961	The Captain's Table Matter	Next week, the fog closing in over a dark abandoned pier in San Diego. A killer on the loose.
4/16/1961	The Latrodectus Matter	Next week, one of the toughest gangs I ever had to deal with; a gang of kids. A rat pack
4/23/1961	The Rat Pack Matter	Next week, a doll, a purple doll and all that goes with it
4/30/1961	The Purple Doll Matter	Unavailable
9/10/1961	The All Wet Matter	Next week, a wild old man, living in — believe it or not — an ancient castle, that is complete with chamber of horrors.

However, a search of radio listings for various newspapers (which included The Washington Post and the Tampa Bay Times) have provided program listing details that change the order of the programs to:

Original Date	Program Title	Newspaper Date
3/12/1961	The Morning After Matter	3/5/1961
3/26/1961	The Informer Matter	3/19/1961
4/9/1961	The Wrong Sign Matter	3/26/1961
4/16/1961	The Latrodectus Matter	4/2/1961
4/30/1961	The Rat Pack Matter	4/9/1961
5/7/1961	The Purple Doll Matter	4/16/1961
4/23/1961	The Latrodectus Matter	4/2/1961
9/10/1961	The All Wet Matter	10/1/1961

The last entry, *The All Wet Matter*, is interesting as an aircheck copy of the 10/1/1961 *Suspense* program *No Hiding Place* starts off with a clip the from the closing of *The All Wet Matter*. The clip includes the teaser for the next week's program and verified cast of *The All Wet Matter*. The air date of this particular *Suspense* program has been confirmed by Dr. Joe Webb.

These are examples of the possible errors in the order of the listings that can crop up without copies of the scripts with the air date indicated. The Hollywood scripts that are available contain the air dates. Once the programs moved to New York City, the ability to track scripts was lost.

Relying on newspaper listings in this era of radio is difficult. Most newspapers listed only series names but not episode titles. Even then, it seemed many editors gave preference to greater details about that week's *Suspense*, possibly because of its anthology style, with different scripts and characters every week. They rarely listed the details of the *Johnny Dollar* episode. In their minds, perhaps, a show based on a continuing character did not warrant the space. It also seems clear that the press releases for the programs were sent weeks in advance of actual broadcast, and that the *Johnny Dollar* plans changed quite often. It was the tail end of the age of big radio network drama and it was clear that CBS executives were less and less concerned about the accuracy of their program listings for these shows.

Given all the information above, I am confident that the program titles and dates in the tables below are correct. Be assured that our research is ongoing, and should new information come to light, it will be available at my website:
(WWW.HUMEALUMNI.ORG/YTJD/ERRATA.HTML).

Table Key:

Program Title: This is the name of the program taken from either the script title page or the name used in the program.

Program Date: This is the date on which the program aired.

Status:
Y = This program is available (typically as an mp3 file).
N = This program does not exist in any form.
P = This program was scheduled but was preempted
S = This program is available as a script and has been read and included in this book.
U = This is an un-produced script.

THE CANONICAL JOHNNY DOLLAR

The Dick Powell Programs

Program Title	Program Date	Status
Milford Brooks III	12/7/1948	Y

The Charles Russell Programs

Program Title	Program Date	Status
The Robert Perry Case (Audition)	1/14/1949	N
The Parakoff Policy	2/18/1949	Y
The Slow Boat from China	2/25/1949	Y
The Robert Perry Case	3/4/1949	Y
Murder is a Merry-Go-Round	3/11/1949	Y
Milford Brooks III	3/25/1949	Y
The Stolen Portrait of the Duke of Massen	4/1/1949	Y
The Case of the Foxy Terrier	4/8/1949	N
The Case of the Hundred Thousand Dollar Legs	4/15/1949	Y
The Case of Barton Drake	4/22/1949	Y
Here Comes the Death of the Party	7/17/1949	S
Who Took the Taxis for a Ride?	7/24/1949	Y
How Much Bourbon Can Flow Under the Bridgework?	7/31/1949	S
Murder Ain't Minor	8/7/1949	Y
Death Takes a Working Day	8/14/1949	S
Out of the Fire, Into the Frying Pan	8/21/1949	Y
How I Turned a Luxury Liner into a Battleship	8/28/1949	S

Program Title	Program Date	Status
The Expiring Nickels and the Egyptian Jackpot	9/4/1949	Y
The Search for Michelle Marsh	9/25/1949	Y
The Fishing Boat Affair	10/1/1949	Y
The Racehorse Piledriver Matter	10/8/1949	Y
Dr. Otto Schmedlich	10/15/1949	Y
Witness, Witness, Who's Got the Witness	10/22/1949	Y
The Little Man Who Wasn't All There	10/29/1949	Y
The Island of Tin-Yutan	11/5/1949	Y
The Melanie Carter Matter	11/12/1949	Y
The Skull Canyon Mine	11/26/1949	Y
Bodyguard to Anne Connelly	12/3/1949	Y
The Circus Animal Show Matter	12/10/1949	Y
Haiti Adventure Matter	12/17/1949	Y
The Department Store Swindle Matter	12/24/1949	Y
The Diamond Protector Matter	12/31/1949	S
The Firebug Hunter Matter	1/7/1950	S
The Missing Chinese Stripper Matter	1/14/1950	S

The Edmond O'Brien Programs

Program Title	Program Date	Status
Death Takes a Working Day	2/3/1950	Y
The SS Malay Trader	2/10/1950	Y
The Gravedigger's Spades	2/17/1950	Y
The Archeologist	2/24/1950	Y
Bodyguard to the Late Robert W. Perry	3/3/1950	Y
Alec Jefferson, the Youthful Millionaire	3/7/1950	Y
The Eighty-Five Little Minks	3/14/1950	Y
The Man Who Wrote Himself to Death	3/21/1950	Y
The Village Scene	3/28/1950	Y
The Big Red Schoolhouse	4/4/1950	Y
The Dead First-Helpers	4/11/1950	Y
The Story of the Ten-O-Eight	4/18/1950	Y
Pearl Carrasa	4/25/1950	Y
The Able Tackett Matter	5/2/1950	Y
The Harold Trandem Matter	5/9/1950	Y
The Sidney Rykoff Matter	5/16/1950	Y
The Earl Chadwick Matter	5/23/1950	Y
The Port-au-Prince Matter	5/30/1950	Y
The Caligio Diamond Matter	6/8/1950	Y
The Arrowcraft Matter	6/15/1950	Y

Program Title	Program Date	Status
The London Matter	6/22/1950	Y
The Barbara James Matter	6/29/1950	Y
The Belo-Horizonte Railroad	7/6/1950	Y
The Calgary Matter	7/13/1950	Y
The Henry J. Unger Matter	7/20/1950	Y
The Tell-All Book Matter	7/27/1950	N
The Blood River Matter	8/3/1950	Y
The Hartford Alliance Matter	8/10/1950	Y
The Mickey McQueen Matter	8/17/1950	Y
The Trans-Pacific Import Export Company, South China Branch	8/23/1950	Y
The Trans-Pacific Import Export Company, South China Branch	8/24/1950	Y
The Virginia Beach Matter	8/31/1950	Y
The Howard Caldwell Matter	9/30/1950	Y
The Richard Splain Matter	10/7/1950	Y
The Yankee Pride Matter	10/14/1950	Y
The Jack Madigan Matter	10/21/1950	Y
The Joan Sebastian Matter	10/28/1950	Y
The Queen Anne Pistols Matter	11/4/1950	Y
The Adam Kegg Matter	11/11/1950	Y
The Nora Falkner Matter	11/18/1950	Y
The Woodward Manila Matter	11/25/1950	Y
The Jackie Cleaver Matter	12/9/1950	P
The Blackburn Matter	12/16/1950	Y
The Montevideo Matter	12/23/1950	S
The Rudy Valentine Matter	12/30/1950	S
The Adolph Schoman Matter	1/6/1951	S
The Port-O-Call Matter	1/13/1951	Y
The David Rockey Matter	1/20/1951	Y
The Weldon Bragg Matter	1/27/1951	S
The Monopoly Matter	2/3/1951	S
The Lloyd Hammerly Matter	2/10/1951	S
The Vivian Fair Matter	2/17/1951	S
The Jarvis Wilder Matter	2/24/1951	Y
The Celia Woodstock Matter	3/3/1951	Y
The Stanley Springs Matter	3/10/1951	Y
The Emil Lovett Matter	3/17/1951	S
The Byron Hayes Matter	3/24/1951	Y
The Jackie Cleaver Matter	3/31/1951	Y
The Edward French Matter	4/7/1951	Y
The Mickey McQueen Matter	4/14/1951	Y
The Willard South Matter	4/21/1951	Y

VIII: The Canonical Johnny Dollar List

Program Title	Program Date	Status
The Month-End Raid Matter	4/28/1951	Y
The Virginia Towne Matter	5/5/1951	Y
The Marie Meadows Matter	5/12/1951	S
The Jane Doe Matter	5/19/1951	S
The Lillis Bond Matter	5/26/1951	Y
The Soderbury, Maine Matter	6/2/1951	Y
The George Farmer Matter	6/9/1951	Y
The Arthur Boldrick Matter	6/16/1951	Y
The Malcolm Wish, M.D. Matter	6/20/1951	Y
The Hatchet House Theft Matter	6/27/1951	Y
The Alonzo Chapman Matter	7/4/1951	Y
The Fair-Way Matter	7/11/1951	Y
The Neal Breer Matter	7/18/1951	Y
The Blind Item Matter	7/25/1951	S
The Horace Lockhart Matter	8/1/1951	Y
The Morgan Fry Matter	8/8/1951	S
The Lucky Costa Matter	8/15/1951	Y
The Cumberland Theft Matter	8/22/1951	S
The Leland Case Matter	8/29/1951	Y
The Rum Barrel Matter	9/12/1951	S
The Cuban Jewel Matter	9/19/1951	Y
The Protection Matter	9/26/1951	Y
The Douglas Taylor Matter	10/6/1951	Y
The Millard Ward Matter	10/13/1951	Y
The Janet Abbe Matter	10/20/1951	S
The Tolhurst Theft Matter	10/27/1951	Y
The Hannibal Murphy Matter	11/3/1951	Y
The Birdy Baskerville Matter	11/10/1951	Y
The Merrill Kent Matter	11/17/1951	Y
The Youngstown Credit Group Matter	12/8/1951	Y
The Paul Barberis Matter	12/15/1951	S
The Maynard Collins Matter	12/22/1951	S
The Alma Scott Matter	12/29/1951	Y
The Glen English Matter	1/5/1952	Y
The Baxter Matter	1/12/1952	S
The Amelia Harwell Matter	7/2/1952	Y
The Yankee Pride Matter	7/9/1952	P
The Henry Page Matter	7/16/1952	S
The Montevideo Matter	7/23/1952	P
The New Bedford Morgue Matter	7/30/1952	S
The Sidney Mann Matter	8/6/1952	S
The Tom Hickman Matter	8/13/1952	S
The Edith Maxwell Matter	8/20/1952	S

Program Title	Program Date	Status
The Yankee Pride Matter	8/27/1952	S
The Montevideo Matter	9/3/1952	S

The John Lund Programs

Program Title	Program Date	Status
The Trans-Pacific Matter (Lund Audition)	11/24/1952	Y
The Trans-Pacific Matter (Lund Audition)	11/28/1952	Y
The Singapore Arson Matter	11/28/1952	S
The James Clayton Matter	12/5/1952	Y
The Elliot Champion Matter	12/12/1952	Y
The New Cambridge Matter	12/19/1952	S
The Walter Patterson Matter	12/26/1952	Y
The Baltimore Matter	1/2/1953	Y
The Thelma Ibsen Matter	1/9/1953	Y
The Starlet Matter	1/16/1953	Y
The Marigold Matter	1/23/1953	Y
The Kay Bellamy Matter	1/30/1953	Y
The Chicago Fraud Matter	2/6/1953	Y
The Lancer Jewelry Matter	2/13/1953	S
The Latourette Matter	2/20/1953	Y
The Underwood Matter	2/27/1953	Y
The Jeanne Maxwell Matter	3/6/1953	Y
The Birdy Baskerville Matter	3/10/1953	S
The King's Necklace Matter	3/17/1953	Y
The Syndicate Matter	3/24/1953	Y
The Lester James Matter	3/31/1953	Y
The Enoch Arden Matter	4/7/1953	Y
The Madison Matter	4/14/1953	Y
The Dameron Matter	4/21/1953	Y
The San Antonio Matter	4/28/1953	Y
The Blackmail Matter	5/5/1953	Y
The Rochester Theft Matter	5/12/1953	Y
The Emily Braddock Matter	5/19/1953	Y
The Brisbane Fraud Matter	5/26/1953	Y
The Costain Matter	6/2/1953	Y
The Oklahoma Red Matter	6/9/1953	Y
The Emil Carter Matter	6/16/1953	Y
The Jonathan Bellows Matter	6/23/1953	Y
The Jones Matter	6/30/1953	Y
The Bishop Blackmail Matter	7/7/1953	S
The Shayne Bombing Matter	7/14/1953	Y

VIII: THE CANONICAL JOHNNY DOLLAR LIST

Program Title	Program Date	Status
The Black Doll Matter	7/21/1953	Y
The James Forbes Matter	7/28/1953	Y
The Voodoo Matter	8/4/1953	Y
The Nancy Shaw Matter	8/11/1953	Y
The Isabelle James Matter	8/18/1953	Y
The Nelson Matter	8/25/1953	Y
The Stanley Price Matter	9/1/1953	Y
The Lester Matson Matter	9/8/1953	Y
The Oscar Clark Matter	9/15/1953	S
The William Post Matter	9/22/1953	Y
The Amita Buddha Matter	9/29/1953	Y
The Alfred Chambers Matter	10/6/1953	Y
The Phillip Morey Matter	10/13/1953	Y
The Allen Saxton Matter	10/20/1953	Y
The Howard Arnold Matter	10/27/1953	Y
The Gino Gambona Matter	11/3/1953	Y
The Bobby Foster Matter	11/10/1953	Y
The Nathan Gayles Matter	11/17/1953	Y
The Independent Diamond Traders Matter	11/24/1953	Y
The Monopoly Matter	12/1/1953	Y
The Barton Baker Matter	12/8/1953	Y
The Milk and Honey Matter	12/15/1953	Y
The Rudy Valentine Matter	12/22/1953	S
The Ben Bryson Matter	12/29/1953	Y
The Fair-Way Matter	1/5/1954	Y
The Celia Woodstock Matter	1/12/1954	Y
The Draminski Matter	1/19/1954	S
The Beauregard Matter	1/26/1954	Y
The Paul Gorrell Matter	2/2/1954	Y
The Harpooned Angler Matter	2/9/1954	Y
The Uncut Canary Matter	2/16/1954	Y
The Classified Killer Matter	2/23/1954	Y
The Road-Test Matter	3/2/1954	Y
The Terrified Taun Matter	3/9/1954	Y
The Berlin Matter	3/16/1954	Y
The Piney Corners Matter	3/23/1954	Y
The Undried Fiddle Back Matter	3/30/1954	S
The Sulphur and Brimstone Matter	4/6/1954	Y
The Magnolia and Honeysuckle Matter	4/13/1954	Y
The Nathan Swing Matter	4/20/1954	Y
The Frustrated Phoenix Matter	4/27/1954	Y
The Dan Frank Matter	5/4/1954	Y
The Aromatic Cicatrix Matter	5/11/1954	S

Program Title	Program Date	Status
The Bilked Baroness Matter	5/18/1954	Y
The Punctilious Firebug Matter	5/25/1954	Y
The Temperamental Tote Board Matter	6/1/1954	Y
The Sara Dearing Matter	6/8/1954	Y
The Paterson Transport Matter	6/15/1954	Y
The Arthur Boldrick Matter	6/22/1954	S
The Woodward Manila Matter	6/29/1954	Y
The Jan Breughel Matter	7/6/1954	Y
The Carboniferous Dolomite Matter	7/13/1954	Y
The Jeanne Maxwell Matter	7/20/1954	Y
The Radioactive Gold Matter	7/27/1954	Y
The Hampton Line Matter	8/3/1954	Y
The Sarah Martin Matter	8/10/1954	S
The Hamilton Payroll Matter	9/5/1954	S
The Great Bannock Race Matter	9/12/1954	S
The Upjohn Matter	9/19/1954	S

The Gerald Mohr Programs

Program Title	Program Date	Status
The Trans-Pacific Matter (Audition)	8/29/1955	Y
The Trans-Pacific Matter (Audition)	8/29/1955	Y

The Bob Bailey Programs

Program Title	Program Date	Status
The Macormack Matter — Ep 1	10/3/1955	Y
The Macormack Matter — Ep 2	10/4/1955	Y
The Macormack Matter — Ep 3	10/5/1955	Y
The Macormack Matter — Ep 4	10/6/1955	Y
The Macormack Matter — Ep 5	10/7/1955	Y
The Molly K Matter — Ep 1	10/10/1955	Y
The Molly K Matter — Ep 2	10/11/1955	Y
The Molly K Matter — Ep 3	10/12/1955	Y
The Molly K Matter — Ep 4	10/13/1955	Y
The Molly K Matter — Ep 5	10/14/1955	Y
The Chesapeake Fraud Matter — Ep 1	10/17/1955	Y
The Chesapeake Fraud Matter — Ep 2	10/18/1955	Y
The Chesapeake Fraud Matter — Ep 3	10/19/1955	Y
The Chesapeake Fraud Matter — Ep 4	10/20/1955	Y
The Chesapeake Fraud Matter — Ep 5	10/21/1955	Y

Program Title	Program Date	Status
The Alvin Summers Matter — Ep 1	10/24/1955	Y
The Alvin Summers Matter — Ep 2	10/25/1955	Y
The Alvin Summers Matter — Ep 3	10/26/1955	Y
The Alvin Summers Matter — Ep 4	10/27/1955	Y
The Alvin Summers Matter — Ep 5	10/28/1955	Y
The Valentine Matter — Ep 1	10/31/1955	Y
The Valentine Matter — Ep 2	11/1/1955	Y
The Valentine Matter — Ep 3	11/2/1955	Y
The Valentine Matter — Ep 4	11/3/1955	Y
The Valentine Matter — Ep 5	11/4/1955	Y
The Lorko Diamonds Matter — Ep 1	11/7/1955	Y
The Lorko Diamonds Matter — Ep 2	11/8/1955	Y
The Lorko Diamonds Matter — Ep 3	11/9/1955	Y
The Lorko Diamonds Matter — Ep 4	11/10/1955	Y
The Lorko Diamonds Matter — Ep 5	11/11/1955	Y
The Broderick Matter — Ep 1	11/14/1955	Y
The Broderick Matter — Ep 2	11/15/1955	Y
The Broderick Matter — Ep 3	11/16/1955	Y
The Broderick Matter — Ep 4	11/17/1955	Y
The Broderick Matter — Ep 5	11/18/1955	Y
The Amy Bradshaw Matter — Ep 1	11/21/1955	Y
The Amy Bradshaw Matter — Ep 2	11/22/1955	Y
The Amy Bradshaw Matter — Ep 3	11/23/1955	Y
The Amy Bradshaw Matter — Ep 4	11/24/1955	Y
The Amy Bradshaw Matter — Ep 5	11/25/1955	Y
The Henderson Matter — Ep 1	11/28/1955	Y
The Henderson Matter — Ep 2	11/29/1955	Y
The Henderson Matter — Ep 3	11/30/1955	Y
The Henderson Matter — Ep 4	12/1/1955	Y
The Henderson Matter — Ep 5	12/2/1955	Y
The Cronin Matter — Ep 1	12/5/1955	Y
The Cronin Matter — Ep 2	12/6/1955	Y
The Cronin Matter — Ep 3	12/7/1955	Y
The Cronin Matter — Ep 4	12/8/1955	Y
The Cronin Matter — Ep 5	12/9/1955	Y
The Lansing Fraud Matter — Ep 1	12/12/1955	Y
The Lansing Fraud Matter — Ep 2	12/13/1955	Y
The Lansing Fraud Matter — Ep 3	12/14/1955	Y
The Lansing Fraud Matter — Ep 4	12/15/1955	Y
The Lansing Fraud Matter — Ep 5	12/16/1955	Y
The Nick Shurn Matter — Ep 1	12/19/1955	Y
The Nick Shurn Matter — Ep 2	12/20/1955	Y
The Nick Shurn Matter — Ep 3	12/21/1955	Y

Program Title	Program Date	Status
The Nick Shurn Matter — Ep 4	12/22/1955	Y
The Nick Shurn Matter — Ep 5	12/23/1955	Y
The Forbes Matter — Ep 1	12/26/1955	Y
The Forbes Matter — Ep 2	12/27/1955	Y
The Forbes Matter — Ep 3	12/28/1955	Y
The Forbes Matter — Ep 4	12/29/1955	Y
The Forbes Matter — Ep 5	12/30/1955	Y
The Caylin Matter — Ep 1	1/2/1956	Y
The Caylin Matter — Ep 2	1/3/1956	Y
The Caylin Matter — Ep 3	1/4/1956	Y
The Caylin Matter — Ep 4	1/5/1956	Y
The Caylin Matter — Ep 5	1/6/1956	Y
The Todd Matter — Ep 1	1/9/1956	Y
The Todd Matter — Ep 2	1/10/1956	Y
The Todd Matter — Ep 3	1/11/1956	Y
The Todd Matter — Ep 4	1/12/1956	Y
The Todd Matter — Ep 5	1/13/1956	Y
The Ricardo Amerigo Matter — Ep 1	1/16/1956	Y
The Ricardo Amerigo Matter — Ep 2	1/17/1956	Y
The Ricardo Amerigo Matter — Ep 3	1/18/1956	Y
The Ricardo Amerigo Matter — Ep 4	1/19/1956	Y
The Ricardo Amerigo Matter — Ep 5	1/20/1956	Y
The Duke Red Matter — Ep 1	1/23/1956	Y
The Duke Red Matter — Ep 2	1/24/1956	Y
The Duke Red Matter — Ep 3	1/25/1956	Y
The Duke Red Matter — Ep 4	1/26/1956	Y
The Duke Red Matter — Ep 5	1/27/1956	Y
The Flight Six Matter — Ep 1	1/30/1956	Y
The Flight Six Matter — Ep 2	1/31/1956	Y
The Flight Six Matter — Ep 3	2/1/1956	Y
The Flight Six Matter — Ep 4	2/2/1956	Y
The Flight Six Matter — Ep 5	2/3/1956	Y
The McClain Matter — Ep 1	2/6/1956	Y
The McClain Matter — Ep 2	2/7/1956	Y
The McClain Matter — Ep 3	2/8/1956	S
The McClain Matter — Ep 4	2/9/1956	Y
The McClain Matter — Ep 5	2/10/1956	Y
The Cui Bono Matter — Ep 1	2/13/1956	Y
The Cui Bono Matter — Ep 2	2/14/1956	Y
The Cui Bono Matter — Ep 3	2/15/1956	Y
The Cui Bono Matter — Ep 4	2/16/1956	Y
The Cui Bono Matter — Ep 5	2/17/1956	Y
The Bennet Matter — Ep 1	2/20/1956	Y

Program Title	Program Date	Status
The Bennet Matter — Ep 2	2/21/1956	Y
The Bennet Matter — Ep 3	2/22/1956	Y
The Bennet Matter — Ep 4	2/23/1956	Y
The Bennet Matter — Ep 5	2/24/1956	Y
The Fathom-Five Matter — Ep 1	2/27/1956	Y
The Fathom-Five Matter — Ep 2	2/28/1956	Y
The Fathom-Five Matter — Ep 3	2/29/1956	Y
The Fathom-Five Matter — Ep 4	3/1/1956	Y
The Fathom-Five Matter — Ep 5	3/2/1956	Y
The Plantagent Matter — Ep 1	3/5/1956	Y
The Plantagent Matter — Ep 2	3/6/1956	Y
The Plantagent Matter — Ep 3	3/7/1956	Y
The Plantagent Matter — Ep 4	3/8/1956	Y
The Plantagent Matter — Ep 5	3/9/1956	Y
The Clinton Matter — Ep 1	3/12/1956	Y
The Clinton Matter — Ep 2	3/13/1956	Y
The Clinton Matter — Ep 3	3/14/1956	Y
The Clinton Matter — Ep 4	3/15/1956	Y
The Clinton Matter — Ep 5	3/16/1956	Y
The Jolly Roger Fraud Matter — Ep 1	3/19/1956	Y
The Jolly Roger Fraud Matter — Ep 2	3/20/1956	Y
The Jolly Roger Fraud Matter — Ep 3	3/21/1956	Y
The Jolly Roger Fraud Matter — Ep 4	3/22/1956	Y
The Jolly Roger Fraud Matter — Ep 5	3/23/1956	Y
The LaMarr Matter — Ep 1	3/26/1956	Y
The LaMarr Matter — Ep 2	3/27/1956	Y
The LaMarr Matter — Ep 3	3/28/1956	Y
The LaMarr Matter — Ep 4	3/29/1956	Y
The LaMarr Matter — Ep 5	3/30/1956	Y
The Salt City Matter — Ep 1	4/2/1956	Y
The Salt City Matter — Ep 2	4/3/1956	Y
The Salt City Matter — Ep 3	4/4/1956	Y
The Salt City Matter — Ep 4	4/5/1956	Y
The Salt City Matter — Ep 5	4/6/1956	Y
The Laird Douglas Douglas of Heatherscote Matter — Ep 1	4/9/1956	Y
The Laird Douglas Douglas of Heatherscote Matter — Ep 2	4/10/1956	Y
The Laird Douglas Douglas of Heatherscote Matter — Ep 3	4/11/1956	Y
The Laird Douglas Douglas of Heatherscote Matter — Ep 4	4/12/1956	Y

Program Title	Program Date	Status
The Laird Douglas Douglas of Heatherscote Matter — Ep 5	4/13/1956	Y
The Shepherd Matter — Ep 1	4/16/1956	Y
The Shepherd Matter — Ep 2	4/17/1956	Y
The Shepherd Matter — Ep 3	4/18/1956	Y
The Shepherd Matter — Ep 4	4/19/1956	Y
The Shepherd Matter — Ep 5	4/20/1956	Y
The Lonely Hearts Matter — Ep 1	4/23/1956	Y
The Lonely Hearts Matter — Ep 2	4/24/1956	Y
The Lonely Hearts Matter — Ep 3	4/25/1956	Y
The Lonely Hearts Matter — Ep 4	4/26/1956	Y
The Lonely Hearts Matter — Ep 5	4/27/1956	Y
The Callicles Matter — Ep 1	4/30/1956	Y
The Callicles Matter — Ep 2	5/1/1956	Y
The Callicles Matter — Ep 3	5/2/1956	Y
The Callicles Matter — Ep 4	5/3/1956	Y
The Callicles Matter — Ep 5	5/4/1956	Y
The Silver Blue Matter — Ep 1	5/7/1956	Y
The Silver Blue Matter — Ep 2	5/8/1956	Y
The Silver Blue Matter — Ep 3	5/9/1956	Y
The Silver Blue Matter — Ep 4	5/10/1956	Y
The Silver Blue Matter — Ep 5	5/11/1956	Y
The Medium, Well Done Matter — Ep 1	5/14/1956	Y
The Medium, Well Done Matter — Ep 2	5/15/1956	Y
The Medium, Well Done Matter — Ep 3	5/16/1956	Y
The Medium, Well Done Matter — Ep 4	5/17/1956	Y
The Medium, Well Done Matter — Ep 5	5/18/1956	Y
The Tears of Night Matter — Ep 1	5/21/1956	Y
The Tears of Night Matter — Ep 2	5/22/1956	Y
The Tears of Night Matter — Ep 3	5/23/1956	Y
The Tears of Night Matter — Ep 4	5/24/1956	Y
The Tears of Night Matter — Ep 5	5/25/1956	Y
The Matter of Reasonable Doubt — Ep 1	5/28/1956	Y
The Matter of Reasonable Doubt — Ep 2	5/29/1956	Y
The Matter of Reasonable Doubt — Ep 3	5/30/1956	Y
The Matter of Reasonable Doubt — Ep 4	5/31/1956	Y
The Matter of Reasonable Doubt — Ep 5	6/1/1956	Y
The Indestructible Mike Matter — Ep 1	6/4/1956	Y
The Indestructible Mike Matter — Ep 2	6/5/1956	Y
The Indestructible Mike Matter — Ep 3	6/6/1956	Y
The Indestructible Mike Matter — Ep 4	6/7/1956	Y
The Indestructible Mike Matter — Ep 5	6/8/1956	Y
The Laughing Matter — Ep 1	6/11/1956	Y
The Laughing Matter — Ep 2	6/12/1956	Y

Program Title	Program Date	Status
The Laughing Matter — Ep 3	6/13/1956	Y
The Laughing Matter — Ep 4	6/14/1956	Y
The Laughing Matter — Ep 5	6/15/1956	Y
The Pearling Matter — Ep 1	6/18/1956	Y
The Pearling Matter — Ep 2	6/19/1956	Y
The Pearling Matter — Ep 3	6/20/1956	Y
The Pearling Matter — Ep 4	6/21/1956	Y
The Pearling Matter — Ep 5	6/22/1956	Y
The Long Shot Matter — Ep 1	6/25/1956	Y
The Long Shot Matter — Ep 2	6/26/1956	Y
The Long Shot Matter — Ep 3	6/27/1956	Y
The Long Shot Matter — Ep 4	6/28/1956	Y
The Long Shot Matter — Ep 5	6/29/1956	Y
The Midas Touch Matter — Ep 1	7/2/1956	Y
The Midas Touch Matter — Ep 2	7/3/1956	Y
The Midas Touch Matter — Ep 3	7/4/1956	Y
The Midas Touch Matter — Ep 4	7/5/1956	Y
The Midas Touch Matter — Ep 5	7/6/1956	Y
The Shady Lane Matter — Ep 1	7/9/1956	Y
The Shady Lane Matter — Ep 2	7/10/1956	Y
The Shady Lane Matter — Ep 3	7/11/1956	Y
The Shady Lane Matter — Ep 4	7/12/1956	Y
The Shady Lane Matter — Ep 5	7/13/1956	Y
The Star of Capetown Matter — Ep 1	7/16/1956	Y
The Star of Capetown Matter — Ep 2	7/17/1956	Y
The Star of Capetown Matter — Ep 3	7/18/1956	Y
The Star of Capetown Matter — Ep 4	7/19/1956	Y
The Star of Capetown Matter — Ep 5	7/20/1956	Y
The Open Town Matter — Ep 1	7/23/1956	Y
The Open Town Matter — Ep 2	7/24/1956	Y
The Open Town Matter — Ep 3	7/25/1956	Y
The Open Town Matter — Ep 4	7/26/1956	Y
The Open Town Matter — Ep 5	7/27/1956	Y
The Sea Legs Matter — Ep 1	7/30/1956	Y
The Sea Legs Matter — Ep 2	7/31/1956	Y
The Sea Legs Matter — Ep 3	8/1/1956	Y
The Sea Legs Matter — Ep 4	8/2/1956	Y
The Sea Legs Matter — Ep 5	8/3/1956	Y
The Alder Matter — Ep 1	8/6/1956	Y
The Alder Matter — Ep 2	8/7/1956	Y
The Alder Matter — Ep 3	8/8/1956	Y
The Alder Matter — Ep 4	8/9/1956	Y
The Alder Matter — Ep 5	8/10/1956	Y

Program Title	Program Date	Status
The Crystal Lake Cabin Matter — Ep 1	8/13/1956	Y
The Crystal Lake Cabin Matter — Ep 2	8/14/1956	Y
The Crystal Lake Cabin Matter — Ep 3	8/15/1956	Y
The Crystal Lake Cabin Matter — Ep 4	8/16/1956	Y
The Crystal Lake Cabin Matter — Ep 5	8/17/1956	Y
The Kranesburg Matter — Ep 1	8/24/1956	Y
The Kranesburg Matter — Ep 2	8/27/1956	Y
The Kranesburg Matter — Ep 3	8/28/1956	Y
The Kranesburg Matter — Ep 4	8/29/1956	Y
The Kranesburg Matter — Ep 5	8/30/1956	Y
The Kranesburg Matter — Ep 6	8/31/1956	Y
The Curse of Kamashek Matter — Ep 1	9/3/1956	Y
The Curse of Kamashek Matter — Ep 2	9/4/1956	Y
The Curse of Kamashek Matter — Ep 3	9/5/1956	Y
The Curse of Kamashek Matter — Ep 4	9/6/1956	Y
The Curse of Kamashek Matter — Ep 5	9/7/1956	Y
The Confidential Matter — Ep 1	9/10/1956	Y
The Confidential Matter — Ep 2	9/11/1956	Y
The Confidential Matter — Ep 3	9/12/1956	Y
The Confidential Matter — Ep 4	9/13/1956	Y
The Confidential Matter — Ep 5	9/14/1956	Y
The Imperfect Alibi Matter — Ep 1	9/17/1956	Y
The Imperfect Alibi Matter — Ep 2	9/18/1956	S
The Imperfect Alibi Matter — Ep 3	9/19/1956	Y
The Imperfect Alibi Matter — Ep 4	9/20/1956	Y
The Imperfect Alibi Matter — Ep 5	9/21/1956	Y
The Meg's Palace Matter — Ep 1	9/24/1956	Y
The Meg's Palace Matter — Ep 2	9/25/1956	Y
The Meg's Palace Matter — Ep 3	9/26/1956	Y
The Meg's Palace Matter — Ep 4	9/27/1956	Y
The Meg's Palace Matter — Ep 5	9/28/1956	Y
The Picture Postcard Matter — Ep 1	10/1/1956	Y
The Picture Postcard Matter — Ep 2	10/2/1956	Y
The Picture Postcard Matter — Ep 3	10/3/1956	Y
The Picture Postcard Matter — Ep 4	10/4/1956	Y
The Picture Postcard Matter — Ep 5	10/5/1956	Y
The Primrose Matter — Ep 1	10/8/1956	Y
The Primrose Matter — Ep 2	10/9/1956	Y
The Primrose Matter — Ep 3	10/10/1956	Y
The Primrose Matter — Ep 4	10/11/1956	Y
The Primrose Matter — Ep 5	10/12/1956	Y
The Phantom Chase Matter — Ep 1	10/15/1956	Y
The Phantom Chase Matter — Ep 2	10/16/1956	Y

Program Title	Program Date	Status
The Phantom Chase Matter — Ep 3	10/17/1956	Y
The Phantom Chase Matter — Ep 4	10/18/1956	Y
The Phantom Chase Matter — Ep 5	10/19/1956	Y
The Phantom Chase Matter — Ep 6	10/22/1956	Y
The Phantom Chase Matter — Ep 7	10/24/1956	Y
The Phantom Chase Matter — Ep 8	10/25/1956	Y
The Phantom Chase Matter — Ep 9	10/26/1956	Y
The Silent Queen Matter — Ep 1	10/29/1956	Y
The Silent Queen Matter — Ep 2	10/30/1956	Y
The Silent Queen Matter — Ep 3	10/31/1956	Y
The Silent Queen Matter — Ep 4	11/1/1956	Y
The Silent Queen Matter — Ep 5	11/2/1956	Y
The Markham Matter	11/4/1956	Y
The Big Scoop Matter	11/11/1956	Y
The Royal Street Matter	11/25/1956	Y
The Burning Carr Matter	12/9/1956	Y
The Rasmusson Matter	12/16/1956	Y
The Missing Mouse Matter	12/23/1956	Y
The Squared Circle Matter	12/30/1956	Y
The Ellen Dear Matter	1/6/1957	Y
The Desalles Matter	1/13/1957	Y
The Blooming Blossom Matter	1/20/1957	Y
The Mad Hatter Matter	1/27/1957	Y
The Ellen Dear Matter — Audition	1/29/1957	S
The Kirby Will Matter	2/3/1957	Y
The Templeton Matter	2/10/1957	Y
The Golden Touch Matter	2/17/1957	S
The Meek Memorial Matter	3/3/1957	Y
The Suntan Oil Matter	3/10/1957	Y
The Clever Chemist Matter	3/17/1957	Y
The Hollywood Matter	3/24/1957	S
The Moonshine Murder Matter	3/31/1957	Y
The Ming Toy Murphy Matter	4/14/1957	Y
The Marley K Matter	4/21/1957	S
The Melancholy Memory Matter	4/28/1957	Y
The Peerless Fire Matter	5/5/1957	Y
The Glacier Ghost Matter	5/12/1957	S
The Michael Meany Mirage Matter	5/19/1957	Y
The Wayward Truck Matter	5/26/1957	Y
The Loss of Memory Matter	6/2/1957	Y
The Mason-Dixon Mismatch Matter	6/9/1957	Y
The Dixon Murder Matter	6/16/1957	Y
The Parley Barron Matter	6/23/1957	Y

Program Title	Program Date	Status
The Funny Money Matter	6/30/1957	Y
The Felicity Feline Matter	7/7/1957	Y
The Heatherstone Players Matter	7/14/1957	Y
The Yours Truly Matter	7/21/1957	Y
The Confederate Coinage Matter	7/28/1957	Y
The Wayward Widow Matter	8/4/1957	Y
The Killer's Brand Matter	8/11/1957	Y
The Winnipesaukee Wonder Matter	8/18/1957	S
The Smoky Sleeper Matter	8/25/1957	Y
The Poor Little Rich Girl Matter	9/1/1957	Y
The Charmona Matter	9/8/1957	Y
The J. P. D. Matter	9/15/1957	Y
The Ideal Vacation Matter	9/22/1957	Y
The Doubtful Dairy Matter	9/29/1957	Y
The Bum Steer Matter	10/6/1957	Y
The Silver Belle Matter	10/13/1957	Y
The Mary Grace Matter	10/20/1957	Y
The Three Sisters Matter	10/27/1957	Y
The Model Picture Matter	11/3/1957	Y
The Alkali Mike Matter	11/10/1957	Y
The Shy Beneficiary Matter	11/17/1957	Y
The Hope to Die Matter	11/24/1957	Y
The Sunny Dream Matter	12/1/1957	Y
The Hapless Hunter Matter	12/8/1957	Y
The Happy Family Matter	12/15/1957	Y
The Carmen Kringle Matter	12/22/1957	Y
The Latin Lovely Matter	12/29/1957	Y
The Ingenuous Jeweler Matter	1/5/1958	Y
The Boron 112 Matter	1/12/1958	Y
The Eleven O'Clock Matter	1/19/1958	Y
The Fire in Paradise Matter	1/26/1958	S
The Price of Fame Matter	2/2/1958	Y
The Sick Chick Matter	2/9/1958	Y
The Time and Tide Matter	2/16/1958	Y
The Durango Laramie Matter	2/23/1958	Y
The Diamond Dilemma Matter	3/2/1958	Y
The Wayward Moth Matter	3/9/1958	Y
The Salkoff Sequel Matter	3/16/1958	Y
The Denver Disbursal Matter	3/23/1958	Y
The Killer's List Matter	3/30/1958	Y
The Eastern Western Matter	4/6/1958	Y
The Wayward Money Matter	4/13/1958	Y
The Wayward Trout Matter	4/20/1958	Y

VIII: The Canonical Johnny Dollar List

Program Title	Program Date	Status
The Village of Virtue Matter	4/27/1958	Y
The Carson Arson Matter	5/4/1958	Y
The Rolling Stone Matter	5/11/1958	Y
The Ghost to Ghost Matter	5/18/1958	Y
The Midnite Sun Matter	5/25/1958	Y
The Froward Fisherman Matter	6/1/1958	S
The Wayward River Matter	6/8/1958	Y
The Delectable Damsel Matter	6/15/1958	Y
The Virtuous Mobster Matter	6/22/1958	Y
The Ugly Pattern Matter	6/29/1958	Y
The Blinker Matter	7/6/1958	Y
The Mohave Red Matter	7/13/1958	Y
The Mohave Red Sequel Matter	7/20/1958	Y
The Wayward Killer Matter	7/27/1958	Y
The Lucky 4 Matter	8/3/1958	Y
The Two Faced Matter	8/10/1958	Y
The Noxious Needle Matter	8/24/1958	Y
The Limping Liability Matter	8/31/1958	S
The Malibu Mystery Matter	9/7/1958	Y
The Wayward Diamonds Matter	9/14/1958	Y
The Johnson Payroll Matter	9/21/1958	Y
The Gruesome Spectacle Matter	9/28/1958	Y
The Missing Matter Matter	10/5/1958	S
The Impossible Murder Matter	10/12/1958	S
The Monoxide Mystery Matter	10/19/1958	S
The Basking Ridge Matter	10/26/1958	S
The Crater Lake Matter	11/2/1958	S
The Close Shave Matter	11/9/1958	S
The Double Trouble Matter	11/16/1958	Y
The One Most Wanted Matter	11/23/1958	S
The Hair Raising Matter	11/30/1958	Y
The Perilous Parley Matter	12/7/1958	S
The Allanmee Matter	12/14/1958	S
The Telltale Tracks Matter	12/28/1958	S
The Hollywood Mystery Matter	1/4/1959	Y
The Deadly Doubt Matter	1/11/1959	Y
The Love Shorn Matter	1/18/1959	S
The Doting Dowager Matter	1/25/1959	Y
The Curley Waters Matter	2/1/1959	S
The Date with Death Matter	2/8/1959	Y
The Shankar Diamond Matter	2/15/1959	Y
The Blue Madonna Matter	2/22/1959	Y
The Clouded Crystal Matter	3/1/1959	S

Program Title	Program Date	Status
The Net of Circumstance Matter	3/8/1959	Y
The Baldero Matter	3/15/1959	Y
The Lake Mead Mystery Matter	3/22/1959	Y
The Jimmy Carter Matter	3/29/1959	Y
The Frisco Fire Matter	4/5/1959	Y
The Fairweather Friend Matter	4/12/1959	Y
The Cautious Celibate Matter	4/19/1959	Y
The Winsome Widow Matter	4/26/1959	Y
The Negligent Nephew Matter	5/3/1959	S
The Fatal Filet Matter	5/10/1959	Y
The Twin Trouble Matter	5/17/1959	Y
The Casque of Death Matter	5/24/1959	Y
The Big H Matter	5/31/1959	Y
The Wayward Heiress Matter	6/7/1959	Y
The Wayward Sculptor Matter	6/14/1959	Y
The Life at Steak Matter	6/21/1959	Y
The Mei-Ling Buddah Matter	6/28/1959	Y
The Only One Butt Matter	7/5/1959	Y
The Frantic Fisherman Matter	7/12/1959	Y
The Will and a Way Matter	7/19/1959	Y
The Bolt Out of the Blue Matter	7/26/1959	Y
The Deadly Chain Matter	8/2/1959	Y
The Lost by a Hair Matter	8/9/1959	Y
The Night in Paris Matter	8/16/1959	Y
The Embarcadero Matter	8/23/1959	Y
The Really Gone Matter	8/30/1959	Y
The Backfire That Backfired Matter	9/6/1959	Y
The Leumas Matter	9/13/1959	S
The Little Man Who Was There Matter	9/20/1959	Y
The Buffalo Matter	10/4/1959	Y
The Further Buffalo Matter	10/11/1959	Y
The Double Identity Matter	10/18/1959	Y
The Missing Missile Matter	10/25/1959	Y
The Hand of Providential Matter	11/1/1959	Y
The Larson Arson Matter	11/8/1959	Y
The Bayou Body Matter	11/15/1959	Y
The Fancy Bridgework Matter	11/22/1959	Y
The Wrong Man Matter	11/29/1959	Y
The Hired Homicide Matter	12/6/1959	Y
The Sudden Wealth Matter	12/13/1959	Y
The Red Mystery Matter	12/20/1959	Y
The Burning Desire Matter	12/27/1959	Y
The Hapless Ham Matter	1/3/1960	Y

VIII: The Canonical Johnny Dollar List

Program Title	Program Date	Status
The Unholy Two Matter	1/10/1960	Y
The Evaporated Clue Matter	1/17/1960	Y
The Nuclear Goof Matter	1/24/1960	Y
The Merry Go Round Matter	1/31/1960	Y
The Sidewinder Matter	2/7/1960	Y
The P.O. Matter	2/14/1960	Y
The Alvin's Alfred Matter	2/21/1960	Y
The Look Before the Leap Matter	2/28/1960	Y
The Moonshine Matter	3/6/1960	Y
The Deep Down Matter	3/13/1960	Y
The Saturday Night Matter	3/20/1960	Y
The False Alarm Matter	3/27/1960	Y
The Double Exposure Matter	4/3/1960	Y
The Deadly Swamp Matter	4/17/1960	Y
The Silver Queen Matter	4/24/1960	Y
The Fatal Switch Matter	5/1/1960	Y
The Phony Phone Matter	5/8/1960	Y
The Mystery Gal Matter	5/15/1960	Y
The Man Who Waits Matter	5/22/1960	Y
The Redrock Matter	5/29/1960	Y
The Canned Canary Matter	6/5/1960	Y
The Harried Heiress Matter	6/12/1960	Y
The Flask of Death Matter	6/19/1960	Y
The Wholly Unexpected Matter	6/26/1960	Y
The Collector's Matter	7/3/1960	Y
The Back to The Back Matter	7/17/1960	Y
The Rhymer Collection Matter	7/31/1960	Y
The Magnanimous Matter	8/7/1960	S
The Paradise Lost Matter	8/14/1960	Y
The Twisted Twin Matter	8/21/1960	Y
The Deadly Debt Matter	8/28/1960	Y
The Killer Kin Matter	9/4/1960	Y
The Too Much Money Matter	9/11/1960	Y
The Real Smokey Matter	9/18/1960	S
The Five Down Matter	9/25/1960	Y
The Stope of Death Matter	10/2/1960	Y
The Recompense Matter	10/9/1960	Y
The Twins of Tahoe Matter	10/16/1960	Y
The Unworthy Kin Matter	10/23/1960	Y
The What Goes Matter	10/30/1960	Y
The Super Salesman Matter	11/6/1960	Y
The Bad One Matter	11/13/1960	Y
The Double Deal Matter	11/20/1960	Y

Program Title	Program Date	Status
The Empty Threat Matter	11/27/1960	Y

The Bob Readick Programs

Program Title	Program Date	Status
The Urned Income Matter	12/4/1960	Y
The Wrong Ending Matter	12/11/1960	S
The Wayward Kilocycles Matter	12/18/1960	Y
The Art for My Sake Matter	12/25/1960	S
The True Love Matter	1/1/1961	S
The Big Date Matter	1/8/1961	Y
The Very Fishy Matter	1/15/1961	Y
The Short Term Matter	1/22/1961	Y
The Death by Jet Matter	1/29/1961	Y
The Planner Matter	2/5/1961	S
The Who's Who Matter	2/12/1961	Y
The Wayward Fireman Matter	2/19/1961	Y
The Two Tired Matter	2/26/1961	S
The Touch-Up Matter	3/5/1961	Y
The Morning After Matter	3/12/1961	Y
The Ring of Death Matter	3/19/1961	Y
The Informer Matter	3/26/1961	Y
The Two's a Crowd Matter	4/2/1961	Y
The Wrong Sign Matter	4/9/1961	Y
The Captain's Table Matter	4/16/1961	Y
The Latrodectus Matter	4/23/1961	Y
The Rat Pack Matter	4/30/1961	Y
The Purple Doll Matter	5/7/1961	N
The Newark Stockbroker Matter	5/14/1961	N
The Simple Simon Matter	5/21/1961	Y
The Lone Wolf Matter	5/28/1961	Y
The Yaak Mystery Matter	6/4/1961	Y
The Stock in Trade Matter	6/11/1961	Y
The Million Dollar Jewelry Matter	6/18/1961	N

The Mandel Kramer Programs

Program Title	Program Date	Status
The Low Tide Matter	6/25/1961	Y
The Imperfect Crime Matter	7/2/1961	Y
The Well of Trouble Matter	7/9/1961	Y

Program Title	Program Date	Status
The Fiddle Faddle Matter	7/16/1961	Y
The Old Fashioned Murder Matter	7/23/1961	Y
The Chuckanut Matter	7/30/1961	Y
The Philadelphia Miss Matter	8/6/1961	Y
The Perilous Padre Matter	8/13/1961	Y
The Wrong Doctor Matter	8/20/1961	Y
The Too Many Crooks Matter	8/27/1961	Y
The Shifty Looker Matter	9/3/1961	Y
The All Wet Matter	9/10/1961	Y
The Buyer and the Cellar Matter	9/17/1961	Y
The Clever Crook Matter	9/24/1961	N
The Double-Barreled Matter	10/1/1961	Y
The Medium Rare Matter	10/8/1961	Y
The Quiet Little Town in New Jersey Matter	10/15/1961	N
The Three for One Matter	10/22/1961	Y
The Bee or Not to Bee Matter	10/29/1961	Y
The Monticello Mystery Matter	11/5/1961	Y
The Wrong One Matter	11/12/1961	Y
The Guide to Murder Matter	11/19/1961	Y
The Mad Bomber Matter	11/26/1961	Y
The Cinder Elmer Matter	12/3/1961	Y
The Firebug	12/10/1961	N
The Phony Phone Matter	12/17/1961	Y
The One Too Many Matter	12/31/1961	Y
The Hot Chocolates Matter	1/7/1962	Y
The Gold Rush Country Matter	1/14/1962	N
The Terrible Torch Matter	1/21/1962	Y
The Can't Be So Matter	1/28/1962	Y
The Nugget of Truth Matter	2/4/1962	Y
The Do It Yourself Matter	2/11/1962	Y
The Takes a Crook Matter	2/18/1962	Y
The Mixed Blessing Matter	2/25/1962	Y
The Top Secret Matter	3/4/1962	Y
The Golden Dream Matter	3/11/1962	Y
The Ike and Mike Matter	3/18/1962	Y
The Shadow of a Doubt Matter	3/25/1962	Y
The Blue Rock Matter	4/1/1962	Y
The Ivy Emerald Matter	4/8/1962	Y
The Wrong Idea Matter	4/15/1962	Y
The Skidmore Matter	4/22/1962	Y
The Grand Canyon Matter	4/29/1962	Y
The Burma Red Matter	5/6/1962	Y
The Lust for Gold Matter	5/13/1962	Y

Program Title	Program Date	Status
The Two Steps to Murder Matter	5/20/1962	Y
The Zip Matter	5/27/1962	Y
The Wayward Gun Matter	6/3/1962	Y
The Wayward Clipper Matter	6/10/1962	S
The All Too Easy Matter	6/17/1962	Y
The Hood of Death Matter	6/24/1962	Y
The Vociferous Dolphin Matter	7/1/1962	Y
The Rilldo Matter	7/8/1962	Y
The Weather or Not Matter	7/15/1962	Y
The Skimpy Matter	7/22/1962	Y
The Four's a Crowd Matter	7/29/1962	Y
The Case of Trouble Matter	8/5/1962	Y
The Oldest Gag Matter	8/12/1962	Y
The Lorelei Matter	8/19/1962	Y
The Gold Rush Matter	8/26/1962	Y
The Doninger Doninger Matter	9/2/1962	Y
The Four C's Matter	9/9/1962	Y
The No Matter Matter	9/16/1962	Y
The Deadly Crystal Matter	9/23/1962	Y
The Tip-Off Matter	9/30/1962	Y

The Unproduced Programs

Program Title	Program Date	Status
The Key to Crime Matter — Pat Fuller Version	10/7/1962	U
The Key to Crime Matter — Phildelphia Version	10/7/1962	U

The Missing Programs

The programs in the table below are those that, after all the dust has settled, do not exist in any audible format. Those entries with a status of "S" exist as scripts and are included in this document.

I have determined that five of the programs below were preempted by baseball games on the east coast.

Program Title	Program Date	Status
The Robert Perry Case (Audition)	1/14/1949	N
The Case of the Foxy Terrier	4/8/1949	N
Here Comes the Death of the Party	7/17/1949	S
How Much Bourbon Can Flow Under the Bridgework?	7/31/1949	S
Death Takes a Working Day	8/14/1949	S
How I Turned A Luxury Liner Into a Battleship	8/28/1949	S
The Diamond Protector Matter	12/31/1949	S
The Firebug Hunter Matter	1/7/1950	S
The Missing Chinese Stripper Matter	1/14/1950	S
The Tell-All Book Matter	7/27/1950	N
The Montevideo Matter	12/23/1950	S
The Rudy Valentine Matter	12/30/1950	S
The Adolph Schoman Matter	1/6/1951	S
The Weldon Bragg Matter	1/27/1951	S
The Monopoly Matter	2/3/1951	S
The Lloyd Hammerly Matter	2/10/1951	S
The Vivian Fair Matter	2/17/1951	S
The Emil Lovett Matter	3/17/1951	S
The Marie Meadows Matter	5/12/1951	S
The Jane Doe Matter	5/19/1951	S
The Blind Item Matter	7/25/1951	S
The Morgan Fry Matter	8/8/1951	S
The Cumberland Theft Matter	8/22/1951	S
The Rum Barrel Matter	9/12/1951	S
The Janet Abbe Matter	10/20/1951	S
The Paul Barberis Matter	12/15/1951	S
The Maynard Collins Matter	12/22/1951	S
The Baxter Matter	1/12/1952	S
The Yankee Pride Matter	7/9/1952	N
The Henry Page Matter	7/16/1952	S
The Montevideo Matter	7/23/1952	P1
The New Bedford Morgue Matter	7/30/1952	S
The Sidney Mann Matter	8/6/1952	S

Program Title	Program Date	Status
The Tom Hickman Matter	8/13/1952	S
The Edith Maxwell Matter	8/20/1952	S
The Yankee Pride Matter	8/27/1952	S
The Montevideo Matter	9/3/1952	S
The Singapore Arson Matter	11/28/1952	S
The New Cambridge Matter	12/19/1952	S
The Lancer Jewelry Matter	2/13/1953	S
The Birdy Baskerville Matter	3/10/1953	S
The Bishop Blackmail Matter	7/7/1953	S
The Oscar Clark Matter	9/15/1953	S
The Rudy Valentine Matter	12/22/1953	S
The Draminski Matter	1/19/1954	S
The Undried Fiddle Back Matter	3/30/1954	S
The Aromatic Cicatrix Matter	5/11/1954	S
The Arthur Boldrick Matter	6/22/1954	S
The Sarah Martin Matter	8/10/1954	S
The Hamilton Payroll Matter	9/5/1954	S
The Great Bannock Race Matter	9/12/1954	S
The Upjohn Matter	9/19/1954	S
The McClain Matter — Ep 3	2/8/1956	S
The Salt City Matter — Ep 2	4/3/1956	S
The Lonely Hearts Matter — Ep 4	4/26/1956	S
The Imperfect Alibi Matter — Ep 2	9/18/1956	S
The Ellen Dear Matter — Audition	1/29/1957	S
The Golden Touch Matter	2/17/1957	S
The Hollywood Matter	3/24/1957	S
The Moonshine Murder Matter	3/31/1957	S
The Marley K Matter	4/21/1957	S
The Glacier Ghost Matter	5/12/1957	S
The Winnipesaukee Wonder Matter	8/18/1957	S
The Fire in Paradise Matter	1/26/1958	S
The Froward Fisherman Matter	6/1/1958	S
The Limping Liability Matter	8/31/1958	S
The Missing Matter Matter	10/5/1958	S
The Impossible Murder Matter	10/12/1958	S
The Monoxide Mystery Matter	10/19/1958	S
The Basking Ridge Matter	10/26/1958	S
The Crater Lake Matter	11/2/1958	S
The Close Shave Matter	11/9/1958	S
The One Most Wanted Matter	11/23/1958	S
The Perilous Parley Matter	12/7/1958	S
The Allanmee Matter	12/14/1958	S
The Telltale Tracks Matter	12/28/1958	S

Program Title	Program Date	Status
The Love Shorn Matter	1/18/1959	S
The Curley Waters Matter	2/1/1959	S
The Clouded Crystal Matter	3/1/1959	S
The Negligent Nephew Matter	5/3/1959	S
The Gruesome Spectacle Matter	9/27/1959	N2
The Magnanimous Matter	8/7/1960	S
The Real Smokey Matter	9/18/1960	S
The Wrong Ending Matter	12/11/1960	S
The Art for My Sake Matter	12/25/1960	S
The True Love Matter	1/1/1961	S
The Planner Matter	2/5/1961	S
The Two Tired Matter	2/26/1961	S
The Purple Doll Matter	5/7/1961	P3
The Newark Stockbroker Matter	5/14/1961	P4
The Million Dollar Jewelry Matter	6/18/1961	P5
The Clever Crook Matter	9/24/1961	N
The Quiet Little Town in New Jersey Matter	10/15/1961	N
The Firebug	12/10/1961	N
The Gold Rush Country Matter	1/14/1962	N
The Wayward Clipper Matter	6/10/1962	S

Notes:
1. The Montevideo Matter broadcast on 7/23/1952 was preempted by the Democratic National Convention.
2. The timeslot for Yours Truly, Johnny Dollar on 9/27/1959 was used to air a special starring Maurice Chevalier. There is no record of a program scheduled for this time and date.
3. The Purple Doll Matter was preempted on the east coast by a baseball game between the NY Yankees and the Washington Senators (source: *Washington Post* and the *New York Times*).
4. The Newark Stockbroker Matter was preempted in Washington by a baseball game with Cleveland, and in New York and Los Angeles by a Yankees game with LA.
5. The Million Dollar Jewelry Matter was preempted in Washington by a baseball game between Washington and Boston.

Index

Numbers in **bold** indicate photographs.

"Able Tackett Matter, The" 115-117, 1259, 1301
"Adam Kegg Matter, The" 157-159, 253, 1264, 1288, 1302
Adams, Bill 1204
Adams, Inge 586
Adams, Mason 1091, 1092, 1115, 1157, 1159
"Adolph Schoman Matter, The" 167-168, 250, 1259, 1288, 1302, 1321
"Alder Matter, The" 629-634, 1285, 1311
"Alec Jefferson, the Youthful Millionaire" 100-101, 1265, 1301
"Alfred Chambers Matter, The" 340-342, 1257, 1305
"Alkali Mike Matter, The" 778-780, 1284, 1314
"All Too Easy Matter, The" 1200-1202, 1283, 1320
"All Wet Matter, The" 1124-1126, 1277, 1298-1299, 1319
"Allanmee Matter, The" 876-877, 1266, 1315, 1322
"Allen Saxton Matter, The" 343-345, 1265, 1305
Allen, Casey 1159, 1186, 1232
Allen, Lynn 59, 80
"Alma Scott Matter, The" 243-245, 313, 1257, 1288, 1303
"Alonzo Chapman Matter, The" 208-209, 1279, 1303
"Alvin Summers Matter, The" 448-452, 1272, 1307
"Alvin's Alfred Matter, The" 973-975, 1264, 1317

"Amelia Harwell Matter, The" 168, 248-250, 1259, 1288, 1303
American Experience 590
Ames, Marlene 84
"Amita Buddha Matter, The" 338-339, 380, 1284, 1305
"Amy Bradshaw Matter, The" 465-468, 1273, 1307
"Archeologist, The" 96-97, 1265, 1301
"Aromatic Cicatrix Matter, The" 403-404, 1262, 1305, 1322
"Arrowcraft Matter, The" 127-128, 1264, 1301
"Art for My Sake Matter, The" 1050-1051, 1270, 1296, 1318, 1323
"Arthur Boldrick Matter, The" 203-204, 415-416, 1259, 1303, 1306, 1322
Arthur, Jack 1212, 1225
Arvan, Jan 51
Audley, Eleanor 384, 465, 526, 576, 752, 765, 800, 824, 858, 885, 896, 985
Aurant, Dick 1238
Averback, Hy 24, 109, 115, 128, 140, 144, 145, 147, 159, 163, 169, 185, 202, 209, 214, 215, 218, 223, 226, 228, 230, 239, 243, 245, 251, 258, 277, 292, 303, 310, 314, 322, 338, 343, 347, 384, 415, 423, 427, 429, 444, 448, 481, 553, 1244
Avery, Gaylord 1184

"Back to the Back Matter, The" 1008-1010, 1258, 1317
"Backfire that Backfired Matter, The" 936-937, 1282, 1316

Backus, Jim 248, 431
"Bad One Matter, The" 4, 1037-1038, 1271, 1317
Baer, Parley 4, 21, 24, 48, 58, 60, 80, 84, 88, 96, 132, 137, 161, 173, 178, 204, 220, 221, 233, 241, 275, 280, 292, 297, 311, 317, 326, 330, 336, 355, 357, 375, 391, 406, 416, 421, 425, 452, 477, 489, 505, 522, 558, 609, 629, 687, 692, 696, 706, 728, 735, 769, 788, 798, 802, 819, 836, 845, 847, 872, 875, 880, 909, 914, 926, 995, 998, 1004, 1029
Bailey, Bob 3, 4, 5, 7, 9, 10, 13, 25, 27, 109, 263, 264, 265, 267, 269, 271, 279, 280, 284, 293, 297, 301, 304, 308, 311, 365, 382, 391, 403, 433, 435-1042, **435**, 1043, 1048, 1051, 1052, 1053, 1237, 1242, 1244, 1245-1250, 1251, 1253, 1254, 1255, 1258, 1260, 1261, 1262, 1263, 1264, 1266, 1267, 1268, 1269, 1270, 1271, 1272, 1273, 1274, 1275, 1276, 1277, 1278, 1279, 1280, 1281, 1282, 1283, 1284, 1285, 1296, 1306-1318
Bainter, Robert (aka Bailey, Bob) 792, 793
Baker, Fay 86
"Baldero Matter, The" 894-896, 1284, 1316
"Baltimore Matter, The" 8, 267-269, 304, 496, 1254, 1290, 1293, 1304
Banks, Joan 107, 306, 745, 945
"Barbara James Matter, The" 130-132, 1270, 1302
Barrett, Michael Ann 101, 530, 600, 674, 677
Barrett, Tony 101, 133, 173, 199, 206, 213, 253, 269, 303, 315, 440, 448, 452, 465, 513, 549, 576, 605, 634, 658, 670, 674, 692, 803, 807, 819, 876, 902, 932, 934, 977, 1000, 1242, 1244
Barrier, Edgar 52, 168, 171, 192, 204, 213, 223, 228, 239, 247, 251, 265, 279, 303, 310, 339, 345, 359, 368, 377, 389, 410, 423, 509, 522, 535, 571, 605, 711, 745, 817, 822, 824, 830, 849, 853, 900, 918, 949, 960, 1006, 1015
Bartell, Harry 24, 103, 127, 128, 465, 493, 500, 540, 544, 553, 567, 576, 590, 594, 619, 629, 634, 653, 658, 662, 692, 698, 702, 717, 720, 726, 741, 754, 756, 764, 769, 778, 780, 795, 796, 800, 815, 828, 833, 835, 844, 858, 863, 866, 877, 879, 892, 894, 898, 910, 914, 931, 938, 947, 951, 963, 967, 973, 978, 993, 998, 1003, 1012, 1015, 1024, 1026, 1040, 1042, 1242, 1244, 1245, 1250
"Barton Baker Matter, The" 357-359, 1283, 1305
"Basking Ridge Matter, The" 867-868, 1262, 1315, 1322
Bates, Jeanne 54, 92, 99, 113, 128, 137, 145, 147, 176, 184, 196, 204, 213, 230, 242, 247, 265, 277, 408, 427, 448, 530, 558, 567, 765
Bauer, Charita 1219
"Baxter Matter, The" 247-248, 1265, 1292, 1303, 1321
"Bayou Body Matter, The" 951-953, 1280, 1216
Bayz, Gus 853, 932, 1031, 1033
Beals, Richard 342, 696, 726, 853, 879, 900
"Beauregard Matter, The" 371-373, 644, 1275, 1289, 1305
Beck, Jackson 907, 1091, 1092, 1121, 1150, 1155, 1204, 1234
"Bee or Not to Bee Matter, The" 26, 1135-1138, 1282, 1319
Begley, Ed 24, 92, 97, 169, 184, 185, 194, 241, 243, 415, 419, 429
Behrens, Frank 1108
Belasco, Leon 812
Bell, Ralph 1046, 1077, 1078, 1087, 1098, 1165, 1173, 1186, 1197, 1219
"Belo-Horizonte Railroad, The" 132-133, 1278, 1302

INDEX

"Ben Bryson Matter, The" 363-365, 653, 1269, 1288, 1305
"Bennet Matter, The" 3, 4, 264, 433, 518-522, 996, 1264, 1292, 1308-1309
Benson, Court 1121, 1123, 1130, 1131, 1146, 1161, 1169
"Berlin Matter, The" 387-389, 1256, 1305
Bernardi, Hershel 991, 1028
"Big Date Matter, The" 1053-1055, 1280, 1296, 1318
"Big H Matter, The" 10, 913, 914-915, 916, 920, 1163, 1266, 1316
"Big Red Schoolhouse, The" 107-109, 535, 1265, 1287, 1292, 1301
"Big Scoop Matter, The" 685-687, 1273, 1313
"Bilked Baroness Matter, The" 404-406, 1261, 1306
"Birdy Baskerville Matter, The" 235-236, 287-288, 1257, 1286, 1303, 1304, 1322
"Bishop Blackmail Matter, The" 317-318, 1271, 1304, 1322
"Black Doll Matter, The" 320-322, 1271, 1305
"Blackburn Matter, The" 163-164, 1275, 1302
"Blackmail Matter, The" 301-303, 1271, 1304
Blaine, Martin 1115, 1141, 1142, 1165, 1197
"Blind Item Matter, The" 213-214, 1303, 1321
"Blinker Matter, The" 842-844, 1278, 1315
Bliss, Ted 284, 384
Blondell, Gloria 103, 119, 218, 253, 277, 493
"Blood River Matter, The" 137-138, 1279, 1302
"Blooming Blossom Matter, The" 10, 702-704, 1267, 1313
"Blue Madonna Matter, The" 890-892, 932, 1263, 1315

"Blue Rock Matter, The" 9, 1176-1178, 1277, 1319
"Bobby Foster Matter, The" 349-351, 1271, 1305
"Bodyguard to Anne Connelly" 77-79, 145, 1255, 1287, 1301
"Bodyguard to the Late Robert W. Perry" 38, 98-99, 1255, 1287, 1301
Boland, Joseph 1227
Boles, Jim 1057, 1074, 1084, 1085, 1141, 1142, 1143, 1144
"Bolt Out of the Blue Matter, The" 927-928, 1264, 1316
"Boron 112 Matter, The" 796-798, 1263, 1314
Botzer, Allen 24, 50, 52, 761, 811
Bouchey, Bill 56, 62, 105, 113, 127, 135, 149, 172, 206, 211, 236, 265
"Brisbane Fraud Matter, The" 306-308, 567, 1260, 1288, 1304
"Broderick Matter, The" 271, 306, 461-465, 1262, 1288, 1307
Brown, Vanessa 88
Bruce, Bob 472, 489, 505, 513, 535, 662, 692, 717, 720, 757, 764, 831, 836, 844
Brundage, Hugh 653
"Buffalo Matter, The" 940-942, 1282, 1316
"Bum Steer Matter, The" 769-771, 1280, 1314
Burke, Walter 92, 99, 107, 121, 123
"Burma Red Matter, The" 1187-1189, 1271, 1319
"Burning Carr Matter, The" 689-692, 1217, 1280, 1313
"Burning Desire Matter, The" 961-963, 1282, 1316
Burns, Allan 1110
Burr, Raymond 99, 111, 119, 137, 140, 149, 155, 159, 179, 181, 188, 197, 211, 226, 228, 238, 242, 253, 273, 277, 700
Bushman, Francis X. 133, 168, 175, 179, 252, 265, 336
Butler, Daws 82, 1238

Butterfield, Herb 51, 65, 86, 105, 130, 137, 149, 161, 174, 178, 181, 182, 189, 192, 196, 199, 200, 202, 223, 233, 242, 245, 248, 250, 265, 267, 318, 331, 339, 357, 373, 397, 440, 505, 530, 535, 605, 609, 670, 704, 711, 720

Buyeff, Lillian 51, 94, 107, 123, 144, 163, 165, 171, 224, 231, 290, 292, 297, 335, 361, 365, 370, 394, 410, 412, 419, 456, 461, 472, 489, 522, 567, 605, 658, 711, 726, 777, 778, 819, 866, 890, 894, 945, 953, 1003, 1021, 1239, 1241, 1242, 1244

"Buyer and the Cellar Matter, The" 1126-1128, 1285, 1319

"Byron Hayes Matter, The" 182-184, 1259, 1302

Cabibbo, Joseph 1184, 1186, 1189, 1193, 1195, 1197

Cagney, Jeanne 430

"Calgary Matter, The" 7, 133-135, 1254, 1302

"Caligio Diamond Matter, The" 125-127, 1268, 1301

"Callicles Matter, The" 308, 562-567, 1260, 1288, 1310

Calvert, Charles 416

Camargo, Ralph 1046, 1061, 1075, 1076, 1119, 1184, 1191, 1208

Campanella, Frank 1169

Campbell, Patsy 1110

"Can't Be So Matter, The" 5, 1157-1159, 1285, 1319

Canel, Pat 1150, 1176

"Canned Canary Matter, The" 965, 998-1000, 1040, 1071, 1276, 1317

"Captain's Table Matter, The" 1082-1085, 1266, 1298, 1318

"Carboniferous Dolomite Matter, The" 5, 421-423, 1261, 1306

Carlson, Dean 1232

"Carmen Kringle Matter, The" 791-793, 1282, 1314

Carpenter, Cliff 1126, 1146, 1148, 1167, 1171

"Carson Arson Matter, The" 826-828, 1285, 1315

"Case of Barton Drake, The" 46-48, 1255, 1300

"Case of the Foxy Terrier, The" 1300, 1321

"Case of the Hundred Thousand Dollar Legs, The" 44-46, 1267, 1300

"Case of Trouble Matter, The" 691, 1215-1217, 1270, 1320

"Casque of Death Matter, The" 912-914, 1274, 1316

Cassar, Barbara 1123, 1146

"Cautious Celibate Matter, The" 904-905, 1263, 1316

"Caylin Matter, The" 489-493, 1279, 1308

"Celia Woodstock Matter, The" 178-179, 367-368, 1283, 1286, 1302, 1305

Chadwick, Bob 1025

Chandler, David 24, 384

Chandler, Freddy 1215

Charles, Milton 290, 293, 295, 303, 306, 309, 311

"Charmona Matter, The" 762-764, 1268, 1314

Chavez, Raul 117

"Chesapeake Fraud Matter, The" 267, 444-448, 1281, 1288, 1306

"Chicago Fraud Matter, The" 277-279, 481, 1257, 1291, 1304

Christy, Ken 82, 140, 317, 367, 368, 401, 440, 485, 553, 851

"Chuckanut Matter, The" 1111-1113, 1284, 1319

"Cinder Elmer Matter, The" 1146-1148, 1285, 1319

"Circus Animal Show Matter, The" 79-80, 1256, 1301

"Classified Killer Matter, The" 380-382, 1261, 1305

"Clever Chemist Matter, The" 715-717, 1275, 1313

"Clever Crook Matter, The" 1128, 1319, 1323

"Clinton Matter, The" 7, 109, 531-535, 1281, 1287, 1292, 1309
"Close Shave Matter, The" 869-870, 1282, 1315, 1322
"Clouded Crystal Matter, The" 892-893, 1279, 1315, 1323
Cole, Robert 1080
"Collector's Matter, The" 1006-1008, 1264, 1317
"Confederate Coinage Matter, The" 749-752, 1275, 1314
"Confidential Matter, The" 365, 649-653, 1262, 1288, 1312
Connors, Chuck 1244
Conrad, William 24, 30, 46, 65, 79, 80, 94, 109, 115, 137, 138, 142, 157, 163, 171, 172, 178, 181, 182, 189, 217, 223, 226, 230, 247, 293, 299, 306, 326, 331, 347, 368, 382, 392, 401, 581, 1238
Conried, Hans 103, 253, 431, 522, 713, 728, 747
Cook, Tommy 571
Corbett, Lois 56, 59, 685
"Costain Matter, The" 308-310, 1263, 1304
Cotsworth, Staats 190
Courage, Alexander 151
"Crater Lake Matter, The" 868-869, 1273, 1315, 1322
Creed, Don 1191
Crenna, Richard 30, 571, 586, 639, 649, 677, 726, 731, 747, 793, 942, 944, 983, 993, 1029, 1033
Croft, Mary Jane 215, 295, 314, 324, 328, 338, 353, 373, 392, 427, 430, 431, 440, 481, 518, 526, 562, 600, 644, 696, 737, 756, 764, 767
"Cronin Matter, The" 465, 472-477, 1277, 1307
Crowder, Connie 84
Crutchfield, Les 25, 317, 365, 370, 373, 391, 403, 444, 461, 477, 485, 493, 509, 518, 526, 562, 571, 585, 594, 614, 624, 644, 653, 670, 1288, 1289
"Crystal Lake Cabin Matter, The" 634-639, 1312

"Cuban Jewel Matter, The" 223-224, 315, 1268, 1303
Cubberly, Dan 153, 155, 159, 161, 163, 164, 165, 185, 187, 194, 196, 206, 208, 211, 219, 221, 222, 224, 226, 230, 231, 233, 235, 236, 242, 243, 245, 247, 248, 257, 258, 260, 262, 264, 265, 267, 269, 271, 273, 275, 277, 279, 280, 282, 284, 286, 687, 689, 692, 694, 695, 696, 697, 700, 702, 704, 706, 708, 710, 711, 713, 715, 717, 719, 720, 722, 724, 726, 728, 729, 731, 734, 735, 737, 739, 741, 743, 745, 747, 749, 751, 763, 765, 767, 769, 771, 773, 775, 776, 780, 782, 784, 787, 788, 790, 793, 794, 796, 798, 800, 801, 803, 805, 807, 809, 811, 812, 815, 817, 818, 821, 822, 824, 826, 828, 830, 831, 864, 865, 866, 868, 869, 870, 872, 873, 875, 876, 877, 879, 880, 882, 883, 885, 886, 888, 890, 891, 892, 894, 896, 898, 900, 902, 904, 905, 907, 909, 910, 912, 913, 915, 916, 918, 920, 922, 932, 934, 935, 943, 945, 947, 949, 951, 953, 954, 956, 958, 959, 961, 963, 964, 965, 967, 968, 1012, 1013, 1195, 1239, 1241, 1250
"Cui Bono Matter, The" 513-518, 1277, 1308
Culver, Howard 82, 121, 138, 174, 275, 377, 394
"Cumberland Theft Matter, The" 219-220, 1259, 1303, 1321
"Curley Waters Matter, The" 885-886, 1270, 1315, 1323
"Curse of Kamashek Matter, The" 27, 644-649, 1268, 1293, 1312
Cusick, Fred 1217
Cutting, Dick 167, 168, 169, 171, 172, 173, 175, 176, 177, 179, 181, 182, 184, 188, 192, 197, 198, 202, 204, 209, 228, 231, 235, 236, 238, 240, 243, 245, 247, 248

"Dameron Matter, The" 297-299, 1263, 1304
Damon, Les 1050
"Dan Frank Matter, The" 401-403, 623, 1257, 1289, 1305
Darnay, Toni 1126, 1133
"Date with Death Matter, The" 7, 886-888, 1270, 1315
"David Rockey Matter, The" 169-171, 1256, 1302
Davis, Charles 235, 338
Dawson, John 24, 439, 440, 448, 456, 465, 472, 481, 489, 496, 505, 513, 522, 530, 535, 549, 558, 567, 581, 599, 600, 685, 694, 702, 710, 719, 1287, 1288, 1289, 1290, 1291, 1292, 1293
Dawson, Sam 25, 500
de Corsia, Ted 92, 99, 113, 125, 133, 223, 286, 373, 410, 658
De Koven, Roger 1065, 1080, 1089, 1090, 1123
"Dead First-Helpers, The" 109-111, 1266, 1301
"Deadly Chain Matter, The" 928-929, 1071, 1258, 1316
"Deadly Crystal Matter, The" 916, 1048, 1230-1232, 1284, 1320
"Deadly Debt Matter, The" 1017-1019, 1280, 1317
"Deadly Doubt Matter, The" 876, 881-882, 1282, 1315
"Deadly Swamp Matter, The" 5, 986-987, 1275, 1317
"Death by Jet Matter, The" 1059-1061, 1296, 1318
"Death Takes a Working Day" 54-56, 90-92, 1265, 1286, 1300, 1301, 1321
"Deep Down Matter, The" 979-980, 1027, 1258, 1317
Deering, Olive 1232
Dehner, John 24, 49, 52, 58, 59, 77, 79, 92, 97, 113, 123, 135, 147, 153, 161, 164, 448, 465, 477, 526, 544, 594, 614, 634, 682, 685, 708, 710, 719, 729, 731, 734, 769, 790, 849, 998, 1026, 1245, 1250
del Valle, Jaime 25, 92, 94, 96, 97, 99, 101, 103, 105, 107, 109, 111, 113, 115, 117, 119, 121, 123, 125, 127, 128, 130, 132, 133, 135, 137, 138, 140, 142, 144, 145, 147, 149, 151, 153, 155, 157, 159, 161, 163, 164, 165, 167, 168, 169, 171, 172, 173, 175, 176, 177, 179, 181, 182, 184, 185, 187, 189, 190, 192, 194, 196, 197, 199, 200, 202, 204, 206, 208, 209, 211, 213, 214, 215, 217, 218, 220, 221, 223, 224, 226, 228, 230, 231, 233, 235, 236, 239, 241, 242, 243, 245, 247, 248, 250, 251, 252, 253, 255, 257, 258, 260, 263, 264, 265, 267, 269, 271, 273, 275, 277, 279, 280, 282, 284, 286, 288, 290, 292, 293, 295, 297, 299, 301, 303, 305, 306, 308, 310, 311, 313, 315, 317, 318, 320, 322, 324, 326, 328, 330, 331, 333, 335, 336, 338, 339, 342, 343, 345, 347, 349, 351, 353, 355, 357, 359, 361, 363, 365, 367, 368, 370, 373, 375, 377, 380, 382, 384, 386, 389, 391, 392, 394, 397, 399, 401, 403, 404, 406, 408, 410, 412, 415, 416, 419, 421, 423, 425, 427, 429, 430, 431, 433, 434, 1239, 1241
"Delectable Damsel Matter, The" 836-838, 1271, 1315
Delmar, Kenny 333
Demetrie, James 1157
Dendrick, Richard 1084, 1085
"Denver Disbursal Matter, The" 8, 815-817, 1274, 1314
"Department Store Swindle Matter, The" 82-84, 1267, 1301
"Desalles Matter, The" 700-702, 1258, 1313
"Diamond Dilemma Matter, The" 809-811, 1270, 1314
"Diamond Protector Matter, The" 36, 84-85, 1255, 1301, 1321
Diamond, Don 52, 77, 290, 361, 394, 410, 412, 419, 431, 452, 468, 485, 509, 540, 594, 605, 629, 634, 677, 830, 893, 847, 951, 963

"Dixon Murder Matter, The" 737-740, 1275, 1313
"Do It Yourself Matter, The" 1161-1163, 1266, 1319
Dobkin, Lawrence 24, 52, 54, 56, 59, 62, 64, 67, 71, 73, 75, 80, 86, 105, 164, 377, 461, 465, 496, 500, 530, 544, 549, 558, 567, 576, 590, 594, 629, 674, 682, 689, 696, 698, 700, 713, 726, 741, 747, 749, 756, 759, 767, 778, 782, 787, 790, 793, 795, 800, 807, 824, 830, 849, 851, 856, 857, 858, 861, 864, 866, 869, 870, 873, 876, 883, 896, 898, 900, 902, 907, 910, 918, 931, 936, 940, 942, 944, 949, 958, 960, 961, 963, 964, 970, 977, 1006, 1013, 1026, 1036, 1038, 1250
"Doninger Doninger Matter, The" 1223-1225, 1272, 1320
Donnelly, Bob 1135, 1137, 1138, 1278
"Doting Dowager Matter, The" 876, 882, 883-885, 1263, 1315
"Double Deal Matter, The" 1000, 1039-1040, 1274, 1317
"Double Exposure Matter, The" 984-985, 1270, 1317
"Double Identity Matter, The" 944-945, 947, 1282, 1316
"Double Trouble Matter, The" 870-872, 1279, 1315
"Double-Barreled Matter, The" 1128-1131, 1271, 1297, 1319
"Doubtful Dairy Matter, The" 767-769, 1281, 1314
Doud, Gil 24, 25, 34, 36, 38, 40, 42, 44, 46, 48, 49, 51, 52, 54, 56, 58, 59, 60, 62, 64, 65, 67, 69, 71, 73, 75, 77, 79, 80, 82, 84, 85, 86, 88, 92, 94, 96, 97, 99, 101, 105, 107, 111, 115, 117, 119, 121, 123, 125, 127, 128, 130, 132, 133, 135, 137, 138, 140, 142, 144, 145, 147, 149, 151, 153, 155, 157, 159, 161, 163, 164, 165, 167, 168, 169, 171, 172, 173, 175, 176, 177, 179, 181, 182, 184, 185, 187, 189, 190, 192, 194, 196, 197, 199, 200, 204, 206, 208, 209, 211, 213, 215, 217, 218, 220, 221, 223, 228, 230, 231, 233, 235, 239, 241, 242, 245, 247, 250, 251, 252, 253, 255, 257, 258, 260, 286, 313, 357, 363, 367, 368, 375, 416, 419, 425, 1238, 1242, 1244, 1286, 1287, 1288, 1289, 1290, 1291
"Douglas Taylor Matter, The" 226-228, 260, 1265, 1289, 1303
Douglas, Hugh 987, 1023
"Dr. Otto Schmedlich" 66-67, 1255, 1301
"Draminski Matter, The" 368-370, 1262, 1305, 1322
Draper, Margaret 1159
Dryanforth, Harold 113
Dryden, Robert 1055, 1057, 1058, 1059, 1067, 1072, 1074, 1076, 1082, 1087, 1089, 1090, 1094, 1096, 1098, 1101, 1113, 1119, 1130, 1131, 1135, 1137, 1138, 1148, 1152, 1153, 1171, 1176, 1191, 1197, 1227
Dubov, Paul 49, 51, 54, 58, 59, 60, 64, 67, 69, 71, 84, 86, 448, 624, 649, 682, 759, 769, 790, 811, 849, 882, 902, 907, 920, 922, 929, 938, 963, 1004, 1021, 1031, 1244
Dudley, Paul 25, 34, 36, 38, 40, 42, 44, 46, 48, 49, 51, 52, 54, 56, 58, 59, 60, 62, 64, 65, 67, 69, 71, 73, 75, 77, 79, 80, 82, 84, 85, 86, 88, 92, 94, 96, 97, 99, 101, 107, 1238, 1286, 1287
"Duke Red Matter, The" 311, 501-505, 1281, 1288, 1308
Duncan, Herb 1163, 1182, 1204, 1221
Dunstedter, Eddie 206, 208, 209, 211, 212, 213, 215, 216, 218, 219, 221, 222, 224, 226, 250, 251, 252, 253, 254, 257, 258, 260, 262, 264, 265, 267, 269, 271, 273, 275, 277, 279, 280, 282, 284, 286, 288, 292, 297, 299, 301, 304, 308, 313, 315, 317, 318, 320, 322, 324, 326, 328, 330, 331, 333, 335, 336, 338, 339, 342, 343, 345, 347, 349, 351, 353, 355, 357, 359, 361, 363, 365, 367, 368, 370, 373, 375, 377, 380, 382, 384, 386, 389, 391, 392, 394, 396, 398, 401, 403, 404, 406, 408,

410, 412, 415, 416, 419, 421, 423, 425, 427, 429, 430, 431, 432, 433, 1239, 1241
"Durango Laramie Matter, The" 807-809, 1263, 1314
DuVal, Joseph 99, 133, 168, 173, 192, 213, 265, 269, 284, 330, 343, 357, 365, 403, 406, 412, 434

Eagles, James 119
"Earl Chadwick Matter, The" 121-123, 1280, 1301
"Eastern Western Matter, The" 819-821, 1279, 1314
"Edith Maxwell Matter, The" 254-255, 1260, 1303, 1322
"Edward French Matter, The" 186-187, 1279, 1302
Edwards, Blake 24, 202, 214, 224, 226, 236, 248, 288, 303, 315, 318, 320, 322, 324, 326, 328, 330, 331, 333, 335, 336, 338, 339, 342, 343, 345, 347, 349, 353, 359, 399, 1286, 1292, 1293
Edwards, Jack 56, 60, 365, 375, 386, 412, 489, 549, 553, 653, 677, 700, 745, 759, 767, 771, 819, 828, 859, 870, 875, 890, 898, 910, 923, 966, 967, 1000, 1010, 1245, 1250
Edwards, Sam 24, 336, 391, 408, 485, 518, 526, 576, 715, 740, 747, 771, 773, 805, 831, 868, 872, 877, 885, 888, 909, 917, 925, 931, 936, 938, 943, 944, 953, 956, 964, 968, 971, 978, 987, 991, 1003, 1006, 1015, 1019, 1022, 1023, 1031, 1038
"Eighty-Five Little Minks, The" 8, 101-103, 233, 710, 1271, 1288, 1301
Eiler, Barbara 465, 505, 549, 670, 715
Eiler, Virginia 155
"Eleven O'Clock Matter, The" 798-800, 1262, 1314
"Ellen Dear Matter, The" 698-700, 991, 1237, 1245-1250, 1284, 1313, 1322
"Elliot Champion Matter, The" 263-265, 433, 522, 1265, 1292, 1304

Ellis, David 24, 88, 105, 111, 1287, 1290
Ellis, Georgia 52, 54, 60, 64, 67, 69, 84, 164
Ellis, Herb 440, 465, 472, 489, 513, 535, 558, 562, 600, 639, 670, 698, 704, 719, 722, 729, 752, 761, 778, 807, 812, 815, 964, 967, 1017, 1031
Ellison, Joan 1113
"Embarcadero Matter, The" 933-934, 1263, 1316
"Emil Carter Matter, The" 245, 312-314, 1257, 1288, 1304
"Emil Lovett Matter, The" 181-182, 1257, 1302, 1321
"Emily Braddock Matter, The" 271, 305-306, 465, 1256, 1288, 1304
"Empty Threat Matter, The" 1041-1042, 1264, 1318
"Enoch Arden Matter, The" 294-295, 1267, 1304
Epstein, Fargo 273
Eric, Elsbeth 1072, 1232
"Evaporated Clue Matter, The" 966-967, 1264, 1317
Everett, Ethel 1152, 1153, 1206, 1229
"Expiring Nickels and the Egyptian Jackpot, The" 4, 59-60, 1258, 1301

"Fair-Way Matter, The" 209-211, 365-367, 1257, 1257, 1286, 1303, 1305
"Fairweather Friend Matter, The" 902-904, 1263, 1316
"False Alarm Matter, The" 982-983, 1280, 1317
"Fancy Bridgework Matter, The" 953-954, 1280, 1316
Farrer, Stanley 172
"Fatal Filet Matter, The" 562, 909-910, 1258, 1316
"Fatal Switch Matter, The" 989-991, 1284, 1317
"Fathom-Five Matter, The" 522-526, 1260, 1309
Fein, Morton 273
Feld, Fritz 380

INDEX

"Felicity Feline Matter, The" 743-745, 784, 1258, 1314
Fennelly, Parker 1106
Fenster, Daphne 273
Fernandez, Peter 907, 1234
"Fiddle Faddle Matter, The" 1106-1108, 1280, 1319
"Final Chapter Matter, The" 13-22
Fine, Morton 25, 273, 389
"Fire in Paradise Matter, The" 800-802, 1264, 1314, 1322
"Firebug Hunter Matter, The" 85-86, 1261, 1301, 1321
Firestone, Eddie 253, 282
"Fishing Boat Affair, The" 62-64, 1268, 1301
Fitzgerald, Neil 1225
"Five Down Matter, The" 1024-1026, 1071, 1276, 1317
"Flask of Death Matter, The" 1003-1004, 1283, 1317
"Flight Six Matter, The" 489, 505-509, 1266, 1308
"Forbes Matter, The" 293, 485-489, 1258, 1289, 1308
Forte, Joe 111
Fortina, Carl 581, 585, 590, 594, 600, 605, 609, 614, 662, 689
Foster, Roger 1189
"Four C's Matter, The" 1225-1227, 1266, 1320
"Four's a Crowd Matter, The" 1212-1215, 1277, 1320
Fox, Gibson Scott 24, 433
Francis, Eugene 1104, 1148, 1150, 1176, 1186
Francis, Ivor 1113, 1137, 1138, 1143, 1144, 1155, 1189, 1210, 1219
Frank, Carl 1055, 1072, 1074, 1123, 1128, 1130, 1131, 1232
Franklin, Paul 25, 715
"Frantic Fisherman Matter, The" 924-925, 1163, 1266, 1316
Frees, Paul 540, 1040
Friedkin, David 25, 273, 389

"Frisco Fire Matter, The" 900-902, 1266, 1316
"Froward Fisherman Matter, The" 834-835, 1191, 1258, 1315, 1322
"Frustrated Phoenix Matter, The" 399-401, 1283, 1305
Fuller, Barbara 477, 496, 505, 549, 600, 634
"Funny Money Matter, The" 741-743, 1263, 1314
"Further Buffalo Matter, The" 4, 942-944, 1282, 1316
Fussell, Sarah 1178

Galen, Hetty 1208, 1215
Garde, Betty 1155
Gaylor, Gerry 389
Gendot, Adrian 24, 682
"George Farmer Matter, The" 201-202, 1265, 1303
Gerson, Betty Lou 67, 79, 82, 456, 513, 1238
Gerstle, Frank 440, 465, 496, 530, 535, 581, 653, 682, 689, 704, 717, 747, 754, 756, 780, 798, 811, 817, 836, 838, 840, 842, 861, 868, 876, 880, 882, 910, 912, 923, 929, 934, 953, 954, 963, 970, 975, 977, 997, 1010, 1017, 1033, 1035, 1244
"Ghost to Ghost Matter, The" 830-831, 1277, 1315
Gibson, John 1208
Gilbert, Joe 149
Gillespie, Jean 1072
Gillian, Bill 1163, 1173
"Gino Gambona Matter, The" 347-349, 1268, 1305
"Glacier Ghost Matter, The" 728-729, 865, 1280, 1313, 1322
"Glen English Matter, The" 245-247, 1267, 1303
Glenn, Roy 24, 311, 326, 590, 694, 987
Gluskin, Lud 172
"Gold Rush Country Matter, The" 1319, 1323
"Gold Rush Matter, The" 1221-1223, 1266, 1320

"Golden Dream Matter, The" 1170-1171, 1266, 1319
"Golden Touch Matter, The" 710-711, 890, 1276, 1313, 1322
Goldsmith, Jerry 704
Gordon, Clark 73, 1238
Gorman, Tom 1121
Gould, Sandra 79, 277, 489, 985
Graham, Tim 82, 161, 178, 185, 199, 241, 399
"Grand Canyon Matter, The" 1184-1186, 1273, 1319
Grant, Bernard 1067, 1091, 1092, 1101, 1176
"Gravedigger's Spades, The" 94-96, 1271, 1301
Gray, Sam 1094, 1108, 1121, 1155, 1157, 1159, 1180, 1180, 1221, 1232
"Great Bannock Race Matter, The" 431-433, 1276, 1306, 1322
Green, Austin 662, 715, 737, 740, 765, 796
Green, Marty 1208
Gregg, Virginia 13, 24, 97, 109, 115, 123, 127, 130, 135, 138, 142, 145, 151, 155, 161, 168, 169, 172, 175, 185, 192, 194, 197, 200, 202, 204, 206, 208, 209, 211, 214, 215, 217, 218, 220, 221, 223, 233, 235, 236, 239, 241, 243, 245, 248, 250, 251, 253, 255, 257, 263, 267, 271, 273, 275, 280, 282, 286, 292, 293, 297, 301, 303, 305, 308, 310, 315, 317, 320, 345, 349, 355, 368, 377, 380, 382, 384, 386, 389, 391, 392, 397, 399, 401, 403, 404, 406, 408, 415, 416, 421, 423, 425, 430, 431, 433, 440, 444, 452, 465, 468, 477, 485, 493, 509, 540, 544, 558, 562, 567, 576, 581, 594, 605, 609, 619, 629, 634, 644, 649, 653, 658, 662, 674, 677, 682, 685, 687, 689, 692, 694, 700, 702, 708, 710, 711, 713, 717, 719, 720, 722, 724, 726, 728, 729, 731, 737, 741, 743, 745, 747, 749, 752, 754, 757, 761, 771, 773, 777, 778, 780, 782, 785, 787, 790, 802, 803, 807, 809, 817, 819, 821, 822, 828, 830, 831, 835, 838, 842, 847, 851, 855, 856, 861, 863, 864, 865, 866, 869, 872, 873, 875, 876, 877, 879, 880, 882, 883, 885, 896, 900, 902, 904, 905, 907, 910, 915, 917, 920, 922, 923, 926, 928, 929, 931, 932, 936, 937, 938, 940, 947, 949, 951, 953, 954, 956, 958, 963, 964, 966, 968, 971, 973, 975, 977, 978, 980, 983, 985, 989, 991, 993, 995, 997, 998, 1000, 1003, 1006, 1008, 1010, 1013, 1015, 1019, 1021, 1026, 1031, 1033, 1035, 1036, 1040, 1042, 1245, 1250
Grey, Bill 105, 121
Griffin, Robert 94, 107, 133, 144, 163, 258, 324, 339, 370, 1239, 1241
Griffis, William 1180
Griggs, John 1084, 1085, 1193
Grimes, Jack 907, 923, 1046, 1059, 1087, 1089, 1090, 1165, 1180, 1189, 1217, 1225, 1234
"Gruesome Spectacle Matter, The" 861-863, 940, 1280, 1315, 1323
"Guide to Murder Matter, The" 1142-1144, 1280, 1319

Haines, Hilda 1119
Haines, Larry 1055, 1077, 1078, 1080, 1082, 1116, 1157, 1212
"Hair Raising Matter, The" 873-875, 1071, 1144, 1277, 1315
Hairston, Jester 326
"Haiti Adventure Matter" 81-82, 124, 1255, 1287, 1301
Halop, Billy 826, 840, 866, 926
"Hamilton Payroll Matter, The" 430-431, 1259, 1306, 1322
"Hampton Line Matter, The" 427-429, 1284, 1306
"Hand of Providential Matter, The" 947-949, 1275, 1316
Hanley, Tom 167, 322, 363, 535, 619, 726, 729, 735, 809, 836, 873, 886, 905, 998, 1004, 1024, 1025, 1031, 1063
Hannes, Art 1046, 1055, 1057, 1059, 1061, 1065, 1067, 1074, 1075, 1077, 1080, 1082, 1084, 1086, 1092, 1094,

1096, 1097, 1101, 1104, 1106, 1108, 1113, 1121, 1123, 1126, 1128, 1130, 1133, 1135, 1137, 1139, 1141, 1144, 1146, 1152, 1156, 1157, 1159, 1161, 1165, 1167, 1169, 1178, 1182, 1186, 1193, 1195, 1197, 1202, 1204, 1206, 1208, 1210, 1214, 1219, 1221, 1225, 1227, 1229, 1232

"Hannibal Murphy Matter, The" 233-235, 1275, 1303

"Hapless Ham Matter, The" 963-964, 1262, 1316

"Hapless Hunter Matter, The" 787-788, 1278, 1314

Hardy, Joe 1210

Harford, Alex 433

"Harold Trandem Matter, The" 117-119, 1257, 1301

Harper, Alec 130

"Harpooned Angler Matter, The" 375-377, 1283, 1305

"Harried Heiress Matter, The" 1001-1003, 1046, 1072, 1176, 1268, 1317

Harris, Stacy 127, 132, 159, 168, 176, 224, 231, 233, 236, 241, 267, 288, 292, 295, 306, 357, 522, 562, 624, 653, 687, 706, 708, 710, 734, 741, 757, 815, 844, 909, 936, 966, 968, 973, 1000, 1015, 1019, 1924, 1033

Hartford Alliance Matter, The 139-140, 1259, 1302

Hartman, Ray (aka Raymond Burr) 179, 181, 188, 189, 206, 211, 226, 228, 238, 239

Hatch, Wilbur 64, 65, 67, 69, 71, 147, 149, 153, 155, 157, 159, 161, 163, 164, 165, 167, 168, 169, 171, 173, 175, 176, 177, 179, 181, 182, 184, 185, 187, 188, 190, 192, 194, 196, 197, 199, 200, 202, 204, 228, 230, 231, 233, 235, 236, 238, 240, 242, 243, 247, 248

"Hatchet House Theft Matter, The" 206-208, 1263, 1303

Hausner, Jerry 65, 873, 949, 995

Hayes, John Michael 24, 103, 109, 113, 710, 1287, 1288, 1292, 1293

"Heatherstone Players Matter, The" 745-747, 1272, 1314

"Henderson Matter, The" 284, 468-472, 1274, 1289, 1307

Hendrickson, Fred 25, 907, 1121, 1155, 1197, 1200, 1202, 1204, 1206, 1208, 1210, 1212, 1215, 1217, 1223, 1225, 1227, 1229, 1232, 1234

"Henry J. Unger Matter, The" 6, 135-137, 1255, 1302

"Henry Page Matter, The" 250-251, 1267, 1303, 1321

Herbert, Wilms 52, 161, 172

"Here Comes the Death of the Party" 48-49, 1275, 1300, 1321

Hill, Ramsey 194, 361

Hill, Sammie 58, 138, 173, 200, 282, 320, 339, 357

"Hired Homicide Matter, The" 956-958, 1281, 1316

Hite, Kathleen 24, 243

Hodge, Al 1189

Hodge, Kenny 1025, 1071

Holland, Bert 553, 567, 614, 662, 685, 713, 787, 886, 892, 951, 1019

Holland, Richard 1061, 1108, 1110, 1182

Holland, Tom 73, 856, 937

"Hollywood Matter, The" 718-719, 1271, 1313, 1322

"Hollywood Mystery Matter, The" 876, 879-880, 1261, 1315

Holmes, Wendell 1098

"Hood of Death Matter, The" 1202-1204, 1264, 1320

Hooper, Mary Ann 863, 864, 1002, 1070, 1072, 1159, 1161

"Hope to Die Matter, The" 783-785, 1263, 1314

"Horace Lockhart Matter, The" 214-215, 1283, 1303

Hosley, Pat 1159

"Hot Chocolates Matter, The" 1153-1155, 1278, 1319

"How I Turned a Luxury Liner into a Battleship" 58-59, 1274, 1300, 1321

"How Much Bourbon Can Flow Under the Bridgework?" 51-52, 1271, 1300, 1321
"Howard Arnold Matter, The" 345-347, 1284, 1305
"Howard Caldwell Matter, The" 146-147, 1256, 1302
Howard, Fred 77
Howell, Jean 311, 324
Hubbard, Irene 190
Huber, Ethel 907, 1046, 1055, 1057, 1059, 1061, 1065, 1067, 1071, 1074, 1075, 1078, 1080, 1082, 1085, 1087, 1089, 1092, 1094, 1096, 1097, 1101, 1104, 1106, 1108, 1110, 1113, 1115, 1116, 1119, 1121, 1123, 1126, 1128, 1131, 1133, 1135, 1137, 1140, 1142, 1144, 1146, 1148, 1150, 1152, 1157, 1159, 1161, 1163, 1165, 1167, 1169, 1171, 1173, 1176, 1178, 1180, 1182, 1184, 1186, 1189, 1191, 1193, 1195, 1197, 1202, 1204, 1206, 1208, 1210, 1212, 1214, 1217, 1219, 1221, 1227, 1229, 1232, 1234
Hughes, Gordon T. 25, 54, 56, 60, 62, 64, 65, 67, 69, 71, 73, 75, 77, 79, 84, 85, 86, 88

"Ideal Vacation Matter, The" 765-767, 1282, 1314
"Ike and Mike Matter, The" 1171-1173, 1281, 1319
"Imperfect Alibi Matter, The" 653-658, 687, 1273, 1312, 1322
"Imperfect Crime Matter, The" 1102-1104, 1277, 1318
"Impossible Murder Matter, The" 864-865, 1280, 1315, 1322
"Independent Diamond Traders Matter, The" 353-355, 1256, 1305
"Indestructible Mike Matter, The" 586-590, 1269, 1310
"Informer Matter, The" 8, 1076-1078, 1274, 1298, 1299, 1318
"Ingenuous Jeweler Matter, The" 795-796, 1274, 1314

"Isabelle James Matter, The" 328-330, 1271, 1305
"Island of Tin-Yutan, The" 5-6, 71-73, 1276, 1301
"Ivy Emerald Matter, The" 1178-1180, 1277, 1319

"J. P. D. Matter, The" 764-765, 1263, 1314
"Jack Madigan Matter, The" 69, 151-153, 253, 1277, 1287, 1302
"Jackie Cleaver Matter, The" 184-185, 1276, 1302
Jacobs, Johnny 609, 704
"James Clayton Matter, The" 261-263, 557, 1272, 1289, 1304
"James Forbes Matter, The" 322-324, 1268, 1305
James, Bill 167, 322, 339, 357, 363, 367, 392, 553, 696, 722, 745, 777, 793, 805, 836, 849, 853, 873, 886, 894, 904, 905, 932, 971, 998, 1004, 1024, 1025, 1031, 1033, 1062, 1063
James, John 729
"Jan Breughel Matter, The" 419-421, 1306
"Jane Doe Matter, The" 196-197, 1272, 1303, 1321
"Janet Abbe Matter, The" 230-231, 1257, 1303, 1321
Janiss, Vivi 49, 275, 477, 481, 496, 634, 692
Janney, Leon 1050, 1065, 1106, 1108, 1128, 1157, 1195, 1223
"Jarvis Wilder Matter, The" 176-178, 1256, 1302
"Jeanne Maxwell Matter, The" 155, 284-286, 423-425, 1259, 1289, 1304, 1306
Jerome, Edwin 811
"Jimmy Carter Matter, The" 898-900, 1254, 1316
"Joan Sebastian Matter, The" 153-155, 286, 425, 1259, 1289, 1302
"Johnson Payroll Matter, The" 859-861, 1282, 1315
Johnson, Lamont 159, 373

Johnson, Raymond Edward 1072, 1104, 1163, 1219
Johnson, Thelma 328
Johnstone, Doug 964, 965, 999, 1032, 1115, 1182, 1183
Johnstone, Jack 9, 10, 13, 15, 21, 24, 24, 25, 26, 435, 440, 444, 448, 452, 456, 461, 465, 468, 472, 477, 481, 485, 489, 493, 496, 500, 505, 509, 513, 518, 522, 526, 530, 535, 540, 544, 549, 553, 558, 562, 567, 571, 576, 581, 585, 590, 594, 600, 605, 609, 614, 619, 624, 629, 634, 639, 644, 649, 653, 658, 662, 666, 670, 677, 682, 685, 687, 689, 692, 694, 696, 697, 700, 702, 704, 706, 708, 710, 711, 713, 715, 717, 719, 720, 722, 724, 726, 728, 729, 731, 734, 735, 737, 740, 741, 743, 745, 747, 749, 752, 754, 756, 757, 759, 761, 763, 765, 767, 769, 770, 771, 773, 775, 776, 778, 780, 782, 785, 787, 788, 790, 793, 795, 796, 798, 800, 802, 803, 805, 807, 809, 811, 812, 815, 817, 819, 821, 822, 824, 826, 828, 830, 831, 833, 835, 836, 838, 839, 842, 844, 845, 847, 849, 851, 853, 855, 856, 858, 859, 861, 863, 864, 865, 866, 868, 869, 870, 872, 873, 875, 876, 877, 879, 880, 882, 883, 885, 886, 888, 890, 891, 893, 894, 896, 898, 900, 902, 904, 905, 907, 909, 910, 912, 913, 915, 917, 918, 920, 922, 923, 925, 926, 928, 929, 931, 932, 934, 935, 937, 938, 940, 942, 944, 945, 947, 949, 951, 953, 954, 956, 958, 959, 961, 963, 964, 965, 966, 967, 968, 970, 971, 972, 973, 975, 977, 978, 980, 982, 983, 985, 987, 989, 991, 993, 995, 997, 998, 1000, 1002, 1003, 1004, 1006, 1007, 1010, 1012, 1013, 1015, 1017, 1019, 1021, 1023, 1024, 1025, 1026, 1028, 1029, 1031, 1033, 1035, 1036, 1038, 1040, 1042, 1046, 1048, 1050, 1051, 1053, 1055, 1057, 1059, 1060, 1061, 1063, 1065, 1067, 1069, 1071, 1072, 1074, 1075, 1078, 1080, 1082, 1085, 1087, 1089, 1092, 1094, 1096, 1098, 1101, 1104, 1106, 1108, 1110, 1113, 1115, 1116, 1119, 1121, 1123, 1126, 1128, 1131, 1133, 1135, 1138, 1140, 1142, 1144, 1146, 1148, 1150, 1153, 1155, 1157, 1159, 1161, 1163, 1165, 1167, 1169, 1171, 1173, 1176, 1178, 1180, 1182, 1184, 1186, 1189, 1191, 1193, 1195, 1197, 1200, 1202, 1204, 1206, 1208, 1210, 1212, 1215, 1217, 1219, 1221, 1223, 1225, 1227, 1229, 1232, 1234, 1235, 1236, 1242, 1244, 1245, 1249, 1250, 1293, 1297
Johnstone, William 24, 79, 103, 115, 127, 151, 155, 163, 167, 179, 196, 241, 253, 257, 258, 293, 299, 305, 318, 322, 335, 338, 343, 357, 363, 365, 367, 380, 384, 386, 397, 399, 406, 412, 421, 425, 1239, 1241
"Jolly Roger Fraud Matter, The" 536-540, 1281, 1309
"Jonathan Bellows Matter, The" 314-315, 1268, 1304
"Jones Matter, The" 315-317, 1257, 1304
Jones, G. Stanley 696, 706, 722, 731, 743, 765, 773, 785, 798, 809, 885, 892, 904, 905, 912, 932, 934, 945, 947, 956, 968, 975, 1004, 1008, 1017, 1021, 1023, 1026, 1042
Jones, Stan 662, 666
Julian, Joseph 907, 1080, 1163, 1180, 1234
Juster, Evelyn 1104, 1133, 1229

Kane, Byron 24, 125, 493, 518, 553, 662, 724, 767, 775, 796, 828, 835, 892, 926
Kane, Michael 1150
"Kay Bellamy Matter, The" 275-277, 1267, 1304
Keane, Teri 1057, 1061, 1077, 1078, 1101, 1150, 1217, 1223
Kearns, Joseph 103, 115, 167, 228, 239, 255, 263, 271, 292, 297, 301, 308, 331, 363, 384, 403, 419, 427, 434, 544, 576, 624, 722, 735, 756, 767, 777, 796, 828, 831, 859, 863, 892, 915, 920, 970, 971, 1238, 1239, 1241

Keith, Richard 780, 1184, 1229
Kemper, Ray 338, 357, 535, 540, 619, 717
Kendrick, Richard 1113
Kern, David 1150
"Key to Crime Matter, The" 1137, 1234-1236, 1282, 1320
Kilburn, Terry 135, 165
"Killer Kin Matter, The" 1019-1021, 1264, 1217
"Killer's Brand Matter, The" 754-756, 1282, 1314
"Killer's List Matter, The" 817-819, 1268, 1314
King, Wally 1071
"King's Necklace Matter, The" 288-290, 1261, 1304
Kinsella, Walter 1227
"Kirbey Will Matter, The" 706-708, 1280, 1313
Kirkpatrick, Jess 96, 391
Kleeb, Helen 931
Kohl, Arthur 1115, 1135, 1159, 1186, 1221, 1229
Kolveg, Pinto 58
Kraft, Chris 117
Kramer, Bill 1165, 1210
Kramer, Mandel 3, 5, 10, 907, 1043, 1057, 1075, 1076, 1080, 1098, 1099-1236, **1099**, 1251, 1253, 1254, 1261, 1262, 1264, 1266, 1267, 1270, 1271, 1272, 1273, 1277, 1278, 1279, 1280, 1281, 1282, 1283, 1284, 1285, 1296, 1297, 1318-1320
"Kranesburg Matter, The" 373, 638, 639-644, 1279, 1289, 1312
Kroeger, Berry 419
Krugman, Lou 24, 51, 54, 125, 137, 165, 206, 248, 377, 416, 431
Kruschen, Jack 49, 51, 58, 105, 111, 133, 151, 163, 175, 214, 224, 231, 257, 440, 485, 530, 553, 571, 581, 662, 694, 698, 717, 734, 782, 793, 815, 826, 840, 859, 900, 938, 1000

Lafferty, Fran 190

"Laird Douglas Douglas of Heatherscote Matter, The" 549-553, 1274, 1309-1310
"Lake Mead Mystery Matter, The" 897-898, 1282, 1316
Lake, Florence 135
"LaMarr Matter, The" 540-544, 1071, 1281, 1309
"Lancer Jewelry Matter, The" 279-280, 1254, 1304, 1322
Lang, Harry 202, 204, 209, 245, 251
"Lansing Fraud Matter, The" 279, 477-481, 1281, 1291, 1307
Lansing, Mary 149, 178, 182, 185, 279, 310, 314, 317, 320, 351, 359, 367, 391, 406, 416
Larch, John 335
"Larson Arson Matter, The" 949-951, 1274, 1316
Latimer, Ed 190
"Latin Lovely Matter, The" 793-795, 1282, 1314
"Latourette Matter, The" 280-282, 1272, 1304
"Latrodectus Matter, The" 1085-1087, 1274, 1298, 1299, 1318
"Laughing Matter, The" 590-594, 1281, 1310-1311
Lawrence, Charlotte 125, 639, 706
Lawrence, Elizabeth 1091, 1092, 1130, 1131
Lawton, Alma 493
Lawton, Donald 394
Lazer, Joan 1206
Lead Audition 1244
Leader, Anton M. 25, 1238
Lee, Earl 125
Leeds, Peter 192, 197, 211, 213, 218, 242, 250, 293, 299, 311, 328, 349, 403, 406, 444, 493, 674, 710, 761, 780, 790, 817, 826, 869, 954, 985, 995, 997
"Leland Case Matter, The" 220-221, 1279, 1303
LeMond, Bob 157, 198, 200
Lenrow, Bernard 190, 1113

"Lester James Matter, The" 292-293, 488, 1258, 1289, 1304
"Lester Matson Matter, The" 334-335, 1257, 1305
"Leumas Matter, The" 937-938, 940, 1285, 1316
Lewis, Abby 1180, 1217
Lewis, Forrest 440, 448, 456, 461, 472, 500, 505, 518, 540, 586, 600, 614, 639, 644, 649, 662, 666, 674, 677, 689, 706, 708, 711, 715, 717, 728, 729, 734, 752, 757, 769, 771, 788, 793, 802, 803, 817, 828, 830, 831, 833, 835, 842, 845, 847, 853, 861, 864, 865, 866, 880, 883, 886, 890, 892, 900, 914, 920, 922, 925, 926, 932, 934, 937, 947, 960, 961, 966, 970, 977, 982, 997, 1000, 1003, 1004, 1008, 1010, 1012, 1015, 1026, 1028, 1031, 1035, 1038
"Life at Steak Matter, The" 918-920, 1258, 1316
Light, Dave 138, 170, 200, 248
"Lillis Bond Matter, The" 197-199, 1266, 1303
"Limping Liability Matter, The" 855-856, 1282, 1315, 1322
Lipton, Bill 1065, 1072, 1077, 1078, 1080, 1096, 1108, 1110, 1133, 1135, 1141, 1142, 1155, 1161, 1173, 1182, 1184, 1193, 1206, 1229
"Little Man Who Was There Matter, The" 938-940, 1282, 1316
"Little Man Who Wasn't All There, The" 69-71, 1283, 1301
"Lloyd Hammerly Matter, The" 8, 174-175, 1265, 1302, 1321
Lloyd, Rita 1115, 1161, 1195, 1221
"London Matter, The" 128-130, 1278, 1302
"Lone Wolf Matter, The" 1092-1094, 1277, 1318
"Lonely Hearts Matter, The" 558-562, 910, 1273, 1310, 1322
"Long Shot Matter, The" 600-605, 1272, 1311

"Look Before the Leap Matter, The" 27, 975-977, 1282, 1317
Lorde, Athena 1050, 1096
"Lorelei Matter, The" 1219-1221, 1277, 1320
"Lorko Diamonds Matter, The" 456-461, 1278, 1307
Lorring, Joan 1057, 1075, 1076, 1082, 1098
"Loss of Memory Matter, The" 734-735, 1258, 1313
"Lost by a Hair Matter, The" 929-931, 1285, 1316
"Love Shorn Matter, The" 875, 876, 882-883, 885, 1282, 1315, 1323
Lovett, Dorothy 62
"Low Tide Matter, The" 1099-1101, 1278, 1318
"Lucky 4 Matter, The" 849-851, 1280, 1315
"Lucky Costa Matter, The" 217-218, 1274, 1303
Lund, John 3, 10, 40, 143, 155, 163, 173, 211, 228, 245, 259-434, **259**, 447, 530, 599, 1043, 1237, 1238-1241, 1251, 1253, 1254, 1256, 1257, 1258, 1259, 1260, 1261, 1262, 1263, 1265, 1267, 1268, 1269, 1271, 1272, 1275, 1276, 1279, 1281, 1283, 1284, 1290, 1304-1306
"Lust for Gold Matter, The" 835, 1189-1191, 1282, 1319
Lynn, Rita 86
Lyon, Charles 250, 251, 252, 253, 254, 288, 290, 292, 293, 295, 297, 299, 301, 303, 304, 306, 308, 309, 311, 313, 315, 317, 318, 320, 322, 324, 326, 328, 330, 331, 332, 335, 336, 338, 339, 342, 343, 345, 347, 349, 351, 353, 354, 357, 359, 361, 363, 365, 367, 368, 370, 373, 375, 377, 380, 382, 384, 386, 389, 391, 392, 394, 396, 398, 401, 403, 404, 406, 408, 410, 412, 415, 416, 419, 421, 423, 425, 427, 429, 430, 431, 432, 433

MacDonald, Dan 1089
MacDonald, Edmond 64, 67, 86, 88

Macdonnell, Norman 25, 49, 51, 52, 58, 59
Mack, Gilbert 190, 1155, 1217
MacKaye, Fred 267, 382, 384
MacLaughlin, Don 1161
"Macormack Matter, The" 8, 436-440, 1254, 1306
"Mad Bomber Matter, The" 1144-1146, 1266, 1319
"Mad Hatter Matter, The" 704-706, 1263, 1213
"Madison Matter, The" 295-297, 513, 1269, 1291, 1304
"Magnanimous Matter, The" 1012-1013, 1282, 1317, 1323
"Magnolia and Honeysuckle Matter, The" 394-397, 1261, 1305
Maher, Wally 127, 130, 151, 155, 176, 204, 247
"Malcolm Wish, M.D. Matter, The" 204-206, 1283, 1303
"Malibu Mystery Matter, The" 856-858, 1284, 1315
"Man Who Waits Matter, The" 4, 7, 995-997, 1261, 1317
"Man Who Wrote Himself to Death, The" 103-105, 1256, 1301
Manners, Joyce 265
Manson, Allan 1096, 1104, 1106, 1123, 1152, 1153
March, Hal 65, 144, 303, 310, 314, 317, 335, 342, 345, 361, 370, 380, 389, 397, 404, 406, 408, 410, 415, 421, 423, 425, 429
"Marie Meadows Matter, The" 195-196, 1283, 1303, 1321
"Marigold Matter, The" 273-275, 1269, 1304
Marino, Amerigo 461, 465, 468, 472, 477, 481, 485, 489, 493, 496, 500, 505, 509, 513, 517, 522, 526, 530, 535, 540, 544, 548, 553, 558, 562, 567, 571, 576, 581, 585, 590, 594, 600, 605, 609, 614, 619, 624, 629, 634, 638, 644, 649, 653, 658, 662, 666, 670, 677, 682, 685, 687, 689, 692, 694, 696, 697, 700, 702, 706, 708, 710, 711, 713, 715, 717, 719, 720, 722, 724, 726, 728, 729, 731, 734, 735, 737, 739, 741, 743, 745, 747, 749, 751, 754, 1250
Marino, Rick 439, 444, 448, 451, 456
"Markham Matter, The" 683-685, 687, 1283, 1313
"Marley K Matter, The" 723-724, 1268, 1313, 1322
Marr, Eddie 215, 265
Marsh, Myra 62
Marshall, Sidney 25, 290, 361, 377, 380, 382, 386, 392, 394, 397, 401, 404, 406, 408, 410, 415, 421, 423, 427, 429, 430, 431
Martin, Ian 1065, 1143, 1144, 1210, 1225
"Mary Grace Matter, The" 773-775, 1270, 1314
"Mason-Dixon Mismatch Matter, The" 735-737, 1275, 1313
Mason, William 1046, 1057, 1135, 1169, 1178, 1180, 1219
Masterson, Paul 64, 65, 67, 69, 73, 77
Mathews, Jimmy 190
"Matter of Reasonable Doubt, The" 581-586, 1255, 1310
Matthews, Grace 1227
Matthews, Jim 923, 925, 926, 928, 929, 931, 937, 938, 940, 942, 943
Matthews, Junius 51, 58, 64, 111, 119, 138, 320, 359, 382, 401, 440, 489, 549, 576, 670, 692, 704, 731, 734, 749, 787, 793, 803, 809, 811, 824, 842, 855, 863, 875, 880, 882, 904, 936, 942, 944, 949, 956, 960, 964, 971, 1012, 1015, 1021
Max, Ed 69, 101, 119, 1238
Maxwell, Bob 907, 1234
"Maynard Collins Matter, The" 242-243, 1256, 1303, 1321
McCallion, James 261, 306, 331, 375, 444, 489, 500, 553, 605, 644, 649, 702, 710, 729, 795, 849, 865, 872, 873, 882, 886, 888, 904, 917, 928, 942, 944, 973, 982, 1010, 1017, 1021, 1033, 1038

"McClain Matter, The" 297, 509-513, 1279, 1291, 1308, 1322
McCluskey, Joyce 99, 265
McCrary, Karen 1210
McGeehan, Pat 97, 113, 196
McGrath, Paul 1189
McGraw, Charles 107
McIntire, John 24, 121, 128, 147, 153, 164, 187, 202, 204, 208, 209, 250, 252, 253, 258, 261, 263, 267, 269, 271, 273, 279, 282, 284, 286, 288, 292, 295, 297, 301, 305, 306, 308, 311, 347, 349, 351, 355, 430, 433, 434, 743, 809, 905
McKennon, Dal 518
McKenny, Bob 10, 946, 947, 1049, 1050, 1206
McLeod, Mercer 1189, 1277
McManus, Kenny 946, 947
McNear, Howard 21, 24, 26, 103, 115, 121, 128, 132, 140, 145, 149, 155, 169, 172, 197, 200, 215, 220, 221, 233, 236, 242, 243, 248, 251, 286, 288, 290, 293, 295, 299, 315, 330, 333, 338, 355, 357, 367, 368, 373, 386, 397, 421, 425, 427, 430, 433, 481, 489, 493, 518, 544, 562, 590, 639, 644, 696, 700, 704, 717, 722, 735, 745, 771, 782, 793, 803, 805, 835, 879, 896, 920, 929, 970, 975, 1013, 1023, 1026
McVey, Tyler 107, 138, 157, 171
Meader, Phil 1089, 1090
"Medium Rare Matter, The" 1130, 1131-1133, 1281, 1319
"Medium, Well Done Matter, The" 6, 571-576, 1133, 1281, 1310
"Meek Memorial Matter, The" 711-713, 1255, 1313
"Meg's Palace Matter, The" 658-662, 1268, 1312
"Mei-Ling Buddah Matter, The" 920, 920-922, 1128, 1285, 1316
"Melancholy Memory Matter, The" 724-726, 1275, 1313

"Melanie Carter Matter, The" 73-75, 1270, 1301
Menken, Shepard 526, 609, 715, 735, 856, 861
Meredith, Lucille 493, 513, 535, 562, 571, 594, 666, 711, 777, 795, 805, 845, 886, 888
Merin, Eda Reiss 119
"Merrill Kent Matter, The" 237-239, 1283, 1303
Merrill, Lou 427, 430, 433, 689, 798, 812, 815, 983, 993, 1024
"Merry Go Round Matter, The" 10, 969-970, 1282, 1317
Metz, Stuart 1115, 1116, 1119, 1148, 1212, 1217, 1223
"Michael Meany Mirage Matter, The" 729-731, 784, 1263, 1313
"Mickey McQueen Matter, The" 23, 140-142, 187-189, 1267, 1302
"Midas Touch Matter, The" 8, 605-609, 707, 1266, 1311
"Midnite Sun Matter, The" 4, 831-833, 1273, 1315
Milano, Frank 1227
"Milford Brooks III" 7, 9, 40-42, 1237-1238, 1260, 1267, 1286, 1300
"Milk and Honey Matter, The" 359-361, 1261, 1305
"Millard Ward Matter, The" 228-230, 1275, 1303
Miller, Bob 653
Miller, Joan 336
Miller, Marvin 342, 423, 440, 452, 456, 465, 472, 496, 522, 530, 567, 581, 600, 619, 670, 710, 713, 737, 761, 785, 811, 821, 855, 859, 883, 910, 914, 936, 958, 985, 993, 997, 1003, 1012, 1023, 1026
Miller, Sidney 69, 86, 137, 153, 167, 176, 185, 192, 218, 226, 230, 236, 248, 253, 273, 288, 295, 343, 363, 382
"Million Dollar Jewelry Matter, The" 1318, 1323
Mind in the Shadows 34

Miner, Jan 190
"Ming Toy Murphy Matter, The" 721-722, 1263, 1313
"Missing Chinese Stripper Matter, The" 87-88, 1255, 1301, 1321
"Missing Matter Matter, The" 863-864, 1282, 1315, 1322
"Missing Missile Matter, The" 10, 945-947, 1050, 1206, 1263, 1316
"Missing Mouse Matter, The" 694-696, 784, 1263, 1313
Mitchell, Shirley 477, 496, 614, 644, 653, 658, 708, 785, 790, 798, 851, 864, 875, 883, 893, 931, 983, 1006
Mitchen, Joan 694
"Mixed Blessing Matter, The" 1166-1167, 1285, 1319
"Model Picture Matter, The" 777-778, 1282, 1314
"Mohave Red Matter, The" 844-845, 1266, 1315
"Mohave Red Sequel Matter, The" 845-847, 1266, 1315
Mohr, Gerald 3, 143, 461, 1237, 1241-1244, 1253, 1254, 1259, 1290, 1306
"Molly K Matter, The" 440-444, 536, 540, 1269, 1306
"Monopoly Matter, The" 172-174, 355-357, 1259, 1286, 1302, 1305, 1321
"Monoxide Mystery Matter, The" 865-866, 1274, 1315, 1322
"Montevideo Matter, The" 164-165, 257-258, 1283, 1287, 1302, 1303, 1304, 1321, 1322, 1323
"Month-End Raid Matter, The" 191-192, 1257, 1303
"Monticello Mystery Matter, The" 1138-1140, 1267, 1319
Moody, Ralph 213, 315, 391, 392, 870, 875, 925, 928, 940, 964, 971, 978, 985, 989, 1042
"Moonshine Matter, The" 977-978, 987, 1275, 1317
"Moonshine Murder Matter, The" 719-720, 1275, 1313, 1322

"Morgan Fry Matter, The" 216-217, 1256, 1303, 1321
"Morning After Matter, The" 1072-1074, 1254, 1298, 1299, 1318
Morrison, Anne 49, 58
Mosley, Donald 902
Moyles, Jack 132, 159, 167, 171, 182, 184, 189, 194, 214, 245, 252, 279, 290, 318, 324, 338, 353, 363, 375, 386, 392, 421, 425, 456, 461, 509, 535, 544, 713, 805, 819, 821, 838, 856, 926, 985, 1017, 1021, 1244
Murcot, Joel 24, 277, 292, 295
"Murder Ain't Minor" 23, 52-54, 1269, 1300
"Murder is a Merry-Go-Round" 38-40, 1273, 1300
Myers, Marty 1208
"Mystery Gal Matter, The" 993-995, 1071, 1258, 1317

"Nancy Shaw Matter, The" 326-328, 1257, 1305
"Nathan Gayles Matter, The" 351-353, 1265, 1305
"Nathan Swing Matter, The" 397-399, 1265, 1305
"Neal Breer Matter, The" 211-213, 1265, 1303
"Negligent Nephew Matter, The" 908-909, 1254, 1316, 1323
"Nelson Matter, The" 330-331, 1257, 1305
Nelson, Frank 314, 320, 322, 347, 351, 359, 403, 416, 685, 694, 708, 715, 726, 737, 740, 761, 773, 775, 807, 809, 822, 826, 833, 883, 898, 907, 983
"Net of Circumstance Matter, The" 893-894, 1280, 1316
Neuman, E. Jack 24, 103, 109, 113, 263, 264, 265, 267, 269, 271, 275, 279, 280, 282, 284, 293, 297, 299, 301, 305, 306, 308, 310, 311, 434, 439, 496, 599, 710, 1239, 1241, 1242, 1244, 1287, 1288, 1289, 1290, 1291, 1292, 1293

"New Bedford Morgue Matter, The" 252, 1257, 1303, 1321
"New Cambridge Matter, The" 265-267, 530, 1272, 1289, 1292, 1304, 1322
"Newark Stockbroker Matter, The" 1318, 1323
"Nick Shurn Matter, The" 481-485, 1278, 1307-1308
"Night in Paris Matter, The" 931-932, 996, 1263, 1316
"No Matter Matter, The" 1227-1229, 1261, 1320
Nolan, Jeanette 121, 128, 147, 153, 157, 159, 161, 164, 167, 168, 182, 187, 199, 202, 204, 206, 208, 209, 228, 235, 239, 242, 243, 245, 247, 250, 252, 253, 258, 261, 263, 267, 269, 271, 273, 282, 284, 286, 288, 295, 301, 305, 306, 308, 311, 339, 342, 343, 347, 349, 351, 353, 355, 357, 363, 365, 412, 416, 535, 553, 586, 600, 614, 731, 737, 740, 741, 782
"Nora Falkner Matter, The" 159-161, 1265, 1302
North, Robert 196, 200
Novello, Jay 71, 84, 97, 132, 165, 171, 226, 247, 258, 261, 277, 301, 308, 333, 345, 349, 361, 370, 394, 399, 406, 419, 423, 430, 433, 434, 456, 461, 540, 581, 700, 719, 722, 1245, 1250
"Noxious Needle Matter, The" 853-855, 1285, 1315
"Nuclear Goof Matter, The" 967-968, 1264, 1317
"Nugget of Truth Matter, The" 1159-1161, 1281, 1319
Nusser, James 24, 69, 107, 142, 164, 169, 172, 179, 184, 185, 197, 247, 251, 275, 280, 303, 305, 320, 331, 339, 353, 359, 368, 403, 408, 415, 429

O'Brien, Edmond 3, 6, 7, 69, 89-258, **89**, 259, 286, 313, 357, 368, 419, 710, 1251, 1253, 1254, 1255, 1256, 1257, 1259, 1260, 1263, 1264, 1265, 1266, 1267, 1268, 1270, 1271, 1272, 1274, 1275, 1276, 1277, 1278, 1279, 1280, 1283, 1301-1304
O'Herlihy, Dan 117, 130, 142, 144, 157, 175, 187, 235, 401
Oates, Edward 1104, 1142
Ocko, Danny 1057, 1075, 1076
Ogilvie, Jack 1067
"Oklahoma Red Matter, The" 310-311, 505, 1281, 1288, 1304
Oland, Cliff 1223
"Old Fashioned Murder Matter, The" 1108-1110, 1277, 1319
"Oldest Gag Matter, The" 1217-1219, 1277, 1320
"One Most Wanted Matter, The" 872-873, 1279, 1315, 1322
"One of the Rottenest Rackets Matter" 1130, 1297
"One Too Many Matter, The" 1150-1153, 1261, 1319
"Only One Butt Matter, The" 922-923, 1261, 1316
"Open Town Matter, The" 27, 403, 619-624, 1266, 1289, 1311
Ortega, Santos 1059, 1094, 1101, 1108, 1130, 1131, 1184, 1189, 1225
Osborne, Reynold 1135, 1139, 1140, 1173, 1215, 1223
Osborne, Ted 119, 123, 135, 140, 174, 179, 196, 214, 217, 224, 231
"Oscar Clark Matter, The" 335-336, 1271, 1305, 1322
Otto, Walter 907, 1121, 1155, 1191, 1212, 1214, 1216, 1223, 1225, 1227, 1229, 1232, 1234
"Out of the Fire, Into the Frying Pan" 56-58, 130, 1259, 1300
Owen, Tudor 117, 123, 130, 144, 165, 179, 187, 197, 208, 326, 404

"P. O. Matter, The" 972-973, 1270, 1317
Paiva, Nestor 224, 231, 290
Palmer, Maria 117, 187
"Paradise Lost Matter, The" 4, 1013-1015, 1272, 1317

"Parakoff Policy, The" 9, 32-34, 1260, 1300
Parkhurst, Doug 1152, 1153
"Parley Barron Matter, The" 740-741, 1279, 1313
"Paterson Transport Matter, The" 413-415, 1261, 1306
Patrick, Lee 161, 172, 184, 255, 397, 415, 429
"Paul Barberis Matter, The" 241-242, 1256, 1303, 1321
"Paul Gorrell Matter, The" 373-375, 1275, 1305
"Pearl Carrasa" 113-115, 1275, 1301
"Pearling Matter, The" 594-600, 1261, 1290, 1311
Pearson, GeGe 71
"Peerless Fire Matter, The" 726-728, 1264, 1313
"Perilous Padre Matter, The" 1115-1116, 1281, 1319
"Perilous Parley Matter, The" 8, 875-876, 882, 885, 965, 1282, 1315, 1322
Perrin, Vic 24, 109, 161, 211, 250, 263, 273, 305, 317, 328, 444, 461, 468, 500, 513, 540, 571, 581, 605, 653, 666, 674, 682, 692, 698, 710, 720, 724, 752, 759, 764, 775, 777, 796, 802, 812, 815, 821, 822, 844, 849, 851, 856, 865, 872, 893, 894, 896, 902, 934, 940, 953, 954, 963, 978, 983, 987, 998, 1008, 1013, 1024, 1026, 1035, 1244
Peters, Ken 530
Petrie, George 1067
Petruzzi, Jack 111, 535, 600
"Phantom Chase Matter, The" 670-677, 1282, 1312-1313
"Philadelphia Miss Matter, The" 1113-1115, 1254, 1319
"Phillip Morey Matter, The" 342-343, 1305
Phillips, Barney 52, 224, 231, 286, 336, 408, 444, 456, 481, 485, 500, 526, 549, 558, 609, 649, 658, 674, 687, 700, 708, 726, 735, 741, 749, 756, 767, 817, 824, 833, 838, 845, 847, 857, 858, 869, 870, 890, 894, 925, 926, 937, 953, 954, 961, 966, 971, 997, 1006, 1019, 1028, 1029, 1040, 1244, 1245, 1250
"Phony Phone Matter, The" 991-993, 1148-1150, 1269, 1279, 1317, 1319
"Picture Postcard Matter, The" 9, 662-666, 1264, 1312
"Piney Corners Matter, The" 389-391, 614, 1279, 1289, 1305
"Planner Matter, The" 1061-1063, 1270, 1296, 1297, 1318, 1323
"Plantagent Matter, The" 265, 527-530, 1262, 1289, 1292, 1309
Polen, Nat 1067, 1152, 1153, 1197
"Poor Little Rich Girl Matter, The" 760-761, 1270, 1314
"Port-au-Prince Matter, The" 82, 123-125, 1287, 1301
"Port-O-Call Matter, The" 168-169, 1265, 1302
Post, Clayton 109, 113, 125, 128, 138, 153, 161, 167, 172, 233, 269, 280, 293, 299, 315, 320, 330, 349, 359, 363, 367, 370, 384, 392, 399, 415, 429
Powell, Dick 3, 7, 9, 42, 1237-1238, 1253, 1254, 1260, 1300
"Price of Fame Matter, The" 802-803, 932, 1264, 1314
Price, Vincent 802, 803
"Primrose Matter, The" 666-670, 1270, 1312
"Protection Matter, The" 6, 225-226, 1257, 1303
"Punctilious Firebug Matter, The" 407-408, 1261, 1306
"Purple Doll Matter, The" 1089, 1298, 1299, 1318, 1323

"Queen Anne Pistols Matter, The" 155-157, 1279, 1290, 1302
"Quiet Little Town in New Jersey Matter, The" 1319, 1323
Quine, Dick 214

"Racehorse Piledriver Matter, The" 64-65, 1269, 1301
"Radioactive Gold Matter, The" 425-427, 1259, 1306
Raeburn, Bryna 1178
Raskyn, Sam 1046, 1133, 1171, 1184, 1186, 1223
"Rasmusson Matter, The" 692-694, 1282, 1313
"Rat Pack Matter, The" 1087-1090, 1262, 1298, 1299, 1318
Readick, Bob 3, 29, 1043-1098, **1043**, 1251, 1253, 1254, 1258, 1260, 1262, 1264, 1266, 1270, 1273, 1274, 1277, 1278, 1280, 1281, 1283, 1284, 1285, 1296, 1297, 1318
"Real Smokey Matter, The" 1023-1024, 1274, 1317, 1323
"Really Gone Matter, The" 934-936, 940, 1282, 1316
"Recompense Matter, The" 1028-1029, 1280, 1317
"Red Mystery Matter, The" 960-961, 1282, 1316
Redfield, William 1077, 1078, 1089, 1090, 1094, 1128, 1139, 1140, 1150, 1173, 1212
"Redrock Matter, The" 997-998, 1266, 1317
Reed, Alan 590, 649, 719, 765, 809, 822, 824, 845, 847, 866, 876, 882, 902, 912, 923, 961
Reid, Elliott 94, 109, 253, 295
Repp, Guy 1072, 1123, 1133, 1155, 1165, 1186, 1221, 1229
"Rhymer Collection Matter, The" 1010-1012, 1271, 1317
"Ricardo Amerigo Matter, The" 497-500, 1274, 1308
Rice, Rosemary 1065, 1212, 1223
"Richard Splain Matter, The" 147-149, 1259, 1302
Richards, Paul 535, 544, 586, 644, 812
"Rilldo Matter, The" 1206-1208, 1279, 1320

"Ring of Death Matter, The" 1074-1076, 1277, 1298, 1318
"Road-Test Matter, The" 382-384, 1258, 1305
"Robert Perry Case, The" 36-38, 99, 1255, 1287, 1300, 1321
Robinson, Bartlett 855, 865, 894, 898, 902, 907, 914, 915, 925, 936, 942, 944, 947, 968, 982, 985, 1003, 1008, 1029
Robinson, Larry 1055, 1206, 1208, 1227
"Rochester Theft Matter, The" 269, 303-305, 496, 1254, 1290, 1293, 1304
Rodman, Victor 331, 368
"Rolling Stone Matter, The" 828-830, 1282, 1315
Ronson, Adele 1139, 140
Rose, Ralph 25, 80, 82
Rost, Elaine 1087
Rowan, Roy 54, 56, 58, 59, 60, 94, 96, 97, 99, 101, 105, 107, 109, 111, 113, 117, 119, 121, 123, 125, 127, 143, 147, 439, 444, 447, 451, 456, 461, 465, 468, 472, 477, 481, 485, 489, 493, 496, 500, 505, 509, 513, 517, 522, 526, 530, 535, 540, 544, 548, 553, 558, 562, 567, 571, 576, 581, 585, 590, 594, 599, 605, 609, 614, 619, 624, 629, 634, 638, 644, 649, 658, 662, 666, 670, 677, 682, 685, 831, 833, 835, 836, 838, 839, 842, 844, 845, 847, 849, 851, 853, 855, 856, 857, 859, 861, 863
"Royal Street Matter, The" 687-689, 1275, 1313
Rubin, Benny 277, 338, 389, 477
"Rudy Valentine Matter, The" 166-167, 362-363, 1260, 1286, 1302, 1305, 1321, 1322
Ruick, Melville 1169, 1212, 1225
"Rum Barrel Matter, The" 222-223, 1275, 1303, 1321
Russell, Charles 3, 6, 7, 31-88, **31**, 89, 124, 130, 153, 1251, 1253, 1254, 1255, 1256, 1258, 1259, 1261, 1263, 1265, 1267, 1268, 1269, 1270, 1271, 1273, 1274, 1275, 1280, 1283, 1300-1301

Ryan, Dick 96, 125, 157, 168, 185, 273, 284, 286, 322, 355, 399, 535, 549, 553
Ryan, Vic 62
Ryf, Robert 25, 452, 468, 619, 639, 658, 666, 677, 687, 756, 767, 778, 782, 790, 800, 807, 819

"Salkoff Sequel Matter, The" 813-815, 1141, 1280, 1314
"Salt City Matter, The" 545-549, 1276, 1291, 1309, 1322
Samuels, Joel 226
"San Antonio Matter, The" 8, 299-301, 456, 599, 1265, 1290, 1293, 1304
San Juan, Olga 101, 181
Sanford, Don 24, 351, 355, 412
Santoni, Renee 1232
Sanville, Richard 25, 34, 36, 38, 40, 42, 44, 46, 48
"Sara Dearing Matter, The" 410-412, 1306
"Sarah Martin Matter, The" 429-430, 1283, 1306, 1322
"Saturday Night Matter, The" 980-982, 1277, 1317
Schoskis, Michael 1212, 1214, 1223
Scott, Janet 169
"Sea Legs Matter, The" 4, 619, 624-629, 1282, 1311
"Search for Michelle Marsh, The" 31, 60-62, 1280, 1301
Seel, Charles 62
Selby, Sarah 115
Sewell, Bud 756, 757, 759, 761
Seymour, John 1110, 1217
"Shadow of a Doubt Matter, The" 1002, 1046, 1174-1176, 1283, 1319
"Shady Lane Matter, The" 391, 610-614, 1277, 1289, 1311
"Shankar Diamond Matter, The" 888-890, 1276, 1315
"Shayne Bombing Matter, The" 318-320, 1257, 1304
"Shepherd Matter, The" 263, 553-558, 1276, 1289, 1310
Sherwood, Madeline 1055, 1204

"Shifty Looker Matter, The" 1121-1123, 1264, 1319
Shipp, Mary 73, 96, 137, 213, 333, 1238
"Short Term Matter, The" 7, 9, 1057-1059, 1272, 1296, 1318
Shoskus, Mike 1155
Shue, Bob 1025
"Shy Beneficiary Matter, The" 5, 781-782, 1282, 1314
"Sick Chick Matter, The" 803-805, 1277, 1314
"Sidewinder Matter, The" 970-971, 1266, 1317
"Sidney Mann Matter, The" 158, 253, 1264, 1288, 1303, 1321
"Sidney Rykoff Matter, The" 119-121, 1260, 1301
"Silent Queen Matter, The" 677-682, 1277, 1313
"Silver Belle Matter, The" 771-773, 1263, 1314
"Silver Blue Matter, The" 567-571, 1271, 1310
"Silver Queen Matter, The" 987-989, 1317
Simes, Eugene 1155, 1223, 1225
Simons, Constance 1210, 1215, 1229
"Simple Simon Matter, The" 1084, 1090-1092, 1281, 1318
"Singapore Arson Matter, The" 228, 259-261, 1265, 1289, 1304, 1322
Singleton, Doris 52, 56, 65, 77
"Skidmore Matter, The" 965, 1182-1184, 1281, 1319
"Skimpy Matter, The" 8, 1210-1212, 1271, 1320
"Skull Canyon Mine, The" 75-77, 1274, 1301
"Slow Boat from China, The" 34-36, 85, 1274, 1300
Smith, Bill 1046, 1067, 1121, 1193, 1215
Smith, Charles B. 24, 689, 696, 706, 713, 722, 726, 731, 737, 740, 745, 752, 773
"Smoky Sleeper Matter, The" 7, 757-759, 1157, 1272, 1314
Smolen, Vivian 1227

Snowden, Eric 235, 257, 261, 404, 544, 649, 694, 754, 885, 890
"Soderbury, Maine Matter, The" 199-200, 1256, 1303
Solow, Larry 1232
Sommers, Jimsey 1182
Sonnenberg, Nellie 1119
Soule, Olan 989, 991
Spaulding, Jean 132
"Squared Circle Matter, The" 696-698, 1075, 1269, 1313
"SS Malay Trader, The" 92-94, 1268, 1301
"Stanley Price Matter, The" 332-333, 1284, 1305
"Stanley Springs Matter, The" 89, 179-181, 1263, 1302
Stanley, Robert 25, 830, 844, 861, 882
"Star of Capetown Matter, The" 4, 614-619, 699, 943, 1278, 1311
"Star of Hades Diamond, The" 36, 85
"Starlet Matter, The" 271-273, 1281, 1304
Stehli, Edgar 757, 865, 954, 1061, 1084, 1085, 1215, 1217
Stephenson, John 155, 220, 221, 318, 333, 339, 380, 489, 505, 513, 702, 728, 788, 980
Sterling, Bill 1050, 1065, 1074
Stevens, Jim 1072, 1121, 1148, 1161, 1176, 1193, 1195, 1217
Stevens, Leith 48, 49, 50, 52, 54, 56, 58, 59, 60, 62, 73, 77, 79, 80, 82, 84, 85, 86, 88, 92, 94, 96, 97, 99, 101, 103, 105, 107, 109, 111, 113, 115, 117, 119, 121, 123, 125, 127, 128, 130, 132, 133, 135, 137, 138, 140, 142, 144, 145
Stevenson, Bob 79, 80, 84, 85, 86, 88, 128, 130, 132, 133, 135, 137, 138, 140, 142, 145, 149, 151, 212, 215, 216, 218
Stewart, Kay 174
"Stock in Trade Matter, The" 1095, 1096-1098, 1285, 1318
"Stolen Portrait of the Duke of Massen, The" 42-44, 1263, 1300

"Stope of Death Matter, The" 1026-1028, 1281, 1317
"Story of the Ten-O-Eight, The" 111-113, 1276, 1301
Stratton Jr, Gil 140, 199, 243, 594, 634, 731, 757, 805, 826, 840, 898, 902, 940, 942, 944, 966, 973
Stratton, Chester 465, 522, 619, 658, 682, 711, 745, 749, 836, 838, 956, 964, 1023, 1035, 1040
Stuart, Kay 111
"Sudden Wealth Matter, The" 958-960, 1282, 1316
"Sulphur and Brimstone Matter, The" 392-394, 1261, 1305
Summers, Jocelyn 1176
"Sunny Dream Matter, The" 785-787, 1282, 1314
"Suntan Oil Matter, The" 10, 713-715, 1277, 1313
"Super Salesman Matter, The" 1035-1036, 1282, 1317
Sweeney, Bob 145, 147, 151, 233, 248, 252, 434
Sweeney, Warren 1171, 1180, 1191
Syms, Sylvia 82
"Syndicate Matter, The" 290-292, 1262, 1304

Tackna, Edith 217
"Takes a Crook Matter, The" 1163-1165, 1285, 1319
Tarplin, Maurice 190, 1091, 1092, 1116, 1119, 1121, 1133, 1167, 1173, 1184
Tatum, Jeanne 481, 544, 549, 586, 619, 624, 639, 694, 719, 740, 771, 775, 780, 793, 833, 840, 858, 864, 868, 880, 883, 905, 920, 963, 1003, 1010, 1031
"Tears of Night Matter, The" 576-581, 702, 1282, 1291, 1310
Tedrow, Irene 92, 472
"Tell-All Book Matter, The" 1302, 1321
"Telltale Tracks Matter, The" 876, 877-879, 1258, 1315, 1322

"Temperamental Tote Board Matter, The" 408-410, 1283, 1306

"Templeton Matter, The" 103, 708-710, 1270, 1288, 1313

"Terrible Torch Matter, The" 1155-1157, 1272, 1319

"Terrified Taun Matter, The" 384-386, 1283, 1305

Thatcher, Leora 1110, 1135, 1165

"Thelma Ibsen Matter, The" 269-271, 306, 465, 1262, 1288, 1304

Thomas, Hugh 96

Thomas, John 1061, 1137, 1138, 1163

Thompson, D. J. 73, 448, 472, 518, 619, 670, 773, 844, 883, 910

Thor, Larry 200, 217, 220, 221, 324, 468, 687, 1244

Thorson, Russell 472, 481, 509, 518, 535, 558, 600, 605, 624, 629, 644, 653, 687, 706, 717, 740, 759, 782, 798, 824, 831, 833, 847, 866, 877, 888, 915, 938, 958, 960, 982, 1000, 1003, 1017, 1019, 1028, 1029, 1033, 1036, 1038

"Three for One Matter, The" 1133-1135, 1269, 1319

"Three Sisters Matter, The" 775-777, 1279, 1314

Tice, Olin 190

"Time and Tide Matter, The" 805-807, 1282, 1314

"Tip-Off Matter, The" 907, 1231, 1232-1234, 1273, 1320

"Todd Matter, The" 8, 269, 304, 493-496, 1264, 1290, 1293, 1308

"Tolhurst Theft Matter, The" 231-233, 1279, 1303

"Tom Hickman Matter, The" 69, 153, 253, 1270, 1287, 1303, 1322

"Too Many Crooks Matter, The" 1119-1121, 1189, 1271, 1319

"Too Much Money Matter, The" 1021-1023, 1264, 1317

"Top Secret Matter, The" 5, 1167-1169, 1277, 1319

"Touch-Up Matter, The" 1069-1072, 1277, 1298, 1318

"Trans-Pacific Import Export Company, South China Branch" 142-144, 1259, 1302

"Trans-Pacific Matter – Part A, The" 1238-1239, 1259, 1290, 1304

"Trans-Pacific Matter – Part B, The" 1240-1241, 1259, 1290, 1304

"Trans-Pacific Matter Part 1, The" 1241-1242, 1259, 1290, 1306

"Trans-Pacific Matter Part 2, The" 1242-1244, 1259, 1290, 1306

Tremayne, Les 649, 687, 735, 764, 775, 840, 842, 917, 923

"True Love Matter, The" 1051-1053, 1055, 1262, 1296, 1318, 1323

Tully, Tom 271, 290, 292, 297, 336, 351, 365, 375, 412, 416

Turner, Fred 1227

Tuttle, Lurene 105, 147, 179, 576

"Twin Trouble Matter, The" 910-912, 1263, 1316

"Twins of Tahoe Matter, The" 1029-1031, 1269, 1317

"Twisted Twin Matter, The" 1015-1017, 1264, 1317

"Two Faced Matter, The" 851-853, 900, 1273, 1315

"Two Steps to Murder Matter, The" 1191-1193, 1284, 1320

"Two Tired Matter, The" 1067-1069, 1284, 1296, 1297, 1318, 1323

"Two's a Crowd Matter, The" 1078-1080, 1285, 1298, 1318

"Ugly Pattern Matter, The" 840-842, 1270, 1315

"Uncut Canary Matter, The" 378-380, 1261, 1305

"Underwood Matter, The" 282-284, 472, 1254, 1289, 1304

"Undried Fiddle Back Matter, The" 391-392, 1261, 1305, 1322

"Unholy Two Matter, The" 964-966, 1281, 1317

Unknown Cast 34, 36, 38, 40, 42, 44, 46, 48, 75, 85, 1048, 1051, 1053, 1063, 1069, 1200, 1202, 1235, 1236
Unknown Producer 1235, 1236
"Unworthy Kin Matter, The" 965, 1031-1033, 1278, 1317
"Upjohn Matter, The" 4, 264, 433-434, 522, 1258, 1292, 1306, 1322
"Urned Income Matter, The" 1002, 1044-1046, 1176, 1273, 1318

"Valentine Matter, The" 301, 452-456, 559, 1272, 1290, 1293, 130
Van Rooten, Luis 1072, 1116, 1165, 1167, 1178
Verdier, Bill 809
"Very Fishy Matter, The" 1055-1057, 1266, 1296, 1318
Victor, Paula 159
Vigran, Herb 24, 56, 500, 567, 576, 590, 704, 728, 747, 752, 793, 821, 842, 849, 853, 856, 869, 879, 888, 909, 918, 923, 929, 940, 945, 953, 967, 973, 977, 997, 1010, 1021, 1026, 1029
"Village of Virtue Matter, The" 824-826, 838, 1258, 1315
"Village Scene, The" 105-107, 1256, 1301
"Virginia Beach Matter, The" 79, 144-145, 1260, 1287, 1302
"Virginia Towne Matter, The" 89, 193-194, 1275, 1303
"Virtuous Mobster Matter, The" 8, 838-840, 1258, 1315
"Vivian Fair Matter, The" 175-176, 1275, 1302, 1321
"Vociferous Dolphin Matter, The" 10, 947, 1050, 1204-1206, 1279, 1320
Vola, Vicki 1155, 1204
"Voodoo Matter, The" 324-326, 1269, 1293, 1305

Wald, John 970, 971, 973, 975, 977, 978, 980, 981, 983, 985, 989, 991, 993, 995, 998, 1000, 1003, 1004, 1006, 1007, 1010, 1015, 1017, 1019, 1021, 1024, 1026, 1028, 1029, 1031, 1033, 1035, 1036, 1038, 1040, 1042
Walsh, George 1242, 1244
"Walter Patterson Matter, The" 265-267, 447, 1260, 1288, 1304
Walters, Joe 754
Warner, Gertrude 1074, 1089, 1090, 1128, 1137, 1138
Warnow, Mark 34, 36, 38, 40, 42, 44, 46
Waterman, Willard 64, 67, 73, 77, 86, 109, 125
"Wayward Clipper Matter, The" 1198-1200, 1284, 1296, 1320, 1323
"Wayward Diamonds Matter, The" 858-859, 1284, 1315
"Wayward Fireman Matter, The" 1065-1067, 1270, 1297, 1318
"Wayward Gun Matter, The" 1195-1197, 1254, 1320
"Wayward Heiress Matter, The" 4, 913, 915-917, 1048, 1232, 1272, 1316
"Wayward Killer Matter, The" 847-849, 1258, 1315
"Wayward Kilocycles Matter, The" 10, 947, 1048-1050, 1206, 1280, 1296, 1318
"Wayward Money Matter, The" 821-822, 1273, 1314
"Wayward Moth Matter, The" 811-812, 1141, 1280, 1314
"Wayward River Matter, The" 835-836, 1258, 1315
"Wayward Sculptor Matter, The" 917-918, 1282, 1316
"Wayward Trout Matter, The" 823-824, 1282, 1314
"Wayward Truck Matter, The" 7, 732-734, 1280, 1313
"Wayward Widow Matter, The" 752-754, 1274, 1314
"Weather or Not Matter, The" 1208-1210, 1280, 1320
Webb, Jane 127, 342, 373, 375
Webber, Peggy 96, 111, 140, 279, 310, 485, 713, 720, 728, 787, 893, 915
Weber, Karl 1178

"Weldon Bragg Matter, The" 171-172, 1263, 1302, 1321
"Well of Trouble Matter, The" 8, 1104-1106, 1277, 1318
Wentworth, Martha 54, 71, 115, 133, 189, 211, 280, 315, 331, 367
"What Goes Matter, The" 1033-1035, 1280, 1317
Whiting, Barbara 215
Whitney, Susan 586
"Who Took the Taxis for a Ride?" 49-51, 1273, 1300
"Who's Who Matter, The" 1063-1065, 1283, 1297, 1318
"Wholly Unexpected Matter, The" 1004-1006, 1282, 1317
"Will and a Way Matter, The" 925-926, 1266, 1316
"Willard South Matter, The" 189-190, 1265, 1302
"William Post Matter, The" 337-338, 1257, 1305
Willway, Lee 694, 895, 896
"Winnipesaukee Wonder Matter, The" 756-757, 1135, 1269, 1314, 1322
Winslowe, Paula 682, 685, 715, 775, 800, 844, 858, 859, 893, 983
"Winsome Widow Matter, The" 10, 905-907, 1234, 1266, 1316
Winters, Roland 609
Wipple, Barbara 1227
"Witness, Witness, Who's Got the Witness" 68-69, 153, 253, 1270, 1287, 1301
Wolcott, Florence 468
Wood, Jean 194
"Woodward Manila Matter, The" 161-163, 417-419, 1257, 1286, 1302, 1306
Wright, Ben 82, 117, 123, 130, 142, 151, 157, 165, 208, 235, 257, 326, 361, 386, 404, 485, 509, 649, 666, 677, 702, 724, 785, 800, 807, 858, 859, 931, 978, 987, 1012, 1042, 1242, 1244
Wright, Stewart 367, 370, 373, 375, 382, 644, 1048, 1051, 1053, 1063, 1069, 1234, 1237, 1244, 1250, 1286
Wright, Will 13, 24, 448, 456, 505, 522, 567, 581, 614, 658, 694, 702, 720, 737, 741, 745, 759, 769, 771, 773, 800, 802, 826, 835, 851, 853, 858, 868, 896, 909, 918, 922, 970, 980, 991, 998, 1242, 1244
"Wrong Doctor Matter, The" 4, 1117-1119, 1281, 1319
"Wrong Ending Matter, The" 916, 1046-1048, 1232, 1260, 1296, 1318, 1323
"Wrong Idea Matter, The" 1180-1182, 1262, 1319
"Wrong Man Matter, The" 955-956, 1263, 1316
"Wrong One Matter, The" 1140-1142, 1280, 1319
"Wrong Sign Matter, The" 1080-1082, 1278, 1298, 1299, 1318

"Yaak Mystery Matter, The" 1094-1096, 1264, 1318
Yafee, Ben 1206
"Yankee Pride Matter, The" 89, 149-151, 255-257, 1279, 1286, 1302, 1303, 1304, 1321, 1322
Yarborough, Barton 94, 175, 230
Young, Carleton 465, 468, 526, 535, 567, 708, 719
Young, Carleton G. 788, 819, 870, 896, 909, 918, 928, 967, 1042
Young, Dave 175, 311
"Youngstown Credit Group Matter, The" 239-241, 1257, 1303
"Yours Truly Matter, The" 748-749, 1282, 1314

Zerbe, Lawson 1059, 1065, 1072, 1077, 1078, 1082, 1087, 1110, 1116, 1119, 1126, 1143, 1144, 1146, 1152, 1153, 1173, 1180, 1182, 1191, 1193
"Zip Matter, The" 1193-1195, 1284, 1320
Zirato, Jr, Bruno 25, 1046, 1048, 1050, 1051, 1053, 1055, 1057, 1059, 1061, 1063, 1065, 1067, 1069, 1072, 1074, 1075, 1078, 1080, 1082, 1085, 1087, 1089,

1092, 1094, 1096, 1098, 1101, 1104,
1106, 1108, 1110, 1113, 1115, 1116,
1119, 1123, 1126, 1128, 1131, 1133,
1135, 1138, 1140, 1142, 1144, 1146,
1148, 1150, 1153, 1157, 1159, 1161,
1163, 1165, 1167, 1169, 1171, 1173,
1176, 1178, 1180, 1182, 1184, 1186,
1189, 1191, 1193, 1195, 1219, 1221

www.ingramcontent.com/pod-product-compliance
Lightning Source LLC
Chambersburg PA
CBHW070327240426
43665CB00045B/1146